Fundamentals of Investments

Fourth Edition

Fundamentals of Investments

Fourth Edition

Richard A. Stevenson
University of Iowa

Edward H. Jennings
Ohio State University

David Loy
Illinois State University

West Publishing Company

St. Paul New York Los Angeles San Francisco

This text was set in Aster by G & S Typesetters. Charlene Brown was the copyeditor. Alice B. Thiede, Carto-Graphics, prepared new art for this edition. The interior was designed by David Corona Design Associates.

The cover photograph was supplied through the courtesy of the New York Stock Exchange. Theresa Jensen designed the cover.

50 W. Kellogg Boulevard
P.O. Box 64526
St. Paul, MN 55164-1003

Library of Congress Cataloging-in-Publication Data

Stevenson, Richard A., 1938–
Fundamentals of investments.

Bibliography: p.
Includes index.
1. Investments. 2. Investment analysis. I. Jennings, Edward H., 1937– II. Loy, David. III. Title.
HG4521.S759 1988 332.6′78 87-31600
ISBN 0-314-65669-3

To our families

About the Authors

Richard A. Stevenson joined the faculty of the University of Iowa in 1967 and is currently Professor of Finance. He chaired the Department of Finance from 1981 through 1986 and is currently serving as the university's Treasurer.

Professor Stevenson received his bachelor's degree from St. Bonaventure University, his M.B.A. from Syracuse University, and his Ph.D. from Michigan State University where he was a Ford Foundation Fellow. He is a Chartered Financial Analyst and a member of the Iowa Society of Financial Analysts. A member of numerous other professional and honorary associations, he is a Past President of the Midwest Finance Association and a Past Director of the Financial Management Association.

He has written *Fundamentals of Finance* (McGraw-Hill, 1980) and *Asset-Liability Management for Credit Unions* (Kendall-Hunt, 1984). He is coeditor, with Susan Phillips, of *Investment Environment, Analysis, and Alternatives* (West, 1977). His articles have appeared in such journals as the *Financial Analysts Journal, Journal of Finance, Accounting Review, Journal of Financial and Quantitative Analysis, Journal of Portfolio Management,* and *Journal of Futures Markets.*

Edward H. Jennings, President of The Ohio State University and Professor of Finance, received his B.S. from the University of North Carolina, his M.B.A. from Western Reserve University (now Case Western) and his Ph.D. from the University of Michigan.

Professor Jennings, a University of Iowa faculty member from 1969 to 1979, also served as Department Chair of Business Administration and Vice President for Finance and University Services. He has held visiting appointments to the University of Hawaii and to the University of Dar es Salaam, where he served as a Rockefeller Foundation adviser on East African management education, assisted in forming a College of Management, and acted as adviser to Tanzania's National Developmental Corporation. A past adviser to the World Bank on loan interest rates for developing countries, he is a member of the American and Western Finance Associations. He was named President of the University of Wyoming in 1979 and became Ohio State's tenth President in 1981.

Professor Jennings has published several articles in academic and professional journals on bonds, common stock, inflation, and other financial topics.

David Loy became a member of the faculty at Illinois State University in 1982 and is currently an Associate Professor of Finance. Professor Loy earned a bachelor's degree in mathematics from Iowa State University and received both his M.B.A. and Ph.D. in finance from the University of Iowa.

He has written *Cases in Managing Financial Resources* (Reston, 1984) (with Ike Mathur), in which he was the first to develop microcomputer-spreadsheet support for financial management case analysis. Professor Loy has received several teaching grants and awards and has worked extensively with the development of computer-supported instructional materials.

He belongs to several honorary associations and is an active participant in both national and regional professional meetings. Articles by Professor Loy have appeared in such journals as the *Journal of Accounting, Auditing and Finance, Management Accounting, The Journal of Cash Management,* and *The International Review of Economics and Business.*

Contents

Preface

Radical changes have occurred in the field of investments during the past twenty years. Many new forms of securities have emerged in response to perceived needs and desires of investors. The structure of the markets in which securities trade has undergone substantial change—especially in the internationalization of these markets. Investors are increasingly aware of expected returns in relation to the risks that need to be assumed in seeking the return. Investment performance measurement gives increasing recognition to risk-adjusted performance. The impact of a given investment on the portfolio of the investor continues to receive great attention. Futures and options are employed to alter the risk and return characteristics of a portfolio to satisfy an investor's unique risk and return desires.

Rationale

This text is designed for the introductory college course in investments. We have attempted to introduce many of the new developments in the field of investments, while retaining enough descriptive material so that the beginning student may become familiar with the various investment alternatives and the investment environment in which they are available. In trying to integrate newer developments with more traditional investment management material, we have attempted to explain the newer developments in a clear and comprehensible manner.

Organization

The book is divided into six general parts. Part 1 (Chapters 1–3) provides basic information with regard to the essentials of investments. Early emphasis is given in Part 1 to the risk-return trade-off, which investors must face. Part 2 (Chapters 4–6) covers the measurement of risk and return along with an introduction to various valuation approaches. Part 3 (Chapters 7–9) provides an approach to the valuation of equity securities. Part 4 (Chapters 10–13) presents an analysis of fixed-income investment opportunities with an introduction to the nature of the innovative activity that has taken place in this type of investment. Part 5 (Chapters 14–17) discusses specialized forms of investments and investment approaches. The final part, Chapters 18–20, examines the essentials involved in planning a portfolio, in managing it, and then in evaluating its performance. Practical portfolio management considerations at the institutional level are considered in this final part.

Flexibility of the Text

The material in this text is presented in a flexible manner so that it may be used in a wide variety of investment courses. Most instructors will probably neither want nor be able to cover adequately all the topics in this book in a quarter or a semester. For example, Chapter 13 deals with fixed-income innovations and investment management strategies and could easily be eliminated without losing continuity. The same is true for Chapter 20 where we consider in some detail the topic of measuring portfolio performance.

Major Changes in the Fourth Edition

A major change in the fourth edition is the addition of David Loy of Illinois State University as a coauthor. Dave brings over ten years of teaching experience to the revision of the text as well as considerable expertise in the area of computer applications in investments. We have made some major organizational changes, which we feel significantly improve both the readability and teachability of the text. The principal changes are as follows:

- The essential character of risk and return in the investments area is presented in Chapter 1 and becomes a theme for the rest of the text.
- We have consolidated much of the descriptive material and reduced the number of chapters from twenty-six in the third edition to twenty in this edition.
- Valuation concepts are examined in detail much earlier in the text so that they can be used in a more comprehensive fashion later in the book.
- In Chapter 13, we have incorporated fixed-income investment management strategies with new material dealing with financial market innovation for fixed-income securities.
- The chapter on futures trading has been refocused and deals exclusively with the use of financial futures for speculative and hedging purposes. An important concept in this material is the ability of

these securities to quickly and efficiently alter the risk and return characteristics of a portfolio.

- The material on investment companies has been reorganized into a separate chapter and includes increased emphasis on the use of closed-end investment companies to achieve specialized investment goals.
- The chapter on global investments has been expanded by including more descriptive material on various foreign markets and types of foreign securities.
- Part 6 has been reorganized into three chapters that take a "before, during, and after" approach to portfolio management. Chapter 18 examines the elements of planning a portfolio. Chapter 19 looks at some aspects of actually managing an institutional portfolio while Chapter 20 presents ways to evaluate performance after the portfolio has been managed for a period of time.

Key Features of the Text

1. A list of KEY TERMS is presented in each chapter so the reader can review the concepts presented in the chapter.
2. A GLOSSARY is presented at the end of the book to help readers quickly find a description of key terms.
3. Each chapter has QUESTIONS at the end. The questions are designed for review purposes as well as to encourage the student to think about situations that may not be covered directly in the text.
4. For those chapters where PROBLEMS are feasible, this revision includes an increased number of realistic problems. Many of these problems are designed so that they can be used with LOTUS 1-2-3 in an easy-to-use format.
5. Fourteen INVESTMENT HIGHLIGHTS are presented throughout the text. Ten of these are new to this edition. These are descriptions of actual situations either experienced or well-known to many investors. Not only will these Investment Highlights reinforce concepts discussed in the text, but they should stimulate student interest in the subject matter and provide a basis for class discussion.
6. Carefully chosen SUGGESTED READINGS are presented at the end of each chapter.

Acknowledgments

With this edition, our debt grows to an increasingly large number of individuals. We have especially benefited from critical and constructive comments given by our professional colleagues. We greatly appreciate the assistance of Sheldon Balbirer, Shyan Bhandari, William Black, Gerald Blum, Keith Boles, Steven Campbell, Eric Chang, Eugene Drzycimski, Timothy Gallagher, Arthur Gudikunst, Elizabeth Hennigar, Thomas Howe, A. James Ifflander, Stanley Jacobs, Paul Jessup, Timothy Johnson, Jaroslaw Komarynsky, Harold Krogh, David Peterson, Mario Picconi, James Rice, Bruce Rubin, Anthony Sanders, Elton Scott, John Shelton, Thomas Stanton, Doug Sweetland, Pochara Theerathorn, David West, and Richard Williams. G. Naidu of Illinois State University provided valuable comments on the chapter on global investing. Over the years, a number of graduate students at the University of Iowa assisted in the collection and organization of data and also provided feedback from the perspective of the student. We especially appreciate the contributions of Kathy Edwards, Barbara Riskedahl, David Spencer, Martin Strabala, Randy Woolridge, Mir Zaman, and Lyle Bowlin. Finally, we would like to express our gratitude to our families and to our colleagues at the University of Iowa, at Illinois State University, and at Ohio State University.

RICHARD A. STEVENSON
IOWA CITY, IOWA

EDWARD H. JENNINGS
COLUMBUS, OHIO

DAVID LOY
NORMAL, ILLINOIS

Part

Investment Essentials

1

The three chapters in this part set the stage for investment decision making. Chapter 1 presents an introduction to the risk and return aspects of investing, including the reasons for investing, the types of investments that are available, and the returns that have been generated in the past by different types of investments. Chapter 2 looks at the organization of the financial markets and how investors may participate in these markets. The types of investment information available and the general usefulness of this information are discussed in Chapter 3.

Chapter 1

Investments: Risk and Return Decisions

Key Concepts

bond
capital appreciation
collateral value
consumption
creditor claim
current income
equity claim
financial assets
inflation
interest rate risk
investment objectives
liquidity
marketability
negotiability
partial ignorance
pension plan
portfolio
principal
purchasing power risk
real assets
real earnings
risk
risk premium
systematic risk
uncertainty
unsystematic risk

Chapter Outline

At the end of 1986, two well-known names appeared on the lists of the ten best and ten worst performers on the New York Stock Exchange for that year. The fourth best performer was Reebok International with a gain of 152.7 percent and the eighth worst performer was Western Union with a decline of 67.7 percent. A maker of trendy athletic shoes, Reebok had a fourfold profit gain in the first nine months of 1986 as compared with its 1985 performance. Western Union, a long-troubled telecommunications firm, tried but failed at a financial restructuring. These two examples show the risks and returns that are possible with investments.

Making prudent and financially rewarding investment management decisions requires the acquisition of knowledge about investment alternatives. With the myriad investment alternatives available in today's complex economic environment, investors must often spend considerable time just learning about investment opportunities. Individuals must also develop the skills needed to evaluate those opportunities. Highly developed skills help in the evaluation of the potential risk and return associated with any investment decision.

Because we cannot be certain about the future, the investment decision that requires giving up some current *consumption* is a risky decision. We know what we can consume now, but any investment alternative we use as a savings vehicle to enhance our future consumption may not fulfill our return expectations. Our future consumption potential may be less than our present purchasing power if investment prices are low when we liquidate. We would incur less risk by consuming now, as the poor performance of Western Union's stock during 1986 illustrates. On the other hand, the Reebok example highlights the rewards made possible by assuming a potential risk that also offers a favorable potential return.

In order to be successful, investors need to develop goals or stated objectives. The first section of this chapter examines *investment objectives.* A number of extremely important policy decisions, such as the optimum percentage of funds to invest in common stocks, are presented. Many of these investment management decisions can be approached by classifying investment alternatives in different ways. These classifications are the subject of the second major section of the chapter. Historical stock and bond returns that investors can use to help predict the future are examined in the third section. Section four introduces the nature of risk. The importance of the investment decision-making process for both individuals and institutions is covered in section five, and section six discusses careers in the investments field.

Seeking Investment Returns

The principal objective in making investments is to earn a return that compensates for the risk of the investment. In order to achieve this main objective for investors experiencing widely varying economic circumstances, a more precise approach to specifying investment goals is often desirable. We will first distinguish between return in the form of current income and return gained through capital appreciation. Next, we will examine investment management objectives such as the safety of principal, liquidity, ease of management, and collateral value.

Income

Investors realize investment income either as *current income* in the form of interest and dividends or as *capital appreciation* in the form of an increase in the security's price. Under some circumstances, current income is either necessary or highly desirable. A retired individual often needs a high level of current income to supplement income from Social Security or other pension plans. Current income is often desirable when an individual or institutional investor is in a very low or zero marginal tax bracket. A marginal tax bracket is the tax rate that applies to the last dollar earned by the taxpayer.

Current investment income may be sacrificed in favor of growth potential. The need for current income for an individual varies greatly depending on such factors as the age, wealth, and noninvestment income of that investor. During an investor's most productive working years, current income may not be an important investment objective. When current consumption needs are satisfied by salary income, growth of principal in the form of capital appreciation often becomes an important investment objective.

Similarly, institutional investors balance the need for current income with the desire for growth in the market value of the investments over time. An endowment fund of a university presents just such an investment goal dilemma. With tuition costs rising at a more rapid rate than the general cost of living, the investment manager of an endowment fund would like to generate a high level of current income. This income could provide matriculating students with financial aid to ease the burden of college expenses. However, if the value of the investments grows too slowly and tuition continues to increase, the fund would be unable to generate adequate financial aid to defray college costs for future students. A university must be careful not to "eat its seed corn."

Safety of Principal

We will define the *principal* of an investment as the amount of the original investment. High-quality investments are those that allow the principal to remain intact. Many investors meet the objective of safety of principal by purchasing high-quality corporate bonds and U.S. Treasury securities. While these types of investments may help to keep the dollar value of the portfolio reasonably constant, *inflation* may reduce its purchasing power. Hence, investors achieve safety of principal only if they seek enough growth in the value of a portfolio to offset changes in the cost of living. A *portfolio* is a combination of all investments (or assets) owned by an individual or an organization.

Liquidity

Liquidity involves two elements from the viewpoint of an investor. The first element relates to the ability to sell an investment quickly at a price close to the last trade for comparable assets. *Marketability* would be a good description of this liquidity attribute, and many assets would meet this qualification. A second element of liquidity is the ability to turn an asset into cash quickly at a value close to the original amount of the investment. Only high-quality investments with short maturities meet this second test of liquidity. As the investment time horizon of the investor becomes shorter, the goal of preserving the original amount of the investment becomes more important.

Ease of Management

The growth of financial institutions specializing in investment management has been rapid in recent years. This growth is a manifestation of the investor's desire to be relieved of the difficult and time-consuming tasks of investment management. The desire for ease of management in investment decisions often varies according to the investment education of the investor and other demands on the investor's time.

Collateral Value

The *collateral value* of investments is another important consideration for some investors. For example, an investor may want to use a margin account to buy securities. In this type of transaction, which is described more fully in the next chapter, investors borrow money to buy securities by pledging the securities in what is known as a margin account at a brokerage firm. If the collateral behind the margin loan increases in value, the investor may be permitted to use that increased collateral value to support a larger loan. Hence, more securities may be purchased. Conversely, if the collateral pledged declines sufficiently in value, more collateral must be pledged or part of the margin loan repaid.

The collateral value of a security is often related to its quality. The higher the quality of an investment holding, the larger the percentage of its value a financial institution will normally loan. Investors who plan to borrow money for any reason in the future may find high-quality collateral an important investment consideration.

Classifying Investment Alternatives

The investment alternatives facing investors can be classified in several ways. These classifications are a reflection of the decisions that investors must make in seeking investment returns. This section examines six different ways of classifying investment alternatives.

Nature of Management

Any investor must determine whether or not to actively manage the investments or to have them managed by another person or institution. This is probably the most important decision an investor will make. If the investor decides to take a self-managed approach to investments, considerable knowledge will need to be obtained. Even if an investor decides to let an institution manage the investments, one needs information in order to make a sound choice regarding the institution doing the managing.

Nature of Asset

As shown in Exhibit 1 – 1, we can classify investments by the nature of the asset. A *financial asset* is a financial claim that is typically represented by a piece of paper such as a common stock certificate. The investor's financial claim will depend on the rights and powers of the various parties creating the claim. In addition to financial assets, many investors also own *real assets* such as real estate, art masterpieces, and antiques. Real assets have intrinsic value to investors, in contrast to the intangible nature of financial assets that have essentially no intrinsic value.

Nature of Claim

We can distinguish two different types of claims: *equity claims* and *creditor claims.* An equity claim represents an ownership interest. Common and preferred stock are the principal financial asset equity claims. A creditor claim exists when you lend money to an individual, a corporation, or other organization. Creditor claims are often called fixed-income or debt securities. Let us examine the equity and creditor nature of financial claims in more detail.

Financial Assets: Equity Claims

Equity claims held by an investor can be identified as being either directly or indirectly held. If you purchase 100 shares of the common stock of General Motors for your account, you become a direct holder of that stock. You share in the good and had fortunes of General Motors. If the automobile market is good, the company's net income may increase. Your dividend income could rise, or the price of the stock could increase. The opposite might occur if the automobile market turns down. If you decide you no longer want to own this stock, you make the decision to sell it. Investors have also been willing to hold common stock in an indirect manner. Mutual funds, examined in Chapter 16, provide investors with a convenient means of buying common stock as well as many other types of securities, with a professional manager making the investment management decisions.

Exhibit 1–1 **An Overview of Major Investment Alternatives**

Real Assets

Real Estate

apartments, office buildings, shopping centers, etc.
personal residences

Collectibles

antiques
art masterpieces
coins
gems
stamps

Financial Assets

Equity Claims

Direct

common stock: shares represent part ownership of a corporation

preferred stock: shares also represent ownership of a corporation, but the shares provide a fixed income and provide the holder with a preferred claim to income and assets

warrant: allows the holder to purchase a fixed number of shares of another security (usually common stock) for a fixed price for a fixed period of time from the company

option: gives the holder the right to buy (or sell) a fixed number of shares from (to) another investor for a fixed price for a fixed period of time

Indirect

investment company: a professionally managed investment portfolio of securities in which investors buy and sell shares or units

Creditor Claims

Provided by financial institutions

savings accounts
certificates of deposit (nonnegotiable)

Provided by the financial market

money market securities: high-quality investments of one year or less in maturity

bankers' acceptances
certificates of deposit (negotiable)
commercial paper
treasury bills

capital market securities: fixed-income securities having a maturity of more than one year

notes
bonds

Financial Assets: Creditor Claims

Another possibility is to invest in a debt security arising out of a debtor-creditor contract. For example, as the holder of a bond issued by a corporation, you are the creditor of that organization and not one of its owners. Of course, you could be the reluctant owner of the corporation's assets should default occur on the contract. Numerous creditor claims exist for the investor to purchase. Consequently, it behooves investors to learn the essentials of investing in creditor claims and the risks associated with this form of investment. To this end, we will now briefly describe some of the more important creditor claims available at financial institutions (such as commercial banks) or in the financial markets.

Financial institutions offer an almost bewildering array of savings accounts and certificates of deposit. These are the creditor claims of the financial institution—the institution has promised to repay the money according to the deposit agreement. These savings alternatives range from daily interest savings accounts to certificates of deposit with maturities of six years or longer. Financial institutions have been quite aggressive in recent years in attempting to attract savings dollars by designing new types of deposit accounts.

The creditor claims available in the financial markets run the gamut from high-quality securities with a maturity of a few weeks or months to low-quality, long-term creditor claims, sometimes known as "junk bonds." Any investor faces the problem of deciding what level of quality and maturity to seek from the many creditor claims available.

Money market securities are relatively high-quality investments with maturities of a year or less and hence are viewed as having characteristics similar to those of money. The best known of the money market securities is a U.S. Treasury bill issued by the federal government. The interest rates on treasury bills vary as general interest rates change in the money market. Other money market investment alternatives include commercial paper, bankers' acceptances, and negotiable certificates of deposit.

A longer-maturity creditor claim known as a *bond* is also available in the financial markets. Most bonds have maturities of five years or longer and tend to differ markedly from money market securities. Bonds are issued by the federal government and its agencies, state and local governments and their agencies, various for-profit corporations such as General Motors, and nonprofit organizations such as hospitals and schools. The potential bond buyer needs to consider the bond's quality, its maturity, the precise nature of the credit claim, and the trend of interest rates.

Nature of Income Stream

An important method of classifying investment alternatives is to sort them according to whether the anticipated current income is fixed or variable. An exciting investment development in recent years has been the growth of numerous types of variable return securities. These investment alternatives, known also as floating rate securities, have an interest rate that varies with general interest rate levels.

Investors often tend to think of equity claims such as common stock as variable return securities because the current income cannot always be determined with certainty and the capital appreciation is especially unpredictable. Likewise, investors tend to think of money market securities and bonds as fixed-income securities because their rate of interest is fixed at the time of issuance. However, the magnitude of interest rate fluctuations that investors have faced in recent years has caused a rethinking of these traditional classifications. The price of fixed-income securities can vary as much as or even more than prices of common stocks, causing substantial capital gains or losses on bonds.

Nature of Collateral

The essential distinction here is between an investment alternative secured by the pledge of an asset and an alternative lacking this pledge. The issuer of the security could pledge either other financial assets or real assets. An ownership position, such as holding common stock, is an unsecured position to the extent that no pledge of specific assets exists. Creditor claims may be secured by a pledge of specific assets, or they may be unsecured. Guarantees of the U.S. government are often highly valued by investors in making choices among investment alternatives.

Nature of Marketability

Investment decision makers are often interested in how easily investments may be liquidated. To be locked into a rapidly deteriorating investment is a most helpless situation. In the context of marketability, we can make two distinctions. First, we should note whether the investment is *negotiable* or *nonnegotiable.* A negotiable investment is one in which title representing ownership of the investment can be legally transferred from one party to another party. Title cannot be legally transferred to another owner in the case of a nonnegotiable investment. A nonnegotiable investment will need to provide the investor with something to compensate for the lack of negotiability. Often this something extra is a rate of return that is higher for a nonnegotiable investment compared to the same quality negotiable investment. However, negotiability may make little difference if that investment has no ready market. Hence, we are interested in whether trading occurs in our investment alternatives. The more active the trading in terms of volume, the better chance we have of getting out of our investment at a reasonable price.

Historical Returns from Stocks and Fixed-Income Securities

The main reason investors study historical rates of return from various types of assets is to use this knowledge to make better asset allocation decisions regarding such fundamental questions as how much should go to common stock investments and how much should be invested in bonds. Investors who forget the lessons of history may be doomed to repeat costly mistakes. By examining historical rates of return, investors may arrive at judgments regarding future rates of return. For example, the annual rate of return for gold during the 1972–82 period was 18 percent versus only 8 percent for common stocks. Based on this information, should investors invest heavily in gold during the next decade? The answer depends on conditions of the projected economic environment. If the next eleven years are expected to be as inflationary and turbulent politically as the 1972–82 period, perhaps gold should be a major asset holding. However, if inflationary pressures are under control and are expected to remain stable in the future, you may not need to purchase a large holding of the "disaster" insurance provided by gold.

Figure 1–1
Wealth Indexes for Investments in the U.S. Capital Markets

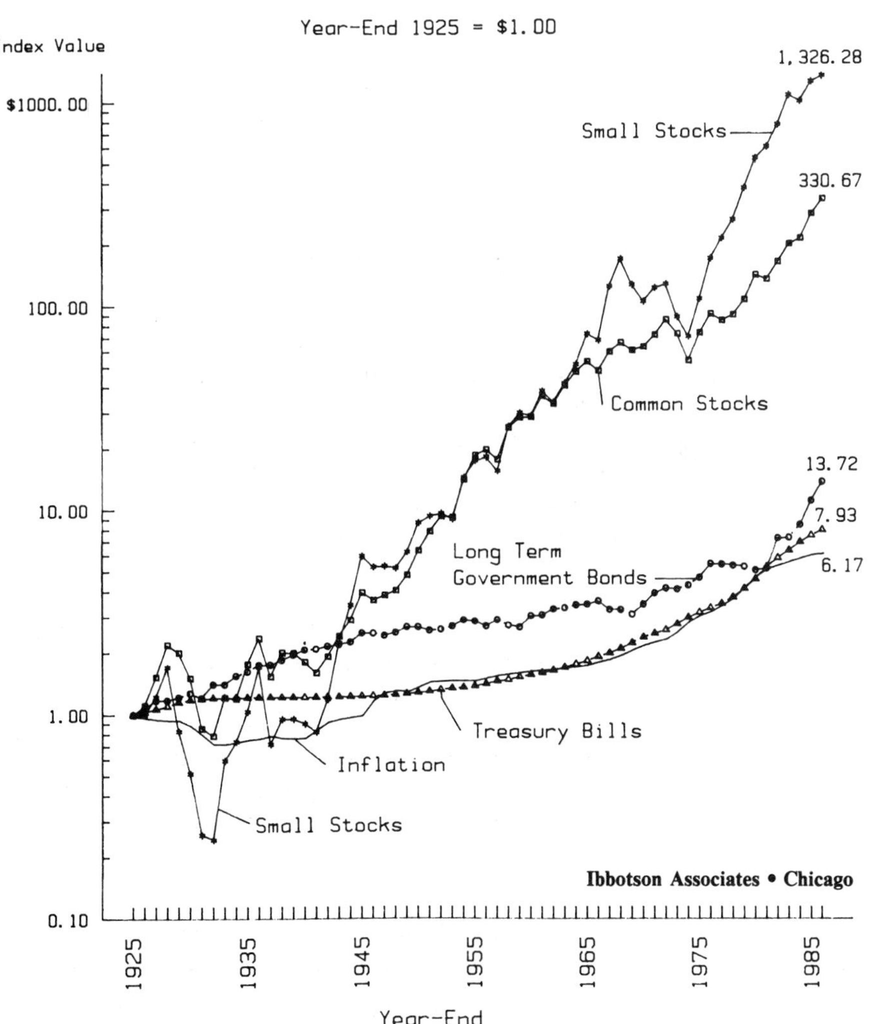

Source: Ibbotson, Roger G., and Rex A. Sinquefield, *Stocks, Bonds, Bills, and Inflation* (SBBI), 1982, updated in *SBBI 1987 Yearbook*, Ibbotson Associates, Chicago.

Table 1–1
Annual Returns, 1972–86, for Various Asset Classes and the Consumer Price Index

	1972 –82	**1983**	**1984**	**1985**	**1986**
Financial Assets					
Common stock	8	23	6	32	18
Long-term U.S. government bonds	6	1	15	31	24
Real Assets					
Oil	30	−7	−2	−1	−32
Gold	18	−15	−19	9	24
Art: old masters	8	17	16	4	5
Consumer Price Index	8	4	4	4	1

Figure 1–1 shows the wealth indexes for various types of investments in the United States capital markets from 1926 through 1986. Studying these performance trends may be helpful in the asset allocation decision. Over long periods of time, common stocks have outperformed the various fixed-income investments and inflation, as represented by the consumer price index. Because any investment could dominate for a period of ten years or less, the investment time horizon is obviously important. The riskiness of common stocks relative to bonds, treasury bills, and inflation is clearly evident from Figure 1–1, which shows percentage changes. The relative riskiness may be an important element in the asset allocation decision.

Table 1–1 shows the compound annual rate of return for the 1972–82 period for various real assets as well as for common stocks, bonds, and the consumer price index. This period was not a good one for the holder of financial assets, but real assets performed well during this inflationary period. After the rate of inflation subsided, financial assets outperformed real assets. This can be noted for the 1983–86 period in Table 1–1. We now have a partial answer to our question regarding the performance of gold versus common stocks during the 1983–1993 period that we raised earlier. For the 1983–86 period, gold provided an average annual return of 0 percent while common stocks returned 20 percent.

What Is Risk?

During 1985, the common stock of The Gap, Inc., went from 20⅝ to 62¾ for an increase of 204 percent. The common stock of Mohawk Data Sciences fell from 10⅞ to 2½ for a decline of 77 percent. During the same year, the general stock market rose about 32 percent. An investor considering the purchase, at the start of 1985, of either The Gap, Inc., or Mohawk Data Sciences probably would not have correctly anticipated either return. This is the essence of risk—the inability to forecast future returns accurately.

We describe this lack of knowledge regarding future events by several different names such as risk, uncertainty, or partial ignorance. *Risk* is a probability factor that can be assigned to a possible outcome when the decision maker knows all possible future outcomes of a given decision. *Uncertainty* exists when the decision maker knows all possible future outcomes but cannot, for whatever reason, assign probabilities to the possible outcomes. *Partial ignorance* is a condition in which some or all of the possible outcomes are unknown.

These definitions are quite arbitrary, and risk and uncertainty are treated in the investment field as though they were synonymous. Actually, every decision probably represents the partial ignorance condition. Clearly, every decision has an element of uncertainty. In the life insurance industry, mortality tables are well-developed and based upon enormous quantities of actual experience. Yet, an individual insures for the unforeseeable future, and the fact that a twenty-year-old female has a life expectancy of fifty-seven years does not necessarily imply that the same condition will exist in the future. In fact, life expectancy has increased markedly during the past century, but this again does not suggest the same increase will occur during the next one hundred years.

The Concept of a Risk Premium

Table 1–2 compares long-term corporate bond and common stock returns for varying periods of time. These historical return data can be used to calculate risk premiums. A *risk premium* is the added return investors

Table 1–2
Corporate Bond and Common Stock Returns, Annual Rates of Return for Selected Periods of Time

Period	Common Stocks	Corporate Bonds
1926–86	12.1%	5.3%
1926–36	8.1	7.1
1937–46	4.4	3.5
1947–56	18.4	1.0
1957–66	9.2	3.3
1967–76	6.6	5.4
1977–86	13.8	10.0
One-Year Period		
Worst: stocks, 1931; bonds, 1969	−43.3	−8.1
Best: stocks, 1933; bonds, 1982	54.0	43.8
Five-Year Period		
Worst: stocks, 1928–32	−12.5	
bonds, 1965–69		−2.2
Best: stocks, 1950–54 and 1951–55	23.9	
bonds, 1982–86		22.4

Source: Stocks, Bonds, Bills, and Inflation, 1987 Yearbook, Ibbotson Associates, Chicago, 1987.

receive (or can reasonably expect to receive) by taking on increasing amounts of risk. Risk premiums can be identified for any two classes of securities. A basic risk premium is the added return that investing in common stocks has produced over a long period of time compared to investing in long-term corporate bonds. During the 1926–86 period, common stocks provided a return of 12.1 percent while long-term corporate bonds yielded 5.3 percent for a risk premium of 6.8 percentage points. Hence, if long-term bonds are yielding 9.0 percent in the market, an investor might reasonably expect common stocks to return 15.8 percent—the current bond yield plus the risk premium. Risk premiums allow investors to consider whether investing in a particular type of security is likely to produce the return estimated. For example, do common stock prices in the market suggest that a 15.8 percent annual return is a reasonable expectation?

Although common stocks have shown long-run superiority, bond returns have been less variable. For example, the worst five-year investment period for bonds was 1965–69 when the average annual return was minus 2.2 percent. While bond returns were generally low compared to stocks, the return in most periods was positive and fluctuated within a narrow range. Apparently, a positive relationship exists between risk and return. Average returns from common stocks were greater than for bonds, but the risk of substantial loss in any one period was greater for stocks than for the high-grade corporate bonds.

Historical returns may not be good forecasting data for short periods of time. The annual total returns for treasury bonds and common stocks for 1984, 1985, and 1986 were as follows:

	1984	**1985**	**1986**
Common stocks	6.3%	32.2%	18.5%
Treasury bonds	15.4	31.0	24.4

As inflation abated during this period, interest rates declined and bond prices went up. The important point is that high-quality bonds provided a better return than common stocks during this three-year period. The volatility of interest rates in recent years has shown that bonds may no longer be the "widow and orphan" securities that many investors believe them to be.

Classifications of Risk

Risk in an investment may be categorized as either systematic or unsystematic, as outlined in Exhibit 1–2. We will also discuss other traditional risk classifications.

Systematic

Systematic risk results from being involved with the market. If an investor invests in common stocks, that investor accepts the possibility that the market may go down or that the economy will do poorly. There is no

Exhibit 1–2 **Two Methods of Risk Classification**

1. *Systematic (Nondiversifiable)*	*Unsystematic (Diversified)*
Risks associated with economy and security market	Risks that are unique to an industry or a company

2. a. Purchasing power (inflation) risk
   b. Interest rate risk
   c. Market risk
   d. Business (industry) risk
   e. Political risk
   f. Psychological risk
   g. Fraud risk

way to diversify away this risk by adding more stocks. Imagine you were a passenger on the Titanic's maiden voyage. Rearranging the Titanic's deck chairs or increasing the number of chairs would not have reduced the risk you assumed by taking a seat on that vessel. However, adding assets other than common stock to a portfolio may help reduce systematic risk.

Unsystematic or Diversifiable

Unsystematic risk is risk that is associated with a particular firm or industry. An investor need not accept this type of risk. A portfolio of sufficient size will be susceptible only to systematic risk. Throughout the generally prosperous period of the early and middle 1980s, the steel industry performed poorly because of obsolete equipment, foreign competition, the availability of alternative materials such as copper and aluminum, and perhaps poor management. Whatever the reasons, the investor in steel stocks experienced the consequences of industry risk despite a good economy. For example, Standard & Poor's steel stock index declined 26.9 percent during the 1980–85 period while the general market went up 55.3 percent. The risk of the individual firm or that risk that is unique to the firm is exemplified by the auto industry since World War II. As a whole, the industry has done well, yet Studebaker, Kaiser, Hudson, and the DeLorean are today footnotes to history.

Risk has traditionally been classified into purchasing power risk, interest rate risk, market risk, business and industry risk, psychological risk, and fraud risk.

Purchasing Power Risk

Purchasing power risk is the possibility that future earnings will not command the goods and services possible with current dollars. A 10 percent investment return during a period when the inflation rate is 10 percent results in the investor being no better off than before in terms of the use of the earnings. The *real earnings* in this case are zero. With an uncertain inflation rate, any investment contains risk even if the investment's monetary return is certain. Hence, a bond issued by the U.S. government is risky even though its monetary return is certain.

We saw that common stocks have done quite well even after the returns are adjusted for inflation, but this favorable outcome requires a long investment horizon. In this context, common stocks are said to be an inflation hedge because they protect the investor from purchasing power risk. Bonds with fixed returns have far more long-run purchasing power risk. Hence, if inflation is expected, the typical advice is to buy common stocks. If deflation is expected, bonds become more desirable. But this advice applies only on average and for long investment horizons.

Interest Rate Risk

Interest rate risk is the potential for loss of principal owing to changes in the general level of interest rates. Suppose an investment promises to pay \$105 at the end of a one-year period. If the interest rate in the market for this quality of investment is 5 percent, the price of the investment is \$100. If the market interest rate changes to 10 percent, the price of the investment should fall to \$95.45.

Interest rate risk is closely related to an investor's time horizon. For a ten-year investment horizon, one may assume that interest rate risk can be avoided simply by purchasing a ten-year bond. Aside from the problems of bonds being callable,[1] a given interest rate can be obtained if and only if the periodic cash proceeds are reinvested at the same interest rate. If a ten-year bond is purchased for \$1,000 and promises to pay \$50 per year in current income, its yield or return will be stated as 5 percent. This assumes that the periodic cash flows are reinvested at a return of 5 percent. If the market interest rates fall below the 5 percent reinvestment rate assumption, the actual return earned on the bond will be less than 5 percent for the ten-year investor. If market interest rates rise, the ten-year return will be somewhat more than 5 percent because periodic interest receipts can be reinvested at more than 5 percent.

Market Risk

Although the impact on an individual security varies, all securities are exposed to market risk. Market risk includes such factors as business recessions or depressions and long-run changes in the tastes and consumption patterns within the economy. In addition to general economic conditions, all securities are influenced by general stock market movements that occasionally are unrelated to the actual performance of the economy. We can see that the concept of market risk is essentially identical to the systematic risk just discussed.

1. A callable bond is one in which the issuer can force redemption of the bond prior to its maturity date. They are discussed in Chapter 10.

Business and Industry Risk

Tastes and preferences change in a dynamic economy. The status of the auto industry in the late 1970s is an excellent example. Consumers expressed a strong preference for smaller cars because of substantial increases in the cost of gasoline. Given this change in preferences, the entire auto industry as well as associated industries needed to revise their product mix. However, by 1987 the real cost of gasoline had declined for five straight years. As a result of this and an improving economy, sales of larger cars increased substantially.

New products and technology also produce dynamic changes. Products with origins external to the industry, as was the case with airlines taking passengers from the railroads, may affect the entire industry. But technology also operates at the production and marketing levels, as exemplified by the use of computers to handle *just-in-time* inventory systems or to perform *real-time* market research using computer scanning devices at grocery checkout lanes.

Political Risk

Political risk may arise from either domestic or foreign sources. Changes in domestic tax laws, such as the elimination of preferential treatment on certain capital gains on investments, are always possible and may have an impact on investments.

Psychological Risk

Success in making investments may be related to an investor's personality. Certain individuals probably should not directly own assets such as common stocks and bonds. Investors who are whiplashed by their emotions may consistently make poor investment decisions. One writer listed the following qualities as being associated with chronic losers in the market: "intellectually lazy, gullible, greedy, irrational, indecisive, prone to extremes of optimism and pessimism, and readily infected by the emotions of the crowd."[2] To the extent that these human traits exist in all individuals, they must be overcome by education and experience if one wishes to achieve investment success. Even the cool-headed investor soon learns that the market has a personality of its own. Fads may exist with regard to certain types of investments such as new issues, energy stocks, gambling stocks, or stock options. The investor needs to keep in mind that these fads may vanish as quickly as they appeared.

2. Charles J. Rolo, "Portrait of the Ideal Investor," *Finance* (July 1967): 32–33.

Fraud Risk

"A fool and his money are soon parted," goes the old saying. How much time an investor spends evaluating business risk, interest rate risk, and all other forms of risk will matter little if the investment being considered is fraudulent. Frauds in the securities business are not unknown. Fortunately, they are uncommon, but when they occur, huge sums of money are often involved.

Can investors avoid possible frauds? Whether a particular investment is an honest venture is difficult to know with certainty, but investors can keep several indicators in mind. Any investment that is being promoted heavily and that appears to promise returns substantially above what one would expect to be reasonable should be seriously questioned by the investor. Additionally, mixing heavy doses of religion or politics with investment decisions may open the door to fraudulent schemes.

Importance of Investment Decisions

Investment decisions are important for many reasons, both for individuals and institutions. A major reason is simply that the assets held by individuals and institutions often represent enormous sums of money. These assets may include the savings of individuals that will provide financial security both during the working years and, more importantly, during the nonworking years of retirement. The private savings plans of individuals and employer-provided pension plans create this financial security blanket. In addition, investments in such places as endowment funds or insurance companies provide a measure of safety for institutions that may face difficult times in the future. This section focuses on the assets controlled by individuals and major financial institutions, with an emphasis on recent asset growth.

Growth of Individuals' Financial Assets

Figure 1–2 shows the substantial increase in the financial assets held by individuals. From 1970 through 1986, the yearly increase in financial assets went from $82 billion to about $500 billion. The total increase in financial assets grew at an annual rate of 12 percent between 1970 and 1986.

Institutional Investment Decisions

Rapid growth in the number and size of institutions managing investment funds has also occurred. This section examines the nature and importance of these institutions, which can be broadly referred to as the financial services industry. We will focus our comments on the growth and importance of life insurance companies and pension funds.

Figure 1–2
Annual Increase in Individuals' Financial Assets, 1970–86

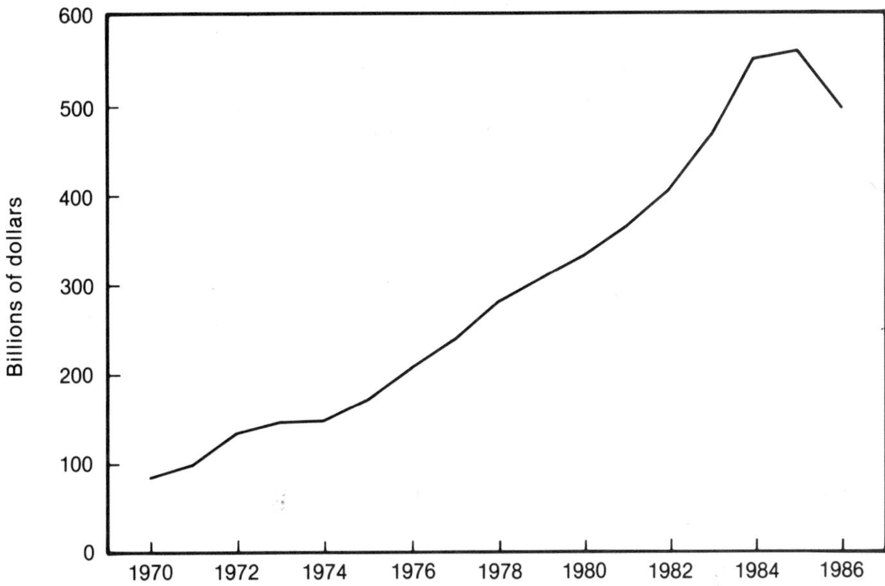

Source: Economic Report of the President, 1986.

Life Insurance Companies

Life insurance companies are important because they manage impressive sums of money. As of year-end 1986, the assets of life insurance companies were over $910 billion.

To the extent that life insurance, in the event of premature death, provides for the possibility of an immediate estate and freedom from worry about the needs of beneficiaries, they allow individuals to invest in other, more risky ventures in pursuit of higher rates of return. In this regard, insurance in force performs in much the same manner as pension fund participation. A pension fund satisfies one's financial obligations during the retirement years, and life insurance aids in satisfying the financial needs of a beneficiary upon the death of the insured.

Pension Plans

We are interested in how pension funds may be classified, their growth, and the impact of pension plans on institutions managing these funds and on the individuals participating in these pension plans. Pension plans may first be classified into public and private plans. Public pension plans are plans administered by federal, state, and local governments as well as the Social Security System. Private pension plans may be either sponsored or individual plans. Sponsorship may be provided by either a for-profit corporation or a nonprofit organization. For example, TIAA-CREF is a pension system whose principal function is to provide pension

Figure 1–3
Annual Increase in Individuals' Financial Assets, 1970–86

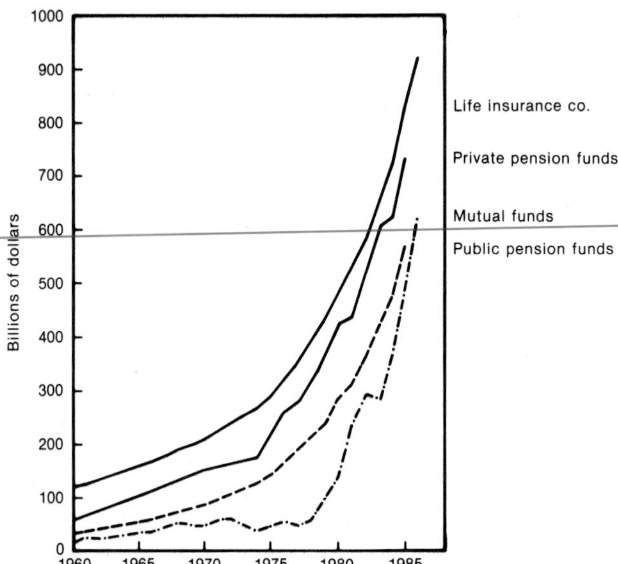

Source: Ibbotson, Roger G., and Rex A. Sinquefield, *Stocks, Bonds, Bills, and Inflation* (SBBI), 1982, updated in *SBBI 1987 Yearbook,* Ibbotson Associates, Chicago.

benefits for the faculties and staffs of colleges and universities, independent schools, and other nonprofit educational institutions. At year-end 1986, 3,813 institutions were participating in TIAA-CREF, and 890,000 participants were accumulating annuity benefits. Another 175,000 participants were receiving annuity benefits. Individual pension plans include Keogh Plans and Individual Retirement Accounts (IRAs).

The rapid growth of pension plans during the past two decades, as shown on Figure 1–3, has profound implications for the financial asset planning done by individual investors as well as for the health of the economy. We can identify three major impacts resulting from this growth in pension plans. First, retirement plans provide substantial amounts of income to retired persons and their dependents. The pension plans help to finance the retirement years of an individual. For many individuals, public and private pension plans represent their main source of retirement income, even though one of the objectives of a life-long investments program is to prevent this situation from occurring.

We have already noted the second impact of the rapid growth of pension plans. To the extent that persons or families experience an increase in their financial well-being as a result of pension plan participation, an "institutional security blanket" is created. This security blanket allows for more risky private investments. A third impact pension plans have is one that is important for the whole economy. Because public and private pension plans have grown rapidly, they have become an important source of capital for corporations, governments, and other organizations needing money from the nation's financial markets. This growth not only fuels the economy but also creates many employment opportunities in the investment management area.

Careers in the Investments Field

The growth noted in most areas of investments and financial services means that good employment opportunities in this field have been generated over the years and will undoubtedly continue to be generated. Four principal areas exist in which one might seek employment: (1) sales, (2) security or market analysis, (3) financial planning and consulting, and (4) portfolio management. Let us briefly examine each of these four areas from the standpoints of education required, potential employers, and other considerations such as certifications that would be desirable.

Sales

The greatest number of potential employment opportunities within the investments field probably exists in the sales area. Typical jobs would be a registered representative or account executive at a brokerage firm or a financial services officer at a financial institution. Although a college degree is probably not essential for these positions, having one should improve one's chances of getting a sales position. Sales positions are often stepping stones to managerial positions within a firm.

Security or Market Analysis

Positions involving security or market analysis are available at such places as commercial banks large enough to have an active trust department, insurance companies, investment banking firms, and investment management advisory companies. An individual could work independently in this area and even publish a newsletter, but might have difficulty establishing a clientele. A master's degree is often required for these positions because a great deal of competition exists for relatively few jobs. In addition, an individual might want to study and obtain a charter from the Institute of Chartered Financial Analysts (C.F.A.).

The Institute of Chartered Financial Analysts was established in 1959. The institute fosters high standards of professional conduct for security analysts and portfolio managers. One vehicle for encouraging professional conduct is the sponsorship and enforcement of a code of ethics including rigorous procedures for dealing with complaints from the public regarding the conduct of a C.F.A.

One of the principal activities of the institute is to prepare and administer a series of three day-long examinations leading to the awarding of the professional designation, C.F.A. The C.F.A. Preliminary Examination (C.F.A. I) examines the tools of economic analysis and the structure of the financial markets, stressing the analysis of investment securities. C.F.A. II deals with applied financial analysis. C.F.A. III tests one's skills in investment management. The emphasis in this examination is on formulating investment policy decisions within the framework of the existing accounting, economic, financial, and legal environment. These three examinations are given once a year and must be passed in order. C.F.A. Examinations II and III have an occupational and experience requirement.

Financial Planning and Consulting

Personal financial planning may well be the fastest growing area in the investments field. A number of individuals and organizations, such as insurance companies, provide financial planning. This service commonly includes a computerized analysis. Relevant details of an individual's current financial status are entered into the computer, and a financial plan to be followed in the future is generated along with specific investment recommendations.

A college degree is normally required for this occupation, and someone having a master's degree is in a much better position to obtain employment. A broad knowledge of the varied aspects that relate to personal financial planning is required. This would range from knowing what investment alternatives are available to understanding legal considerations in estate planning. In order to enhance the professional status of this activity, a program of study leading to the awarding of the professional designation Certified Financial Planner (C.F.P.) has been established.

Portfolio Management

The field that may be the most exciting to many individuals is portfolio management. We have noted that the amount of money under institutional management has been growing very rapidly, and someone must manage these funds. A college degree is probably required for this area, and a master's degree is often essential for landing the job, but one's staying power will depend on the performance of the portfolio under management. This is a highly competitive field. If your portfolio performs poorly, you are likely to lose your job.

Management of a common stock portfolio may seem to be the more glamorous profession, but employment opportunities within the fixed-income area can be as interesting, given the variability of interest rates in recent years. In addition, the importance of such investments as municipal bonds and the development of many new forms of fixed-income investments and fixed-income management strategies have stimulated new interest in what was formerly viewed as a rather dull area of portfolio management.

Summary

Investing is an activity of risks and returns. Investors take on risk to earn a return on their investments that is higher than can be earned from so-called riskless investments such as treasury bills. To accomplish the goal of earning a relatively high return, an essential task for investors is to develop investment objectives so that an informed decision can be made regarding risk and return trade-offs. How much current income is desired, and can some of the current income be sacrificed to attempt to achieve price appreciation? How safe an investment is desired? Does the investor want to manage the investments, or should a professional manager perform this task? These are just a few examples of the questions that investors must consider in deciding on the appropriate risk and return combination.

Risk is a somewhat elusive concept, which is one reason why making good investments is so difficult. We can distinguish between diversifiable and nondiversifiable risk. Diversifiable risk, also called unsystematic risk, can effectively be eliminated by purchasing enough different investments. Clearly, investment mix is a critical element of investment success. Nondiversifiable risk, also called systematic risk, cannot effectively be eliminated by buying more of the same type of asset. If an investor owns only common stock and the stock market goes down, the investments will probably not produce a positive rate of return. Buying different types of assets may be somewhat helpful in reducing the impact of systematic risk. In virtually all situations, the importance of investors carefully examining the period of time for which investments can be prudently made is fundamental. Determining an investment time horizon will help the investor identify the proper degree of risk.

Suggested Readings

BAUMAN, W. SCOTT. *Performance Objectives of Investors.* Occasional Paper Number 2. Charlottsville, VA.: Financial Analysts Research Foundation, 1975, 29–50.

BERNSTEIN, PETER L. "What Rate of Return Can You Reasonably Expect?" *Journal of Finance* (May 1973): 273–82.

GRAUER, ROBERT, and NILS HANKANSSON. "A Half-Century of Returns on Levered and Unlevered Portfolios of Stocks, Bonds, Bills, With and Without Small Stocks." *Journal of Business* (April 1986): 287–318.

IBBOTSON ASSOCIATES, INC. *Stocks, Bonds, Bills and Inflation: 1987 Yearbook.* Chicago: Ibbotson Associates, 1987.

SOLDOFSKY, ROBERT M. "Risk and Return for Longterm Securities: 1971–1982." *Journal of Portfolio Management* (Fall 1984): 57–64.

WILSON, JACK W., and CHARLES P. JONES. "A Comparison of Annual Common Stock Returns: 1871–1925 with 1926–86." *Journal of Business* (April 1987): 239–58.

Questions

1. Define investment. Why do people invest?
2. What are the factors an investor might consider when setting investment goals? Briefly explain why these factors are important.

3. What are the basic differences between real and financial assets from an investment standpoint?

4. Explain the general types of financial assets available to investors.

5. The return from an investment can come from current income or from capital appreciation. Under what circumstances would it be more desirable to have the major portion of the return come in the form of capital appreciation? Current income?

6. What is the importance of the consumer price index (or inflation) in the investment decision?

7. Why is the time horizon an important concept in investment management decisions?

8. Human emotions can be a critical aspect in investment decisions. Why may it be important to try to compensate for the outcome of decisions made involving human emotions?

9. Both public and private pension plans have grown rapidly in recent years.
   (a) Of what significance is this institutional growth in planning for financial security in retirement years?
   (b) What has been the impact of the growth of pension plan holdings?

10. Based on the historical evidence presented in the chapter regarding the return earned on common stocks, what would you use at the present time as the appropriate discount rate in calculating the present value of a stock? What factors other than the historical evidence might cause you to alter your discount rate?

11. Bonds have earned a long-term rate of return substantially below the long-term rate of return earned from common stock investments. Therefore, the logical conclusion is that bonds have no place in the portfolio of an investor. Do you agree? Why or why not?

12. Risk can normally be classified into risk that can be diversified away and risk that is a part of the system and cannot be diversified away. Give some examples of each type of risk.

13. Do you think any relationship exists for the individual investor between market risk and psychological risk?

14. What is the nature of a risk premium? Of what value is the concept to the investor at any given point in time?

Chapter 2

Investor Participation in Financial Markets

Key Concepts

agent transaction
best efforts offering
bid-asked spread
block
blue-sky law
brokerage commission
call loan rate
capital market
cash account
competitive bidding
discount brokerage house
diversification
fourth market
initial margin
intrastate offering
investment banking
limit order
maintenance margin
margin account
margin call
market order
match
money market
NASD
negotiated commission
negotiated underwriting
odd-lot
organized exchange
over-the-counter market
primary market
principal transaction
registration by coordination
registration by qualification
restricted account
rights offering
round-lot
seat
secondary distribution
secondary market
short sale
SIPC
specialist
standby underwriting
stock ahead
stop buy order
stop order
syndicates
third market
underwriter
uptick

Chapter Outline

The economic strength of the United States is partially the result of strong and efficient financial markets. In a broad sense, a financial market includes all financial transactions between a user of funds and a supplier of funds. For example, when you place funds in a local financial institution such as a bank, a savings and loan association, or a credit union, you engage in a financial market transaction in the broad meaning of the term. When you borrow from a financial institution, a financial transaction is involved. However, for many aspects of this book, a narrower view of financial markets is appropriate. Much of our discussion of financial markets will be confined to relatively long-term, impersonal financial instruments such as stocks and bonds. These long-term securities trade in the *capital market* in contrast to securities with a maturity of a year or less (short-term). The market for short-term securities is known as the *money market.*

Functions of Financial Markets

The basic function of a financial market is to bring buyers and sellers together so that transactions can occur. In bringing buyers and sellers together, the financial markets provide liquidity, allow for diversification on the part of investors, and assist in the allocation of capital by allowing for price discovery.

To Provide Liquidity and Marketability

The potential for resale of an asset is an important aspect of a financial market transaction. As noted in Chapter 1, *liquidity* is the ability to turn an asset into cash quickly without a significant change from the current market price. A second and often very important attribute of liquidity is that the proceeds from the sale closely approximate the amount originally invested. For example, daily interest savings accounts and treasury bills possess both of these liquidity characteristics to a significant degree.

Marketability is the ability to resell an asset without encountering an extended delay. Highly liquid assets are typically assets that also have a high degree of marketability. Investors need to be concerned with the relative degree of marketability of an asset as well as its liquidity. Real estate and many other real asset holdings are much less liquid than most stocks and bonds. Well-developed financial markets provide marketability because of the activities of market makers.

To Allow for Diversification

Financial markets assist the *diversification* goals of investors along the dimensions of size, maturity, and quality. Investors can choose to purchase a small portion of a stock or debt issue of an organization rather than large amounts of stock or bonds. To the extent that financial markets offer already well-diversified portfolios in relatively small units, such as in the situation of the investment companies discussed in Chapter 16, the goal of diversification is more easily achieved. In a similar manner, the financial market offers investors an array of investment alternatives of widely varying maturity and quality especially for fixed-income securities.

To Assist in Capital Allocation

The price of money is the interest rate charged on debt securities or the anticipated rate of return in the case of common stocks. The forces of supply and demand within the financial sector of the economy determine this price. The price in turn serves to allocate scarce capital resources among the potential users. Of course, legislatively determined actions, such as interest rate ceilings, can also influence this allocation process.

Understanding Market Activities

Agents versus Principals

One of the difficulties in understanding the nature of transactions in the financial markets is that transactions occur in different forms. In addition, these different transactions could be handled by the same party acting in a different capacity each time. Because of these considerations, we distinguish between an agent transaction and a principal transaction.

An *agent transaction* occurs when a third party acts only to facilitate the transaction between the two main parties (i.e., the agent's "best effort" is given). For example, a real estate firm typically acts as an agent when bringing the buyer and the seller together so that a transaction can occur. In an agent transaction, the third party *does not have* any capital at risk. The real estate firm does not normally purchase a house from the seller and then attempt to find a buyer for the house.

In a *principal transaction,* the third party *does have* capital involved in the transaction. If the real estate firm actually purchased the house from the seller and then attempted to find a buyer, the firm would then be a principal in the transaction. In such a case, title to the house has passed from the seller to the real estate firm. The real estate firm now owns the house, has money tied up in the transaction, and is taking the risks associated with the ownership of the house. Of primary concern is the fact that the real estate firm, as a principal in the transaction, may have difficulty finding a buyer for the house and may lose money when the sale is finally made.

The efficient functioning of the financial markets is largely the result of organizations willing to act as principals in transactions. On most of the organized exchanges, a *specialist,* a type of market maker, acts as a principal and is charged with maintaining an orderly market. This means the specialist's function is to buy when no one else wants to buy and to sell when no one else wants to sell. Over the long run, the specialist should make money for providing this economic function by selling shares for more than their purchase price. In other words, the specialist makes money as a result of the *spread* between the purchase price and the selling price.

The specialist system is not without its problems. With the growth of institutional trading over the years in the financial markets, the specialists on the New York Stock Exchange sometimes appear overwhelmed by the trading activity and the volatility of the market. For example, in December 1982 the small specialist firm of Rothenberg Stuart experienced marketmaking problems with the Warner Communications Inc. stock assigned to it. After a negative financial projection for Warner's Atari unit, Rothenberg Stuart was deluged with sell orders and halted all trading in Warner Communications from 3:16 P.M. one day until after 3 P.M. the next day. However, Jefferies & Co., a brokerage firm on the West Coast that was not a member firm of the New York Stock Exchange, traded Warner during this period.

Not only did Rothenberg Stuart appear to have inadequate capital to continue its marketmaking function during this period but it also had to seek help to handle the paperwork generated by the order flow. In response to this event, the New York Stock Exchange established a Good Samaritans specialist squad consisting of six of the largest specialist firms. This group of specialists has agreed to assist smaller specialist firms with both personnel and capital should events similar to the Warner Communications episode occur again.

Primary versus Secondary Markets

A *primary market* is a market in which the users of capital obtain funds directly. The cash involved in the transaction is taken directly into the asset structure of the user organization. *Investment* occurs, in the economist's meaning of the term, in as much as the organization will probably use the funds productively to construct a building, buy machinery, or to increase its sales capacity. For example, when General Motors issues a *new* stock or bond, the cash goes directly to GM to spend as the needs of the business dictate. The new transaction occurs in the primary market.

The *secondary market* involves transactions in which the ultimate user of funds is not involved. In the secondary market, trades occur among investors in previously issued financial instruments. The secondary market might even be described as a market for "used" securities. By far the vast majority of capital market transactions occur in the secondary market.

Secondary markets exist in a modern economy to allow investors to commit funds to an enterprise without sacrificing the potential of recovering the investment at some unknown future date (short of liquidating the firm). If an investor requires funds, the common stock can be sold in the secondary market without directly affecting the operation of the firm. The firm can obtain long-term funds while the investor can commit funds for virtually any period of time.

Investment Highlight

Home Shopping Network (A Fad without a Fizzle?)

This investment highlight details the risks and rewards from investing in a new retailing concept.

Description

In May 1986, a Clearwater, Florida, company named Home Shopping Network went public at a price of $18 a share. Adjusted for subsequent three-for-one and two-for-one splits, the shares in early 1987 sold for almost $40 a share versus an adjusted issue price of just $3 a share. What caused this tremendous price increase?

Home Shopping sells discount merchandise via cable television, and some investors thought that this innovation would have a dramatic impact on retailing in the United States. For the quarter ending November 1986, sales increased 319 percent from the year before, and net income was up 258 percent. With 86 million shares outstanding, Home Shopping had a market value of over $3 billion versus assets of about $170 million.

Home Shopping planned to acquire ten UHF television stations and did acquire Baltimore Federal Financial, a financially troubled thrift institution, for $40 million. Home Shopping also planned a bid for C.O.M.B., a competitor, although this merger was later called off. Could recent, fast growth along with plans for acquisitions support a market capitalization for this company that was about equal to that of CBS?

Things started to simmer down when it was reported in the press that Home Shopping had experienced a 65 percent return rate on some furs that had been improperly cured. By mid-June 1987, the price of Home Shopping had declined to about 16. The price for the prior twelve months had ranged from 11⅛ to 47.

Conclusion

Investors who invest in new concepts through "fad" stocks may be taking on great potential price volatility. As a result, investors have to be nimble in order to make a profit and avoid substantial losses because stocks like Home Shopping can decline in price very quickly.

Primary Markets: Investment Banking

Investment banking is the business of either selling securities for a customer such as a corporation or helping to arrange for long-term sources of capital from financial institutions such as insurance companies. Investment banking may be viewed as either public or private. Investors are concerned with the public investment banking function because this process generates the new securities that become available for public sale. It should be noted that investment bankers sometimes offer for sale large blocks of already outstanding stock in what is known as a *secondary distribution.* The important area of private investment banking deals with the role of the investment banker acting as a liaison between organizations needing funds and financial institutions having loanable funds. The remainder of our discussion deals with public investment banking.

Investment bankers are responsible for the issuance of enormous amounts of new issues over the course of a year. Some investment banking firms, such as Merrill Lynch, do an extensive retail business and are well known to the average investor. Other investment banking firms, such as Salomon Brothers, do relatively little retail brokerage business but deal mainly with institutional clients.

Functions of the investment banker The investment banker may perform several functions in selling new securities. Investment bankers perform a *marketing function* for the issuer of securities by seeking buyers for the securities being offered for sale. To accomplish adequately the marketing of large issues of securities, investment bankers will often form *syndicates.* Normally, an originating investment banker will have primary responsibility for the issue, and syndicate members will agree to sell specific quantities of the security being marketed. When the issue is sold (or has failed), the syndicate is dissolved.

Investment bankers may act either as agents or as principals in any given transaction. If an investment banker acts as a principal, the investment banker actually purchases the issue from the firm and attempts to resell it. In this instance, the investment banker guarantees that the selling firm will receive the proceeds of the sale after the investment banker's fee and expenses. The investment banker in this principal transaction is often called an *underwriter.* We will refer to this transaction as the standard form of underwriting. The underwriter has capital at risk and may stand to lose a substantial sum of money if the issue proves to be a poor seller. As in most selling endeavors, if the merchandise is selling poorly, a clearance sale is held.

When an investment banker acts only as an agent, the transaction is called a *best efforts offering.* The investment banker does not take title to the issue, as occurs in the standard form of underwriting, but only agrees with the firm issuing the securities to give the best possible effort in marketing the securities. The investment banker in a best efforts offering does not stand to lose any risk capital. However, some injury to the investment banker's reputation might result if the issue does not sell well. In general, purchase of a best efforts offering tends to be quite risky for the investor. After all, the investment banker is not even willing to accept the risk of a successful offering.

The investment banker performs two other functions for an organization. The investment banker acts in an *advisory capacity* to the organization contemplating the sale of securities. As a specialist in financial market activities, the investment banker should be in a position to offer much useful advice regarding such matters as the form of the proposed issue, the timing of the sale of the issue, the terms that need to be placed on the issue to increase its marketability, and the size of the investment banking syndicate needed.

The investment banker also performs what is known as the *origination function* by constantly looking for smaller businesses that might benefit from "going public" by selling their common stock to the general public. In this connection, an investment banker may serve as an informal advisor to smaller companies and help nurture them to the point when it appears prudent for them to obtain additional capital by going public.

Types of investment banker offerings Another method of classifying an underwriting is to determine whether it is negotiated or is the result of a competitive bidding process. In a *negotiated underwriting,* the issuer and the investment banker discuss what the offering should be like and what the terms of the issue should be (including the price). A satisfactory agreement is reached before the offering is made.

In *competitive bidding,* the organization establishes the terms of the issue except for the price and announces that bids will be accepted up to a deadline set by the organization. The underwriting syndicate that offers the best price wins the issue and attempts to resell it at a profit. Competitive bidding is normally used only by those organizations required to do so by law or by their regulatory authority. This means that the vast majority of competitively bid offerings are made by firms in the public utility industry and by governmental borrowers.

A negotiated offering gives the investment bankers more time to sell the issue than tends to be true for an issue sold under competitive bidding. The investment bankers also have a better opportunity to tailor the terms of the issue to current capital market conditions with a negotiated issue. The major criticism of a negotiated sale is that it may increase the cost of obtaining the needed funds due to the absence of competition among investment bankers.

Another form of investment banking offering is known as *standby underwriting.* A company required by its corporate bylaws to offer stock to its shareholders under a pre-emptive right provision before offering the stock to the general public will often enter into a standby underwriting agreement with an investment banker. Stock is offered to the current stockholders first so that they may have an opportunity to retain their proportionate ownership of the firm. In a standby underwriting, the investment banker attempts to sell those shares not purchased by the firm's present shareholders.

The investment banker's compensation in a *rights offering* normally comes in two parts. A flat fee, in the nature of an insurance premium, is received for all the shares offered. A second fee, essentially a marketing fee, may be received for those shares eventually sold by the investment banker.

Secondary Markets: Organized Exchanges

An *organized exchange* provides a fixed location at which trading in various securities occurs. The New York Stock Exchange (NYSE) is the major organized stock exchange. The American Stock Exchange (AMEX) is also a national stock exchange. In addition, regional stock exchanges exist. We will examine the NYSE in detail because it is an important part of the U.S. securities markets and because the operations of other exchanges are quite similar to that of the NYSE.

New York Stock Exchange The NYSE is by far the largest of the organized exchanges in the United States. The dominance of the NYSE is the reason it is called the "Big Board." A membership in the NYSE is represented by one of its 1,366 *seats*. Most owners of seats on the NYSE are associated with brokerage firms, and most brokerage firms will have several partners who are members.

To obtain a seat on the NYSE, an individual must first find a member willing to sell a seat. In general, the price of a seat closely parallels the volume of trading and price changes of stocks listed on the exchange. Finding a seat for sale is not all that must be done before one can trade on the floor of the NYSE. A prospective member must have approval of the Board of Governors of the NYSE. This group consists of ten directors chosen from member firms, ten chosen from outside the securities industry, and the chairperson of the NYSE. An application is approved on the basis of the applicant's demonstrated financial strength and reputation within the financial community.

Each listed stock trades at an assigned post on the floor of the NYSE. When an order to buy or sell 100 shares or a multiple of 100 shares is received on the floor of the exchange, the brokerage firm's representative takes that order to the post where the stock is traded. If other brokerage firm representatives are present at the post with orders to buy or sell that same stock, the auction market will begin and a trade eventually executed between two brokerage firm representatives on behalf of their customers. Suppose a sell order arrives at the trading post and no orders are present to buy the particular stock at a price reasonably close to the price of the last trade. The specialist assigned to that stock will participate in the transaction by purchasing the stock.

Securities must be listed in order to be traded on the NYSE. Rather stringent requirements must be met for listing. These requirements deal with the earnings of the firm, the value of its assets, and the market value of its stock. In addition, at least 1.1 million publicly held shares must be outstanding, and these must be owned by at least 2,000 shareholders each owning 100 shares or more, or 2,200 shareholders owning any amount if the average monthly trading volume for the most recent six months is 100,000 shares or more. The firm must also demonstrate a national interest in its shares, conduct business in a stable industry with reasonable prospects for expansion, and provide reasonable assurance that the firm will maintain its relative position in the industry. Just because a firm is able to meet the listing requirements does not mean that the firm is either well managed or will be a good investment. Listing is not a guarantee of quality, profitability, or economic efficiency.

The general listing standards discussed apply to firms when they obtain their initial listing. However, the NYSE reserves the right to review and "delist" the shares of a corporation at any time. A temporary delisting known as a suspension occurs when trading in a given common stock is likely to get out of control because of an injection of very favorable or unfavorable news. Suspensions can be for a few hours or for several weeks. Delisting is much more serious and typically will be considered by the NYSE only when the total market value of the stock falls below a minimum of $2.5 million and a maximum of $5 million, depending on the level of stock prices. Delisting will also be considered if the public holds less than 600,000 shares or if less than 1,200 shareholders owning at least 100 shares each remain. However, delisting does not automatically occur when the above conditions are met. Delisting is not undertaken lightly. Another possibility is for the Securities and Exchange Commission to delist a security.

The American Stock Exchange and regional exchanges The American Stock Exchange (AMEX) is the second largest national securities exchange in the United States. It is often referred to as the "Little Board" in contrast to the NYSE. Its method of trading and form of organization are quite similar to those of the NYSE. The AMEX provides a national exchange market for those firms that do not qualify for NYSE listing, in as much as the AMEX's listing requirements are less stringent.

Regional exchanges, such as the Midwest Stock Exchange, the Pacific Stock Exchange, the Philadelphia-Baltimore-Washington Stock Exchange, and the Boston Stock Exchange, trade in securities that are listed on the NYSE, plus stocks in which interest is primarily local. For example, General Motors, a NYSE-listed stock, trades on the Midwest Stock Exchange. Pacific Resources trades only on the Pacific Stock Exchange.

Secondary Markets: Over-the-Counter, Third Market, and Fourth Market

In contrast to the organized exchanges, the *over-the-counter market* is not physically located in any one place. Rather, the over-the-counter market is better characterized as a communications network that facilitates the trading of securities not traded on the organized exchanges.

For each security traded in the over-the-counter market, one or more brokerage firms make a market in the security. In making a market, the brokerage firm holds an inventory of the security and buys for that inventory or sells from the inventory in order to provide liquidity to the market. In effect, the marketmaker brokerage firm acts as a principal in the market. For example, a common stock might trade in the over-the-counter market at $13 bid and $13½ asked. This price quotation does not indicate that every market maker was willing to buy 100 shares at $13 per share and sell 100 shares at $13.50. The amount of *spread* between the *bid* and the *asked* price depends on the number of market makers actively trading in this stock (competition), the number of shares outstanding and readily available for trading, and the actual trading volume for the stock. The price quotations given by the various market makers in this common stock might differ slightly from this reported quotation. Consequently, in executing an order for a customer, more than one market maker is normally contacted in an attempt to obtain the best price for the customer. For certain small over-the-counter issues, only one market maker may be available.

Third market As institutional trading in stocks increased during the 1960s, some financial institutions became increasingly disenchanted with having their transactions executed on the NYSE. Two factors appear to account for this development. First, until December 1968, no volume discounts existed on the NYSE. One would pay 100 times as much in brokerage commissions to have an order of 10,000 shares executed as one did to have a 100-share order executed. Thus, some institutions sought to find an alternative market offering lower transaction costs. Second, considerable dissatisfaction with the execution of large trades on the NYSE was expressed in terms of the price received. As previously mentioned, some institutions felt that the specialist system was not adequate to accommodate the quick purchase or sale of a large number of shares, which was desired by the institutions.

When an economic need exists, someone is usually ready to fill that need if it can be done at reasonable profit. Hence, a rationale existed for the development of a third market. Firms such as Weeden & Company were formed to handle institutional transactions in NYSE-listed stocks, but off the floor of the exchange. The third market makers act as principals in that they will buy stock for their own account when it is offered to them by an institution. They will attempt then to resell this stock to other institutions at a higher price as soon as possible. For example if the last trade of IBM on the NYSE was at $115 per share, a third market maker may be willing to buy 100,000 shares from an institution at $114½ net. This means that the institution will receive a check for $11,450,000, because no commission is paid on trades occurring on a net basis. The seller must determine if the third market maker's quotation of $114½ per share is better than could be realized on the NYSE after deducting commissions. Similar transactions occur on the sell side. The third market marker might be willing to sell 100,000 shares of IBM at $115½ net.

Fourth market The fourth market is similar to the third market except that no firm acts as a principal in the transaction. An institution desiring to sell stock can enter the necessary information into a computer under a code name and wait to see if a *match* registers. The computer acts only as an agent in the case of INSTINET, a system presently operating. Firms that wish to buy stock can also interrogate the computer to see what is for sale. The two institutions then get together to work out pricing details. The main drawback is that no one may be willing to buy the firm's stock for a considerable period of time, and this can be unfavorable in a period of rapidly falling prices.

Types of Transactions

We can classify orders in several different ways. Exhibit 2–1 shows a basic classification scheme, which we will use in the discussion that follows.

Odd-Lots, Round-Lots, and Blocks

On the floor of the major exchanges, trading normally occurs only in 100-share multiples known as *round-lots*. For example, an order to buy or sell 100 shares of AT&T common stock could be executed on the floor of the

Exhibit 2–1 **Classification of Orders**

Classification Category	*Types of Orders*
1. Quantity	odd-lot round-lot block trade
2. Price	market limit short
3. Time	market limited time period (i.e., good till cancelled)
4. Method of Payment	cash margin

NYSE. This order might also be executed on a regional exchange or in the over-the-counter market, depending on the brokerage firm handling the order. An investor desiring to enter an order for less than 100 shares gives the brokerage firm what is known as an *odd-lot* order. An order to buy or sell 140 shares of AT&T consists of both a round-lot and an odd-lot.

A transaction of 10,000 or more shares is known as a *block* trade. The number of blocks traded is a measure of the activity of institutional investors in the stock market. As we noted previously, institutions often trade blocks in the third and fourth markets in order to gain commission discounts or other price advantages.

Market Order

A *market order* instructs the broker's representative to obtain the best possible price available at the time the order reaches the market where the security is traded. This may be the price at which the last trade took place, or it may be higher or lower. In addition, the specialist may or may not participate in the trade. Let's look at an example to see what might happen.

If you call your broker regarding an order for AT&T, your broker may inform you that the last trade for AT&T common was at $24¼. You may also ask your broker to provide you with the current quotation in AT&T. Your broker replies, "$24⅛ bid, $24⅜ asked." This means that the specialist or other investors are willing to buy at least 100 shares at $24.125 per share and are willing to sell at least 100 shares at $24.375 per share. You might also ask for the size of the price quotation. The reply might be something like "5 by 10." This means that 500 shares are being sought at $24⅛ and 1,000 shares are being offered at $24⅜.

You decide to place a buy order for 100 shares of AT&T at the market, and your order is transmitted to the floor of the exchange. Your broker's representative goes to the trading post where AT&T is traded. If another broker on the floor has an order to sell at least 100 shares of AT&T at the same time that your order arrives, these two brokers may execute a transaction by auction bidding. Let's assume that they settle on a price of \$24¼—identical to the last trade. On the other hand, if no one wants to sell 100 shares of AT&T at a price close to the most recent trade, your broker will buy the 100 shares from the specialist at \$24⅜. It normally takes two or three minutes from the time an order is entered for it to reach the trading post where the stock is traded. Prices may have moved up or down in that time—especially in a stock that is being actively traded.

Limit Order

A *limit order* restricts the broker in the execution of the order to a specified price. You could have entered an order to buy 100 shares of AT&T at \$24 per share. This order would also go to the floor of the exchange. If your broker's representative cannot find anyone willing to sell 100 shares of AT&T at \$24, the broker will leave the order with the specialist. One of the specialist's functions is to maintain a book showing all limit orders that could not be filled when they arrived at the trading post. Should the price of AT&T decline from \$24¼ as a result of investors' desire to sell AT&T stock, your order to buy 100 shares of AT&T stock may be filled. However, if other limit orders were placed in the book ahead of yours (*stock ahead*), they would be filled first. Even if the stock trades at \$24, your order might not be filled.

To prevent a conflict of interest, a specialist must fill orders from the book before acting as a principal in the transaction because the specialist is charged with maintaining a fair and orderly market. The specialist would not be doing this if the price dropped sharply on small volume because the only order to buy in the specialist's book was at \$22. In this instance, the specialist would be obligated to buy the stock offered for sale at a higher price to maintain a fair and orderly market.

Limit orders may be valid for varying periods of time, depending on the wishes of the customer. Limit orders may be placed on a GTC basis—good till cancelled. They may also be made to expire at the end of the day, the end of the week, and so on. The time dimension of the limit order is up to the investor, but discretion should be used. Market prices may change rapidly as new information becomes available. A limit order may be executed at a price that turns out to be unattractive to the investor simply because the limit order could not be changed in time. In addition, some brokerage houses may charge higher commissions for limit orders to compensate for the extra work involved.

In summary, the basic function of a limit order is to establish a maximum price in a purchase transaction and a minimum price in a sale transaction. When buying, the limit order is typically placed below the market. A limit order to sell is typically placed above the market. Limit orders are more common for securities traded on an exchange than for those traded over-the-counter. Monitoring the over-the-counter market to insure proper order execution becomes more difficult.

Stop Order

A *stop order* is a special type of limit order to sell entered to protect profit on a security or to limit the amount of loss on a security. Stop orders to buy are discussed in the next section dealing with short sales. If an investor bought 100 shares of AT&T at $24¼ and the price rose to $29, the investor might decide to enter the following order: Sell 100 AT&T at $28½ stop. Should the price of AT&T fall to $28½ or less, this order would immediately become a market order to be executed at the best price available. If the sale subsequently occurs at $28¼, the investor has realized a profit on the complete transaction. This type of order would be entered if the investor thought AT&T would go up in price, but wanted to protect the profit.

Essentially the same rationale would hold if the investor bought 100 shares of AT&T at $22¼ and wanted to limit the amount of potential loss. The investor might place the following order: Sell 100 AT&T at $21 stop. This order would become a market order if AT&T dropped to $21 or below. The investor would suffer a small loss but may have sold at the beginning of a sustained decline. However, the investor may have been sold out on a minor downward price fluctuation just prior to a major upward movement in the price of AT&T.

Short Sale

In a *short sale,* stock is sold by the customer hoping the stock will decline in price. The customer does not own the stock being sold short, so the brokerage firm must borrow stock in order to make delivery of the shares sold.[1] The brokerage firm will borrow the stock from the account of another customer or perhaps from another brokerage firm. When a customer opens a margin account, the margin account agreement allows the brokerage firm to lend the securities in the account for short sale purposes. Normally, stock can be borrowed for an indefinite period of time, although the customer must eventually replace the borrowed stock and close out the transaction. The short seller must also reimburse the account from which the stock is borrowed for any dividends paid on the stock during the short sale period. At times, entering into a short sale of a security is not possible because of the inability of the brokerage firm to find shares available to borrow for the purpose of making delivery.

Suppose an investor visits Disney World and decides to look at the common stock of Disney as a possible investment. Upon investigation, the investor come to the conclusion that, at the existing price of $120 per share for Disney, the stock is substantially overvalued. Naturally, the stock should not be purchased, but it could be sold short in anticipation

1. The customer can sell short a stock that is owned. This is known as "selling short against the box." See: Theodore F. Whitmarsh, "When to Sell Securities Short Against the Box," *Financial Analysis Journal* (May–June 1972): 80–81ff, for a description of this investment technique.

of a market correction of this perceived overvaluation. The investor's brokerage firm says that Disney stock is available for shorting. An order is entered to sell 100 shares of Disney short at the market. This order can be executed only under certain conditions to be discussed below, but let us assume that the order is filled at $120 per share.

The investor must eventually purchase 100 shares of Disney to replace the stock originally borrowed. The investor has strong convictions and waits until Disney is selling for $26 per share to "cover" the short sale. The investor then buys 100 shares of Disney for $2,600. The total transaction, excluding commissions and other transaction costs, may be summarized in the following manner:

Sold short 100 Disney at $120	+$12,000
Bought 100 Disney at $26	− 2,600
Net gain on the transaction	+$ 9,400

The Disney transaction produced a fine profit for the investor. However, when the stock was shorted at $120, the potential for loss was virtually unlimited should the stock advance in price. The higher the price of Disney stock, the greater the investor's loss. To alleviate this problem, the investor could have placed a *stop buy order.* An order to buy 100 shares of Disney at $125 stop would become a market order should Disney sell for $125 or higher. The investor would then have covered the short sale at a small loss.

To prevent investors from selling stock short to drive prices down in order to buy the stock back at depressed levels (called a "bear raid"), rules exist regarding the circumstances under which short sales are allowed. A short sale can be made only on a trade in which the price of the stock advances or when the last change in price was an advance if the trade on which the short sale takes place is unchanged from the previous transaction. An advance in price is called an *uptick.* Thus, a short sale can occur on an uptick or on a zero plus uptick. A zero plus uptick simply means the situation of no price change on the trade but that the previous change was an uptick.[2]

Cash and Margin Account Orders

An account may be settled by two basic methods. If an investor purchases a security, the investor is normally expected to pay for the purchase on or before the fifth business day following the transaction. Likewise, the brokerage firm is to pay the customer any proceeds from a sale on the fifth business day following the sale. Instead of paying cash for a security (a *cash account*), the investor could elect to open a margin account with the brokerage firm and enter a margin account order.

2. Because of the ability to effectively sell short in the options market (covered in Chapter 14), changes in the short sale rules are being considered by the Securities and Exchange Commission. The rules may eventually be eliminated.

A *margin account* order is one in which the purchaser of the security uses borrowing power. To open a margin account, most brokerage houses require that the investor deposit $2,000 in the account, although some brokerage houses require a higher deposit.[3] To enter a margin account order, the investor need only specify that the transaction is to be made in the margin account previously opened.

If an investor buys 100 shares of stock on margin for a total of $6,200, the investor will pay for a portion of the stock and the brokerage firm will borrow the remaining amount on behalf of the investor. The 100 shares of stock will remain in the account and will be used as collateral for the loan. How much can the investor borrow? That depends on what the *initial margin* requirement is at the time of the purchase. The Federal Reserve Board sets initial margin requirements as part of its selective credit control authority. The amount of initial margin required has varied from 40 to 100 percent of the amount of the transaction since 1934. If the initial margin were 60 percent, the investor could borrow 40 percent of the amount of the purchase as shown in the following example:

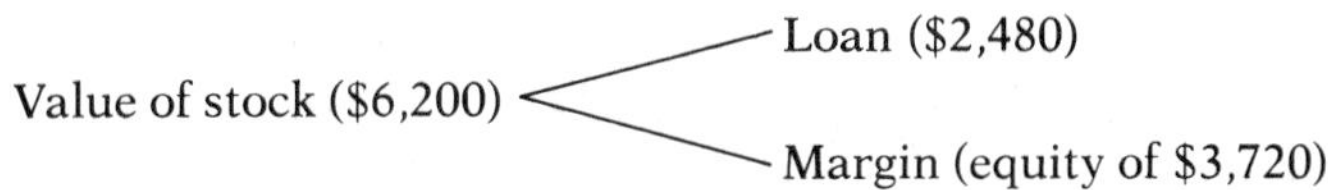

The investor may borrow $2,480 and needs to deposit $3,720 margin. This margin deposit becomes the equity the investor has in the transaction. The amount of equity becomes important should the value of the common stock decline. For example, the NYSE sets what is known as a *maintenance margin* requirement for NYSE-listed stocks. The investor is required to place additional funds in the account if the equity in the account falls to less than 25 percent of the value of the securities in the account. The request for an additional deposit of funds is known as a *margin call.* Although the NYSE maintenance margin requirement is 25 percent, individual brokerage firms often set a higher requirement for their customers to prevent a customer from violating the NYSE maintenance margin requirement.

To see how margin transactions work, let us assume that the common stock we bought, the only security in the margin account, begins to decline in price. At a price of $50, we have the following situation:

Loan ($2,480)
Value ($5,000)
Margin (equity of $2,520)

The account shown above with $5,000 worth of securities is known as a *restricted account,* because the equity is now only 50.4 percent. The customer is not required to put up additional margin, but neither can the customer purchase additional stock on margin without putting up more equity.

At what point will the investor be required to deposit additional margin? This can be calculated fairly easily by allowing the market value of

3. The investor could deposit securities having a loan value of $2,000. With a 50 percent initial margin, $4,000 of securities would have a loan value of $2,000.

the security in the account to equal x. The investor will be required to deposit additional margin when the equity in the account falls below $.25x$. Therefore, we have the following situation:

Value (x) — Loan ($2,480)

— Margin (equity of $.25x$)

We can solve the following equation:

$$\begin{aligned} x &= \$2{,}480 + .25x \\ .75x &= \$2{,}480 \\ x &= \$3{,}307 \end{aligned}$$

If the value of the 100 shares falls below $3,307, the customer will receive a margin call requesting the deposit of additional funds. The brokerage firm might require that the equity be restored to 30 percent. If the investor does not meet the margin call, securities will be sold to liquidate the loan. All the securities in an investor's margin account are normally valued together to determine if a margin call is required.

Assume that the stock value falls to $32 and a margin call is issued to restore the equity to 30 percent. The dollar amount of the margin call can be determined as follows:

Required equity	= $3,200 × .3	= $960
less existing equity	= $3,200 − $2,480	= $720
Margin call		= $240

The margin call of $240 is used to repay a portion of the margin loan. This repayment leads to the following results:

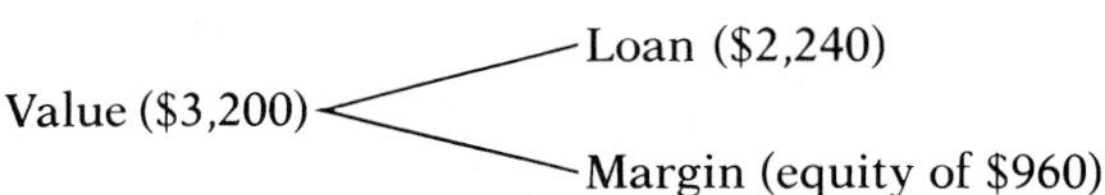

Other aspects of margin accounts may be important. An investor with excess equity in a margin account can use that account as a source of borrowing. For example, assume an investor wants to purchase a new car costing $9,000. The investor's margin account contains securities worth $30,000, and a margin loan of $5,000 exists. A telephone call to the broker allows the investor to borrow the $9,000 using the margin account securities as collateral. Of course, interest is paid on the margin account borrowing whether used to purchase securities or to fund investor expenditures such as a car.

The interest rate paid on margin accounts is known as the *call loan rate,* and an indication of this rate is published in the *Wall Street Journal.* Paying interest on money borrowed to purchase securities may be either favorable or unfavorable, depending on the relationship between the return on the margin securities and the margin interest rate paid. If you can earn more on the security than you are paying on the margin loan, you are in a favorable position.

The margin interest rate also tends to change frequently. If interest rates are increasing, your margin account may receive the "old one-two punch." This could easily happen if rising interest rates result in falling

Exhibit 2–2 **Margin Account Examples with Changing Interest Rates and Stock Prices**

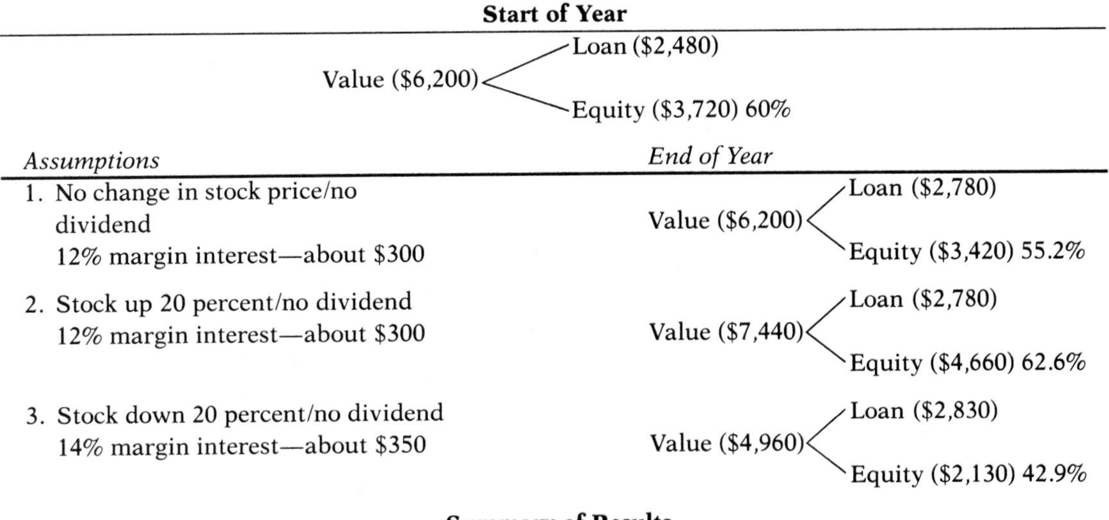

Summary of Results

Example	*Stock Return*	*Pre–Tax Equity Change*
1.	0%	$3,720 to $3,420 or −8.1%
2.	+20	3,720 to 4,660 or +25.3
3.	−20	3,720 to 2,130 or −42.7

stock and bond prices. Let's use our original example to see the joint impact of paying interest on the margin account and having the price of the common stock change. We will use one year as our time period in Exhibit 2–2, and interest is added to the amount of the loan. Example 1 in this exhibit shows a zero stock return, but a decline of 8.1 percent in the margin account equity. Interest rates stayed at an average of 12 percent during the year. Example 2 shows the results of an increase in the stock price with the average margin interest rate constant at 12 percent. Because we made 20 percent on the stock but paid only 12 percent interest, our equity grew faster than the price of the stock. Example 3 shows the impact of a fall in the price of the stock coupled with rising interest rates. With a 20 percent decline in the price of the stock and a rise in the average interest paid to 14 percent, the equity in the account declined 42.7 percent during the year.

The rules applying to margin accounts are complex, and many of the more complicated transactions that could occur have not been mentioned. For example, short sales are typically done in a margin account. An investor should make absolutely certain he or she understands the margin rules existing in any individual member firm, as these do tend to differ slightly. In addition, having a broker borrow for the investor via a margin account is a very impersonal transaction. If a margin call is not satisfied, the investor is sold out. If the investor had borrowed directly from a bank, other considerations might be important, such as the investor's credit rating and the value of his or her business to the bank. Other arrangements with the banker might be made to avoid having to sell a security in order to liquidate a loan. In fact, the banker may even be willing to make an unsecured loan.

Commission Rates

A *brokerage commission* is the basic fee charged by a broker for buying and selling securities as the customer's agent. This may be a negotiated commission or one established by a *fixed schedule of commission rates.* Prior to May 1, 1975, the commission structure established by the NYSE and approved by the SEC applied. At the present time, all stock transactions are subject to commissions that are determined by discussions between the customer and the brokerage firm. Any investor may theoretically negotiate commissions with a brokerage firm, but the commissions that are actually charged for small transactions tend to be determined by the firm.

A *discount brokerage house* does not generally provide the range of services offered by many full-service brokerage firms. If an investor does not need many of these services, a discount brokerage firm provides an alternative at a lower commission cost. For the investor who wants the research provided by a full-service brokerage firm and the advice given by a broker, the higher fees may be worthwhile. The full-service firms will often grant discounts on commissions to their good customers when a request is made. Table 2–1 presents a comparison of a representative discount firm's commissions for selected trades with the rates existing at a representative full-service brokerage firm. Both commission rates are one-way rates in that they apply when both buying and selling stocks.

Trades in low-priced stocks have a relatively higher percentage commission than do trades in high-priced stocks. For example, $6,000 spent to buy 100 shares of a $60 stock means a discount commission of .42 percent of the value of the trade, but the same $6,000 spent to buy 200 shares of a $30 stock means a commission equal to .83 percent. The transaction costs involved in excessive trading activities tend to make the broker

Table 2–1
Representative Brokerage Commissions Rates for a Full-Service and a Discount Brokerage Firm

Number of Shares	Price per Share	Full-Service Rates	Percent of $ Value	Discount Rates	Percent of $ Value	Dollar Difference from Using Discount Firm
100	$12	$ 40.22	3.35%	$ 35.00	2.08%	$ 5.22
100	60	92.00	1.53	52.00	.87	40.00
200	30	126.62	2.11	58.00	.97	68.62
400	5	88.37	4.42	54.00	2.70	34.37
500	50	372.45	1.49	100.00	.40	272.45
1,000	10	251.66	2.52	90.00	.90	161.66
2,000	20	580.98	1.45	170.00	.43	410.98

richer and the stockholder poorer. The investor might want to plan to hold stocks for a fairly long time in order to reduce the impact of commissions.

Bonds are traded on both the organized exchanges and in the over-the-counter market. The majority of bonds trade in the over-the-counter market, including government and corporate bond issues. The *Wall Street Journal* reports the daily prices of corporate bonds traded on the NYSE, the ASE, and the Pacific Stock Exchange. Not all corporate bonds are listed on an exchange, but some of the bonds that are listed are actively traded.

The commission rates for bonds differ from those applying to stocks. In addition, many brokerage firms have specific rules that apply to commissions on corporate bonds with which investors should become familiar before placing an order. In general, the one-way commission per corporate bond is between $2.50 and $10, depending on the number of bonds in the transaction. Some brokerage firms charge $2.50 for the purchase or sale of corporate bonds of short maturity regardless of the number of bonds purchased, while other brokerage firms have a specified minimum charge (such as $20) per order.

Tax Considerations

The Tax Reform Act of 1986 is the most comprehensive tax law revision since 1954. This legislation has many implications for investors, although the law generally simplifies many tax aspects. This section examines tax goals for investors in light of the 1986 legislation and highlights those investments that still give rise to important tax considerations.

The Tax Reform Act of 1986 had two basic purposes. First, it attempted to broaden the base of taxable income by eliminating many special provisions in the tax code, such as the provision that allowed a portion of the gain from a security held for a specified period of time to escape taxation. The base was also broadened by eliminating some of the itemized personal deductions that previously applied to investors. The ability to make a deduction from taxable income for contributions to an Individual Retirement Account was also substantially curtailed. Second, the legislation lowered the marginal tax rate that applied to taxable income. The marginal tax rate determines the percentage a taxpayer will have to pay on each additional dollar of income received. To help accomplish this marginal rate reduction, the law established two marginal tax brackets in lieu of the fourteen brackets that previously existed.

Investor Tax Goals and the 1986 Act

The basic goal of an investor is to obtain the best after-tax rate of return on any investment consistent with the risk assumed in making that investment. Actions taken with regard to obtaining tax-exempt income and making sure the lowest possible marginal tax rate applies to taxable income may be crucial to achieving a favorable rate of return.

Tax-Exempt Income

Successful investors attempt to receive income in a form that does not subject it to taxation. We will see later that this involves several considerations. However, one of the most important may involve the acceptance by the investor of a lower before-tax rate of return.

Lowest Tax Rate on Ordinary Income

If an investor must receive investment income in a fully taxable form (ordinary income), the next desirable goal is to have that income taxed at the lowest possible rate. Tax planning may help to reduce the total amount of income subject to taxation, and this could involve the timing of the recognition of that income for tax purposes. A taxpayer might be interested in deferring the recognition of taxable income until a future tax year when that income could be taxed at a lower marginal tax rate.

Tax-Exempt and Tax-Deferred Income

This section examines three examples of how an investor might find it advantageous to obtain either tax-exempt income or to defer the recognition of taxable income.

Municipal Bonds

As will be seen in more detail in Chapter 11, the interest income received from many bonds issued by state and local governmental bodies is exempt from federal taxation. These bonds are quite popular with taxpayers in a relatively high marginal tax bracket. The yields on these tax-exempt bonds tend to be somewhat lower than for taxable bonds of comparable quality, so the effective after-tax yield from both types of bonds, given the investor's marginal tax bracket, must be calculated. The nature of this calculation is presented in Chapter 11.

Timing of Income Recognition

Timing the realization of income so that it is not taxed or is taxed at a low marginal tax rate is often possible. An interesting example in view of the Tax Reform Act of 1986 deals with the interest income from federal government Series EE bonds. This interest income is not taxed until it is received by the investor when the bond is cashed in, unless the taxpayer elects to be taxed on an accrued interest basis rather than on a cash receipt basis. Under the accured interest basis, the taxpayer calculates the amount of interest earned during a given tax year and reports it as taxable income that year.

Consider the situation of an eight-year-old child. The parents of this child have been saving money for this child in anticipation of college expenses. They currently have $20,000 invested and receive $1,600 in interest income in the child's name. Under the Tax Reform Act of 1986, unearned income, such as interest income, in excess of $1,000 is taxed at the parent's marginal tax rate unless the child is at least fourteen years of age. By buying Series EE bonds for the child and holding them for at least six years, two benefits are received. First, the taxes on the interest income are deferred until the bonds are cashed. Second, the income realized after the child becomes fourteen is now all taxed at his or her marginal tax rate, which will probably be lower than the parents' rate.

Tax-Deferred Pension Contributions

Company-sponsored pension plans, Keogh plans for self-employed individuals, and Individual Retirement Accounts (IRAs) may all provide a means of deferring taxes. With some company plans, employers allow their employees to contribute to pension plans and to avoid paying tax on these contributions until the funds are received as retirement benefits. The taxable salary of the individual is reduced by the amount of the tax-deferred contributions. The result is a lower taxable income for the employee. To be sure, the tax must be paid when the retirement benefits are received. But this may be many years later, and the individual's taxable retirement income may be less than that earned during his or her working years.

A tax-deferral incentive known as a Keogh plan exists for self-employed individuals. Money contributed to these plans is not taxed in the year of the contribution nor is a current tax assessed on income earned by the investment of the contributions. Taxes are assessed when retirement benefits are taken from the Keogh plan. Retirement benefits may start at age 59½ and must start by age 70½. Premature benefit distributions, except in cases such as death and disability, are subject to the regular tax rate plus a ten percent penalty tax on the amount of the distribution.

The Tax Reform Act of 1986 substantially altered the rules that apply to IRAs. The taxable income feature of these retirement plans was previously available to every individual with earned income such as wage income. The 1986 law established a dollar standard for eligibility for deducting IRA contributions from taxable income. For example, joint tax returns with earned income over $40,000 start losing the ability to make tax-deductible IRA contributions, and this ability is entirely lost at $50,000 and over. However, any individual may still make a nondeductible IRA conbtribution up to the limit specified in the law and be able to defer taxes on any income earned over the years on the IRA's assets.

Regulatory Aspects

Regulation of the securities industry occurs at three different levels—at the state level, at the federal level, and by the industry itself. Regulation at the state level started in 1911 in Kansas, and the state laws are known as *blue-sky laws* because they were conceived to prevent an individual from buying a "piece of the blue sky." The dominant regulatory authority at the federal level is the SEC. Self-regulatory activities in the industry are also an element of the total regulatory environment. These three major areas of regulation will now be discussed.

State Blue-Sky Laws

The philosophy behind state regulation is characterized by a paternalistic regard for the purchaser of securities. The key words applying to state regulation of securities are *fair, just,* and *equitable.* The administrator of any individual blue-sky law has considerable power to stop the sale of a security within the borders of the state if the sale is not deemed in the best interest of the state's residents.

State security laws generally provide for the following types of regulation:

1. Antifraud provisions.
2. Requirements for the registration of dealers and security salespersons.
3. Requirements for the registration of nonexempt issues.

Certain types of securities are exempt from the provision requiring that securities sold within the state be registered with the appropriate regulatory agency. Issues of the federal government are exempt in all states, as are state and local bonds. Securities issued by public utilities regulated either by the state itself with regard to rates and charges or by a federal or state commission are exempt from registration. In addition, most states exempt securities listed on specific stock exchanges on the presumption that disclosure concerning the business activities of these concerns is adequate.

If a security is being registered with the SEC under the Federal Securities Act of 1933, it may be registered in a given state under a *registration by coordination* provision existing in most blue-sky laws. The firm simply files copies of the registration material required by the SEC plus supplementary material required by the state. If the required material has been on file at least ten days, the state registration becomes effective when the federal registration becomes effective. Of course, the state securities regulator can deny the registration of the security in any given state during the period of time prior to the effective date of the federal registration.

All nonexempt securities must become registered in the state in which they will be sold by a procedure known as *registration by qualification.* The state regulatory agency examines the material supplied to it and either approves or denies the sale. At times, a firm will plan to sell stock only within the borders of one state. This type of offering is known as an *intra-state offering* and may be purchased only by residents of that state.

From the viewpoint of investment companies, the important fact is that blue-sky laws vary from state to state. They may deal with such matters as sales procedures, sales charges, operating costs, and diversification policies. Some mutual funds have decided not to register their shares for sale in all states because of the legal and administrative work involved. Hence, some investment opportunities may not be available to residents of certain states—especially states with relatively small populations.

Federal Securities Acts

Starting with the Securities Act of 1933, several significant pieces of federal legislation have been passed regarding the securities industry. The regulatory philosophy at the federal level is quite different from that at the state level. Federal law requires fair and adequate disclosure of information concerning the financial conditions of the issuing company and of information regarding the management and business of the firm. An old joke suggests that the federal government does not care if people invest in a hole in the ground as long as they are not told, without supporting geological data, that it really is a gold mine.

Securities Act of 1933

This important law is sometimes referred to as the "truth-in-securities" act. It requires the registration of new issues of securities except for exempt issues such as those of the U.S. government. Issues must normally be registered for at least twenty days before they may be offered to the public so that the SEC staff may review the registration material.

The law requires that a prospective purchaser of a new security be provided with a prospectus describing the issue and the company. Prior to the effective date of the registration, a prospective purchaser is given what is known as a preliminary prospectus, or "red herring." This preliminary prospectus is complete with the possible exception of the price at which the security will be offered. The name red herring comes from the fact that a statement is printed in red ink on the face of the prospectus stating that the registration statement has not yet become effective and the security may not be sold nor may offers to buy be accepted until the registration does become effective. The preliminary prospectus gives a prospective buyer a means of deciding whether or not the security being offered for sale would be a desirable investment. If the answer is affirmative, the investor can give the brokerage firm an indication of interest in the security.

In March 1982, the SEC put Rule 415 into effect. This rule allowed companies to register the securities they planned to issue over the next two years all at one time. Then, when a firm wanted to sell some of these securities, it took them "off the shelf." Hence, this form of registration is known as shelf registration. While many companies are eligible for shelf registration, it attracts those larger companies that plan to sell securities frequently.

Securities Exchange Act of 1934

The Securities Exchange Act of 1934 is the second of the New Deal laws dealing with the securities industry. The act is important for a number of reasons. It established the SEC as the federal agency having responsibility for the administration of the various federal laws dealing with the securities industry. The Securities Act of 1933 had given regulatory authority to the Federal Trade Commission.

The 1934 act is concerned with the manner in which the securities markets work. The SEC is charged with attempting to keep the markets free of manipulative practices. All significant exchanges in the United States are required to register with the SEC. The SEC is also given authority with regard to many of the general trading practices and policies of the exchanges. From time to time, the SEC has sponsored studies in an attempt to determine if general trading rules and practices need changing.

As a result of this law, insiders are required to file reports concerning their trading activities. Insiders are defined as officers and directors of the firm or any beneficial owner of more than 10 percent of the company's outstanding stock of any registered class. The intent of this provision is to make public the trading activities of parties that may have access to inside or privileged information. Public disclosure of trading activities should act as a deterrrent to fraudulent or manipulative trading by insiders.

The Investment Company Act of 1940 and 1970 Amendments

The investment company concept suffered a severe blow during the 1930s. The Investment Company Act of 1940 helped to restore the trust of the American public in the concept of the investment company and began a new era in that concept. This renewed trust aided the tremendous growth investment companies have experienced in the past four decades. Congress felt investment companies were important from a public policy standpoint. Hence, the objectives of the 1940 act were formulated within a public policy framework. The act mentions the possibility of domination and control of other companies by an investment company, the vital impact investment companies have on savings flows into the capital markets, and the difficulties of state regulation, given the wide geographic distribution of investment company shareowners.

The 1940 act and the Investment Company Amendments Act of 1970, in conjunction with the Securities Act of 1933 require that investment companies desiring to sell shares to the public file certain information with the SEC via a registration statement. Following an examination by the SEC of the information submitted, a prospectus is printed. The following items represent the more common items that are disclosed in the prospectus:

1. The objectives of the fund and its general investment policies.
2. Restrictions regarding investments of the investment company. These vary and should be studied by a potential investor. Typical restrictions relate to the use of borrowed money, short sales, participation in underwritings of securities, purchase of real estate or commodities, and the size of individual portfolio holdings.

3. The management of the fund.
4. Management fees and the methods by which they are determined.
5. Past performance of the investment company.
6. Methods by which the shares of the investment company may be purchased and redeemed.
7. Special services offered by the investment company.
8. Taxation of the fund's income.
9. Audited financial statements including the composition of the portfolio.

The Securities Investor Protection Act of 1970

In the late 1960s, the securities industry started to suffer severe problems. Trading volume in stocks expanded rapidly, and many brokerage firms found that they were unable to handle the increased volume with their facilities. Many brokerage firms also discovered a tendency to be short of capital, especially in view of the large expenditures that would be required for computers in order to process the blizzard of paperwork the high trading volume was generating. Experienced back office personnel to handle the trading volume also proved difficult to hire.

As a result of these developments, undesirable events began to occur. Customers were often forced to wait months to receive stock certificates that had previously been delivered in weeks. Dividend checks were sometimes late in arriving, as was payment for securities sold. While some brokerage firms suffered relatively little from these problems, the general crush of back office problems, with the resulting increase in costs, forced some brokerage firms to go bankrupt. The NYSE had a trust fund to help a bankrupt brokerage firm achieve an orderly liquidation, but concern that the trust fund would not be adequate because brokerage firms were failing at a fairly rapid rate was growing. Some market observers feared that a crisis of confidence somewhat similar to the situation in the 1930s would occur.

As a result of these events, Congress in late 1970 passed the Securities Investor Protection Act. This law established a government agency, the Securities Investor Protection Corporation (*SIPC*), to insure brokerage accounts against the failure of a brokerage firm in much the same manner as the Federal Deposit Insurance Corporation insures accounts at commercial banks. The SIPC insures accounts at brokerage firms up to $100,000. Some brokerage firms have added privately purchased supplemental insurance coverage.

Self-Regulatory Activities

Several organizations within the securities industry are concerned with the regulation of the industry. The National Association of Securities Dealers (NASD), the exchanges themselves, and various professional groups such as the Institute of Chartered Financial Analysts discussed in Chapter 1 are all engaged in self-regulatory activities.

The NASD has a membership of over 4,000 dealers in securities. A code of fair practice has been developed by the NASD and is enforced by a district committee structure. Because no NASD member may transact business with a nonmember except on the same price basis as on a transaction with the general public, the NASD has substantial power over its members. A securities dealer needs to be able to obtain wholesale prices from other NASD members rather than retail prices in order to compete effectively with other dealers.

The exchanges themselves have considerable authority in the area of trading practices. The exchanges continually monitor the performance of specialists to determine if they are fulfilling the task of maintaining a fair and orderly market. We previously mentioned the fact that a new member to the NYSE must be carefully screened by the Board of Governors of the Exchange. The exchange also has rules regarding the capital requirements of broker-members.

Summary

The financial markets in highly developed countries are complex. They must perform in many diverse ways in order for the economies of these countries to function properly. Financial markets provide investors with the opportunity to purchase marketable assets and to diversify. By providing market participants the ability to discover a consensus forecast of the price of an asset, financial markets function in their role of allocating scarce capital in an efficient manner.

Financial markets may be classified into primary and secondary markets. Primary markets involve the sale of securities for the first time. The proceeds after investment banking commissions are paid go to the issuing organization. The proper functioning of the primary market is crucial to the growth and development of an economy. Trading occurs in the secondary market so that organizations can achieve long-term financing while individual investors may commit funds for shorter periods. Good secondary markets are necessary before investors will seriously consider participating in many primary market activities.

In viewing the activities of participants in the financial markets, we distinguish between an agent transaction and a principal transaction. An agent performs service at the request of the customer and is normally paid a commission for performing that service. An agent has no risk capital tied up in the transaction. A principal in a transaction has money invested in the transaction. Title to the asset passes to the principal along with the risk that goes with the ownership.

Investors need to understand the various types of orders that may be placed for the purchase or sale of a security. These orders may be classified by the quantity to be purchased or sold, the price at which the trade is to be executed, the time when the order is to be executed, and the method of paying for the purchase or receiving proceeds from the sale. Commissions may represent a significant percentage of the value of a transaction and should be carefully considered by the investor. Excessive trading activity will increase brokerage commissions and should be avoided. The investor will also want to consider the tax aspects involved with investing in various types of securities. While the Tax Reform Act of 1986 substantially reduced certain tax advantages for investors, some types of securities, such as municipal bonds, still possess important tax features.

Regulation of the financial markets occurs at the state level, at the federal level, and as a result of the self-regulatory activities of market participants. State laws are known as blue-sky laws and are generally concerned with whether the proposed offering is in the best interests of the residents of the state. Federal regulation, on the other hand, is based on the doctrine of fair and adequate disclosure.

Suggested Readings

BRANCH, BEN, and WALTER FREED. "Bid-Asked Spreads on the AMEX and the Big Board." *Journal of Finance* (March 1977): 159–63.

CONDON, KATHLEEN A. "Measuring Equity Transaction Costs." *Financial Analysts Journal* (September–October 1981): 57–60.

GRUBE, R. CORWIN, O. MAURICE JOY, and DON B. PANTON. "Market Response to Federal Reserve Changes in the Initial Margin Requirement." *Journal of Finance* (June 1979): 659–74.

HOPEWELL, MICHAEL H. and ARTHUR L. SCHWARTZ JR. "Temporary Trading Suspensions in Individual NYSE Securities." *Journal of Finance* (December 1978): 1355–73.

HOWE, JOHN S., and GARY SCHLARBAUM. "SEC Trading Suspension: Empirical Evidence." *Journal of Financial and Quantitative Analysis* (September 1986): 323–33.

JACOB, NANCY, and RICH PETIT. "Research Output and Capital Market Efficiency Under Alternative Commission Rate Structures." *Journal of Financial Research* (Winter 1978): 45–60.

KENNAN, MICHAEL. *Profile of the New York Based Security Industry.* New York University, Center for the Study of Financial Institutions, Monograph 1977–3.

MCENALLY, RICHARD W., and EDWARD A. DYL. "The Risk of Selling Short." *Financial Analysts Journal* (November–December 1969): 73–76.

PEAK, JUNIUS. "The National Market System." *Financial Analysts Journal* (July–August 1978): 25–33ff.

SANGER, GARY C., and JOHN J. MCCONNELL. "Stock Exchange Listings, Firm Value, and Security Market Efficiency: The Impact of NASDAQ." *Journal of Financial and Quantitative Analysis* (March 1986): 1–16.

SCHWERT, G. WILLIAM. "Stock Exchange Seats as Capital Assets." *Journal of Financial Economics* (January 1977): 51–78.

STOLL, HANS R. "The Pricing of Security Dealer Services: An Empirical Study of NASDAQ Stocks." *Journal of Finance* (September 1978): 1153–72.

———. *The Stock Exchange Specialist System: An Economic Analysis.*

New York University, Salomon Brothers Center for the Study of Financial Institutions, Monograph 1985–2.

WHITMARSH, THEODORE F., "When to Sell Securities Short Against the Box." *Financial Analysts Journal* (May–June 1972): 80–81ff.

Questions

1. Define a financial market. Briefly discuss the functions of a financial market.
2. What is the difference between an agent transaction and a principal transaction?
3. In what financial market transactions does the brokerage firm (investment banker) act as a principal?
4. What major functions does an investment banker perform for an organization wishing to sell securities? Are these functions always performed?
5. It has been suggested that a good secondary market is required for an efficient primary market to exist. Discuss the validity of this contention.
6. GDV Inc. and Metro Airline both trade on the over-the-counter market. On the same day, the price quotation for GDV Inc. was $18¼ bid and $20¼ asked, and the quotation was $9¾ bid and $10 asked for Metro Airline. What, in your opinion, are the factors that contributed to the differences in "spread" between the two stocks?
7. What is the nature of a third market transaction? How does it differ from a fourth market transaction?
8. In what ways can orders to buy or sell stock be classified?
9. What are the potential dangers in using limit orders to buy or sell securities?
10. What are the important tax goals in making investments? Has the importance of these goals increased or diminished during the 1980s?
11. What is the difference between a cash account and a margin account?
12. Are short positions riskier than long positions? Why?
13. Distinguish between an initial margin and a maintenance margin requirement.
14. Would you agree that the greater the percentage difference between the initial and maintenance margins, the less the risk of getting a margin call?
15. What is the difference between the regulatory philosophy regarding securities sales at the state and at the federal level?

16. What is SIPC, and why was it established?

17. If an investor is having difficulties with an account at a brokerage firm in either order execution or record keeping, what do you think the investor should do about it?

Problems

1. Melissa sells short 100 shares at $60 and *covers* the short sale one year later at $48. Ignoring commissions, how much has she gained or lost on this transaction?

2. Henry has a margin account containing the following securities:

Description	Cost per Share	Current Price per Share
200 shares of Gold, Inc.	$50	$30
100 shares of General Axle	70	90

(a) If the initial margin requirement was 60 percent and Henry borrowed all that he could, what is Henry's current equity in the account assuming the amount of money borrowed is unchanged?

(b) Can Henry purchase additional securities without depositing more margin money in the account?

(c) If the maintenance margin requirement is 30 percent, when will Henry receive a margin call?

(d) If the brokerage firm requires Henry to restore his equity to 35 percent to satisfy the margin call made when the equity fell to 30 percent, how much cash will Henry need to deposit?

3. The initial margin requirement is 60 percent. You are planning to buy 400 shares of a stock selling at $75 a share and hold that stock for one year. Ignoring taxes, commissions, interest expense, and potential margin calls, show in detail the impact in terms of equity change if the price of your stock rises to $100 or falls to $40 assuming (a) you pay cash for the stock and (b) you buy using the maximum amount of leverage available.

4. Rework Problem 3 assuming you must pay interest on the amount of your loan at the call loan rate.

(a) Assume the call loan rate is 12 percent for your one-year investment period.

(b) Assume the call loan rate starts at 12 percent, but due to rising interest rates, averages 14 percent for the one-year investment period.

5. Julie wants to invest $10,000 and receive the highest after-tax return. She is in the 28 percent marginal tax bracket and has the following equally risky alternatives to consider:

(a) A certificate of deposit that pays 9 percent annual interest, producing taxable income of $900.

(b) A municipal bond that pays 7 percent, producing nontaxable income of $700.

Which investment should she choose, a or b?

6. George is comparing two stocks, both selling for $30 per share. One stock, the Hi Yield Company, will pay a dividend of $3 this year; its price is expected to stay at the current level of $30. The other stock, the Grow Company, will pay no dividend, but its price is expected to increase by 10 percent this year. George's income is subject to a 28 percent tax rate.

(a) Which is the best investment?

(b) At the end of the year, George sells the Hi Yield Company stock and receives $30. He also receives a $3 dividend payment that is taxed at 28 percent. At the end of the year, he sells the Grow Company stock and receives $33, realizing a $3 capital appreciation that is taxed at 28 percent.

If George did not sell the stock at the end of the year but left his money invested for another year, which would be the best investment based on the following information?

Hi Yield Company: George does the following:

(1) Sells the stock for $30 at the end of year two.

(2) Receives a $3 dividend at the end of year one, pays taxes on the dividend, and reinvests the remainder for year two to earn at a 10 percent rate.

(3) Receives the reinvested amount from step 2 plus a 10 percent return at the end of year two and pays taxes on the 10 percent return amount.

(4) Receives a $3 dividend at the end of year two and pays taxes on the dividend.

Grow Company: George sells the stock for $36.30 at the end of year two and immediately pays taxes on the $6.30 capital appreciation. Notice that the $36.30 price represents a 10 percent growth in the stock price from $33 to $36.30 in year two.

Chapter 3

Sources of Investment Information

Key Concepts

Dow Jones Industrial Average
equally weighted index
market indexes
New York Stock Exchange composite
Standard & Poor's 500
Value Line index
value-weighted index
Wilshire 5000

Chapter Outline

For many investors, the critical aspect of an investment decision lies in the information available with which to make wise and thoughtful trade-offs among alternatives. Good investments are often not made simply because the person is unaware of them or did not have sufficient information to determine the risk and potential return. This chapter discusses some of the more important sources of information concerning investment opportunities.

The amount of information available to the investor is enormous. The quality of the information and of the investment advice given by investment advisory services varies widely, and we cannot hope to cover all the potential sources of investment information. More importantly, the cost of obtaining the information may be prohibitive when the cost of obtaining the additional information is greater than the added return or reduced risk achieved by obtaining the information.

This chapter discusses only financial information publicly available at a nominal cost or free in libraries available to investors. Consequently, much of our discussion concentrates on information routinely supplied through the financial press. The first section examines the sources of price information available to the investor. This section is brief in that later chapters discuss this topic for specific securities. Therefore, only a general discussion is given here, and the reader is referred to exhibits in other chapters for specific examples of the reporting of prices. The next section discusses market indexes, which allow the investor to ascertain how the market is doing. Section three examines some of the investment advisory services and brokerage house reports available, and section four describes various business, academic, and government periodicals. Section five introduces other sources of information, including data available from companies, from the federal government, and from computerized information sources.

Price Information

Most major daily newspapers include a financial section that reports the prices of stocks, bonds, and other publicly traded securities. Perhaps the most complete daily report is provided by the *Wall Street Journal,* a national financial newspaper that publishes not only financial news but also general news of importance to the investor. In addition, it provides opinions of noted financial experts and a daily analysis of the various markets where financial instruments trade. For many investors, the *Wall Street Journal* is required reading.

The New York Stock Exchange composite price quotations given in Exhibit 3–1 for selected securities are taken from the *Wall Street Journal* of May 15, 1987, and describe transactions that occurred on the May 14, 1987 the preceding trading day. Many other newspapers have similar reports. To read these reports requires knowledge of certain terminology. Let's look at the various columns reporting the activity of the security to interpret their meaning. Our discussion does not include all possible items an investor may encounter but includes most of the major items.

Exhibit 3–1 NYSE Composite Security Trading Report, May 14, 1987

52 Weeks High	52 Weeks Low	Stocks	Div.	Yld %	P-E Ratio	Sales 100s	High	Low	Close	Net Chg.
35¼	16	AirbFrt	.60	1.7	14	820	u36	34⅝	35½	+¾
11¾	10	AsiaPc n		. . .	. . .	1195	10⅛	d9¾	9¾	−¼
46	34¾	BellSo s	2.20	5.8	11	3361	38⅛	37⅝	38⅛	+⅜
58½	38¾	DaytHd	.92	2.2	12	x3407	43⅞	42½	42½	−¾
92⅜	65⅞	GMot	5.00e	5.6	12	5363	89¾	88	88½	−1
3⅝	1	GalHou		. . .	. . .	1745	3½	3⅛	3½	+⅜
61¾	36	Maytag	1.60a	2.9	19	498	55¼	54⅛	55¼	+⅝
83½	68½	OhEd pf	7.36	10.2	. . .	z750	75	72½	72½	. . .
29⅞	18⅛	SpectP		. . .	217	121	24	23	23⅞	. . .
66	33½	TootRl	.40b	.8	17	334	56¾	50½	57½	−6

Notes

a–also extra or extras
b–annual rate plus stock dividend
d–indicates a new 52-week low
e–declared or paid in preceding 12 months
n–new issue in the past 52 weeks
pf–preferred stock
s–stock split in last 52 weeks
u–indicates a new 52-week high
x–ex-dividend or ex-rights
z–sales in full

Source: Wall Street Journal, May 15, 1987. Reprinted by permission,

Item	Discussion
52 weeks High-Low	These two columns report the highest and lowest prices for the security during the preceding 52 weeks plus the current week. However, the current trading day is not included. Airborne Freight's common stock had a daily high of $35.25 per share and a low of $16 but reached a new 52-week high of $36 on May 14, 1987, as indicated by the "u" next to the price. In a similar fashion, Asia Pacific's stock touched a new 52-week low (indicated by the "d") of $9.75 on May 14.
Stocks Div.	These two columns show the company name, the type of security being reported upon, and the dividend. The Spectra-Physics common stock pays no dividends. The dividend figure given is the annualized dividend based on the latest quarterly or semiannual dividend declaration unless otherwise noted, as in the case of General Motors. The "a" for Maytag indicates an extra dividend and the "e" for General Motors is the amount of dividends paid in the last 12 months. Other exceptions are footnoted with the explanations noted at the end of the price report.
Yld %	This column shows the yield on the security obtained by dividing the dollar dividend figure by the closing price for the trading day.

P-E Ratio	The P-E ratio column shows the price paid for each dollar of earnings per share reported by the company during the previous 12 months. Galveston Houston operated at a loss for the previous 12 months so no P-E ratio is reported. Bell South is selling for about 11 times earnings per share, while Spectra-Physics is selling for 217 times earnings per share. Low earnings per share, such as in the case of Spectra-Physics, result in high P-E ratios that may have little meaning. In addition, simply taking the earnings per share for the past four quarters and calculating a P-E ratio does not capture any trends that may be occurring. If earnings are moving strongly upward or declining sharply, the investor would want to know about these trends and judge the P-E ratio accordingly.
Sales 100s	The number of shares traded that day in 100s is reported in this column except for a few inactively traded securities in which the actual number of shares traded (indicated by a "y" or a "z") is reported, as shown for the Ohio Edison preferred stock. The trades reported include trades on the NYSE as well as the Midwest, Pacific, Philadelphia, Boston, and Cincinnati stock exchagnes as well as those reported by the National Association of Securities Dealers and Instinet. An "x" in this column indicates the security traded ex-dividend or ex-rights that day. The Dayton Hudson stock traded ex-dividend on May 14, meaning investors buying that stock that day will not receive the 23-cent dividend, while investors who purchased the previous day will receive the dividend.
High Low Close	These prices present the high price the security traded at during the day, the lowest price, and the closing price representing the last transaction during the trading day.
Net Chg.	This final column represents the change in the closing price from the close of the last trading day the security traded. For example, the price of Maytag common stock increased $.625 a share from the previous trading day it traded. When a stock goes ex-dividend, as Dayton Hudson did on May 14, the net change is not the difference between the two closing prices. An investor who purchased Dayton Hudson on May 13 was entitled to a dividend of 23 cents a share. The stock closed on May 13 at $43½. The investor purchasing this stock on May 14 is not entitled to the dividend. Hence, the stock should fall in price by about ¼, or 25 cents a share. Dayton Hudson closed on May 14 at $42½, so the financial press reported this as a change of −¾ for the day because ¼ of the $1 decline was the result of the ex-dividend.

Knowing these details on reporting transactions, you can determine the activity of any stock on the NYSE. The American Stock Exchange and other exchanges report transactions in the same fashion except that fewer details are given for the regional exchanges. However, stocks traded over-the-counter are reported in two different ways, depending on whether they are on the NASDAQ National Market List, which reports like the NYSE, or on the regular over-the-counter list.

GV Medical is not on the NASDAQ National Market List, and its trading activity is reported as follows:

Stock & Div.	Sales 100s	Bid	Asked	Net Chg.
GV Medical	385	11¾	12	−½

We saw in Chapter 2 that the over-the-counter market is a negotiated market compared to the auction market system of the organized exchanges. As such, the prices reported for over-the-counter securities such as GV Medical are not prices that actually occurred but are representative bids and asked quotations at the close of the trading day. The bid price is the price that dealers are willing to pay, and the asked price is the price at which dealers are willing to sell. The net change is the change in the bid price from the previous trading day.

Reports of transactions in bonds follow essentially the same format as that for stocks, with some exceptions. Chapters 10, 11, 12, and 13 discuss bonds in detail including bond quotations. These quotations include the description of the bond, providing its coupon rate and maturity date. The volume, high, low, close, and net change for the day are also reported, just as they are for listed stocks.

The *Wall Street Journal* and several other major dailies also report prices of other financial instruments. These data include the prices of the many and varied bond issues of the federal government, the value of mutual fund shares, price and transaction data for commodities, the prices of stocks sold on some foreign markets, the value of foreign currencies, and the prices of options on common stock that are available to investors. We will not discuss these price quotations now, because they require an explanation of the securities themselves.

Market Indexes and Activity Measures

Types of Indexes and Activity Measures

In addition to prices, the *Wall Street Journal* and other daily newspapers report other statistics the active investor follows closely. Perhaps the most important of these data are the various *market indexes* and activity measures that allow the investor to obtain a summary of daily price and market activity. Exhibit 3–2 shows part of the *Wall Street Journal's* summary of trading activity for May 14, 1987, as reported in the next day's paper.

Exhibit 3–2 Market Trading Statistics, May 14, 1987

Major Indexes

High	*Low*	*(12 Mos)*	*Close*	*Net Ch*	*% Ch*	*12 Mo Ch*	*%*	*From 12/31*	*%*
Dow Jones Averages									
2405.54	1758.18	30 Industrials	2325.49	− 4.19	− 0.18	+ 550.81	+31.04	+ 429.54	+22.66
976.04	709.13	20 Transportation	976.04	+ 8.55	+ 0.88	+ 199.54	+25.70	+ 168.87	+20.92
227.83	181.15	15 Utilities	x203.82	− 1.79	− 0.87	+ 21.48	+11.78	− 2.19	− 1.06
893.21	682.86	65 Composite	x873.36	+ 0.19	+ 0.02	+ 183.93	+26.68	+ 136.34	+18.50
New York Stock Exchange									
171.08	132.61	Composite	165.76	+ 0.06	+ 0.04	+ 30.47	+22.52	+ 27.18	+19.61
207.48	151.44	Industrials	202.42	+ 0.08	+ 0.04	+ 46.24	+29.61	+ 42.31	+26.43
80.85	67.64	Utilities	72.65	− 0.01	− 0.01	+ 4.55	+ 6.68	− 1.12	− 1.52
144.29	105.58	Transportation	144.92	+ 1.01	+ 0.70	+ 25.24	+21.09	+ 27.27	+23.18
164.56	138.01	Finance	147.05	− 0.15	− 0.10	− 0.66	− 0.45	+ 7.00	+ 5.00
Standard & Poor's Indexes									
301.95	229.91	500 Index	294.24	+ 0.26	+ 0.09	+ 59.81	+25.51	+ 52.07	+21.50
349.49	254.26	400 Industrials	342.46	+ 0.38	+ 0.11	+ 80.55	+30.76	+ 72.53	+26.87
237.92	176.16	20 Transportation	237.92	+ 1.80	+ 0.76	+ 40.64	+20.60	+ 40.65	+20.61
124.04	100.74	40 Utilities	109.42	− 0.13	− 0.12	+ 7.82	+ 7.70	− 2.87	− 2.56
31.51	26.16	40 Financials	27.94	− 0.07	− 0.25	− 0.12	− 0.43	+ 1.02	+ 3.79
NASDAQ									
439.64	343.67	OTC Composite	422.65	+ 0.74	+ 0.18	+ 36.90	+ 9.57	+ 73.82	+21.16
465.16	339.13	Industrials	454.53	+ 0.74	+ 0.16	+ 61.18	+15.55	+ 105.20	+30.12
471.52	399.10	Insurance	417.03	+ 0.56	+ 0.13	− 16.44	− 3.79	+ 12.89	+ 3.19
526.64	392.38	Banks	480.90	+ 1.40	+ 0.29	+ 63.19	+15.13	+ 68.37	+16.57
188.21	146.10	Nat. Mkt. Comp.	180.62	+ 0.32	+ 0.18	+ 16.71	+10.20	+ 31.58	+21.19
177.26	127.41	Nat. Mkt. Indus.	173.40	+ 0.29	+ 0.17	+ 25.76	+17.45	+ 40.83	+30.80
Others									
342.23	255.72	AMEX	336.93	+ 0.35	+ 0.10	+ 64.86	+23.84	+ 73.66	+27.98
1686.9	1212.6	Fin. Times Indus.	1684.2	+ 3.7	+ 0.22	+ 381.6	+29.30	+ 370.3	+28.18
24651.44	15674.03	Nikkei Stock Avg.	24651.44	+288.25	+ 1.18	+8726.75	+54.80	+5950.14	+31.82
273.86	218.79	Value-Line	263.89	+ 0.36	+ 0.14	+ 25.76	+10.82	+ 38.27	+16.96
3014.73	2344.89	Wilshire 5000	2923.47	+ 1.16	+ 0.04	+ 493.95	+20.33	+ 488.52	+20.06

Most Active Issues

NYSE	*Volume*	*Close*		*Ch*
Amer T&T	3,848,500	26⅜	+	¼
AllegisCp	3,510,100	71½	+	1⅞
NatSemi	3,039,300	14⅞	+	⅛
vjTexaco	2,020,900	36¼	+	¾
CenteriorEn	1,792,100	16⅜	−	⅝
Navistar	1,705,200	7⅞	+	⅛
WstCoNA	1,621,700	1¾	+	⅜
PacGE	1,490,000	19¾	−	¾
GenMills	1,456,800	54⅛	+	3⅛
HewlettPk	1,423,900	64¼	+	1
RangerOil	1,366,800	61	+	⅜
IBM	1,346,300	165⅛	−	1⅛
USX Corp	1,306,900	32	+	⅛
SFeSouPac	1,217,600	44⅞	+	⅜
RJR Nab	1,136,400	51⅛	+	2

Diaries

NYSE	*Thur*	*Wed*	*Wk Ago*
Issues traded	1,990	2,002	1,978
Advances	769	761	811
Declines	776	838	782
Unchanged	445	403	385
New highs	57	63	98
New lows	36	24	24
Adv Vol (000)	83,545	86,199	113,123
Decl Vol (000)	51,384	69,091	80,414
Total Vol (000)	152,040	170,970	215,200
Block trades	3,046	3,404	4,216

Source: Wall Street Journal, May 15, 1987. Reprinted by permission,

Market Indexes

Exhibit 3–2 shows the four Dow Jones averages: industrials, transportation, utility, and composite. Investors need to understand the meaning of data such as the *Dow Jones Industrial Average* (DJIA). The DJIA consists of thirty common stocks, including many large and prominent firms such as Eastman Kodak, Exxon, Sears, and Texaco. These firms do not make up a random sample of NYSE-listed stocks. Although this may suggest that the DJIA is not representative of the NYSE, it does not necessarily follow that fluctuations in the DJIA do not follow those of the market in general. Actually, the DJIA appears to be a reasonably good barometer of market activity.

The DJIA is not really an average. The average price of a stock is nowhere near the value of the DJIA (about 2,300 in May 1987). The actual average price of the stocks in the DJIA is approximately $60. The reason for this difference is the manner in which the DJIA is adjusted for stock splits and stock dividends. A stock split is a method used by firms to reduce the per share price of their stock. For example, a two-for-one split means that a stockholder with 100 shares owns 200 shares after the split. The firms simply double the shares outstanding. In theory, the price of the share of stock should fall to half its previous price, since nothing has happened to the earning power of the firm. The price may not in fact drop by 50 percent, but it will drop substantially. If nothing is done, the DJIA, if it includes that security, will also show a drop. Hence, the split must be taken into account by an adjustment made when calculating the average. The DJIA adjusts for the split by reducing the divisor when the average is figured.

The Dow Jones Transportation Average (DJTA) is composed of twenty large firms engaged in air, rail, and truck transportation. The Dow Jones Utility Average (DJUA) comprises fifteen gas and electric utilities but does not include American Telephone & Telegraph, which is included in the DJIA. The Dow Jones Composite (DJC) consists of the sixty-five stocks included in the DJIA, DJTA, and DJUA. Each average has its special use, but when investors refer to the Dow index, they are invariably speaking of the DJIA. All the Dow Jones averages are price-weighted indexes of market behavior. Hence, the highest priced stocks are the most influential in the movement of the Dow Jones average. For example, in early March 1979, DuPont sold for about $134 a share and accounted for about 11 percent of the value of the DJIA. A pending three-for-one stock split would reduce DuPont's price. This split would make DuPont the tenth most important stock in the DJIA, accounting for only about 4 percent of the DJIA's value.

As one might expect in a competitive economy, other firms publish market indexes and, without exception, each major index is broader than the Dow Jones market averages. Another popular market index is *Standard & Poor's 500* stock index, known simply as the S&P index. This index contains 500 common stocks listed on the NYSE, and like the Dow Jones indexes, the 500 stocks are large and well-known companies.

The S&P index is what is known as a *value-weighted index*. It is the ratio of the total market value of the 500 securities on the particular day to the total market value of the same securities during the base period,

1941–43. Total market value is the sum of the market price times the number of shares outstanding for each security. This ratio is multiplied by 10 in order to make the index roughly comparable to the average price of stocks when the current index was formed in 1957. However, current index values are no longer representative of the average price of a share of stock. The S&P index need not make any explicit adjustments for splits and stock dividends because they will not affect total market value.

Interpreting the S&P index is straightforward. As noted, the base period is 1941–43, when the value of the index was 10. By May 1987, common stocks had increased in value approximately 29.4 times over the forty-five years (S&P 500 equal to approximately 294).

Like Dow Jones, Standard & Poor's publishes an industrial index (S&P 400), a utility index, and a transportation index in addition to indexes for about ninety separate industries. However, the most widely used index is the 500 stock index, which is quite useful in that S&P also publishes earnings, dividends, sales, operating income, working capital, and several other financial variables of the companies in the index, all of which can be related directly to the index.

A relative newcomer to the list of market indexes is the *NYSE composite.* This index is constructed in nearly the same manner as the S&P index except that it contains all of the securities listed on the NYSE, rather than just 500. The NYSE also reports indexes for groups such as utilities in addition to its composite index. Its base period is December 1965, and the ratio of market values is multiplied by 50 instead of 10.

Several other indexes exist, including the New York Times index, the Value Line index, the Wilshire 5000 and the NASDAQ OTC index. The American Stock Exchange also compiles an index, which is the only index of AMEX stocks. Its method of construction (average of all price changes in dollars and cents) means that the index has a tendency to go up faster and down slower than more conventional indexes. For this reason, the AMEX index is used rather infrequently as a market index. The NYSE, the S&P, and even the DJIA are probably superior market guides even for the investor interested in the AMEX. The *Value Line* composite average gives *equal weight* to each stock and avoids the heavy emphasis on large companies with big market values. The *Wilshire 5000* Equity Index is prepared by Wilshire Associates of Santa Monica, California. This index is composed of 5000 stocks. As such, it is the broadest of all stock indexes and is roughly the total market value of all shares outstanding. In effect, it is a market value-weighted index much like the S&P 500.

Activity Measures

Exhibit 3–2 shows several activity measures. The stock market data bank section gives the number of issues traded along with several measures of which way these issues moved in price. In the trading activity section, the trading volume of advancing and declining stocks for various markets is given. Elsewhere in the *Wall Street Journal,* the total volume for each market is presented.

Criticisms of Indexes

Except for the AMEX index, we have avoided judgments thus far as to the value of the indexes discussed. But each index may be criticized in specific terms. For example, the DJIA is not broad enough. It covers mostly mature blue-chip companies and gives too much weight to high-priced stocks. Exhibit 3–3 shows the stocks in the various Dow Jones averages in 1987. As a result, the price movements of a few high-priced stocks may significantly affect the movements of the DJIA.

To settle these criticisms, a comparison of indexes is necessary. In this context, we discuss three comparisons:

1. The extent to which the indexes move together.
2. The extent to which the volatility of the indexes is similar.
3. The similarity of the rates of return implied by movements in each of the indexes.

On the first point, the evidence seems to indicate that the choice of a particular index for price movements over long periods of time is not cru-

Exhibit 3–3 **Stocks in the Dow Jones Averages**

Thirty Stocks Used in the Dow Jones Industrial Average

Allied Signal	Exxon	Phillip Morris
Alcoa	General Electric	Primerica
American Express	General Motors	Procter & Gamble
American Telephone	Goodyear	Sears
Bethlehem Steel	IBM	Texaco
Boeing	International Paper	USX
Chevron	McDonalds	Union Carbide
CocaCola	Merck	United Technologies
DuPont	Minnesota M&M	Westinghouse
Eastman Kodak	Navistar	Woolworth

Twenty Stocks Used in the Dow Jones Transportation Average

AMR Corp.	Consolidated Freight	Piedmont Aviation
Allegis	Delta Airlines	Ryder Systems
American Presidential	Federal Express	SantaFe SP
Burlington Northern	Leaseway Trans.	TWA
CSX	NWA	Union Pacific
Canadian Pacific	Norfolk Southern	US Air
Carolina Freight	Pan Am Corp.	

Fifteen Stocks Used in the Dow Jones Utility Average

American Elec. Power	Consolidated Nat. Gas	Panhandle Eastern
Centerior Energy	Detroit Edison	Peoples Energy
Columbia Gas	Houston Industries	Phila. Electric
Commonwealth Edison	Niagara Mohawk Pr.	PS Enterprise
Consolidated Edison	Pacific G&E	Southern Cal. Edison

Table 3–1
Movements in Several Market Indicators Year Ending May 14, 1987

	Percentage Change during Previous Twelve Months
Broad Indexes	
DJ composite	26.68
S&P 500	25.51
NYSE composite	22.52
Value Line	10.82
Wilshire 5000	20.33
AMEX	23.84
NASDAQ OTC composite	9.57
Industrial Indexes	
DJ industrial	31.04
S&P 400 industrial	30.76
NYSE industrial	29.61
NASDAQ OTC industrial	15.55
Other Indexes	
DJ transportation	25.70
NYSE transportation	21.09
DJ utilities	11.78
NYSE utilities	6.68
NYSE financial	−.45
NASDAQ OTC insurance	−3.79
NASDAQ OTC banks	15.13

Source: Exhibit 3–2.

cial. When movements in the value of a given index are compared with movements in the value of other indexes, the results are quite similar.

Table 3–1 reorganizes some of the percentage changes for market indexes presented in Exhibit 3–2. Clearly, the various market indicators do not always move together. However, two important points should be made about Table 3–1. First, the "action" during the twelve-month period examined was not in the over-the-counter market; rather, it was concentrated among stocks listed in the DJIA and S&P 500 indexes. Second, the performance by industry category varied widely. Utility stocks were not good investments during this period, nor were the NYSE financial companies. Both of these points serve to illustrate the importance of deciding what securities should be purchased and what should be sold.

In terms of the volatility of the index, we encounter a similar situation, at least for the more widely used market indexes. The volatility of the DJ composite, the S&P 500, and the NYSE composite is roughly comparable. This is true for the twelve-month period shown on Table 3–1. Over-the-counter stocks in general did poorly, as investors apparently favored higher quality issues.

The third criterion, similarity of rate of return, is not so easy to push aside. For example, IBM was dropped from the DJIA in 1939 and AT&T was added. One estimate of the impact of this substitution was that at the end of 1965 the DJIA would have been nearly double the actual level if IBM had remained in the index. IBM was put back in the DJIA in 1979 along with Merck as substitutes for Chrysler and Esmark. In 1982, American Express was substituted for Manville. Other substitutions since 1939 have apparently also served to keep the DJIA at a lower level than would be true if the substitutions had not been made. In this sense, the DJIA may "underestimate" the rates of return available in the market.

Investment Advisory and Brokerage House Services

The astute investor must evaluate and assimilate information regarding individual firms, and literally hundreds of sources of information about these individual companies exist. For many investors, the quickest and often least expensive sources are large brokerage houses that offer a wide variety of investment information. The services include providing summary financial data and detailed analyses of companies, industries, and the economy. Exhibit 3–4 is a report published by Dain Bosworth on National Computer Systems. Most brokers are happy to supply the investor with as much detail as is desired, and the investor should not be shy about asking to be supplied with relevant informaton. However, the broker eventually expects something in return and hopes for the opportunity to execute transactions. In essence, the size and frequency of trades may influence some brokerage houses regarding the quantity of information supplied.

Several information services that may be valuable are available from private sources. The cost of these services may not be justified given the size of a person's portfolio, but many libraries carry one or more of the more important information services. Three frequently used services are published by Moody's, Standard & Poor's, and Value Line.

Moody's annually publishes a set of massive volumes known as *Moody's Manuals.* These books contain considerable information for literally thousands of firms. The data typically include a brief history of the firm, a description of the business, at least (and frequently more than) two years of financial statements, explanations of the details of the capital structure, and in many cases some analytical work using many of the ratios to be discussed in Chapter 9. Next to the annual report of a company, Moody's is probably the most complete source of readily available information about a company. At the same time, *Moody's Manuals* do not comment on the quality of a particular firm for which information is reported. Subscriptions are also available to *Moody's Bond Survey, Moody's Stock Survey,* and the *Handbook of Widely Held Common Stocks.* Each of these publications is informative and makes qualitative judgments about future prospects.

Standard & Poor's publishes *S&P Corporation Records,* which covers much the same material as *Moody's Manuals.* The data are somewhat less complete than Moody's, but are still quite acceptable. In fact, the brevity

Exhibit 3–4 Brokerage House Research Report

ResearchMemo

An informal and timely discussion of topical interest. 12/86

BUY

NATIONAL COMPUTER SYSTEMS (NASDAQ-NLCS)
(Recent Price: $14 3/8)

52-Week Price Range	Earnings Per Share 1986	1987E	1988E	P/E 1987E	1988E	Div.	Yield	# Shares Outstanding (millions)
$24-$17	$0.89	$0.92	$1.20	15.6x	12.0x	$0.20	1.4%	18.8

SUMMARY AND RECOMMENDATION

National Computer's stock has softened due in part to the loss of investment tax credits (ITCs) causing a negative comparison in the third quarter and small earnings growth for the expected year. However, the fundamental businesses remain strong and should continue showing 20% growth over the next three to five years. The stock is at historic low relative valuations and provides us with what we believe to be a unique buying opportunity. **PURCHASE IS STRONGLY RECOMMENDED** targeting 30% appreciation in 1987 to the high teens, with good growth potential thereafter.

HIGHLIGHTS

HISTORIC LOW VALUATIONS - National Computer is currently priced at almost a 30% discount (based on our $1.20 estimate) to the market versus a five-year historical premium averaging close to 50%. The stock has traded at a premium to the market for the last ten years.

IMPRESSIVE HISTORICAL RESULTS - Over the previous five years, revenue and earnings have shown compound growth in excess of 35% and 25%, respectively, and return on equity has averaged over 20%. The stock has split eight of the last ten years, and dividends have increased every year but one since first paid in 1976.

FUNDAMENTALS ARE STRONG BUT HIDDEN BY ITC - A $0.05 investment tax credit reversal in the third quarter resulted in a down quarter, causing investor nervousness. However, ignoring ITC earnings altogether, the quarter's earnings would have been up 23% relative to last year. Likewise, this year (estimated at $0.92 versus $0.89), which will show only a moderate earnings gain, would show a 23% gain ($0.86 versus $0.70) if ITC earnings were removed.

DOMINATES A HIGH-GROWTH MARKET - National Computer dominates the optical mark recognition market in educational testing. We believe this market is maybe 30% penetrated and growing at better than 25% per year. The Company is currently attacking the low-end of the market with stand-alone units being placed in individual school buildings. These units are "loaned" for a forms commitment of

Source: Dain Bosworth, Inc.

$800 per year, with the cost of the unit being recouped before that year is out. Competition comes from Scantron (NASDAQ - SCNN), a much smaller company (estimated FY1987 sales of $33 million) which is strong in the small systems and has virtualy no penetration in the high-end market.

Besides education, there are numerous other markets where NLCS is continually developing applications for scanners and forms. An example would be Avon, which eliminated 600 data entry jobs, and now scans 300,000 32-page order books every two weeks. Other large potential markets include foreign (currently less than 1% of revenues) where a recent acquisition in Germany gives NLCS a good foothold, and government where about 50 U.S. agencies are supplied with scanning products and services.

ALMOST 70% OF REVENUE IS RECURRING - Scanning forms, maintenance and service fees, software leases and operating lease revenue is recurring, making earnings very predictable. National Computer's growth generally entails upfront investments in developing applications and markets, and in effect creates annuities consuming high margined forms and paying rental and maintenance fees. Because of this, any slowing of growth should translate into higher profitability.

LEASING - Representing about 25%-30% of revenues, we believe leasing has been overemphasized with the loss of investment tax credits, which contributed $0.19 last year and will add only $0.06 this year. However, tax advantages are not critical to computer peripheral operating leases and this is still a solid business. We believe management has been conservative in recognizing lease income and furthermore will begin to slow the growth of leasing, thus causing higher margins and cash generation.

OUTLOOK AND VALUATION

Our estimate for the fourth quarter of $0.33 will bring the year to $0.92 versus $0.89 last year. Fiscal 1986 is projected to generate $1.20 EPS on revenues of $310 million. We expect that as the year progresses, investors will focus more on operating results versus the leasing company (and the ITC issue), and will value NLCS at least in line with the market. Comparisons will be mildly positive in the first two quarters (due to $0.05 of ITC earnings recognized in each quarter this year) and turn quite strong in the second half. A 16 P/E multiple and our expectation of $1.20 EPS provides our target for next year of $19.

We believe the bad news is out and that downside is minimal at current valuations and upside substantial as next year unfolds.

We view National Computer as an excellent long-term investment and recommend **PURCHASE** for growth-oriented investors.

Clinton H. Morrison
(612) 371-2863
December 18, 1986

100 DAIN TOWER • MINNEAPOLIS, MINNESOTA 55402 • (612) 371-2728

Exhibit 3–5 Value Line Analysis

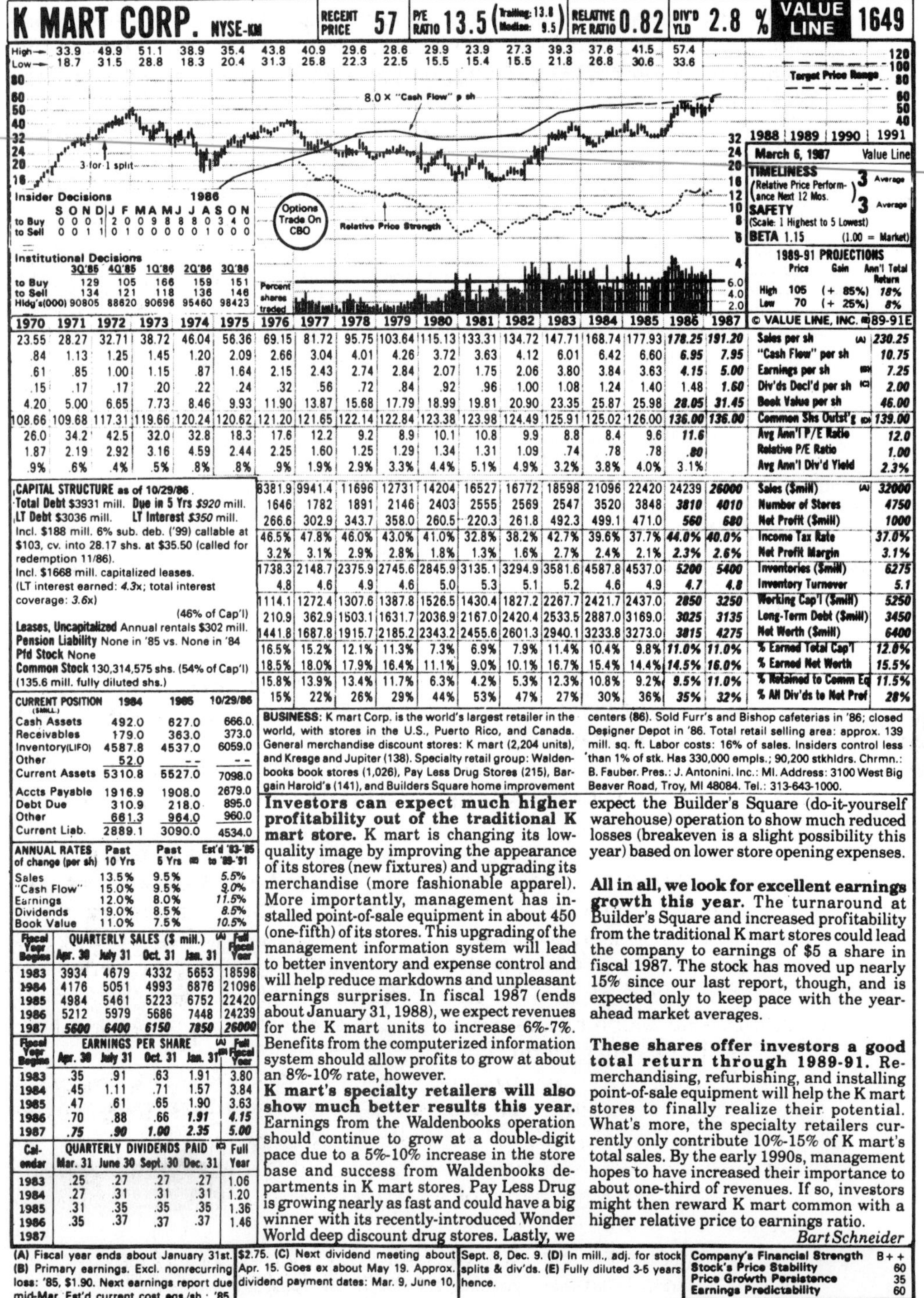

K MART CORP. NYSE-KM

RECENT PRICE 57 | P/E RATIO 13.5 (Trailing: 13.8 Median: 9.5) | RELATIVE P/E RATIO 0.82 | DIV'D YLD 2.8 % | VALUE LINE 1649

Insider Decisions

	S	O	N	D	J	F	M	A	M	J	J	A	S	O	N
					1986										
to Buy	0	0	0	1	2	0	0	9	8	8	8	0	3	4	0
to Sell	0	0	1	1	0	1	0	0	0	0	0	1	0	0	0

Institutional Decisions

	3Q'85	4Q'85	1Q'86	2Q'86	3Q'86
to Buy	129	105	166	159	151
to Sell	134	121	118	136	146
Hldg's(000)	90805	88620	90696	95460	98423

March 6, 1987 Value Line

TIMELINESS (Relative Price Performance Next 12 Mos.) 3 Average

SAFETY 3 Average (Scale: 1 Highest to 5 Lowest)

BETA 1.15 (1.00 = Market)

1989-91 PROJECTIONS

	Price	Gain	Ann'l Total Return
High	105	(+ 85%)	18%
Low	70	(+ 25%)	8%

1970	1971	1972	1973	1974	1975	1976	1977	1978	1979	1980	1981	1982	1983	1984	1985	1986	1987	© VALUE LINE, INC.	89-91E
23.55	28.27	32.71	38.72	46.04	56.36	69.15	81.72	95.75	103.64	115.13	133.31	134.72	147.71	168.74	177.93	178.25	191.20	Sales per sh (A)	230.25
.84	1.13	1.25	1.45	1.20	2.09	2.66	3.04	4.01	4.26	3.72	3.63	4.12	6.01	6.42	6.60	6.95	7.95	"Cash Flow" per sh	10.75
.61	.85	1.00	1.15	.87	1.64	2.15	2.43	2.74	2.84	2.07	1.75	2.06	3.80	3.84	3.63	4.15	5.00	Earnings per sh (B)	7.25
.15	.17	.17	.20	.22	.24	.32	.56	.72	.84	.92	.96	1.00	1.08	1.24	1.40	1.48	1.60	Div'ds Decl'd per sh (C)	2.00
4.20	5.00	6.65	7.73	8.46	9.93	11.90	13.87	15.68	17.79	18.99	19.81	20.90	23.35	25.87	25.98	28.05	31.45	Book Value per sh	46.00
108.66	109.68	117.31	119.66	120.24	120.62	121.20	121.65	122.14	122.84	123.38	123.98	124.49	125.91	125.02	126.00	136.00	136.00	Common Shs Outst'g (D)	139.00
26.0	34.2	42.5	32.0	32.8	18.3	17.6	12.2	9.2	8.9	10.1	10.8	9.9	8.8	8.4	9.6	11.6		Avg Ann'l P/E Ratio	12.0
1.87	2.19	2.92	3.16	4.59	2.44	2.25	1.60	1.25	1.29	1.34	1.31	1.09	.74	.78	.78	.80		Relative P/E Ratio	1.00
.9%	.6%	.4%	.5%	.8%	.8%	.9%	1.9%	2.9%	3.3%	4.4%	5.1%	4.9%	3.2%	3.8%	4.0%	3.1%		Avg Ann'l Div'd Yield	2.3%
						8381.9	9941.4	11696	12731	14204	16527	16772	18598	21096	22420	24239	26000	Sales ($mill) (A)	32000
						1646	1782	1891	2146	2403	2555	2569	2547	3520	3848	3810	4010	Number of Stores	4750
						266.6	302.9	343.7	358.0	260.5	220.3	261.8	492.3	499.1	471.0	560	680	Net Profit ($mill)	1000
						46.5%	47.8%	46.0%	43.0%	41.0%	32.8%	38.2%	42.7%	39.6%	37.7%	44.0%	40.0%	Income Tax Rate	37.0%
						3.2%	3.1%	2.9%	2.8%	1.8%	1.3%	1.6%	2.7%	2.4%	2.1%	2.3%	2.6%	Net Profit Margin	3.1%
						1738.3	2148.7	2375.9	2745.6	2845.9	3135.1	3294.9	3581.6	4587.8	4537.0	5200	5400	Inventories ($mill)	6275
						4.8	4.6	4.9	4.6	5.0	5.3	5.1	5.2	4.6	4.9	4.7	4.8	Inventory Turnover	5.1
						1114.1	1272.4	1307.6	1387.8	1526.5	1430.4	1827.2	2267.7	2421.7	2437.0	2850	3250	Working Cap'l ($mill)	5250
						210.9	362.9	1503.1	1631.7	2036.9	2167.0	2420.4	2533.5	2887.0	3169.0	3025	3135	Long-Term Debt ($mill)	3450
						1441.8	1687.8	1915.7	2185.2	2343.2	2455.6	2601.3	2940.1	3233.8	3273.0	3815	4275	Net Worth ($mill)	6400
						16.5%	15.2%	12.1%	11.3%	7.3%	6.9%	7.9%	11.4%	10.4%	9.8%	11.0%	11.0%	% Earned Total Cap'l	12.0%
						18.5%	18.0%	17.9%	16.4%	11.1%	9.0%	10.1%	16.7%	15.4%	14.4%	14.5%	16.0%	% Earned Net Worth	15.5%
						15.8%	13.9%	13.4%	11.7%	6.3%	4.2%	5.3%	12.3%	10.8%	9.2%	9.5%	11.0%	% Retained to Comm Eq	11.5%
						15%	22%	26%	29%	44%	53%	47%	27%	30%	36%	35%	32%	% All Div'ds to Net Prof	28%

CAPITAL STRUCTURE as of 10/29/86
Total Debt $3931 mill. **Due in 5 Yrs** $920 mill.
LT Debt $3036 mill. **LT Interest** $350 mill.
Incl. $188 mill. 6% sub. deb. ('99) callable at $103, cv. into 28.17 shs. at $35.50 (called for redemption 11/86).
Incl. $1668 mill. capitalized leases.
(LT interest earned: 4.3x; total interest coverage: 3.6x)
(46% of Cap'l)
Leases, Uncapitalized Annual rentals $302 mill.
Pension Liability None in '85 vs. None in '84
Pfd Stock None
Common Stock 130,314,575 shs. (54% of Cap'l)
(135.6 mill. fully diluted shs.)

CURRENT POSITION ($MILL.)	1984	1985	10/29/86
Cash Assets	492.0	627.0	666.0
Receivables	179.0	363.0	373.0
Inventory(LIFO)	4587.8	4537.0	6059.0
Other	52.0	--	--
Current Assets	5310.8	5527.0	7098.0
Accts Payable	1916.9	1908.0	2679.0
Debt Due	310.9	218.0	895.0
Other	661.3	964.0	960.0
Current Liab.	2889.1	3090.0	4534.0

ANNUAL RATES of change (per sh)	Past 10 Yrs	Past 5 Yrs (B)	Est'd '83-'85 to '89-'91
Sales	13.5%	9.5%	5.5%
"Cash Flow"	15.0%	9.5%	9.0%
Earnings	12.0%	8.0%	11.5%
Dividends	19.0%	8.5%	8.5%
Book Value	11.0%	7.5%	10.5%

Fiscal Year Begins	QUARTERLY SALES ($ mill.) (A) Apr. 30	July 31	Oct. 31	Jan. 31	Full Fiscal Year
1983	3934	4679	4332	5653	18598
1984	4176	5051	4993	6876	21096
1985	4984	5461	5223	6752	22420
1986	5212	5979	5686	7448	24239
1987	5600	6400	6150	7850	26000

Fiscal Year Begins	EARNINGS PER SHARE (A)(B) Apr. 30	July 31	Oct. 31	Jan. 31	Full Fiscal Year
1983	.35	.91	.63	1.91	3.80
1984	.45	1.11	.71	1.57	3.84
1985	.47	.61	.65	1.90	3.63
1986	.70	.88	.66	1.91	4.15
1987	.75	.90	1.00	2.35	5.00

Cal-endar	QUARTERLY DIVIDENDS PAID (C) Mar. 31	June 30	Sept. 30	Dec. 31	Full Year
1983	.25	.27	.27	.27	1.06
1984	.27	.31	.31	.31	1.20
1985	.31	.35	.35	.35	1.36
1986	.35	.37	.37	.37	1.46
1987					

BUSINESS: K mart Corp. is the world's largest retailer in the world, with stores in the U.S., Puerto Rico, and Canada. General merchandise discount stores: K mart (2,204 units), and Kresge and Jupiter (138). Specialty retail group: Waldenbooks book stores (1,026), Pay Less Drug Stores (215), Bargain Harold's (141), and Builders Square home improvement centers (86). Sold Furr's and Bishop cafeterias in '86; closed Designer Depot in '86. Total retail selling area: approx. 139 mill. sq. ft. Labor costs: 16% of sales. Insiders control less than 1% of stk. Has 330,000 empls.; 90,200 stkhldrs. Chrmn.: B. Fauber. Pres.: J. Antonini. Inc.: MI. Address: 3100 West Big Beaver Road, Troy, MI 48084. Tel.: 313-643-1000.

Investors can expect much higher profitability out of the traditional K mart store. K mart is changing its low-quality image by improving the appearance of its stores (new fixtures) and upgrading its merchandise (more fashionable apparel). More importantly, management has installed point-of-sale equipment in about 450 (one-fifth) of its stores. This upgrading of the management information system will lead to better inventory and expense control and will help reduce markdowns and unpleasant earnings surprises. In fiscal 1987 (ends about January 31, 1988), we expect revenues for the K mart units to increase 6%-7%. Benefits from the computerized information system should allow profits to grow at about an 8%-10% rate, however.

K mart's specialty retailers will also show much better results this year. Earnings from the Waldenbooks operation should continue to grow at a double-digit pace due to a 5%-10% increase in the store base and success from Waldenbooks departments in K mart stores. Pay Less Drug is growing nearly as fast and could have a big winner with its recently-introduced Wonder World deep discount drug stores. Lastly, we expect the Builder's Square (do-it-yourself warehouse) operation to show much reduced losses (breakeven is a slight possibility this year) based on lower store opening expenses.

All in all, we look for excellent earnings growth this year. The turnaround at Builder's Square and increased profitability from the traditional K mart stores could lead the company to earnings of $5 a share in fiscal 1987. The stock has moved up nearly 15% since our last report, though, and is expected only to keep pace with the year-ahead market averages.

These shares offer investors a good total return through 1989-91. Remerchandising, refurbishing, and installing point-of-sale equipment will help the K mart stores to finally realize their potential. What's more, the specialty retailers currently only contribute 10%-15% of K mart's total sales. By the early 1990s, management hopes to have increased their importance to about one-third of revenues. If so, investors might then reward K mart common with a higher relative price to earnings ratio.

Bart Schneider

(A) Fiscal year ends about January 31st. (B) Primary earnings. Excl. nonrecurring loss: '85, $1.90. Next earnings report due mid-Mar. Est'd current cost egs./sh.: '85, $2.75. (C) Next dividend meeting about Apr. 15. Goes ex about May 19. Approx. dividend payment dates: Mar. 9, June 10, Sept. 8, Dec. 9. (D) In mill., adj. for stock splits & div'ds. (E) Fully diluted 3-5 years hence.

Company's Financial Strength	B++
Stock's Price Stability	60
Price Growth Persistence	35
Earnings Predictability	60

Factual material is obtained from sources believed to be reliable, but the publisher is not responsible for any errors or omissions contained herein.

Source: *Value Line Investment Survey*, March 6, 1987, p. 1649. © 1987 Value Line, Inc.

may be an advantage during an investor's initial screening of possible investment opportunities. Standard & Poor's also publishes the *Stock Guide* and the *Bond Guide,* which present summary information on thousands of firms and are useful as references to find data for major financial variables. S&P also publishes *The Outlook* and the *Stock Market Encyclopedia,* which are informative and offer opinions on the future prospects of the firms evaluated.

The Value Line Investment Survey is another excellent reference service, but the information here is typically more analytical than strictly informative. *Value Line* reviews more than 1,600 firms quarterly. Exhibit 3–5 is a recent report from *Value Line* on K Mart. In addition to a wealth of financial and descriptive information, *Value Line* provides the investor with a quality judgment for each stock reviewed: A numerical score from 1 to 5 is assigned to stocks for (a) the expected price performance during the next twelve months and (b) the stocks' rank for safety. *Value Line* also gives estimated price performance for the coming three- to five-year period. Additionally, *Value Line* presents industry data and analysis, special stock recommendations, and an analysis of the economy.

Periodicals

Business and Academic Publications

Financial information is not the only information required by the wise investor. A wealth of qualitative information exists and is typically found in one of several daily, weekly, or monthly publications. We previously mentioned the *Wall Street Journal.* It carries financial reports, qualitative business news, general world and national news, and analyses of business and economic conditions.

The Dow Jones Company publishes *Barron's National Business and Financial Weekly,* or simply *Barron's,* in addition to the *Wall Street Journal.* Each week *Barron's* includes an in-depth analysis of three or four companies and industries, designed strictly as an analysis of investment possibilities. *Barron's* also contains a good statistical section covering the previous week's market activities, including all the organized exchanges, the over-the-counter market, the bond markets, the commodity markets, mutual funds, and general economic information.

The *Wall Street Transcript* was started in 1963. This weekly publication presents verbatim and without comment reports issued by many brokerage firms, as well as corporate news items. Another potentially useful feature of this publication is the "Roundtable," in which experts in a given area, such as energy or the mobile home industry, discuss their views on the future.

Forbes, published twice a month, contains industry and company articles on a regular basis. Columnists provide analyses of the market from several different perspectives. The first January issue contains a complete ranking of firms by industry and profitability. The second August issue contains a complete evaluation of the various mutual funds available.

Also of some interest to the investor are *Financial World*, the *Magazine of Wall Street* and *Dun's Business Month*. Like *Forbes*, these concentrate on analysis rather than mere factual reporting.

One of the most difficult tasks for the investor is the determination of the quality of a company's management. *Fortune* is a valuable source of information in making this assessment. This magazine often carries detailed articles on a firm's top management people and how they make critical decisions. *Fortune* also has a personal investing section in which specific investment topics are discussed.

Business Week, a weekly general business publication, is a quick way for the average investor to keep abreast of general developments within the economy. In its special issues, *Business Week* discusses topics of great importance to the investor. The topics include such areas as the role of debt usage in all sectors of the economy, the investment outlook for the coming year, and the role of the multinational corporation.

Many other sources of market and financial information are published regularly, and most investors are unable to subscribe to or read all of the publications. Consequently, it is often wise to check one or two popular and complete business periodical indexes available in many libraries, such as the *Business Periodicals Index* or the *F&S Index of Corporations and Industries*. Both can be used as basic reference sources to discover the location of articles about a company, an industry, or any general subject of interest to the investor.

Several academic periodicals are also available to help the investor keep abreast of recent investment concepts. The *Financial Analysts Journal* is published bimonthly and contains analytical articles on the economy, investment management, and investment analysis. Many sophisticated and complex mathematical techniques are summarized and evaluated in this publication. A quarterly publication, the *Journal of Portfolio Management*, has numerous articles that are relevant to practical investment decisions. Its great advantage lies in presenting complex topics in clear and concise terms. Among the many other academic journals concerned with investments are the *Journal of Finance*, the *Journal of Financial and Quantitative Analysis*, the *Journal of Financial Economics*, and the *Journal of Business*. Each presents articles on recent developments and typically concentrates on theory, using considerable amounts of mathematics and statistics.

Government and Private Economic Publications

Several sources of economic data are available from both private sources and the federal government, and are designed to assist the investor in the analysis of general economic conditions. Two prominent government publications are the *Survey of Current Business* and the *Federal Reserve Bulletin*. Both are published monthly and contain articles about and analyses of the economy as a whole and by sector, as well as considerable quantities of statistical data. The twelve federal reserve banks also publish monthly bulletins that discuss general business and monetary conditions. These bulletins vary widely in the subjects covered and in their usefulness for investors.

Much economic forecasting uses leading indicators of the business cycle. For the novice and experienced investor alike, a good source of information about the course and interpretation of economic indicators is the *Business Conditions Digest,* published monthly by the Department of Commerce. Economic forecasts can also be found in the *Annual Report* of the President's Council of Economic Advisors.

Other Sources of Information

Annual Reports to Stockholders

Before investing in a security, an investor would be wise to obtain the company's annual report, which is available on request from the company. Modern annual reports are generally quite complete and informative. Of course, one should remember that they are published by the firm and that they attempt to place the firm in the best possible light, given the regulatory and financial reporting limitations on the firm.

Registration Statements and Prospectuses

In addition to annual reports, detailed company information may be obtained from registration statements required when securities are registered for public trading and prospectuses published when a new issue of securities is offered for sale. Although these sources contain a wealth of information, the investor may find the amount of information and the manner in which it is presented somewhat overwhelming. This tends to be especially true for prospectuses issued in conjunction with complex mergers.

Routine SEC Filings

Associated with the required information that companies must supply are several reports that must be routinely filed with the SEC. The 8-K is a monthly report designed to disclose any changes in such things as voting rights, capitalization, legal problems, and management financial interests in the transactions of the firm. The 10-Q report is an unaudited quarterly financial statement. The 10-K is a detailed annual financial report of the firm. This report must be audited and contains virtually all the financial information that even the most sophisticated investor should need. Companies will often send the investor a copy of the 10-K report.

Computerized Information Banks

The relatively low cost of personal computers and printers along with the availability of communications software and modems has opened up new data sources for investors. In addition to current market quotations for stocks, bonds, commodities, and other types of investments, database information is available for such items as current and historical news items, historical price information, annual report information, SEC filings, proxy statement information, such as the names, ages, titles, and compensation of company officers and directors, and even the transcripts of the four most recent shows of the popular television program *Wall Street Week.*

Two principal computer financial information databases are *The Source* and the *Dow Jones News/Retrieval Service.* Computer owners typically pay a one-time connect fee and usage rates based on the time of day and the database accessed. Individuals in the larger cities in the United States are typically able to dial either a local TELENET or TYMNET telephone number and log-on to the computer having the database.

The *Value Line Investment Survey* has a database available on slightly over 1,600 common stocks. Available on a monthly basis for a personal computer, this database allows investors to quickly identify stocks that meet or exceed standards specified by the investor. Exhibit 3–6 is the result of one such screening of the April 1987 *Value Line Database.* Eight stocks out of 1,604 survived the six specified screening hurdles such as a beta of 1.0 or less and a current dividend yield equal to or greater than 5 percent. Having the ability to screen a database allows investors to identify stocks for additional consideration. Investors can also quickly and easily change the hurdle standards to see what happens to the list of surviving companies. In a similar fashion, Exhibit 3–7 is a computer screening of one industry classification, specialized retailers, for the purpose of a comparison of firms within that industry. The data items shown on both Exhibits 3–6 and 3–7 were selected from thirty-two items available for screening and comparison purposes.

Summary

Information is the key ingredient in an investment decision. Much information or advice is available at no cost, which is what some of it is worth, especially if it comes in the form of a "hot tip" from a barber or beautician or some similar source. However, many free publications are available from brokerage houses, financial institutions, the Federal Reserve System, and similar sources that can be of value to the investor.

Other information and advice are not free. In these cases, the cost must be related to the benefits to be realized from using the particular source of information. These benefits should appear in the form of better investment decisions than would be the case without the information. The investor should be discriminating in the choice of information and advice purchased, recognizing that both time and money are limited resources.

Exhibit 3–6 Computer Screening of Value Line Data

Data: Apr 1987

Company Name	Time-liness	Fin'l Strgth	Price Stabil	Beta	Recent Price	Current P-E	Current Yield	% Return Net Worth	5-Yr EPS Growth	5-Yr Div Growth	Prj EPS Growth	Prj Div Growth	Prj 3-5 Yr Return
BALTIMORE G&E	3	A+	100	0.70	32.875	10.4	5.8	13.5	9.0	5.5	5.0	6.5	10
CENTRAL & SW	3	A+	100	0.80	35.250	9.2	6.6	13.9	7.5	6.0	6.0	6.0	9
EASTERN UTIL	3	B	80	0.75	35.125	11.5	6.5	13.9	9.0	3.5	7.5	6.5	13
ENERGEN CORP.	3	B++	90	0.45	21.250	12.5	5.2	8.5	2.0	5.0	9.0	6.0	9
GRT NORTH IRON	3	NA	45	0.65	28.000	8.8	8.7	34.4	-2.0	-4.0	4.5	6.5	10
INDIANA ENERGY	3	B++	100	0.60	34.250	10.4	6.4	12.7	8.5	8.0	3.5	6.0	10
MINNESOTA P&L	2	A	95	0.75	28.125	10.3	5.9	14.4	7.5	6.0	7.0	7.5	12
TUCSON ELEC PWR	3	A	90	0.65	60.750	12.7	6.0	14.9	14.0	13.0	5.5	7.5	9
Averages	2.9	A	88	0.67	34.453	10.7	6.4	15.8	6.9	5.4	6.0	6.6	10

Screening Criteria:

Timeliness Rank	<= 3
Beta	<= 1
Current P-E Ratio	<= 15
Current Yield (%)	=> 5.0
Prj Divd Growth	=> 6.0
Prj 3-5 Yr Av Return	=> 9

Sort Variable:

Company Name Ascending Sort

Exhibit 3–7 **Computer Screening of Value Line's Classification of Specialized Retailers**

Data: Apr 1987

Company Name	Time-liness	Fin'l Strgth	Price Stabil	Beta	Recent Price	Current P-E	Current Yield	% Return Net Worth	5-Yr EPS Growth	5-Yr Div Growth	Prj EPS Growth	Prj Div Growth	Prj 3-5 Yr Return
FABRI-CENTERS	3	B	45	0.85	11.500	23.5	2.4	1.7	-6.0	11.0	16.5	4.0	17
FUR VAULT	2	B++	30	1.10	11.875	20.5	1.7	15.4	24.0	NA	31.5	58.5	21
GEN'L NUTRITION	3	B	10	1.00	6.625	24.5	2.4	6.8	6.5	59.0	4.5	4.5	16
HEILIG-MEYERS	3	B	30	1.05	34.375	22.6	1.0	11.1	14.0	16.0	19.5	20.5	11
HOUSE OF FABRIC	3	B	35	1.05	15.000	12.0	3.2	7.7	26.5	14.0	8.5	8.5	19
MELVILLE CORP	3	A+	70	1.20	73.750	15.5	2.4	19.9	13.0	13.0	13.0	11.0	10
NEW PROCESS	3	B+	30	1.00	30.000	13.9	3.9	25.2	18.5	17.0	7.5	6.5	6
STD BRAND PAINT	3	B++	55	1.05	24.375	16.1	2.5	9.3	4.5	10.5	7.0	8.5	12
TANDY CORP.	2	A	35	1.25	50.500	16.5	1.0	17.8	23.5	NA	15.5	NA	16
Averages	2.8	B+	38	1.06	28.667	18.3	2.3	12.8	13.8	20.1	13.7	15.3	14

Screening Criteria:

Timeliness Rank	<= 3
Industry Code	= 5600
Current Yield (%)	=> 1.0

Sort Variable:

Company Name Ascending Sort

Suggested Readings

BUTLER, HARTMAN L., JR, and J. DEVON ALLEN. "The Dow Jones Industrial Average Reexamined." *Financial Analysts Journal* (November–December 1979): 23–30.

GROTH, JOHN C. "Investor Objectives, Stock Recommendations, and Abnormal Returns." *Quarterly Review of Economics and Busines* (Summer 1978): 55–72.

GROTH, JOHN C., WILBER G. LEWELLEN, GARY G. SCHLARBAUM, and RONALD C. LEASE. "An Analysis of Brokerage House Securities Recommendations." *Financial Analysts Journal* (January–February 1979): 32–40.

HARTMAN, L. BUTLER, JR., and RICHARD F. DEMONG. The Changing Dow Jones Industrial Average." *Financial Analysts Journal* (July–August 1986): 59–62.

RUDD, ANDREW. "The Revised Dow Jones Industrial Average; New Wine in Old Bottles?" *Financial Analysts Journal* (November–December 1979): 57–63.

WOODWELL, DONALD R. *Automating Your Financial Portfolio: An Investor's Guide to Personal Computers.* Homewood, IL: Dow Jones-Irwin, 1983.

Questions

1. The price-to-earnings ratio reported in the financial press should be carefully evaluated by investors. Why is this true?

2. The Booklet Corporation's common stock goes ex-dividend $.50 per share today. Yesterday, the closing price was $32½. If today's closing price is $32¼, what will the *Wall Street Journal* price quotations for today show as the net price change for the stock?

3. What does the NYSE security trading report tell about
   (a) trading volume?
   (b) percentage of the firm's stock traded each day?
   (c) expected dividends per share for the coming year?
   (d) the P-E ratio?

4. What are the major differences in construction of the DJIA, the S&P 500, the NYSE composite, and the Wilshire 5,000 Equity Index? How do their constructions influence their performance measurement as demonstrated in Table 3–1?

5. Where might one go to find information regarding
   (a) the state of the general economy?
   (b) the movements of business cycle indicators?
   (c) industry information?
   (d) company information?
   (e) interest rates for various types of fixed-income securities?

6. In Table 3–1, the DJ composite went up 26.68 percent, but the

NYSE composite went up 22.52 percent. What is your explanation of this difference?

7. In 1979, Chrysler's common stock was deleted from the Dow Jones Industrial Average and replaced by another company. The annual price movements of the DJIA and Chrysler's common stock for the 1980–82 period are as follows:

Year	DJIA	Chrysler
1980	14.9%	−27.8%
1981	−10.2	−30.8
1982	19.6	425.9

(a) What, in your opinion, was the impact of replacing Chrysler in the DJIA?

(b) Given the relatively low price of Chrysler during these years and the method of weighting used in constructing the DJIA, what change would you make in your answer to part *a*?

8. In what ways might the dividend per share and the dividend yield values as published in the financial press be misleading?

9. Identify some ways in which data bases of information regarding stock can be screened. In your opinion, what is the major purpose an investor accomplishes by such screening?

Problems

1. From the monthly index values for the S&P 500 and the S&P 40 Financial Index for a recent period of two and one-half years, show the monthly percentage changes in the indexes.

(a) Discuss the movements of the indexes.

Month	S&P 500	Financials	Month	S&P 500	Financials	Month	S&P 500	Financials
12/84	167.24	18.80						
1/85	179.63	20.67	1/86	211.78	26.63	1/87	274.08	29.63
2/85	181.18	20.98	2/86	226.92	29.19	2/87	284.20	30.93
3/85	180.66	20.60	3/86	238.90	31.02	3/87	291.70	29.79
4/85	179.83	21.25	4/86	235.52	28.84	4/87	288.36	28.12
5/85	189.55	22.93	5/86	247.35	30.12	5/87	290.10	27.94
6/85	191.85	23.30	6/86	250.84	29.75	6/87	304.00	29.46
7/85	190.92	22.44	7/86	236.12	27.98			
8/85	188.63	21.78	8/86	252.93	30.37			
9/85	182.08	20.55	9/86	231.22	26.80			
10/85	189.82	22.60	10/86	243.98	27.59			
11/85	202.17	24.24	11/86	249.22	27.42			
12/85	211.28	25.72	12/86	242.17	26.92			

(b) Update the monthly series from July 1987 to the present time. Compare the movements in the series before and after July 1987.

2. For the 1972–86 period, look at the annual percentage changes of the DJIA, S&P 500, NYSE Composite, ASE Value Index, and

NASDAQ Composite. Compare these indexes in the following contexts.

(a) Do the indexes move together?
(b) To what extent are the indexes similar regarding volatility?
(c) How similar are the rates of return implied by the indexes?
(d) Update the indexes to the end of last year.

Year	DJIA	S&P Composite	NYSE Composite	ASE Value Index	NASDAQ Composite
1972	1,020	118.05	64.48	64	133.72
1973	850	97.55	51.82	45	92.19
1974	616	68.56	36.13	30	59.82
1975	852	80.19	47.64	42	77.62
1976	1,003	107.46	57.88	55	97.88
1977	831	95.10	52.50	64	105.05
1978	805	96.11	53.62	75	117.98
1979	838	107.94	61.95	123	150.83
1980	963	135.76	77.86	174	202.34
1981	875	122.30	71.11	160	195.84
1982	1,046	141.24	81.03	170	232.41
1983	1,258	165.34	95.18	223	278.60
1984	1,211	167.24	96.38	204	247.35
1985	1,547	211.28	121.58	246	324.93
1986	1,896	242.17	138.58	263	348.83

3. The Dow Jones Industrial Average is a price-weighted index in which the *market prices* of 30 selected stocks are summed and divided by an appropriate divisor. The Standard and Poor's 500 Composite Index is a market-value weighted index in which the *market values* of 500 selected stocks are added. This sum is then divided by the market value of 500 selected stocks in a base period. Finally, the resulting ratio is multiplied by 10 to arrive at the quoted index figure.

(a) Calculate both a price-weighted index and a value-weighted index for the four stocks, Grow, Deca, Slow, and Vary. Use 1980 as the base year, and assign both indexes a value of 10 in 1980. (Hint: The price-weighted index has a divisor of 18.8.)

	Market Values				Closing Prices			
Year	Grow	Deca	Slow	Vary	Grow	Deca	Slow	Vary
1980	100	28	51	180	40	56	17	75
1981	110	26	57	144	44	52	19	80
1982	120	24	63	180	48	48	21	75
1983	130	22	69	144	52	44	23	70
1984	140	20	75	180	56	40	25	75
1985	150	18	81	144	60	36	27	80
1986	160	16	87	180	64	32	29	75

(b) What differences do you observe in the way the indexes change over time?

(c) Why do these differences occur?

Part

Risk and Valuation Concepts

2

Risk and return are the twin cornerstones in virtually any investment decision. Investors almost always have to make trade-offs between risk and return. In seeking to earn a higher return, investors must necessarily take on greater risk. This part of the text examines risk and valuation concepts in considerable detail. Chapter 4 presents a discussion of the risk and return measures with which investors need to be acquainted. Chapter 5 examines the fundamental approach to making investments, with emphasis on how investors make judgments about whether or not securities are undervalued. The technical approach to investment timing decisions is also presented in this chapter. The final chapter in this part looks at various asset pricing models. The general valuation concepts presented are important because they represent one way of using the historical rates of return examined earlier.

Chapter 4

Risk and Return Measures

Key Concepts

alpha
arithmetic holding period return
beta
characteristic line
coefficient of determination
correlation
correlation coefficient
correlation matrix
covariance
deviation
dispersion
expected return
firm specific risk component
geometric mean return
histogram
investment process
market portfolio
market risk component
normal distribution
portfolio return
present value concept
probability distribution
range of returns
standard deviation
state of nature
statistical independence
time value of money
variance
wealth relative

Chapter Outline

Chrysler's common stock provides an outstanding example of investment risk. In 1976, an investment in Chrysler's common stock would have earned a return of 104.2 percent. During the next five years, however, Chrysler provided its investors with a negative return in each year. A dollar invested in Chrysler's stock at the beginning of 1977 was worth only 20 cents by the end of 1981. Miraculously, in 1982 the stock rebounded from 3⅜ per share to end the year at 17¾—a 425.9 percent increase. By April 1987, the stock price had risen even further to an equivalent $57 per share (after adjusting for a 3-for-2 stock split)—an astonishing increase of 1,589 percent in just five years. These dramatic examples of historical returns show risk operating on both the upside and downside.

Investors have a wide range of potential alternatives from which to choose when deciding to invest. To aid in this selection, measures are needed to gauge the degree of risk taken in attempting to earn a given return. Investors rely to a considerable extent on the variability of past returns to help them make this critical risk-return judgment. To the extent that history repeats itself, past return patterns, often represented as statistical measures, can be useful in deriving estimates of future returns and their variability. When making these judgments, all available information should be taken into consideration including, but not limited to, the historical patterns of returns. Usually, investors combine historical statistics along with subjective projections to make forecasts of future returns.

We begin this chapter with a discussion that carefully lays out the sources of return and the processes used in return measurement. As we proceed through the chapter, we will examine the measurement of risk at three separate levels: (1) as a single investment, (2) in a portfolio context, and (3) in a capital market context.

The Investment Process

The *investment process* involves making a trade-off between expected returns and the risk of not achieving those returns. In Chapter 1 we noted several sources of risk, including market risk, interest rate risk, price level risk, and business risk. Now, we will examine measures of risk formulated in the same manner as the measurement of heat or distance or time. The analogy to a physical phenomenon such as heat is appropriate if we recognize that temperature is not heat. Temperature is merely a measure communicating relative differences in heat and has no necessary relationship to the cause of heat or lack of heat (cold). In a similar fashion, a risk measure should not be thought of as risk or a cause of risk but merely as a technique to distinguish among assets with differing degrees of risk. Although our discussion is built around the measurement of risk for common stock, the concepts apply as well to all other types of investments.

Exhibit 4–1 shows a data set for selected securities. Annual returns for the common stock of Chrysler, A&P, IBM, and U.S. Tobacco are given along with the Standard and Poor's 500 stock index for the 1967–86

Exhibit 4–1 **Annual Rate of Return Data, Selected Investments**

	Chrysler	*A&P*	*IBM*	*U.S. Tobacco*	*S&P 500*
1967	89.4%	14.3%	70.0%	47.8%	24.0%
1968	3.1	30.3	1.3	−31.0	11.1
1969	−35.0	−20.6	16.9	−26.2	−8.5
1970	−16.8	6.7	−11.5	49.4	4.0
1971	4.4	−18.5	7.5	45.2	14.3
1972	46.4	−19.6	21.1	−54.1	19.0
1973	−58.7	−46.6	−21.9	−21.1	−14.7
1974	−44.6	−10.6	−29.7	11.7	−26.5
1975	39.7	44.1	37.4	45.2	37.2
1976	104.2	34.1	28.0	38.9	23.8
1977	−33.6	−37.5	1.6	22.6	−7.2
1978	−25.0	−33.7	13.4	9.9	6.6
1979	−19.4	50.0	−9.1	12.2	18.4
1980	−27.8	−39.1	10.8	22.3	32.4
1981	−30.8	−26.2	−11.1	29.2	−4.9
1982	425.9	112.9	75.3	54.4	21.4*
1983	55.6	48.5	30.6	71.0	22.5
1984	18.0	30.6	4.3	0.2	6.3
1985	48.8	37.3	29.9	−4.9	32.2
1986	22.6	9.3	−20.0	32.9	18.5

*Note the strong bull market that started in 1982 and continued through the end of 1986.

period. The risk and return measures to be discussed in this chapter are calculated for the data in Exhibit 4–1, and the results are recorded in Table 4–1.

Return Measurement

A starting point for a discussion of return measurement must be the *time value of money.* This central concept in finance simply means that dollars received at the present time have more value than those to be received at some future date. The time value of money discussion leads naturally into the measuring of returns and the *present value concept.*

Time Value of Money

Suppose the authors asked a group of individuals to read this book for a fee of $100 each. In accepting this task, the individuals would have the opportunity to receive the fee immediately upon completion of the reading or one year after completion. The individuals undoubtedly would prefer immediate acceptance of the fee.

Table 4–1
Risk and Return Measures, Various Securities, 1967–86

	Chrysler	A&P	IBM	U.S. Tobacco	Equally Weighted Portfolio	S&P 500
Return measures						
Arithmetic	28.3%	8.3%	12.2%	17.8%	16.6%	11.5%
Geometric	6.8	1.4	9.1	12.5	10.8	10.2
Risk measures						
Range of returns						
High	425.9	112.9	75.3	71.0	170.2	37.2
Low	−58.7	−46.6	−29.7	−54.1	−19.1	−26.5
Variance	10,793	1,635	779	1,072	1,900	287
Standard deviation	103.9	40.4	27.9	32.7	43.6	16.9
Beta	2.6	1.2	1.0	0.6	1.4	1.0
Alpha	−1.7	−5.7	0.4	10.8	1.0	—
R Squared	.18	.26	.39	.10	.28	1.0

If instead the individuals were offered a fee of \$100 if taken immediately or \$110 in one year, a few would accept the larger sum. Setting the sum at \$120 in one year would induce even more individuals to accept the future payment. Given the opportunity to receive a \$500 future payment, almost all individuals would prefer \$500 in one year to \$100 immediately. This phenomenon is known as the time value of money.

To evaluate different types of investment opportunities, investors must be able to calculate today's value of a sum to be received in the future. Likewise, investors must be able to determine what amount will be received at some future date if a dollar amount is invested today, to earn at a known, positive rate of interest. The procedures to calculate these values are reviewed in the appendix to this chapter.

Calculation of Arithmetic Holding Period Returns

To make wise investment decisions and to judge the performance of past investments, investors need to be able to measure the returns on their investment holdings over various periods of time. Usually, the return is measured by the *arithmetic holding period return* (HPR) and is calculated as follows:

$$R_1 = \frac{(P_1 - P_0) + D_1}{P_0} \qquad (4.1)$$

end - beginning

where R_1 = return for period 1
P_0, P_1 = beginning- and end-of-period price, respectively
D_1 = cash flows (dividends paid) during period 1

The return calculation considers the capital gain or loss plus any dividend (or interest income in the case of a fixed-income security). $E(R_1)$ is

Exhibit 4–2 **1986 Quarterly Price and Dividend Data, Selected Securities**

		*Chrysler**	*A&P*	*IBM*	*U.S. Tobacco*	*S&P 500*
4th 1985		31.08	21⅞	155½	34⅞	211.28
1st 1986		46	24	149⅛	33⅝	238.90
2nd 1986		38⅛	26¼	146½	42⅝	250.84
3rd 1986		36	21½	134½	41	231.32
4th 1986		37	23½	120	44⅜	242.17
Quarterly	$.25	1st–3rd				
dividends	$.35	4th	$.10/Q	$1.10/Q	$.49/Q	$2.05/Q e

*Adjusted to show Chrysler's 3-for-2 split stock in March 1987.
e–estimated as the average quarterly dividend over the year.

Table 4–2
1986 Return Measures Using Quarterly Data, Various Securities

Quarter	Chrysler	A&P	IBM	U.S. Tobacco	S&P 500
1st 1986	48.8%	10.2%	−3.4%	−2.2%	14.0%
2nd 1986	−16.6	9.8	−1.0	28.2	5.9
3rd 1986	−4.9	−17.7	−7.4	−2.7	−7.0
4th 1986	3.8	9.8	−10.0	9.4	5.6
1986 actual*	22.6	9.3	−20.0	32.9	18.5
1st quarter annualized	390.2	47.5	−12.9	−8.5	69.5

*Annual returns are subject to a slight rounding error.

used in place of R_1 in equation 4.1 whenever the expected return is to be calculated instead of the historical return.

Consider the end-of-quarter price and quarterly dividend information for Chrysler, IBM, A&P, U.S. Tobacco, and the S&P 500 index, as shown in Exhibit 4–2. The 1986 return for Chrysler is calculated as follows:

$$R_{1986} = \frac{(37.00 - 31.08) + 1.10}{31.08} = \frac{5.92 + 1.10}{31.08} = 22.6\%$$

For the first quarter, the return is determined as follows:

$$R_{1-1986} = \frac{(46.00 - 31.08) + 0.25}{31.08} = \frac{14.92 + 0.25}{31.08} = 48.8\%$$

The 48.8 percent gain in the first quarter can be converted into an equivalent annual return figure by applying equation 4.2:

$$(1 + \text{HPR})^m - 1 \qquad (4.2)$$

where m = number of periods per year

$$(1 + 0.488)^4 - 1 = (4.902) - 1 = 390.2\%$$

Table 4–2 shows the returns on the four stocks for (1) each quarter of 1986, (2) the actual 1986 holding period return, and (3) the annualized

1986 return based on the first quarter data only. The first quarter's annualized return appears to be a poor indication of the actual annual return.

Return Measurement Problems

Annual HPRs can be calculated with relative ease, but we start having difficulties when determining returns for more than one period. Returns over several periods are generally reported as measures of the average return per period. Earlier in this chapter, Exhibit 4–1 showed the annual HPRs over the 1967–86 period for four different stocks and the S&P 500 index. If average annual HPRs are calculated for ten- and twenty-year periods, we can observe how the choice of the investment interval and averaging technique can affect the resulting measure of average return. Table 4–3 displays the arithmetic and geometric mean HPRs of the four stocks and the S&P 500 index for the 1967–86 and 1977–86 periods.

Arithmetic Mean

The arithmetic mean annual return can be found by adding the HPRs for every year over the investment period and dividing by the number of years. As a measure of average return, the arithmetic mean HPR is unsatisfactory in many situations. To see why, consider investing in a common stock that pays no dividend, has an initial price of $10, grows to $20 in the first year, and declines to $10 in the second year. At the end of the second year, the return on the investment is zero. Notice that the return in the first year is 100 percent and in the second year is −50 percent. The average of these returns is 25 percent, but the investor is no better off. The correct measure of annual return is zero and is calculated by the geometric mean formula.

Geometric Mean Return

The geometric mean measures the time-weighted rate of return. The formula for the geometric mean is as follows:

Table 4–3
Average Annual Returns for Differing Holding Periods

	Chrysler	A&P	IBM	U.S. Tobacco	S&P 500
Arithmetic returns					
1967–86	28.3%	8.3%	12.2%	17.8%	11.5%
1977–86	43.4	15.2	12.6	25.0	14.6
Geometric returns					
1967–86	6.8	1.4	9.1	12.5	10.2
1977–86	18.2	10.8	9.7	20.6	14.7

$$G = \prod_{j=1}^{n} W_j^{1/n} \tag{4.3}$$

where G = the geometric mean
j = the jth period
n = the number of periods
$\prod_{j=1}^{n}$ = means to multiply n times
W_j = the *wealth relative* (1 + HPR) in period j
$1/n$ is an exponent meaning to take the nth root

The geometric mean can be determined as shown in Exhibit 4–3. IBM's 1985 and 1986 returns are used for the example.

Under what circumstances would the arithmetic mean rate of return be satisfactory? An arithmetic mean annual rate of return is approximately correct when all annual rates are between plus and minus 15 percent per year. For example, if the period returns are 11 and 2 percent, the arithmetic mean is 6.5 percent, while the geometric mean is 6.4 percent. The quality of the arithmetic mean estimate deteriorates as the annual returns become large. The arithmetic mean overstates positive returns and understates negative returns. The geometric mean of −11 percent and −2 percent is approximately −6.6 percent as compared to the arithmetic mean of −6.5 percent.

Exhibit 4–3 Geometric Return Calculation

1. Convert each annual return (HPR) into an annual wealth relative, W_j. W_j can be defined in either of two ways: (1) one plus the HPR or (2) the ratio of the ending to beginning wealth. The 1986 wealth relatives are as follows:

$$W_{1986} = 1 + \frac{(P_{1986} - P_{1985}) + D_{1986}}{P_{1985}} = \frac{P_{1986} + D_{1986}}{P_{1985}}$$

IBM's 1985 and 1986 wealth relatives are given below:

$$W_{1985} = 1 + (.299) = 1.299 \qquad W_{1986} = 1 + (-.200) = .800$$

2. Find the product of all period wealth relatives:

$$\prod_{j=1}^{n} W_j = W_1 \times W_2 \times W_3 \times \cdots \times W_n$$

For IBM, the product of W_{1985} and W_{1986} is 1.0392.

$$\prod_{j=1}^{n} W_j = (1.299) \times (.800) = 1.0392$$

3. Calculate the mean wealth relative, W, by taking the nth root of the result obtained in step 2. In the IBM example, n equals two periods; therefore, W is the square root of 1.0392 and equals 1.0194.

4. Subtract 1 from the mean wealth relative, W, to yield the geometric mean, G. For IBM, the geometric mean is 1.94 percent ($G = W - 1 = 1.0194 - 1 = .0194$), and the arithmetic mean is 4.95 percent.

Estimating Expected Returns

Investors make decisions based on what they think will happen to a security's returns over the time period their money is to be invested. These estimates of a security's returns are based on a combination of factors, some of which are historical returns, economic data, and investors' insights. Some investors will estimate a single, most likely return, while others will foresee a range of possible return outcomes. An investor in the latter group, for example, might be able to specify a return estimate in case the company has a good year, another in case the company has an average year, and a third in case the company has a bad year. The various cases are often referred to in investment discussions as *states of nature.* The investor may be unsure about which kind of year the company will have but can roughly assign probabilities or chances for each state occurring. A graph showing the association between the return estimates and their probabilities of occurrence is a *histogram.* Usually, returns are divided into even intervals over the likely range of expected returns. Then, the probability of a return falling in each interval is shown on the graph with a bar or pie-wedge shape. The histogram is a representation of the investor's estimate of the *probability distribution* for the returns on an investment.

Once the probability distribution has been estimated, the investor can determine the mean outcome or expected return for the security. The expected return can be represented by equation 4.4.

$$E(R) = \sum_{h=1}^{q} R_h F_h \tag{4.4}$$

where $E(R)$ = the expected return in investment period
q = the number of possible outcomes or states
h = the specific outcome or state
$\sum_{h=1}^{q}$ = means to add q times
R_h = the return if h occurs
F_h = the probability of h occurring

The *expected return* on an investment is a probability-weighted average of the likely returns the investor foresees over the investment period. IBM's expected return can be estimated as 13 percent under the following assumed business conditions, returns, and probabilities.

Business Conditions	**Return** R_h	**Probability** F_h	$R_h F_h$
Good year	35%	.3	10.5%
Average year	13	.5	6.5
Bad year	−20	.2	− 4.0
		Expected return =	13.0%

Along with the expected return, investors need to be able to determine the degree of risk being undertaken when making an investment. Most investors value consistency in the anticipated returns. Each of the situations shown in Figure 4–1 promises investors a different return and risk combination.

Investment A is typical of the return pattern of a U.S. Treasury bill, for which the expected return is close to 5 percent. Investment B also offers investors an expected return of 5 percent, but it is riskier than Investment A because of the greater possibility that the actual return will vary from 5 percent. With Investment C, the riskiest situation, investors get a chance at a higher expected return than for A or B but at a greatly increased level of variability in possible returns. Investors need to develop measures that will distinguish between the increasing riskiness of the investments, such as in going from Investments A to B to C. They also need to develop measures to distinguish between investments with different combinations of risk and expected return, as between A and B, A and C, or B and C. We will examine the concept of total variability of return as the first step in developing our discussion of risk measurement.

Measuring Total Variability of Return

If all of an investor's money is placed in a single security, then the investor's future income and wealth will depend on the variability of the returns for the one security. Because risk is such an important element in the investment decision, investors should attempt to perform relatively complete and sophisticated risk analyses. One way to conduct these analyses is to measure the variability of returns over time. Two of these measures are (1) the range of returns and (2) the variance or standard deviation.

Figure 4–1
Probability Distributions for Hypothetical Securities

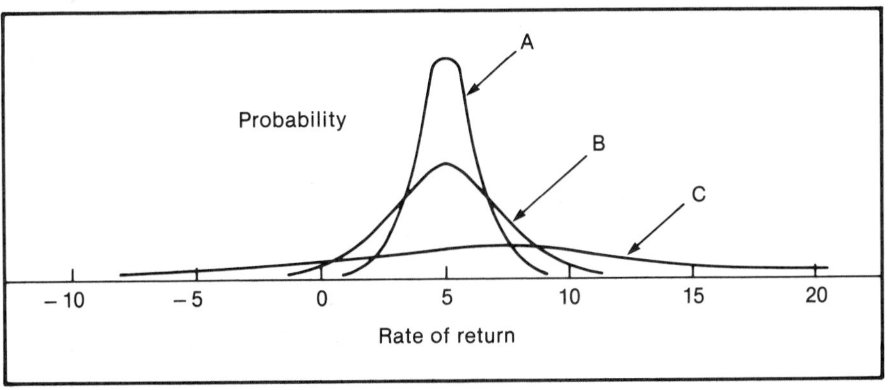

Range of Returns

The simplest measure of risk is to determine the *range of returns* from a given investment alternative by looking at the difference between the highest and lowest annual returns. In Table 4–1, the annual high and low returns were shown for each of four investment alternatives. IBM and U.S. Tobacco appear to be the least risky securities if we concentrate on the difference between the highest and the lowest annual returns. Likewise, Chrysler appears to be the most risky investment as both its highest and lowest annual returns exceed those of the other investment alternatives.

One difficulty with using the range of returns is that investors cannot say that various securities have specific degrees of risk based on an examination of the high and low annual returns. The range says nothing about the distribution of the annual returns that fall between the highest and lowest figures. Hence, investors need a better measure of risk for investment alternatives that includes the possibility of all returns and not just the extremes.

Variance and Standard Deviation

The *dispersion* of historical returns can be described by the way the returns are spread around the mean return. Referring to Table 4–3, we can see that the arithmetic mean return for the S&P 500 over the 1977–86 period was 14.6 percent. We find in Exhibit 4–1 that the return in 1986 was 18.5 percent. The return in 1986 was above the ten-year mean return by 3.9 percent (18.5 − 14.6). The difference between the individual return and the mean return is called the *deviation* from the mean and is defined as follows:

$$U_j = R_j - \bar{R} \tag{4.5}$$

where U_j = deviation of the jth period return from its mean
R_j = return in the jth period
$\bar{R}$ = mean return over the investment period

The first step in measuring dispersion of returns is to calculate the deviation for each of the historical returns. The deviations for the S&P 500 annual returns for 1977–86 are given in column 4 of Table 4–4.

After determining the deviations from the mean, the next step in measuring dispersion is to aggregate the individual deviations. The average of the individual deviations (U_js) will always equal zero because the mean, $\bar{R}$, is simply the number for which the sum of the deviations is zero. To circumvent this problem, we can square each deviation to get U_j^2 (which will always be positive), and then average the squared deviations. The resulting measure of dispersion is called the *variance*, and the steps required to calculate it are shown in Table 4–4. Column 5 gives the results from squaring each deviation in column 4. The sum of the squared deviations, 1,753.28, is shown at the bottom of column 5. To find the average squared deviation, we divide 1,753.28 by 9, the number of squared deviations *less one*. We divide by 9 instead of 10 because we are using

Table 4–4
Variance and Standard Deviation for S&P 500, 1977–86

Year		Annual Rate of Return (R)	Mean ($\bar{R}$)	Deviation from Mean (U)	Squared Deviation (U^2)
(1)		*(2)*	*(3)*	*(4)*	*(5)*
1977		−7.2	14.6	−21.8	475.24
1978		6.6	14.6	−8.0	64.00
1979		18.4	14.6	3.8	14.44
1980		32.4	14.6	17.8	316.84
1981		−4.9	14.6	−19.5	380.25
1982		21.4	14.6	6.8	46.24
1983		22.5	14.6	7.9	62.41
1984		6.3	14.6	−8.3	68.89
1985		32.2	14.6	17.6	309.76
1986		18.5	14.6	3.9	15.21
Sum	=	146.2			1,753.28
Mean	=	14.6			
			Variance = 1,753.28/(10 − 1)		= 194.81
			Standard deviation = $\sqrt{194.81}$		= 13.96

sample data and not population data. The variance for the S&P 500 over the period 1977–86 is 194.81.

The procedures for determining the sample variance for security returns can be summarized by the following formula:

$$V = 1/(n - 1)\sum_{j=1}^{n}(R_j - \bar{R})^2 = 1/(1 - n)\sum_{j=1}^{n} U_j^2 \qquad (4.6)$$

where V = the sample variance

If we are working with expected returns instead of historical returns, the variance can be calculated by multiplying each squared deviation, U_h^2, by its associated probability of occurrence, F_h. Taking the example from Figure 4–1, we can calculate the variance for the hypothetical distribution of IBM's returns to be 363.0, as shown in Table 4–5.

Table 4–5
Variance for Hypothetical Expected Returns for IBM

Business Conditions	Return	Mean	Deviation		Probability	
	R_h	R	U_h	U_h^2	F_h	$U_h^2 F_h$
Good year	35%	13%	22%	484%	.3	145.2
Average year	13	13	0	0	.5	0.0
Bad year	−20	13	−33	1,089	.2	217.8
					Variance =	363.0

To the extent that the dispersion of returns and risk are roughly identical concepts, risk can be gauged by measures of deviation. The appropriate measures of deviation are the variance and standard deviation. The *standard deviation* is found by taking the square root of the variance. Therefore, we can easily translate from one risk measure into the other. Chrysler is clearly the riskiest stock in Table 4–1 if we focus on past variance as the measure of risk. IBM appears to be the least risky because it has the lowest variance.

The purpose for estimating the historical mean and variance is to enable investors to make inferences about the underlying mean and variance for the population of historical returns and to combine these sample estimates with other information to derive estimates of future expected return and variance. If investors expect the future to depart substantially from the present and past experience and they can predict the future direction of change, the sample estimates of variance and mean should be adjusted to take into account the new information.

By recalling our elementary statistics, we can show the usefulness of variance as a risk measure when used in an investment decision. If the probability distribution of security returns is *normal,* it would appear as the symmetrical, bell-shaped curve shown in Figure 4–2. This familiar curve is uniquely described by two numbers, the mean and the variance. Therefore, knowing the expected value and the variance is all the information investors need to describe the distribution of expected returns if they are normal. Given that investors generally dislike risk (are risk averse) and returns are normally distributed, then their investment decisions can be made on the basis of expected value and variance alone.

Either variance or standard deviation can be used to measure risk. One application of the standard deviation allows a rigorous interpretation of the dispersion of returns. Given a normal distribution, about 95 percent of the actual returns over long periods of time should fall within a range of plus or minus two standard deviations of the mean. Refer back to Table 4–4 for the ten years of historical returns for the S&P 500 index. Its arithmetic mean is 14.6 percent, and its standard deviation is 13.96 percent. Therefore, about 95 percent of the S&P 500 index's actual returns over time should fall between −13.3 percent and 42.5 percent. The greater the standard deviation, the greater the range of possible returns.

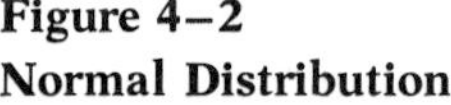
Figure 4–2
Normal Distribution

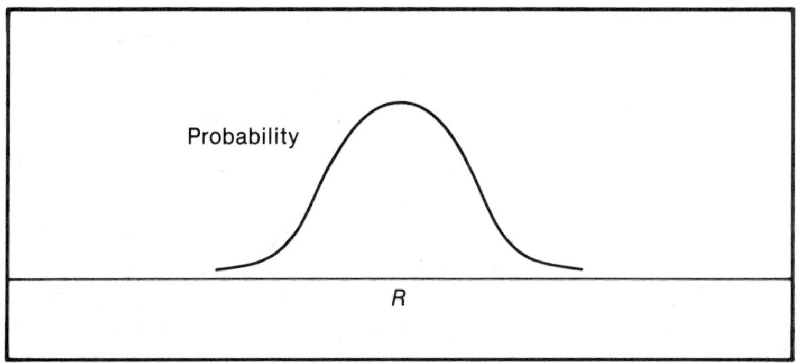

The larger the number of past observations (annual returns in this case) available for calculating the mean and standard deviation, the more confidence investors should have in the results obtained. Because the S&P 500 mean and standard deviation calculated in Table 4–4 were based on only ten yearly returns, the usefulness of the resulting mean and standard deviation needs to be considered when making predictions about future S&P 500 returns. Are there unusual returns or statistical outliers in the ten-year period? For example, is the 1982–86 bull market typical of market performance over prior periods in history? Should investors project the higher average 14.6 percent return from 1977–86 into the future or the lower average 11.5 percent return from 1967–86?

So far we have used annual returns as the measure of performance and analyzed their changes over long periods of time. Often, investors calculate monthly returns and evaluate them over shorter periods, usually five years. If the investment horizon is short, less than five years, for example, investors should consider calculating risk measures using monthly returns as opposed to annual returns.

Do actual returns in the financial markets have a normal, bell-shaped distribution? The available evidence suggests that the distributions of annual returns for common stocks are not normal. One reason for the lack of normality for annual data is that the distributions are limited on the downside. The maximum loss is 100 percent, while gains can range upward without limit. Instead of being normal, common stock returns belong to a family of statistical distributions of which normal is a member, but the actual distribution of returns is of a character in which variance has no meaning. In other words, common stock distributions resemble distributions whose dispersion cannot be measured by variance.

Security returns for short periods, such as daily, weekly, and monthly returns, are very close to being normally distributed. For periods of a month or shorter, the possibilities of large gains and losses are unlikely, so the bias against large losses is of little consequence.

Variance is still widely used by investors as a measure of risk even though common stock returns are not normally distributed. The reason lies in the fact that, while deviations from normality clearly exist, the difference between a normal distribution and the actual distribution of returns is small. It is so small that decisions made using variance are, for practical purposes, no different than decisions made using a dispersion measure in keeping with the actual distribution.

Measuring Systematic Variability for a Portfolio

Our study of riskiness has so far concentrated on analyzing individual financial assets. The focus now switches to measuring the risk of a portfolio. A *portfolio* can be defined as the combination of all real and financial assets held by an investor for investment purposes. Most individuals and institutions own many different types of securities and real assets. Examples of investments in real assets would include physical assets such as real estate, antiques, and coins. Although care must be taken in selecting individual assets, the welfare of investors depends on how well their portfolios perform.

Risk and Return Relationships

The key dimensions of portfolio performance are expected return and risk. When building portfolios, investors need to know what will happen to a portfolio's risk and return as individual securities are added. The *portfolio return* can be defined as a weighted average of the returns earned over the investment period by the individual securities held in the portfolio. The weighting factor would be the relative dollar amounts invested in each of the securities. For example, if in 1967 an investor had placed equal dollar amounts in Chrysler, A&P, IBM, and U.S. Tobacco stocks, the portfolio would have earned a 16.6 percent average annual return by 1987 (see Table 4–1). Given the average returns on the four securities, respectively, the portfolio return, R_p, is as follows:

$$R_p = 28.3(1/4) + 8.3(1/4) + 12.2(1/4) + 17.8(1/4) = 16.6\%$$

The next question investors need to address is how the returns from various assets might be expected to vary with each other over time. In the following hypothetical example, we demonstrate the impact of comovement between security returns on portfolio risk.

Assume an investor has to choose from among securities A, B, and C when forming a portfolio and believes the economy will be either in a recessionary, normal, or booming state with the probabilities of these states happening equal to 20, 60, and 20 percent, respectively. Also, assume the investor can estimate the returns for the three securities in each of the three economic states, and these return estimates are shown in Table 4–6. Let us observe what happens to the rate of return when the investor constructs two portfolios: one with 50 percent each in securities A and B, and the other with 50 percent each in securities A and C.

Most investors would agree that securities A and C individually are more risky than security B. However, by combining equal amounts of se-

Table 4–6
Three Securities: Hypothetical Expected Return and Variance

		Expected Return				
Future	*Proba-*	**Securities**			**Portfolios**	
Economy	*bility*	*A*	*B*	*C*	*AB*	*AC*
Recession	.20	80%	6%	−60%	43.0%	10%
Normal	.60	10	5	10	7.5	10
Boom	.20	−60	4	80	−28.0	10
Expected return		10%	5%	10%	7.5%	10%
Variance		1,960	.4	1,960	504.1	0

Note: The variance and mean were calculated using the procedures outlined earlier in Table 4–5.

Figure 4–3
Correlation Examples

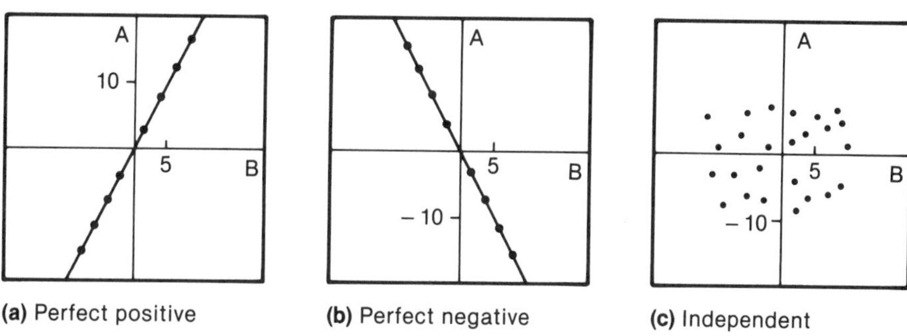

(a) Perfect positive **(b)** Perfect negative **(c)** Independent

curities A and C, the risk presented to the investor from owning each security individually is eliminated. Combining the almost riskless security B with risky security A achieves considerable reduction in the risk associated with A but not to the extent produced when combining securities A and C. The difference in the risk-reducing potential of the individual security combinations shown in Table 4–6 is explained by the nature of the differences in their correlations.

The Concept of Correlation

Correlation measures the degree to which the returns on two securities move together. Often the concept of correlation is conveyed by describing three extreme cases: perfect positive correlation, perfect negative correlation, and no correlation (independence). Figure 4–3 gives examples of these three degrees of correlation.

Positive Correlation

Perfect positive correlation means the return from one asset is directly related to the return from a second asset. If the return on security A goes up by 10 percent and the return on security B goes up by 5 percent, the return on security A will always change by twice the percentage change of security B. The relationship is perfect in that knowledge of the return on one asset will tell us, without error, exactly the return on the second asset. Although perfect correlation does not exist between actual security returns, some positive correlation between assets may be found.

The greater the positive correlation, the less will be the risk-reducing properties for a given combination of securities, and perfect positive correlation will provide no risk reduction. As an example of nearly perfect correlation, consider the impact of forming a portfolio with two electric utility common stocks. Over time, the correlation between the returns on these two stocks will not be perfect, but the returns will likely share a high degree of positive correlation. Very little risk reduction will be achieved by splitting the investments in a portfolio between the two stocks. A high positive correlation for the two utility stocks will occur because the companies are in the same industry, face comparable operating and financial problems, and are strongly affected by interest rate risk.

Statistical Independence

Two securities are *statistically independent* if a knowledge of one security's return tells us nothing about the second security's return. In effect, the price movements of the two securities will appear to be influenced by entirely different events. Combining two securities showing statistical independence will result in more risk reduction than with two positively correlated securities. Past patterns of security returns showing statistical independence tend to be somewhat rare.

Negative Correlation

Perfect diversification is in theory possible with securities that have perfect negative correlation. Two securities would exhibit *perfect negative correlation* if knowledge of the return from one security tells us all we need to know about the return from the second security and if the changes in their returns are always opposite in direction. For example, if the return from one security increases, the return from the second security decreases. By combining equal amounts of two securities with perfect negative correlation and equal variances, we could produce a portfolio with zero variance such as with portfolio AC in Table 4–6. Combining two securities with negative correlation will provide more risk reduction than securities with positive correlation or statistical independence.

Correlation Measures

Three related techniques commonly used to measure the degree of correlation between securities are (1) the covariance, (2) the correlation coefficient, and (3) the beta coefficient. We will discuss the first two correlation measures in this section along with the correlation matrix and the coefficient of determination. The beta measure will be taken up later in this chapter.

Covariance between Two Securities

This is the most frequently used measure to show the degree of association between the returns for two securities. Investors often calculate historical covariance between securities and use it to help forecast expected covariance, correlation, and systematic risk.

To illustrate the measurement of the historical covariance, we will analyze the monthly returns listed in Table 4–7 for Chrysler and A&P, re-

Table 4–7
Covariance: Chrysler and A&P, 1986 Monthly Stock Returns

	Chrysler Return	$U_{C,j}$	A&P Return	$U_{A,j}$	$U_{C,j} \times U_{A,j}$
(1)	*(2)*	*(3)*	*(4)*	*(5)*	*(6)*
1/86	−1.07%	−3.45	−4.11%	−5.10%	17.6
2/86	23.04	20.66	9.58	8.59	177.5
3/86	22.25	19.87	4.92	3.93	78.1
4/86	−21.20	−23.58	7.19	6.20	−146.2
5/86	2.76	.38	−2.93	−3.92	−1.5
6/86	3.02	.64	5.53	4.54	2.9
7/86	−6.23	−8.61	−2.95	−3.94	33.9
8/86	8.39	6.01	.49	−.50	−3.0
9/86	−6.45	−8.83	−15.69	−16.68	147.3
10/86	6.94	4.56	3.95	2.96	13.5
11/86	2.27	−.11	8.99	8.00	−.9
12/86	−5.14	−7.52	−3.09	−4.08	30.7
					Sum = 349.9
	Mean = 2.38%		Mean = .99%		
	Variance = 150.5		Variance = 52.1		
		Covariance = 349.9/(12−1) = 31.8			

spectively. The process by which the covariance is calculated is not obvious to most investors, so we will explain how covariance is determined.

First, the deviations for each security, $U_{C,j}$ and $U_{A,j}$, must be calculated for every period. The mean monthly returns for Chrysler and A&P were 2.38 and 0.99 percent, respectively. Using January as the example, Chrysler's deviation was −3.45 percent (column 3), which is the January return of −1.07 (column 2) minus 2.38 (the mean return). In like manner, A&P's January deviation was −5.10 (column 5). The process must be repeated for every month for both securities.

Second, for a given month, the deviations for the two stocks are multiplied together. Column 6 shows the product for January, 17.6, from multiplying −3.45 times −5.10. The product can be referred to as the cross-product deviation. The rest of column 6 records the cross-product deviations for the remaining months.

The third step requires that the cross-product deviations be summed for all months and the total divided by the number of months *less one.* The resulting number is the degree of covariance for the two securities. For Chrysler and A&P, we have the covariance equal to 349.9 divided by 11, which equals 31.8.

The equation for determining the covariance between two security returns from historical data can be stated as follows:

$$V = 1/(n - 1) \sum_{j=1}^{n} U_{A,j} U_{B,j} \qquad (4.7)$$

where V = sample covariance

Figure 4–4
Correlation: Chrysler and A&P, 1986 Monthly Stock Returns

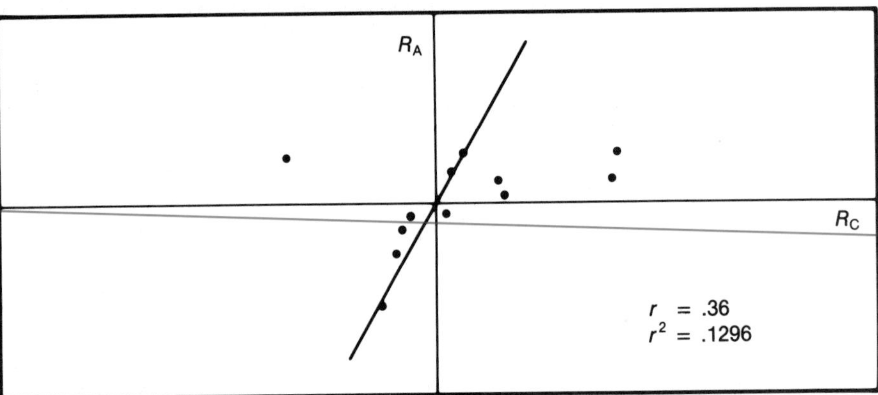

Correlation Coefficient

The covariance and correlation coefficient are closely related measures. Once we have found the covariance between two securities, we can calculate the correlation coefficient, given that we have already determined their respective standard deviations. The correlation is found by applying equation 4.8.

$$r_{AB} = \text{Cov}(R_A, R_B)/(S_A \cdot S_B) \qquad (4.8)$$

where r_{AB} = the correlation coefficient for securities A and B
S_A, S_B = the standard deviations for securities A and B, respectively

Applying equation 4.8, we can see that the correlation between the monthly stock returns for Chrysler and A&P is .36. See Figure 4–4.

$$r_{CA} = 31.8/(12.3 \cdot 7.2) = .36$$

The correlation of .36, as displayed in Figure 4–4, indicates a low degree of positive correlation between the two stocks. The values for r will range between -1 for perfect negative correlation, to 0 for no correlation, to $+1$ for perfect positive correlation.

Correlation Matrix

The correlation coefficient provides investors with one measure showing the strength of the relationship between two variables. The *correlation matrix* shows the correlation for *each pair of securities* in a portfolio. Table 4–8 shows the correlation matrix for the 1967–86 period for the four securities in Table 4–1. The correlation matrix allows investors to obtain an indication of the potential risk-reducing ability of each security. For example, based on historical patterns, adding IBM to U.S. Tobacco to form a portfolio would be one of the combinations that provides the most risk reduction because these two securities have a relatively low correlation (r = .3155). On the other hand, adding Chrysler and A&P stock to form a

Table 4–8
Correlation Matrix, Selected Securities, 1967–86 Annual Data

	Correlation Matrix			
	Chrysler	*A&P*	*IBM*	*U.S. Tobacco*
Chrysler	1.0000			
A&P	.7665	1.0000		
IBM	.7562	.5877	1.0000	
U.S. Tobacco	.3606	.3812	.3155	1.0000

Note: The correlations between each of the stocks and the S&P 500 are

	Chrysler	*A&P*	*IBM*	*U.S. Tobacco*
S&P 500	.4270	.5095	.6223	.3140

portfolio would provide weak risk reduction as calculated by $r = .7665$ for the way the returns on these two securities move together.

When examining the correlation matrix, an investor should keep two important considerations in mind. First, the risk of any resulting portfolio may be inappropriate for the investor. Second, in focusing on the risk of the portfolio, the investor should not ignore what is happening to the return at the same time.

Coefficient of Determination

Squaring the correlation coefficient, r, yields the coefficient of determination, r^2. The *coefficient of determination* gives the percent of the fluctuations of one security's returns explained by knowing the other security's returns. Using the correlation coefficients from Table 4–8, we can show that if we know the returns for Chrysler, we can explain 57 percent ($.756^2$) of the fluctuation in the returns for IBM. On the other hand, we can explain only 10 percent ($.3140^2$) of the fluctuation in U.S. Tobacco's returns by knowing the returns on the S&P 500. The coefficient of determination is important because it provides investors with a good measure of the strength of the co-movement between stock returns. Its maximum value will be one, and its minimum value will be zero.

To this point, we have discussed the risk-reduction achieved when forming portfolios with only two securities. Next, we will expand the discussion to look at portfolios formed with many securities.

Diversification Aspects

How many securities need to be in a portfolio before most of its unsystematic risk is diversified away? Studies generally show that by combining approximately eight to sixteen randomly selected stocks, most of the unsystematic risk of the portfolio may be eliminated.

Figure 4–5
Risk and Portfolio Size

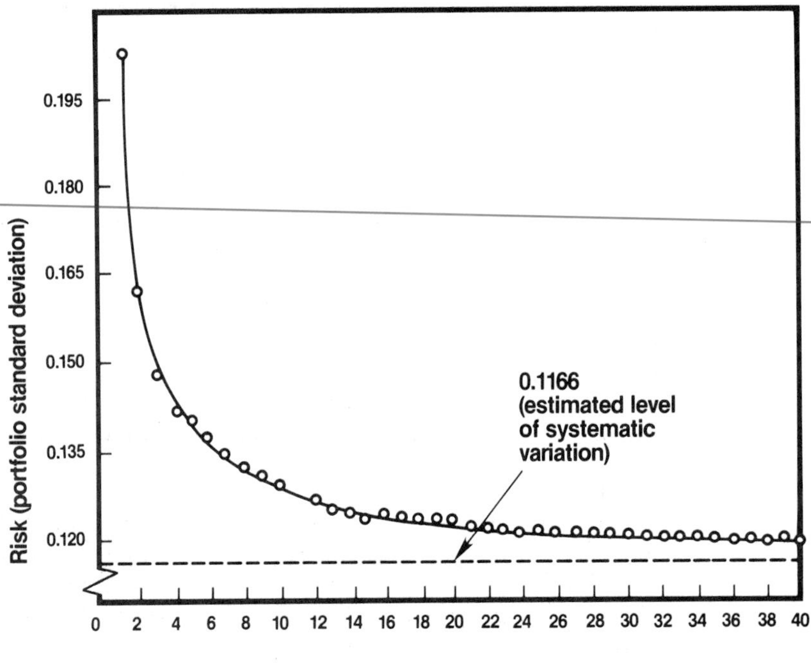

Source: John L. Evans and Stephen H. Archer, "Diversification and the Reduction of Dispersion: An Empirical Analysis," *Finance* (December 1968): 761–67.

An important point to be noted from Figure 4–5 is the difference between diversifiable risk and nondiversifiable risk. Figure 4–5 demonstrates that diversifiable risk can be eliminated quite easily by simply buying enough different kinds of common stock. This process is known as "naive" diversification.

Variability and the Market Portfolio

The *market portfolio* is defined as a portfolio consisting of all assets with each asset's weight in the portfolio being equal to its market value relative to the market value of all assets. The assets would include financial assets such as stocks and bonds as well as real assets such as houses, art masterpieces, automobiles, and human capital. All unsystematic risk is eliminated for the market portfolio, and its returns respond only to market-wide influences. In other words, the systematic risk for the aggregate of all real and financial assets is the variability of the market portfolio.

Hence, if we measure the correlation between a stock and the market portfolio, we are measuring *the stock's systematic risk.* The risk of any stock is its contribution to the risk of the market portfolio *as measured by*

Figure 4–6
Covariance: Chrysler and the S&P 500, 1986 Monthly Returns

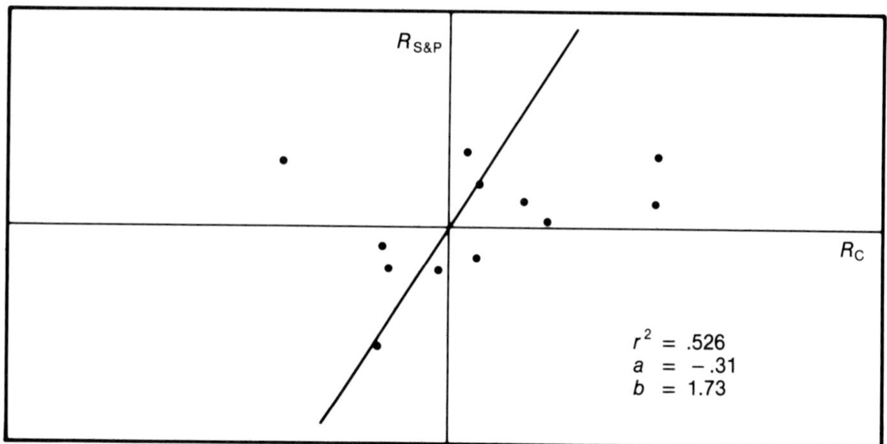

the covariance between the returns of the stock and the returns of all assets. Not all stocks respond by the same degree to a change in the overall market. Once we find the individual stock's systematic risk, however, its return can be separated into two basic components: the *market component* and the *firm specific component.*

The complication here is that although all assets should be considered in the market portfolio, valuation and return measurement problems for many of these assets are insurmountable. As a way around this problem, investors often use the returns on a broad-based market index, such as the S&P 500 index, as a reasonable approximation for the return performance of the market portfolio.

Figure 4–6 shows the degree of correlation between Chrysler's monthly common stock returns and those of the S&P 500 stock index for 1986. Most of the monthly return pairs are clustered in the first and third quadrants of the figure, indicating positive correlation. If we calculated the covariance between Chrysler's returns and the S&P 500 index's returns, it would turn out to be 45.82, and the variance of the S&P 500 index returns would be 26.49. The procedures used to calculate the covariance between Chrysler and the S&P 500 index are the same as those used to show the measurement of covariance between Chrysler and A&P except the S&P 500 returns are substituted for the A&P returns.

$$\text{Cov}(R_C, R_{S\&P}) = 504.00/(12 - 1) = 45.82$$

The Market Model and the Characteristic Line

The relationship between any two variables can be specified as a model showing the way we think their values should change together over time. Theoretically, stock returns (on average) and market portfolio returns should move together proportionally or as if related by a straight line. The formal statement of this association is given in equation 4.9 and is called the *market model.* This equation describes the return for a single investment period *j*.

$$\tilde{R}_{k,j} = \hat{a}_k + \hat{b}_k(\tilde{R}_{M,j}) + \tilde{E}_{k,j} \qquad (4.9)$$

where $\tilde{R}_{k,j}$ = security *k*'s return during period *j*

$\hat{a}_k$ = security *k*'s constant return, known as *alpha*

$\hat{b}_k$ = co-movement measure for security *k*'s return and the market portfolio's return, known as *beta*

$\tilde{R}_{M,j}$ = the market portfolio's return during period *j*

$\tilde{E}_{k,j}$ = the difference between $\tilde{R}_{k,j}$ and the actual return for period *j*, known as the error term

The market model simply says that if the market return is known for a given period, the stock's return should equal alpha plus the product of the market return times beta. For example, given that the estimates of alpha, 10.8, and beta, .6, based on twenty years of annual returns as shown in Table 4–1, are the correct market model values and that the S&P 500 earned 18.5 percent in 1986, then in 1986 U.S. Tobacco's stock should have earned:

$$10.8 + .6(18.5) = 21.9\%$$

The actual return in 1986 was 32.9 percent, so the market model's error term was 11 percentage points.

If on average the association between stock returns is something other than what we have specified in the market model, another model would be more appropriate to explain how the returns on securities are related. A more appropriate model would consistently provide better predictions of security returns by having smaller error terms. If the market model correctly represents the association between returns on securities and the market portfolio, the next step in our evaluation of the risk and return for individual securities is to estimate a_k and b_k. The line with the parameters, a_k and b_k, that we estimate for an individual security is called its characteristic line.

Estimating the Characteristic Line

The first step in estimating a security's alpha and beta parameters is to define the data on which the estimates are to be made. Should daily, weekly, monthly, or yearly stock returns be used? Should the data be collected for one, five, ten, twenty, or sixty years? The investor must consider many complex factors in setting up the data to estimate the alpha and beta parameters, some of which depend on the investment horizon, the availability of data, and statistical design issues. These topics are the subject of more advanced discussions in investment analysis. Let us assume that the investor can identify the "appropriate" data and use it to assess the alpha and beta parameters of a security.

Given the appropriate data, we can estimate a_k and b_k by taking a ruler and drawing a line between the points in Figure 4–6 so as to approximate the average co-movement between the individual $R_{k,j}$ and $R_{M,j}$

pairs. From elementary statistics, we know the line that best fits the relationship between two variables is found by the method of regression analysis. Applying regression analysis to pairs of returns for security k and the market index will yield the estimates for a_k and b_k.

Alpha and Beta Estimates for Securities

The statistical equations used to estimate a_k and b_k for a set of data are given below by equations 4.10 and 4.11. They are called the *normal* equations in statistics.

$$b_k = \text{Cov}(R_k, R_M)/V_M \tag{4.10}$$

where $\text{Cov}(R_k, R_M)$ = the covariance between security returns and market index portfolio returns

V_M = the variance of the market index portfolio returns

The beta estimate is the slope of the line that best fits the plot of the return pairs for the stock and the market over time, and it is a measure of the stock's systematic variability with the market portfolio. The variance of the S&P 500 index monthly returns in 1986 was 26.48, and the covariance between Chrysler's returns and the S&P 500's returns was 45.82. Applying equation 4.10, the beta based on the 1986 monthly returns can be shown to be:

$$b_C = 45.82/26.48 = 1.73$$

A beta of 1.73 means that if investors expect the market to increase by 10 percent, they should expect that *on average* Chrysler's return will increase by 17.3 percent (1.73 times 10 percent).

The intercept term estimate, a_k, is also of importance to investors who are attempting to forecast future stock returns.

$$a_k = \bar{R}_k - b_k\bar{R}_M \tag{4.11}$$

The alpha estimate can be interpreted as the rate of return that would be earned on an investment independent of the market return. Given that in 1986 the average monthly returns on the S&P 500 and Chrysler were 1.56 and 2.38 percent, respectively, then the alpha for Chrysler can be determined by applying equation 4.11 as follows:

$$a_C = 2.38 - 1.73(1.56) = -.31\%$$

From the historical analysis of a security's returns, investors can derive estimates of the expected return on the basis of the systematic risk and constant term. The equation for a security's expected return, given the return on the market index, is called the *characteristic line* and is stated by equation 4.12.

$$E(R_{k,j}) = a_k + b_kR_{M,j} \tag{4.12}$$

The characteristic line for Chrysler's stock based on the 1986 monthly returns is given by:

$$E(R_{C,j}) = a_C + b_CR_{M,j} = -.31\% + 1.73R_{M,j}$$

If we take a longer perspective and state the characteristic line using alpha and beta estimates derived from the 1967–86 period (from Table 4–1), we have the following:

$$E(R_{C,j}) = -1.7\% + 2.6R_{M,j}$$

Clearly, our assessment of Chrysler's systematic risk will differ substantially depending on whether we use the one-year or the twenty-year estimate. The investor must exercise judgment in deciding what statistical information to use and how to combine it with other information to come up with estimates of expected returns.

We can now distinguish between Chrysler, A&P, IBM, and U.S. Tobacco as to which is the riskiest on the basis of their historical beta estimates. Over the 1967–86 period, Chrysler is the riskiest with an estimated beta of 2.6, while U.S. Tobacco is the least risky with an estimated beta of .6. On the basis of the beta estimates alone, Chrysler would be classified by investors as a high-risk stock, A&P and IBM as average-risk stocks, and U.S. Tobacco as a defensive or low-risk stock.

r and r^2

How much actual returns deviated from the predicted values on the characteristic line can be measured by a statistical error term. Often, the error term is presented in percentage terms as the coefficient of determination, r^2. The coefficient of determination breaks the security's total return variability into (1) the percent explained by the characteristic line and (2) the percent attributed to the residual error. Applying equation 4.8, correlation coefficient for Chrysler and the S&P 500 based on the monthly returns in 1986 is determined to be:

$$r_{C,S\&P} = 45.82/(12.27 \cdot 5.15) = .725$$

The coefficient of determination then is calculated by squaring r:

$$r^2_{C,S\&P} = .725^2 = .526$$

Finally, we can give an answer to the question about how much of a stock's total risk is market risk and how much is firm specific risk. For Chrysler, we break down total risk as follows:

Market risk component = 52.6%

Firm specific component = 47.4%

Alpha and Beta Estimates for Portfolios

Once we have estimated alpha and beta for each security in a portfolio, we can take a shortcut to calculate the portfolio's alpha and beta estimates. For example, the alpha and beta values for an equally weighted portfolio of Chrysler, IBM, A&P, and U.S. Tobacco based on the 1967–86 period can be determined as follows:

	Alpha	Beta
Chrysler	−1.7	2.6
A&P	−5.7	1.2
IBM	.4	1.0
U.S. Tobacco	10.8	.6
Portfolio	3.8/4 = 1.0	5.4/4 = 1.4

Portfolio alpha and beta estimates are the weighted averages of the alpha and beta estimates, respectively, for the individual securities.

Summary

Any measurement technique for determining the rate of return from an investment needs to consider the time value of money. Based on the concept of compound interest, the time value of money allows us to examine any investment in a present value framework. The price we are willing to pay for any investment should be the present value of all future cash flows.

The investor will need to discount anticipated future cash flows at the appropriate discount rate that reflects the rate of return desired by the investor, given the nature of the investment's anticipated risk. For common stocks, the cash flows will come from dividends and the estimated selling price of the security. The investor will need to examine such factors as management skills, marketing opportunities, and the general economic environment in estimating future dividends and the selling price at the end of the investment holding period.

In assessing the anticipated return from any investment, investors need to attempt to measure the risk that will be assumed in order to earn the anticipated return. Variance was chosen as the appropriate measure of risk for two reasons. First, most investors agree that risky assets have a large dispersion or a wide range of possible returns. If dispersion is our intuitive concept of risk, variance is the relevant risk measure because variance measures dispersion. Second, if returns are close to being normally distributed, all we need to know to make investment decisions is the mean and the variance. By taking the square root of the variance, we obtain the standard deviation, which is a powerful statistical tool for portfolio risk management. It indicates the percentage of the fluctuation in one price series that is "explained" by the movement of a second price series.

In combining securities into portfolios, investors need to be concerned with both the return and risk dimensions of the resulting combination. The concept of correlation allows us to consider the nature of the risk and return trade-offs that result. By combining securities whose returns have either a low positive correlation or a negative correlation, investors can achieve more risk reduction than by combining securities having relatively high return correlations. In essence, investors need to focus on the return achieved per unit of risk assumed.

Symbols Used in This Chapter

P	Price or value at a point in time
R	Holding period return
D	Dividend or interest payment
m	Number of periods per year
G	Geometric mean
j	jth period, time index
n	Total number of periods
W_j	Wealth relative in period j, equals 1 + holding period return
$E(R)$	Expected return over a future period
q	Total number of possible outcomes or states
h	hth outcome or state, states of nature index
F	Probability distribution for outcomes
U	Deviation of the return from its mean
$\bar{R}$	Mean return over the investment period
V	Sample variance
S	Sample standard deviation
k	kth security, security index
p	Specific portfolio, portfolio index
r	Correlation coefficient between securities' returns
Cov	Covariance between two securities' returns
r^2	Coefficient of determination
a	Alpha estimate
b	Beta estimate
E	Error term
alpha	Intercept
beta	Slope
i	Annual rate of return
0	Beginning (origin) of period
∞	Infinity
Π	Product of
Σ	Sum of
A	Present value of an annuity
PMT	Equal periodic annuity payment
Z	Future value of an annuity

Suggested Readings

ALTMAN, EDWARD I., and ROBERT A. SCHWARTZ. "Common Stock Price Volatility Measures." *Journal of Financial and Quantitative Analysis* (January 1970): 603–625.

BREALEY, RICHARD A. *An Introduction to Risk and Return from Common Stocks*, Second Edition. Cambridge, MA: MIT Press, 1983.

HAUGEN, ROBERT A. "Do Common Stock Quality Ratings Predict Risk?" *Financial Analysts Journal* (March–April 1979): 68–71.

IBBOTSON, ROGER G., LAURENCE B. SIEGEL, and KATHRYN S. LOVE. "World Wealth: Market Values and Returns." *Journal of Portfolio Management* (Fall 1985): 4–23.

KANDEL, SHMUEL, and ROBERT F. STAMBAUGH. "On Correlations and Inferences About Mean-Variance Efficiency." *Journal of Financial Economics* (March 1987): 61–90.

LAKONISHAK, JOSEF, and ALAN C. SHAPIRO. "Stock Returns, Beta, Variance and Size: An Empirical Analysis." *Financial Analysts Journal* (July–August 1984): 36–41.

MODANI, NAVAL K., PHILIP L. COOLEY, and RODNEY L. ROENFELDT. "Stability of Market Risk Surrogates." *Journal of Financial Research* (Spring 1983): 33–40.

Modigliani, Franco, and Gerald A. Pogue. "An Introduction to Risk and Return." *Financial Analysts Journal* (March–April and May–June 1974): 68–80 (Part I) and 69–86 (Part II).

Pinches, George E., and William R. Kinney, Jr. "The Measurement of the Volatility of Common Stock Prices." *Journal of Finance* (March 1971): 119–125.

Rosenblum, Harvey, and Steven Strongin. "Interest Rate Volatility in Historical Perspective." *Economic Perspectives,* Federal Reserve Bank of Chicago, (January–February 1983): 10–19.

Schweser, Carl, Robert M. Soldofsky, and Tom Schneeweis. "The Meaning of the Mean." *Journal of Portfolio Management* (Summer 1979): 23–27.

Singleton, J. Clay, and John Wingender. "Skewness Persistence in Common Stock Returns." *Journal of Financial and Quantitative Analysis* (September 1986): 335–41.

Soldofsky, Robert M., and Dale F. Max. Holding Period Yields and Risk-Premium Curves for Long-Term Marketable Securities: 1910–1976. New York University, Center for the Study of Financial Institutions, Monograph 1978–2.

Statman, Meir, and Neal Ushman. "Another Look at Bonds versus Stocks." *Journal of Portfolio Management* (Winter 1987): 33–38.

Questions

1. Why does money have a time value?
2. How do you calculate the arithmetic mean? Under what circumstances is the arithmetic mean a poor method of measuring rates of return over time?
3. Making investment decisions involves a trade-off between what two fundamental variables?
4. If one recommends that variance be used to measure risk, discuss whether or not it is necessary to relate variance to such important items as interest rate risk, purchasing power risk, and business risk.
5. Critically examine the reasons why variance or standard deviation might be used to measure the risk of financial assets. Can you cite any evidence that suggests the validity of variance to measure risk?
6. Define and interpret the following:
   - **(a)** standard deviation
   - **(b)** perfect correlation
   - **(c)** covariance
   - **(d)** correlation coefficient
   - **(e)** coefficient of determination

7. Why is covariance such an important concept for the investor when considering the selection of a portfolio of financial assets?

8. Why is it necessary to introduce the coefficient of determination in order to interpret the meaning of the covariance statistic?

9. What is the importance of probability distributions of returns in making investment decisions? What is the nature of the probability distribution that would apply to a risk averter as opposed to a risk seeker?

10. Discuss the importance of the correlation matrix in considering appropriate investments.

11. What role does the size of the portfolio play in achieving the benefits of diversification? What other factors do investors need to consider besides the number of securities in the portfolio?

12. What does the characteristic line tell investors?

Problems

1. Teresa told Wally that she had invested $10,000 three years ago and that on average her money had tripled each year. For example, it quadrupled the first year, tripled the second year, and doubled the third year.

   Wally was impressed by her surprisingly good investment luck and said, "Wow, Teresa, you must have $270,000 by now since your money tripled on average each year for three years." Teresa replied, "Well, not exactly, Wally. You see, I only have $240,000."

   Wally asked, "Oh, what happened to the additional $30,000, Teresa? Did you lose it?"

   What should Teresa tell Wally?

2. Suppose you are given a $1 lottery ticket with a chance to win $10 million. If the odds of having the winning numbers are less than one in a billion and someone offers you a dime for your ticket, would you take the dime? Why or why not?

3. Allicia bought 100 shares of IBM stock at the end of 1985 for $155.50 per share. During 1986, she received $4.40 per share in dividends, and at the end of 1986, she sold the stock for $120 per share.

   (a) What was Allicia's holding period return for 1986?

   (b) What would have been her holding period return if she had been able to sell the stock for $220 per share instead of $120 per share?

4. Merck Company's year-end stock prices and annual dividends per share for the eight-year period, 1979–86, are given below. Calculate the seven annual holding period returns over the 1980–86 period. What is the average holding period return on Merck's com-

mon stock for the 1980–86 period using the arithmetic mean approach?

Year	Price	Dividend	Year	Price	Dividend
1979	$36.125	$ .95	1983	$45.188	$1.40
1980	42.375	1.15	1984	47.000	1.50
1981	42.375	1.30	1985	68.500	1.60
1982	42.313	1.40	1986	123.875 *	1.90 *

* Prices and dividends have been adjusted for the effect of a two-for-one split in 1986.

5. For the data in Problem 4, calculate the geometric mean return for Merck over the 1980–86 period. Are the geometric mean return and the arithmetic average return equal? Which estimate would be a better measure of the mean return for the 1980–86 period? Why?

6. IBM's adjusted annual dividends and end-of-year stock prices are given for the 1979–86 period.

Year	Price	Dividend	Year	Price	Dividend
1979	64.375	3.44	1983	122.00	3.71
1980	67.875	3.44	1984	123.125	4.10
1981	56.875	3.44	1985	155.50	4.40
1982	96.25	3.44	1986	120.00	4.40

(a) Calculate the annual holding period return for each year.

(b) Calculate the average annual growth in the stock price for the 1980–86 period.

(c) Calculate the average annual dividend yield for the 1980–86 period.

(d) Calculate the arithmetic mean return and the geometric mean return for the 1980–86 period.

7. The annual holding period returns for Merck, Texas Instruments, Walt Disney, and Western Union are given in the following table.

Year	Merck	Texas Instruments	Walt Disney	Western Union	S&P 500
1977	−16.3%	−26.9%	−16.3%	−7.4%	−7.2%
1978	24.9	11.3	2.6	−2.8	6.6
1979	9.6	12.5	13.0	51.0	18.4
1980	20.5	39.5	15.8	18.6	32.4
1981	3.1	−31.7	3.9	56.3	−4.9
1982	3.2	69.7	23.3	26.1	21.4
1983	10.1	4.5	−14.9	−15.1	22.5
1984	7.3	−12.3	16.1	−73.2	6.3
1985	49.1	−10.0	90.5	41.4	32.2
1986	83.6	13.9	54.0	−67.7	18.5

(a) Calculate the mean, variance, and standard deviation for each of the four stocks. Compare the results with the corresponding values for the S&P 500.

(b) Rank the desirability of these securities using the means and standard deviations.

8. For the data in Problem 7, calculate the covariance between the annual rates of return for Merck and Walt Disney over the 1977–86 period. Determine the correlation coefficient and the coefficient of determination. Give an interpretation of what the correlation coefficient implies about the historical association between returns on the two securities.

9. Ralph foresees five possibilities for next year's economy, states A through E, and he formulates probability estimates associated with the likelihood that each state will occur. He considers investing in one of three stocks, GG, JJ, or KK, and derives expectations about the returns on these stocks for each state of the economy. The following table shows these expectations.

State of the Economy	Returns R_{GG}	R_{JJ}	R_{KK}	Probabilities P_i
A	−.10	−.25	.15	.1
B	−.05	−.05	.10	.2
C	.00	.15	.00	.4
D	.10	.45	−.05	.2
E	.15	.55	−.10	.1

(a) If Ralph rates the desirability of security returns for GG, JJ, and KK on the basis of their means and standard deviations, how do the three securities rank? On the basis of the standard deviations, which is the riskier security?

(b) If Ralph places 50 percent of his money in GG and 50 percent in JJ, what is the resulting portfolio's expected return and standard deviation for the next year?

10. In Problem 9, $\bar{R}_{GG} = \bar{R}_{KK}$ and $\sigma_{GG} = \sigma_{KK}$.

(a) If Ralph invests 50 percent of his money in GG and 50 percent in KK, what is the portfolio's expected return and standard deviation for the next year?

(b) Calculate the covariance and correlation coefficient between GG and JJ, between GG and KK.

11. What is your interpretation of the following correlation matrix?

Company	Merck	Texas Instruments	Walt Disney	Western Union
Merck	1			
Texas Instruments	.1314	1		
Disney	.7497	.1144	1	
Western Union	−.3168	.0692	.0406	1

12. General Electric Company's monthly prices and dividends for the first twelve months in 1986 are as follows:

Month	Month Ending Price	Dividend	Month	Month Ending Price	Dividend
12/85	72.75		7/86	73.00	
1/86	70.875		8/86	78.625	
2/86	77.50	.58	9/86	71.875	.58
3/86	78.00		10/86	76.25	
4/86	78.125		11/86	83.00	
5/86	79.75	.58	12/86	86.00	.63
6/86	81.00				

(a) What is the annualized return for the stock based on its performance in the first quarter? The second quarter? The third quarter? The fourth quarter? What is the annual return based on the full-year data?

(b) What problems do you foresee with annualizing returns based on short-interval data?

13. Refer back to the data given in Problem 7. Assume that in 1977 Mary held a portfolio with 50 percent invested in Merck and 50 percent invested in Walt Disney. At the end of each year, the value of the portfolio was recalculated, and the investments in Merck and Disney were returned to the proportions of 50 percent each.

(a) What was the holding period return on the portfolio in each year from 1977 through 1986? What was the arithmetic mean return on the portfolio for the entire ten-year period? How did this mean return compare with the mean return on each stock?

(b) Calculate the standard deviation for the portfolio, and compare it with the standard deviation for each stock.

(c) Comment on the degree of diversification that Mary achieved by combining Merck and Walt Disney stock.

(d) If Mary added more stocks to the portfolio, what would most likely happen to the portfolio's standard deviation? Which stock, Western Union or Texas Instruments, would provide the most diversification for her portfolio if combined with Merck and Walt Disney stock? (Hint: Use the data in Problem 11 to help you make a choice.)

14. You are given the following results of the regression analysis comparing the returns for Jordan Corporation with the S&P 500.

alpha	−10%
beta	1.75
correlation coefficient	65%

(a) If you expect the return on the S&P 500 for next year to be 18 percent and the return on the risk-free asset to be 7 percent, what return do you expect on the Jordan Corporation?

(b) If the actual return on the Jordan Corporation next year is 5 percent, what would you say caused the error in the forecast?

15. Refer back to the data given in Problem 7.

(a) Graph the return pair for each year over the period, 1977–86, for Merck and the S&P 500. Using your own judgment, draw a line that best represents the points on the graph. What is the slope of your line? Where does it cross the vertical axis? How closely related are the returns on Merck and the S&P 500?

(b) Calculate the characteristic line for Merck, and compare the calculated beta with the slope of the line on your graph.

(c) What percentage of the variability of the return for Merck is systematic risk?

16. Calculate the characteristic lines for the remaining three securities in Problem 7 using a regression program. Compare the results for these three securities with the results found for Merck in Problem 15.

(a) Rank the stocks in terms of their systematic risk.

(b) Graph the characteristic lines using the alpha and beta estimates you derived with regression analysis.

(c) Given that the return on the risk-free security averaged 9.6 percent over the 1977–86 period, what are the implications of the alpha estimates you calculated for the three stocks?

17. You are constructing a portfolio that will consist of five investments, Dayton Hudson, General Motors, Allegis, Southern Bell, and gold coins. The expected beta for each investment is listed below. Assume the $140,000 portfolio is invested in the five securities as follows:

	Beta	Market Value
Dayton Hudson	1.2	$25,000
General Motors	1.1	20,000
Allegis	1.3	30,000
Southern Bell	0.7	15,000
Gold Coins	0.1	50,000

(a) What is the portfolio beta?

(b) How would you suggest the portfolio composition be changed if you anticipated a *bear* market?

(c) What would happen to the portfolio beta if you replaced the investment in gold coins with an investment in Deb Shops, a stock with a beta of 2.0?

Appendix

Time Value of Money

Investment analysis requires that investors be able to compare and combine investment values that occur at different points in time. The procedures used to compare money values over time are the future and present value calculations. The *future,* or *compound value,* is the amount that a sum will equal in the future if interest is compounded on a periodic basis. Compounding means that the *interest earned in a period and not paid out* will earn interest itself in future periods.

Compound Interest Calculations

To understand compound interest problems, we can look at a savings account example. If a savings institution states that it pays 6 percent interest, an investor will expect a \$100 deposit to grow to \$106 by the end of one year. As a matter of common practice, interest rates are expressed in annual terms as a percentage of the initial investment.

$$P_1 = \$100(1 + .06) = \$106$$

In general, for a one-year investment, the future amount will equal the principal plus the accumulated interest:

$$P_1 = P_0(1 + i) \qquad (4A.1)$$

where P_1 = the future value at the end of 1 period
P_0 = the present value (at time 0)
i = the compound interest rate for the period

Now, suppose the initial \$100 savings account is held for two years. How much money will be available at the end of the two-year period? The answer is given by:

$$P_2 = \$100(1 + .06)(1 + .06) = \$112.36$$

During the first year, the 6 percent return generated \$6 on the \$100 deposit. During the second year, the 6 percent return generated \$6.36 *on the \$106.00 in the account at the start of the second year.* During the second year the depositor earned \$6 on the initial deposit of \$100 and \$.36 on the \$6 interest earned but left in the account from the first year. This is the essence of compound interest.

The above procedure can be generalized so that the future sum for any number of compounding periods can be determined. This is shown below as equation 4A.2.

$$P_n = P_0(1 + i)(1 + i)(1 + i) \ldots (1 + i)$$

$$P_n = P_0(1 + i)^n \qquad (4A.2)$$

where P_n = the value of the investment at the end of n periods
n = the number of periods

In the two-year example above, P_2 will be as follows:

$$P_2 = \$100(1 + .06)^2 = \$100(1.1236) = \$112.36$$

Frequently, a savings institution will advertise an annual rate of return compounded for other than annual periods. The basic compounding equation still applies and can be restated in the following manner:

$$P_n = P_0[1 + (i/m)]^{mn} \qquad (4A.3)$$

where m = the number of compounding periods in a year

The examples presented in Exhibit 4A–1 show the initial \$100 compounded semiannually, quarterly, and monthly for a period of four years at an annual rate of 6 percent.

Some banks advertise that interest is paid continuously on money left in the account. The future sum of an amount deposited where interest is compounded continuously can be determined by the equation 4A.4:

$$P_n = P_0e^{in} \qquad (4A.4)$$

where e is the exponential function, base e, and $e^1 = 2.71828$

The interest factor $(1 + i/m)^{mn}$ becomes e^{in} when interest is compounded continuously. Continuing with the example above, the future sum of \$100 at the end of 4 years, compounded continuously at 6 percent annually, is calculated as follows:

$$P_4 = \$100e^{.06(4)} = \$100e^{.24}$$

$$= \$100(1.2712) = \$127.12$$

Exhibit 4A–1 Future Value Calculations: Compounding Periods

Semiannually	*Quarterly*	*Monthly*
$P_8 = 100(1 + .06/2)^{4(2)}$	$P_{16} = 100(1 + .06/4)^{4(4)}$	$P_{48} = 100(1 + .06/12)^{4(12)}$
= \$126.68	= \$126.90	= \$127.05

Nominal versus Effective Rate (Annual Percentage Return)

When deposits are compounded more frequently than annually, a distinction is made between the nominal rate and the effective rate. The *nominal rate* is simply the advertised rate. The *effective rate*, or annual percentage return (APR), equals the following:

$$\text{effective rate} = (1 + i/m)^m - 1 \qquad (4A.5)$$

For a 6 percent annual rate, the effective rate is 6.09 percent semiannually $(1 + .06/2)^2 - 1$, 6.14 percent quarterly $(1 + .06/4)^4 - 1$, and 6.17 percent monthly $(1 + .06/12)^{12} - 1$.

Present Value Calculations

The *present value* is the amount that a future value will equal today when discounted at a rate of i percent per period. Alternatively, the present value can be defined as the amount of money that would have to be invested initially to earn at a given rate so as to produce a given amount at the end of the investment period.

Recall that equation 4A.2 can be used to determine the value of an investment at the end of n periods:

$$P_n = P_0(1 + i)^n$$

Using simple algebra, the equation can be restated in the present value form to solve for P_0. Dividing both sides of equation 4A.2 by $(1 + i)^n$ yields equation 4A.6.

$$P_0 = P_n \frac{1}{(1 + i)^n} = P_n(1 + i)^{-n} \qquad (4A.6)$$

Thus, an investor expecting to receive $116.64 at the end of two years and desiring to earn an 8 percent return compounded annually will need to deposit $100 initially as determined below:

$$P_0 = \frac{\$116.64}{(1 + .08)^2} = \$116.64(.8573) = \$100$$

The $100 is the present value of the future receipt $116.64.

To give another example, an investment producing $90 at the end of four years will have a present value of $61.47 if the investor desires a 10 percent return compounded annually. Using equation 4A.6, the present value of the $90 future receipts is determined as follows:

$$P = \$90 \frac{1}{(1 + .10)^4} = \$90(1 + .10)^{-4}$$

$$= \$90(.6830) = \$61.47$$

The term $(1 + i)^{-n}$ is commonly referred to as the discount factor. For the above example, the discount factor $(1 + .10)^{-4}$ equals 0.6830.

Present and Future Value Calculations for Annuities

An investment that promises a constant payment in each period is called an *annuity*. Many investment opportunities either require a constant annual investment or offer to pay a constant annual amount for several years into the future. We present three examples showing how to evaluate investments that have part or all of their returns in the form of an annuity.

One example of a typical investment decision is the purchase of a bond. Suppose an investor considers purchasing a bond that pays $75 at the end of each of the next three years plus $1,000 face value (return of principal) at the end of the third year. Suppose further that the return on similar bonds is currently 9 percent compounded annually. What price should be paid for this bond? The investor should be willing to pay the present value of all future bond payments, discounted at a 9 percent rate of return.

Exhibit 4A–2 illustrates the required present value calculations. Columns 1 and 2 show the year and the receipts for that year, respectively, and column 3 is the discount factor. Column 4 is the product of the payment times the discount factor and represents the present value of each annual cash receipt or payment. The bond's value is made up of two components, the present value of the constant annuity (the $75-per-year interest payment) and the present value of the single payment at maturity (the $1,000 principal value). The total present value, $962.05, is the price of the bond required for the investor to reach a 9 percent return. If the actual price in the market were more than $962.05, the investor would earn less than 9 percent. A price lower than $962.05 would generate a return greater than 9 percent. The only difference between our hypothetical bond calculations and the price calculations made by bond investors is that actual calculations utilize semiannual payments and we assumed annual payments in this example.

Using Present Value Tables

Present value calculations such as those presented in Exhibit 4A–2 are usually facilitated by the use of present value tables. These tables can be found in Appendix A–1 at the end of the book. Appendix A–1 is simply a

Exhibit 4A–2 Present Value Calculation: Hypothetical Bond

Year	Payment Received at End of Year	Discount Factor $(1 + i)^{-n}$ $i = 9\%$	Present Value
(1)	*(2)*	*(3)*	*(4)*
1	$75	.9174	$68.80
2	75	.8417	63.13
3	1,075	.7722	830.12
		Total Present Value =	$962.05

Exhibit 4A–3 Present Value Calculation: Hypothetical Bond

Year	Payment Received at End of Year	Discount Factor 9%	Present Value
1–3	$ 75	2.5313	$189.85
3	1,000	.7722	772.20
		Total Present Value =	$962.05

compilation of various values of equation 4A.6, $1/(1 + i)^{-n}$. Each column represents a separate value of i, and each row, a separate value for n. For example, the discount factor of .7722 in Exhibit 4A–2 can be found in Appendix A–1 under the column labeled *9%* and the row labeled *3*. This is the present value of $1 received in three years at a 9 percent discount rate, or rate of return.

Often, present value calculations can be shortened even further. Whenever periodic payments are constant, we do not need to multiply each payment by its corresponding discount factor. We can instead simply sum the present value factors and multiply this sum by the constant annual payment. Equation 4A.7 shows this procedure.

$$A_n = \text{PMT} \sum_{j=1}^{n} (1 + i)^{-n} \tag{4A.7}$$

where A_n = the present value of an annuity of n payments
PMT = the constant periodic payment

An example of this process is given in Exhibit 4A–3, where the present value of the hypothetical bond is calculated in the shorter manner. The yearly $75 payment (annuity) is multiplied by the sum of the three discount factors. This product is added to the present value of the bond's $1,000 face value received in the third year.

To facilitate this calculation, Appendix A–2 at the end of the book shows discount factor sums for various returns and various periods. The first row in Appendix A–2 is a duplicate of the first row of Appendix A–1. Each additional row in Appendix A–2 is generated by adding the next period's discount factor from Appendix A–1 to the number in the previous row in Appendix A–2. In our example, the 2.5313 present value factor may be found in the third row under the column labeled *9%*.

Algebraically, the values in the present value column of Appendix A–1 can be summed to arrive at the corresponding value in Table 4A–2. The equation to determine the present value of an annuity of $$R$ per period for n periods is given as follows:

$$A_n = \text{PMT} \frac{1 - (1 + i)^{-n}}{i} \tag{4A.8}$$

Although we do not prove the relationship here, equation 4A.8 follows directly from equation 4A.7 if we recognize that the interest component in equation 4A.7 is the sum of a geometric interest rate series. The interest component in equation 4A.8 is an equivalent statement of the geometric series sum.

The present value of any constant stream of payments can be determined using equation 4A.8. For example, if an investor wants to receive an annuity of \$10,000 per year for 20 years when money can earn 7.3 percent per year, an investment of \$103,514 will be required. The calculation is as follows:

$$A_{20} = \$10{,}000 \, \frac{1 - (1 + .073)^{-20}}{.073} = \$10{,}000 \, \frac{1 - .2443}{.073}$$

$$= \$10{,}000(10.3521) = \$103{,}521$$

A second example of a typical investment is the purchase of preferred stock. Suppose an investor is considering the purchase of a share of preferred stock that promises to pay dividends of \$50 per year, forever. Suppose further that the return on similar preferred stock is 10 percent. What price should be paid for this preferred stock? The investor should be willing to pay the present value of the \$50 perpetual annuity, discounted at a 10 percent rate. With the number of annuity payments extending to infinity, for example, setting n to infinity in equation 4A.8, the value of a perpetual annuity becomes the following:

$$A_\infty = \frac{\text{PMT}}{i} \tag{4A.9}$$

In the second example, the present value of the preferred stock to the investor is \$500.

$$A_\infty = \frac{\$50}{.10} = \$500$$

A third example of a typical investment situation involves finding the future accumulated sum of a periodic annuity, such as an individual retirement account or an insurance endowment program. Suppose an investor considers depositing \$10,000 into a retirement program at the end of each year for the next ten years. Furthermore, suppose that the program offers to pay 10 percent per year. At the end of ten years, how much will be accumulated in the retirement account? The investor should calculate the sum of the compound future value of the ten payments.

As with the present value of an annuity, the calculations needed to determine the sum on an annuity can be shortened. In this case, the future value of an annuity can be written as equation 4A.10.

$$Z_n = \text{PMT} \sum_{j=1}^{n} (1 + i)^n$$

$$= \text{PMT} \, \frac{(1 + i)^n - 1}{i} \tag{4A.10}$$

where Z_n = the future value of an annuity of n payments

In the above example, the accumulated future value of the retirement account will be \$159,374.

$$Z_{10} = \$10{,}000 \, \frac{(1 + .10)^{10} - 1}{.10} = \$10{,}000 \, \frac{2.5937 - 1}{.10}$$

$$= \$10{,}000(15.9370) = \$159{,}370$$

Most financial calculators have programmed function keys for future and present value problems, including both the present and future value of an annuity.

Problems

1. Jane is considering a savings deposit in three different banks. Which bank should she choose if the banks pay interest as follows?

   Bank A = $5\frac{1}{2}$ percent compounded semiannually
   Bank B = $5\frac{3}{8}$ percent compounded quarterly
   Bank C = $5\frac{1}{4}$ percent compounded monthly

   Jane plans to keep her money in the bank for one year.

2. A bond is currently selling for $500 in the market. It pays zero percent interest annually, and its $1,000 principal amount is repaid at maturity in ten years. What is this bond's annual rate of return?

3. A $1,000 bond pays $100 interest annually at the end of each year and has fifteen years remaining until it matures. At maturity, the $1,000 is returned to the investor. What would an investor who desires a twelve percent return be willing to pay for this bond?

4. John's broker calls and informs him that a new bond offering is currently being made at par ($1,000 per bond). John is promised $100 yearly in interest income for every bond he purchases, and the bonds mature in thirty years. John knows that interest rates have been volatile in recent years and is concerned about the bond investment should he have to sell sometime prior to the maturity date.

   (a) What would happen to the price of his bond if interest rates immediately increased to 12 percent?

   (b) Suppose John sells the bonds after holding them for only three years. Including interest payments received over the three-year period, how will John do if interest rates fall to 8 percent in the market? Rise to 14 percent?

5. Maura Walther is considering two options: (1) planting trees on some land she owns or (2) selling the land. She could sell the land for $1,500 an acre now. On the other hand, she estimates that the land would be worth $4,000 an acre in twenty years if she plants the trees. If she wants a 12 percent return from holding the land, what should she do?

6. When the time comes, Harry Smith wants to provide a college education for his son, who is now two years of age. He would like to have $40,000 when his son is eighteen. To enable him to have this future amount, Harry wants to make common stock investments now and feels a 10 percent annual compounded rate of return is a reasonable expectation. How much must he invest now in order to pay for his son's education?

7. In Problem 6 above, instead of investing everything today, how much money—in fifteen equal annual installments beginning at the end of the current year—must Harry invest in order to meet the goal? Assume the last payment is made at the end of the fifteenth year when his son is seventeen.

8. Joe is considering several different investment opportunities and is analyzing the cash flows and prices for each. His investment horizon is ten years, and all tax issues are ignored in his analysis.

   (a) A zero coupon bond (a bond that pays no interest) matures in ten years, at which time it pays Joe $1,000. Currently, bonds of the same risk class are providing investors with a yield to maturity of 12 percent. Determine the price for this zero coupon bond.

   (b) A preferred stock issue pays Joe a constant annual dividend of $8 per share and is viewed as being perpetual. The preferred stock is currently being discounted at 13 percent in the market. Determine the price for this preferred stock.

   (c) A bond pays Joe 12 percent interest at the end of every year and matures in 10 years, at which time it pays Joe the $1,000 par value. At the moment, the bond's yield to maturity is 14 percent. Determine the price for this bond.

   (d) A company pays all of its earnings as dividends. Joe receives an annual dividend of $1.20 that is expected to continue far into the future. The stock is not expected to grow in value over the next ten years, and Joe plans to sell it in ten years for the same price as he paid today. Given that the market requires a 14 percent return on this investment, determine the price Joe would pay today.

9. Jenny buys a new sports car for a price of $25,000 and makes a $10,000 down payment. How much are the monthly payments if her car loan requires thirty-six equal monthly installments and the interest rate is 1 percent per month?

10. Billy wants to be a millionaire. If Billy starts today and invests $30,000 every year, how long will it take to achieve his goal if his funds are invested to earn 10 percent annually? (Ignore taxes and commissions.)

16

9, 12

Chapter 5

Valuation Approaches: Fundamental and Technical Analysis

Key Concepts

- advance-decline line
- asset value method
- book value
- confidence index
- constant growth model
- discount rate
- dividend yield
- Dow Theory
- efficient market hypothesis
- fundamental analysis
- intrinsic value
- leverage
- multiple growth model
- P/E ratio
- present value method
- price pattern
- price-to-book value ratio
- quality of earnings
- relative value method
- resistance level
- support level
- sustainable growth model
- technical analysis
- technical indicator
- turnover

Chapter Outline

Fundamental Analysis

Technical Analysis: Investment Timing

Summary

Valuation approaches for determining the prices of securities can be separated into three categories: fundamental analysis, technical analysis, and asset pricing models. Fundamental analysis attempts to determine the *intrinsic* or long-run value for a share of stock based on the capitalization of its income stream. Investors can profit from trading strategies keyed to exploit differences between a stock's current market price and its intrinsic value. Technical analysis is the study of trends in security prices and market data for the purpose of detecting patterns in the movement of stock prices. Investors can profit from trading strategies based on temporary stock price adjustments. In Chapter 6, we develop two asset pricing models that can be used in determining the return investors should earn for bearing systematic risk. On the basis of the asset pricing models, investors can identify opportunities in which systematic risk is being mispriced.

Fundamental Analysis

Fundamental analysis is the process of identifying securities that are under- or overvalued at a point in time. In the quest for extraordinary returns, the fundamental analyst attempts to "uncover" these special situations by applying a variety of appraisal techniques. Three commonly used techniques of fundamental analysis are the present value, relative value, and asset value methods.

Present Value Method

The essence of the various present value models used to value common stock is that the price of a stock is simply the present value of its future dividend stream. The present value is determined by applying the appropriate *discount rate* to the expected future dividends. We will assume for the moment that investors know what rate should be applied when discounting the income stream from a common stock, and this appropriate rate is the stock's required rate of return. The required return should include the risk-free rate plus premiums reflecting the riskiness of the future dividend stream.

In a more general manner, we can use all future cash receipts rather than only dividends when determining the value of any security. For example, the future receipts for a fixed-income investor will be the interest payments plus the estimated selling price of the security.

Consider an investment in a common stock for a one-year holding period. The investor will receive dividends, if any are paid, and the selling price. The initial price should be the present value of these payments as follows:

$$P_0 = \frac{D_1}{1 + i} + \frac{P_1}{1 + i}$$

where P_0, P_1 = the beginning and ending prices, respectively

D_1 = the dividends received during year or period 1
i = the return required by investors

The price of a common stock for any investment period can be given by an extension of the above equation as follows:

$$P_0 = \frac{D_1}{(1+i)} + \frac{D_2}{(1+i)^2} + \frac{D_3}{(1+i)^3} + \cdots + \frac{P_n}{(1+i)^n} \qquad (5.1)$$

where P_n = the ending or selling price
n = the number of periods or years of the investment

This equation assumes that the dividend payment is made at the close of each period. The assumption is strictly for convenience and does not alter the basic nature of equation 5.1. The equation applies to any common stock investment. If the investor's expected holding period is very small or zero, then the current price is dominated by the selling price at the end of the holding period. If the holding period is very long or dividends are very large, the current price, P_0, may be determined primarily by the dividend portion of receipts. Accordingly, this model is applicable to so-called growth stocks paying little or no dividends as well as to high-dividend-paying stocks.

The terminal price, P_n, in equation 5.1 is the present value of all future returns expected beyond the close of the nth period. The sale price, P_n, for one investor will equal the present value of the dividends and eventual selling price the next investor expects to receive from owning the stock. When the final price of the stock is pushed far enough into the future, its present value approaches zero. Under these circumstances, the current price of any common stock can be given by equation 5.2, which emphasizes the importance of dividends in the valuation process.

$$P_0 = \frac{D_1}{(1+i)^1} + \frac{D_2}{(1+i)^2} + \cdots + \frac{D_n}{(1+i)^n} \qquad (5.2)$$

$$= \sum_{j=1}^{\infty} \frac{D_j}{(1+i)^j}$$

where j = the jth period (the time index)

Constant Growth Model

Equation 5.2 can be simplified even further if, as is the case in many instances, future dividends are related in some functional manner to the present dividend. Suppose the present dividend of a firm is \$1, and the dividend next year is expected to be \$1.05. Let us look at the implication of having future dividends grow at a rate of 5 percent annually. The dividend in the first year, D_1, becomes:

$$D_1 = D_0(1+g) = \$1(1+.05) = \$1.05$$

where g = the annual growth rate in dividends

Assume the dividend in the second and subsequent years is expected to continue growing at the rate established in the first year. The dividend in the second year becomes $D_0(1 + g)^2$, the dividend in the third year becomes $D_0(1 + g)^3$, and so on for each year thereafter. At a 5 percent growth rate, a \$1 current dividend will grow to \$1.1025 in two years (\$1.05²) and to \$1.1576 in three years (\$1.05³). Under these circumstances, the current price of the common stock as described in equation 5.2 may be restated as given in equation 5.3:

$$P_0 = \sum_{j=1}^{\infty} \frac{D_0(i + g)^j}{(1 + i)^j} \tag{5.3}$$

If we assume that the growth rate is constant and less than the required rate of return, i, the price of the stock reduces to equation 5.4:

$$P_0 = \frac{D_1}{i - g} \tag{5.4}$$

For example, assume that three different investors are considering the purchase of a common stock that pays a dividend of \$1.50 and has an expected dividend growth rate of 6 percent. Investor A wants a minimum 10 percent return, investor B wants a minimum 8 percent return, and investor C wants a minimum 12 percent return. As shown below, A should be willing to pay no more than \$37.50, and the theoretical maximum prices for B and C are \$75 and \$25, respectively.

	Investor A (i = 10%)	**Investor B (i = 8%)**	**Investor C (i = 12%)**
$P =$	$\frac{1.50}{.10 - .06}$	$\frac{1.50}{.08 - .06}$	$\frac{1.50}{.12 - .06}$
$=$	\$37.50	\$75.00	\$25.00

In order to use equation 5.4, we are required to make the following assumptions about the conditions of the marketplace:

1. A known and constant growth rate of dividends, g
2. A constant rate of return, i
3. A rate of return that is greater than the growth rate, $i > g$
4. An infinite time horizon for the market as a whole, $j \to \infty$

Although the practicality of these assumptions is surely questionable, the constant growth model does capture the fundamental factors to be considered when determining the value of a common stock. Essentially, the investor's task becomes one of estimating future dividends either in absolute values, equation 5.2, or by establishing a growth rate for dividends, equation 5.4. Once either of these has been determined, the present value of the stock will depend on the *rate of return the investor requires* in order to satisfy specific utility, risk, and opportunity cost characteristics.

The risk characteristics of the anticipated dividend stream are taken into account by investors when the required rate of return is established. From Chapter 4, we learned that a variety of techniques are available for incorporating risk into the evaluation of security returns. In the remainder of Chapter 5, we will assume that investors estimate the risk premium based on personal judgments or by deriving them from risk premiums associated with comparable investments. In Chapter 6, we will describe two different techniques that are often used to make these risk premium estimates.

The dividend valuation model just developed in no way suggests that other factors will not operate in determining the price of a given stock. Such factors as stock popularity and rumors about various company policies may have their effects, but in general these aspects of common stock investment are short lived. Such items as earnings growth, quality of management, financial integrity, and general economic conditions, however, *will* influence the price of a common stock because they affect its fundamental value, as determined by the dividends of the firm, both now and in the future. Many facets of a company become important to the investor as these variables influence the firm's dividend-paying ability.

Multiple Growth Model

One of the important assumptions made in using equation 5.4 is that the dividend grows at a constant, perpetual rate. Quite often, companies in the early stages of development have exceptionally high growth rates. After the company matures, these rates decline and stabilize at lower levels. To capture these different stages of dividend growth, we need to evaluate the stages separately. For example, assume an investor wants to receive an 18 percent return from an investment that promises a current dividend of \$1.50. The dividend is expected to grow for three years at 20 percent per year, for two years at 15 percent per year, and annually after that at a constant rate of 10 percent. The value of the dividend stream is as follows:

$D_1 = (1 + .20)\ \$1.50 = \$1.80$	$\$1.80\ (.8474)$	=	\$ 1.53
$D_2 = (1 + .20)\ \$1.80 = \$2.16$	$\$2.16\ (.7182)$	=	1.55
$D_3 = (1 + .20)\ \$2.16 = \$2.59$	$\$2.59\ (.6086)$	=	1.58
$D_4 = (1 + .15)\ \$2.59 = \$2.98$	$\$2.98\ (.5158)$	=	1.54
$D_5 = (1 + .15)\ \$2.98 = \$3.43$	$\$3.43\ (.4371)$	=	1.50
$P_5 = (1 + .10)\ \$3.43 = \$3.77$	$[\$3.77/(.18 - .10)](.4371)$	=	20.60
			\$28.30

Notice that the value of the 10 percent, constant growth dividend stream beginning in year 6 can be calculated as a single value, P_5, in year 5 by using equation 5.4 as follows:

$$P_5 = D_6/(i - g) = \$3.77/(.18 - .10) = \$47.13$$

The final value of the stock is the sum of its individual growth components. Often, instead of using equation 5.4, investors will calculate a selling price for the stock at some future date and discount that future value back to the present time. The future value is usually determined by multiplying the future earnings level by a long-run average price-to-earnings per share ratio (usually referred to as the price-earnings or *P/E ratio*).

Relative Value Approach

Relative valuation methods determine such basic information as the firm's P/E ratio, the return on stockholders' equity (ROE), the dividend yield

(*D/P*), and the growth rates for both dividends and earnings. These figures are then compared to the market in general, to the industry, and to firms within the industry. As we stated earlier, the idea is to find companies that appear to be relatively over- or undervalued.

Stocks for companies with a high potential for future growth in earnings will usually have higher P/E ratios than stocks for companies with low or no growth potential. Similarly, companies with higher variability of their earnings and dividend streams will have lower P/E ratios than those with lower variability. Different relative P/E ratios for stocks tend to reflect the positions of companies with respect to their industry and the overall market on the basis of key characteristics, such as earnings growth, dividend payout, leverage, return on equity, and risk levels. An average stock with average performance would likely have its earnings capitalized at the P/E ratio for the average stock in the market. Investors frequently take data from several time periods when determining the relative value of a stock. Often, data from the current and several past years are examined and combined with data on expectations about future years.

Exhibit 5–1 **Relative Valuation Example: Market, Industry, and K mart**

	Market	Industry	K mart
	Multiplier		
Price-earnings ratio (P/E)			
current (1987)	17.1	17.5	13.9
past five-year average	12.1	11.2	9.6
	Percent		
Return on stockholders' equity (ROE)			
current (fiscal 1986)	13.0	15.3	14.8
past five-year average	12.9	15.4	14.3
	Percent		
Historical five-year growth rates			
dividends per share (DPS)	7.6	16.9	8.5
earnings per share (EPS)	6.7	16.6	8.0
	Percent		
Projected five-year growth rates			
dividends per share (DPS)	8.7	13.7	8.5
earnings per share (EPS)	15.7	17.9	11.5
	Percent		
Dividend yield			
current (1987)	2.3	1.4	2.9*
past five-year average	3.7	3.3	3.8

*These calculations are based on the May 6, 1987, stock price for K mart of $40¼, after taking into account a three-for-two stock split. These dividend estimates are derived by annualizing the first quarter dividend and amount to $1.16 per share on a post-split basis.

Source: Value Line Investment Survey, various editions, 1986–87, and K mart Corporation, *1986 Annual Report*.

Exhibit 5–1 is an example of how the relative valuation of a stock might be done. The stock for the K mart Corporation has been chosen for the demonstration, and the *Value Line* data are reported for key performance measures (1) in fiscal 1986, (2) during the prior five-year period, and (3) as projected for the future five-year period. (See Exhibit 3–5 for the *Value Line* report on K mart.) To establish a basis of comparison, *Value Line* averages for the retail trade industry and the overall market are also presented. To make the industry averages conform more closely to K mart's circumstances, only retailing firms that had earnings yields greater than 1 percent were included in the data set.

According to this analysis, K mart seems to be valued less favorably than the industry and the market in general. Although we would want to look at other data, such as those discussed in detail in Chapters 7 through 9, we can make the following general observations regarding Exhibit 5–1:

1. The P/E ratio is lower for K mart than for the industry and the market. In other words, investors can "buy" earnings at lower prices from K mart than from the industry and the market. Note that this industry's current P/E ratio is slightly higher than the market average.
2. The ROE for fiscal 1986 is slightly lower for K mart than for the industry. Both K mart and the retailing industry have higher ROE measures than the market.
3. Over the prior five-year period, K mart's dividends per share (DPS) and earnings per share (EPS) grew approximately 1 percentage point faster than the corresponding market figures. However, K mart's dividends per share and earnings per share grew at substantially lower rates than those of the industry, around one-half the corresponding rates. *Value Line*'s forecasts of future earnings and dividend growth for K mart are below both the industry and the market averages. K mart is not expected to keep up with the industry or market in the future.
4. K mart's *dividend yield* (D/P) is slightly higher than for the industry and the market yields. If we add the current dividend yield to the expected growth in DPS to obtain an estimate of the future total return, we get:

$$
\begin{aligned}
i = D/P + g &= 2.3 + 8.7 = 11.0 \quad \text{Market} \\
&= 1.4 + 13.7 = 15.1 \quad \text{Retailing industry} \\
&= 2.9 + 8.5 = 11.4 \quad \text{K mart}
\end{aligned}
$$

On the basis of the *Value Line* estimates, the future expected return on K mart appears to be well below the industry's return and a little above that of the general market.

Asset Value Approach

An *asset value approach* focuses mainly on the value of the tangible assets owned by a firm. Investors examine such things as the value of the firm on a per-share basis as revealed by the company's accounting records or

Figure 5–1
Price-to-Book Value for S&P 400 Industrial Average, 1950–86

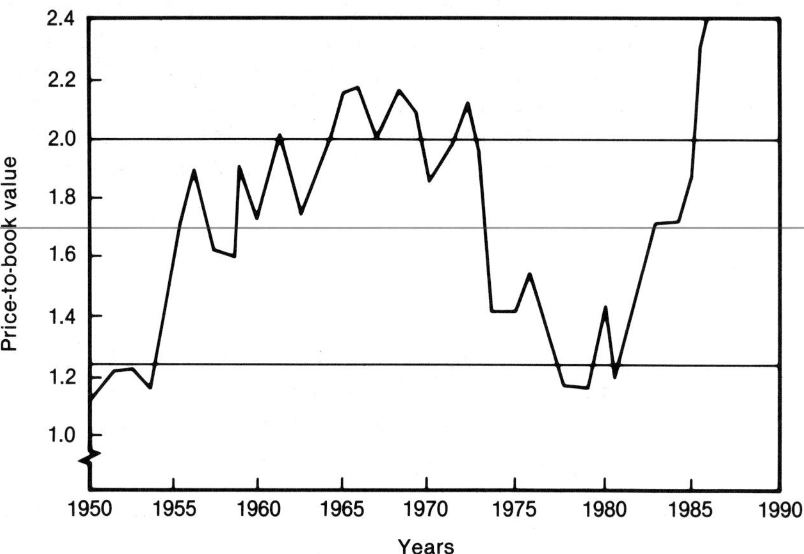

by its cash assets. Investors essentially seek to buy physical assets at a bargain price—perhaps in the hope that another company will want to merge with that company at a later date and at a much higher price.

Figure 5–1 shows the *price-to-book value ratio* for the Standard and Poor's Industrial Average of 400 stocks for the 1950–86 period. Although accounting considerations have an impact on the *book value* of the S&P 400 index, this measure seems to be of help to investors. Using arbitrary standards of 2.00 to 1.25 as measures of over- and undervaluation, we see that undervalued periods were evident in the early 1950s and during the 1978–81 period. The market appeared to be overvalued in 1960, in the mid to late 1960s, in 1972, and in 1986. The long bull market starting in May 1982 can be seen in the rise in the ratio to above 2.00 in 1986.

For K mart, the price-to-book value ratio in early 1987 was 2.05 ($40.25/$19.66), which is close to the industry average of 2.4. By historical standards, K mart's stock price does not appear to be undervalued in comparison to the value of its underlying assets.

Sustainable Growth Model

In order for dividends to grow at a steady pace, several phases of the firm's operations must expand in unison and be unconstrained. The concept of *sustainable growth* focuses on the ability of a company to establish and maintain a balanced growth rate and is supported by several underlying foundation concepts. First, an equity base is assumed to be needed to support future growth. Second, additional equity in the form of a new common stock offering is assumed to be unobtainable. The second assumption implies that the future net income growth is a function of the future rate of return on stockholders' equity and the amount of earnings retained in the business.

The third foundation is based on the assumption that growth can occur only to the extent that the equity base expands. In other words, if all the earnings are paid out in dividends and new stock is not sold, growth cannot occur. Implicit in this discussion is the idea that the present debt and equity mix used for the firm is close to the optimal capital structure. For example, future debt issues should only be made in proportion to new equity growth.

Growth Rate Estimate

We will use the fiscal 1986 annual report for K mart to analyze its sustainable growth. The growth in net income that is sustainable under the assumptions just noted is given by equation 5.5.

$$g = \text{ROE} \times (1 - \text{DPS/EPS}) \tag{5.5}$$

where g, ROE, DPS, and EPS are as defined previously in this chapter

Using the fiscal 1986 figures for K mart, we get a sustainable growth rate of 9.6 percent using the 14.8 percent ROE for K mart in 1986 as reported in Exhibit 5–1.

$$\begin{aligned} g &= \text{ROE} \times (1 - \text{DPS/EPS}) \\ &= .148 \times (1 - .35) = .096 \text{ or } 9.6\% \end{aligned}$$

The ROE is in turn a function of a number of factors as shown in the following equation, with K mart's 1986 data used for the example.[1] (See Exhibits 9–2 and 9–3 for the fiscal 1986 *K mart Annual Report* data.)

$$\begin{aligned} \text{ROE} &= \text{Margin} \times \text{Turnover} \times \text{Leverage} \times \text{Tax adjustment} \\ &= \frac{\text{Earnings before taxes}}{\text{Revenue}} \times \frac{\text{Revenue}}{\text{Total assets}} \times \frac{\text{Total assets}}{\text{Net worth}} \times (1 - \text{tax rate}) \\ &= \frac{1{,}040}{23{,}812} \times \frac{23{,}812}{10{,}578} \times \frac{10{,}578}{3{,}939} \times (1 - .440) \\ &= .0437 \times 2.251 \times 2.685 \times .560 \\ &= .148 \text{ or } 14.8\% \end{aligned} \tag{5.6}$$

By breaking down the ROE into four components, we can examine each component to see whether the value calculated for 1986 seems representative of what the future might hold. In this manner, we can get a better idea of whether or not a substantial number of shares of common stock will need to be sold in the near future. K mart has not had a sizable

1. To be consistent with the way *Value Line* data are presented, ROE is calculated as net income divided by end-of-year net worth. In Chapter 9, we show an alternative measure for ROE in which beginning net worth is used in place of ending net worth.

sale of new shares since 1972; the firm has been able to handle its growth without issuing new shares of stock.

Let us now look at the impact of each individual component on K mart's return on equity (ROE). In our review of the components, we will suggest when changes are likely to occur in future periods.

Margin

K mart's before-tax margin is higher than in any year in the previous five-year period except 1983, when the margin was 4.7 percent. For 1986, the before-tax margin of 4.37 percent translates into an after-tax margin of 2.45 percent. In early 1987, K mart announced intentions to streamline its operations by closing or selling subsidiaries with unprofitable and low-profit performance records. The sustainable growth calculation of 14.8 percent may be low as related to the future if K mart can maintain profit margins on its streamlined operations. In this regard, we examine *Value Line*'s profit margin projections for the 1989–91 period below. *Value Line* remarked that "remerchandising, refurbishing, and installing point-of-sale equipment will help the K mart stores to finally realize their potential."[2]

Turnover

The turnover figure of 2.251 seems to be a little low if the new point-of-sale equipment improves the company's inventory control procedures. In the past, inventory turnover, the critical component in the estimation of turnover ratios for merchandising companies, has been stable from year to year. If inventory turnover is improved, the estimate of sustainable growth could be raised slightly.

Leverage

K mart took on considerable long-term debt between 1972 and 1986 for the purpose of financing new stores. The number of stores in operation rose from 1,183 in 1972 to 3,700 in 1986. During that period, long-term debt usage increased from \$23.4 million to a peak of \$3.1 billion. However, in 1986 K mart began reducing its debt levels and finished the year at the \$2.6 billion level. Continuing with its restructuring moves in 1987, K mart sold 116 Kresge and 22 Jupiter stores to Woolworths. Apparently, K mart built up debt capacity so that leverage should not be a limiting factor to its sustainable growth. A reasonable estimate of the future asset-to-net worth ratio might be in the 2.3 range.

---

2. *Value Line Investment Survey,* report dated March 6, 1987, p. 1,649.

Tax Adjustment

The tax rate can be expected to decline from the 44 percent level of 1986 to around a 37 percent level in future years. This tax reduction should follow as a consequence of the implementation of the 1986 Tax Reform Act.

Projections

Value Line anticipated that earnings would grow at an 11.5 percent annual rate from the 1983–85 period to the 1989–91 period. Let us briefly examine the *Value Line* estimate for the 1989–91 period to see how much new equity financing might be needed. *Value Line* expected an after-tax profit margin of 3.2 percent and a tax rate of 37 percent. This translates into a before-tax margin of 5.1 percent [3.2/(1 − .37)]. Making the assumption that the asset-turnover ratio will increase to around 2.3 and the asset-to-equity ratio will decline to around 2.3, we estimate the future ROE to be approximately 17 percent.

$$\begin{aligned} \text{ROE} &= \text{Margin} \times \text{Turnover} \times \text{Leverage} \times \text{Tax adjustment} \\ &= .051 \times 2.3 \times 2.3 \times (1 - .37) = .170 \end{aligned}$$

Using *Value Line*'s estimate of the company's future dividend payout rate of 28 percent, we calculate a growth rate of 12.2 percent.

$$g = .17 \times (1 - D/E)$$
$$g = .17 \times (1 - .28) = .122 \text{ or } 12.2\%$$

Value Line indicated that earnings were expected to grow at an 11.5 percent annual rate from the 1983–85 period to the 1989–91 period, which is very close to our 12.2 percent estimate. What would need to happen to prevent K mart from realizing an earnings growth rate in the 12 percent range?

Several possibilities exist. The most significant would be that the profit margins could be lower than anticipated, and the turnover rate could decrease instead of increasing. A widespread economic downturn, especially in personal consumption expenditures, could have a substantial negative impact on these two ratios. A higher tax rate or dividend payout ratio would also reduce K mart's growth rate. *Value Line* estimated that K mart's sales will grow to almost $32 billion by the 1989–91 period, for an average annual increase of slightly more than 6 percent. We can only question how long the earnings of a major retailer can be expected to grow at a rate almost twice that of its growth in sales.

Let us project the total equity financing needs for the future based on *Value Line*'s estimate for K mart's sales in the 1989–91 period of $32 billion. With the asset-turnover rate at 2.3, K mart will need to maintain about $14 billion in assets ($32/2.3). Financing these assets at the leverage factor of 2.3 would mean having approximately $6 billion in equity financing ($14/2.3). Will K mart be able to obtain this level of equity financing solely on the basis of retaining earnings from operations?

By projecting K mart's future earnings (Exhibit 5–2), we can see if financing with retained earnings is a reasonable expectation. If *Value*

Exhibit 5–2	Hypothetical Equity Position, K mart Corporation, 1991		
Year	*Sales Growing at 6% (millions)*	*After-tax Earnings 3.2% of Sales (millions)*	*Retained Earnings 72% of After-Tax Earnings (millions)*
1986	$23,812	—	—
1987	25,240	$ 807.7	$ 581.5
1988	26,755	856.2	616.4
1989	28,360	907.5	653.4
1990	30,062	962.0	692.6
1991	31,865	1,019.68	734.2
Accumulation of Retained Earnings			$3,278.1
Beginning Equity, January 28, 1987			3,939.0
Total Equity Available January 31, 1991			$7,217.1

Line's estimate is accurate and earnings grow at a much faster rate than sales, K mart would not need to finance its expansion with new equity issues in the near future.

Quality of Earnings

Throughout our discussion on valuation models, little has been said concerning the potential need to adjust earnings or cash flow values because of accounting considerations. The phrase *quality of earnings* essentially refers to whether the accounting method used to record a given type of transaction is conservative or liberal. An investor may downgrade the quality of a company's earnings on the basis of the practices a company uses for a few individual items.

A general feeling prevails that the higher the quality of earnings, the higher the price-earnings ratio of the firm. For example, a security having earnings per share of $2 might sell for $24 if its earnings are perceived as high quality. The stock might sell for only $16, however, if the quality of its earnings is considered low. Several factors seem to explain this relationship between quality of earnings and valuation.

Earnings over time seem to be more predictable and less volatile if the quality of earnings is relatively high. Investors dislike uncertainty and are willing to pay for relative certainty. In addition, the future dividend-paying ability of the firm should be related to its earnings quality. Quality of earnings is a concept that is difficult to define precisely. However, Exhibit 5–3 conveys some of the general considerations.

A policy board consisting of accounting professionals, security analysts, and academic researchers has provided leadership in the development of accounting standards. The Financial and Accounting Standards Board (FASB) periodically reviews accounting practices and prepares discussion memorandum on emerging accounting problems. After careful discussion and review, the FASB issues statements to be used as guidelines in the preparation and interpretation of financial reports.

Exhibit 5–3 **Accounting Issues and Quality of Earnings**

Item	*High-Quality Earnings*	*Low-Quality Earnings*
Inventory	LIFO method: current costs are matched closely with current revenues	FIFO method: old costs (the first ones in) are matched against current revenues, thus overstating profits
Pension funds	Funds are fully funded for the actuarially determined benefits	Funds are substantially underfunded to meet the actuarially determined benefits (essentially, the fund is on a pay-as-you-go basis)
Depreciation	Methods use relatively short depreciation lives and accelerated methods for financial reporting to stockholders	Methods use relatively long depreciation lives and a straight-line method for financial reporting
Source of income	From operations	From financial transactions—such as gains from early extinguishment of debt, selling at a discount

Summary of Fundamental Analysis

We examined four valuation approaches: the present value models, the relative value technique, the asset value technique, and the sustainable growth model. The present value models are probably the most important tools in evaluating the price of any investment because the price should be the present value of all the future cash flows from that investment. For common stocks, this implies that the basic source of returns is from the dividends paid by the firm, although capital gains and losses may be equally important. Investors should analyze factors such as earnings, management skill, and product demand to see how they may be expected to influence future dividends.

The sustainable growth model incorporates the joint impact of profitability and the dividend retention rate. The higher the profitability of the firm and the lower the dividend payout rate, the faster the firm can grow without resorting to selling new common stock. The sustainable growth model pinpoints possible bottlenecks to a company's dividend growth potential.

From fundamental analysis, investors can derive trading strategies that say to buy (or sell) whenever the intrinsic value is greater (or less) than the market price. Next, we turn to technical analysis, which evaluates the timing of investment decisions based on short-run market characteristics.

Technical Analysis: *Investment Timing*

Investment timing has a variety of meanings. Primarily, it means to selectively purchase securities when they are inexpensively or favorably priced and to sell securities when their prices are relatively high, in anticipation of an eventual price decline. Investors make timing decisions regarding individual financial assets, real assets, and the market as a whole. In reference to common stocks, investment timing usually means making purchases during depressed market conditions and selling during periods when the market has become overextended. In cases of fixed-income securities, timing relates to expected interest rate movements and the proper choice of which fixed-income maturity to purchase or sell. Investors may decide to disregard investment timing and to follow an investment program that alleviates the need for making such decisions. However, investors who wish to time their investments to take advantage of anticipated price movements may find technical analysis to be a useful tool.

The Nature of Technical Analysis

Technical analysis represents a methodology for forecasting short-run fluctuations in the prices of individual securities and the market in general. Technical analysis is not restricted to common stocks, but many of its applications are directed at common stocks or the common stock market. The forecasting techniques, by and large, attempt to determine existing supply and demand conditions. The emphasis on supply and demand differs from the emphasis on financial and real factors, which is the focus of fundamental investment analysis.

In its purest sense, technical analysis is not concerned with fundamentals. If excess demand exists for the shares of a particular stock, the technician will consider the stock to be an outstanding purchase candidate and will not worry about its fundamental characteristics. Usually, technical analysts assume that the market has already taken into account the fundamental factors that affect stock valuation.

Technical analysis procedures emphasize short-run price fluctuations and the timing of purchases and sales. For example, the technical analyst may advise against the purchase of a security simply because of supply and demand considerations, whether or not the security has long-term profit potential. The analyst may be able to predict that the security will sell for a lower price in the near future. In this case, the investor would be advised to time his or her purchase when a more favorable price is available. Technical analysis is designed to forecast temporary changes in the supply or the demand of a security.

Classification of Technical Indicators

Two types of technical indicators exist: (1) pattern formations and (2) measures of sentiment or behavior. Many attempts to measure supply-demand relationships are based primarily on isolating patterns in the fluctuation of stock prices or other market statistics. By attempting to use pattern recognition, technical analysts rely upon empirical observations. If a particular pattern reappears several times and consistently forecasts a particular price movement, technicians will use that pattern even if a theoretical justification is absent for the price move that follows. Ideally, a technician would prefer both theoretical and empirical justification, but a historical record of consistent forecasts is enough to admit a particular indicator to the technician's arsenal of forecasting techniques. The second classification of technical indicators, those that measure sentiment or behavior, are either general in nature or attempt to measure the sentiment or behavior of particular investors.

Multiple Indicators

By its very nature, technical analysis must rely on a wide variety of supply and demand indicators. A particular price pattern may have an outstanding forecasting record but may appear infrequently. To be useful, a forecasting technique must not only demonstrate reliability but also appear frequently enough to isolate most supply-demand shifts. Since many technical indicators by themselves do not frequently signal a price movement, technical analysts may rely on several indicators.

Many pricing situations are caused by interactions among several technical indicators. Most analysts do not claim a given pattern will always forecast a particular price move. Instead, they hold that the observed pattern in an indicator must be interpreted in conjunction with patterns in one or more indicators. Technical analysts are often criticized when a particular technique does not forecast properly. The incorrect forecast may result from a failure to recognize the interaction of the particular pattern with other technical indicators. Even if technical analysts do recognize the interactions of various technical indicators, incorrect signals are sometimes given, as no technique is infallible. Consequently, as far as possible, technicians make forecasts on the weight of evidence produced by several indicators.

Accuracy of Forecasts

Determining the forecasting accuracy of a particular indicator may be difficult. One obstacle is the problem of obtaining enough observations to attach statistical validity to an empirical test of a particular indicator. Two correct forecasts during the past twenty years are insufficient to allow any conclusions regarding the reliability of a particular pattern. Likewise, an incorrect forecast does not suggest that a forecasting technique should be discarded. Appropriate conditions of interaction may have been absent or the error may have been statistically insignificant. Because technical analysts rely on interaction among several indicators, direct testing of a particular indicator may not be possible.

The result of these and other empirical testing difficulties is that the reliability of technical analysis has been and continues to be tested indirectly. The indirect tests concentrate on an examination of (1) whether price patterns actually exist and (2) the extent to which technicians actually earn returns in excess of those available to investors who do not use technical analysis. If predictable patterns exist, technical analysis may have validity. If investors earn excess profits using technical analysis, the methods must be useful. The tests generally go under the name of the *efficient market hypothesis,* which is designed to examine several characteristics of our capital markets, including technical analysis. The efficient market hypothesis has been divided into three separate forms labeled (1) the weak form, (2) the semi-strong form, and (3) the strong form.

The *weak form* testing of the efficient market theory is directed at the information contained in the price behavior of a given common stock. In the weak form, price predictions cannot be made by using the pattern of historical prices. If the weak form is valid, we should find that the price change in one period is statistically independent of the price change in any other period.

The *semistrong form* states the price of a stock should reflect all publicly available information. The empirical tests of the semistrong form concentrate on how stock prices adjust to new information when the information becomes public. If the price adjustment is rapid and complete, we have support for the efficient market hypothesis.

The *strong form* of the efficient market theory states that stock prices reflect all information, both public and private. The private information usually referred to is insider information. The tests of the strong form are indirect in the sense that they seek to determine if groups of investors earn "excess" profits. If investors exist who systematically beat the market on a risk-adjusted basis, we have evidence that the strong form of the efficient market hypothesis is not valid. If one can profit in some regular fashion from the use of insider information, the market is inefficient. To prevent the inefficiencies that would be caused by insider trading, laws exist to eliminate the profits from this form of trading and penalties exist for those breaking the law.

Technical analysis encounters problems, both in its use and empirical validation, when investors attempt to recognize patterns in security prices or other market statistics. A particular pattern may be an accurate reflection of the future, but the technical analyst often has difficulty determining if the pattern is developing or has actually appeared. As with any statistical approach, the technical patterns are never perfect in the sense that it is clear and obvious as to what is occurring. One technician's chart may suggest a particular pattern, but ambiguities can always arise and another technical analyst may not "see" the pattern. Moreover, a particular pattern may have an excellent forecasting record, but recognition of the pattern often comes too late for the technician to take advantage of the forecast.

Literally hundreds of technical indicators are actively used, and hundreds of systems of indicators are employed by investors. Access to inexpensive and extensive financial data bases with desktop computers has made possible the development of numerous technical indicators for use in timing stock price and market movements. So many indicators are available, in fact, that we cannot even begin to discuss all the more popular ones. Instead, we will simply present a sampling of some well-known technical indicators with no suggestion that the techniques presented are better than others that are actively employed.

Price Patterns

Usually, technical analysts attempt to detect what the market is doing by observing *price patterns.* Virtually all price patterns used in technical analysis are related to breakthroughs around resistance or support levels. A *resistance level* is the price at which selling pressures are expected to appear. A *support level* is the price at which substantial buying is expected to become evident. Technicians speak of head-and-shoulders formations, pennants, wedges, triangles, gaps, and so on. All these labels refer to separate patterns that can be observed in a chart showing the price movements of a particular stock or the market.

Detecting Patterns

Each pattern has a specific interpretation, but all interpretations are based on breakthroughs above or below previous resistance or support levels. For example, Figure 5–2 shows a chart of the DJIA for early 1975. The DJIA formed a classic pattern known as a head-and-shoulders formation. The shoulders of a formation provide the base or support level,

Figure 5–2
Head-and-Shoulders Formation, Dow Jones Industrial Average, First Quarter, 1975

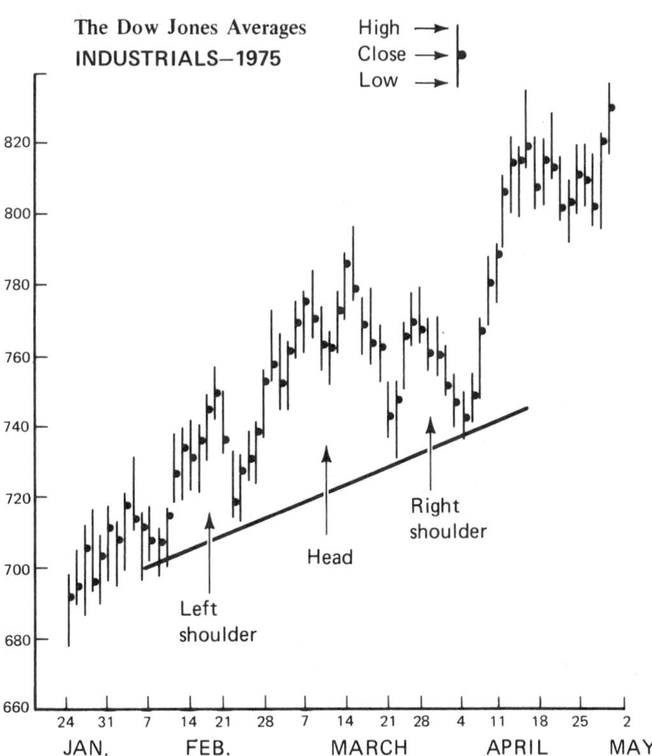

Source: Wall Street Journal, May 20, 1987, p. 63. Reprinted by permission, © Dow Jones & Company, Inc. All Rights Reserved.

Figure 5–3
Price Chart for the DJIA, November 1986–May 1987

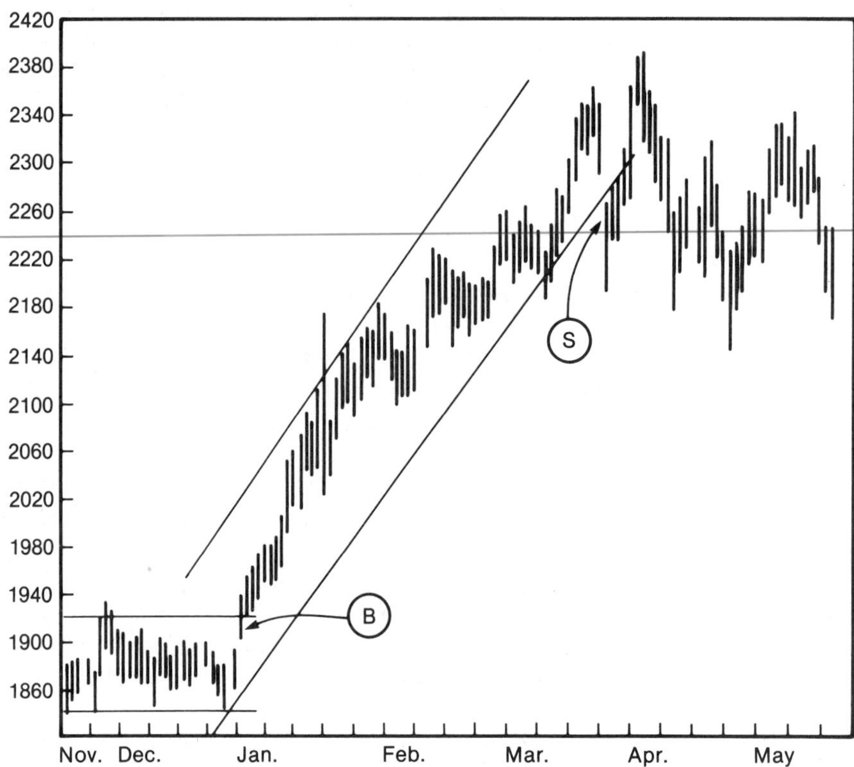

Source: Wall Street Journal, May 2, 1975, p. 31. Reprinted by permission, © Dow Jones & Company, Inc. All rights reserved.

which is typically called the neckline. When the price declines and breaks through the neckline from the right shoulder, a strong sell signal is given.

In Figure 5–2, the DJIA did not move through the neckline. Hence, a strong buy signal was given to market technicians. Had the DJIA broken through the neckline (about 740 on the DJIA) during the week of April 4, 1975, the head and shoulders pattern would have indicated a strong signal for a market decline.

Figure 5–3 gives a view of the DJIA for the late 1986 and early 1987 period—continuing a bull market that had been operating for the previous five years. During the months of November and December 1986, the DJIA established what is known as a sideways channel between 1840 and 1920. The top line of the channel represents a resistance level, and the bottom line of the channel represents a support level.

Market technicians look for breakouts from the channel to indicate buying or selling opportunities. A breakout occurred during the first week in January 1987 when the DJIA closed higher than the resistance level (indicated by *B* on Figure 5–3) and gave a buy signal. In the meantime, an uptrend channel started in late December and continued into early March. The downside breakout occurred in late March and is indicated by the letter *S*. This provided a sell signal to investors. However, the market recorded what appeared to be a wide-ranging sideways channel between the 2220 to 2400 levels in April and May 1987; the sell signal may have been premature.

Literally scores of price patterns are employed as technical indicators. We should remember that technical indicators are generally based on recurring patterns in the price of a stock or the market. The forecasts generally come from breakthroughs above and below support or resistance levels.

Dow Theory

One of the best-known and oldest of stock market indicators is the Dow Theory. The primary object of the Dow Theory is to forecast major changes in the trend of the stock market. Casual observation of the fluctuations in any of the market indexes shows that long periods of time occur when the general trend of the market is upward (a "bull" market) or downward (a "bear" market). Whether we are in a bull or a bear market, fluctuations often occur in the opposite direction. The trend may be upward, but every bull market has its reversals, as does every bear market. The Dow Theory is supposed to forecast when the reversals become permanent and the trend changes direction.

Figure 5–4 presents a hypothetical chart of the Dow Jones Industrial Average during a major bull market. The trend is upward, but on four occasions declines may be observed. The first three declines did not equal the previous advances. The fourth decline is more serious. The decline is greater than the previous advance, and the index breaks through a previously established support level—the bottom of the previous decline.

Figure 5–4
Hypothetical Dow Theory Sell Signal

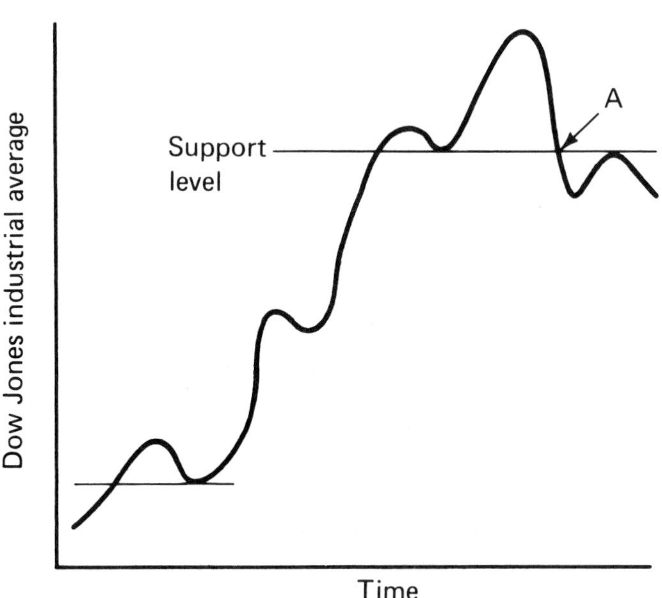

When the DJIA breaks through the support level, the Dow Theory holds that the bull market is finished and a bear market is beginning. In Figure 5–4, point *A* is the sell signal. If the market goes through point *A*, the Dow theorist sells. If the market does not go through point *A*, the bull market is expected to continue. The signal given in Figure 5–4 is not complete in that most users of the Dow Theory require confirmation of the signal by the Dow Jones Transportation Average (DJT). In other words, a sell signal is not complete until a similar breakthrough is observed in the DJT. The beginning of a bull market is predicted in exactly the same fashion when a breakthrough on the upside is observed.

The Dow Theory is popular mainly because it gave a sell signal a few weeks before the 1929 stock market crash. Its record since that time has been mixed, with the greatest difficulty being the lateness of the predictions. Quite often, by the time the DJT confirms the sell signal, 80 to 90 percent of the bear market has already passed. Instead of a leading indicator, the Dow Theory frequently turns out to be a lagging indicator of general market trends. The predictions are often accurate but come too late to be of use as a trading signal.

An application of the Dow Theory can be made to the market performance between November 1986 and May 1987 as shown in Figure 5–3. A support level was established in December at a level of 1900, followed by another in February at 2220. Following an upward move to the 2350 level in March, a modest reversal occurred in April as the DJIA fell back to the 2220 support level. An upward trend then ensued as the market moved to the 2340 level. The support level was re-established in April at about the 2220 level. If the DJIA failed to hold at this level, technical analysts might anticipate that the market would fall to the previous support level. If the market should pass through the 2220 support, investors could be in for a long slide to the next major support level at 1900.

General Sentiment or Behavioral Indicators

Technical analysts do more than merely examine patterns in the price of a stock. They also study two groups of general sentiment indicators: (1) momentum figures and (2) trading activity measures for special groups of investors, such as short-sellers, option traders, and odd-lotters. The general sentiment indicators show the use of data other than price patterns in detecting changes in price movements.

Volume Data

One of the most widely used momentum indicators is the volume of trading in a particular stock or the market. Volume is defined as the number of shares that exchange hands during a particular time period. The interpretation of volume statistics is often complex; however, a general rule is that heavy volume indicates a continuation of recent price trends and light volume implies a reversal. For example, if the market moves up on light volume, the technician will forecast a decline. On the other hand, movement down on light volume suggests subsequent upward price movements.

The primary exception to the tendencies just noted comes on what are known as key or important reversal days. A major market or stock decline often begins with a very rapid price increase on a given day, accompanied by heavy volume. Correspondingly, a major price advance is often preceded by a rapid price decline on a particular day, accompanied by heavy volume. These key reversal days are the exception to the general rule that heavy volume signals a continuation of the previous price direction while light volume indicates a reversal.

Advance-Decline Line

The strength or weakness of the market is also judged by changes in the advance-decline line. Each day, the financial press reports the number of stocks on the NYSE that had price increases (advances) and the number that experienced price declines. Technical analysts use these statistics to construct an advance-decline line, which is a daily chart of the cumulative net advances or declines. The advance-decline line ignores the magnitude of price changes and concentrates only on the cumulative number of stocks that are gainers versus losers.

If we begin our chart on a day with 700 advances and 500 declines, our first point would be 200. If on the following day 650 advances and 550 declines occur, the next point would be 300, or the sum of the net advances on the first two days.

The advance-decline line is often referred to as a breadth-of-the-market indicator because its basic function is to determine whether a particular market movement is sufficiently general and strong to be sustained. For example, if the market is moving upward as measured by one of the several market averages but the advance-decline line is flat or even declining, the indication is that the upward movement will shortly come to an end. The market is moving upward, but more stocks are declining than are advancing, suggesting that the general increase is concentrated in relatively few securities. If the advance-decline line moves up rapidly, the forecast would be for the upward trend of the market to continue. In essence, the advance-decline line is an indication of how widespread a particular market fluctuation happens to be. The more widespread a particular move, the stronger it is likely to be.

In addition to the strength of a market movement, the advance-decline line is also employed as a leading indicator. The termination of a bear market is often preceded by increases in the number of stocks showing gains. Correspondingly, an increase in the number of stocks showing declines frequently signals the end of a bull market. Hence, the advance-decline line should begin to increase prior to the beginning of a bull market and begin to decline prior to the beginning of a bear market.

Figure 5–5 illustrates the performance of the advance-decline line during the 1984 through early 1987 period. As can be observed from the chart, the advance-decline line confirmed the upward market movement at each stage of the bull market since 1984. In January 1987, the advance-decline line increased as the S&P 500 index increased, confirming the continuation of the long bull market into the first part of 1987.

Investment Highlight

Joseph Granville (The Comeback of "Broadway Joe")

This highlight discusses the roller-coaster performance of a well-known technical analyst.

Description

Joe Granville has a checkered, albeit flamboyant, career as a technical analyst using at least seventeen different technical indicators in making his predictions. His long-term track record of forecasting movements in the Dow Jones Industrial Average was good prior to August 1982. During that period, his investment seminars often mixed show business with investments. He has appeared in a Moses costume, letting his "followers" touch him. In April 1980, he changed his outlook from bearish to bullish the day before the Dow started a strong upward movement. On January 6, 1981, he advised the subscribers to his market letter to sell all their stock, which "caused" the Dow to fall 23.80 points on then-record volume of 92.9 million shares. He based this advice partially on the fact that the number of stocks selling above their 200-day moving average price had stopped rising. To Granville, this indicated the Dow was losing momentum and was ready to fall.

However, in August 1982, he called a rise in the Dow a "sucker's rally" and missed the longest and strongest bull market in history. Granville remained adamantly bearish as the Dow moved from about 800 in August 1982 to 1,675 in February 1986, and the cheers turned to jeers. In 1986, he became strongly bullish again and switched to recommending high-risk option positions. By the first quarter of 1987, Granville's investment advisory letter was once again perched on top of the performance roller coaster as reported by the *Gilbert Financial Digest*. See "Greatly Exaggerated: Joe Granville Is Alive, Well and (Gasp!) No. 1," *Barron's* (May 11, 1987): 13.

Conclusion

What happened to Granville's ability to predict the market? For missing the 1982 bull market, critics suggested his ego interfered with his judgment. Granville said he was playing too much golf and had forgotten to do his homework. As for the comeback, Granville suggested that he had returned to diligently following his technical indicators. Apparently, even investors who follow technical analysis would be wise to keep in mind the fundamentals of the market and to be aware of both the past successes and the past failures from using these procedures.

Figure 5–5
Advance-Decline Volume Line versus the S&P 500, 1984–87

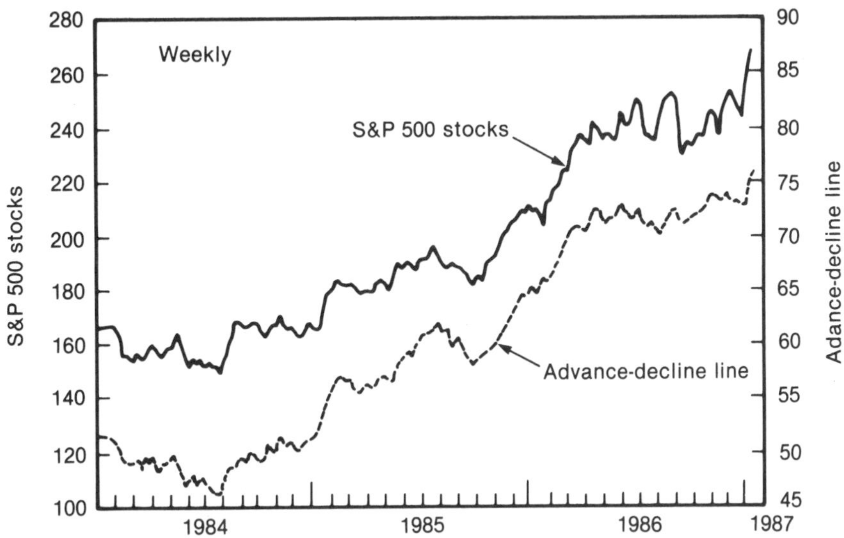

Source: The Outlook, Standard and Poor's Corporation (February 4, 1987): 939.

Other Indicators

We will briefly mention four more indicators that are favored by technicians. They are the confidence index, odd-lot trading, mutual fund liquidity, and put-call volume index.

Barron's publishes weekly a leading measure of general market fluctuations called the *confidence index* (CI). The CI is defined as follows:

$$\text{Confidence index} = \frac{\text{High-grade corporate bond yield (10 bonds)}}{\text{Lower-quality corporate bond yield (40 bonds)}}$$

High-grade corporate bonds should always yield less than low-grade ones. Thus, the CI should be less than one. If bond investors are optimistic about the future, the difference between the yields on high- and low-grade bonds becomes smaller, and if they are pessimistic, the difference becomes greater. A rising CI suggests that professionals managing very large bond portfolios are becoming optimistic, and a declining CI indicates pessimism.

Odd-lot indexes are designed to determine what less sophisticated investors feel about the future of the market. These indexes are based on the idea of "contrary opinion." The general thought underlying this view is that small investors, who deal primarily in odd-lot transactions (purchases and sales of less than 100 shares at a time), are unsophisticated in making investment decisions and typically are wrong regarding the future. Thus, odd-lot investors will buy heavily at market tops and sell at market bottoms. If this is true, odd-lot purchases should be expected to increase relative to odd-lot sales prior to the end of a bull market. Likewise, the end of a bear market should be preceded by an increase in odd-lot sales relative to odd-lot purchases. Technicians taking this "contrarian approach" to investment timing decisions want to discover what the odd-lot investors are doing and then do the opposite.

The odd-lot index is the ratio of odd-lot sales to odd-lot purchases. As the index begins to decrease, the contrarian expects a decline in the market to begin shortly. As it increases, the contrarian expects the end of a bear market. We should emphasize that the odd-lot index is normally interpreted on the basis of changes rather than the absolute level. Long periods of time exist when odd-lot purchases exceed odd-lot sales and vice versa. We should also note that most technicians consider the odd-lot index to be a far better predictor of market tops than market bottoms.

The liquidity of mutual funds is sometimes used to measure the sentiment of mutual fund managers. From monthly data compiled by the Investment Company Institute, technical analysts can determine the percentage of cash and equivalents, such as short-term U.S. government securities, relative to the total assets of mutual funds.

Technicians feel that the greater the liquidity position of mutual funds, the more bullish is the market because this cash represents buying power that can force prices up when the cash is finally committed to stock investments. Likewise, a low level of liquidity is seen as a bearish indicator because mutual funds have no reserve buying power and investors may even start to restore their liquidity by selling stocks. Liquidity positions between about 6 and 10 percent are considered normal, above 10 percent is often viewed as a bullish signal, and below 6 percent is considered bearish. For example, in late 1986—just prior to enactment of the 1986 Tax Reform Act and the rally of January 1987—the average liquidity ratio of mutual funds exceeded 10.2 percent, providing a bullish signal to the market.

Of the many new indicators, we will mention just one. With the emergence of option trading as a very popular investment, technical analysts have begun to follow the activities of option traders by means of the put-call volume ratio. This ratio compares the volume of put options to call options and is viewed as a contrary opinion measure of short-term stock market movements. A put is an option that allows the investor at any time for a limited period to sell a stock at a price established in the put contract. Investors buy puts with the expectation that the stock price will decline. A call is an option that allows investors at any time for a limited period to buy a stock at a price established in the call contract. Investors buy calls with the expectation that the stock price will increase.

Behind technical analysts' thinking in using the put-call volume ratio is the idea that option traders are usually wrong about market swings. If the volume of puts relative to calls is high, option traders believe that the market will decline, which signals, to the technician, that the market should increase.

Summary of Technical Analysis

Technical analysis attempts to predict future price changes strictly on the basis of past price changes and indicators of market sentiment. Most often, technical analysis has a short-run emphasis and is used for timing security purchases and sales. We examined a few of the many technical indicators used to forecast market and common stock price fluctuations, although we have barely scratched the surface of this topic.

In our discussion, we said relatively little about whether the technical indicators examined have validity when making forecasts. As noted in the chapter, the direct testing of an individual indicator's forecasting power is difficult because of the interactions that are possible between the various indicators. Hence, the validity of technical analysis remains to be determined indirectly within the broader context of how efficiently markets price securities.

Summary

We examined four basic approaches to valuation in this chapter: the present value approach, the relative value approach, the asset value approach, and the sustainable growth model. The present value models maintain that the price of any investment should be the present value of all the future cash flows from that investment. For common stocks, this implies that the basic source of returns is from the dividends paid by the firm. For fixed-income securities, the interest and principal payments are the relevant cash flows. Relative value models focus on the pricing of a particular security in light of the market's current valuation of comparable assets. The asset valuation approach examines the value of the tangible assets owned by the firm, either as recorded on the books or as adjusted by security analysts for price changes over time. However, intangible assets, such as patents or strong product brand names, may often be of considerable value.

The sustainable growth model is a potentially useful analytical technique. This model incorporates the impact of the profitability of the firm with the dividend retention rate. The higher the profitability of the firm and the lower the dividend payout rate, the faster that firm can grow without resorting to the sale of new common stock to raise additional equity. The sustainable growth model also breaks the return on stockholders' equity into the component parts of margin, turnover, leverage, and the tax rate. Forecasting the future values for these various components is often valuable.

Technical analysis attempts to predict future price changes strictly on the basis of past price changes or an interpretation of indicators of investor sentiment. To the investor who believes in the efficient market theory, technical indicators are of little value. We examined a few of the many technical indicators used to forecast market and common stock fluctuations, but our analysis was certainly not complete. Determining the forecasting validity of any technical indicator is complicated by the interpretation of that individual indicator as well as its interaction with other technical indicators. Multiple technical indicators are often examined in making investment timing decisions.

Suggested Readings

ARNOTT, ROBERT D. "Relative Strength Revisited." *Journal of Portfolio Management* (Spring 1979): 19–23.

BAESEL, JEROME, GEORGE SHOWS, and EDWARD THORP. "Can Joe Granville Time the Market?" *Journal of Portfolio Management* (Spring 1982): 5–9.

BANZ, ROLF W. "The Relationship between Returns and Market Value of Common Stocks." *Journal of Financial Economics* (March 1981): 3–18.

BISHOP, GEORGE W., JR. *Charles H. Dow and the Dow theory.* New York: Appleton Century Crofts, 1960.

BOWLIN, LYLE L., and MICHAEL ROZEFF. "Do Specialists' Short Sales Predict Returns?" *Journal of Portfolio Management* (Spring 1987): 59–63.

CHANG, ERIC, and J. MICHAEL PINEGAR. "Risk and Inflation." *Journal of Financial and Quantitative Analysis* (March 1987): 89–99.

DAIGLER, ROBERT T., and BRUCE D. FIELITZ. "A Multiple Discriminant Analysis of Technical Indicators on the New York Stock Exchange." *Journal of Financial Research* (Fall 1981): 169–82.

DEBONDT, WERNER F. M., and RICHARD THALER. "Does the Stock Market Overreact?" *Journal of Finance* (July 1985): 793–808.

DIMSON, ELROY, and PAUL MARSH. "An Analysis of Brokers' and Analysts' Unpublished Forecasts of UK Stock Returns." *Journal of Finance* (December 1984): 1257–92.

DOWEN, RICHARD J., and W. SCOTT BAUMAN. "The Relative Importance of Size, P/E and Neglect." *Journal of Portfolio Management* (Spring 1986): 30–35.

FARRELL, JOHN L., JR. "The Dividend Discount Model: A Primer." *Financial Analysts Journal* (November–December 1985): 16–25.

GRANT, DWIGHT. "Market Timing: Strategies to Consider." *Journal of Portfolio Management* (Summer 1979): 41–46.

HARRIS, L., and E. GUREL. "Price and Volume Effects Associated with Changes in the S&P 500 List: New Evidence for the Existence of Price Pressures." *Journal of Finance* (September 1986): 815–29.

HUIZINGA, JOHN, and FREDERIC S. MISHKIN. "Inflation and Real Interest Rates on Assets with Different Risk Characteristics." *Journal of Finance* (July 1984): 699–711.

JAMES, C., and R. O. EDMISTER. "The Relationship Between Common Stock Returns, Trading Activity and Market Value." *Journal of Finance* (September 1983): 1075–86.

KARPOFF, JONATHAN M. "The Relationship Between Price Changes and Trading Volume: A Survey." *Journal of Financial and Quantitative Analysis* (March 1987): 109–126.

———. "A Theory of Trading Volume." *Journal of Finance* (December 1986): 1069–88.

LAKONISHOK, JOSEF, and SEYMOUR SMIDT. "Trading Bargains in Small

Firms at Year-End." *Journal of Portfolio Management* (Spring 1986): 24–29.

LANE, MORTON. "Fixed-Income Managers Must Time the Market." *Journal of Portfolio Management* (Summer 1979): 36–40.

LERNER, EUGENE M., and POCHARA THEERATHORN. "The Returns of Different Investment Strategies." *Journal of Portfolio Management* (Summer 1983): 26–28.

LERRO, ANTHONY J., and CHARLES B. SWAYNE, JR. *Selection of Securities: Technical Analysis of Stock Market Prices,* 2d ed. Morristown, NJ: General Learning Press, 1974.

LEVY, ROBERT A. "Conceptual Foundation of Technical Analysis." *Financial Analysts Journal* (July–August 1966): 83–89.

MALKIEL, BURTON G. *A Random Walk Down Wall Street,* 4th ed. New York: W. W. Norton & Co., 1985.

NAGORNIAK, JOHN J. "Thoughts on Using Dividend Discount Models." *Financial Analysts Journal* (November–December 1985): 13–15.

PENMAN, STEPHEN H. "A Comparison of the Information Content of Insider Trading and Management Earnings Forecasts." *Journal of Financial and Quantitative Analysis* (March 1985): 1–18.

———. "The Predictive Content of Earnings Forecasts and Dividends." *Journal of Finance* (September 1983): 1181–1200.

PFEIFER, PHILIP E. "Market Timing and Risk Reduction." *Journal of Financial and Quantitative Analysis,* December 1985, 451–459.

RANSON, R. DAVID, and WILLIAM G. SHIPMAN. "Institutional Buying Power and the Stock Market." *Financial Analysts Journal* (September–October 1981): 62–68.

REINGANUM, MARC R. "Abnormal Returns in Small Firm Portfolios." *Financial Analysts Journal* (May–April 1981): 52–56.

SENCHACK, A. J., JR., and JOHN D. MARTIN. "The Relative Performance of the PSR and PER Investment Strategies." *Financial Analysts Journal* (March–April 1987): 46–56.

SMIRLOCK, MICHAEL, and LAURA STARKS. "A Further Examination of Stock Price Changes and Transaction Volume." *Journal of Financial Research* (Fall 1985): 217–25.

SORENSEN, ERIC H., and DAVID A. WILLIAMSON. "Some Evidence on the Value of Dividend Discount Models." *Financial Analysts Journal* (November–December 1985): 60–69.

SUMMERS, LAWRENCE. "Does the Stock Market Rationally Reflect Fundamental Values?" *Journal of Finance* (July 1986): 591–601.

TREYNOR, JACK L., and ROBERT FERGUSON. "In Defense of Technical Analysis." *Journal of Finance* (July 1985): 757–773.

WHITFORD, DAVID T., and FRANK K. REILLY. "What Makes Stock Prices Move?" *Journal of Portfolio Management* (Winter 1985): 23–30.

Questions

1. How would an investor go about determining the appropriate rate of return that should be expected from an investment?

2. If Sara Edwards desires a total return (dividend and capital gains) of 15 percent from investing in common stocks, what are the implications for Sara of investing in the local utility having a 10 percent dividend yield versus a growth stock having only a 3 percent dividend yield?

3. The perpetual dividend valuation model is as follows:

$$P_0 = \frac{D_1}{i - g}$$

How could an investor use this model to ascertain how the stock market is going to move in the next year or two?

4. Discuss four ways a firm can increase its after-tax return on equity. Illustrate your discussion with an example.

5. Grocery chains typically have low profit margins, yet their ROE is significantly high. Does this seem logical? Why?

6. What importance should the investor give to the relationship between the market price and book value for a given investment? Does this importance vary from investment type to investment type?

7. What factors should an investor consider in making an assessment of the quality of a firm's earnings?

8. Distinguish the major differences between technical and fundamental analysis for stock selection.

9. What is the basic purpose of technical analysis?

10. Why would technical analysts be tempted to use more than one technical indicator?

11. Technical analysts rely heavily upon the concepts of support and resistance levels.
    - **(a)** Why does the technical analyst consider these levels to be so important?
    - **(b)** Can you offer a rationale for using support or resistance levels on the basis of investor psychology?

12. Robert Stovall has recommended the use of what he calls the GM Bellwether Theory to time market investments. If General Motors common stock continues to hit new highs or new lows over a four-month period, the market will continue in the same direction. For example, if GM hit a new low on July 1, a buy signal noting the end of the bear market would not be given until four months had passed (November 1) without a new low for GM. What do you think is the rationale behind this technical indicator?

13. An article in *Forbes* of June 20, 1983, suggested using the Rule of 20 as a technical indicator. You add the rate of inflation to the P/E

ratio for the Dow Jones Industrial Average. If the total is substantially below 20, such as 16 or 17, the market is still undervalued. If the total is in the range of 20 or 21, the market is likely overvalued. At the time the article was written, the total was 15.8 consisting of a P/E ratio of 12.8 and an inflation rate of 3 percent. The value of 15.8 is the second lowest total since 1961. Did this technical approach work? What could cause it to fail to correctly predict the trend of the market?

14. David Bostian (*Business Week,* November 1, 1982) uses what he calls his "hysteria premium." He examines real interest rates and finds them in the range of 6 to 8 percent. He maintains that anything above that represents hysteria. Hence, he argues that stock prices could increase. Discuss the linkages involved in Bostian's line of reasoning.

Problems

1. Cindy wants to purchase Dina Company common stock and estimates dividends per share for the next five years as follows: $2.00; $2.15; $2.25; $2.45; and $2.75. She also estimates that the Dina Company stock will sell for $85 a share at the end of the fifth year. What will be the rate of return if Dina Company stock sells for $50 now?

2. Todd Company paid a $2 dividend per share last year. The dividend is expected to grow at 6 percent per year in the future. Given the current state of the market, Jim desires a 16 percent rate of return for stock of this risk level. What would he be willing to pay for the Todd Company stock?

3. In 1986 J. C. Penney paid out 35 percent of its earnings as dividends. The company's return on equity was 8 percent. Both of these values represent typical historical values and are reasonable estimates of future values. What is the estimated growth rate of net income for J. C. Penney?

4. For 1986, The Limited, Inc., earned $1.21 per share and paid a dividend of $0.16 per share. The Limited's return on equity was 29.1 percent. *Value Line* estimates its growth in earnings for the period from 1983–85 to 1989–91 at 35.5 percent.

   (a) Assuming no major changes in operations and financing, can The Limited obtain the anticipated growth rate of 35.5 percent?

   (b) If step a indicates that the 35.5 percent growth rate is unattainable, what changes would you suggest to The Limited's management so as to increase the growth rate?

5. As of the end of December 31, 1986, the average dividend per share for the S&P 500 index was $8.22 for the prior twelve months. Assuming that (a) the dividend per share growth will be 14 percent for the next five years and 10 percent for years six through ten and

(b) the value of the index at the end of the tenth year will be equal to twenty-five times the S&P 500 dividend value at that time, what is the present value of the S&P 500 index if investors want a 16 percent rate of return? If the index is at 253, is the market overvalued or undervalued according to your calculations?

6. IBM paid out 56 percent of its earnings in 1986 and earned 14 percent on stockholders' equity. What will be its expected growth rate under these circumstances assuming no new common stock financing?

7. In 1987, *Value Line* expects IBM's future growth in earnings to be 15.5 percent.

(a) Determine the various components of IBM's return on equity from the following information:

Margin = 9.3%
Revenue = $51,250 million
Total assets = $57,814 million
Net worth = $34,374 million
Average tax rate = 36.0%

(b) If your answer to part a is less than 16 percent, what can IBM do in terms of its return on equity components to finance the higher rate of growth? In addition to reducing the dividend payout ratio, which component seems the most feasible to you for producing a higher growth rate?

8. As of July 1987, the following rates existed:

Estimated inflation for the coming year = 4%
Treasury bills (26 weeks) = 7%
Long-term corporate bonds = 9.5%

(a) Calculate the expected rate of return for common stocks from each of these rates using historical risk premiums from the 1926–86 period.

Inflation
Treasury bills
Long-term corporate bonds

(b) What rate would you use? Under what circumstances?

9. Butterfly Valve Company stock sells at $55 per share, and its current dividend is $2.50 per share. Investors expect future dividends to grow at a constant, perpetual rate, and they currently require a 16 percent return on the stock. What is the implied dividend growth rate?

10. On November 20, 1986, Goodyear Tire and Rubber Company (GT) issued a press release announcing that the company would undergo a major restructuring of its operations. Calculate the value for the common stock of the "new" Goodyear using the data in the table below. Use two methods, one of which must be the dividend discount model ($P = D/i - g$). Show all calculations and support all assumptions. (Excerpted with permission from the 1987 Level II examination, The Institute of Chartered Financial Analysts.)

	"New" Goodyear	Firestone	Goodrich	S&P 500
Current price	*	$29.00	$45.00	$250.00
Current dividend	$ 1.60	$ .80	$ 1.56	$ 8.80
Normalized ROE	18%	8%	9%	13%
Implied growth rate	*	5.3%	5.3%	6.5%
Forecast 1987 EPS	$ 5.60	$ 2.35	$ 3.80	$ 17.50
Current P/E	*	12.3	11.8	14.3
10-year average P/E (as a % of the S&P 500)	not applicable	70%	65%	100%
Debt to total capitalization	80%	19%	33%	38%
Stock beta (estimated)	1.4	1.0	1.1	1.0
	Risk-free rate of return			7.5%
	Expected return on market			13.5%

* To be determined.

Chapter 6

Asset Pricing Models

Key Concepts

- alpha
- anomalies
- arbitrage pricing theory
- beta
- borrowing portfolio
- capital asset pricing model
- capital market line
- efficiency criterion
- efficient frontier
- equilibrium
- indifference curve
- inefficient portfolio
- lending portfolio
- market portfolio
- reward-to-risk ratio
- risk aversion
- risk-free asset
- risk-free rate
- riskless arbitrage
- risk-neutral investors
- risk-seeking investors
- security market line
- standard deviation
- systematic risk factor
- utility
- variance

Chapter Outline

Modern investment analysis focuses on how the financial markets price the relationship between return and risk. Two models, the *capital asset pricing model* (CAPM) and the *arbitrage pricing theory* (APT), provide innovative ways for investors to measure the return and risk characteristics of a portfolio. An important intuition in modern investment analysis is that covariability of an asset's return with the return on other assets, rather than total variability, is the critical risk factor from the perspective of risk-averse investors holding well-diversified portfolios. The CAPM transforms this intuition into a model of asset pricing, while the APT extends the basic insight gained from the CAPM model into a more general framework.

Both CAPM and APT are based on two fundamental principles: (1) the efficiency criterion and (2) the arbitrage law. We will begin by discussing the efficiency criterion. Throughout the chapter, we will show the importance of the arbitrage law in the pricing of assets.

Modern Portfolio Analysis

Harry Markowitz introduced the basic portfolio analysis concepts in 1952 and laid the groundwork for modern portfolio theory. His theory helps investors solve the practical problem of choosing the "best" portfolio. Underlying his theory are several simplifying assumptions about the behavior of investors: (1) They make single-period decisions based on a portfolio's expected return and variance only, (2) they all have the same estimates of a security's return distribution, and (3) they are free from taxes and transaction costs. The benefit of making these assumptions is in narrowing the investment problem to a few key issues.

The Efficiency Criterion

Investors have an extremely large number of risky securities and portfolios from which to choose when making investment decisions. What guidelines and decision rules should they use in deciding among the available alternatives? Generally, we find that *investors like high returns but dislike risk.* If this is so, a procedure can be defined that reduces the number of investment candidates to the most desirable few. From this point on, an individual security can be viewed as a portfolio consisting of one security. The procedure, known as the *efficiency criterion,* can be stated in either of the following ways:

1. Select the highest-return portfolio for any given level of risk
2. Select the lowest-risk portfolio for any given rate of return

To show how the efficiency criterion operates, assume that an investor must choose from a set of investment opportunities as shown in Figure 6–1. Applying the efficiency criterion to the investment opportunity set, we can show that portfolio X is inferior to portfolio Y, in that X's risk

Figure 6–1
Hypothetical Opportunity Set Comparing Risk and Return

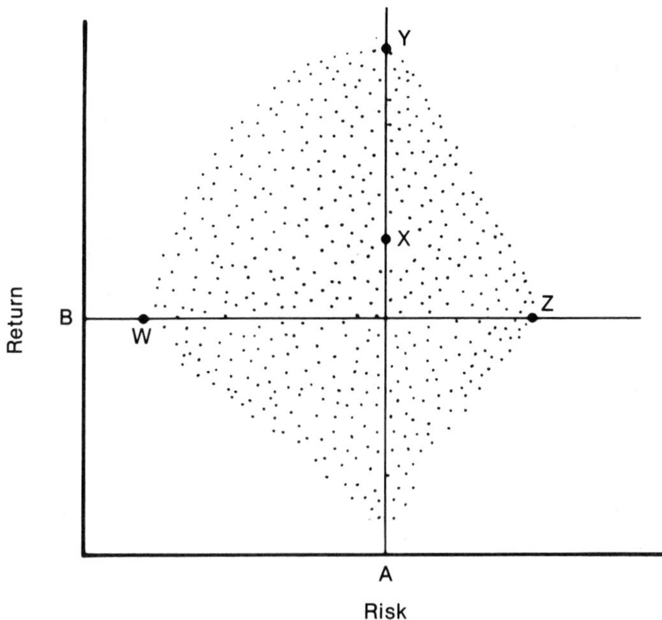

equals Y's risk but Y's expected rate of return is higher. Portfolio Y is the best possible portfolio for risk level A. Note that with the rate of return held constant, portfolio W is preferable to portfolio Z. Both portfolios earn rate of return level B, but by holding portfolio W, the investor takes on much less risk in earning that return. Portfolio W is the best possible portfolio for return level B. Both portfolios Y and W are efficient portfolios because the investor does not expect to do better than these portfolios.

The Efficient Frontier

Use of the efficiency criterion allows investors to determine all efficient portfolios and form what is known as an *efficient frontier.* The efficient frontier can be described as the best possible set of portfolios in the sense that they *all have the minimum level of variance for their given level of return.* These portfolios are sometimes referred to as *mean-variance efficient portfolios* and are indicated in Figure 6–2 by the upper left boundary of the entire set of portfolios. Investors can concentrate on selecting one portfolio from the efficient frontier and ignore all other "inferior" portfolios.

The shape of the efficient frontier implies the existence of a positive relationship between return and risk. This relationship is expressed by the often-repeated advice that in order to obtain higher returns, investors must accept more risk. In general high-risk investments produce higher returns than low-risk investments. Why then do investors not invest in very high-risk investments? The fundamental reason is that although in-

Figure 6–2
The Efficient Frontier

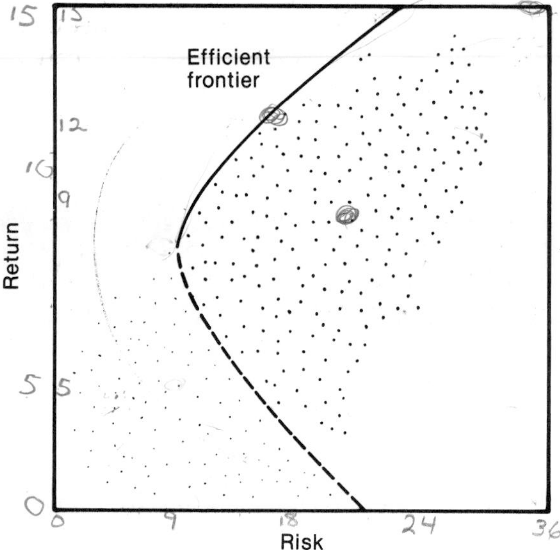

vestors expect high returns from high-risk investments, increased variability can forestall these high and positive returns.

Risk Preferences

Figure 6–2 shows that application of the efficiency criterion results in the efficient frontier. The efficient frontier highlights the superior investment opportunities, but it does not indicate which portfolio any individual investor should own. Utility theory, taken from the basic economic concepts of consumer choice, can help the investor select the one "best" portfolio from among the efficient portfolios.

Investors seek high investment returns for the *utility,* or want-satisfying power, that investing provides. Most investors seek more money to provide more want-satisfying power. On the other hand, the utility of a given quantity of money is a highly individual matter. Wealth is often of vital importance. A millionaire may attach very little utility to $1,000. But a student working to finance a college education may find that $1,000 has a large amount of want-satisfying power. Age and education may be factors that influence differences in investors' attitudes toward the utility of money.

Investors can be classified into three major groups with regard to their desire to undertake risky investments: (1) risk averters, (2) risk neutrals, and (3) risk seekers. *Risk aversion,* the most common type of behavior evidenced by investors, is characterized by what is known as a diminishing marginal utility of return. This means that as the risk-averse investor earns more return, the added returns provide decreasing amounts of added satisfaction. Such an investor prefers receiving \$100,000 over receiving \$10,000, but not by ten times as much. Put another way, to the risk-averse investor, the utility of \$2 is greater than the utility of \$1, but the utility of the first dollar received is greater than the utility of the second dollar.

For the *risk-neutral investor,* the second dollar received has as much utility as the first dollar received. The risk-neutral investor demonstrates constant marginal utility of return. Gambling is typical of the *risk-seeking investor,* who possesses increasing marginal utility of return. Neither the risk-neutral nor the risk-seeking investor is typical of the vast majority of investors. Most discussions about portfolio selection ignore the risk-neutral and risk-seeking investor, and we will follow that practice.

The relationship indicating the trade-offs made by risk-averse investors between return and risk can be shown on a graph as an indifference curve. The *indifference curve* connects all the return and risk combinations that the investor identifies as having the *same level of utility.* The shape of the indifference curve varies from one investor to the next. Figure 6–3 presents a set of indifference curves for the risk-averse investor. For example, indifference curve I shows all the return-risk combinations with an equivalent level of satisfaction for the investor. Investments Y and Y′ have different return and risk characteristics but provide the investor with the same amount of want-satisfying power. The saucer shape of the indifference curve reflects the risk-averse investor's diminishing marginal utility of return.

The set of indifference curves shown in Figure 6–3 is called an indifference map. The best investment strategy is to select the portfolio that falls on the highest indifference curve. By highest, we mean the utility curve that has the highest value on the vertical axis in Figure 6–3. For example, portfolio X will be preferred to portfolio Y because a higher return is achieved for the same risk level. In a similar fashion, portfolio Z will be preferred to both portfolios X and Y′ because the same return level is earned at a lower risk level.

Figure 6–3
Hypothetical Indifference Curves: Risk-Averse Investor

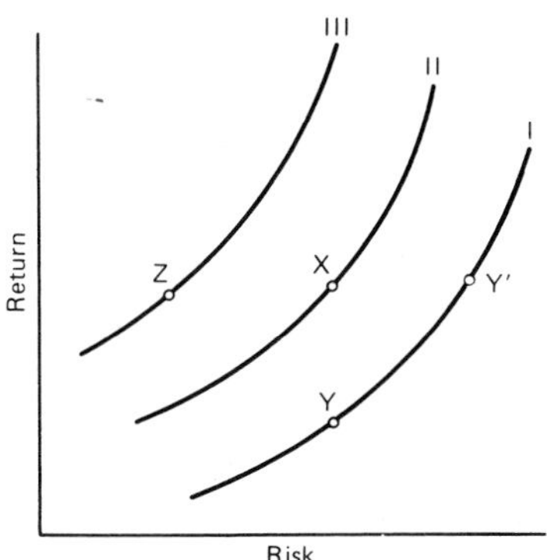

Selecting Mean-Variance Efficient Portfolios

The introduction of indifference curves allows the investor to select, from among the mean-variance efficient portfolios, the portfolio with the highest level of utility. We can show the investor's optimal choice graphically in Figure 6–4 by superimposing the indifference curves of Figure 6–3 on the efficient frontier of Figure 6–2. The investor will want to own the portfolio that falls on the highest attainable indifference curve because this choice will provide the most want-satisfying power. In Figure 6–4, the optimum portfolio is portfolio X. Any other portfolio, such as Y or Y′, will lie on a lower indifference curve and provide less utility than portfolio X. Portfolio Z, although more desirable, is unattainable and therefore should be ignored.

Investors may not actually think of indifference curves and the efficient frontier in practice, but these concepts provide guidelines that can help investors achieve their objectives. Most investors seek to own the best possible portfolio in terms of the anticipated rate of return and the risk they are willing to assume in seeking the return. As a result, these investors will tailor-make portfolios to fit their own return-risk preferences—some investors will own low-risk portfolios that promise low returns, while others will own high-risk portfolios that promise high returns.

Although Markowitz introduced the mathematical concepts of modern portfolio theory in 1952, his work was virtually ignored until the middle 1960s because it was difficult to use. His procedures for identifying the efficient portfolios involve calculating portfolio variances and selecting the minimum-variance portfolio at each level of return. To calculate the variance of a portfolio, the values for a correlation matrix must be estimated, with a row and a column for each security being considered. In Chapter 4, we showed that for a small portfolio of 4 stocks, the

Figure 6–4
Hypothetical Optimum Portfolio Selection

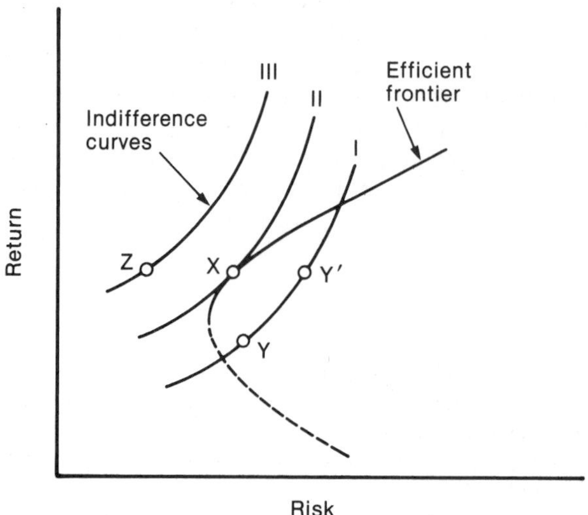

correlation matrix consisted of 6 elements (see Table 4–8). To calculate the variance of a 100-security portfolio, estimates of 4,950 correlation coefficients would be needed.

Simplifying the Portfolio Selection Problem

Fortunately, a technique exists to simplify the estimation problem encountered in performing the Markowitz analysis.[1] The simplification is based on an assumption about the nature of the co-movement between security returns. Security returns are assumed to move together *only* because they respond to the same common influence, *as captured by their correlation with the market portfolio.*

The *market portfolio* was defined in Chapter 4 as the portfolio consisting of all real and financial assets, with each asset's weight in the portfolio being equal to its market value relative to the market value of all assets. The variability of the market portfolio is simply the aggregate of the co-movement between the returns on all pairs of assets.

If the only co-movement between security returns is assumed to be caused by the market portfolio, industry conditions or special market segment factors such as tax status should have *no influence* on how security returns relate to each other. Once the common influence of the market portfolio is removed, the movement of security prices should not be related. Investors often use the returns on a broad-based market index, such as the S&P 500, as a proxy for the market portfolio.

Let us see how reasonable this assumption is for an equally weighted portfolio consisting of Chrysler, A&P, IBM, and U.S. Tobacco. The correlation matrix for these four securities was presented in Table 4–8. After removing the correlation between securities common to the S&P 500 market index, the correlation matrix should be approximately described by diagonal and zero values.[2]

Table 6–1 shows that, with the market influence removed, all except two pairs, Chrysler-A&P and Chrysler-IBM, have correlation terms reasonably close to zero. To the extent that security returns are correlated on the basis of influences not captured by the market index, the simplifying assumption can lead to an underestimation of a portfolio's variance.

After making the simplifying assumption, the estimation of variance for a 100-security portfolio reduces to finding 100 expected returns, 100 security variances, 1 market index variance, and 100 correlations—1 between each security and the market index. Next, we will develop the CAPM and see how it helps investors choose the optimal portfolio.

1. Developed independently by Sharpe, Lintner, and Mossin.

2. The correlation between securities due to the market index can be estimated by (1) multiplying the betas of the two securities times the market portfolio variance and then (2) dividing the result by the product derived from multiplying the standard deviations of the two securities.

Table 6–1
Correlation Matrix with Market Index Influence Removed

	Chrysler	A&P	IBM	U.S. Tobacco
Chrysler	1			
A&P	.5532	1		
IBM	.4988	.2822	1	
U.S. Tobacco	.2288	.2248	.1268	1

The Capital Asset Pricing Model

The capital asset pricing model (CAPM) is an economic model that describes the pricing of securities in financial markets. It takes the original Markowitz assumptions and adds the assumption that investors can borrow and lend at a *risk-free interest rate.* This assumption allows investors to form new portfolios consisting of risky securities combined with a single, riskless security. The resulting combined portfolios are the focus of the CAPM analysis.

The Risk-Free Asset and the Market Portfolio

The *risk-free asset* can be defined as an investment having a zero variance and a zero covariance with other securities. U.S. Treasury bills come close to being riskless and are often used as a proxy for the risk-free asset. Treasury bills represent the short-maturity debt of the U.S. government.

The availability of a risk-free asset has some important consequences for portfolio analysis. Combining the risk-free asset with the market portfolio produces a portfolio with the following features:

$$R_d = X_m R_m + (1 - X_m) R_f \quad \text{and} \quad S_d = X_m S_m$$

where R_d = the combined portfolio's return
X_m = the percentage invested in the market portfolio
R_m = the market portfolio's return
R_f = the risk-free security's return
S_d = the combined portfolio's standard deviation
S_m = the market portfolio's standard deviation

In Figure 6–5, the risk-free asset is combined with the market portfolio M. The straight line between R_f and M represents the return-risk relationship for all combinations of the risk-free asset and the market portfolio.

A portion of the original efficient frontier was eliminated by introducing the risk-free asset. Without a risk-free asset, any asset or portfolio lying on the efficient frontier between A and M is efficient and could be purchased by a risk-averse investor. However, with the addition of the risk-free asset, an investor who desires the return-risk combination of

Figure 6–5
The Efficient Frontier with a Risk-Free Asset

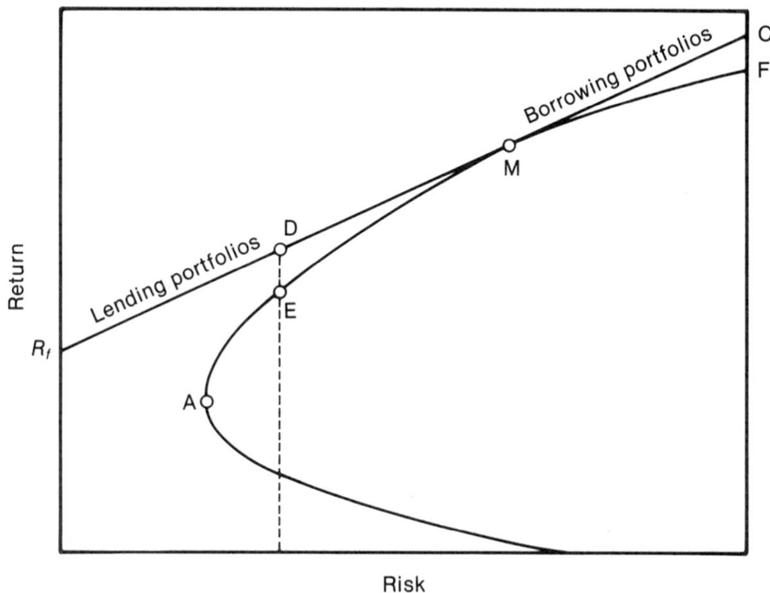

portfolio E would be better advised to purchase D instead. Portfolio D consists of part risk-free asset and part risky portfolio M. Compared to portfolio E, portfolio D has the same risk but a higher expected return. Hence, according to the efficiency criterion, portfolio E is inefficient relative to D. By combining the risk-free asset with the market portfolio, we have created a new efficient frontier represented by the line R_fC, which passes through portfolio M.

A portfolio in the portion of the newly created efficient frontier from R_f to M is referred to as a *lending portfolio* because part of the investor's portfolio consists of treasury bills. When the investor purchases treasury bills, this is effectively a loan by the investor to the U.S. government. Beyond portfolio M through point C, the investor is said to hold a *borrowing portfolio.* All of the investor's funds have been invested in portfolio M, and added funds have been borrowed (perhaps in a margin account) at the risk-free rate. The total investment in portfolio M amounts to more than 100 percent of the investor's own funds.

The assumption made in Figure 6–5 that the lending rate is equal to the borrowing rate is not realistic. In March 1987, for example, three-month treasury bills were yielding about 5.5 percent, but the basic margin loan rate was 7.5 percent. Although convenient, the equal borrowing and lending rate assumption is not necessary. A "riskless" portfolio (minimum variance, zero beta) consisting of risky assets can be substituted for the risk-free asset in the CAPM model with the benefit that any investor can buy or sell short the zero-beta portfolio. The zero-beta form of the CAPM provides the same general implications about return and risk relationships in the market as the original CAPM.

The Capital Market Line

The *capital market line* (CML) is the new efficient frontier created by combining the risk-free asset with the market portfolio. This new efficient frontier can be represented as follows:

$$E(R_p) = R_f + \sigma_p \frac{E(R_m) - R_f}{\sigma_m} \tag{6.1}$$

where $E(R_p)$ = the expected return on an efficient portfolio
R_f = the return on the risk-free asset
σ_p = the standard deviation of the portfolio's return
σ_m = the standard deviation of the market's return
$E(R_m)$ = the expected return on the market

Equation 6.1, representing the capital market line (CML), is shown in Figure 6–6. Notice that the equation for the CML is stated in terms of expected returns. The CML shows the return and risk relationship for *fully diversified portfolios with no unsystematic risk.* The vertical axis for Figure 6–6 is the expected portfolio return, and the horizontal axis is the risk measure (σ_p/σ_m) of the portfolio. This risk measure represents the systematic risk of an efficient portfolio.

The CML contains portfolios that are efficient in the sense that they have only systematic risk, and no higher expected return is possible for the risk taken on. One particular portfolio of risky assets that should be on the efficient frontier is the market portfolio.

The implications of the CML are that virtually all investors, regardless of their risk preferences, should own a combination of the market portfolio and the risk-free asset. Investors can adjust their holdings by either borrowing or lending, if they want to alter their risk position away from that of the market portfolio. The one major exception is that a

Figure 6–6
The Capital Market Line (CML)

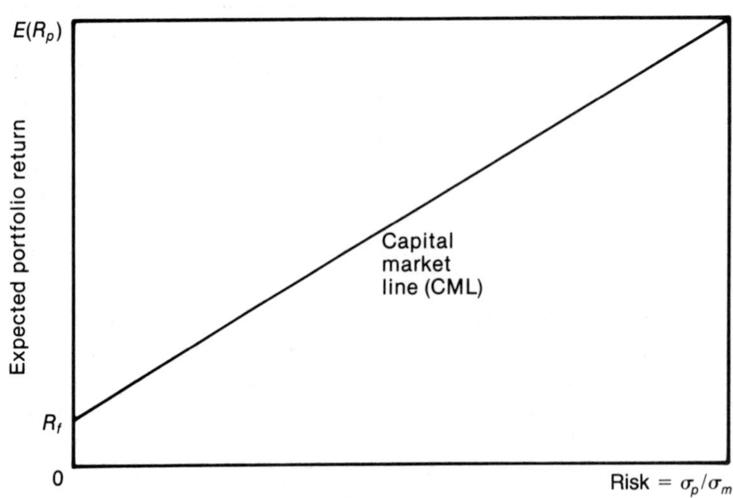

highly risk-averse investor may have a portfolio containing only treasury bills. In contrast, an aggressive investor will borrow money to purchase the market portfolio.

The Security Market Line

A pricing relationship between return and risk for efficient portfolios is suggested by the CML. The relevant risk measure in the case of the CML is the *standard deviation* of the expected returns for efficient portfolios. The CML does not say anything directly about the relationship between expected returns and risk of inefficient portfolios (or individual securities). By *inefficient portfolios,* we mean those that have unsystematic risk—risk not eliminated through diversification. The pricing relationships between return and risk for inefficient portfolios can be derived from the co-movement between the market portfolio, M, which lies on the CML, and the securities that comprise the inefficient portfolios. These pricing relationships, which we do not attempt to derive in this text, are described by the *security market line* (SML).

Security Pricing Relationships

The SML says that the required expected rate of return of an asset is proportional to its covariance with the return on the market portfolio. When markets are in equilibrium, $E(R_k)/\text{Covariance}(R_k,R_m)$, the *reward-to-risk ratio* is identical for all assets. Under these conditions, all assets are "held" in the market portfolio. Let us ask for a moment, what will happen if markets are not in equilibrium, and for example, a security is not included in the market portfolio because its reward-to-risk ratio is not the same ratio as for all other securities? The answer is that investors will be able to engage in *riskless arbitrage* to obtain a positive return without investing any capital.

Arbitrage may be defined as the simultaneous buying and selling of assets or their equivalents at prices that momentarily differ. A *pure arbitrage* process also requires that the arbitrageur takes no risk and invests no capital in seeking to gain a return from price differentials. Security prices can be said to be *in equilibrium* when no arbitrage profits are possible.

Arbitrage operates in the CAPM because securities having the same expected reward-to-risk ratio are perfect substitutes. By perfect substitutes, we mean that investors price only one aspect of securities, the reward-to-risk ratios, and that securities with the same ratio are for pricing purposes identical and can be substituted for each other at equal value.

Any time a price differential exists, arbitrageurs will come into the market and trade the price gap between the equivalent securities or portfolios. For example, assume that an investor has the opportunity to buy a

Figure 6–7
The Security Market Line (SML)

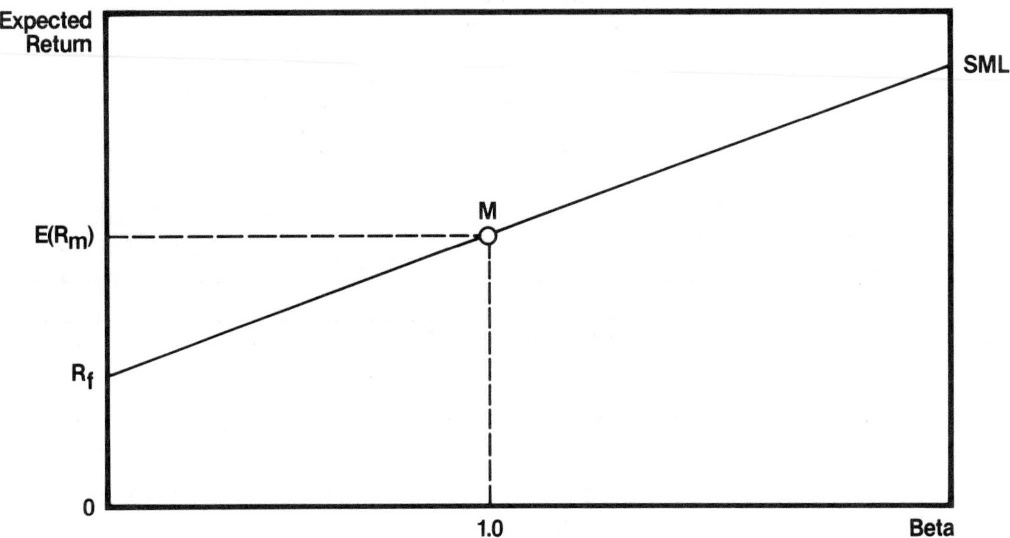

security with a reward-to-risk ratio equal to 1.5 while the other securities in the market portfolio have a ratio equal to 1.3. Security A will reward investors with 1.5 units of return for 1 unit of *systematic risk.* This is a superior return to the one offered by the market portfolio assets, which are rewarding the investor only 1.3 units of return for each unit of systematic risk. Therefore, investors will sell the market portfolio short and use the funds to buy security A until the yield differential disappears. With the simultaneous selling of the market portfolio and the purchasing of security A, the investor gains .2 units of return for no risk and no capital investment. This is an example of the *law of arbitrage* operating to make capital market prices converge to one price for a unit of risk.

If security prices are in market equilibrium, all security and portfolio returns should lie on the SML despite the fact that the portfolios may not be fully diversified. The SML in Figure 6–7 relates the expected returns on various assets, including both individual securities and portfolios, to the level of systematic risk.

The equation for the SML is as follows:

$$E(R_k) = R_f + \beta_k[E(R_m) - R_f] \qquad (6.2)$$

where $E(R_k)$ = the expected return on security k
R_f = the return on the risk-free asset
β_k = the beta for security k, which in turn
= covariance $(R_k, R_m)/\sigma_m^2$
$E(R_m)$ = the expected return on the market portfolio
σ_m^2 = the variance of the market portfolio's return

The *beta* of the market is defined as equal to 1.0. A beta of less than 1.0 for a security (or portfolio) indicates the security's returns are less variable than those of the market. Likewise, a beta greater than 1.0 indicates the security's returns are more variable than those of the market.

In Chapter 4, we showed how to obtain estimates of beta using the linear regression method. We reported the regression estimates b_k of β_k and a_k of α_k for the characteristic line estimates on four stocks over the 1967–86 period as follows:

Stock	a_k	b_k	$\bar{R}_k$
	Based on Annual Returns, 1967–86		
Chrysler	−1.7	2.6	28.3
A&P	−5.7	1.2	8.3
IBM	.4	1.0	12.2
U.S. Tobacco	10.8	0.6	17.8
	Average Annual Market Returns and Risk-Free Returns		
S&P 500	0.0	1.0	11.5
T-bills	7.2	0.0	7.2

From the data for the S&P 500 and the average return on treasury bills over the 1967–86 period, we can derive an estimate of the SML as shown in Figure 6–8. The historical average annual returns, $\bar{R}_k$, and beta estimates, b_ks, for the four stocks are also plotted in Figure 6–8 to give an indication of how closely the characteristic line estimates approximate the SML estimates of expected return.

Because b_k is an estimate subject to statistical sampling error, we can expect it to equal β_k only by chance. To get an idea of how good an estimate b_k is of β_k, we can look at the coefficient of determination, r^2. If r^2 is low, we may not put much faith in the b_k value. Hence, any difference between a security's actual return and the return that is predicted by the SML for its level of β_k can be caused by having an error in our estimate b_k of β_k. The differences may also be caused by a number of other factors

Figure 6–8
Beta Estimates for Four Securities versus the SML

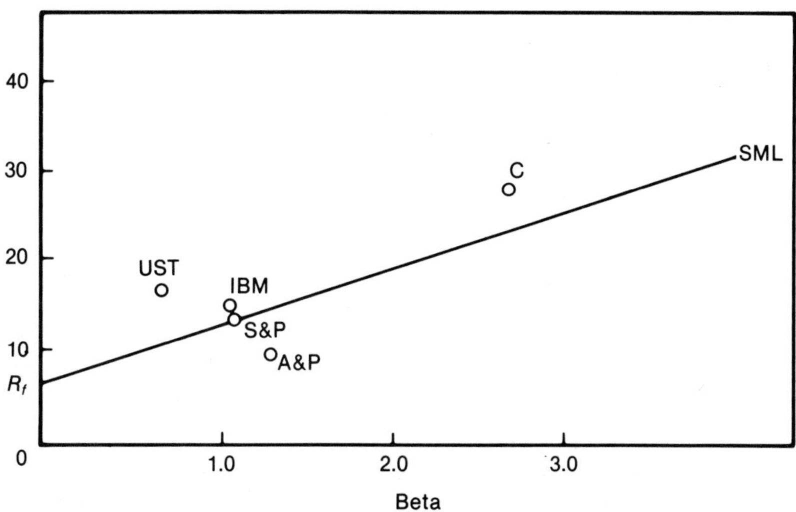

Figure 6–9
Security Market Line, 1926–86, 1977–81, and 1982–86

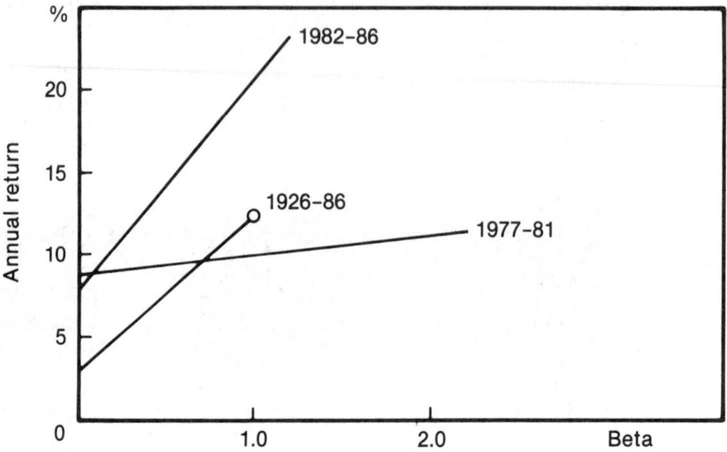

such as (1) the CAPM being an incorrect representation of security pricing, (2) the S&P 500 index being a poor representation of the market portfolio, and (3) the security being mispriced by the market.

Figure 6–8 shows that the estimated average returns for U.S. Tobacco and Chrysler are above the SML. IBM is close to it, and A&P is below it. Generally, the expected returns for portfolios of securities will more closely fit the SML returns than will the returns for individual securities. This occurs because the errors in estimating individual security betas tend to cancel out when portfolios are formed. The r values for each of the b_k estimates are quite low (for example, from Table 4–1, we have them as .18, .26, .39, and .10, respectively). So, we only have very rough estimates of the betas for these four stock returns.

Historical SMLs and Factors Influencing SMLs

Figure 6–9 shows three different SMLs—one for the period 1926–86, the second for the period 1977–81, and a third for the 1982–86 period. An investor might be tempted to rely on the SML, but an examination of the 61-year period from 1926 through 1986 shows that the SML is not static. The intercept, the return on the risk-free asset, will vary as interest rates change. Interest rates were high relative to historical averages during the 1979–84 period but declined to long-term historical levels in 1985 and 1986. The slope of the SML also changes over time because of changes in the risk-bearing attitudes of investors in aggregate. Note that in Figure 6–9 the slope of the SML in the 1982–86 period is almost identical to the slope for the 61-year period.

Figure 6–10 shows what might happen to the SML if investors change their outlook toward the economy and if the risk-free interest rate changes. Panel A of Figure 6–10 shows that when investors are less optimistic, they will want to earn higher returns than usual because of their greater

Figure 6–10
Potential Changes in the Security Market Line

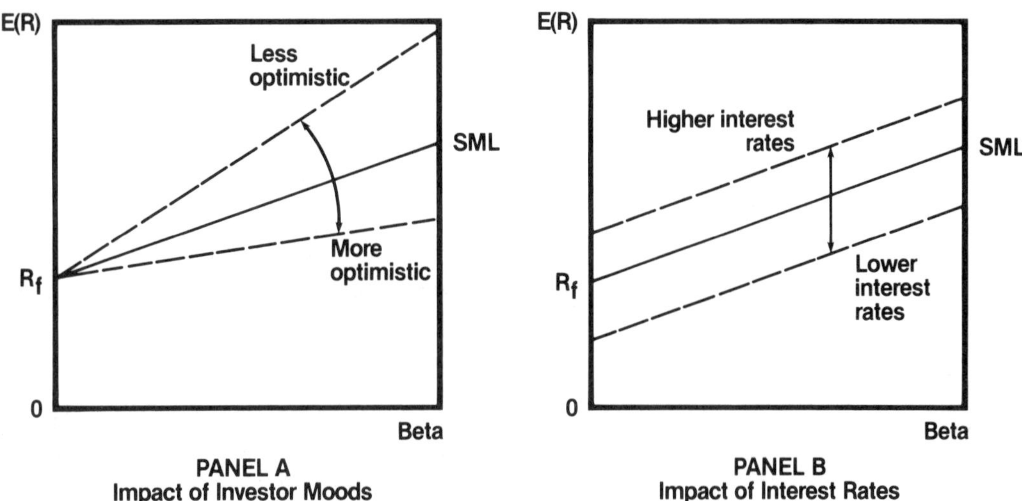

uncertainty. If investors become more optimistic and, hence, more certain about what the future will bring, they may be willing to settle for lower expected returns for a given amount of risk. Panel B shows that interest rate changes will simply shift the SML up or down.

Interpretation of the SML

The CAPM, as visualized by the SML in Figure 6–7, shows that the higher the beta the greater the expected return and vice versa. Why not maximize the beta in order to maximize the expected rate of return? Indeed, if investors knew with certainty that the return on the market would exceed the risk-free rate, the optimal strategy would be to maximize beta.

$$R_f + \beta_p(R_m - R_f) = R_p \tag{6.3}$$

The SML equation, as restated above, shows that the return on a portfolio is a combination of the risk-free rate, the market risk premium, and the portfolio's beta. Whether the market has a positive or negative excess return $(R_m - R_f)$ is important to the portfolio return. To see beta's influence on the return from the portfolio, suppose an investor purchases an S&P 500 index fund on margin so that the beta is 2.0. Borrowing to buy the index portfolio always produces a beta greater than 1.0 and lending produces a beta of less than 1.0. What will be the return on the portfolio with a beta of 2.0?

The answer depends on the risk-free rate and the market performance during the investment period. The tabulation in Table 6–2 gives the result achieved by this high-risk portfolio for the period 1978–86. Notice especially the portfolio performance when the market goes up as it did in 1982 through 1986, when it is relatively stable as it was in 1978, and when it goes down as it did in 1981. The actual treasury bill rate for

Table 6–2
Predicted Portfolio Returns, 1978–86

Year	T-bill	Risk Premium	Beta		Predicted Return	
	R_f	$R_m - R_f$	High	Low	R(High)	R(Low)
1978	7.2	6.6 − 7.2 [−0.6]	2.0	.5	6.0	6.9
1979	10.4	18.4 − 10.4 [8.0]	2.0	.5	26.4	14.4
1980	11.2	32.4 − 11.2 [21.2]	2.0	.5	53.6	21.8
1981	14.7	−4.9 − 14.7 [−19.6]	2.0	.5	−24.5	4.9
1982	10.5	21.4 − 10.5 [10.9]	2.0	.5	32.3	16.0
1983	8.8	22.5 − 8.8 [13.7]	2.0	.5	36.2	15.6
1984	9.9	6.3 − 9.9 [−3.6]	2.0	.5	2.7	8.1
1985	7.7	32.2 − 7.7 [24.5]	2.0	.5	56.7	20.4
1986	6.2	18.5 − 6.2 [12.3]	2.0	.5	30.8	12.4
Mean	9.6	17.6 [7.4]			24.5	13.4
Std. Dev.	2.6	11.6			24.4	5.4

Portfolio returns = $R_p = R_f + \beta_p(R_m - R_f)$

each year is used. Similar calculations are presented for a low-risk portfolio with a beta of .5.

In strong bull market years such as 1980 and 1985, the return for bearing the risk of a portfolio with a beta of 2.0 was 53.6 and 56.7 percent, respectively. A return of 11.2 percent could have been obtained in 1980 by simply investing in treasury bills, but only 7.7 percent would have been earned in 1985. During 1981, however, the return for taking on the high-risk beta of 2.0 was −24.5 percent. In that year, the portfolio actually declined 9.8 percent (twice the market decline of 4.9 percent), but because treasury bills yielded 14.7 percent, the investor was 24.5 percent worse off compared to simply purchasing treasury bills. In a similar fashion, the investor got a lower return with the .5-beta portfolio in the bull markets of 1980 and 1985 compared to the high-beta portfolio. On the other hand, the low-beta portfolio was less battered by the bear market of 1981 than was the high-beta portfolio.

In stock market terminology, a high-beta portfolio is referred to as an aggressive portfolio and a low-beta portfolio as a defensive portfolio. For the strong bull market period running from 1982 into 1987, the investor would have done well with a high-beta portfolio. Investors anticipating bull markets tend to shift to high-beta stocks, and those anticipating bear markets shift to low-beta stocks for the obvious reasons shown in Table 6–2.

Practical Aspects of the Capital Asset Pricing Model

Using the CAPM for investment purposes requires that the theoretical implications of the model be applicable to everyday investment decisions. A number of factors must be considered before we can reach a conclusion regarding the practical value of the CAPM. These factors relate to the reasonableness of the assumptions and the accuracy of estimating the risk-free rate, beta, and market return.

Reasonableness of the Assumptions

The original CAPM has undergone considerable reformulation. The remakings of the CAPM have attempted to state more reasonable assumptions about investors and markets. Extended discussions of these topics are found in advanced treatments of security analysis. However, the practical implications of one revision of CAPM are particularly interesting for investors. If investors are faced with different tax rates, they will again need to "tailor-make" individual portfolio choices to achieve the highest level of individual want-satisfying power. The personal portfolio choice must take into account the return, risk, and tax implications for each portfolio possibility. The market portfolio may or may not be desirable for an individual investor. Next, we will discuss some of the empirical issues surrounding CAPM.

Estimating the Risk-Free Rate

The CML and SML shift as the risk-free rate changes over time. As a result, the investor is not relieved of the thorny problem of forecasting interest rates for varying periods of time. For example, we can see in the second column of Table 6–2 how variable interest rates on ninety-day treasury bills have been from year to year during the 1978–86 period. An investor using the CAPM model for investment purposes still needs to be concerned with interest rate risk.

Estimating Beta

One of the more difficult tasks for an investor using the CAPM is to come up with a reliable estimate of beta. On an abstract level, beta is easy to envision, but on a practical level, its measurement is difficult. The beta value we are seeking is for the future, but we usually resort to the evaluation of historical data (e.g., estimating the characteristic line) in order to forecast future betas. When using historical betas for decisions regarding the future, we must understand what, if any, relationship exists between past and future betas.

Reliability of Historical Betas

Both Marshall Blume and Robert Levy examined the question of the relationship between historical betas and future betas. Blume dealt with annual periods, and Levy used weekly data. Selected results are given in

Table 6–3
Relationship between Past and Future Betas for Various Time Periods

	Coefficient of Determination between Past and Future Betas		
Securities in Portfolio	*7-Year Periods*	*52-Week Periods*	*13-Week Periods*
1	.38	.24	.13
4(5)*	.69	.59*	.38*
10	.84	.73	.51
20(25)*	.91	.88*	.70*
50	.96	.95	.80

*Number of securities in portfolio, Levy study.

Sources: Marshall E. Blume, "On the Assessment of Risk," *Journal of Finance* (March 1971): 1–10, and Robert A. Levy, "On the Short-Term Stationarity of Beta Coefficients," *Financial Analysts Journal* (November–December 1971): 55–62.

Table 6–3. By analyzing all common stocks listed on the NYSE from 1926 to 1968, Blume found a tendency for high betas to decline toward one and for low betas to increase toward one. An explanation for this tendency is that younger growth companies mature and older mature companies seek growth through diversification. A more general explanation is that this is another example of a statistical phenomenon known as the tendency for values to return to their mean.

Method of Estimation

The estimation of beta requires analyzing historical data, and this can be accomplished by many different techniques. Consequently, the resulting beta estimates may vary considerably. Some of the major factors that may change are (1) the time period being examined, (2) the frequency of price observations, (3) the frequency with which trades occur, and (4) the market index being used as a proxy for the market. For example, in Chapter 4 we presented two estimates of beta for Chrysler stock: (1) using annual returns over 1967–86, beta = 2.6, and (2) using monthly returns in 1986, beta = 1.73. Betas on inactively traded securities are probably less reliable than betas based on actively traded ones. Finally, to the extent that different market indexes, as examined in Chapter 3, do not all move together, betas calculated using different indexes will vary.

For large portfolios of about twenty-five securities and up, these problems may not matter much. However, for the investor holding ten securities, the coefficient of determination might vary greatly from the .84 Blume found, depending on the method used to measure betas.

Beta Forecasting Services

As a result of the widespread use of betas in security analysis and portfolio management, numerous beta forecasting services have thrived. The various services engage in a wide variety of forecasting practices to ar-

Table 6–4
Beta Values for Selected Industries

Industry	Mean Beta	Low Beta	High Beta
Securities brokerage	1.58	.90	1.90
Savings and loans	1.53	.90	1.95
Computers and peripherals	1.38	1.05	1.85
Air transport	1.17	.90	1.45
Hotel/Gaming	1.10	.65	1.35
Auto and truck	1.10	.65	1.50
Broadcasting/Cable TV	1.04	.85	1.20
Gold/Diamond	.98	.90	1.10
Home appliance	.96	.65	1.40
Cement	.91	.65	1.05
Machine tool	.91	.60	1.25
Tobacco	.86	.60	1.00

Source: Means calculated from *Value Line Investment Service,* various issues, February to April 1987.

rive at their beta estimates. These services are provided by companies such as Value Line, Merrill Lynch, and Wells Fargo Investment Advisors.

As an example, the *Value Line Investment Advisory Service* uses weekly observations over five years and compares stock returns to the NYSE Composite Index when calculating beta values. The Value Line betas are adjusted for the tendency of betas to regress toward the mean. Table 6–4 shows the mean Value Line beta for selected industry groups. Notice the betas are clustered in a range between .8 and 1.6. Barr Rosenberg and James Guy have provided forecasts of "fundamental" betas in which the systematic risk estimates for securities are adjusted to reflect underlying fundamental characteristics of the securities. Wells Fargo Investment Advisors have developed a system to include both historical and expectational data in estimating betas.

Estimating the Market Return

Probably the most important estimate an investor needs to make when using the CAPM is the market return expected over the investment horizon. In Chapter 7, we will examine some techniques that can be used to estimate future market index values. Who could have predicted in 1980–82 that the Dow Jones Industrial Average would reach the 2400 level by early 1987? At the same time, this is precisely why portfolio theory places such heavy emphasis on risk measurement. If we knew for sure that the market would increase by 20 percent over the next year, we should buy the highest beta portfolio available and, on average, enjoy a great deal of success.

Risk Level Selection

After arriving at an estimate of the market return, the next important step is for the investor to establish the portfolio's risk level in terms of its beta. Poor performance in a given year hurts even if the termination of the investor's time horizon is several years away. On the other hand, taking on risk can provide important benefits. Consider the ending value of a \$10,000 investment made in either a .9 or a 1.1 beta portfolio for the 1926–86 period. Since the market risk premium ($R_m - R_f$) was positive in this period, a high-beta portfolio would give the higher returns. For example, the portfolio returns for the 1926–86 period can be calculated as follows, using the Ibbotson-Sinquefield data examined in Chapter 1:

$$\begin{aligned} R_p &= R_f + b_i(R_m - R_f) \\ &= 0.035 + 0.9(0.121 - 0.035) = 0.1124 \\ &= 0.035 + 1.1(0.121 - 0.035) = 0.1296 \end{aligned}$$

The low-beta portfolio (.9) produced an annual return of 11.24 percent while the high-beta portfolio earned 12.96 percent.

An investor placing the initial \$10,000 in a high-beta portfolio would have an accumulated wealth position after sixty-one years of

$$\$10{,}000\ (1 + .1296)^{61} = \$10{,}000\ (1692.019) = \$16{,}920{,}190$$

Alternatively, an investor placing the \$10,000 in a low-beta portfolio would have accumulated

$$\$10{,}000\ (1 + .1124)^{61} = \$10{,}000\ (663.620) = \$6{,}636{,}200$$

The \$10,000 initial investment would have been worth \$10,283,990 more after sixty-one years when placed in the high-beta rather than the low-beta portfolio.

Concept of Alpha

Does the CAPM negate the perspectives we gained in the last chapter about fundamental analysis? If the CAPM can provide the value of an asset in the form of a return, why is it necessary to bother with the complex task of security analysis?

The CAPM does not imply that individual securities will not produce returns greater than the return projected by the CAPM. In Figure 6–8, the return from investing in U.S. Tobacco from 1967 through 1986 was greater than one might have anticipated based on the risk-free rate and the general market performance during the period. The CAPM merely says that, *on the average,* actual returns will correspond to the predictions of the model. An investor with superior stock selection skills, a good sense of market timing, or superior information should do better than predicted by the CAPM. An investor is not prevented from obtaining a return in excess of what is implied by the risk assumed. Naturally, an investment could also fall short of the return estimated by the CAPM.

The primary objective of the security analyst is to discover an underpriced security where the calculated price of the security is greater than its current price. How does this valuation process fit into portfolio theory? A measure of the excess return derived from picking undervalued portfolios *or* the excess loss from picking overvalued portfolios can be obtained by comparing the actual returns with the average return for the portfolio's beta level, as shown by the SML. For example, taking the 1967–86 data for U.S. Tobacco given earlier in this chapter, we can calculate the return for U.S. Tobacco using the SML as follows:

$$\text{SML: } R_f + \beta_j(R_m - R_f) = 7.2 + 0.6(11.5 - 7.2) = 9.78\%$$

The actual average return for U.S. Tobacco for the period was 17.8 percent, for an excess return of 8.02 percent (17.8 − 9.78). The excess percent returns for the other three securities were: Chrysler 9.82, IBM .4, and A&P −4.26. The excess return is often referred to as the stock's *alpha*. It is related to the a_j measure we calculated for the characteristic line as follows: alpha $= a_j - R_f(1 - b_j)$

The CAPM: Empirical and Theoretical Issues

CAPM holds that a strong, positive relationship should exist between systematic risk, as measured by beta, and the expected return for stocks. Although we cannot measure expected returns, the next best course is to concentrate on the relationship between actual returns earned and the risk taken to earn those returns. Three questions are generally raised when tests of the CAPM are made.

1. Is there a positive and linear association between beta and return?
2. Is the intercept of the SML equal to the risk-free rate, using the short-term treasury bill rate as a proxy?
3. Is beta the only factor that explains differences in security returns, or are there other factors not captured by the beta that explain security return differences?

Typically, studies are conducted on portfolios of securities instead of securities directly because of the large statistical errors associated with individual beta estimates. These studies usually involve two stages. First, historical betas are calculated for securities, and these securities are combined into portfolios. The portfolio return characteristics, especially beta, are then inspected to see if the portfolio betas and returns are approximately linearly related, as would be shown by the SML.

Two major studies on the association between security returns and beta were by Black, Jensen, and Scholes (BJS) and by Fama and MacBeth. In the BJS study, portfolio returns (less the risk-free return) were regressed against portfolio betas for several historical time periods. In general, they found that portfolio returns and beta were linearly related. However, in one time period, the relationship was negative and not positive as CAPM would require. Also, their estimate of alpha did not appear to approximate the short-term, treasury bill rate. Fama and MacBeth attempted to extend the BJS study and generally supported the overall findings. They tended to rule out other mathematical forms of the market model as being superior to the CAPM formulation.

On the other side of the research issue, many studies identified *anomalies* or results from studies that would be inconsistent with the way the CAPM explains return differences. The major anomalies evolved out of studies into extra-market factors that explained security return differences unrelated to the market portfolio (see Table 6–1). Three examples of the major anomalies are as follows:

1. Price-earnings effect. Low P/E stocks report higher returns than high P/E stocks, and the differences are not explained by the SML.
2. Small firm effect. Small size firms earn higher risk-adjusted returns than large firms.
3. Calendar effect. Extraordinary returns are earned on stocks in January, during the early part of the month, and during certain days of the week, whereas the SML says that returns should be time independent.

Along with research concerning market anomalies, new models and theories were developed to replace or improve upon the market model. Empirical tests were conducted to identify whether factors in addition to the market index help to explain security return differentials. Of the new approaches, the multiple-factor models have gained the most popularity in recent years.

The strongest criticism of the CAPM does not come from its empirical weakness but from its theoretical weakness. In a 1977 article, Richard Roll questioned whether the CAPM was at all testable, asserting that the market portfolio is not measurable. He indicated that the various index portfolios used in the empirical research as proxies for the market portfolio are not equivalent to the market portfolio, as specified in the CAPM. He argued that we have no way of knowing if the betas calculated with the market index portfolio represent the systematic risk that is being priced in the markets.

The perspectives gained from the CAPM and the SML have made possible the performance evaluation of professional portfolio managers and have allowed investors a framework for formally analyzing risk and return relationships between securities. Although heavily criticized on both theoretical and empirical levels, the CAPM still remains as the foundation to the understanding of more complex relationships that exist among security returns.

Arbitrage Pricing Theory

Arbitrage pricing theory (APT) provides a general theory for the pricing of capital assets. Whereas CAPM attributes all systematic risk to a single factor, the market portfolio, the APT holds that the return on a security should equal the risk-free rate plus a combination of risk premiums, including one risk premium for each systematic risk factor. With APT, systematic risk can be caused by one, two, or many factors.

A Multifactor Model of Asset Pricing

APT can be described as a multifactor model of asset pricing. The sources of systematic risk can be varied, ranging from economy-wide factors, such as movements in the general level of stock prices, changes in interest rates, inflation, and tax laws, to industry-specific factors, such as the vulnerability of an industry to foreign competition or changes in federal health, safety, and pollution standards. The level or index of the factor can be represented by a symbol O_L, where L identifies the factor. One factor could be related to changes in the level of the general stock market, where $O_{S\&P}$ could be the return on the S&P 500. Unlike CAPM, with the APT, the systematic market index factor, if it is a risk component, is not the *only* factor and does not represent the market portfolio. It is simply one of many possible systematic risk components explaining differences in the returns of some securities. Examples of indexes for other factors might be the change in an index of monthly oil prices or the change in monthly 90-day treasury bill yields.

Each factor has a risk premium associated with it that is linearly related to expected returns. By linearly related, we mean that an arbitrage pricing line similar to the SML can be drawn for each systematic risk factor. For every security, we can measure its sensitivity, $b_{k,L}$, to each systematic risk factor L. This sensitivity factor is analogous to the beta in the CAPM model, except with APT we have a beta for each factor that might affect a security's return.

According to the APT, under very general assumptions about investor behavior, the expected return on any security should equal

$$E(R_k) = \sum_{L=1}^{l} b_{k,L}E(O_L) \tag{6.4}$$

where $E(R_k)$ = the expected return on security k
L = the Lth factor (the factor index)
l = the number of factors
$E(O_L)$ = the expected level of factor L
$b_{k,L}$ = the sensitivity of security k to factor L

Underlying the APT are the assumptions necessary for making unlimited arbitrage possible. The market model for the APT described in equation 6.4 has l factors, with the pricing effects of each factor being added together in a linear relationship.

As with the CAPM, the arbitrage process is at the heart of the model. The APT assumes that investors are rational in the sense that they avoid bearing unsystematic risk. As with the CAPM, the financial markets do not reward the investor for any unsystematic risk of the security or portfolio returns. Unlike the CAPM, the APT does not require the existence of the market portfolio nor are investors' utility curves as narrowly defined.

Arbitrage and the Law of One Price

The law of one price states that two perfect substitutes must sell at the same price. What makes the APT work is the assumption that arbitrageurs will exploit all opportunities where equivalent riskless security positions offer different yields. By perfect substitutes, we mean securities or portfolios with the *same sensitivity to a systematic risk factor.*

To see how the APT operates, let us assume that three securities A, B, and C with sensitivities to factor 1 (change in interest rates) are equal to $b_{A,1} = .8$, $b_{B,1} = 1.2$, and $b_{C,1} = 2.0$, respectively. Furthermore, assume that investors' expected returns for interest rate risk are 2 percent for security A, 8 percent for security B, and 12 percent for security C. Arbitrageurs can engage in activities to guarantee a riskless return if this situation should occur. Assume that the risk-free rate is 6 percent, and we have the following:

$$R_A = 6 + .8(2) = 7.6\%$$

$$R_B = 6 + 1.2(8) = 15.6\%$$

$$R_C = 6 + 2.0(12) = 30\%$$

An investor can duplicate security B's level of systematic risk caused by sensitivity to the changes in interest rates by combining two-thirds of security A with one-third of security C to form portfolio AC. For example, $b_{AC,1} = 2/3(.8) + 1/3(2.0) = .533 + .667 = 1.2$. The expected return for portfolio AC, with $b_{AC,1}$ equal to 1.2 is

$$\text{Portfolio (AC)} = 2/3(7.6) + 1/3(30) = 5.1 + 10 = 15.1\%$$

Arbitrageurs would sell short portfolio AC and buy security B with the proceeds as long as any positive return differential remains. The action of the short selling of A and C combined with the buying of B will cause prices on all three securities to change, until finally the security returns are in equilibrium, which means that they are all on the same return-to-sensitivity ratio for the interest rate risk factor.

A linear association can be found between a security's sensitivity to a factor and the risk premium earned on that factor. A major difficulty with the APT is in identifying the systematic risk components in the market. For this purpose, statistical factor analysis procedures are often used to derive systematic risk components from samples of returns for portfolios.

Empirical Issues

Numerous empirical studies have attempted to identify these fundamental, systematic factors in the market. Such factors as market return, dividend yield, capitalization rates, and industry groupings have been found to be priced by the market in some studies. On the basis of research to this point, no factor has been consistently found, except possibly a general market factor, to be priced by the market. The empirical evidence gives only weak support to the APT model.

What insight can the investor gain from the CAPM and the APT approaches to security valuation? From our discussion, two key issues have emerged. Investors should diversify broadly to achieve efficient investment performance and be rewarded for whatever systematic risk they are undertaking. Second, arbitrage operates to eliminate unsystematic risk and equate prices for securities that have identical levels of systematic risk components.

Summary

As the number of securities being considered for a portfolio increases, the number of covariance terms becomes too large to make the covariance approach to portfolio selection practical. We solve this covariance problem by introducing an "index" security. By allowing the investor to borrow or lend at the risk-free rate, the efficient frontier reduces to a single risky portfolio, and risk can be altered by borrowing or lending. This single risky "security" is commonly known as the market portfolio, which contains all assets in proportion to their respective market values.

In the capital asset pricing model, the risk-return relationship of the efficient frontier reduces to a linear relationship between the portfolio return and the beta or risk of the portfolio. Beta measures the variability of a security or an asset relative to the variability of the market. Betas are often useful to investors, but they should be understood and not misused. One way to obtain an estimate of the future beta is to calculate the historical beta for the security or portfolio and assume the future beta will be equal to the historical beta. While historical betas for individual securities are unreliable estimates for future betas, the usefulness of historical beta estimates improves greatly as securities are combined to form portfolios.

Selection of the appropriate risk level is a personal matter depending directly on the investor's aversion to risk. While the risk measures resulting from the capital asset pricing model are useful, the investor should consider the financial consequences of portfolio losses, the manner in which performance is to be measured, and the ability to watch a portfolio decline in value without panic. Over long periods of time, small differences in beta may generate large differences in wealth. While the expected rewards from high-risk investing may be great, the investor must be willing to accept the possibility of severe temporary losses.

Arbitrage pricing theory (APT) was developed to provide an alternative to the capital asset pricing model. APT is essentially a multifactor pricing model in which systematic risk is related to one or more pricing factors. These factors could change from security to security and could include such factors as interest rate movements, inflation, energy prices, tax changes, foreign exchange fluctuations, and the regulatory or antitrust environment. One of the major criticisms against the capital asset pricing model is that it may be impossible to test empirically, and APT tends to suffer from the same problem.

Symbols Used in This Chapter

- R return
- S standard deviation
- V variance
- X percent of security in portfolio
- σ population variance
- $E(R)$ expected return
- R_f risk-free rate
- R_m return on market portfolio
- R_p return on portfolio
- b_j beta for jth security
- O value of factor index
- L a factor index
- l the number of factors
- $b_{k,L}$ the sensitivity of security k to factor L

Suggested Readings

AUERBACH, ROBERT D. "Politics and the Federal Reserve." *Contemporary Policy Issues* (Fall 1985): 43–58.

BARRY, CHRISTOPHER, and STEPHEN BROWN. "Limited Information as a Source of Risk." *Journal of Portfolio Management* (Winter 1986): 66–72.

BLACK, FISCHER. "Noise." *Journal of Finance* (July 1986): 529–43.

BLUME, MARSHALL E. "Betas and Their Regression Tendencies." *Journal of Finance* (June 1975): 787–95.

———. "Betas and Their Regression Tendencies: Some Further Evidence." *Journal of Finance* (March 1979): 265–67.

BROWN, DAVID P., and MICHAEL GIBBONS. "A Simple Econometric Approach for Utility-Based Asset Pricing Models." *Journal of Finance* (June 1985): 359–82.

BROWN, DAVID P., and MARK WEINSTEIN. "A New Approach to Testing Asset Pricing Models." *Journal of Finance* (June 1983): 711–44.

BROWN, STEPHEN J., and JEROLD B. WARNER. "Measuring Security Price Performance." *Journal of Financial Economics* (November 1980): 205–58.

CHEN, NAI-FU, RICHARD ROLL, and STEPHEN ROSS. "Economic Forces and the Stock Market." *Journal of Business* (July 1986): 383–403.

CHO, D. CHINHYUNG. "On Testing the Arbitrage Pricing Theory: Inter-Battery Factor Analysis." *Journal of Finance* (December 1984): 1485–1502.

DHRYMES, PHEOBUS. "The Empirical Relevance of Arbitrage Pricing Models." *Journal of Portfolio Management* (Summer 1984): 35–44.

DHRYMES, PHEOBUS, IRWIN FRIEND, and N. BULENT GULTEKIN. "A Critical Reexamination of the Empirical Evidence on the Arbitrage Pricing Theory." *Journal of Finance* (June 1984): 323–46.

DYBVIG, PHILIP H., and STEPHEN A. ROSS. "Tax Clienteles and Asset Pricing." *Journal of Finance* (July 1986): 751–63.

EVANS, JOHN L., and STEPHEN H. ARCHER. "Diversification and the Reduction of Dispersion: An Empirical Analysis." *Journal of Finance* (December 1968): 761–67.

Ferson, Wayne E., Shmuel Kandel, and Robert F. Stambaugh. "Tests of Asset Pricing with Time-Varying Expected Risk Premiums and Market Betas." *Journal of Finance* (June 1987): 201–220.

Fuller, Russell H. *Capital Asset Pricing Theories—Evolution and New Frontiers.* Charlottesville, VA: Financial Analysts Research Foundation, 1981.

Gibbons, Michael R. "Multivariate Tests of Financial Models: A New Approach." *Journal of Financial Economics* (March 1982): 3–27.

Gibbons, Michael R., and Wayne Ferson. "Testing Asset Pricing Models with Changing Expectations and an Unobservable Market Portfolio." *Journal of Financial Economics* (June 1985): 217–36.

Hawkins, David F., and Walther J. Campbell. *Equity Valuation: Models, Analysis and Implications.* New York: Financial Executives Research Foundation, 1978.

Keim, Donald. "Size Related Anomalies and Stock Return Seasonability: Further Empirical Evidence." *Journal of Financial Economics* (June 1983): 13–32.

Levy, Robert A. "On the Short-Term Stationarity of Beta Coefficients." *Financial Analysts Journal* (November–December 1971): 55–62.

Patell, James, and Mark Wolfson. "The Timing of Financial Accounting Disclosures and the Intraday Distribution of Security Price Changes." *Journal of Financial Economics* (June 1984): 223–52.

Rogolski, Richard J., and Seha M. Tinic. "The January Size Effect: Anomaly or Risk Measurement." *Financial Analysts Journal* (November–December 1986): 63–70.

Roll, Richard. "Ambiguity When Performance Is Measured by the Securities Market Line." *Journal of Finance* (September 1978): 1051–70.

Rosenberg, Barr. "The Capital Asset Pricing Model and the Market Model." *Journal of Portfolio Management* (Winter 1981): 5–16.

Sharpe, William. "Bonds versus Stocks: Some Lessons from Capital Market Theory." *Financial Analysts Journal* (November–December 1973): 74–80.

———. "Factor Models, CAPMs, and the APT." *Journal of Portfolio Management* (Fall 1984): 21–25.

Trzcinka, Charles. "On the Number of Factors in the APT." *Journal of Finance* (June 1986): 347–68.

Questions

1. Explain in your own words why the riskiness of a single security may be completely irrelevant to the investor's decision to buy or sell the security.
2. What is meant by the efficiency criterion and the efficient frontier? How do these two concepts relate to each other?
3. Why is it necessary to establish an efficient frontier prior to arriving at an investment decision?

4. Discuss the general criterion used to select the optimum or best portfolio from the set of efficient portfolios. Why might the optimum portfolio of one investor be different from the optimum portfolio of another investor?
5. What is an efficient market? What conditions need to be present for an efficient market to exist?
6. Explain why the introduction of the risk-free asset eliminates the need for covariances and reduces the portfolio decision to one of borrowing or lending on a theoretical basis.
7. Discuss the difference between lending and borrowing portfolios.
8. The security market line changes over time. How does it change with respect to changes in interest rates and investor moods?
9. In equilibrium, all assets lie on the security market line. What will happen to a security (in a disequilibrium case) that lies above the SML?
10. Discuss why it is ordinarily unwise to purchase a portfolio that contains diversifiable risk. Under what conditions should the investor accept diversifiable risk?
11. Beta has become a well-known measure of risk. Discuss how accurate past estimates of beta are compared to future betas, and show how adjustments can be made to better estimate beta.
12. Define the term *alpha* and discuss how alpha relates to security analysis.
13. In portfolio performance evaluation, why is the return on the market portfolio considered a benchmark?
14. What is riskless arbitrage, and why is it important to the understanding of valuation models?
15. What is a market anomaly, and why is this concept important to an understanding of security and market valuation models?
16. Briefly describe the arbitrage pricing model and the role the *law of one price* plays in the development of that model.

Problems

1. Which one of the following portfolios *cannot* lie on the efficient frontier as described by Markowitz?

Portfolio	Expected Return	Standard Deviation
Y	15%	36%
X	5	7
W	9	21
Z	12	15

(Excerpted with permission from the 1987 Level I examination, The Institute of Chartered Financial Analysts)

2. Assume the following formula:

Adjusted beta = (.75 times historical beta) + .25

Calculate the adjusted betas for the following three stocks given their historical beta measures.

Superdog, Inc., with a historical beta of .35
Mean-Median, Inc., with a historical beta of .97
Charge, Inc., with a historical beta of 1.82

3. The Uptrend Company is currently paying a dividend of $2 per share, which is expected to grow indefinitely at a 6 percent annual rate. The company's stock has a beta of 1.5. Given that the expected market return is 15 percent and the risk-free rate is 7 percent, what should be the price of the Uptrend Company stock?

4. The risk level an investor assumes may make a big difference in the return realized on a portfolio depending on what the market does during the period. Determine what difference the risk level makes to a portfolio of $100,000 for the following situations:

(a) Market annual return of 7.0 percent, risk-free rate of 3.0 percent, a twenty-year investment period, and a beta of either .8 or 1.1.

(b) Market annual return of 4.0 percent, risk-free rate of 7.0 percent, a five-year investment period, and a beta of either .8 or 1.1.

5. The returns and standard deviations based on the 1970–86 period for well-diversified portfolios of various securities are listed in the following table. Plot the returns versus the standard deviations for these portfolios. On the basis of these data, produce a free-hand drawn straight line approximating the capital market line. From these data, what do you infer about the nature of risk and return over the period? What is an approximate value for the slope of the capital market line?

Security Portfolio	Mean Return	Standard Deviation
Treasury bills	7.8%	2.9%
Long-term government bonds	9.8	12.6
Long-term corporate bonds	10.4	13.3
Common stocks	12.0	17.5
Small stocks	17.7	25.8

6. Using the following data, plot each stock's expected return versus the market portfolio's expected return, and graphically show each stock's position on the security market line. The risk-free rate is expected to be 7 percent, and the market return is expected to be 14 percent.

Stock	Expected Beta
IBM	1.1
GM	1.2
Allegis	1.3
Southern Bell	0.7

7. As a portfolio manager of a large pension fund, you are given the following five-year forecasts by your staff economist:

Expected annual inflation rate	4%
Expected real interest rate	4%
Expected return on market portfolio	15%

The investment planning horizon for the pension fund is five years.

(a) Draw the security market line, indicating the expected returns for stocks with beta values of −.5, 0, .5, 1, 1.5, and 2, respectively.

(b) Assume that the economist returns in two months and says she underestimated the inflation rate by 2 percent. How would the security market line change? Draw the new security market line. How does change in expected inflation affect the expected risk-free rate? How does it affect the expected return on the market portfolio?

(c) Assume that the economist returns in another two months and suggests that investors have become less willing to purchase common stock and are demanding higher risk premiums to compensate for the risk. She estimates that the expected return on the market portfolio has now increased to 20 percent. Show the new security market line with the higher market risk premium and the higher inflation rate.

8. What is your interpretation of the following correlation matrix? The matrix represents the correlation between each of the stocks with the common influence of the market portfolio removed.

	Merck	Texas Instruments	Walt Disney	Western Union
Merck	1			
Texas Instruments	.0173	1		
Walt Disney	.5621	.0131	1	
Western Union	.1004	.0048	.0016	1

9. Brad has determined that two factors affect security prices: The interest-rate factor and the oil-price factor. Over the investment horizon, Brad expects the risk premiums to be 2 percent for the interest-rate factor and 3.5 percent for the oil-price factor. Assume that he is considering three stocks that have estimated beta coefficients showing their sensitivity to the two factors as follows:

Factor	Factor Sensitivity or Beta		
	Firm D	**Firm E**	**Firm F**
Interest rate	1.5	.2	.5
Oil price	.6	1.2	1.0

Assume the risk-free rate is 6 percent.

(a) What are the expected returns for firms D and E?

(b) Assume that the expected return for firm F is independently determined to be 14 percent. Should Brad want to buy stock F or sell it short? Why?

10. Martha has chosen to invest in an efficient portfolio of risky stocks that offers a return of 10 percent and a standard deviation of 35 percent. As an alternative, Andy suggests that she can obtain the same return at a lower level of risk by investing part of her funds in the market portfolio and the remainder in a risk-free asset. Assume that Martha can both borrow and lend unlimited funds at the risk-free rate.

(a) Given that the market portfolio offers a 16 percent return with a 44 percent standard deviation and the risk-free rate is 8 percent, what *superior* portfolio earning 10 percent would Andy recommend for Martha?

(b) If Martha had chosen a portfolio of risky stocks offering a 20 percent return and a 75 percent standard deviation, what portfolio should Andy recommend that would provide the 20 percent return at less risk?

Part

Equity Valuation

3

The three chapters in this part follow what is sometimes called the funnel approach to security valuation. We begin by examining the economy and then gradually narrow the focus down to an industry and finally to a specific company. Chapter 7 covers the macroeconomic considerations that are important to investors. This material highlights the various components of Gross National Product. Investors are able to monitor business cycle indicators to determine the health of the economy from an investment standpoint. Chapter 8 presents the factors investors can consider in examining an industry to determine its growth potential. Chapter 9 presents security analysis as it is applied to common stock investments. Much of the discussion presented in these chapters is also relevant for later chapters—especially those dealing with investment in fixed-income securities.

Chapter 7

Analysis of the Economy

Key Concepts

- business cycle
- business cycle indicator
- capital expenditures
- coincident indicator
- consumer price index
- crowding out
- disposable personal income
- federal deficit
- fiscal policy
- gross national product
- Index of Industrial Production
- inventory-to-sales ratio
- lagging indicator
- leading indicator
- monetary policy
- money supply
- personal consumption expenditures
- population growth
- productivity
- real growth rate

Chapter Outline

If, at the end of 1981, an investor had foreseen that the stock market in general was undervalued and had placed $100,000 in a mutual fund that replicated the performance of the S&P 500 stock index, the stock would have been worth approximately $300,000 by early 1987. For the five-and-one-quarter year period, the stock market's annual real return adjusted for changes in the consumer price index was 20 percent while the real gross national product (GNP) grew at only a 2.5 percent rate. Investors who foresaw two important economic developments would have been rewarded handsomely. These developments were the beginning of a long, uninterrupted period of economic growth and the capitalizing of earnings on common stocks at much higher price-earnings (P/E) levels.

The first question investors face when deciding to buy or sell stock is whether the overall stock market is under- or overvalued at that time. During the period beginning in 1982 and continuing into 1987, many investment analysts severely undershot the target in forecasting the growth of stock prices. They judged that the stock market was overvalued, based on assessments made of future economic growth, corporate earnings projections, and historical stock market capitalization rates. Some analysts recommended that investors shift out of equities, and in some cases, even take short positions. These recommendations came at times when the S&P 500 systematically rose to new heights, passing through the 200, 230, 260, and finally the 300 levels. Investors who followed these analysts' recommendations missed out on most of the longest bull market in modern stock market history.

Nature of Economic Analysis

Economic analysis is the first stage in the security analysis process. It centers around two important activities: (1) estimating the long-run economic growth in the economy and (2) predicting the turning points in the *business cycle.* Returns on most securities closely follow the performance of the general economy. Interest rate movements are tied to the growth of the economy. High interest rates normally occur during boom periods, and low interest rates are more often associated with low or negative rates of economic growth. The level of market interest rates is a primary determinant of bond prices for any given quality bond. As we discussed in Chapter 6, the returns on most securities are positively correlated with the aggregate level of economic activity as reflected by the performance of the market portfolio of risky securities. We use as a proxy for the market portfolio the returns on the S&P 500 stock index.

We begin our discussion by estimating the index level for the S&P 500 based on a forecast of long-run economic growth. Then, we investigate the major factors underlying economic growth. Finally, we look at ways investors can attempt to predict turning points in economic cycles as well as stock market cycles.

To analyze the growth factors for a specific common stock, investors need to go beyond the general economic outlook and focus on industry and market segments that have growth rates differing from the overall economy. Companies within the specific industry or market segments that have unique elements of growth must be identified. Chapter 8 discusses the analysis of the growth potential for specific industries, and Chapter 9 examines the manner in which investors analyze the growth prospects of a specific company.

Forecasting the Market: *The Constant Growth Approach*

The significance of the growth factor on security valuation can be seen by recalling equation 5.4.

$$P_0 = \frac{D_1}{i - g}$$

where P_0 = the value of the stock
D_1 = the expected dividend
i = the rate of return desired
g = the expected rate of growth in dividends

The constant growth model can be applied as a starting point when trying to determine whether the stock market in general is under- or overvalued. Let us apply the model to evaluate the S&P 500 on May 20, 1987, when the index was at the 280 level. The average dividend on the S&P 500 for 1986 was approximately $8.22.

One reasonable estimate of i, the required return on common stocks, might be in the 14 percent area. The 14 percent rate would consist of a 3 percent *real growth rate,* a 6 percent inflation rate, and a 5 percent equity-risk premium. In 1987, economists forecasted long-term GNP growth in real terms around 3 percent. Treasury bonds yielded 9 percent, reflecting a 6 percent (9 − 3) expected long-term inflation rate. A study by Brigham, Shome, and Vinson reported that on average equity securities carried a 5.6 percent risk premium above long-term treasury bond yields, and the premium was relatively stable over the 1966–83 period, ranging from 3.75 percent to 6.92 percent.[1] In 1987, the stock market appeared to be requiring an equity risk-premium slightly below the long-run average value—somewhere in the area of 5 percent.

Growth rates for dividends over the 1964–86 period averaged 1.2 percent in real terms. Over the same period, real GNP growth averaged approximately 2.6 percent annually, or 1.4 percent above the dividend growth rate. Future dividend growth could be estimated to be around 7.6 percent as follows: 3 percent real growth + 6 percent inflation rate − 1.4. The 7.6 percent dividend growth rate, 14 percent discount rate, and $8.22 dividend level can be combined to produce a price estimate for the S&P 500 of 138.

$$P = \frac{8.22(1 + .076)}{.14 - .076} = 138$$

1. Brigham, Shome, and Vinson, "The Risk Approach to Measuring a Utility's Cost of Capital," *Financial Management* (Spring 1985): 33–45.

Clearly, what we have calculated using the constant growth formula is approximately one-half the actual level of the S&P 500 index at the time. The higher market value is attributable to additional factors. Changes in structural, tax, and demographic factors in the economy during the last half of the 1980s could lead to a change in the historical relationship between dividend growth and overall economic growth. A second set of estimates might predict that dividends would grow at the same 9 percent rate as forecasted for the GNP and that the required return on common stock might drop to 13 percent. On this basis, the constant growth model generates a market price estimate of 224.

$$P = \frac{8.22(1.09)}{.13 - .09} = 224$$

This market price estimate is far below the actual market level of 280 in May 1987.

We might ask what growth rate is implied by the market when the price of the S&P is at 280. The implied growth rate can be derived from the constant growth equation. Solving for g, we have the following:

$$280 = \frac{8.22(1 + g)}{.14 - g} \qquad g = 10.7\%$$

The high implied growth rate indicates that the market anticipated a very positive economic environment. To gain additional insight into economic growth, investors can perform a more complete analysis of the economy and its sectors.

Composite Economic Analysis

Investors often examine past growth rates for several of the more important economic variables to arrive at reasonable expectations regarding future stock market growth rates. An investigation of economic growth generally includes at a minimum the following three factors: (1) the expected changes in the current population and its age distribution, (2) the role of the government in fostering economic growth, and (3) the behavior of corporations with regard to expenditures on plants, equipment, and inventories.

GNP and Industrial Production

Figure 7–1 shows inflation-adjusted *gross national product* (GNP) from 1889 through 1986. GNP is the dollar value of all final goods and services produced in the economy. Although the long-term growth rate of the economy as measured by the GNP series has been in the neighborhood of 3.5 percent, this growth has been somewhat erratic.

Table 7–1 contains a breakdown of the GNP rates of growth for the economy from 1840 through 1986. With the exception of the decades of

Figure 7–1
A Century of Economic Growth

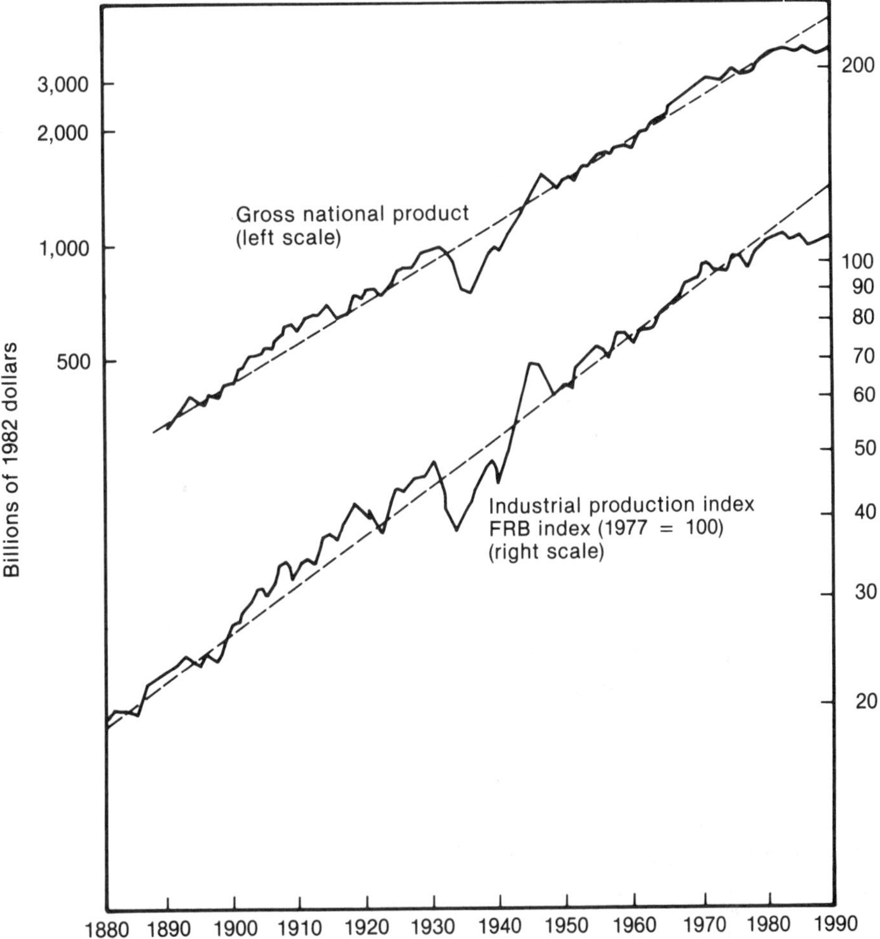

Source: David H. McKinley et al., *Forecasting Business Conditions* (New York: American Bankers Association, 1965), p. 16. Updated using Department of Commerce data.

1860–69 and 1930–39, the growth of the economy over ten-year periods has been at a fairly constant rate, fluctuating in the range of 2.6 percent to 5 percent per year. Economic growth rates in the 1970s and 1980s have been sluggish, averaging at the lower end of the range of historical growth, around 2.6 to 3 percent.

The *Index of Industrial Production* is shown in Figure 7–1 for the period from 1880 through 1986. This index has the same general growth trends as the GNP series, but its fluctuations are more pronounced. This greater volatility of industrial production relative to GNP will probably continue in future years as the usually stable service activities, which are included in GNP but not in industrial production, become an even more important part of the U.S. economy.

In summary, the past growth of the economy, adjusted for changes in the price level, has averaged about 3.5 percent per year. Because this historical record covers more than a century, it serves as a benchmark for

Table 7–1
Real GNP Growth, 1840–1986, Annual Percentages

1840 to 1986 3.5%	1840 to 1880 4.0%	1840s	4.2%
		1850s	5.0
		1860s	2.0
		1870s	5.0
	1880 to 1920 3.5%	1880s	3.7
		1890s	4.0
		1900s	3.7
		1910s	2.6
	1920 to 1970 3.4%	1920s	4.0
		1930s	1.4
		1940s	4.3
		1950s	3.2
		1960s	4.0
		1970s	2.3
		1980–86	3.6

Sources: Simon Kuznets, *Economic Growth and Structure* (New York: W. W. Norton & Co., 1965), p. 305, and *1987 Economic Report of the President.*

future growth projections. Past trends indicated a long-term growth expectation for the economy of at least 3 percent. However, future growth projections must consider past trends as only a starting point. The contemporary federal deficit situation demonstrates the problems that may be encountered when making future forecasts on the basis of historical projections.

Components of GNP

Investors interested in forecasting future economic growth need to look at the major components of GNP. These are (1) personal consumption expenditures, (2) gross private domestic investment, (3) government purchases of goods and services, and (4) net exports of goods and services. In addition, investors should examine the breakdown of investment in terms of fixed investment and changes in business inventories. Figure 7–2 shows the growth of GNP components from 1960 through 1986.

Personal Consumption Expenditures

During the 1960–86 period, inflation-adjusted *personal consumption expenditures* ranged from 60 to 66 percent of GNP. Because this is a sizable part of GNP, investors need to give special attention to consumer expenditures and expectations. Of concern are issues such as how long an eco-

Figure 7–2
Components of Real GNP, 1960–86

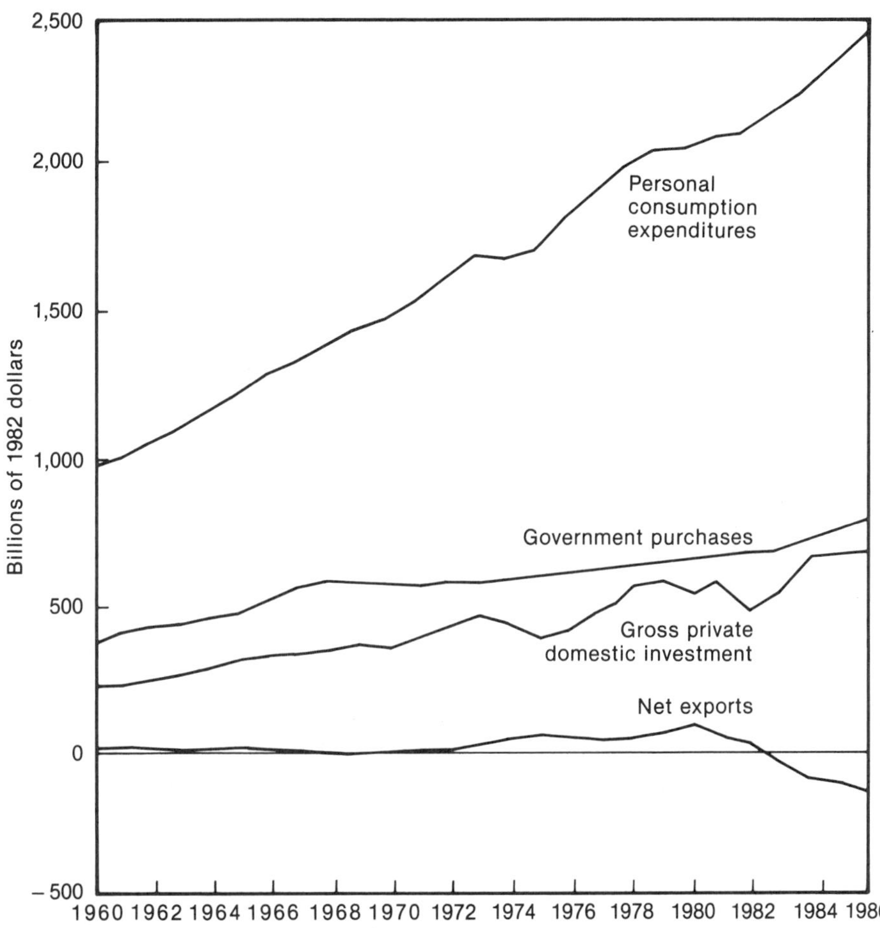

Source: U.S. Department of Commerce.

nomic expansion can be based on increases in personal consumption and how changes in tax laws may affect consumer levels.

Strong growth of real consumption spending was the main driving force for GNP growth in the 1982–86 period. Real personal consumption expenditures as a percentage of GNP reached their highest level since 1962, and 1949 before that. The longest economic expansion in modern U.S. history began in 1982 and continued at a moderate pace into 1987.

Figure 7–3 shows that the ratio of consumer installment debt to *disposable personal income* increased sharply from 1983 to 1987. Consumers used borrowing to support the record level of purchases. At the same time that consumer demand was rising, interest rate levels were declining, providing even further incentive to support spending by borrowing. In general, investors need to be aware that consumer demand tends to be very volatile and that changes in consumer demand appear to be a cause of major shifts in the balance of trade, consumer borrowing, and inflation.

Figure 7–3
Ratio of Consumer Installment Credit to Disposable Income

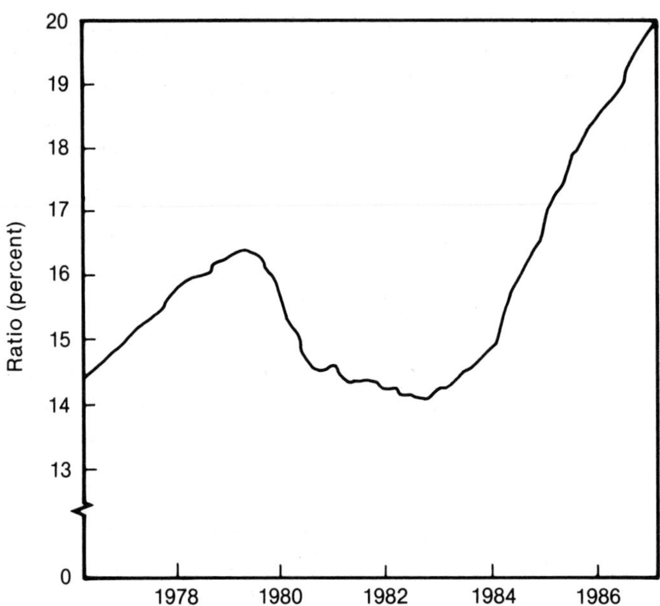

Sources: U.S. Department of Commerce and Council of Economic Advisers.

Fixed Investment

The federal government is concerned with the level of spending for plants and equipment because this is a powerful economic stimulant. Huge sums of money must be spent to replace and modernize obsolete equipment. As the economy benefits from ever higher levels of technology, our stock of capital goods becomes both larger and shorter lived. The following quotation, issued by the Reagan administration, captures the essence of the government's market-based approach to investment activities:

> These [economic] projections [for 1988–92] reflect the Administration's policies to promote long-term, noninflationary growth by encouraging investment in physical and human capital and improvements in productive technology. The Administration believes that creating an economic environment that provides strong incentives for work and production is the best policy for promoting investment and productivity growth. Reducing disparities in the rate of taxation on different economic activities contributes to this result by encouraging resources to be allocated to activities where they can be used most productively.[2]

Direct government support for capital investments was eliminated by the 1986 Tax Reform Act (TRA), which discontinued provisions for investment tax credits on new *capital expenditures* by businesses and individuals.

2. *1987 Economic Report of the President,* p. 61.

Inventories

Businesspeople plan their inventories in light of anticipated sales. If these sales do not materialize, inventories must be reduced to a level consistent with the actual volume of sales. Inventories for the total economy are large. Consequently, small changes in the rate of inventory accumulations may cause important adjustments in the economy. At year-end 1986, manufacturing and trade inventories valued at book value were estimated at $502 billion. If, instead of adding to inventories at a 3 percent annual rate, businesspeople decided not to increase their inventories, the result would be a reduction in spending for inventories by $15 billion. This reduction would have a sizable impact on the overall level of GNP for the period.

Investors can monitor statistics that indicate whether or not inventory levels are satisfactory. Figure 7–4 shows changes in business inventories during the 1983–86 period as indicated by quarterly changes in inflation-adjusted business inventories. The reduction in inventories during the final quarter in 1986 reflected consumer responses to the enactment of the 1986 Tax Reform Act. After 1986, sales taxes on consumer purchases were not tax deductible, so many consumers moved their planned purchases ahead to 1986. Inventory levels again accumulated in the first part of 1987 as corporations rebuilt their inventories and as consumer and government demand lagged behind the earlier levels.

Figure 7–5 shows the relationship between inventory levels and industrial production in a more direct fashion, that is, through the inflation-adjusted manufacturing and trade *inventory-to-sales ratio* for the 1980–86 period. The ratio rose in 1980 as the economy stagnated. The imbalance between inventory and sales brought about efforts by businesses to reduce their inventories. This reduction took place in the last half of

Figure 7–4
Quarterly Change in Non-Farm Business Inventories

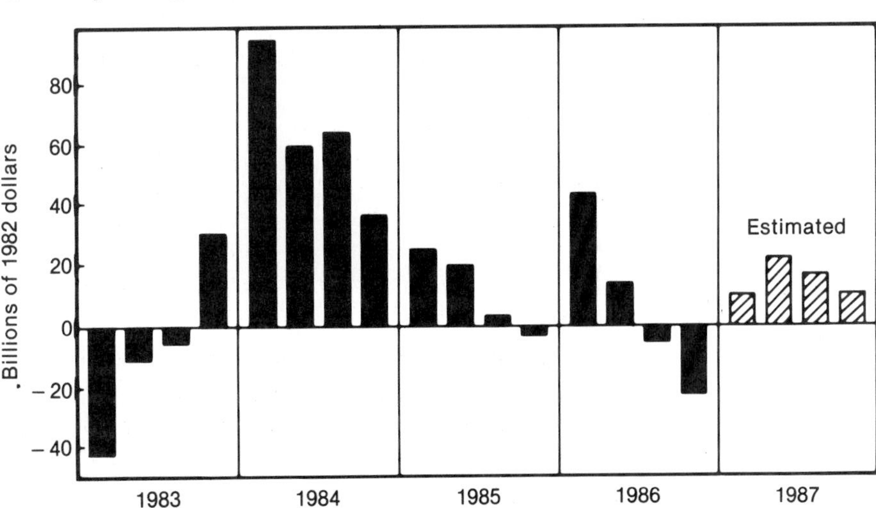

Source: U.S. Department of Commerce

Figure 7–5
Real Inventory/Sales Ratio and Industrial Production

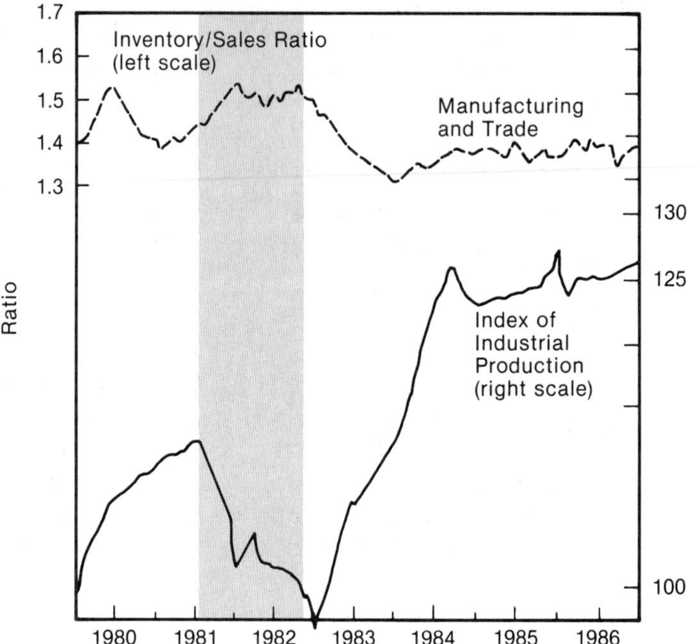

Sources: U.S. Department of Commerce and Board of Governors of the Federal Reserve System.

1980 and the first half of 1981. However, the anemic economic recovery in 1981 resulted in a rapidly increasing inventory/sales ratio and another bout of inventory liquidation in 1982. Following the 1982 liquidation, the inventory/sales ratio settled into a narrow range as economic growth continued at a steady rate into 1987. The industrial production ratio reflects the economic expansion in the 1982–86 period as it increased steadily throughout 1983 and leveled out in the 1984–86 period.

Figure 7–5 shows that the Index of Industrial Production appears to move inversely with the inventory/sales ratio. In other words, changes in inventory levels have a great deal to do with changes in industrial production. If inventories get relatively high compared to sales, a fairly pronounced decline in industrial production can be anticipated. One can readily see why investors monitor closely the rate of change in inventory investment.

Government Purchases of Goods and Services

Figure 7–6 shows the growth of inflation-adjusted government purchases of goods and services for the 1960–86 period. These purchases, which included federal, state, and local expenditures, grew at an annual compound growth rate of 2.5 percent. The growth pattern for recent years is quite different from that of the entire 1960–86 period. From 1982 to 1986, real federal purchases grew at a rate of 6.2 percent, compared to just 2.1 percent for state and local purchases.

The tabulation below shows real growth rates for both federal defense and non-defense purchases for the 1972–77, 1977–82, and 1982–86 periods.

Real Growth Rates for Federal Purchases of Goods and Services

	Defense	Non-defense
1972–77	−2.2%	4.2%
1977–82	3.7	1.3
1982–86	4.3	1.5

Opportunities are often presented to those investors able to anticipate shifts in government spending patterns. Investors who had anticipated a shift toward defense spending could have made money buying defense-related stocks during the Reagan administration.

An important consideration in projecting government expenditures is the impact of such initiatives as the Gramm-Rudman-Hollings (GRH)

Figure 7–6
Government Purchases of Goods and Services, 1960–86

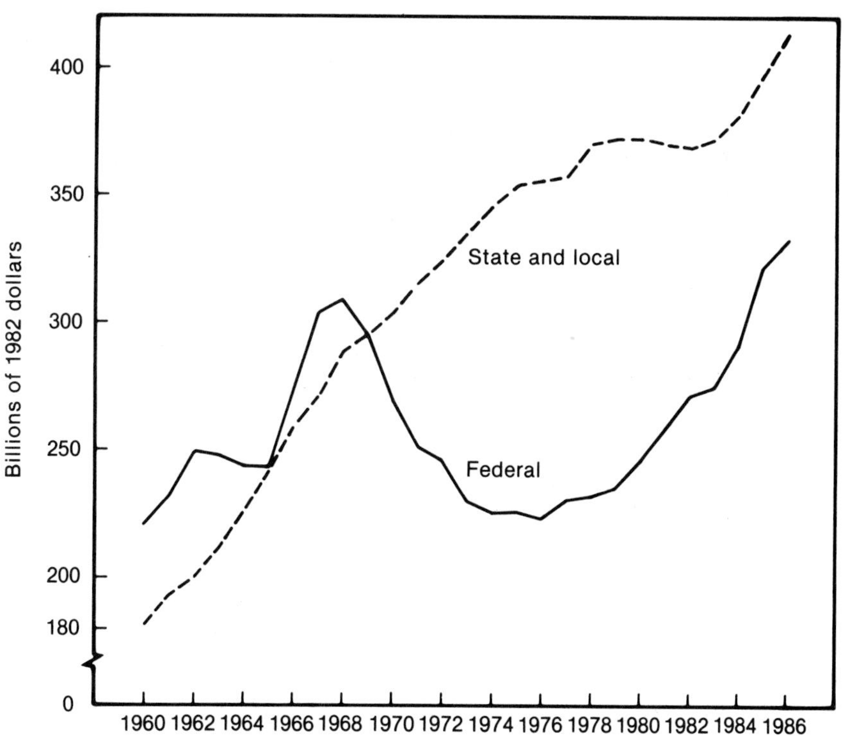

Source: U.S. Department of Commerce.

Act, which required Congress to achieve annual targets for deficit reduction and a balanced budget by 1991. The 1987 budget deficit is projected at a $50 billion lower rate than the 1986 deficit. Future deficit reductions are projected to be derived from reductions in federal spending rather than tax increases, although skeptics are plentiful on this issue.

Net Exports of Goods and Services

Net exports accounted for −4.6 percent of real GNP in 1986. The trend in the net export position is dramatic for the 1982 through 1986 period. Beginning with a slight surplus of exports over imports in 1982, the U.S. economy moved rapidly into a net importer position, with the net import amount approximately doubling every year. U.S. companies that were heavily dependent on industrial or agricultural exports for much of their business suffered during the 1982–85 period as the dollar appreciated against other currencies. U.S. goods were at a relative price disadvantage in the international markets. In 1986 and 1987, the value of the dollar declined against major world currencies, which made U.S. goods more price competitive.

Influences on GNP

Gross National Product is influenced in three basic ways. Two of these, fiscal and monetary policy, involve government action or intervention in various forms. The third influence on GNP is demographic in nature, including such factors as changes in population, labor force, and productivity. Consequently, this influence tends to be longer term. All three factors are important for investors to consider.

Fiscal Policy

Fiscal policy is the way the government handles its finances. The revenue side of fiscal policy has mainly to do with taxation by the federal government. The expenditure aspects of fiscal policy involve actions taken by the federal government to increase or reduce the amount of money it spends. Both of these aspects are important, but it is not always possible to separate them. In this section, we discuss examples of fiscal policy that are important to the investor, although a comprehensive analysis of the implications of federal, state, and local budgets is beyond the scope of this book.

In 1929, federal, state, and local purchases of goods and services amounted to $8.8 billion, or 8.5 percent of GNP. By 1986, these purchases amounted to $874 billion, or 21.1 percent of GNP. With all governmental

Figure 7–7
Federal Surpluses and Deficits, 1960–88

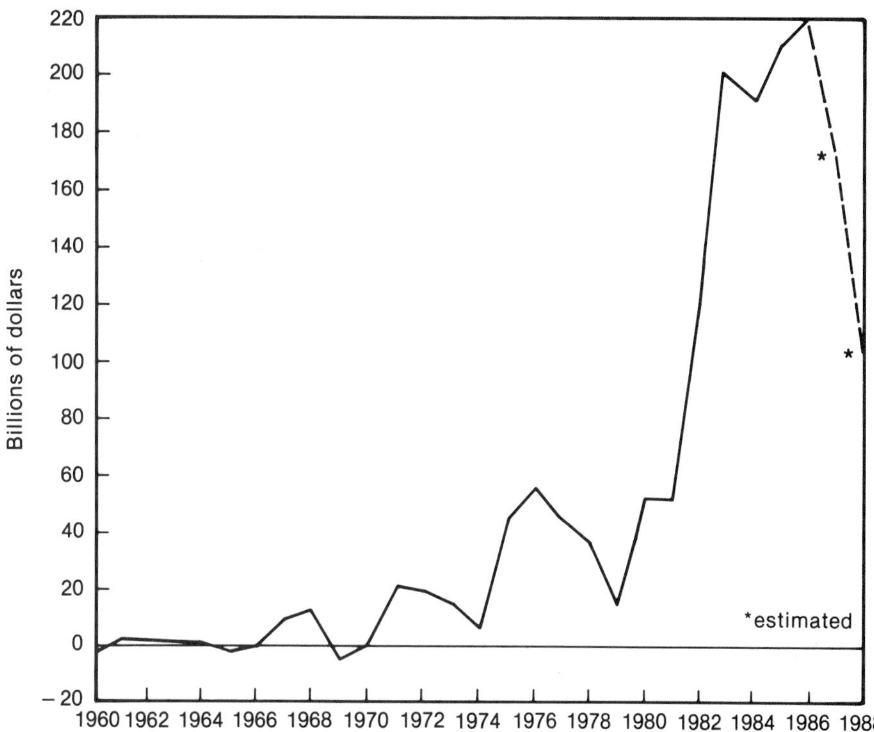

Source: 1987 Economic Report of the President, p. 331.

spending commanding over 21 percent of GNP, changes in government spending have profound economic consequences.

Figure 7–7 shows the federal surpluses or deficits as reported in the national income and product accounts for fiscal years from 1960 through 1988. The values of fiscal years 1987 and 1988 are estimates that are subject to revision. In 1986, the annual *federal deficit* amounted to 5.3 percent of GNP.

Concern over the size of the federal deficit prompted Congress to pass the Gramm-Rudman-Hollings Act in 1985. The potential impact of the act on economic activity was described by President Reagan as follows:

> Meeting the GRH deficit targets for 1988 and later fiscal years will not be an easy task, even with the continuation of reasonably strong economic growth and with further moderation of inflation and interest rates. . . . The projected reductions . . . imply that to reach a balanced Federal budget, the combined share of all other categories of Federal expenditures must decline from 15.7 percent of GNP in 1986 to roughly 12.5 percent in 1991.[3]

3. Ibid., p. 71.

Investors should develop an assessment of the consequences of balanced federal budgets. If federal programs are drastically cut back, state and local governmental expenditures could be expected to rise as these governmental units acquire the responsibility for funding some programs previously included in the federal budget. A drastic cutback in federal spending would have major consequences for those industries dependent on federal funds, for example, health care and education.

At issue in the controversy surrounding the size of the federal deficit is the effect that financing the growing debt has on economic activity. The federal government obtains funds to finance the shortfall between expenditures and tax receipts by borrowing in the financial markets. By doing so, the federal government must compete with other borrowers for available funds. The demand for funds pushes up interest rates, which serves to crowd out private sector borrowers from the financial markets. The *crowding out* results in a lower level of domestic capital formation and economic growth in the private sector.

Let us now examine some federal tax policies to illustrate the importance of fiscal policy for investors. The 1986 Tax Reform Act was a major reform in tax legislation and contained many provisions. For individual taxpayers, the major provisions of the law were to lower the maximum effective tax rate on income, to reduce the number of tax brackets, and to eliminate the differential tax rates between income and capital gains. Some tax loopholes were closed, and a selected group of deductions were eliminated. Interest expenses, except on owner-occupied residential mortgages, were eliminated as tax deductions, drastically affecting nonresidential real estate investment activities.

Another section of the tax act of 1986 changes the depreciation guidelines for individuals and corporations. As mentioned earlier, investment tax credits were eliminated for new investment expenditures. Also, depreciation methods underwent major revisions as asset lives were redefined and acceleration techniques revamped.

Monetary Policy

Monetary policy deals with the management of the nation's *money supply* by the Federal Reserve System. The relationship between changes in the money supply and stock prices has been the subject of considerable research and debate in recent years. Can future stock prices be determined by examining current money statistics? How do investors define money supply? This section examines the importance of changes in the money supply. Although much research has been conducted on the relationship between money supply and stock prices, the nature and specification of any relationship is still not completely settled.

Several investigators have found what they believe to be a long-term relationship between changes in the money supply and changes in stock prices. The most generally accepted definition of the money supply, known as M2, is the sum of time and demand deposits at commercial banks, and currency held by the public. Often, the money supply series is seasonally adjusted. Investigators feel that the change in money supply is an important factor explaining changes in the general level of prices and corporate income. The changes in corporate income in turn have a major influence on the level of stock prices.

Beryl Sprinkel examined the relationship between changes in the rate of growth of the money supply and stock prices.[4] In *Money and Markets,* he argued that stock prices lead business cycle peaks by an average of five to six months. In addition, growth in the money supply leads business cycle peaks by fifteen to sixteen months, on the average. After conducting a similar study of cyclical downturns, Sprinkel concluded that "changes in monetary growth lead changes in stock prices by an average of about nine months prior to a bear market and by about two or three months prior to bull markets."[5]

Sprinkel also looked at how well investors would have done over the long run if they had based their investment decisions on an examination of changing money supply growth. From 1918 to 1970, he maintained, investors "would have participated in all bull markets" but "would have avoided most bear markets."[6] In recent years, however, it would have been critical for the investor to recognize a reduction of the lead time of monetary changes compared to stock prices for bear market periods. We should note that another study questions the relationship between money and stock prices. The conclusion of this study is that the relationship is weak, and if one exists, it is more likely that the stock market leads the money supply![7] The money supply is important, but the specific relationship beween money supply and stock prices remains open to question.

For many years, M1 was the focus of monetary policy controls as the Federal Reserve attempted to target the level of the money supply. M1 is defined as the nation's currency, travelers' checks, demand deposits, and other checkable deposits. With deregulation of the banking system, a structural change occurred in the way individuals kept their money balances; they shifted their funds from noninterest to interest-bearing checking accounts. M1 does not include these deposits, whereas M2, a more reliable measure of money supply, includes interest-bearing accounts and time deposits. In 1987, Paul Volcker, then Chairman of the Federal Reserve Board, announced that the "Fed" was no longer targeting money supply growth on the basis of M1 because M1 had become an unreliable measure.

Numerous factors besides the rate of change in the money supply need to be considered by investors. For instance, tax changes may not be correctly accounted for by using money supply data. Money matters, but it may not be the only thing that matters.

---

4. Beryl Sprinkel, *Money and Stock Prices* (Homewood, Illinois: Richard D. Irwin, 1964); Sprinkel, *Money and Markets* (Irwin, 1971); and Sprinkel and Robert J. Genetski, *Winning With Money: A Guide for Your Future* (Dow Jones-Irwin, 1977).
5. Sprinkel, *Money and Markets,* p. 221.
6. Ibid., p. 25.
7. Michael S. Rozeff, "Money and Stock Prices: Market Efficiency and the Lag in Effect of Monetary Policy," *Journal of Financial Economics* (September 1974): 245–302.

Population and Productivity

Two of the principal determinants of long-run economic growth from the supply side are *population growth* and increases in *productivity*. On the demand side, changes in the population also have a major impact on the composition and amount of goods demanded. What is the best projection of population growth in the United States and the world? Will certain industries benefit from a slower rate of population growth while others are hurt? These questions indicate the vital significance population data can have for investors.

Investors should be aware of important developments in the areas of population growth and distribution. Figure 7–8 shows selected population statistics. The graph on the left shows the fertility rate since 1940; and columns on the right illustrate the age distribution of the U.S. population as of 1986 and a projection for the year 2030.

The fertility rate in the United States has declined over the last half of the century and has stabilized at a low 1.8 figure. This rate is the number of children the average woman will have during her child-bearing years. A fertility rate of 2.1 children per female is considered the replacement level that will result in zero population growth once a stable population distribution is achieved. If the fertility rate continued at the rate of recent years, zero population growth would occur in the United States about the year 2030. After that, the population would start to decline.

The population will continue to grow in the near future even though the fertility rate is below the replacement level because a relatively large number of women are in their child-bearing years. The "baby boomers"

Figure 7–8
Selected Population Statistics

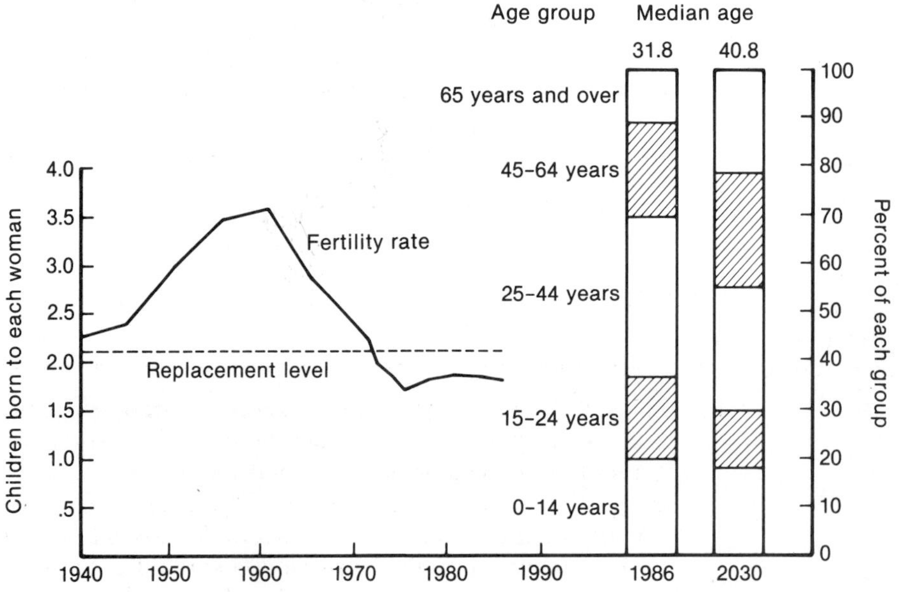

Source: U.S. Census Bureau.

are having babies, although they are waiting longer to have them and are having fewer than their parents had.

The U.S. population is expected to become progressively middle-aged with a median age of 40.8 by the year 2030. Corporations will need to adapt to this changing age distribution. For example, in the 1980s, many television advertisements switched to themes aimed at drawing the attention of the middle-aged viewers. Anti-wrinkle cream appears to be a growth product line.

In the 1990s, as the "baby boomers" grow older, the relative number of people in the 25–44 and 45–64 age groups will increase substantially. These are two important age groups for many reasons. First, a larger percentage of the population will be in the labor force. This is especially true when consideration is given to the increasing participation of women in the labor market. The economy will have to grow at a reasonable rate in future years just to provide employment for new entrants into the labor force. Second, the increase in the 25–44 year age bracket falls in the family formation years. During these years, families spend heavily for housing, consumer durables such as furniture and automobiles, and for many expensive luxury items such as vacations and recreational equipment. The 45–64 year age group is also important because they will have the money to save so that the economy's capital expenditures can be financed.

Along with a decrease in the birthrate, the average number of persons per household has tended to decrease steadily over the years. For example, the average family size declined from 3.33 persons in 1960 to 2.69 persons in 1985. The declining family size, coupled with a well-educated population, means that the per capita income for the family unit should increase markedly. In addition, evidence indicates that persons living alone are becoming a significant market for some goods and services such as owner-occupied housing. These developments should provide the impetus for continued and relatively sustained growth in economic activity in the years ahead. In short, a much higher standard of living per person should result. A lower birthrate may be detrimental to specific industries, but the economy should prosper.

The 1987 Economic Report of the President provided an estimate of economic growth in real GNP of 3.5 percent between 1987 and 1992. The estimate indicated that real economic growth would be produced by increases of 1.5 percent in productivity and 2 percent in the labor supply.

Impact of the Economy on Investment Decisions: *Using Business Cycle Indicators*

Although it is interesting to follow the components of GNP and to think about the impact of fiscal and monetary policy, investors need to use economic data to forecast such crucial variables as interest rates and stock prices. This section examines one such source of economic data as provided by *business cycle indicators* and discusses their predictive ability.

For many years, the National Bureau of Economic Research (NBER) has conducted studies investigating the behavior of various economic indicators and the business cycle. On the basis of these studies, the NBER has classified specific statistical series as being either *leading, lagging,* or roughly *coincident indicators.* Each of these series is charted, and the results are published monthly by the U.S. Department of Commerce in *Business Conditions Digest.*

In addition to calculating individual indicators, the NBER has developed three composite measures of economic activity, one for each of the leading, lagging, and coincident groups of indicators. Figure 7–9 shows

Figure 7–9
Composite Indicators

CYCLICAL INDICATORS

COMPOSITE INDEXES AND THEIR COMPONENTS

Chart A1. Composite Indexes

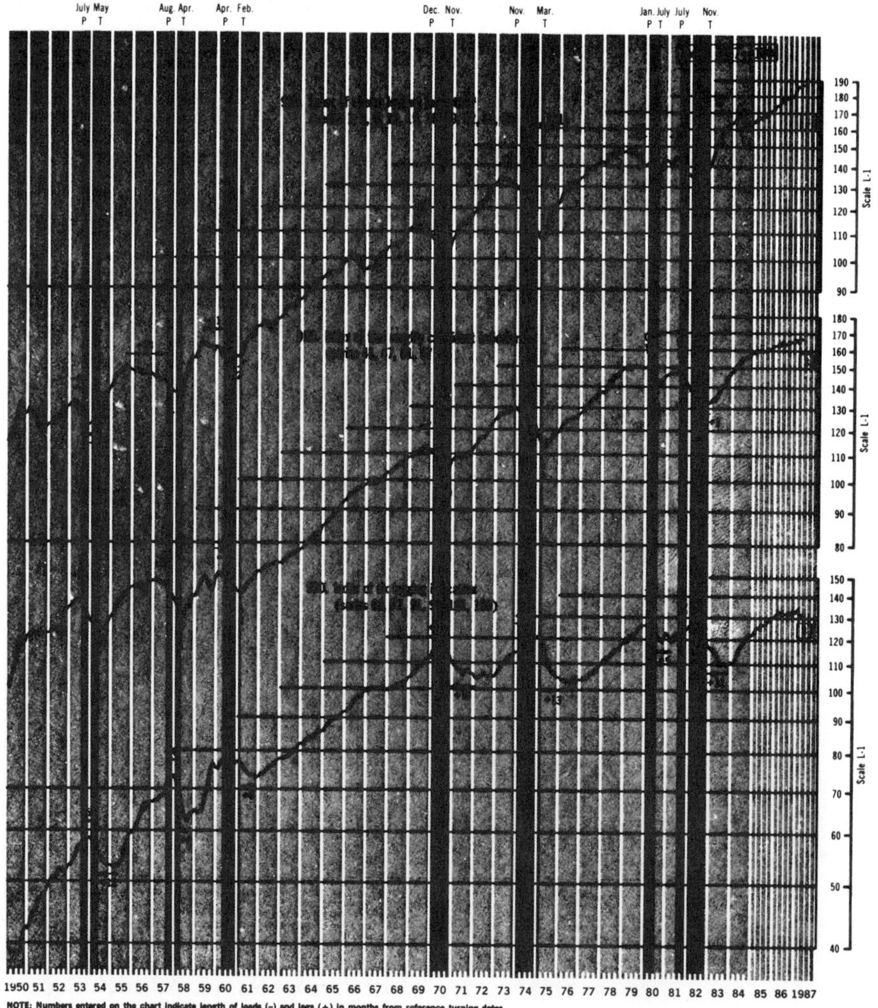

NOTE: Numbers entered on the chart indicate length of leads (–) and lags (+) in months from reference turning dates.
[1] Beginning with data for January 1984, series 12 has been suspended from this index.
Current data for these series are shown on page 60.

10 APRIL 1987 BCD

Source: Business Conditions Digest

Table 7–2
Short List of Eleven Leading Economic Indicators

I. Capital investment commitments	Contracts and orders, plant & equipment
	Housing permits
II. Inventory investment and purchasing	New orders, consumer goods & materials
	Change in inventory, on hand & ordered
	Vendor performance, reported slower deliveries
	Changes in sensitive material prices
III. Sensitive financial flows	Money balance (M2)
	Change in credit outstanding
IV. Profitability	Common stock prices
V. Marginal employment adjustments	Average workweek, manufacturing
	Initial unemployment claims (inverted)

the three composite indicators and their movements since 1950. The composite indicators show the average movement in the components underlying the series. In other words, all leading indicators do not move together at the same time.

The leading indicator series is undoubtedly the most useful of the statistical series for investors. Table 7–2 shows what is known as the "short list" of leading indicators, as revised in March 1987. Unfortunately, the index of the eleven (previously, twelve) leading indicators, as shown in Figure 7–9, does not always act in a similar fashion over each business cycle. Historically, the index gives from three to twenty-three months warning of a coming recession, with a mean lead time of ten months. A problem appears when trying to decide when a true downturn in the index of leading indicators occurs as opposed to a false signal or a temporary downturn. In 1966, for example, the index of leading indicators declined most of the year, as shown on Figure 7–9, but the economy went through a period of sluggish growth rather than an officially designated recession. Notice that the index of four roughly coincident indicators for 1966 and 1967 showed no decline comparable to the decline of the leading indicator index in 1966. Also, the index of leading indicators dipped slightly in the first part of 1984, but no economic downturn followed.

Although the index of leading indicators appears to have a reasonable lead time with regard to downturns, its lead time for forecasting the upturns shown in Figure 7–9 is much shorter. The range of lead times for the upside ranged from one to six months with a mean upside lead time of three months. This short lead time plus the usual interpretation problems may cause difficulties for investors. For example, in mid-1974, an investor might have come to the conclusion that the recession was almost over because the extent of the decline in the index of leading indicators was already about the same as for the previous recessions. However, the recession was only half over. Indeed, from July 1, 1974, to December 31, 1974, the S&P 500 index went from 97.37 to 76.47—a decline of 21.5 percent. The market then went up rapidly, and the S&P 500 hit 93.54 on March 31, 1975. This value on March 31 represented 70 percent of the index's total gain for the year. Would an investor following the index of leading indicators have been able to benefit from most of this three-month gain? Clearly, investors need to rely on other information in addition to the index of leading indicators.

Summary

From a review of past economic trends in the U.S. economy, investors can reasonably expect long-term future growth, probably in the 2 to 3 percent range. This general conclusion is supported by examining population and age distribution statistics. The high percentage of the population in the more productive years means a larger labor force and a greater tendency toward consumption, as young families fulfill needs for such fundamental items as housing, transportation, and clothing. The actions of the government, especially in the areas of fiscal and monetary policy, are important in formulating more accurate predictions of economic activity. Of particular importance is resolution of the federal deficit problem, either through changing taxation or fiscal policies.

Despite the likelihood for good economic growth and a favorable investment environment, caution needs to be exercised. Circumstances exist which have the potential to alter this growth picture. International trade imbalances could bring about a series of political and economic changes that would affect the level and composition of domestic activities.

Suggested Readings

Bernstein, Peter L., and Theodore H. Silbert. "Are Economic Forecasters Worth Listing To?" *Harvard Business Review* (September–October 1984): 32–40.

Cornell, Bradford. "Money Supply Announcements and Interest Rates: Another View." *Journal of Business* (January 1983): 12–24.

Gramley, Lyle E. "The Effects of Exchange Rate Changes on the United States Economy." *Business Economics* (July 1985): 40–44.

Kling, John L. "Predicting the Turning Points of Business and Economic Time Series." *Journal of Business* (April 1987): 201–38.

Lynge, Morgan J., Jr. "Money Supply Announcements and Stock Prices." *Journal of Portfolio Management* (Fall 1981): 40–43.

Meadows, Donella H. et al. *The Limits to Growth.* New York: Universe Books, 1972. This is often referred to as the Club of Rome Study.

Mennis, Edmund A. "The Practical Uses of Economic Analysis in Investment Management." In *The Economic Framework for Investors.* Charlottesville, VA: The Financial Analysts Research Foundation, 1975, 43–56.

MESAROVIC, MIHAJLO, and EDMUND PESTEL. *Mankind at the Turning Point.* New York: Dutton/Readers' Digest, 1974. This is the second Club of Rome Study.

PEARCE, DOUGLAS K., and V. VANCE ROLEY. "Stock Prices and Economic News." *Journal of Business* (January 1985): 49–67.

ROZEFF, MICHAEL S. "Money and Stock Prices: Market Efficiency and the Lag in Effect on Monetary Policy." *Journal of Financial Economics* (September 1974): 245–302.

SPRINKEL, BERYL W., and ROBERT J. GENETSKI. *Winning With Money: A Guide to Your Future.* Homewood, IL: Dow Jones-Irwin, 1977.

Questions

1. What are the major activities with which investors are concerned from the standpoint of economic analysis?

2. Is it reasonable to expect a relationship to exist between stock price movements and economic activities? Why or why not?

3. Suppose someone states that stock prices typically turn before the economy does. Can you explain this phenomenon?

4. A principal concern for investors has been the deficit in the federal budget. Why is the deficit so important to investors? Suppose federal expenditures are reduced by $10 billion to bring down the deficit. What would be the consequences of such an act to the investors?

5. With a declining birth rate in recent years, the expectation is that the U.S. population will become increasingly middle-aged. Of what significance is this to the investor?

6. An extremely important consideration in recent years for the investor forecasting the future of the economy is attempting to determine what will happen to interest rates both in the short run and in the long run. Why is this forecast of interest rates of concern to the investor in stocks and in fixed-income securities?

7. Some analysts argue that inventory considerations were a fundamental cause of the relatively severe 1981–82 recession. What is it about inventories that lead to certain economists to relate inventory adjustment to recessions?

8. Concern has been expressed that the major industrialized countries in the world have business cycles that are increasingly uniform. The result could be a synchronized slump leading to a worldwide depression. Do you think this will happen? Why or why not?

9. Give examples of leading, lagging, and coincident indicators. Why do you think these are classified as such? Discuss.

10. Do you think investors should be very interested in the personal consumption component of GNP? Why or why not?

11. Figure 7–3 relates consumer installment debt to disposable personal income. What concerns might you have as an investor about this figure as of the end of 1986? What information is missing from this graph that might alter your concerns?

Problems

1. Assume that between 1980 and 1984, the money GNP increased from $2,632 trillion to $3,661 trillion and that the appropriate index of prices increased from 178 to 223. What is the GNP for 1984 in terms of the base year prices? (Excerpted with permission from the 1987 Level I examination, The Institute of Chartered Financial Analysts.)

2. For the 1972–86 period, look at the annual percentage changes in the key economic indicators in Table P7-1. All indicators are stated on a current dollar basis. Compare these indexes in the following context.

   (a) Do the indexes move together?

   (b) To what extent are the indexes similar regarding volatility?

   (c) How similar are the average percentage growth rates implied by the indexes?

   (d) To what extent do the economic indexes move with the stock index?

   (e) How do the average growth rates for the economic indexes compare with the growth rates in the stock indexes?

Table P7–1

Year	Nominal GNP ($ billions)	CPI (%)	Disposable Income ($ billions)	Corporate Profits ($ billions)	Treasury Bill Rates (%)	S&P 500 ($)
1972	1,158	3.4	802	92	3.8	118
1973	1,295	8.8	904	105	6.9	98
1974	1,397	12.2	980	106	8.0	69
1975	1,529	7.0	1,084	99	5.8	90
1976	1,706	4.8	1,186	128	5.1	107
1977	1,890	6.8	1,309	139	5.1	95
1978	2,156	9.0	1,463	199	7.2	96
1979	2,414	13.3	1,642	197	10.4	108
1980	2,629	12.4	1,822	182	11.2	136
1981	2,958	8.9	2,042	190	14.7	122
1982	3,069	3.9	2,181	159	10.5	141
1983	3,305	3.8	2,340	225	8.8	165
1984	3,765	4.0	2,671	265	9.9	167
1985	3,998	3.8	2,828	281	7.7	211
1986	4,206	1.1	2,972	300	6.2	242

Source: Federal Reserve Bulletin, various issues.

3. For the data in Problem 2, adjust the nominal GNP and disposable personal income factors to remove the effects of inflation. What were the changes in real GNP and real personal income over the period?

4. A starting point in the analysis of securities is to forecast the general level of stock market prices.
   (a) Forecast the S&P 500 index value for one year and three years into the future. Be sure to include in your analysis a discussion of the inflation rate, real economic growth rate, and the relationship between economic growth and dividend growth.
   (b) Compare your forecast with the current level of the S&P 500. To what do you attribute the differences between your forecast and the actual level of the index?
   (c) What is the implied growth rate for the S&P 500 at the current time?

5. Figure 7–1 shows that the Index of Industrial Production and real GNP have the same general growth trends historically. In the 1980–86 period, both indexes of economic growth showed declines from historical growth trends. Update the graph since 1986, and interpret the nature of the relationship between the two measures. Has real economic growth continued to lag behind historical levels?

6. Figure 7–2 reports the trends in the real GNP components for the period 1960–86. In 1986 several trends were apparently emerging as personal consumption expenditures reached all-time high levels and net exports reached record low levels. Update the graph with data since 1986. Have personal consumption expenditures continued in the 60 to 66 percent range? Have imports continued to increase relative to exports? Has the ratio of consumer installment credit relative to disposable income continued above the 20 percent level? Interpret how these changes affect economic growth.

7. Collect current data on quarterly changes in nonfarm business inventories. How has the inventory/sales ratio moved relative to the Index of Industrial Production since 1986? Interpret what you think the current levels of these measures indicate about industrial production in the near future.

8. Collect current data on the short-list of leading economic indicators. At what stage of the economic cycle do you think we are currently situated? Which leading indicators support your position? Which leading indicators do not support your position?

Chapter 8

Industry Analysis

Key Concepts

decline phase
growth phase
income elasticity
index of consumer sentiment
industry capacity
industry growth trend
infancy
international factor
life cycle analysis
maturity
P/E ratio
political factor
restructuring
social factor
use per capita

Chapter Outline

The analysis of an industry is a logical follow-up to the analysis of the economy. In performing the industry analysis, investors attempt to trace economic developments within specific industries. For example, what affect would a long-term increase in energy prices have on the transportation industry? Would the competitive positions of railroads, airlines, and automobiles change as a result of this long-term development?

This chapter discusses an approach investors may take in analyzing the growth prospects of an industry. Because growth potential varies considerably from one industry to the next, a separate analysis should be conducted of each industry for which an investment is under consideration. New industries are born, and old industries stagnate. In addition to the growth patterns, investors need to identify factors that are relevant in assessing the future growth, return, and risk of a specific industry. For example, is the industry especially sensitive to interest rate risk? To political risk? To foreign competition?

The analysis of industries is not without its problems, however. Being able to define just what constitutes an industry can be difficult. For example, one must decide whether an industry is defined by its products, factor inputs, labor, capital base, technology, or some other features. Even if investors are able to define industries in a meaningful way, very few major U.S. companies operate in just one industry. Most companies are diversified and operate in several different industries at the same time. Therefore, analysis of a specific industry may be only partially useful as an input to the analysis of a diversified company. The growth of conglomerates is a development that makes industry analysis more complex. As a matter of fact, many firms are currently classified in the conglomerate "industry," which is not really an industry but a group of firms having no dominant characteristics in common other than a widely diversified product line.

We begin the chapter by discussing the role of *life cycle analysis* in evaluating industries. Building on the life cycle discussion, we review eight basic considerations that should be taken into account when conducting an analysis of an industry. Finally, a study of the general retail merchandising industry is presented in the last part of the chapter.

Life Cycle Analysis

Just as individuals are born, grow to become adults, and die, so do industries. A convenient framework to use in beginning the analysis of an industry is the life cycle curve, as shown in Figure 8–1.

Stages of the Cycle

The stages of the life cycle curve are commonly known as *infancy, growth, maturity,* and *decline.* Each of these stages can be described by a certain set of conditions.

Figure 8–1
Life Cycle Curve

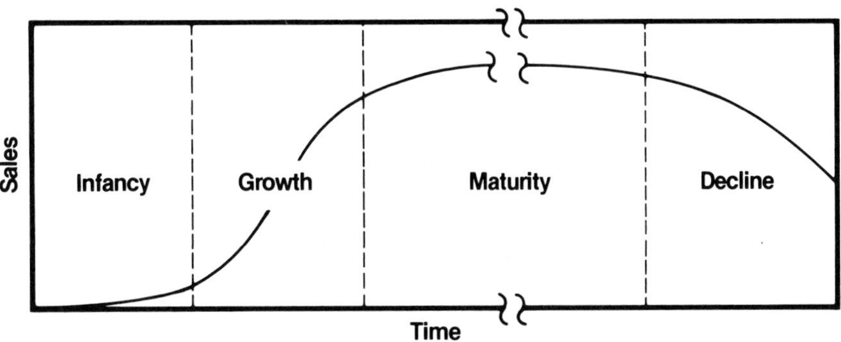

Infancy

The first stage refers to the birth of a new industry or a new product. At this stage, the products have no competition of any importance. The public must be educated to the use of the products manufactured by this industry. Normally, a limited number of product models are available, and prices tend to be quite high, although promotional discounts may be used. The birth of the computer industry and the introduction of photocopy machines are good illustrations. Investors generally incur extremely high risk by making investments in infant industries or in relatively small companies with a major product in its infancy.

Growth

The second stage is recognized by the rapid increase in the sales of the industry or product. Aggressive competitors begin to enter the scene, and a heavy emphasis may be placed on advertising. More models of the product will be available. Prices will be adjusted to create a mass market. The rapid growth of the personal computer industry during the early 1980s is a classic example. From the investor's viewpoint, a substantial reshuffling of industry participants occurs during this period. Investors need to identify those companies with managerial and financial resources to survive this very competitive period.

Maturity

In the third stage, competition is likely to be relatively stable, and market shares are unlikely to change much over time from company to company. Advertising is used extensively, as are dealer promotions. Considerable attention is given to cost cutting within the industry. Sales tend to grow slowly compared to the growth of GNP. The automobile and steel industries are probably reasonable examples of mature industries, but timing is an important factor because these industries tend to be cyclical.

Decline

In the final stage sales grow at a rate substantially less than GNP or experience an absolute decline. Normally, a decline occurs in the number of competitors in the industry. Firms make a definite attempt to eliminate unprofitable products. Prices are set to maintain profit margins, and less concern is given to market shares. To identify precisely which industries are in the decline stage is difficult, but those industries serving the agricultural sector would seem to qualify. Also, industries catering to the high school age and younger markets would seem to qualify in the near future, solely on the basis of the change in the age distribution of the population, discussed in the previous chapter.

Implications of Life Cycle Analysis

Each stage of the life cycle has definite risks for investors. By classifying companies according to their place on the life cycle curve, investors can estimate whether a particular security is reasonably priced. Investors can also get an indication of the risk involved in buying securities in a given industry.

Although investors probably should avoid investing in companies serving declining industries, stocks in well-managed companies bought at a reasonable price could prove to be good investments. Investors can get an extraordinary return by investing in a portfolio of declining industry stocks if the market discounts the industry at too severe a rate.

Figure 8–2 shows some of the difficulties involved in applying the life cycle concept, with Honeywell, Inc., as our example. The data for both the 1986–87 and the 1989–91 periods are *Value Line* estimates. Revenues per share declined in both 1971 and 1976, but recovered after three years. In 1976, investors might have suspected that Honeywell was in the maturity stage, but the firm had good growth in the 1976 through 1979 period. Figure 8–2 also shows Honeywell's earnings per share for the 1966–91 period. The earnings per share showed a slow growth between 1966 and 1973, a decline in 1974, and rapid growth between 1975 and 1979. After 1979, Honeywell's earnings showed little growth and remained flat into 1987. *Value Line* projected only moderate earnings growth throughout the 1989–91 period.

Figure 8–1 shows a rigid life cycle curve, however, the exact shape of the curve may vary and can be influenced by actions of a firm's management. Introducing new products or improving present products are methods used to make the growth phase last longer. Abandoning unprofitable products or merging to acquire either new managerial talent or new technology may also be useful in extending the growth phase.

Basic Industry Considerations

In addition to specifying where an industry is on the life cycle curve, investors need to take into account many other factors such as the social,

Figure 8–2
Honeywell, Inc., Data 1966–91

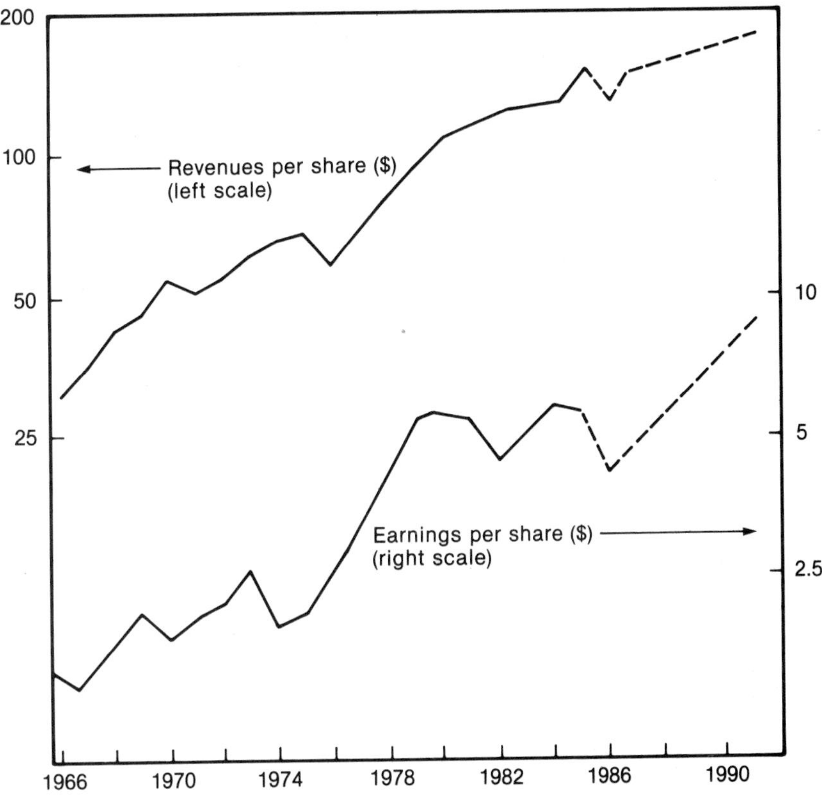

political, and economic environment. Some factors, such as past industry growth trends and the nature of the products, are closely related to the analysis of the life cycle even though they can be studied separately. We will study the economic factors first, then follow with a discussion of the social and political factors.

Industry Characteristics: Economic

In this section, we describe five important economic features that investors need to look at when evaluating an industry's investment potential.

Past Industry Growth Trends

Just as investors should examine the past growth trends of the economy, the past trends for an industry also should be reviewed. Any recent change in growth relative to past growth rates will help investors to determine where the industry might be located on the life cycle curve.

Figure 8–3 provides a view of the rapid growth in the number of cable television subscribers from 1965 to 1985. The industry's growth ap-

Figure 8–3
Cable TV Subscribers

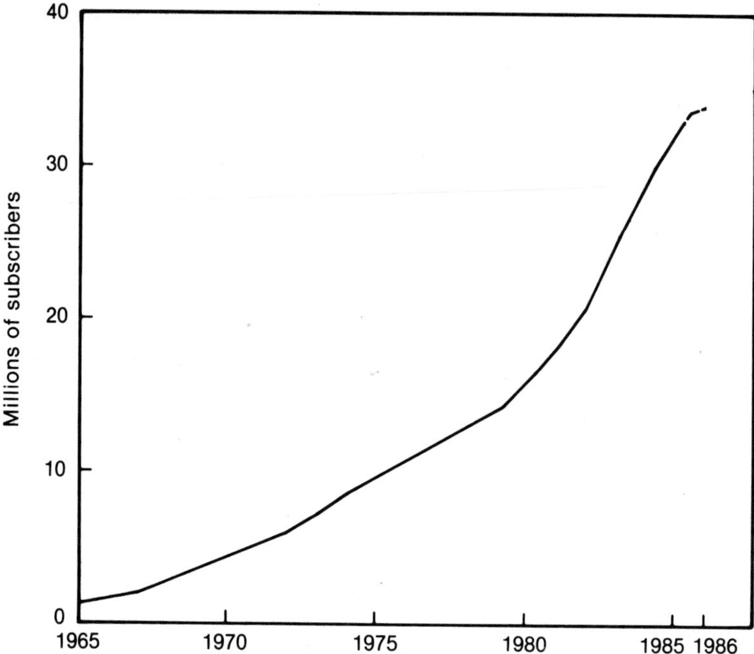

Source: U.S. Statistical Abstract, various issues.

peared to be unaffected by general economic conditions. By 1986, the rapid growth phase for the cable television industry was apparently at an end, as an obvious limit existed to the possible number of cable television subscribers. As the end of the growth period approached, many cable operators slowed their expansion of facilities and concentrated on adding new services to existing cable lines.

Supply and Demand

Investors need to determine the supply and demand situation within any given industry. Has the demand been increasing? Where is the basic source of the demand? Does the industry have enough capacity to accommodate future expected demand, or does excess demand exist? This question may be of critical importance. For example, demand in the electric utility industry has been fairly predictable over the years. In recent years, the rate of growth in demand has slowed and this reduction appears relatively permanent. Regulatory commissions may be reluctant to allow a fair rate of return on excess capacity because rates would need to be raised. Hence, the profits of an individual utility could suffer.

Nature of Products

One aspect of the demand for the products of an industry concerns the nature of those products. Products of companies in growth industries

Investment Highlight

Aldus (A "Hot" New Issue)

Aldus, the fifteenth century Venetian printer who invented italic type and founded the first modern publishing house, is also the name of a company selling shares in a new public offering.

Description

The first Italian edition of Virgil was published in 1501 in a style of type later to become known as italics. These days, people want to use their personal computers to publish. Enter Aldus Corporation and its PageMaker computer program listing for $695, and we have the ingredients for a much-desired initial public offering.

Established in 1984 and generally acknowledged as the industry leader and coiner of the phrase *desktop publishing,* Aldus produces computer software that allows individuals who are relatively unsophisticated about computers and page layout procedures to produce printed material such as newsletters, directories, and manuals, using either an Apple Macintosh computer or an IBM computer.

Aldus and its investment bankers originally anticipated that its 2.2-million-share initial public offering would sell for between $14 and $16 a share. However, the growth of Aldus was exceptional in its short history, with sales quadrupling in the first quarter of 1987 versus the same quarter a year before. The offering price was increased to $20 a share shortly prior to the sale, and the shares closed at $35.75 in over-the-counter trading at the end of the first trading day in what could be described as frenzied market activity.

For the year ended March 31, 1987, Aldus earned 31 cents a share. This means the company sold for over 64 times its earnings for the past year based on its initial offering price, and over 115 times its earnings on the basis of its price at the end of trading on the first day. The market obviously anticipates great growth in sales and earnings for this company.

Conclusion

Investors are fortunate when they are able to participate in a resoundingly successful initial public offering such as that of Aldus Corporation on June 16, 1987. However, one cannot help but wonder if this type of spectacular price performance is a signal that the end of the five-year-old bull market is near. After all, the DJIA had risen from about 800 to over 2,400 during that period. Time will tell.

often exhibit increasing *use per capita.* Until recent years, more and more high school students decided to go to college, making the business of providing college educations a growth industry. As the century comes to an end, personal computers will increasingly occupy a central place in the lives of the U.S. population, resulting in greater use per capita.

Besides increased use per capita, investors need to determine if a mass market truly exists for the products of any industry or industry segment. Xerox found a mass market for its dry process copier and became one of the great growth companies of the past two decades. Apple Computer found a mass market for its personal computers. Sony introduced the beta video recorder and created a whole new industry. If a mass market does not exist, the firm or industry may have difficulty in producing a quality product at a competitive price.

Investors should attempt to determine whether the products of any industry are capable of long-run technological improvement. If the continued technological upgrading of an industry is promising, the industry will be able to meet competitive challenges from other industries and from foreign competitors. The miniaturization of electronic components has allowed continued long-term growth for the computer industry. IBM is an example of a company for which technological upgrading has been favorable.

The life expectancy of a product may be of concern and is related to its per capita use. In the hospital supply field, disposable products have created a mass market, resulting in increased use per capita. More profitable investment opportunities may become evident in future years as machine-produced goods continue to be substituted for those made with expensive, on-site labor.

Relationship to Income Levels

A reasonably precise method of determining the nature of products is to relate changes in the use of the product to changes in the income level of the consuming group. Economists refer to this relationship as the *income elasticity* of the product. A product is income elastic when the volume of sales goes up and down at a faster rate than the up and down fluctuations in the consumer's income. A product that is income inelastic will experience changes in demand that are lower than the consumer's relative changes in income. Investors often refer to a product or industry that is inelastic as "recession proof." Can the demands of the consumer be postponed, or do they need to be fulfilled on a regular basis? Is the product a luxury or a necessity?

Items that take a relatively minor part of an individual's total income are considered to have an inelastic income demand function. In other words, changes in income levels leave demand for these products virtually unchanged. Items in this category include chewing gum, cigarettes, and newspapers. Other items accounting for a larger percentage of the consumer's budget may also be relatively recession proof. Items such as alcoholic beverages could fall into this category.

Figure 8–4 presents per capita cigarette consumption for the 1972–85 period as well as per capita disposable personal income. Cigarette consumption is apparently income inelastic in that increases in income levels do not result in more cigarette consumption. Other considerations, such as health concerns, are potential causal factors. This is true despite the fact that a regression between the two data series shown on Figure 8–4 results in the following regression equation:

$$\text{Cigarette consumption} = 4{,}416 - .0678 \text{ per capita disposable personal income}$$

Even though the r^2 for this equation is .80, more valid ways of forecasting cigarette consumption can probably be discovered.

Figure 8–4
Per Capita Cigarette Consumption and Per Capita Disposable Personal Income, 1972–85

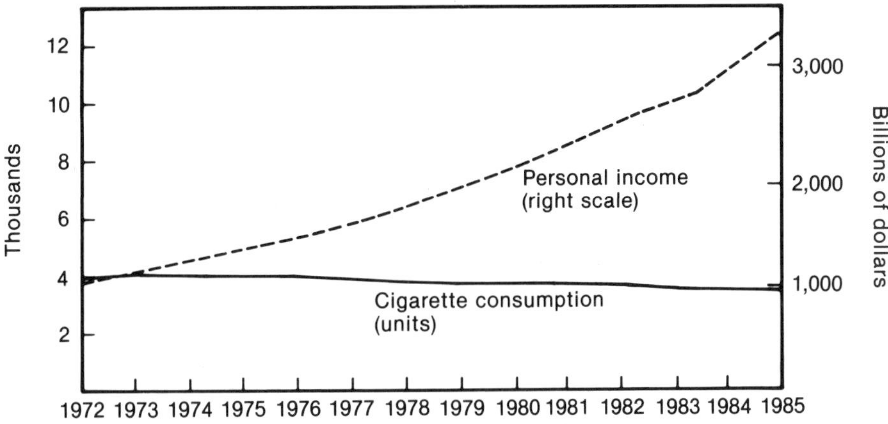

Source: U.S. Department of Commerce.

Industry Capacity

The physical capacity of an industry may be a vital factor in its investment outlook. Often a relationship can be found between the prices charged for a product and the percentage of capacity utilized. The cement industry during the 1960s and 1970s provides an excellent example of this relationship. Industry capacity expanded rapidly in the early 1960s, resulting in substantial excess capacity. Each company in the industry seemingly built enough capacity to accommodate expected increased demand for the entire industry for the next several years. The result was that virtually every company in the industry had excess capacity because of overexpansion of plants and equipment.

Industry Characteristics: Political and Social

In this section, we will present several important social and political perspectives that investors need to consider in evaluating an industry's future prospects. The political factors are divided into domestic and international issues.

Domestic Political Factors

Political factors influence an industry in many ways. The degree of industry regulation by government is one consideration. Industries such as public utilities, banking, and transportation are influenced a great deal by government regulations of rates charged, routes served, and types of services provided. Investors must be aware when any changes in the regulatory environment occur and must decipher the impact of the changes on industry profitability and growth.

The airlines in the late 1970s became subject to much less regulation by the Civil Aeronautics Board in such matters as routes and fares. As a result, many airlines experimented with promotional fares to increase their profits. However, Braniff overexpanded after the deregulation of the industry and was forced to file for bankruptcy in 1982. The industry has continued to experience major reshuffling and failures as the competitive factor continues to be an important ingredient to the future of an industry that has too many planes and too many routes.

International Considerations

Political factors of the international scene can be just as influential as domestic factors when analyzing an industry. As modern communication networks effectively shrink the size of the world, investors must give added attention to international considerations. Over the years, U.S. corporations have had property confiscated by foreign governments. At times, adequate compensation has been received. At other times, compensation has been either too little or nonexistent. Investors who purchase securities in firms operating in politically sensitive areas of the world need to examine the nature of the firms' diversification.

On a more positive note, foreign markets can provide an enlarged arena for growth in various industry groups. Conversely, some industries face increasingly strong competition from foreign producers, as imports command an increasing percentage of the U.S. market. Industries that produce steel, automobiles, optical goods, and electronics have not fared well against foreign competitors. How will international trade agreements between the United States and the industrialized foreign countries, such as Japan, affect specific domestic industry groups?

Investors have recently had to add a new concern regarding international trade to their worries. Fluctuating exchange rates and rapid currency revaluations make the international market very volatile. Firms may make or lose money merely as a result of currency fluctuations, and the prices of goods may change in a relative manner. As the dollar gets more expensive, in terms of other currencies, U.S.-produced goods become less price competitive. Likewise, as the dollar gets cheaper and is devalued relative to foreign currencies, U.S. goods become more price competitive.

Figure 8–5 shows U.S. agricultural exports for the 1970–85 period. In 1970 the U.S. share of the world grain market was 38 percent, and this share grew to 58 percent by 1979. The main reason for the decline in exports in 1982–85 was the strong U.S. dollar relative to other currencies. Hence, U.S. grains became relatively expensive compared to foreign sources of supply.

Social Changes

Social change may be one of the more important considerations in the analysis of an industry. Many recent changes in the consumption patterns of individuals have apparently resulted from *social factors.* Such trends as the movement toward smaller families, as noted in the previous chap-

Figure 8–5
U.S. Agricultural Exports, 1970–1985

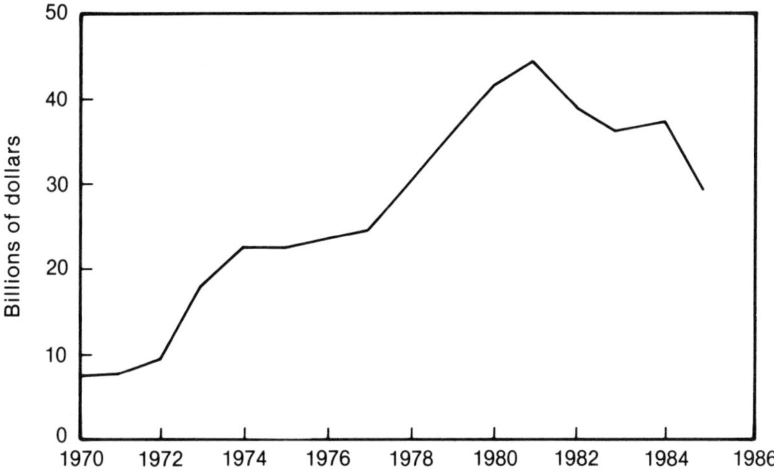

Source: U.S. Department of Commerce.

Table 8–1
U.S. Consumption of Alcoholic Beverages Per Capita in Gallons

		Distilled Spirits	Beer	Wine	Total
1965		1.5	16.0	1.0	18.5
1970		1.8	19.2	1.3	22.4*
1975		2.0	22.2	1.7	25.9
1980		2.0	25.2	2.1	29.3
1981		2.0	25.6	2.2	29.8
1982		1.9	25.4	2.2	29.5
1983		1.8	25.2	2.2	29.3*
1984		1.8	24.9	2.3	29.1*
1985		1.7	23.4	2.5	27.6
Change	1965–85	.6%	1.9%	4.7%	2.0%
per	1970–80	1.0	2.8	4.9	2.7
year	1980–85	−3.2	−1.5	3.5	−1.2

*Rounding error.

Source: U.S. Statistical Abstract, various issues.

ter, more leisure time, and changing emphasis on materialistic goals may have profound investment ramifications. Smaller families may result in decreased demand for the products of the toy and baby industries. The trend toward more leisure time in the future may create or wipe out entire industries.

Tastes appear to change slowly, but changing tastes may create excellent investment opportunities. The alcoholic consumption of Americans has shifted away from heavy spirits such as bourbon to lighter spirits such as vodka and gin. Along with these changes in tastes has come the increasing consumption of wine. The consumption figures in Table 8–1 show the changing tastes of the American consumer in this regard. Table 8–1 also reveals a noticeable decline in the per capita consumption of alcohol, although it remained above pre–1980 levels.

General Retail Merchandising: *An Industry Analysis*

This section presents a description and analysis of the general retail merchandising industry. In the first part, the composition of the industry by firm type is described and the place of the industry on its life cycle curve is indicated. Then, an analysis of several key data series is presented, indicating the relationships between economic variables and industry performance. In the second part, a brief analysis of the general retail merchandising industry is conducted. The analysis draws on the background statistics reported in the first part of this section. We will continue our security analysis process at the company level in Chapter 9 with an examination of K mart, a leading company in the retail merchandising industry.

Industry Description

Retailing is a service industry containing a number of different types of retailers. Excluding such retailers as drug stores, we can distinguish three main types of retail outlets.

1. *Department stores.* These retail outlets specialize in apparel, other soft goods, and furniture. They are generally interested in increasing the quality and fashion element of their goods. Examples of department stores include R. H. Macy and Marshall Field.
2. *Specialty stores.* These retail outlets concentrate on one type of merchandise such as apparel, jewelry, or shoes. The retail units tend to be relatively small and offer considerable sales assistance. Examples of this type of outlet include Tandy (Radio Shack) and Zale Jewelry.
3. *National general merchandise retailers.* These are the large national retailing operations such as Sears, J. C. Penney, and K mart. They offer a broad line of merchandise, concentrating on staple items that have relatively low fashion appeal. However, the quality and fashion appeal of some of their items have increased over the years.

Restructuring

The merchandising industry underwent major restructuring and consolidation in the 1980s as it reached the maturity phase. Exhibit 8–1 lists the top twenty general merchandise chains, as of 1985, along with their sales volume and number of stores. The structural changes in the industry occurred as a number of large merchandise chains were acquired through leveraged-buyout activities, merged with other companies, or re-

Exhibit 8–1 Top Twenty General Merchandise Chains, 1985

	1985 Stores	*1985 Sales ($ billions)*	*Percent Change 1984–85 Sales*
1. Sears	799	24.4	–.7
2. K mart	3,848	22.4	6.3
3. J. C. Penney	1,909	13.7	2.2
4. Dayton Hudson	1,206	8.8	9.8
5. Wal-Mart	882	8.5	32.0
6. Federated	477	8.2	2.6
7. F. W. Woolworth	5,822	6.0	3.9
8. Montgomery Ward	315	5.4	–17.1
9. May Department Stores	2,074	5.1	8.9
10. Melville	5,574	4.8	12.0
11. Associated Dry Goods	346	4.4	6.8
12. R. H. Macy	95	4.4	7.5
13. Allied Stores	665	4.1	4.1
14. Zayre	985	4.0	26.5
15. Carter Hawley Hale	284	4.0	6.8
16. Tandy Corporation	9,117	2.8	2.4
17. Household Merchandising	n.a.*	2.8	–4.9
18. Service Merchandise	328	2.5	52.5
19. The Limited	2,353	2.4	77.7
20. Best Products	213	2.2	9.9

*n.a. means not available.

Source: Chain Store Age, General Merchandise Edition, June 1986.

organized to avoid hostile takeover attempts. Examples of these activities were the leveraged buyout of R. H. Macy, the merger of May Department Stores and Associated Dry Goods, and the split-up of Carter Hawley Hale. Accompanying the merger and buyout activities were substantial reorganization and consolidation of many other firms in the industry. These consolidations were brought about to improve operating and managerial efficiencies for the various chains.

Maturity Stage

Two long-term trends, typical of the maturing stage, became especially troubling for the industry: overstoring and sluggish demand. For many years, retail merchandise chains expanded by opening new stores. Standard and Poor's stated:

> According to *Shopping Center World,* the total number of shopping centers in the U.S. surged 93% between 1972 and 1984, sharply outpacing population growth, while shopping space square footage grew by more than 200%.[1]

1. Standard & Poor's, *Industry Surveys,* Retailing, January 22, 1987, p. 81.

A statistic related to capacity utilization is the dollar sales per square foot of retail space. The National Retail Merchants Association reported that the real sales dollar per square foot had declined in 1985 to below the 1975 level. The figure had declined from $142 to $135 sales per square foot in the 1984–85 period alone.[2]

Changes in Consumer Tastes

Although overall demand grew to record levels, sluggish demand was evident in many areas of general retailing in the 1980s, especially for the large major retail chains. For the future, two economic factors brought out in Chapter 7 will have a major impact on the industry demand: (1) a decline in population growth and (2) an increase in the average age of the U.S. population. With aging, consumption patterns are expected to shift away from fads and fashions to services and health products. This should produce less demand for the products traditionally sold by retail chains.

Marketing analysts forecast future sales growth in the retailing area to be limited to around 2.4 percent annually. As the level and nature of demand changes, the number of different types of retail merchants is expected to increase. Significant developments may possibly take place in the areas of at-home television shopping networks, warehouse clubs, and deep discount stores. Industry analysts predict a major shakeout to occur as the industry adjusts to its excess store capacity and adapts to the changing markets.

Operating Characteristics

Retail merchants are in many ways similar to airlines and other high fixed-cost service industries. Because of the high fixed-cost of facilities and labor, the firms in the industry must operate at fairly high break-even levels, which makes them subject to considerable operating risk. Because demand for retail merchandise is generally sensitive to economic conditions, the profitability for the industry can undergo wide swings. The relationships between economic data and industry profitability are brought out in the next section.

Relevant Industry Data

Retail sales during the 1971–85 period and the profitability of sales by general merchandise retailers are presented in Figure 8–6. Sales by all types of retail stores have increased steadily over the years. The net income as a percentage of sales for general merchandise chains suffered as a result of the recession of 1980–81 but rebounded somewhat throughout

2. Ibid., p. 80.

Figure 8–6
Retail Sales and Profitability of General Merchandise Retail Companies, 1971–85

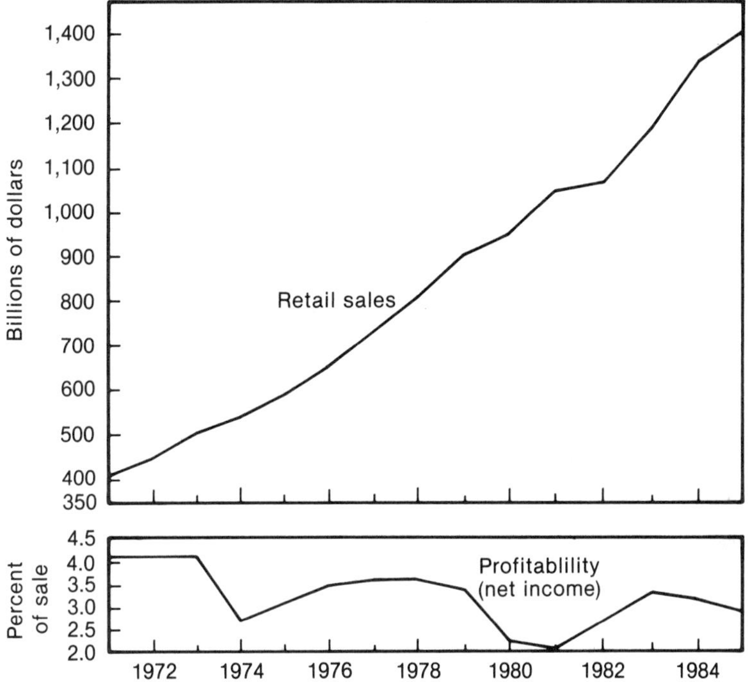

Source: U.S. Department of Commerce.

the 1982–85 period. During the 1982–85 period, the industry fared much better as personal consumption expenditures fueled economic growth. Figure 8–7 provides an indication of the close association between percentage changes in general merchandise sales and disposable personal income between 1973 and 1986. The vertical scales in the figure are both semilog so as to bring out the relationship between the percentage changes of the two variables. Also shown in the figure is *Value Line*'s forecast of these two factors to the year 1990.

Sales volume increases are important to the profitability of the general retail merchandise chains, and not surprisingly, the industry's profitability has grown and should be expected to continue to grow with sales growth. However, any economic downturn in the near future would severely hurt industry profitability.

One convenient way to discern consumer attitudes is to follow the Conference Board's *Index of Consumer Sentiment.* Figure 8–8 shows the Confidence Index, which measures the sentiment of consumers during the period. The huge decline in consumer confidence in 1980 and the resurgent growth in 1982 through 1986 are clearly displayed in Figure 8–8. Many economic and industry analysts have interpreted the declining confidence ratio as experienced at the end of 1986 and continuing in 1987 to be a sign that consumer demand was softening. If so, general merchan-

Figure 8–7
General Merchandise Sales versus Disposable Income

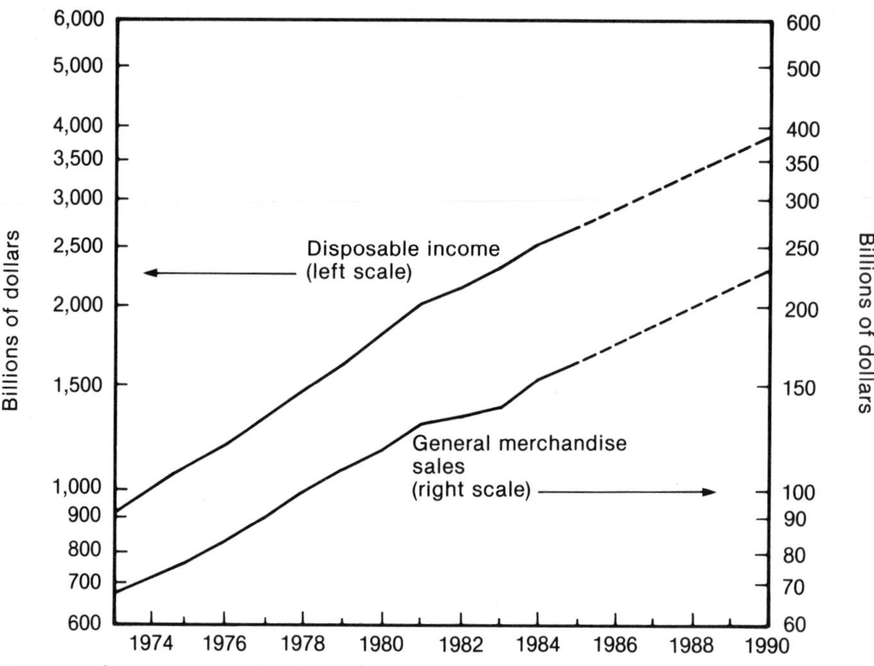

Source: Value Line, report dated March 6, 1987, p. 1,633.

Figure 8–8
Index of Consumer Sentiment, 1979–86

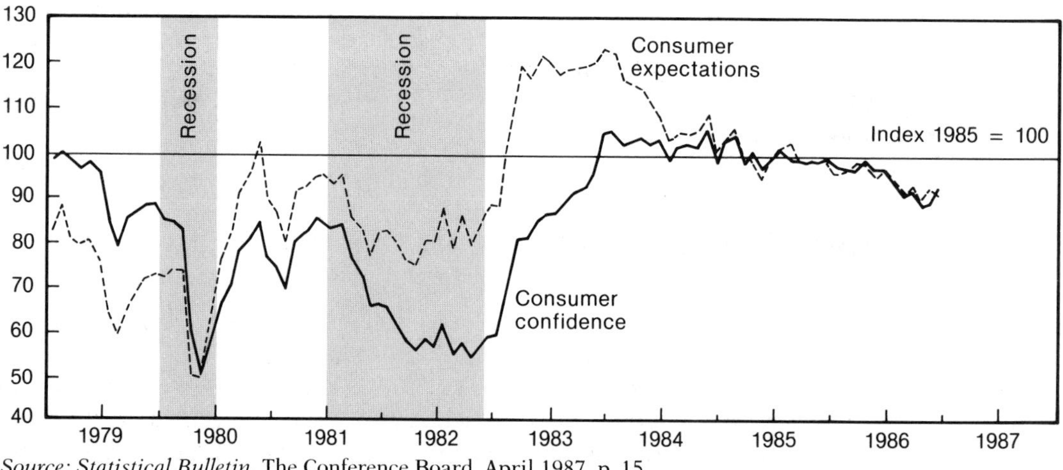

Source: Statistical Bulletin, The Conference Board, April 1987, p. 15.

dise retailers could anticipate a mild drop in their rate of increase in sales and profitability.

Two additional indicators of retail sales demand are the amounts of personal savings and consumer credit. To the extent that consumers decide to save less and spend more, retail sales should increase. Likewise,

Figure 8–9
Savings, Installment Debt, and Retail Sales, 1980–86

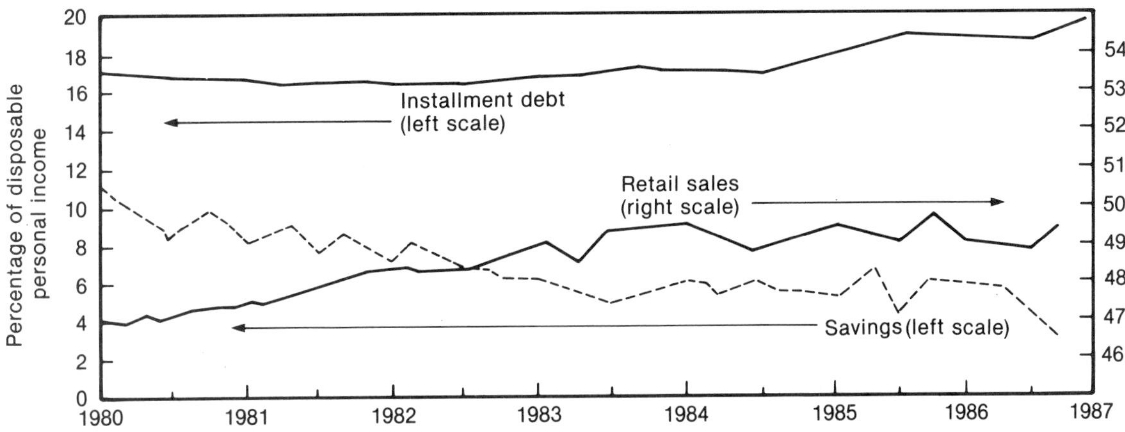

Source: U.S. Department of Commerce.

consumers borrow more to support increased demand for goods and services. To the extent that consumers have not overextended themselves, further purchases through credit expansion are possible. If consumers are overextended, on average, then a period of consumer defaults and repayments would be expected, with a corresponding falling off in retail sales. Figure 8–9 presents personal savings expressed as a percentage of disposable personal income for the 1980–86 period. One important aspect of this data series is the decline in savings that occurred during the 1980–83 period and again in 1986. As individuals reduced their rate of savings and increased consumption, the profitability of the general retail merchandising chains improved. Figure 8–9 also indicates that installment debt as a percent of personal income rose to a record high 20 percent in 1986. Significant increases in interest rates could have a dampening effect on consumer credit and could provide an incentive for personal savings increases.

Growth Analysis for Retail Merchandising Industry

Industry analysis is aided in recent years by the availability of large data bases on which investors can easily access industry data. Exhibit 8–2 contains the *Value Line* data base sorted on the retailing industry code and reporting eleven key variables. At the bottom of the listing are the corresponding industry average figures for the thirty-four firms identified to be in the industry as of May 1987.

To provide a basis of comparison for the *Value Line* industry data, the average values for key ratios were derived from the Value Line data base for their entire listing of over 1,600 stocks. A comparison of the retailing industry averages with market data is presented in Table 8–2. Industry growth, like economic growth, can be evaluated by using many different techniques. We will use several techniques to reach by consensus an esti-

Exhibit 8–2 **Value Line Data Screen for the Retailing Industry, 1987**

Data: May 1987

Company Name	Sales	Current P-E	Current Yield	% Return Net Worth	5-Yr EPS Growth	5-Yr Div Growth	Prj EPS Growth	Prj Div Growth	Prj 3-5 Yr Return	Price/ Bk Val	Beta
ALEXANDER'S	520.1	NA	0.0	3.5	NA	NA	19.0	0.0	-4	2.77	0.80
AMES DEPT STRS	1449.0	21.5	0.5	11.0	24.0	14.5	22.5	24.0	27	2.20	1.05
CARSON PIRIE	1301.9	17.3	1.8	8.7	2.0	2.0	15.0	12.0	8	1.86	0.85
CARTER HAWLEY	3977.9	19.4	2.0	7.7	-18.0	2.5	46.5	1.0	15	3.39	1.05
CHARMING SHOPPE	391.6	25.6	0.5	24.9	20.0	22.5	32.0	22.5	14	11.05	1.60
DAYTON HUDSON	8793.4	15.8	2.2	14.6	16.5	10.5	14.5	8.0	19	2.11	1.20
DEB SHOPS	147.1	18.7	1.1	26.5	NA	NA	20.5	36.0	15	7.04	1.90
DILLARD DEPT ST	1851.4	14.3	0.4	13.4	37.0	12.0	22.0	26.5	23	1.96	1.05
DOLLAR GENERAL	564.8	15.6	2.2	4.0	26.0	29.0	6.5	15.5	24	1.83	1.15
FAMILY DOLLAR	487.7	15.4	1.7	21.6	25.5	24.0	16.0	17.5	29	3.38	1.15
FEDERATED DEPT	9978.0	15.1	3.2	10.6	8.0	7.0	7.0	5.5	8	1.67	1.15
GAP (THE), INC.	647.3	26.1	1.0	22.7	18.0	15.5	33.5	42.0	7	12.50	1.25
HECK'S INC.	523.3	NA	0.0	NA	NA	8.5	NA	NA	35	0.38	0.80
HUDSON'S BAY CO	5271.6	NA	2.4	NA	NA	-10.0	NA	0.0	21	0.83	0.75
JAMESWAY CORP.	523.2	15.0	0.6	9.5	11.5	18.0	16.0	16.5	16	1.98	1.45
K MART CORP.	22420.0	13.2	2.9	14.4	8.0	8.5	11.5	8.5	12	2.31	1.20
LIMITED INC.	2387.1	27.1	0.6	36.0	61.0	64.0	35.5	41.0	12	18.17	1.45
MAY DEPT.STORES	5027.6	16.1	2.6	14.8	13.0	11.5	10.5	10.0	11	2.51	1.05
MERCANTILE STS	1880.0	13.2	1.6	15.1	16.5	17.5	11.5	13.0	7	2.38	1.05
MERRY-GO-ROUND	164.1	15.6	0.0	20.9	31.0	NA	13.5	0.0	10	4.20	1.30
NICHOLS (S.E.)	310.0	10.2	0.0	8.9	16.5	NA	-0.5	0.0	12	0.63	1.40
NORDSTROM, INC.	1301.9	26.0	0.7	15.9	17.5	18.0	24.5	21.5	7	6.44	1.10
PENNEY (J.C.)	14740.0	13.3	3.1	12.2	8.0	6.0	8.5	4.5	7	1.66	1.10
PETRIE STORES	1160.8	15.0	2.4	16.3	3.5	4.5	18.0	10.0	20	2.86	1.05
PIC 'N' SAVE	303.3	19.9	0.0	26.1	24.5	NA	21.0	0.0	16	6.40	1.30
REGIS CORP.	151.6	18.6	1.2	23.1	NA	NA	14.0	22.0	14	4.75	1.00
ROSES STORES'B'	1009.2	15.3	1.1	12.6	22.5	15.5	20.0	15.5	18	2.52	0.65
SEARS, ROEBUCK	44281.5	13.8	3.8	10.4	11.5	5.5	9.5	5.5	13	1.53	1.30
STOP & SHOP	3689.1	16.9	2.3	7.5	19.5	15.0	13.0	9.5	14	1.90	1.20
SYMS CORP.	215.2	15.8	0.0	19.2	24.5	NA	14.0	0.0	13	3.53	1.05
WAL-MART STORES	8451.5	30.4	0.4	25.5	41.0	40.5	27.5	29.5	10	12.23	1.30
WICKES COS.	2806.2	12.5	0.0	2.9	-35.0	NA	19.0	0.0	31	0.87	1.15
WOOLWORTH(F.W.)	5958.0	13.9	2.7	14.5	-2.0	3.0	16.0	13.5	9	2.61	1.10
ZAYRE CORP.	4036.0	15.4	1.6	15.6	28.0	75.0	14.5	20.5	21	2.38	1.25
Averages	4609.5	17.5	1.4	15.3	16.6	16.9	17.9	13.7	15	3.97	1.15

mate of future growth for the industry. To begin the analysis, we note that past industry growth had been moderate over the previous five-year period. Table 8–2 shows that industry earnings grew at an average .9 percent faster than market earnings, while industry dividends almost doubled the market dividend growth rate.

Table 8–2
Comparison of Key Ratios, Retailing Industry versus Market

Ratio	Retailing	Overall Market
1987 data		
Return on net worth	15.3%	13.0%
Dividend yield	1.4%	2.3%
Price/book value	4.0 times	2.6 times
Price-earnings ratio	17.5 times	17.1 times
Beta	1.15	1.0
Debt/total capital	40%*	31%
Past five-year growth		
earnings per share	16.6%	15.7%
dividends per share	16.9%	8.7%
Future five-year growth		
earnings per share	17.9%	15.7%
dividends per share	13.7%	8.7%
average return	15%	13%

*Not reported in Exhibit 8–2.

Source: Value Line, data screen, 1987.

In 1987, the industry return on net worth was 15.3 percent, and its dividend yield was 1.4 percent. This implies that the market was expecting substantial capital appreciation from the industry, on the order of 13.9 percent. By comparison, the average stock in the market had a 2.3 percent dividend yield and an expected capital appreciation of 10.7 percent.

Over the 1978–86 period, industry sales grew from $537 billion to $1,086 billion, according to Standard & Poor's composite industry data. The average annual sales increase was 9.2 percent compared to only a 2.2 percent growth in real GNP. Consumer spending was not likely to increase at such a high rate relative to GNP growth in future years. Although future sales growth would probably not repeat the rapid growth of the 1978–86 period, *Value Line* estimated the future earnings and dividend growth for the retailing industry to approximate the historical performance and to outperform the overall stock market averages.

In Chapter 5, we calculated an estimate of the market required rate of return using *Value Line* data. The required return for the average stock in the industry was determined as follows:

$$i = D_1/P + g = 1.4\% + 13.7\% = 15.1\%$$

The corresponding estimate for the overall market was derived as follows:

$$i = D_1/P + g = 2.3\% + 8.7\% = 11.0\%$$

The average industry stock was expected to yield a 4.1 percentage point premium above the market average. We can ask if this is consistent with the systematic risk of the average industry stock, as measured by the industry beta of 1.15. Given the industry beta, the required return should be:

$$R_{\text{Retail}} = 9\% + 1.15(14\% - 9\%) = 14.75\%$$

Figure 8–10
Price-Earnings Ratio, Retail Index versus S&P 500, 1970–86

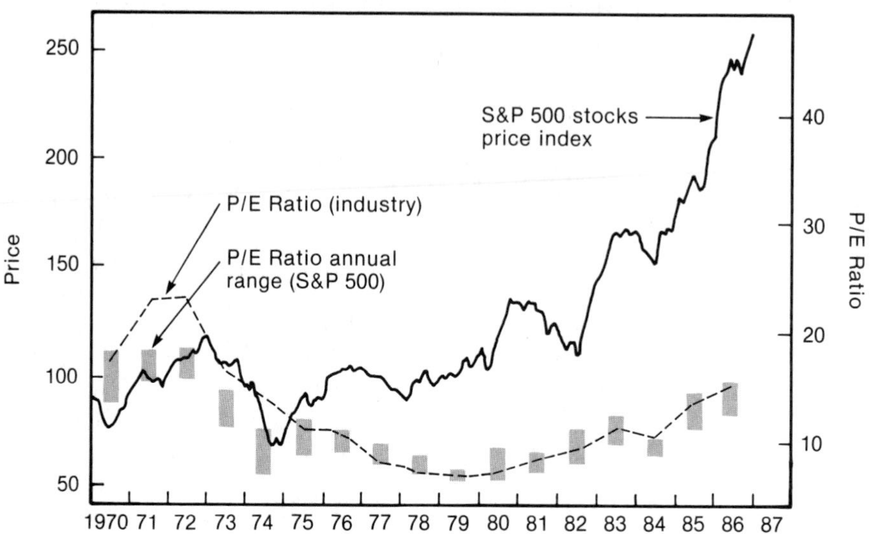

Source: Standard & Poor's *The Outlook,* January 4, 1987, p. 974 and *Industry Surveys,* "Retailing," January 22, 1987, p. R104.

The 14.75 percent estimate is very close to the *Value Line* estimate of 15.1 percent.

Another measure frequently used in analyzing an industry is its average *price-earnings ratio* (P/E ratio). Figure 8–10 displays the relationship between the industry and overall stock market average price-earnings ratio for the period between 1970 and 1987. To give perspective as to the relative position of the stock market, the S&P 500 index levels are presented in the figure along with the price-earnings data. Industry earnings appear to have been valued at about the average price-earnings ratio for all stocks over the 1970–86 period. Looking back at Exhibit 8–2 to see the price-earnings ratios for selected firms in the retailing industry leads to the discovery that two distinct subgroups of firms were worth further inspection. One group of firms, including Wal-Mart, The GAP, and The Limited, had high past earnings-growth rates and were being capitalized at high price-earnings multiples. On the other hand, the larger, more established national chains, such as Sears, J. C. Penney, and K mart, had much lower earnings growth, and their price-earnings ratios were at the lower end of the industry rankings. Whereas the larger firms appeared to have reached a maturity stage, the newer, more aggressive marketers were expanding sales rapidly and capturing greater market shares.

Overall, the industry growth appears to be tied very closely with overall growth in the economy. As long as the economy has stable growth at moderate rates, the retailers can benefit from the use of high operating leverage and moderate financial leverage. With a beta not significantly different from the market, the future returns for the industry stocks should closely approximate the market.

Summary

In this chapter, we examined two major topics. First, we examined the major factors accounting for the future growth of an industry. Second, we examined the general merchandising industry as an example of the application of these factors.

In looking at the future growth potential of an industry, often a useful starting point is to attempt to locate the industry on its life cycle curve. Four stages of the life cycle were examined. These are: (1) infancy, (2) growth, (3) maturity, and (4) decline. In helping to determine the proper life cycle stage of any given industry, examining the past growth of the industry is important. While past growth allows the investor to form preliminary expectations regarding future growth, other factors are also important. These other factors include the nature of the product, the supply, demand, and capacity relationships existing in the industry, political and social considerations, and international developments within the industry. The analysis of specific industries serves as a starting point for the analysis of companies within the industry.

Suggested Readings

"America Rushes to High Technology for Growth." *Business Week,* March 28, 1983, 84–90.

BURKHEAD, J. GARY, WILLIAM W. HELMAN, and JOHN B. WALKER, "Company Report Guideline." In Richard A. Stevenson and Susan M. Phillips (eds.), *Investment Environment, Analysis, And Alternatives.* St. Paul, Minn.: West Publishing Co., 1977, 123–134.

CHENEY, HARLAN L. "The Value of Industry Forecasting As an Aid to Portfolio Management." *Appalachian Financial Review* (Spring 1970): 331–39.

KING, BENJAMIN. "Market and Industry Factors in Stock Price Behavior." *Journal of Business* (January 1966): 139–190.

LATANE, HENRY A., and DONALD L. TUTTLE. "Profitability in Industry Analysis." *Financial Analysts Journal* (July–August 1968): 51–61.

LIVINGSTON, MILES. "Industry Movements of Common Stocks." *Journal of Finance* (June 1977): 861–74.

REILLY, FRANK K., and EUGENE DRZYCIMSKI. "Alternative Industry Performance and Risk." *Journal of Financial and Quantitative Analysis* (June 1974): 423–46.

WENGLOWSKI, GARY M. "Industry Profit Analysis—A Progress Report and Some Predictions." *The Economic Framework for Investors,* Charlottesville, VA: The Financial Analysts Research Foundation, 1975, 19–30.

Questions

1. What are the stages in the life cycle of a firm or an industry?

2. Companies are often concerned with avoiding the final stage of the life cycle. As an investor, how would you identify those firms that are making an attempt to avoid this stage?

3. The utility industry has many problems of both a supply and a demand nature. Discuss the nature of these various problems and their significance to the investor.

4. How would you determine whether the demand for a given product is income elastic? Give some examples of products that you think would fall into this category.

5. The investor should examine the per capita use of products. However, certain products face natural barriers to sustainable increases in use per capita. What is the nature of these barriers, and what products are most vulnerable to the impact of these barriers?

6. Interest rate changes have a varying impact on different industries. What would you expect the impact of rising interest rates to be on the following?
   (a) housing
   (b) traveler's check industry
   (c) retailing
   (d) soft drinks
   (e) savings and loan associations

7. By referring to the charts and figures in the chapter, identify the key variables that should influence the performance of the general retail merchandising stocks over the next three years.

8. One of the factors an investor should examine in an industry is the current political environment. What political problems currently exist for both international and domestic petroleum producers and for U.S. commercial banks?

Chapter 9

Company Analysis

Key Concepts

acid-test ratio
activity ratios
balance sheet
book value
capitalization ratio
common size financial statement
current ratio
current yield
debt-to-asset ratio
diversification
dividend policy
efficiency ratios
FIFO
financial planning
income statement
inventory turnover
leverage ratios
LIFO
liquidity ratios
management's grand design
market required rate of return
production planning and control
profitability ratios
quality of management
ratio analysis
receivables turnover
research and development
return on assets
return on equity
return on sales (revenue)
statement of changes in financial position
statement of retained earnings
tax reconciliation
technical insolvency
times-interest-earned ratio

Chapter Outline

Investors want to examine in detail both the qualitative and quantitative aspects of investment decisions before buying or selling securities. In this chapter, we set up a checklist of the qualitative and quantitative items that should be considered when making investment decisions. The qualitative aspects include assessing (1) the quality of a firm's management, (2) the nature of the products or services provided, and (3) the growth potential as reflected by past performance and current planning efforts. Investors' qualitative judgments should be validated by quantitative analysis, such as a financial statement analysis that includes the calculation of key financial ratios. The final step in the process is to decide on the suitability of this investment in light of the conclusions reached in the previous steps.

We will present the items on the checklist in the same order that investors would ordinarily examine them. Actually, investors probably telescope many of the individual steps that we will discuss and effectively do many things at the same time. Before launching into a full-scale qualitative and quantitative analysis of a security, investors should conduct an initial assessment of how the security is currently being valued by the financial markets.

An Initial Assessment

A few factors should be considered prior to making a detailed investment analysis. These factors relate to the current and historical valuation of the common stock, its current yield, its potential rate of return, its beta estimate, its market required rate of return, and its marketability.

Current and Historical Valuation

The price-earnings (P/E) ratio for K mart is calculated below, using the May 6, 1987, stock price of $40¼ (after adjusting for a pending three-for-two stock split) and the 1986 earnings per share of $2.84 (from continuing operations). On that date, investors were willing to pay about $14.17 for each $1 of K mart's earnings.

$$\text{P/E ratio} = \frac{\text{Price per share}}{\text{Earnings per share}} = \frac{\$40\tfrac{1}{4}}{\$2.84} = 14.17$$

With regard to the P/E ratio, the following questions are worthwhile additions to the checklist:

1. How does the current P/E ratio compare with historical P/E ratios for the company?
2. What is the trend of earnings per share?
3. How does the P/E ratio compare with the performance of other firms in the same industry?

Figure 9–1
P/E Ratios: S&P 500 versus K mart, 1970–87

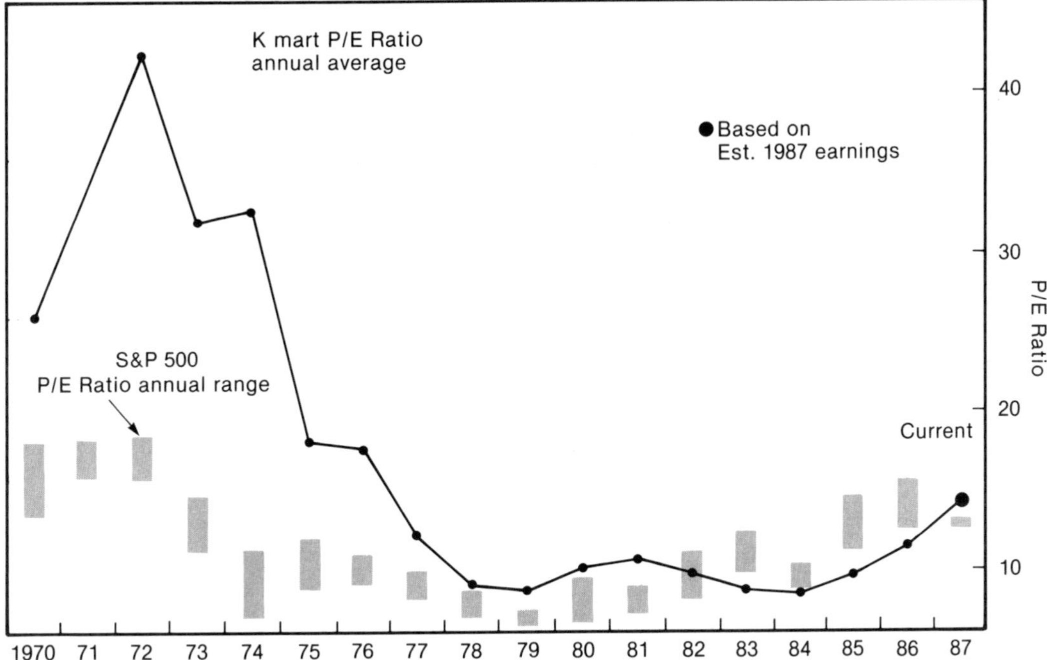

Source: Standard & Poor's *The Outlook,* January 14, 1987, and *Value Line,* March 6, 1987, p. 1649.

Figure 9–1 shows the P/E ratio for K mart relative to the P/E ratio for the S&P 500 in the 1970–87 period. Between 1981 and 1983, the P/E ratio for K mart stock dropped below the S&P 500 average P/E ratio. However, by early 1987, a dollar of K mart's earnings appeared to be valued almost the same as a dollar of earnings from the average of the S&P 500 stocks.

Current Yield and Potential Rate of Return

The *current yield* is calculated by dividing the dividend per share by the market price per share. In March 1987, K mart declared an increase in its quarterly dividend from \$.25 to \$.29 per share. At the \$.29 quarterly dividend level, the annual current yield became 2.9 percent.

$$\text{Current yield} = \frac{\text{Dividend per share}}{\text{Market price per share}} = \frac{\$1.16}{\$40\frac{1}{4}} = .029 \text{ or } 2.9\%$$

The current yield for K mart was relatively low. Investors who held the common stock must have expected to achieve substantial capital gains and receive increased dividends. The following questions should be added to the checklist for consideration by potential investors:

1. What is a reasonable total return (dividend yield plus capital appreciation) from holding a stock of this risk class or beta level?

2. Is it reasonable to expect enough growth in the stock price to produce the capital appreciation needed to achieve the desired total return? For example, assume investors wanted a total return of 14.8 percent (to be derived later in the chapter) from holding K mart stock. With a 2.9 percent current dividend yield, investors would need an 11.9 percent increase in price each year (ignoring any potential dividend increases) to achieve the desired 14.8 percent total rate of return. The calculation follows:

$$\begin{aligned} i &= D_0/P + g \\ 14.8\% &= 2.9\% + g \\ g &= 11.9\% \end{aligned}$$

Current Risk Assessment and Market Required Rate of Return

One of the key steps in valuing a security is to determine its *market required rate of return.* We have discussed several methods for estimating the required rate of return in previous chapters, based on the capital asset pricing model, the constant growth model, the sustainable growth model, and the risk-premium-above-bond-yield method. Also, we have shown how to get estimates for the risk-free rate, the market return, beta, and growth. No single approach for determining required returns is best all the time, and most investors use a combination of techniques to arrive at required return estimates.

The market's current risk assessment of the stock can be indicated by estimating its beta or systematic risk component. The beta estimate can be derived from a variety of sources. Investors can calculate a beta using their own data bases and statistical techniques. Alternatively, beta forecasts are provided regularly by many financial service organizations, such as *Value Line* and Merrill Lynch. For K mart, the *Value Line* beta estimate was 1.15. A historical beta, calculated by regressing annual holding period returns for the 1968–86 period for K mart and the S&P 500, turned out to be 1.20. Potential investors could derive a market-based required rate of return for K mart by using the beta estimate of 1.15 or by using some other beta measure.

In Chapter 7, the expected market return (from the 1987 perspective) was estimated to be about 14 percent and the risk-free return to be about 9 percent. Using these figures, we can calculate the required return for K mart based on its systematic risk (its security market line value) as follows:

$$\begin{aligned} R_{KM} &= R_f + \beta_{KM}(R_m - R_f) \\ &= 9\% + 1.15(14\% - 9\%) \\ &= 14.8\% \end{aligned}$$

We can take the required return from the security market line, R_{KM}, and use it in the constant growth model to estimate the implied growth rate for K mart stock. Given that the required return, i, is equal to R_{KM}, which equals 14.8 percent, and the current dividend equals \$1.16, then the implied growth rate for K mart can be derived as follows:

$$R_{KM} = i = D_1/P + g$$
$$.148 = \$1.16(1 + g)/\$40.25 + g$$

Solving for g, we have

$$g = .116 \text{ or } 11.6\%$$

How can we determine whether the growth estimate is a reasonable one? One way is to compare our implied growth estimate with growth estimates derived from other sources, such as from security analysts' forecasts. Standard and Poor's publishes a periodical called the *Earnings Forecaster* that reports forecasts by various security analysts of earnings and earnings growth for major corporations. The 11.6 percent growth rate we have calculated is almost identical to *Value Line*'s estimated growth in earnings of 11.5 percent. Another way is for investors to derive their own estimates. Later in this chapter, we present a discussion on measuring the level and variability of earnings growth for a firm.

Marketability Aspects

Investors should not purchase a common stock, or any investment for that matter, without considering the nature of the market in which the stock is traded, its trading activity, and the ownership of the stock. In considering the ease of buying and selling the stock, the following checklist of questions is useful:

1. How many shares does the firm have outstanding? K mart had 124,494,346 common shares outstanding as of January 28, 1987.
2. How closely held are the firm's shares? Is a large percentage of the stock held by the original founders or other investors not likely to be buying or selling stock? In effect, investors are interested in the "floating supply" of stock that is reasonably available for day-to-day trading. K mart is a widely held company with a large trading volume.
3. Where is the stock traded? If traded in the over-the-counter market, what is the spread between the bid and asked prices? A large spread is an indication of limited trading volume in the stock. K mart's stock is listed on the NYSE.
4. What is the average daily or weekly trading volume? Does the price of the stock change relatively quickly in response to small changes in trading activity? K mart's stock price tends to move in small price increments from trade to trade.

Quality of Management

To a considerable extent, judgment is required of investors in determining the *quality of management,* and this is an arduous task reflecting subjective analysis. Furthermore, a judgment regarding the quality of management requires more than just a study of the people running a particular company. The actual performance of the management relative to the opportunities available must be carefully analyzed. Despite the many problems that may be encountered, investors must still make the effort to judge the quality of management. In this section, we suggest several critical viewpoints to be used in judging management quality. Several factors to consider are the management's grand design, educational background and experience, depth, track record, and planning activities.

Management's Grand Design

Does the management have a reasonable plan or *grand design* for the company's future? Careful and thoughtful consideration about the future is one of the major characteristics of successful management. Investors need to be satisfied that management can answer the following questions: Has management established a long-range plan? Are policies written so that employees can refer to them when handling situations that occur in the day-to-day affairs of the business? Is the firm recruiting top-notch young managerial talent, and is it willing to pay the price to obtain the services of these people?

Annually, *Fortune* surveys nearly 6,000 corporate executives, outside directors, and financial analysts and asks them to rate the 200 largest U.S. corporations with regard to their ability to attract, develop, and keep talented people. In the 1987 report, *Fortune* rated Merck as the best company to work for, with J. P. Morgan and Boeing in second place and third place, respectively. BankAmerica was ranked as the worst for this characteristic. LTV and American Motors were rated only slightly better than BankAmerica.

Education and Experience

One of the most useful ways to form opinions about the educational background and experience of management is to have actual personal contacts with members of the management team. However, when personal contact is not possible, valuable insights can often be gained from suppliers, bankers, and customers. Fortunately for investors, many top management people are evaluated in a variety of publications, including *Fortune, Business Week,* the *Wall Street Journal, Forbes,* and the *New York Times.* The firm's annual report is another source of information about the educational background and experience of management.

Depth and Track Record of Management

Does the firm's management have a plan of succession or orderly transfer of control at some future date? Many companies have been criticized as

Investment Highlight

ShowBiz Pizza Place (Brock Hotel Offers Pizza with Pizzazz)

The mixture of entertainment and eating has always held the potential for profitable operations. This investment highlight shows the importance of planned growth and market saturation.

Description

Brock Hotel Corporation owns 80 percent of ShowBiz Pizza Place, which uses computer-controlled lifesize, animated characters and video games to entertain customers while they wait for their pizzas. From a low of 3⅝ in 1980, Brock Hotel's common stock hit a high of 17½ in mid-1982. However, Brock's quarterly earnings per share for 1981 and 1982 were as follows:

	Q1	Q2	Q3	Q4
1981	.07	.17	.19	.16
1982	.17	.19	.30	(.11)

The deficit of 11 cents a share in the fourth quarter of 1982 was not well received by the market because this deficit made earnings per share for 1982 come in at 55 cents a share, unchanged from what they were in 1979. One of the problems seems to have been extremely rapid expansion. The number of ShowBiz outlets grew from 7 at the end of 1980 to 142 at the end of 1982. Robert Brock stated: "If I had to do it over again, I would build only two or three restaurants in Kansas City instead of five." See "Pigging Out," *Fortune* (April 4, 1983): 12. The combined result of this rapid expansion and the economic recession continued to take its toll. During the first half of 1983, Brock continued to lose money and the stock was at 8⅝ as of July 1983.

Conclusion

ShowBiz Pizza Place apparently saturated the market in some of its retail territories. Offering a pizza/entertainment concept whose purchase consumers could easily postpone during difficult times made the firm vulnerable to recessions. In addition, this concept possibly had a relatively short product life, as customers got tired of the animated characters.

"one-man shows." These companies may suffer if the one person who runs the company decides to resign, becomes stagnant in the position, or is no longer capable of keeping up with the competition. Without advancement opportunities, the company may have difficulty in hiring and retaining competent senior management personnel.

The true test of the quality of management is the long-term record produced for the stockholders of the firm. Investors should be able to infer much about the quality of management by studying financial statements. To be sure, not everything of significance is revealed in the financial statements, but they do represent a good check on evaluations based on other factors. Direct evidence will generally be very difficult for investors to acquire.

Planning Efforts

In order to achieve long-run objectives, the management must develop strategic plans for each of the firm's functional areas. This section concentrates on the planning efforts of the firm in the areas of financial planning, marketing, production planning and control, and diversification.

Financial Planning

Investors need to observe the appropriateness of such items as the profit margin on sales, the capital structure, and the liquidity level. Although the actual financial ratios for each company will vary over time and the acceptable levels for these ratios will vary from industry to industry, trends can certainly be noted. A reason for conducting a financial statement analysis is to provide investors with evidence of good financial planning.

The *dividend policy* is a significant part of a firm's financial planning effort. In fiscal 1986, K mart paid out 35.2 percent of its earnings from continuing operations as dividends. Whether K mart's dividend payout ratio was appropriate depended on such factors as the firm's anticipated growth rate and its liquidity position. The dividend payout percentage shown below is based on K mart's fiscal 1986 dividends and earnings.

$$\text{Dividend payout percentage} = \frac{\begin{array}{c}\text{Dividends}\\ \text{per share}\end{array}}{\begin{array}{c}\text{Earnings}\\ \text{per share}\end{array}} = \frac{\$1.00}{\$2.84} = .352 \text{ or } 35.2\%$$

Marketing Efforts

The marketing effort is critical to the success or failure of most firms. Investors must determine whether present marketing efforts are effective and whether plans are being made to meet the marketing challenges of the future. Many of the more successful marketing efforts that promote new products or services are carefully constructed, with major emphasis being placed on selecting the proper distribution channel. Once the channel is selected, a firm must ensure that the channel is filled with sales. The Investment Highlight for Merck indicates that the company has been successful in cultivating a quality image for its drug manufacturing business.

Production Planning and Control

For a manufacturing firm, the orderly flow of goods through the production process is essential to a sound business operation. The proper planning and control of production has several dimensions, the most important of which is the careful analysis and forecasting of future demand. Once this has been accomplished, production capacity must be made available so that future demand can be met.

Investment Highlight

Merck & Co. (A Quality Image)

This highlight shows the importance of a quality product line, corporate planning focus, and sound marketing.

Description

For its first four years, the *Fortune* annual survey of corporate executives voted IBM as the most-admired U.S. corporation. In 1987, IBM was replaced as number one by Merck & Company, a New Jersey-based pharmaceutical company. Merck's president, P. Roy Vangelo, designed the company to have the leading research group in the industry with a purpose of exploiting recent discoveries in medical science. Since the early 1980s, Merck has produced a flood of innovative prescription drugs from its research labs. In 1987 alone, Merck introduced five new products in the United States: treatments for hypertension, ulcers, and urinary tract infections, a multipurpose antibiotic, and a hepatitis B vaccine. In an industry in which research has been described as a crap shoot, Merck has amassed an enviable record of successes.

One key to Merck's accomplishments has been the concentration of company efforts on pharmaceuticals. While other companies diversified their product lines, Merck created an excellence in marketing programs and pharmaceutical research and development. Industry analysts comment that no other company has all the pieces of the biotechnology puzzle "so well put together." For example, Merck has the largest and best-trained sales force in the industry. Salespeople port lap-top computers that are programmed with up-to-date medical research, and they use them in their presentations to physicians. President Vangelo insists that his representatives try to gain a physician's trust by making balanced comparisons between Merck's products and those of competitors. See "Merck Has Made Biotech Work," *Fortune* (January 19, 1987): 59, 60, 64, for more details.

Merck's performance has also caught the attention of the stock market. From the beginning of 1986 through the first half of 1987, the stock price increased over 150 percent, trading at around 171 by late June 1987.

Conclusion

Merck has cultivated a quality image as the leading biotech firm. An industry pace-setting research and development effort combined with an astute marketing effort has made the company the industry leader and the country's most respected corporation. Unlike many other pharmaceutical companies, Merck has concentrated its energies, resources, and products in prescription drugs and has "put it all together" in this high-risk industry.

An example of the problems that can arise in the production planning process is provided by the electric utilities industry. At one time, demand for electricity could be estimated with reasonable accuracy and for fairly long periods. Figure 9–2 shows the annual U.S. electric power production for the 1955–86 period. From 1955 through 1973, production

Figure 9–2
U.S. Electric Power Production, 1955–86

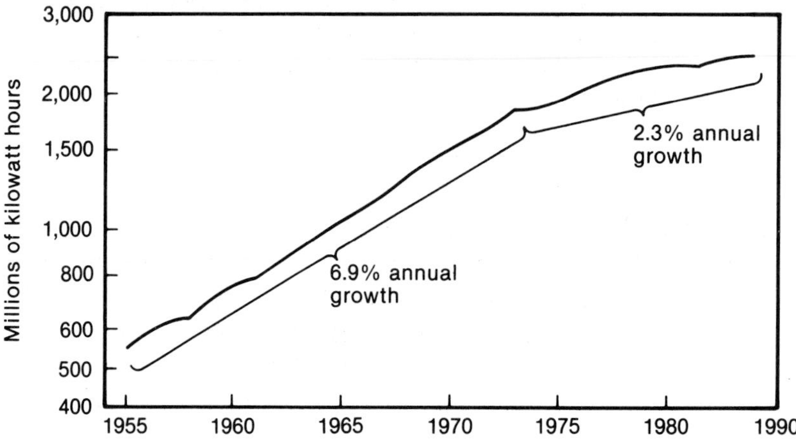

Source: U.S. Statistical Abstract, various issues.

grew at 6.9 percent per year with only very slight deviations from the trend line. Then, from 1973 through 1986, production slowed to increase at a rate of only 2.3 percent per year. If growth had continued at 6.9 percent per year, production in 1986 would have been 4.4 billion kilowatts instead of the 2.5 billion kilowatts actually produced.

Construction of an electric generating plant takes several years to complete. Therefore, long-range planning is vital for electric utility companies. Several utilities found themselves with excess capacity as power plants planned in the early 1970s came on line in the late 1970s and early 1980s. These plants caused problems for all of the parties involved—managements, utility rate commissions, consumers, and bondholders and stockholders. Managements filed for politically unpopular rate increases to cover the costs incurred in building the excess capacity. The North American Electric Reliability Council expects growth in generating capacity to increase at an average rate of only 1.6 percent per year through 1994. Load factors (representing capacity utilization) for the industry should move up slowly to 62 percent by 1994 from 61.3 percent in 1985.

Another dimension of production planning and control deals with the physical handling of raw materials and finished goods inventories. For a retailing firm such as K mart, the careful control of inventory reduces the need to have large price markdowns of seasonal merchandise. K mart installed point-of-sale terminals for the first time in 1987 to allow for better control of merchandise pricing and inventory control.

Diversification

Management's grand design should ideally include judicious expansion through acquisitions, which need to be carefully planned. R. J. Reynolds, a major producer of cigarettes, conducted a successful diversification effort in recent years. With the cash generated from profitable cigarette operations, the company diversified into the food industry by acquiring Nabisco. As a result, the combined firm, RJR Nabisco, compiled a respectable earnings growth record in recent years. American Brands, U.S. Tobacco, and other tobacco firms also successfully diversified into other areas.

Product and/or Service Analysis

Chapter 8 presented the life cycle framework for analyzing the various stages of growth for an industry. This approach is certainly relevant for identifying the various growth stages for individual firms as well. Investors should seek answers to many questions regarding the firm's products and/or services. At what stage of the life cycle are the firm's products? Are new products and models continually being introduced to offset the slower sales growth of more mature products? In the case of a retailing firm, does the firm have a sound marketing concept? Is the marketing concept updated to reflect changes of a demographic, social, or economic nature in the marketplace? Are the new services that consumers desire being introduced and marketed aggressively?

Nature and Diversity of Products

In an old but still relevant article, Jeremy Jenks enumerates the characteristics commonly found for the products of growth companies. Because these characteristics seem as useful today as they were in 1947, we list them below.

1. Direct price competition is moderate. (This was certainly true for Apple Computer in its early history. A firm's ability to increase prices to recover higher production costs is generally directly related to the degree of price competition for its products.)
2. The product can be produced at low cost compared to other methods of production.
3. The product can be produced in quantity and with uniform quality. (This is similar to the increasing use per capita standard developed in the previous chapter.)
4. The market for the products should be broad. A large number of potential customers should exist. (This aspect of product demand has an international dimension today.)
5. The product has special features or uses to distinguish it from competing products. (Polaroid's success with the field of instant photography is a good example of this generalization.)
6. The product is frequently protected by patents or by superior managerial know-how. (In the case of computer software, for example,

Investment Highlight

Texas Instruments (An "Air-Pocket" Stock)

This highlight shows how unexpected bad news can have a rapid and pronounced impact on the price of a stock. Additionally, the highlight reveals the impact price discounting can have on the profitability of a firm's product.

Description
On Friday, June 10, 1983, Texas Instruments (TI) disclosed that it would have a second quarter loss of approximately $100 million. This announcement came as a shock to investors and security analysts. Delayed in the opening of trading on Monday, June 13, TI's common closed at 118¼, down 39½ from its close on Friday.

Although shareholders were given a hint at TI's annual meeting in April that price cutting was harming the profitability of its computer, the 99/4A, the size of the write-down was not anticipated. TI initiated the price-cutting battle in August 1982 when it offered a $100 rebate that dropped the computer base price to $199. Commodore International retaliated, and TI was forced to sell the 99/4A for $99, or $15 to $20 below the estimated manufacturing cost.

TI has long had problems in the area of consumer electronics. Ming Li of Prescott Ball & Turben stated: "We had always been leery of the consumer electronics part of TI's business, but we did not expect this kind of a fiasco." *Business Week* (June 27, 1983): 88. Personal computer sales have expanded rapidly, but TI apparently expected more growth than occurred and was not able to make enough profit on the software and auxiliary equipment to overcome the loss on the basic hardware.

Conclusion
TI's strategy of rapid price-cutting failed to increase the size of the market (or TI's market share) enough to overcome the lack of profits on the computer. Shareholders were given some early warning signals, although faint, that TI could have trouble. The industry scenario, in light of the fact that TI's stock had risen from 70⅝ in early 1982, should have tempered investor enthusiasm. See "How Texas Instruments Shot Itself in the Foot," *Business Week* (June 27, 1983): 26, and "Texas Instruments and the Analysts: Love Was Blind," *Business Week* (June 27, 1983): 88.

consideration must be given to how enforceable the patents or licensing arrangements are when copyable products are sold to the public.)

The factors listed above refer primarily to the nature of the product. Investors should also consider whether the firm has the proper mix of products and/or services. Of concern is whether a firm has plentiful, low-cost, and reliable sources of supply because shortages have occurred on occasion in recent years.

An important intangible factor is the firm's reputation for producing quality products or giving superior service. The company making Maytag washers, for example, publicizes the reputation of its products for dependable and long-lived service. Publications such as *Consumer Reports* can assist investors by helping them to arrive at informed decisions regarding the quality associated with a firm's products.

Research and Development Programs

To remain competitive, a firm must continually invest money in *research and development* (R&D) programs. Investors need to examine the magnitude of a firm's R&D effort and determine its financial impact. Comparisons of R&D expenditures between firms and industries can be made on the basis of total dollars or as a percentage of sales (or some other suitable measure such as net income). R&D is clearly a very important consideration in high-technology industries such as electronics. In looking at the financial impact of R&D expenditures, investors should attempt to ascertain the sales and profitability of recent additions to the product line.

Table 9–1 provides data on R&D expenditures as a percentage of sales for various industry groups for 1986. R&D expenditures vary widely from industry to industry and also from company to company within an industry. High-technology industries, including producers of office equipment, spend the greatest percentage on R&D. Most of the major computer manufacturers spend in the 3 to 9 percent range. For example, Apple Computer spent 6.7 percent for R&D in 1986, up from a low 3.8 percent in 1985. The companies in the food industries have low R&D expenditures. For these industries, marketing expenditures are perhaps more critical for investors to examine.

Table 9–1
Research and Development Expenditures for Selected Industries, as a Percentage of 1986 Sales

Industry	High	Low	Average
Aerospace	6.7%	1.3%	4.5%
Automotive	4.0	0.8	3.7
Chemicals	7.6	0.3	4.1
Drugs	37.6	1.3	7.8
Electronics	14.7	0.5	4.4
Food and beverages	5.4	0.1	0.9
Fuel	2.6	0.2	0.8
Information processing	20.9	3.3	8.3
Leisure time	9.2	0.5	5.9
Machinery	17.0	0.3	3.3
Steel	2.5	0.4	0.5
Textiles and apparel	2.0	0.4	0.8

Source: "Research Spending Is Building Up to a Letdown," *Business Week*, June 22, 1987, pp. 139–160.

An Examination of Past Growth

We previously noted the need to observe management's track record. Investors need to assess the trend and consistency of sales, earnings, and dividends. As we have stated before, investors appear to value consistency. They need to see how well management has performed in all kinds of economic environments.

Figure 9–3 shows the dollar value of sales, earnings per share, and dividends per share for K mart from 1969 through 1986. The data are plotted on a semilog scale in order to show percentage changes. Table 9–2 reinforces the impression given by Figure 9–3 that the company has had a strong and reasonably consistent record of growth.

Investors must use a past growth record such as K mart's only as a beginning point in forecasting what the future will bring. K mart has performed well in the past, and investors could expect that it will continue

Figure 9–3
K mart Earnings per Share, Sales, and Dividends per Share, 1969–86

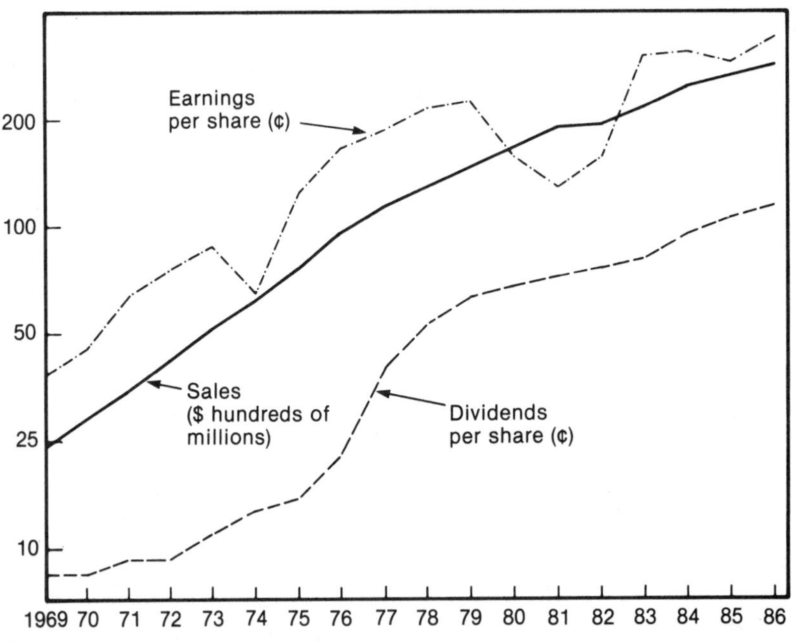

Source: Various K mart Annual Reports.

Table 9–2
K mart Corporation, Selected Statistics

			Compound Annual Rate of Growth		
	1969	*1986*	*1969–76*	*1976–86*	*1969–86*
Sales ($ millions)	2,185	24,152	21.2%	11.2%	15.2%
Earnings per share	$.347	$2.84	22.2	7.1	13.2
Dividends per share	$.089	$1.00	12.3	16.7	15.3

Source: Various K mart *Annual Reports.*

Table 9–3
Correlation Matrices for Various Companies, 1970–86

		Year	Earnings per Share	Dividends per Share
General Motors	Year	1.000		
	Earnings per share	.283	1.000	
	Dividends per share	.025	.706	1.000
IBM	Year	1.000		
	Earnings per share	.933	1.000	
	Dividends per share	.976	.922	1.000
Allegis	Year	1.000		
	Earnings per share	.039	1.000	
	Dividends per share	.220	.117	1.000
K mart	Year	1.000		
	Earnings per share	.900	1.000	
	Dividends per share	.977	.883	1.000

Figure 9–4
Earnings and Dividends per Share, K mart and Allegis, 1970–86

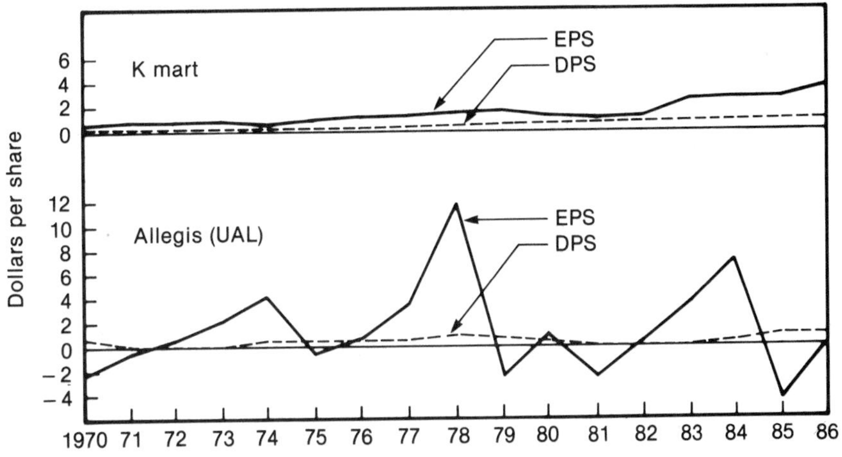

to perform well in future years if the industry outlook is as favorable as we noted in Chapter 8.

Table 9–3 shows the correlation matrices for selected variables for General Motors, International Business Machines, Allegis Corporation (UAL), and K mart. Annual values for earnings per share and dividends per share for the 1970–86 period were taken from *Value Line.* In the analysis of the data, the years were numbered consecutively, starting with one for 1970 and ending with seventeen for 1986, to give a sense of time to the correlations. The correlations for GM and Allegis indicate considerable instability. For example, the correlation, r, between the year variable and earnings per share for Allegis is .039, or an r^2 with time of .001. This low value indicates virtually no consistent trend over time, as Figure 9–4 clearly demonstrates. On the other hand, the correlation for K mart of .900, or an r^2 of .810, reveals a reasonably consistent trend, as can be seen in Figure 9–4.

Table 9–3 contains other interesting aspects. The relationship between earnings per share and dividends per share for General Motors is relatively high, with an r of .706. However, because earnings per share are very unstable (an r of .283) over time, forecasting dividends per share becomes difficult on the basis of trend analysis. The dividends per share over time for IBM are highly correlated with earnings per share; r is .922. Because earnings per share for IBM are fairly predictable over time, dividends also become fairly predictable. In essence, statistical forecasting methods such as regression analysis and projection of trend lines may be useful *if historical relationships are stable and investors expect the nature of the relationship in the future to be similar to that of the past* for the particular company.

Financial Statement Analysis

The financial markets in the last quarter of the century can be described as "dynamic." Investors continue to survey the markets looking for undervalued assets, unexploited opportunities, takeover candidates, turnaround situations, bankruptcy candidates, unused debt capacity, leverage buyout possibilities, and so on. Many investors conduct financial statement analysis as an early step in their search for profitable investment opportunities.

Our brief review of financial statement analysis will concentrate on three topics: (1) the various types of financial statements that are available to investors, (2) the general nature and quality of information contained in financial statements, and (3) financial ratio analysis. *Ratio analysis* takes the information presented in financial statements and presents it in a format that allows investors to derive a composite view of a company's performance as well as to identify possible difficulties or problem areas. Three categories of ratios are presented: (1) liquidity and activity, (2) leverage and capital structure, and (3) profitability-efficiency.

Types of Financial Statements

The three major types of financial statements are the balance sheet, the income statement (including the statement of retained earnings), and the statement of changes in financial position (commonly referred to as the sources and uses statement).

Balance Sheet

The balance sheet represents the position of the firm at a point in time. Its two major sections report (1) the assets of the firm and (2) the liabilities and shareholders' equity. Exhibit 9–1 shows the consolidated balance

Exhibit 9–1 K mart Balance Sheet

CONSOLIDATED BALANCE SHEETS

(Millions)	January 28, 1987	January 29, 1986
Assets		
Current Assets:		
Cash (includes temporary investments of $296 and $352, respectively)	**$ 521**	$ 627
Merchandise inventories	**5,153**	4,537
Accounts receivable and other current assets	**390**	363
Total current assets	**6,064**	5,527
Investments in Affiliated Retail Companies	**317**	293
Property and Equipment–net	**3,594**	3,644
Other Assets and Deferred Charges	**603**	527
	$10,578	$9,991
Liabilities and Shareholders' Equity		
Current Liabilities:		
Long-term debt due within one year	**$ 4**	$ 15
Notes payable	**296**	127
Accounts payable–trade	**2,207**	1,908
Accrued payrolls and other liabilities	**639**	624
Taxes other than income taxes	**223**	218
Income taxes	**162**	198
Total current liabilities	**3,531**	3,090
Capital Lease Obligations	**1,600**	1,713
Long-Term Debt	**1,011**	1,456
Other Long-Term Liabilities	**315**	345
Deferred Income Taxes	**182**	114
Shareholders' Equity	**3,939**	3,273
	$10,578	$9,991

See accompanying Notes to Consolidated Financial Statements.

Source: K mart Corporation *1986 Annual Report.*

sheet from K mart's *1986 Annual Report*. The balance sheet is *consolidated* because combined accounts of the company and its subsidiaries are reported.

Exhibit 9–1 indicates that K mart's total assets as of January 28, 1987, were $10.6 billion. The firm financed these total assets either by incurring a liability (debt) or by obtaining capital from its shareholders (equity). Of K mart's total liabilities amounting to $6.6 billion, $3.1 were long-term liabilities and $3.5 billion were current liabilities. K mart's stockholders invested $3.9 billion in the firm, including both the price originally paid for the shares (common stock plus capital in excess of par value) and income retained by the firm for use in the business.

Income and Retained Earnings Statement

Exhibit 9–2 shows the consolidated statements of both current and retained earnings from K mart's *1986 Annual Report*. For the fiscal year ending January 28, 1987, K mart sales and other revenues were $24.152 billion. Total costs and expenses of doing business were $23.124 billion, resulting in pre–tax earnings of $1.028 billion. The company paid $458 million in income taxes, or 44.6 percent of pre–tax earnings. After adjusting for discontinued operations and extraordinary items in the net amount of a $12 million credit, net earnings available for the common stockholders were $582 million. K mart's statement of retained earnings is also shown in Exhibit 9–2. For fiscal 1986, the company added $389 million to retained earnings ($582 million net income less $193 million dividends) and thereby increased the total at the end of the fiscal year to $3.347 billion.

K mart's *1986 Annual Report* presented the statement of changes in financial position for the latest two years. In Exhibit 9–3, we have reproduced this statement of changes in financial position. Investors find this statement useful for indicating the direction of change in certain financial variables. Any major shifts in a company's financing structure or asset utilization can often be identified by inspecting sources and uses statements.

Quality of the Financial Statement

Financial statements are the basic raw material from which investors analyze a firm's performance and future prospects. Investors recognize, however, that a financial statement published by a firm is sometimes an ambiguous source of information. Ambiguities result because considerable leeway is allowed in the techniques and accounting principles that can be employed to prepare the balance sheet and income statement. Selection of a particular accounting technique is not typically related to corporate dishonesty or attempts to deceive investors. Rather, a basic disagreement may exist over how some information should be reported. In other situations, a conflict may exist between the way transactions are recorded as dictated by accounting principles and the way economic val-

Exhibit 9–2 K mart Income and Retained Earnings Statement

CONSOLIDATED STATEMENTS OF INCOME

	Fiscal Year Ended		
(Millions, except per-share data)	January 28, 1987	January 29, 1986	January 30, 1985
Sales	**$23,812**	$22,035	$20,762
Licensee fees and rental income	**234**	223	206
Equity in income of affiliated retail companies	**83**	76	65
Interest income	**23**	23	39
	24,152	22,357	21,072
Cost of merchandise sold (including buying and occupancy costs)	**17,258**	15,987	15,095
Selling, general and administrative expenses	**4,936**	4,673	4,268
Advertising	**581**	554	543
Interest expense:			
Debt	**171**	205	147
Capital lease obligations	**178**	181	184
	23,124	21,600	20,237
Income from continuing retail operations before income taxes	**1,028**	757	835
Income taxes	**458**	285	332
Income from continuing retail operations	**570**	472	503
Discontinued operations (Note B)	**28**	(251)	(4)
Extraordinary item (Note I)	**(16)**	–	–
Net income for the year	**$ 582**	$ 221	$ 499
Earnings per common and common equivalent share:			
Continuing retail operations	**$ 2.84**	$ 2.42	$ 2.58
Discontinued operations	**.14**	(1.27)	(.02)
Extraordinary item	**(.08)**	–	–
Net income	**$ 2.90**	$ 1.15	$ 2.56
Weighted average shares outstanding	**201.5**	197.4	197.3

See accompanying Notes to Consolidated Financial Statements.

The consolidated statements of income for prior periods have been restated for discontinued operations.

Per share amounts and weighted average shares outstanding have been adjusted to reflect the three-for-two stock split declared March 24, 1987.

Source: K mart Corporation *1986 Annual Report.*

Exhibit 9–2 *(continued)*

CONSOLIDATED STATEMENTS OF SHAREHOLDERS' EQUITY

($ Millions)	Common Stock Shares	Common Stock Amount	Capital in Excess of Par Value	Retained Earnings	Treasury Shares	Foreign Currency Translation Adjustment	Total Shareholders' Equity
Balance at January 25, 1984	**188,866,208**	**$126**	**$293**	**$2,569**	**$**	**$ (48)**	**$2,940**
Net income for the year				499			499
Cash dividends declared, $.84 per share				(155)			(155)
Common stock sold under stock option and employees' savings plans and conversion of debentures	1,178,232	1	20				21
Purchase of 2,517,750 treasury shares, at cost					(51)		(51)
Foreign currency translation adjustment						(20)	(20)
Balance at January 30, 1985	**190,044,440**	**127**	**313**	**2,913**	**(51)**	**(68)**	**3,234**
Net income for the year				221			221
Cash dividends declared, $.92 per share				(176)			(176)
Common stock sold under stock option and employees' savings plans and conversion of debentures	1,478,041	1	30				31
Foreign currency translation adjustment						(37)	(37)
Balance at January 29, 1986	**191,522,481**	**128**	**343**	**2,958**	**(51)**	**(105)**	**3,273**
Net income for the year				582			582
Cash dividends declared, $1.00 per share				(193)			(193)
Three-for-two stock split		67	(67)				–
Common stock sold under stock option and employees' savings plans	2,792,834	2	63				65
Common stock issued for conversion of debentures	7,867,995	5	181				186
Reissue of 666,328 treasury shares for employees' savings plan			8		14		22
Foreign currency translation adjustment						4	4
Balance at January 28, 1987	**202,183,310**	**$202**	**$528**	**$3,347**	**$(37)**	**$(101)**	**$3,939**

Common stock, authorized 250,000,000 shares, $1.00 par value.

Ten million shares of no par value preferred stock with voting and cumulative dividend rights are authorized but unissued. Currently there are no plans for its issuance.

See accompanying Notes to Consolidated Financial Statements.

Cash dividends declared and common stock shares have been adjusted to reflect the three-for-two stock split declared March 24, 1987 [Note C].

Source: K mart Corporation *1986 Annual Report.*

Exhibit 9–3 K mart Statement of Changes in Financial Position

CONSOLIDATED STATEMENTS OF CHANGES IN FINANCIAL POSITION

	Fiscal Year Ended		
(Millions)	**January 28, 1987**	**January 29, 1986**	**January 30, 1985**
Cash Provided by (Used for):			
Operations			
Income from continuing retail operations	**$ 570**	$ 472	$ 503
Noncash charges (credits) to earnings:			
Depreciation and amortization	**377**	344	289
Deferred income taxes	**58**	90	14
Undistributed equity income	**(23)**	(23)	(16)
Increase in other long-term liabilities	**52**	44	35
Other–net	**13**	20	9
Total from continuing retail operations	**1,047**	947	834
Discontinued operations			
Gain (loss) from discontinued operations	**28**	(251)	(4)
Cash provided by discontinued operations	**214**	–	–
Items not affecting cash–net	**(95)**	249	17
Total from discontinued operations	**147**	(2)	13
Extraordinary item	**(16)**	–	–
Cash provided by (used for) current assets and current liabilities:			
(Increase) decrease in inventories	**(677)**	387	(792)
Inventories of acquired companies	**–**	(336)	(214)
Increase (decrease) in accounts payable	**312**	(9)	200
Other–net	**(59)**	215	(122)
Total	**(424)**	257	(928)
Financing			
Increase in long-term debt and notes payable	**169**	563	646
Reduction in long-term debt and notes payable	**(452)**	(310)	(17)
Obligations incurred under capital leases	**31**	18	44
Reduction in capital lease obligations	**(80)**	(77)	(77)
Common stock issued	**259**	31	21
Reissuance (purchase) of treasury stock	**14**	–	(51)
Net cash provided by (used for) financing	**(59)**	225	566
Dividends Paid	**(187)**	(171)	(151)
Investments			
Additions to owned and leased property	**(583)**	(561)	(646)
Owned property of acquired companies	**–**	(156)	(94)
Proceeds from the sale of property	**36**	40	62
Increased investment in affiliated retail companies	**(8)**	(107)	(3)
Other assets and deferred charges of acquired companies	**–**	(317)	(151)
Other–net	**(59)**	(20)	(38)
Net cash used for investments	**(614)**	(1,121)	(870)
Net Increase (Decrease) in Cash	**$ (106)**	$ 135	$ (536)

See accompanying Notes to Consolidated Financial Statements.
Certain prior year amounts have been restated for the effect of discontinued operations.

Source: K mart Corporation *1986 Annual Report.*

ues change in a firm. In still other cases, the financial community may not know how to reflect certain situations in financial statements. Instead of listing possible problem areas, we present an example of one problem that will suffice as a warning to unwary investors who are inclined to accept the data given in financial statements as correct and unambiguous.

A contemporary problem of considerable importance concerns the treatment of inventories and the effect of this on the cost of goods sold. Suppose a firm sells 100 units of its product at $15 per unit to produce gross sales of $1,500. Exhibit 9–4 compares two legitimate methods to account for the value of the inventory. The LIFO (last-in, first-out) technique places the cost associated with the last items purchased into the cost-of-goods-sold account. Under FIFO (first-in, first-out), the cost associated with the last items purchased is included in the ending inventory account and the cost associated with the first items purchased is included in the cost-of-goods-sold account.

Exhibit 9–4 shows income statements using each inventory method. With LIFO, the firm has a net profit of $50, but with FIFO, the reported profit is $70. The FIFO technique generates an increase in profit of 40 percent, even though physically the inventory is identical. In other words, this firm can increase its reported profits by 40 percent merely by using FIFO instead of LIFO. The effect on earnings is tied directly to price changes associated with the firm's purchases. As prices increase, FIFO will typically report larger profits. This inventory example underscores the fact that accounting data do not always provide a clear picture of the financial condition of the firm.

Exhibit 9–5 is an analysis from Standard and Poor's *Outlook* that discusses four accounting items of special importance in annual reports during the 1980s. Debt-equity swaps, LIFO inventory liquidations, restructured operations, and foreign currency translations are examined for their impact on reported earnings. Investors should be careful to recog-

Exhibit 9–4 **Earnings with LIFO and FIFO**

	Income Statement Using			
	LIFO		*FIFO*	
Sales—100 @ $15		$1,500		$1,500
Cost of goods sold				
Beginning inventory, 10 @ $10	$ 100		$ 100	
Purchases, 50 @ $11	550		550	
50 @ $12	600		600	
	$1,250		$1,250	
Ending inventory	100 (10 @ $10)		120 (10 @ $12)	
		1,150		1,130
Gross profit		$ 350		$ 370
Other expenses		300		300
Net profit		$ 50		$ 70

FOUR KEY ITEMS ANALYZED

Annual Reports: Don't Overlook Special Items

With annual reports arriving in the mail almost daily, investors may be tempted to scan each one quickly, then lay it aside.

The chairman's letter, financial highlights and the glossy product photos usually get most of the shareholder's attention. But the reports contain a lot of vital information, often tucked away in financial footnotes, that is well worth spending some time to dig out. This is especially true with respect to special or non-recurring charges or credits that may either have lowered or have enhanced 1982's reported results.

Over the past year, four types of items had a major effect on many companies' reported earnings—debt-equity swaps, LIFO inventory liquidations, restructured operations and foreign currency translations. Each is briefly discussed below.

Debt-equity swaps, a popular technique for retiring long-term debt and reducing interest payments, helped many companies spruce up reported earnings last year. Some companies that obtained sizable non-recurring earnings gains via debt-for-equity swaps were ALLIED CORP. ($1.24 per share), U.S. STEEL ($0.87), ARA SERVICES ($0.43), TEXTRON ($0.28) and HERCULES ($0.25). While a few companies, such as HERCULES, treated the gain as an extraordinary item, most included the gain in operating income.

In each case, the company bought back a sizable volume of older, low-coupon bonds at a deep discount from face value, posting the difference to earnings and paying for the bonds mainly with newly issued common stock. Since the company didn't pay cash for any of the bonds, but swapped equity for them instead, the transaction was tax-free.

LIFO inventory liquidations. Reductions of inventories valued under the LIFO method generally bolstered operating earnings last year. Under the LIFO (last in, first out) method, the latest inventory costs charged against sales tend to approximate the cost of replacing the goods. LIFO thus eliminates the lag effect of the widely used FIFO (first in, first out) method in which the costs of the oldest inventory costs are matched first against current sales, thereby tending to overstate reported earnings during a period of rapid inflation.

While LIFO tends to reduce inventory profits during periods of rising prices, it can have the opposite effect when inventories are being liquidated. When a company pares inventory on a large enough scale, it digs into older, lower-cost layers of inventory. As sales are made, these "frozen" older costs are matched against higher current prices, buoying earnings.

LIFO inventory profits were substantial last year for many companies in the chemical, tire, textile, oil and steel industries. TEXACO and GULF, for example, both drew down oil and gas inventories at a rapid rate in 1982, in the face of a deepening oil glut. The inventory liquidation yielded a $503 million earnings benefit to TEXACO, accounting for about one-third of the company's 1982 net income. GULF reduced its LIFO-valued inventories by 32 million barrels in 1982, thereby adding $360 million to earnings, more than enough to offset the losses incurred in the company's U.S. marketing and refining operations.

In the tire industry, GOODYEAR slashed domestic inventories, increasing its net income by $51 million, or $0.69 a share. Without the inventory profits, earnings would have been off by 17%; instead, they were essentially the same as those of 1981.

Restructured operations. Owing to the business slump, many companies, particularly in such cyclical industries as steel, farm equipment and mining, realigned their operations in 1982, closing down marginal facilities or selling off assets that did not fit well with managements' long-term strategies. Some restructurings were minor, involving no more than the elimination of one or two outmoded plants. Others were more fundamental. In some cases, an entire division was sold; in others, a line of business was eliminated.

While the shedding of cash-draining operations may have positive investment implications for the long term, current earnings are often battered by the substantial one-time charges against income.

Investors need to be alert to such charge-offs, since they tend to distort reported earnings and may significantly affect other financial and investment yardsticks such as a company's net worth or debt-equity ratio.

BETHLEHEM STEEL, for example, sustained a net loss of $1.5 billion in 1982, two-thirds of which was due to a non-recurring charge relating mostly to the shut-down of obsolete steel-making plants. By eliminating 16% of its steel-making capacity, the company will be able to devote more of its resources to modernizing those remaining facilities that have the best prospects for future profitability.

Under current accounting rules, the financial impact of major restructurings must be clearly identified in a company's financial statements and related footnotes. If the restructuring or "asset redeployment" program involves the disposal or discontinuance of a complete line of business—even a relatively small segment—the results must be segregated, under the heading "discontinued operations." In this case, "earnings

Exhibit 9–5 *(continued)*

Annual Reports

from continuing operations" become the reported profits on which most investors will focus.

The divestment of partial lines of business may also give rise to non-recurring losses, but these write-offs usually don't receive as full-disclosure as discontinued operations. Ordinarily, these items will be described in the footnotes to financial statements. If the adjustments are large enough, they will also be separately identified in the income statement.

RALSTON PURINA is a case in point. In the fiscal year ending September 1982, the diversified food company incurred a $92 million charge ($0.87 per share) from the sale of its unprofitable tuna vessels and European pet food businesses. Since the company is remaining in the seafood and pet food businesses, the transaction was not considered a discontinued operation. But in the same year, RALSTON decided to phase out its entire mushroom operations, writing off an additional $0.18 a share. Last year's earnings of $0.87 a share, however, only reflect non-recurring losses only from the tuna and pet food activities.

Other companies that had sizable non-recurring restructuring charges in 1982 (on a per share basis) were NATIONAL STEEL ($12.26), AMF ($0.85), IC INDUSTRIES ($1.49), and BELL & HOWELL ($3.80).

Such write-offs typically include much more than the net book value of property, plant and equipment, adjusted for estimated sales or scrap value. Personnel costs associated with discontinued operations can also be substantial. Besides accrued salaries and severance payments, companies must absorb the present value of unfunded pension costs. In BETHLEHEM STEEL'S case, some $700 million of the $1 billion restructuring write-off related to employment costs.

Foreign currency translations. A change in the accounting rule governing foreign currency gains and losses benefited the reported earnings of many companies in 1982. The new accounting guideline, known as FASB Statement 52, requires companies with international operations to place certain types of foreign currency translation gains or losses directly in the shareholders' equity account of the balance sheet, rather than in the income statement. Since the dollar was strong relative to most foreign currencies last year, many companies experienced sizable unrealized currency translation losses. Under the former accounting rules, these losses would in most cases have reduced net income, but last year their absence tended to boost earnings from international activities.

The new accounting rule, however, did not help those companies with large operations in countries with highly inflationary economies, such as Mexico and Brazil. They were hard-hit by the sharp declines that occurred in the exchange rate of the peso and cruzeiro.

FASB 52 stipulates that companies doing business in "hyperinflationary" economies—those experiencing inflation rates of 100% of more over a three-year period—must absorb any foreign exchange losses in current earnings, whether they are realized or not. When a hyperinflationary country devalues its currency, as Mexico did three times last year, U.S. companies' earnings are reduced in two ways. First, profits from ongoing operations shrink because each unit of local currency translates into fewer dollars. Secondly, the value of monetary assets and liabilities must be marked down and the charge taken against earnings each quarter, depending on how rapidly the local currency declines.

This double-barrelled adverse impact was largely felt by multinational companies in consumer goods and packaged foods fields. In a number of cases, it offset the positive effect of the accounting rule on reported results from operations in less-inflationary economies. Among the companies whose results were severely penalized by Latin American currency problems were CELANESE ($5 a share), GILLETTE ($0.56), MOHASCO ($1.59) and AVON PRODUCTS ($0.30).

Source: The Outlook (Standard & Poor's Corporation).

nize the importance of accounting practices on reported earnings and to determine what affect, if any, the conditions and their reporting have on security prices.

Common Size Financial Statements

Because of the size differences among firms, investors often reduce the major financial statements to a common size by converting the statements to percentage terms. This conversion allows the investor to conveniently compare one company in an industry with other companies in the same industry. Also, it allows investors to observe potentially significant trends that may have developed within the firm over the years.

Ratio Analysis

The analysis of financial statements involves the calculation of ratios in order to get a composite picture of a firm's financial performance and health. Potential investors are interested in both the absolute level of the ratios and their trends over time. Comparing ratios for different companies in the same industry is often useful in determining whether any particular company differs substantially from industry norms. We will examine various ratio classifications, including liquidity, leverage, activity, and profitability-efficiency.

Although investors seldom agree on what ratios should be measured and how individual ratios should be calculated, we present a set of ratios commonly used for conducting financial statement analyses. Investors must be careful when comparing the ratios they calculate with those published by the financial services, such as *Value Line*, to make sure that the ratios are defined in exactly the same manner. Otherwise, any comparison, as with industry averages, will be of little value.

Interpretation of financial ratio data demands that the investor have a good deal of skill. Financial statement analysis is in some ways similar to solving a puzzle. Each ratio provides a look at a small part of the puzzle, but its true importance is not known until the whole picture is put together. Investors want to deduce from ratio analysis a picture of the "health" of the firm at a point in time. We arrive at the composite view by combining insights gained from each of the individual parts.

Exhibit 9–6 reports the key financial ratios for the retailing industry, based on the average ratios derived from twelve representative companies. K mart's ratios are also represented so that its performance can be compared with the industry. The data for calculating the ratios presented in this section are taken from the fiscal 1986 reports for K mart as presented in Exhibits 9–1 and 9–2.

Exhibit 9–6 **Financial Ratios: K mart versus Retailing Industry**

Financial Ratio	*Industry*	*K mart*
Liquidity		
Current	2.49 ×	1.72 ×
Quick	1.20 ×	.26 ×
Activity		
Inventory turnover	6.86 ×	3.6 ×
Average collection period	6.9 days	5.8 days
Leverage		
Debt to total assets	45.5%	62.8%
Times financial charges earned	4.47 ×	3.95 ×
Profitability-efficiency		
Return on revenue	10.5%	5.7%
Return on total assets	16.4%	13.8%
Return on equity	17.0%	17.8%

Liquidity and Activity Ratios

Liquidity and activity ratios are concerned with the firm's management of its working capital position. Liquidity ratios measure the firm's ability to meet its obligations out of the cash account or by using assets that will be converted to cash within a relatively short period of time. The four ratios we will examine are the current ratio, the acid-test or quick ratio, the inventory turnover ratio, and the average collection period.

Current Ratio

The current ratio is determined by dividing current assets by current liabilities. K mart's current ratio was 1.72.

$$\text{Current ratio} = \frac{\text{Current assets}}{\text{Current liabilities}} = \frac{\$6{,}064}{\$3{,}531} = 1.72$$

Acid-Test Ratio

The acid-test ratio is determined by dividing current assets (excluding inventory) by total current liabilities. Inventory is the least liquid of the current assets, and by excluding it from the liquid asset category, a more restrictive definition of the firm's ability to meet current liabilities can be obtained. K mart's acid-test ratio was determined as follows:

$$\text{Acid-test ratio} = \frac{\begin{array}{c}\text{Current assets}\\ \text{less inventory}\end{array}}{\text{Current liabilities}} = \frac{\$911}{\$3{,}531} = .26$$

The low .26 ratio reflects the common practice by K mart of financing merchandise inventory with trade credit and is not likely an indication of a liquidity problem.

Evidence of good financial management in other aspects of the firm will also lessen our concern about the level of cash. One of the questions investors need to consider is how the firm is managing its assets. Are inventories under good control? Is inventory "fresh" or has slow-moving inventory accumulated? Are accounts receivable being collected within a reasonable period of time? These and similar questions can be answered with the assistance of activity ratios that measure inventory turnover and average collection period.

Inventory Turnover

Inventory turnover measures the speed with which inventory moves from acquisition and manufacture to the ultimate sale. It is calculated by dividing the cost of goods sold by the average inventory during the period for which the ratio is being calculated. Ideally, we would prefer to have an average inventory figure based on weekly or monthly data, although these data are not often available to investors. The following calculation uses the average of the fiscal, year-end figures for 1985 and 1986 to calculate K mart's inventory turnover figure:

$$\text{Inventory turnover} = \frac{\text{Cost of goods sold}}{\text{Average inventory}}$$

$$= \frac{\$17{,}258}{(\$5{,}153 + \$4{,}537)/2} = 3.6 \times$$

When compared with industry averages, K mart's turnover ratio was low. This is inconsistent with the past company strategy of pushing for relatively high turnover and placing low markups on merchandise.

Accounts Receivable Turnover

This ratio is calculated by dividing the sales figure by the average of the accounts receivable. Ideally, we should use only credit sales, but this figure is not usually available. Instead, we have to use total sales. We will use the average of the 1985 and 1986 fiscal year-end accounts receivable figures in the turnover ratio calculation because we do not have interim report data.

$$\text{Receivables turnover} = \frac{\text{Sales}}{\text{Average accounts receivable}}$$

$$= \frac{\$23{,}812}{(\$390 + \$363)/2} = 63.2 \times$$

If the receivables turnover figure is divided into 365 days, the result is the average collection period; for K mart, this amounted to 5.8 days.

$$\text{Average collection period} = \frac{\text{365 days}}{\text{Annual receivables turnover}} = \frac{365}{63.2} = 5.8 \text{ days}$$

Comparisons between firms within the retailing industry are difficult to make on the basis of the receivables turnover ratios because several of the companies make sales only on a cash or a bank credit card basis.

Leverage and Capital Structure Ratios

Leverage ratios provide a means of examining the use and impact of debt within a firm. Capital market conditions have reinforced investors' concerns about the need to have financial flexibility. The investing public has become aware of quality considerations, and securities of poor quality have come under increased scrutiny by investment analysts and financial market regulators.

In this section, we examine three measures of leverage. These are the composition of the firm's capital structure, the debt-to-asset ratio, and the times-interest-earned ratio.

Capitalization Ratio

A useful starting point when analyzing a firm's use of debt is to calculate the percentage breakdown of the capital structure. In this calculation, investors are interested in the sources of financing for the firm's long-term capital. The calculation below gives K mart's capital structure as of January 28, 1987:

Long-term debt	$1,011
Total common stockholders' equity	3,939
Total long-term capital	$4,950

Of K mart's capital structure, 20.4 percent is in the form of long-term debt. Whether this is a prudent figure depends on many different factors. Some of these factors include the amount of short-term debt the firm is using, the amount of interest relative to net income, the stability of its revenues and earnings, the past and expected growth of income for the firm, the maturity structure of the long-term debt, and the use of leases. Not included in the capital structure breakdown is the amount of short-term debt a firm is using. This amount is included in some of the other leverage measures we will now examine.

Debt-to-Asset Ratio

A measure that tells inventors what percentage of the firm's assets are being financed by various forms of debt is called the debt-to-asset ratio. To derive this ratio, we add the balance sheet amounts for all the categories of debt and divide the result by the total assets. The debt-to-asset ratio indicates that approximately 62.8 percent of K mart's assets were financed by debt of all types, which included leases.

$$\text{Debt-to-asset ratio} = \frac{\text{Total debt}}{\text{Total assets}} = \frac{\$6{,}639}{\$10{,}578} = 62.8\%$$

In comparison to the industry average ratio of 45.5 percent, K mart made greater use of leverage than the typical retailing firm in 1986. The major difference between K mart and the industry occurred because K mart had more short-term debt relative to other financing sources than other retailing firms in the industry sample.

Times-Interest-Earned Ratio

One of the fundamental calculations investors can make is to determine the relationship between the income earned by the firm and the interest charges that must be paid. This relationship is commonly called the times-interest-earned ratio. The ratio is often calculated on a before-tax basis, although it can be and often is calculated after taxes. We restrict our discussion to the before-tax method because interest is a before-tax deduction. The times-interest-earned ratio for K mart was 8.05 times.

$$\text{Times interest earned} = \frac{\text{Earnings before interest and taxes}}{\text{Interest expense}} = \frac{\$1{,}377}{\$171} = 8.05\times$$

K mart's coverage was substantial, as earnings could have declined to roughly 12 percent (1/8.05) of the 1986 level before the firm would be technically insolvent. *Technical insolvency* occurs when earnings are not sufficient to meet the firm's debt obligations. Two points need to be made, however. First, the interest coverage figure does not include other fixed financial obligations such as lease payments. K mart's interest expense for capital lease obligations was $178 million in 1986. When this amount is added to the interest expense for debt of $171 million, the times-fixed-financial-charges-earned figure would decline to 3.95 times ($1,377/$349). In comparison to the industry, K mart's fixed financial charges coverage was somewhat below the average of 4.47 times.

The second point deals with the relationship between the ability of a firm to carry the burden of debt and the profitability of the firm. As we saw in Chapter 5, K mart is a profitable firm when measured by the rate of return on stockholders' equity. This profitability and a relatively low dividend payout percentage combined make K mart's debt burden quite manageable.

Profitability-Efficiency Ratios

We group *profitability* and *efficiency ratios* together for discussion purposes because they are really two different ways of examining the same basic aspects of a firm. If a firm is efficiently managed, it tends to be profitable. Likewise, a profitable firm tends to be efficiently managed. Hence, investors should reach the same general conclusion concerning the quality of management by looking at either type of ratio. We should note, however, that an efficient firm is not necessarily profitable nor is the profitable firm necessarily efficient.

The profitability ratios we will examine are the rate of return on revenue, the rate of return on assets, and the rate of return on stockholders' equity. The rate of return on revenue and assets will be examined on a before-interest and before-tax basis. This will provide a better picture of the efficiency or *earning power* of the assets and will allow the separation of asset efficiency from the firm's use of financial leverage. The rate of return on stockholders' equity will be examined on an after-interest and after-tax basis in an attempt to measure profitability from the stockholders' point of view.

Return on Revenue

To avoid the influence of financial leverage and extraordinary items, the return on revenue is calculated by taking the ratio of *earnings before interest and taxes* (EBIT) to revenue. K mart achieved a return on revenue of 5.7 percent.

$$\text{Return on revenue} = \frac{\text{Earnings before interest and taxes}}{\text{Sales (or revenue)}}$$

$$= \frac{\$1{,}028 + \$171 + \$178}{\$24{,}152}$$

$$= \frac{\$1{,}377}{\$24{,}152} = 5.7\%$$

Return on Assets

The return on assets is also expressed on a before-interest and before-tax basis and is the ratio of EBIT to the total assets held at the beginning of the year. The return on assets for K mart was 13.8 percent.

$$\text{Return on assets} = \frac{\text{EBIT}}{\text{Total assets (start of period)}} = \frac{\$1{,}377}{\$9{,}991} = 13.8\%$$

Return on Equity

We come to the measure of profitability that most directly relates to the prosperity of the common stockholder. The return on stockholders' equity (ROE) is the ratio of earnings after taxes to the stockholders' equity *at the beginning of the year.* Because we want to measure the earning power available to the common stockholder, preferred stock and preferred dividends are excluded. For the same reason, the calculation is on an after-interest and after-tax basis. K mart's ROE was 17.8 percent.

$$\text{Return on equity} = \frac{\text{Earnings after taxes}}{\text{Stockholders' equity at start of period}} = \frac{\$582}{\$3{,}273} = 17.8\%$$

A return of 17.8 percent was adequate, but before drawing any conclusions, a comparison with past performance as well as with the performance of other firms in the same industry should be made. The 1983–87 boom in consumer spending caused a significant rise in profitability for the retailing industry, and K mart was not left out. K mart's ROE figure was .8 percent above the industry average. In comparison to historical levels, the 1986 ROE was the highest achieved by K mart since the late 1970s.

Tax Reconciliation

Calculation of the tax rate has a use in financial statement analysis. If this figure falls substantially below the applicable federal tax rate, the investor may need to do some additional investigation in the form of a *tax reconciliation.*

The corporate tax rate before 1987 for larger corporations was approximately 46 percent. Therefore, an effective tax rate below the 46 percent figure indicated that some of the income was not fully taxable. For income beginning in 1987, the applicable tax rate for larger corporations should fall in the 35 to 37 percent range. In addition, special tax laws may exist, as in the case of the petroleum industry, that tend to reduce the effective tax rate. Although the Tax Reform Act of 1986 led to tax simplification in many areas, it contained many special provisions and conditions. Investors should be aware that the tax laws remain very complex and that effective tax rates for a given corporation can be difficult to reconcile.

Exhibit 9–7 shows a tax reconciliation presented in K mart's *1986 Annual Report*. The investor is presented with information showing reasons why the effective tax rates for the three most recent years were less than the 46 percent rate stated in the law. Notice that investment tax credits declined in 1986 owing to the repeal of this item by the 1986 Tax Reform Act.

Book Value

Book value is the summation of the contributions over time made by shareholders to the firm. To calculate book value per share, the stockholders' equity is divided by the number of shares outstanding. For example, K mart's *1986 Annual Report* stated the shareholders' equity (book value) per share at $19.66 as of January 28, 1987.

Of what importance is the book value per share to the investor? The answer to this question depends primarily on the industry classification of the company being analyzed. For many industrial companies, the relationship between the market price of the company's stock and the book value per share is not very meaningful. Based on K mart's stock price range of $44½ to $28¾ in the 1986–87 period, price exceeded book value by 2.26 to 1.46 times. On May 6, 1987, K mart's common stock sold at $40¼ per share, a price over twice its book value. This stock was probably not selling primarily on the basis of book value considerations.

For firms in the financial service field and for public utilities, book value per share assumes a greater degree of importance. For banks, insurance companies, and investment companies, investors should take note of the book-value-to-market-value relationship as a part of a complete investment analysis of the firm. Because the assets of the financially based firms could be liquidated at a price close to the value carried on the company's books, the book value may have some bearing on market value. This does not imply that an investor should necessarily buy securities in these financial areas from the firm with the lowest ratio of market price to book value, only that consideration should be given to the historic relationship between book and market price.

The Composite View of K mart

On the basis of the financial statement analysis for K mart, what composite picture emerges, if any? K mart was in a period of prosperity in

Exhibit 9–7 Tax Reconciliation for K mart, 1986

(H) Income Taxes

Components of income from continuing retail operations before income taxes follow:

(Millions)	**1986**	1985	1984
U.S.	**$ 951**	$710	$800
Foreign	**77**	47	35
Total	**$1,028**	$757	$835

The provision for income taxes consists of:

(Millions)	**1986**	1985	1984
Current:			
Federal	**$ 320**	$148	$265
State and local	**57**	38	49
Foreign	**23**	9	4
Deferred:			
Excess of tax over book depreciation	**46**	51	45
LIFO inventory	**(4)**	48	6
Lease capitalization	**(10)**	(12)	(13)
Other	**26**	3	(24)
Total income taxes	**$ 458**	$285	$332

A reconciliation of the company's effective tax rate for continuing retail operations to the federal statutory rate follows:

(Millions)	**1986**	1985	1984	**1986**	1985	1984
Federal statutory rate	**$473**	$348	$384	**46.0%**	46.0%	46.0%
State and local taxes, net of federal tax benefit	**31**	21	27	**3.0**	2.8	3.2
Tax credits	**(15)**	(43)	(46)	**(1.4)**	(5.7)	(5.6)
Equity in income of affiliated retail companies subject to lower tax rates	**(31)**	(31)	(26)	**(3.0)**	(4.1)	(3.1)
Other	**–**	(10)	(7)	**–**	(1.4)	(.8)
Total income taxes	**$458**	$285	$332	**44.6%**	37.6%	39.7%

The amounts shown on the consolidated balance sheets for deferred income taxes result principally from the difference between financial statement and income tax depreciation, reduced by the effect of accounting for certain leases as capital leases. At January 28, 1987 and January 29, 1986, the net amount of current deferred taxes included in accrued payrolls and other liabilities was $5 million and $35 million, respectively.

Investment credits were $4 million in 1986, compared with $26 million and $33 million in 1985 and 1984, respectively. The decrease in investment credits in 1986 is primarily due to their repeal under the Tax Reform Act of 1986.

Undistributed earnings of subsidiaries, which are intended to be permanently reinvested, totaled $220 million at January 28, 1987.

Source: K mart Corporation *1986 Annual Report.*

1986, helped by high levels of consumer spending. The company experienced a low inventory turnover and low profit margins that generated a less than average return on assets when compared to the industry. By using higher than average levels of debt, K mart benefited from the positive use of leverage. Taken together, these factors helped K mart to achieve a level of return on equity just equal to the industry average. Low liquidity ratio levels reflected K mart's use of short-term debt to finance inventories and should not pose problems for K mart, considering the many long-term financial resources that are available to it.

Summary

This chapter develops a framework for investing in common stock. In this endeavor, determining the growth potential of the company and the quality of management are vital tasks for the investor. Although the quality of management is to some extent a subjective evaluation, many items can be considered with regard to both the quality of management's past record and the growth potential of the firm and its products. Investors need to determine the philosophy of management with regard to the future of the business. Another important consideration is the education and experience of management personnel as well as their past performance record. The past growth record serves as a starting point for projection into the future.

Investors are expressing renewed interest in financial statement analysis. Three basic types of financial statements were examined: (1) the balance sheet, (2) the income statement along with the statement of retained earnings, and (3) the statement of changes in financial position. Common size financial statements were suggested as a means of adjusting for differing sizes of firms.

Different types of ratios were examined. The types and the actual ratios examined under each type are summarized below:

Liquidity Ratios and Activity Ratios

$$\text{Current ratio} = \frac{\text{Current assets}}{\text{Current liabilities}}$$

$$\text{Acid-test ratio} = \frac{\text{Current assets less inventory}}{\text{Current liabilities}}$$

$$\text{Inventory turnover} = \frac{\text{Cost of goods sold}}{\text{Average inventory}}$$

$$\text{Accounts receivable turnover} = \frac{\text{Sales (Credit)}}{\text{Average accounts receivable}}$$

Leverage Ratios and Capital Structure

$$\text{Debt-to-asset ratio} = \frac{\text{Total debt}}{\text{Total assets}}$$

$$\text{Times interest earned (before taxes)} = \frac{\text{Earnings before interest and taxes}}{\text{Interest expense}}$$

Profitability-Efficiency Ratios

$$\text{Return on revenue} = \frac{\text{Earnings before interest and taxes (EBIT)}}{\text{Revenue}}$$

$$\text{Return on assets} = \frac{\text{EBIT}}{\text{Total assets}}$$

$$\text{Return on stockholders' equity} = \frac{\text{Earnings after taxes}}{\text{Stockholders' equity}}$$

Suggested Readings

BENESH, GARY A., and PAMELA P. PETERSON. "On the Relationship Between Earnings Changes, Analysts' Forecasts and Stock Price Fluctuations." *Financial Analysts Journal* (November–December 1986): 29–39.

BERNSTEIN, LEOPOLD A., and JOEL G. SIEGEL. "The Concept of Earnings Quality." *Financial Analysts Journal* (July–August 1979): 72–75.

CRAIG, DARRYL, GLENN JOHNSON, and MAURICE JOY. "Accounting Methods and P/E Ratios." *Financial Analysts Journal* (March–April 1987): 41–45.

DUTTER, PHILIP H. "Quality of Management." *Financial Analysts Journal* (March–April 1969): 105–108.

ESTEP, TONY. "Security Analysis and Stock Selection: Turning Financial Information into Return Forecasts." *Financial Analysts Journal* (July–August 1987): 34–43.

FURTADO, EUGENE P. H., and MICHAEL S. ROZEFF. "The Wealth Effects of Company Initiated Management Changes." *Journal of Financial Economics* (March 1987): 147–60.

JENKS, JEREMY C. "Investing in Growth Stocks." *The Analysts Journal* (2d quarter 1947): 38–53.

MAGEE, JOHN F. "Assessing a Company's Technological Program." *Financial Analysts Journal* (July–August 1982): 56–59.

MIEDICH, STANLEY J., and RONALD MELICHER. "Corporate Sales Growth Rates and Stockholder Returns: A Risk-Return Market Analysts." *Review of Business and Economic Research* (Spring 1985): 35–44.

MODOK, N. D. "Corporate Planning and the Securities Analyst." *Financial Analysts Journal* (September–October 1974): 51–54ff.

PRUITT, STEPHEN W., and DAVID R. PETERSON. "Security Price Reactions Around Product Recall Announcements." *Journal of Financial Research* (Summer 1986): 113–22.

REGAN, PATRICK J. "The 1929 Cloud." *Financial Analysts Journal* (July–August 1987): 4–10.

SIEGEL, JOEL G. "The 'Quality of Earnings' Concept—A Survey" *Financial Analysts Journal* (March–April 1982): 60–68.

WOOLRIDGE, J. RANDALL. "The Information Content of Dividend Changes." *Journal of Financial Research* (Fall 1982): 237–47.

Questions

1. In analyzing quality of management, the management goals should be clear and consistent with a "grand design." What would an investor look for to ascertain whether or not this is true in any given company?

2. The size of a company is often cited as an important consideration because some managers seem able to effectively manage a relatively small company but lose control as the firm becomes larger. How would an investor determine whether management will be able to cope with this *critical size* consideration?

3. Define the current yield from an investment. How does the current yield relate to the potential rate of return from an investment?

4. In determining an adequate rate or return to be achieved from an investment, what is the role of the investment's beta?

5. The proper role of diversification in the long-run growth of a firm is important to the investor. From material contained in the standard financial reference sources, evaluate the diversification effort R. J. Reynolds made in acquiring Nabisco.

6. The Bland Company has a P/E ratio in 1988 that was well below industry and market averages. What should an investor look for before using the P/E information in an investment decision?

7. Why might the trading volume of a particular common stock be an important factor to consider in an investment decision?

8. In July 1987, the *Wall Street Journal* reported that Chrysler's P/E ratio was 6, and that the P/E ratio for General Motors was 12. What could account for these differences?

9. What is the relative importance of the research and development expenditures for the chemical industry as opposed to the textile industry? As a potential investor, would you be interested in buying a textile firm that has R&D expenses as a percentage of sales that are significantly above the industry average?

10. Why is it important to examine a firm's capital structure and calculate the debt component and the equity component? Do you feel that this calculation is more important in the 1980s than it was ten to fifteen years ago? Support your position.

11. Some financial analysts feel that it is not sufficient for the investor to examine only the breakdown of the firm's capital structure. What other related items could the investor examine to provide more information regarding the firm's debt-paying ability?

12. What problems might one foresee for a firm that has turnover ratios substantially below the industry average?

13. The quality of a firm's earnings is important for investment purposes. What is meant by the quality of earnings? Give some examples.

Problems

1. The following data for Ohio Edison are for the 1973–82 period:

Year	Earnings per Share	Dividends per Share	Year	Earnings per Share	Dividends per Share
1973	$2.14	$1.59	1978	$1.19	$1.76
1974	1.71	1.65	1979	1.80	1.76
1975	1.95	1.66	1980	1.52	1.76
1976	2.14	1.67	1981	2.10	1.76
1977	1.97	1.72	1982	1.89	1.76

   (a) Calculate the dividend payout ratio for each year. What are your conclusions or concerns regarding this ratio?

   (b) Determine the compound annual growth rate for earnings and dividends per share for the 1973–82 period.

   (c) What do you infer from the above data?

2. The following data for IBM are as reported over the 1970–86 period. Calculate the growth rate for each year and the compound annual growth rate for the entire period. In addition, plot the data on semi-log paper to check for the consistency of growth.

Year	Sales per Share	Earnings per Share	Dividends per Share
1970	$13.10	$ 1.78	$ .96
1971	14.32	1.88	1.04
1972	16.38	2.21	1.08
1973	18.73	2.70	1.12
1974	21.37	3.12	1.39
1975	24.09	3.34	1.63
1976	27.05	3.99	2.00
1977	30.74	4.58	2.50
1978	36.14	5.32	2.88
1979	39.18	5.16	3.44
1980	44.90	6.10	3.44
1981	49.08	5.63	3.44
1982	57.04	7.39	3.44
1983	65.79	9.04	3.71
1984	74.98	10.77	4.10
1985	81.34	10.67	4.40
1986	84.49	7.81	4.40

3. Let 1970 equal 1 and 1986 equal 17. Do a linear regression showing how both earnings per share and dividends per share change over time for Litton and Eastman Kodak. Calculate the correlation coefficients when performing these regressions. Then, prepare a matrix displaying the correlation coefficients for the two companies.

	Litton		Eastman Kodak	
Year	EPS	DPS	EPS	DPS
1970 (1)	$1.41	$ .00	$2.50	$1.32
1971 (2)	.99	.00	2.60	1.34
1972 (3)	(.19)	.00	3.39	1.39
1973 (4)	.80	.00	4.05	1.81
1974 (5)	(1.08)	.00	3.90	1.99
1975 (6)	.73	.00	3.80	2.06
1976 (7)	.15	.00	4.03	2.07
1977 (8)	1.23	.00	3.99	2.10
1978 (9)	(2.40)	.00	5.59	2.33
1979 (10)	4.50	.23	6.20	2.90
1980 (11)	6.99	1.04	7.15	3.20
1981 (12)	7.46	1.25	7.66	3.50
1982 (13)	7.54	1.47	7.12	3.55
1983 (14)	5.41	1.67	2.27	2.37
1984 (15)	6.47	1.90	3.81	2.37
1985 (16)	7.20	1.50	1.46	2.37
1986 (17)	2.52	.00	1.66	2.44

4. Calculate the effective tax rate for SCM Corporation for the 1973–78 period according to the following information taken from the firm's *1978 Annual Report:*

($ millions)	1973	1974	1975	1976	1977	1978
Income before income taxes and extraordinary losses	32.2	49.1	42.9	55.6	69.3	51.5
Income taxes	13.9	21.5	15.0	25.2	31.9	13.9

If the effective tax rate seems low in any given year, what would you do to discover the cause? Would it really matter to you as a potential investor?

5. The following are balance sheet items for Litton Industries for the 1978–82 period. Calculate the current ratio and the acid-test ratio for each year, and give your opinions regarding what the trend of these ratios means for Litton's overall corporate strategic planning.

($ millions)	1978	1979	1980	1981	1982
Cash/marketable securities	93	410	788	1,094	1,043
Accounts receivable	638	628	699	784	749
Inventory	563	503	633	578	674
Total current assets	1,524	2,081	2,462	2,758	2,747
Total current liabilities	1,479	1,479	1,660	1,805	1,621

6. Total Petroleum's net profit, long-term debt, and net worth (stockholders' equity) are shown in the following table for the 1976–84 period.

   (a) Calculate the ratio of long-term debt to long-term debt plus net worth. What conclusions do you draw from this ratio?

(b) In view of the net profit figures, do you have any added concerns regarding the level of debt? Justify your concerns by calculating the after-tax return on net worth for each year.

($ millions)	1976	1977	1978	1979	1980	1981	1982	1983	1984
Net profit	10	15	17	30	48	(64)	13	(31)	11
Long-term debt	70	85	84	69	278	358	349	313	203
Net worth	117	131	168	307	358	281	283	285	288

7. From the following figures for Towle Manufacturing for the 1978–85 period, calculate and comment on the following:
   (a) Times interest earned
   (b) Ratio of long-term debt to long-term debt plus net worth

($ millions)	1978	1979	1980	1981	1982	1983	1984	1985
Interest expense	$ .94	$3.99	$7.29	$10.28	$11.89	$13.78	$19.15	$14.52
Income taxes	3.45	6.55	9.35	9.23	3.53	6.50	−11.36	.82
Net profit	3.50	6.94	9.57	10.83	5.81	1.76	−15.60	−67.24
Long-term debt	$ 8.5	$34.7	$66.5	$70.2	$76.8	$89.7	$88.0	$41.8
Net worth	34.0	42.8	46.3	63.4	85.7	82.7	63.9	(0.9)

8. Houston Industries' earnings per share and dividends per share for the 1971–86 period were as follows:

Year	Earnings per Share	Dividends per Share	Year	Earnings per Share	Dividends per Share
1971	$1.89	$ .86	1979	3.23	1.57
1972	2.07	.91	1980	3.14	1.79
1973	2.03	.93	1981	3.14	1.99
1974	1.95	1.00	1982	1.62	2.16
1975	1.95	1.04	1983	3.54	2.28
1976	2.67	1.07	1984	3.85	2.44
1977	2.94	1.24	1985	4.42	2.60
1978	2.81	1.41	1986	3.81	2.76

   (a) Calculate and comment on the dividend payout ratio in terms of whether you think it is appropriate for a utility company.
   (b) In Houston Industries' *1982 Annual Report,* the following statement was made: "Houston Industries' net income and earnings per share would have been up thirty-six percent and sixty-three cents, respectively, had it not been for disappointing regulatory treatment accorded the canceled Allen's Creek nuclear plant." Houston took a charge against income of $168 million in the quarter ending December 1982. Calculate Houston Industries' growth rate in earnings per share for the 1971–82 and 1982–86 periods with and without adjusting for the extraordinary chargeoff. Calculate the growth rate for dividend per share for the same periods. What are your conclusions regarding which earnings per share value to use for 1982?

9. Mr. George, your director of research, has assigned you to examine the possibility of purchasing the common stock of the United States Tobacco Company. This company is the dominant producer of moist smokeless tobacco, a form of oral tobacco, which has become increasingly popular during the 1970s and 1980s. This business, whose principal brand names include Copenhagen and Skoal, accounts for an estimated 95 percent of the firm's earnings, and almost all volume is generated in the United States where the company has an 85 percent market share. Because of this high market share, the company institutes more than adequate price increases on a regular basis. Profit margins, therefore, are extremely high.

Because your investment firm is small and resources are limited, basic research is purchased from a large Wall Street research department. George instructs you to use this research, which is shown in Tables P9–1 through P9–7. However, this research must be expanded somewhat to make a final decision, and you are asked to complete the analysis as follows:

Table P9–1
Balance Sheet ($ Millions)

Assets	**1985**	**1986**
Current & equivalents	$ 24.1	$ 31.5
Other current assets	198.3	219.0
Total current assets	$222.4	$250.5
Fixed assets, net	$244.4	$263.7
Goodwill	1.3	1.0
Total assets	$468.1	$515.2
Liabilities & shareholders' equity		
Current liabilities	$ 55.7	$ 61.0
Deferred income taxes	32.0	44.4
Long term debt	57.0	47.1
Total liabilities	$144.7	$152.5
Shareholders' equity	$323.4	$362.7
Total liabilities & shareholders' equity	$468.1	$515.2

Table P9–2

1986 Income Statement ($ millions)		**1986 Other Data ($ millions, except per share data)**	
Revenues	$518.0	Earnings per share	$ 1.79
Total expenses	323.3	Depreciation	16.2
Pretax income	$194.7	Additions to fixed assets	35.5
Taxes	90.8	Dividends paid	54.7
		Amortization of goodwill	0.3
Net income	$103.9	Common stock purchased	9.9

Table P9–3
Historic Income Statement Data ($ Millions)

	Revenues	Income Before Interest and Taxes	Interest Expense	Income Before Taxes	Taxes	Net Income	Earnings per Share
1986	$518.0	$200.3	$5.5	$194.7	$90.8	$103.9	$1.79
1985	480.0	177.1	5.9	171.2	77.7	93.5	1.64
1984	443.8	165.1	5.1	159.9	76.2	83.7	1.43
1983	382.8	141.2	4.7	136.5	65.9	70.6	1.21
1982	320.4	110.3	6.6	103.7	48.4	55.3	1.01
1981	280.2	92.3	3.6	88.7	43.0	45.7	.84
1980	265.8	80.7	5.1	75.5	37.8	37.7	.70
1979	233.3	67.7	6.9	60.7	28.7	32.0	.60
1978	205.9	59.0	4.8	54.2	26.4	27.8	.53
1977	181.0	49.5	3.8	45.7	21.4	24.3	.47
1976	166.4	42.1	3.4	38.7	19.3	19.4	.38
Compound annual growth rates							
1976–86	12%	17%	5%	18%	17%	18%	17%

Table P9–4
Historic Asset and Equity Analysis (in $ Millions)

	Average Total Assets	Revenues/ Average Total Assets	Average Total Equity	Net Income as % of Average Total Equity	Average % Debt/ Total Capital
1986	$496.0	1.04	$347.5	30%	75%
1985	438.3	1.10	302.2	31	73
1984	390.7	1.14	270.6	31	79
1983	352.8	1.08	239.4	30	75
1982	306.8	1.04	202.2	27	74
1981	272.0	1.03	173.8	26	75
1980	252.5	1.05	151.9	25	73
1979	230.1	1.01	133.3	24	71
1978	197.7	1.04	117.3	24	69
1977	166.7	1.09	102.8	24	69
1976	145.8	1.14	89.6	22	66

(a) The profit growth of the United States Tobacco Company has been excellent. George understands that there are five important sources of corporate internal earnings growth. Identify these *five* sources, and from the data appearing in Tables P9–3, P9–4, and P9–5, state whether each *has* or *has not* contributed to the profit progress of United States Tobacco Company over the past ten years.

(b) From his long investment experience, George is aware that

Table P9–5
Historic Dividend and Retained Earnings Data ($ Millions)

	Dividends	Retained Earnings	Payout Ratio		Dividends	Retained Earnings	Payout Ratio
1986	$54.7	$49.2	53%	1980	$18.9	$18.8	50%
1985	47.8	45.7	51	1979	16.4	15.6	51
1984	40.5	43.2	48	1978	14.1	13.7	51
1983	32.5	38.2	46	1977	12.3	12.1	50
1982	25.7	29.6	46	1976	9.5	9.9	49
1981	21.9	23.8	48				

Table P9–6
Historic Unit Volume Trends—Moist Smokeless Tobacco (Millions of Cans)

1986	463	1983	426	1980	344	1977	267
1985	476	1982	392	1979	323	1976	237
1984	464	1981	364	1978	295		

1976–1986 Compound annual growth rate = 7%

Table P9–7
Valuation Data

	United States Tobacco	S&P 500
Recent price	$27.00	290
Book value per share	$ 6.42	
Liquidation value per share	$ 4.90	
Replacement costs of assets per share	$ 9.15	
Anticipated 1987 dividend per share	$ 1.20	
Estimated annual growth in dividend per share	10.0%	
Required return	13.0%	
Estimated 1987 earnings per share	$ 2.40	$16.50
Price-earnings ratio based on 1987 EPS	11.3	17.6
Estimated 1987 dividend per share	$ 1.20	$ 8.75
Dividend yield based on 1987 dividend	4.4%	3.0%
Estimated annual growth in earnings and dividends	10.0%	7.0%

stock price performance can be affected by a company's stage of development or position in its "life-cycle of profits." List the *four* stages of development in the "life-cycle of profits," and explain the revenue, profit margin, and earnings characteristics of each stage. Also, using the data shown in Tables P9–1 through P9–7, identify United States Tobacco's current position in this model for each of the three characteristics.

(c) Using only the data provided in Table P9–7, briefly discuss whether the common stock of United States Tobacco Company *is* or *is not* attractively priced based on each of three different valuation models.

(Excerpted with permission from the 1987 Level I examination, The Institute of Chartered Financial Analysts)

Part

Fixed-Income Investing

4

The art of fixed-income investing has become increasingly important in recent years. High and variable interest rates have created the potential for large total returns—both positive and negative—as capital appreciation and losses became more common with fixed-income investments. Additionally, many new types of fixed-income securities have been created by financial market participants. In this part of the text, we discuss the general concepts of fixed-income investing and examine the attractiveness of many of the new types of fixed-income securities.

Chapter 10 presents the basic aspects of fixed-income investing. Chapter 11 examines money market securities and government bonds. Corporate bonds and preferred stocks are considered in Chapter 12. The reasons for the tremendous amount of innovative activity in the fixed-income area in recent years are presented in Chapter 13. An essential element of this chapter is a discussion of how the traditional risk-return trade-off for fixed-income securities can be altered either by changes in the provisions of the bond itself or by investment strategies.

Chapter 10

Fixed-Income Investment Concepts

Key Concepts

acceleration clause
after-acquired clause
balloon payment
basis point
bearer bond
bond
bond table
call premium
call provision
collateral trust bond
coupon rate
current yield
debenture
deferred call
duration
equipment trust certificate
expectations hypothesis
guaranteed bond
indenture
interest rate risk
liquidity hypothesis
market segmentation hypothesis
maturity
money market securities
mortgage bond
note
purchasing power risk
registered bond
sinking fund
subordinated debenture
term structure of interest rates
trustee
yield curve
yield-to-maturity

Chapter Outline

Features of Fixed-Income Securities
Importance of Fixed-Income Investing
Risks and Decisions in Fixed-Income Investing
Summary

Safe, but stuffy. If that's what you think fixed-income securities are, you had better change your mind! In 1982, long-term corporate bonds gave investors a total return of 43.8 percent versus only 21.4 percent for common stocks. Long-term corporate bonds outperformed common stocks in both 1984 and 1986. How about down markets? In 1974, investors in long-term corporate bonds lost only 3.1 percent compared to a loss of 26.5 percent for common stocks. In 1979, when stocks returned 18.4 percent, bonds lost 4.2 percent. Evidently, in any given year, an investor can do better or worse in bonds than in common stocks.

This chapter examines the importance of fixed-income securities to investors, including basic concepts of fixed-income investing and the decisions that investors face. The first section examines the features of fixed-income securities. The second highlights the growing importance of fixed-income investing. A discussion of the risks and decisions involved in fixed-income investing is presented in section three.

Fixed-income securities provide the holder with a fixed or constant dollar amount of interest during the anticipated lifetime of the security. Alternatives include opportunities to invest for from a few days to forty years or more. Short-term, relatively high-quality investment opportunities with maturities of one year or less are known as *money market securities.* Fixed-income securities in the one-to-ten-year range are often referred to as *notes. Bonds* are generally defined as fixed-income securities with maturities of ten years or longer. These time distinctions are somewhat arbitrary, and investors customarily categorize fixed-income securities as either short-term or long-term investment opportunities, with one year as the dividing line. Hence, we will use the term *bond* to refer to any long-term promissory note given under the official seal of the issuing debtor. Figure 10–1 provides a framework for thinking about fixed-income securities when they are jointly classified by investment quality and maturity.

Features of Fixed-Income Securities

To be a successful fixed-income investor requires a sound understanding of the basic features of these securities. A particular feature may be quite important to the return that is realized from holding a given bond. In addition, much innovation has occurred in recent years with regard to fixed-income securities. This innovation means investors should know the importance of "plain vanilla" bond features in order to appreciate the significance of innovative features. The major features of a fixed-income security relate to the way interest is paid, when owners can expect their principal back, and what collateral backs the security.

Indentures and Trustees

The typical non-U.S. fixed-income security is created under what is known as an *indenture,* the legal document spelling out the obligations and terms

Figure 10–1
Classification System for Fixed-Income Securities

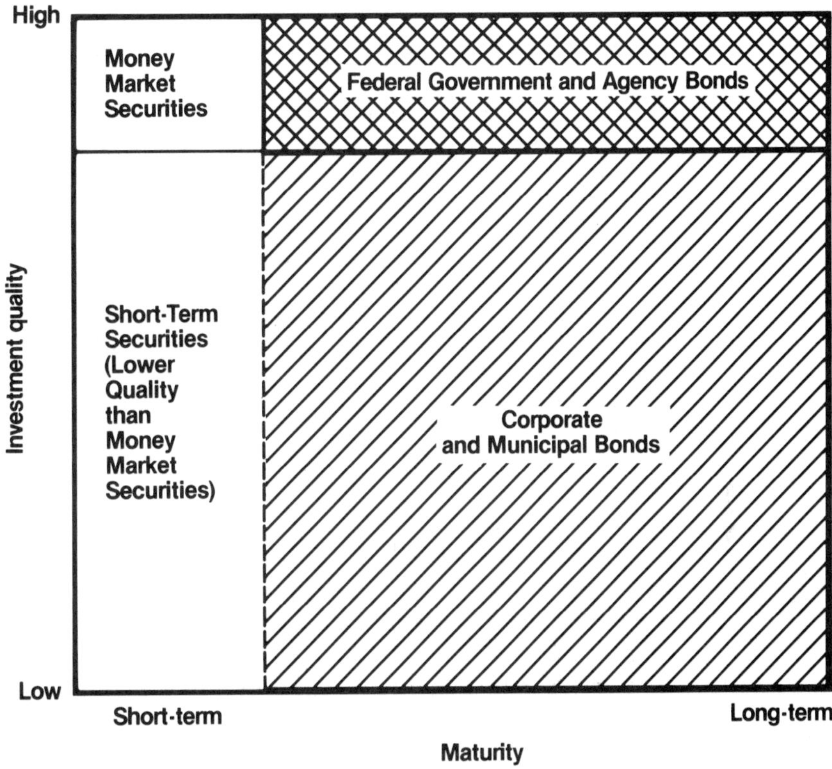

of the borrowing. An indenture is the contract between the borrower and its creditors. It stipulates the total amount of the borrowing, the number of bonds to be issued, the date of interest payments, and other crucial features of the contract.

In practice, interest and principal payments called for under the indenture are not made directly to the bondholder by the borrower but to an intermediary called a *trustee,* usually a commercial bank. The trustee is responsible for payment of interest and principal to the holder of the security, and is also responsible for enforcement of the bond indenture. If a debtor fails to live up to any part of the indenture, it is the responsibility of the trustee to take whatever action is necessary on behalf of the bondholders. Widespread bond ownership would make any violation of the indenture difficult to enforce without a trustee.

Interest Payments

The indenture stipulates the interest payments to be made at a fixed or determinable rate. This rate is called the *coupon rate* and determines the amount of money the bondholder will receive on each interest payment date. If a bond issue has a coupon rate of 7 percent, this means that the bondholder will receive $7 per year per $100 of face value, or $70 per year for a $1,000 bond. Within the context of bond yields, the term *basis point* is often used. A basis point is one-hundredth of one percentage point. Thus, a bond selling to yield 8 percent would have a yield of 800 basis points. The term is used most often when considering changes in the yield-to-maturity, which we discuss later in this chapter. If yields increase from 8 to 8.25 percent, we note the change with the statement that the yield has increased 25 basis points.

The typical bond pays interest semiannually, with the timing of the semiannual payment stated in the indenture. The usual arrangement is for the first payment to be made six months after the date of original issue and every six months thereafter. Thus, for a bond issued in February, the coupon payments would be made in August and February. The method of interest payment depends on how the indenture stiulates legal ownership. Bond ownership is evidenced in two basic ways: *bearer bonds* and *registered bonds*. No record of ownership exists for a bearer bond. The investor collects interest by simply removing the appropriate coupon from the bond certificate and redeeming it. In practice, interest coupons are redeemed through a bank in much the same way that checks are cashed. The principal is collected in the same fashion. Registered bonds are similar to stock certificates. The owner's name is recorded, and a check for each interest payment is sent directly to the owner. Present government regulations require that all new bonds issued be registered so that both principal and interest payments may be tracked by the Internal Revenue Service.

Maturity Dates

The principal repayment date, stated in the indenture, refers to the date when all of the bonds are to be retired and is usually called the *maturity date*. However, a maturity date of February 15, 2001, such as for an existing AT&T bond, does not necessarily mean that the corporation will retire all the bonds on February 15, 2001. It simply means that all the bonds must be paid off by then, using one of several repayment techniques. Call provisions and the operation of sinking funds may effectively shorten the maturity of a given bond.

Call Provisions

A bond with a *call provision* enables the issuer to repay the debt prior to the maturity date. Such bonds are said to be callable. If the bond is called, the investor is obligated to return the bond to the issuer, at which time the issuer repays the principal. The investor has no choice in the matter because the call provision is written into the indenture. If the investor retains the bond, no additional interest payments are realized.

The call provision often requires the issuer to pay a premium if the bond is called. The indenture will stipulate this *call premium* in the form of a price that must be paid when the bond is called. If bonds are callable at 105, the investor will receive $1,050 for each $1,000 bond (if called). In this case, the call premium is 5, or $50 per $1,000 bond. The call premium is usually not constant over the life of the bond, but typically declines as the bond gets closer to maturity. The investor should determine whether a given bond is callable and the terms of the call price by consulting such sources as Moody's *Manuals* or the S&P *Bond Guide.*

A borrower is unlikely to call outstanding bonds unless new bonds can be sold at a lower interest rate to replace the called bonds. With call provisions existing in most corporate bond issues, corporations will not hesitate to call the bonds when interest rates decline substantially. The result is that the bond investor loses some of the benefits of a decline in interest rates because of the operation of the call provision.

Even if the issuer does not call the bonds, the investor will not reap the entire benefit of a price increase resulting from a decline in interest rates. Given a call feature and an interest rate decline, the bond market is unlikely to value a bond at a price much above the call price. For example, a twenty-year 8 percent bond should sell for over $1,200 if the market interest rate is 6 percent. However, given a call price of $1,050, the price of the bond will tend not to exceed $1,050. The risk of a call prevents the bond price from moving higher, as would be the case without the call provision.

In essence, a call provision is a great benefit to the issuer and a major disadvantage to the investor. If interest rates increase, the investor has either a capital loss or an opportunity loss if the bonds are held to maturity. If interest rates decline, the capital gain or opportunity gain that would accrue to the investor is reduced by the call provision.

In times of high interest rates, the investment community frequently insists on what is called a *deferred call* provision. The deferred call is identical to the ordinary call except that the borrower may not call the bonds until several years after the date of issue. For example, a bond issue may be callable five or ten years after the date of issue. The deferred call is actually a compromise between the bond issuer and the investor. It provides some of the advantages of a callable bond to the issuer, while allowing the investor to hold the bond for a specified, minimum period of time. In a similar manner, high call premiums represent a compromise designed to make bonds more attractive to investors.

A borrower is sometimes willing to accept a deferred call because without it investors would require a higher rate of interest. Generalizing about how much more interest the borrower would be required to pay is difficult because it depends on what the investment community thinks will happen to interest rates after the bond has been issued. If a good chance exists that interest rates will increase, the call provision will not be very expensive. If, on the other hand, the investment community believes that interest rates may fall sharply, it will demand considerable payment for a call provision and typically insist on either a deferred call or a very high call premium. In recent years, the deferred call of five to ten years has become popular.

Sinking Funds

Closely associated with the call provision is the *sinking fund* provision of the bond indenture. Contrary to its name, a bond with a sinking fund does not require the borrower to establish a fund of money with which to repay the principal at maturity. Rather, the sinking fund is a method of repaying a portion of the bond issue prior to the maturity date. The sinking fund works on the same principle as any sort of installment loan. With corporate bonds, the sinking fund is established in the indenture as a payment schedule. The typical payment arrangement calls for partial payment each year so that a portion of the principal has been retired by the maturity date. At maturity, the corporation is required by the bond indenture to make a final *balloon payment*. For example, a firm may sell a $50 million bond issue with a twenty-year maturity. The indenture may establish an annual sinking fund payment of $2 million at the start of the sixth year with a balloon payment of $20 million at maturity. Like any installment plan, the credit risk is reduced as time goes by because the payments gradually reduce the principal and interest obligation.

A corporate bond with a sinking fund presents a problem to the investor. The problem lies in the method of satisfying the sinking fund. A $50 million bond issue will contain 50,000 separate $1,000 bonds, and each bond will have the same maturity in the typical corporate bond issue. In our example, the sinking fund provision would require that 2,000 bonds be retired at the beginning of each year starting with the sixth year, but would not stipulate which of the 50,000 bonds were to be retired in any given year. In practice, the sinking fund can be satisfied in one of two ways. The bonds may be purchased in the market at the current market price. Alternatively, the trustee can select 2,000 bonds at random and notify the owners that these bonds have been selected. A holder of a registered bond would be notified by mail. The notice of a call for redemption of bearer bonds would appear in the financial press (i.e., the *Wall Street Journal*). The owners of these 2,000 bonds must return them and receive the call price as stipulated in the indenture.

Which call alternative will the firm select? If it selects the bonds at random, the amount paid will be the call price stipulated in the indenture. If the firm purchases the bonds in the market, the price will be the market price. Obviously, the market purchase alternative will be selected when the market price is below the call price. The market price will be below par if interest rates have increased since the issue date. In effect, an increase in interest rates allows the firm to retire $2 million face value of bonds per year for less than $2 million.

If interest rates decline and the market price exceeds the sinking fund call price, the firm will satisfy the sinking fund requirement with a call for the appropriate number of bonds. We again face the problem encountered with a general call provision. The difference is that only a portion of the issue will be retired as a result of the call. Nevertheless, the bond price is unlikely to increase to its theoretical market price. The sinking fund requirement will prevent the price from increasing much above par (if that is the sinking fund call price) with an interest rate decline because an investor may face a call. In addition, a sinking fund provision effectively shortens the maturity of a corporate bond issue.

Collateral

An important feature of bonds is the collateral behind them. If a bond has collateral, the bond investors as a group have a claim to the assets described in the indenture if and when the bonds are in default. The collateral can be sold and the proceeds of the sale used to satisfy the debt obligation. However, an issuer that has defaulted on its bonds is having serious financial problems and these problems usually result from an inability of the collateral to produce sufficient earnings to satisfy the financial obligations. If the problems are permanent, the market value of the collateral will be low. The "best collateral" is an asset capable of producing a wide variety of products or of being used in many ways. Specialized assets are much less valuable as collateral because their value depends entirely on one product or process. Collateral is to be preferred in any debtor-creditor situation, but it may do little to reduce the risk of loss of principal in a given default.

The types of collateral are many and varied. Often the characteristics of the collateral dictate the label attached to a particular bond. A *debenture* is a bond issue with no collateral. A *subordinated debenture* is a bond the holder of which, in the event of liquidation, has a claim that is subordinated (inferior) to the claims of some or all other creditors. The subordinated debenture holder is usually inferior in rank to other bondholders. In addition, the claim may also rank behind that of the issuer's general creditors. The nature of the subordination is stated in the bond indenture. A *mortgage bond* is a bond that is secured by a lien on the property of the issuer. The lien is usually confined to specified real property. The typical mortgage arrangement is a lien on all real property. The mortgage bond may also contain an *after-acquired clause* stipulating that any real property acquired after the bonds have been issued will come under the mortgage agreement. The intent of the after-acquired clause is to maintain the bondholder's relative position in growth situations.

Mortgage bonds may be *senior* or *junior;* the distinction preassigns which bonds have first claim in the event of a default. The senior mortgage bonds must be completely paid off from the sale of the assets prior to any payment to the junior mortgage bondholders. The value of the junior claim will be related to the market value of the assets in the event of bankruptcy. If the senior claim is $50 million and the market value of the collateral is $200 million, $150 million is available for the junior claim. The market value to be used is the collateral's market value, given bankruptcy.

Collateral trust bonds are bonds backed by other stocks and bonds. The stocks and bonds are frequently the financial securities of one or several of the borrower's subsidiaries or simply the financial investments of the issuer. The quality of the collateral is directly related to the fortunes of the firm(s) whose securities are being used as collateral.

The Carolina, Clinchfield and Ohio Railway has a bond outstanding that is a *guaranteed bond.* The payment of the principal, interest, and sinking fund is unconditionally guaranteed, jointly and severally, by the Seaboard Coast Line Railroad Company and the Louisville & Nashville Railroad Company. If the issuing firm cannot pay the interest, principal, or sinking fund payments, the two railroads guaranteeing the bond will do so.

Another form of mortgage bond is the *equipment trust certificate,* where the bonds are backed by specific equipment or machinery. These generally high-quality securities are frequently used by railroads and airlines—the equipment is the rolling stock of the railroad or the airplanes of the airline. The unique feature of equipment trust certificates is that the trustee of the bond retains legal title to the equipment until the bonds have been paid in full. For example, plaques on many railroad freight cars show a bank as trustee owner. Consequently, a compelling reason exists to meet the financial obligations of the bonds because the trustee can prevent use of the equipment at any time without the necessity of obtaining a court order. For a firm in the transportation business, the use of equipment is essential to continued operation.

Importance of Fixed-Income Investing

Fixed-income securities are an important investment alternative for a number of reasons. High yields are possible at certain times. The proper timing of the purchase of certain types of fixed-income securities may provide the investor with substantial capital gains. Risk reduction potential and tax aspects may be important to many investors when purchasing fixed-income securities. Finally, money market securities with their short maturities and good liquidity may provide a useful "parking place" for money waiting to enter either the stock market or the long-term bond market. Let's examine the importance of these various reasons for fixed-income investing in more detail.

Availability of High Returns

There used to be an adage in Wall Street that an interest rate of ten percent would draw money from the moon. That was prior to recent years, when ten percent returns have been more common. However, high interest rates may be available from time to time that provide the investor with the opportunity to earn a favorable rate of return for the risk taken. Figure 10–2 shows the interest rates available to the investor on high-quality corporate bonds for the 1960–86 period. In certain years, such as 1969–70, 1975, and 1980–82, interest rates reached high levels and provided investors with potentially excellent fixed-income security buying opportunities.

Figure 10–2
S&P Composite AA Bond Yields, 1960–86

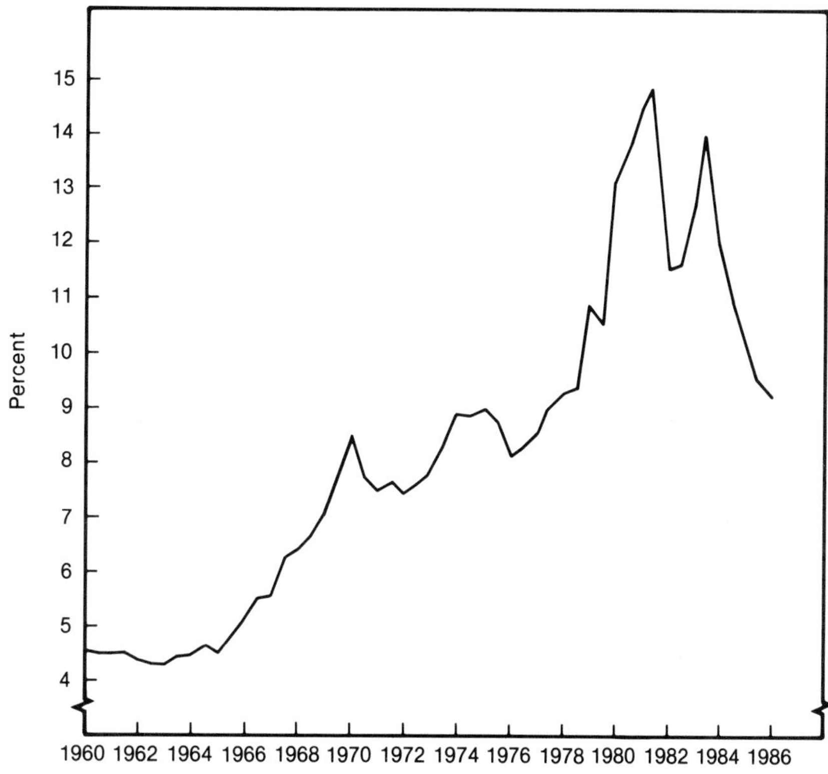

Potential for Capital Appreciation and Loss

The years in Figure 10–2 that show high historical interest rates may not have provided investors with the golden opportunities that one would first imagine because of the risks involved in fixed-income investing. Fixed-income securities are subject to *interest rate risk.* The seemingly high interest rates noted in Figure 10–2 for 1969 appeared to provide investors with the opportunity to "lock in" historically high interest rates by purchasing long-term bonds. After all, interest rates as high as that had not been seen for at least four decades. Subsequently, even higher interest rates occurred in 1975 and 1980–82 and produced capital losses for investors who purchased seemingly high-yield long-term bonds in 1969. For example, an investor buying Dow Chemical's new 7¾ percent bond to mature in 1999, issued on July 10, 1969, would have paid $1,000 for each bond. The 7¾ percent yield probably seemed high at the time of purchase. Yet higher interest rates in 1983 resulted in this bond selling for $710 at mid-1983.

The brighter side of interest rate risk is that interest rate fluctuations provide the investor with an opportunity to make capital gains from investing in fixed-income securities. For example, the Dow 7¾ percent bond sold for $935 in December 1986, an increase of 31.7 percent from mid-1983.

Risk-Reducing Potential

Although fixed-income securities come in all varieties with regard to risk, the risk of a common stock portfolio may be reduced by investing in fixed-income securities. U.S. government bonds and high-quality corporate bonds provide an investor with the opportunity for low-risk investing. We will have some additional observations on the risk of fixed-income investing and how to assess and manage that risk later in the book.

Tax Aspects

Chapter 11 deals with government bonds issued by all levels of government. A portion of that chapter is devoted to examining state and local bond issues, which are commonly referred to as municipal bonds. We noted in Chapter 2 that municipal bonds provide the investor with the opportunity to obtain interest income not taxed by the federal government. For certain bonds and for certain individuals, municipal bond interest may be exempt from state and local income taxes as well.

Liquidity Aspects

Many short-term fixed-income securities provide investors with the opportunity to earn a reasonable return and still have liquidity. Short-term U.S. government securities and others with similar characteristics provide the investor with a good place to invest idle funds while searching for other good investments. Institutions, as well as individuals, can adopt a defensive strategy and buy short-term highly liquid securities when the market seems to be near its peak.

Risks and Decisions in Fixed-Income Investing

In some ways, fixed-income investing is easy. The investor simply needs to determine if the interest rate offered on a given fixed-income investment is sufficient for the quality of the debt obligation, its maturity, and any significant features regarding its marketability. In other ways, fixed-income investing is difficult. The investor must often deal with rapidly fluctuating interest rates and an almost bewildering array of new types of provisions attached to fixed-income securities. Let's first examine the concept of return as applied to fixed-income securities and then we can look at the risk aspects associated with quality, maturity, and marketability.

Yields on Fixed-Income Securities

Several yield or return concepts are associated with fixed-income investing. One return concept is what the investor actually earns on the investment during the time period it is held. This is a very relevant return for the investor, but it can be calculated only after the security is sold. For example, suppose you purchase a bond paying 10 percent interest for $1,000. If you sell this bond for $950 a year later, you would have earned only 5 percent on this bond investment. You made a 10 percent interest return, but lost 5 percent of the bond's value when you sold a year after purchase. Two other important yield concepts are the current yield and the yield-to-maturity.

Current Yield

Interest payments on a bond are made at the coupon rate. The bond used as our example for the realized rate of return has a coupon rate of 10 percent. For a $1,000 bond, the investor would expect to receive $100 a year in interest payments. The $100 is determined by multiplying the coupon rate by the $1,000 principal amount of the bond. The current yield is calculated as follows:

$$\text{Current yield} = \frac{\text{Annual coupon rate (amount) of interest}}{\text{Current price of the bond}}$$

For the 10 percent bond, the current yield is 10 percent ($100 divided by $1,000). An investor buying this bond a year later at $950 would have a current yield of 10.53 percent, determined by dividing $100 by the price of $950. Current yields may provide the investor with a poor idea of what the return from a given bond will actually be if the bond has potential for capital gains or losses during its anticipated lifetime.

Yield-to-Maturity

The yield-to-maturity is the discount rate that equates the present value of the future cash flows (interest payments plus principal repayment) with the current price of the bond. For the bond selling at $1,000 and expected to be redeemed by the issuer at $1,000, the current yield and the yield-to-maturity are identical. However, the yield-to-maturity will differ from the current yield if the bond sells at a discount or a premium from the anticipated redemption price (principal amount, in most instances).

Many investors use a book containing *bond tables* like the one presented in Exhibit 10–1 to determine a bond's yield-to-maturity. Sophisticated financial calculators or computers can also do the job quickly. A book of bond tables contains prices for a large number of maturities, coupon interest rates, and yields-to-maturity. If our 10 percent bond had

Exhibit 10–1 Portion of a Page from a Bond Table

10%				Years and Months				
Yield	*18–6*	*19–0*	*19–6*	*20–0*	*20–6*	*21–0*	*21–6*	*22–0*
6.00	144.33	144.98	145.62	146.23	146.82	147.40	147.96	148.51
6.20	141.48	142.08	142.66	143.22	143.76	144.29	144.80	145.29
6.40	138.71	139.26	139.78	140.29	140.79	141.27	141.73	142.18
6.60	136.02	136.51	136.99	137.46	137.91	138.34	138.76	139.17
6.80	133.40	133.85	134.28	134.70	135.11	135.50	135.88	136.25
7.00	130.86	131.26	131.65	132.03	132.40	132.75	133.09	133.42
7.20	128.38	128.75	129.10	129.44	129.77	130.08	130.39	130.69
7.40	125.97	126.30	126.62	126.92	127.21	127.50	127.77	128.03
7.60	123.63	123.92	124.20	124.47	124.74	124.99	125.23	125.46
7.80	121.36	121.61	121.86	122.10	122.33	122.55	122.76	122.97
8.00	119.14	119.37	119.58	119.79	119.99	120.19	120.37	120.55
8.10	118.06	118.27	118.47	118.66	118.85	119.03	119.20	119.37
8.20	116.99	117.18	117.37	117.55	117.72	117.89	118.05	118.20
8.30	115.93	116.11	116.29	116.45	116.62	116.77	116.92	117.06
8.40	114.89	115.06	115.22	115.37	115.52	115.66	115.80	115.93
8.50	113.86	114.02	114.17	114.31	114.44	114.57	114.70	114.82
8.60	112.85	112.99	113.13	113.26	113.38	113.50	113.62	113.73
8.70	111.85	111.98	112.10	112.22	112.33	112.44	112.55	112.65
8.80	110.86	110.98	111.09	111.20	111.30	111.40	111.50	111.59
8.90	109.89	110.00	110.10	110.19	110.29	110.37	110.46	110.54
9.00	108.93	109.02	109.11	109.20	109.28	109.36	109.44	109.51
9.10	107.98	108.07	108.15	108.22	108.29	108.36	108.43	108.49
9.20	107.05	107.12	107.19	107.26	107.32	107.38	107.44	107.49
9.30	106.13	106.19	106.25	106.30	106.36	106.41	106.46	106.51
9.40	105.22	105.27	105.32	105.37	105.41	105.46	105.50	105.54
9.50	104.32	104.36	104.40	104.44	104.48	104.51	104.55	104.58
9.60	103.43	103.47	103.50	103.53	103.56	103.59	103.61	103.64
9.70	102.56	102.58	102.61	102.63	102.65	102.67	102.69	102.71
9.80	101.69	101.71	101.72	101.74	101.75	101.77	101.78	101.79
9.90	100.84	100.85	100.86	100.86	100.87	100.88	100.88	100.89
10.00	100.00	100.00	100.00	100.00	100.00	100.00	100.00	100.00
10.10	99.17	99.16	99.15	99.15	99.14	99.13	99.13	99.12
10.20	98.35	98.34	98.32	98.31	98.29	98.28	98.27	98.26
10.30	97.54	97.52	97.50	97.48	97.46	97.44	97.42	97.41
10.40	96.74	96.71	96.69	96.66	96.64	96.61	96.59	96.57
10.50	95.96	95.92	95.89	95.85	95.82	95.79	95.77	95.74
10.60	95.18	95.13	95.09	95.06	95.02	94.99	94.95	94.92
10.70	94.41	94.36	94.31	94.27	94.23	94.19	94.15	94.12
10.80	93.65	93.60	93.55	93.50	93.45	93.41	93.36	93.32
10.90	92.90	92.84	92.79	92.73	92.68	92.63	92.59	92.54

nineteen years to go to maturity when purchased for $950, the bond tables indicate that the yield-to-maturity for a 10 percent bond with nineteen years to maturity is 10.62 percent. This is determined by reading across the top row to the nineteen-year maturity for a 10 percent coupon, and down that column until we reach a price of $95.00 ($950 per $1,000 bond). We see that a price of $95.13 equates to a yield of 10.60 percent and a price of $94.36 equates to a yield of 10.70 percent. Interpolation between these two values results in the return of 10.62 percent.

In some cases, calculating an approximate yield-to-maturity that is acceptable for most investment decisions is possible. The approximate yield-to-maturity calculation considers both the interest income and the annual capital gain or loss and relates these to the average investment in the fixed-income security. Using the approximate yield-to-maturity formula for the 10 percent bond that sells for $950 and has nineteen years to final maturity results in an approximate yield-to-maturity of 10.53 percent. This approximate yield-to-maturity is in contrast to the yield-to-maturity of 10.62 percent from the bond table. The approximate yield-to-maturity formula works reasonably well for bonds selling between about $900 and $1,100, but gives an increasingly inaccurate answer as the premium or discount from par widens. This yield deviation becomes larger because the average investment calculation becomes more inaccurate and does not reflect the compounding that actually occurs.

$$\begin{aligned}\text{Approximate yield-to-maturity} &= \frac{\text{Interest income} + (\text{Capital gain or loss} \div \text{Years to maturity})}{(\text{Price} + \text{Redemption value}) \div 2} \\ &= \frac{\$100 + (\$50 \div 19)}{(\$950 + \$1{,}000) \div 2} \\ &= \$102.63 \div \$975 = 10.53\%\end{aligned}$$

Risk Elements in Fixed-Income Investing

The yield-to-maturity needs to be related to the quality of the fixed-income investment, its maturity, and its marketability aspects. The investor might have to adjust the yield-to-maturity for any tax factors. The yield-to-maturity calculations assume that the investor will hold the bond to maturity and that all interest payments and principal will be paid by the issuing firm when due. The assumption is also made that *all interest received will be reinvested at the yield-to-maturity.* The assumption may not hold and, if not, the return will be different from that expected. The possibility of return variability is, of course, the risk of corporate bond investment.

Quality

The quality of fixed-income alternatives varies enormously from very high-quality U.S. government securities to very low-quality corporate bonds, sometimes referred to as "junk bonds." One of the important decisions facing an investor is what quality fixed-income investment alternative is the best by any given time. Part of the answer to the quality choice question goes back to the risk preferences of the investor, but part of the question relates to the anticipated price movements of various quality bonds. Low-quality corporate bonds might be expected to increase in price much more than high-quality corporate bonds if the economy is about to enter a prosperous period after just having been in a recession. What we are speaking about here is the business risk assessment that any potential bondholder needs to make.

Bond indentures typically contain an *acceleration clause* stipulating that if an interest payment is missed, the entire debt becomes due immediately. In practice, repayment of the principal is not possible. Hence, a defaulted bond normally continues to be traded while the firm, the courts, and the bondholders seek a settlement. Settlement of defaulted bonds frequently requires years, and the final outcome is often unsatisfactory for the corporate bondholder.

Another aspect of the quality decision relates to the type of fixed-income security purchased. Chapter 12 examines convertible bonds in depth. These bonds allow the holder to convert the fixed-income security to common stock if circumstances make this a proper course of action. Convertible bonds tend to be more risky than nonconvertible bonds. One study resulted in the following betas for samples of various quality bonds during the 1960–75 period. Quality was measured by bond ratings (described in detail in Chapter 12), and the beta was calculated by comparing the bond fluctuations against the S&P 500 stock index:[1]

Type of Bond		Beta
BBB	Nonconvertible bond (medium quality)	.31
BBB	Convertible bond	.62
BB	Convertible bond (relatively speculative)	.69
B	Convertible bond (quite speculative)	1.00

The beta of the lowest quality convertible bonds was 1.00, indicating that the risk present in these bonds was equal to the risk present for common stocks in general. An investor thinking he or she is buying a relatively low-risk, fixed-income security would be quite disappointed in the subsequent market action of low-quality convertible bonds because of the large business risk element in these securities. As a solution to the quality choice question, many fixed-income investors simply decide they will not hold a fixed-income security below a predetermined quality level. Naturally, this limits the risk of fixed-income investing but also tends to limit the return potential.

1. Robert M. Soldofsky, Richard A. Stevenson, and Susan M. Phillips, "Convertible Securities: New Issues, Conversions, and Performance Record," *Investment Environment, Analysis, and Alternatives, A Book of Readings* (ed., Stevenson and Phillips) (St. Paul, MN: West Publishing Company, 1977), p. 210.

Maturity and Duration

Fixed-income investors need to be aware of the relationship between maturity (or its companion concept, duration) and interest rate risk. The basic relationship is that the longer the maturity, the greater the interest rate risk. Duration—an alternative method of looking at the life of a fixed-income investment—is the average number of years it takes to receive the present value of all future payments, including both periodic interest payments and the principal repayments. As a present value concept, duration is sensitive to the time pattern of the cash flows received from a fixed-income security. Not only is duration a useful way of looking at the effective life of a fixed-income investment but it is also an important element in some investment management strategies.

Exhibit 10–2 shows a duration calculation for three different bonds. All of these bonds have a final maturity of five years, but they have different coupon interest rates and different sinking fund provisions designed

Exhibit 10–2 Duration Examples

	Year 1	*Cash Flow* 2	*Present Value at 7% (Bond A) and 14% (Bonds B and C)* 3	*Present Value of Cash Flow* 4	*Present Value as % of Price* 5	*Product* 1×5
Bond A						
	1	70	.933	65.45	.065	.065
	2	70	.873	61.11	.061	.122
	3	70	.816	57.12	.057	.171
	4	70	.763	53.41	.054	.216
	5	1,070	.713	762.91	.763	3.815
				1,000.00	1.000	4.389 years
Bond B						
	1	140	.8772	122.81	.123	.123
	2	140	.7695	107.73	.018	.216
	3	140	.6750	94.50	.094	.282
	4	140	.5921	82.89	.083	.332
	5	1,140	.5194	592.12	.592	2.960
				1,000.05	1.000	3.913 years
Bond C						
	1	140 + 0	.8772	122.81	.123	.123
	2	140 + 0	.7695	107.73	.108	.216
	3	140 + 200	.6750	229.50	.229	.689
	4	112 + 200	.5921	184.74	.185	.739
	5	84 + 600	.5194	355.27	.355	1.776
				1,000.05	1.000	3.543 years

to partially retire the issue before its final maturity. The three bonds and their duration calculations are as follows:

Bond A: This is a bond paying 7 percent, or $70 per year, based on its par value of $1,000. Exhibit 10–2 presents the duration when it was originally issued using present value factors based on 7 percent and interest payments that are assumed to occur at the end of the year. As you can see from Exhibit 10–2, over 76 percent of the bond's price is the result of the cash flow in year five. The duration, or present value life of the bond, is 4.389 years.

Bond B: This bond was issued when market interest rates were 14 percent and pays $140 a year in interest. Only 59 percent of its price is the result of the cash flow received in year five becaue the periodic interest payments are $140 a year rather than the $70 for Bond A. Bond B's duration is only 3.913 years.

Bond C: This bond is the same as Bond B except that the issuer is required to redeem 20 percent of the issue in both years three and four. As these principal repayments of $200 are received, the dollar amount of subsequent interest payments declines. Only 35 percent of this bond's price results from the fifth year cash flow. Likewise, Bond C's duration is only 3.543 years rather than 3.913 years for Bond B because Bond B did not require partial redemption prior to the end of the fifth year.

Exhibit 10–3 is a portion of a duration table for a bond carrying a 12 percent interest rate. This duration table shows the duration for this bond assuming different final maturities and assuming investors face various market yields. For example, a twenty-five-year, 12 percent bond has a duration of 7.88 years if market yields for this quality bond are also at 12 percent. Three things are evident from Exhibit 10–3 and from Table 10–1, which shows durations for selected interest rates and maturity combinations.

Exhibit 10–3 Portion of a Duration Table

Bond Duration					**Years and Months**							**12%**
Yield	*21–0*	*22–0*	*23–0*	*24–0*	*25–0*	*26–0*	*27–0*	*28–0*	*29–0*	*30–0*	*35–0*	*40–0*
4.00	11.47	11.82	12.16	12.49	12.82	13.13	13.44	13.74	14.03	14.31	15.64	16.81
4.20	11.36	11.70	12.03	12.36	12.67	12.97	13.27	13.56	13.84	14.12	15.38	16.50
4.40	11.26	11.59	11.91	12.22	12.52	12.82	13.11	13.38	13.66	13.92	15.13	16.19
4.60	11.15	11.47	11.78	12.09	12.38	12.67	12.94	13.21	13.47	13.73	14.89	15.89
4.80	11.04	11.36	11.66	11.95	12.24	12.51	12.78	13.04	13.29	13.53	14.64	15.60
5.00	10.93	11.24	11.53	11.82	12.09	12.36	12.62	12.87	13.11	13.34	14.40	15.31
5.20	10.83	11.12	11.41	11.69	11.95	12.21	12.46	12.70	12.93	13.15	14.17	15.02
5.40	10.72	11.01	11.29	11.55	11.81	12.06	12.30	12.53	12.75	12.97	13.93	14.74
5.60	10.62	10.90	11.17	11.42	11.67	11.91	12.14	12.36	12.58	12.78	13.70	14.47
5.80	10.51	10.78	11.04	11.29	11.53	11.76	11.99	12.20	12.40	12.60	13.48	14.20
6.00	10.41	10.67	10.92	11.16	11.40	11.62	11.83	12.04	12.23	12.42	13.25	13.93
6.20	10.31	10.56	10.80	11.04	11.26	11.47	11.68	11.87	12.06	12.24	13.03	13.67
6.40	10.20	10.45	10.68	10.91	11.12	11.33	11.53	11.71	11.89	12.07	12.82	13.42
6.60	10.10	10.34	10.57	10.78	10.99	11.19	11.38	11.56	11.73	11.89	12.60	13.17
6.80	10.00	10.23	10.45	10.66	10.86	11.05	11.23	11.40	11.56	11.72	12.39	12.92

Exhibit 10–3 *(continued)*

Bond Duration						**Years and Months**						**12%**
Yield	*21–0*	*22–0*	*23–0*	*24–0*	*25–0*	*26–0*	*27–0*	*28–0*	*29–0*	*30–0*	*35–0*	*40–0*
7.00	9.90	10.12	10.33	10.53	10.73	10.91	11.08	11.25	11.40	11.55	12.19	12.68
7.20	9.80	10.01	10.22	10.41	10.60	10.77	10.94	11.09	11.24	11.38	11.99	12.45
7.40	9.70	9.90	10.10	10.29	10.47	10.63	10.79	10.94	11.08	11.22	11.79	12.22
7.60	9.60	9.80	9.99	10.17	10.34	10.50	10.65	10.79	10.93	11.06	11.59	12.00
7.80	9.50	9.69	9.88	10.05	10.21	10.37	10.51	10.65	10.77	10.90	11.40	11.78
8.00	9.40	9.59	9.76	9.93	10.09	10.23	10.37	10.50	10.62	10.74	11.22	11.57
8.20	9.30	9.48	9.65	9.81	9.96	10.10	10.23	10.36	10.47	10.58	11.03	11.36
8.40	9.21	9.38	9.54	9.70	9.84	9.97	10.10	10.22	10.33	10.43	10.85	11.16
8.60	9.11	9.28	9.44	9.58	9.72	9.85	9.97	10.08	10.18	10.28	10.68	10.96
8.80	9.02	9.18	9.33	9.47	9.60	9.72	9.83	9.94	10.04	10.13	10.50	10.77
9.00	8.92	9.08	9.22	9.36	9.48	9.60	9.71	9.81	9.90	9.99	10.34	10.58
9.20	8.83	8.98	9.12	9.25	9.36	9.47	9.58	9.67	9.76	9.84	10.17	10.39
9.40	8.74	8.88	9.01	9.14	9.25	9.35	9.45	9.54	9.62	9.70	10.01	10.21
9.60	8.64	8.78	8.91	9.03	9.14	9.23	9.33	9.41	9.49	9.56	9.85	10.04
9.80	8.55	8.69	8.81	8.92	9.02	9.12	9.20	9.28	9.36	9.43	9.69	9.87
10.00	8.46	8.59	8.71	8.81	8.91	9.00	9.08	9.16	9.23	9.29	9.54	9.70
10.20	8.37	8.50	8.61	8.71	8.80	8.89	8.96	9.04	9.10	9.16	9.39	9.54
10.40	8.29	8.40	8.51	8.61	8.69	8.77	8.85	8.91	8.98	9.03	9.25	9.38
10.60	8.20	8.31	8.41	8.50	8.59	8.66	8.73	8.80	8.85	8.91	9.10	9.23
10.80	8.11	8.22	8.32	8.40	8.48	8.55	8.62	8.68	8.73	8.78	8.97	9.08
11.00	8.03	8.13	8.22	8.30	8.38	8.45	8.51	8.56	8.61	8.66	8.83	8.93
11.20	7.94	8.04	8.13	8.20	8.28	8.34	8.40	8.45	8.50	8.54	8.70	8.79
11.40	7.86	7.95	8.03	8.11	8.17	8.23	8.29	8.34	8.38	8.42	8.57	8.65
11.60	7.78	7.86	7.94	8.01	8.08	8.13	8.18	8.23	8.27	8.31	8.44	8.52
11.80	7.69	7.78	7.85	7.92	7.98	8.03	8.08	8.12	8.16	8.19	8.31	8.38
12.00	7.61	7.69	7.76	7.83	7.88	7.93	7.97	8.01	8.05	8.08	8.19	8.25
12.20	7.53	7.61	7.67	7.73	7.79	7.83	7.87	7.91	7.94	7.97	8.07	8.13
12.40	7.45	7.52	7.59	7.64	7.69	7.74	7.77	7.81	7.84	7.86	7.96	8.01
12.60	7.37	7.44	7.50	7.55	7.60	7.64	7.68	7.71	7.74	7.76	7.84	7.89
12.80	7.30	7.36	7.42	7.47	7.51	7.55	7.58	7.61	7.63	7.66	7.73	7.77
13.00	7.22	7.28	7.33	7.38	7.42	7.45	7.49	7.51	7.54	7.56	7.62	7.66
13.20	7.14	7.20	7.25	7.29	7.33	7.36	7.39	7.42	7.44	7.46	7.52	7.55
13.40	7.07	7.12	7.17	7.21	7.24	7.28	7.30	7.32	7.34	7.36	7.41	7.44
13.60	7.00	7.05	7.09	7.13	7.16	7.19	7.21	7.23	7.25	7.26	7.31	7.34
13.80	6.92	6.97	7.01	7.05	7.08	7.10	7.12	7.14	7.16	7.17	7.21	7.23
14.00	6.85	6.89	6.93	6.97	6.99	7.02	7.04	7.05	7.07	7.08	7.12	7.13
14.20	6.78	6.82	6.86	6.89	6.91	6.93	6.95	6.97	6.98	6.99	7.02	7.04
14.40	6.71	6.75	6.78	6.81	6.83	6.85	6.87	6.88	6.89	6.90	6.93	6.94
14.60	6.64	6.68	6.71	6.73	6.75	6.77	6.79	6.80	6.81	6.82	6.84	6.85
14.80	6.57	6.60	6.63	6.66	6.68	6.69	6.70	6.72	6.72	6.73	6.75	6.76
15.00	6.50	6.53	6.56	6.58	6.60	6.61	6.63	6.64	6.64	6.65	6.67	6.67

Source: Reprinted from *Duration Tables,* Publication No. 761 (Boston, MA.: Financial Publishing Company, 1980).

Table 10–1
Durations for Various Bonds

		Duration in Years	
Coupon Rate (%)	*Market Rate (%)*	*10-Year Bond*	*40-Year Bond*
5	5	7.79	17.23
	10	7.13	10.36
	15	6.44	6.83
10	5	6.93	15.60
	10	6.23	9.80
	15	5.54	6.69
13	5	6.61	15.19
	10	5.92	8.67
	13	5.51	7.64
	15	5.24	6.66

Source: Duration Tables for Bond and Mortgage Portfolio Management. Publication No. 761 (Boston, MA.: Financial Publishing Company, 1980).

1. Lengthening the maturity has little duration impact after about twenty or twenty-five years. For example, Exhibit 10–3 shows that duration increases only .37 years (7.88 versus 8.25) for the 12 percent bond as the final maturity increases from twenty-five to forty years.
2. Fluctuating interest rates can have great impact on the duration of a given bond. A rising interest rate reduces duration and a falling interest rate increases duration. For example, the duration of a 10 percent forty-year bond issued at par is 9.8 years. This duration falls to 6.69 years if the market interest rate increases to 15 percent.
3. The trend over the years toward rising interest rates shown on Figure 10–2 impacts on the durations of fixed-income securities. A 5 percent, forty-year bond issued in 1966 when market interest rates were about 5 percent had a duration of 17.23 years. However, a 13 percent, forty-year bond issued during the 1981–82 period when market interest rates were about 13 percent had a duration of only 7.64 years. The moral is this: As interest rates have risen, the commitment involved in buying a long-term bond, as measured by duration, has steadily become shorter. This is an important concept for fixed-income investment management strategies and will be developed in Chapter 13.

Term Structure of Interest Rates

A *yield curve* is a useful graphic representation of the relationship between the yield-to-maturity and the maturity date for fixed-income securities of a given risk class. Figure 10–3 shows the yield curve that existed at various dates for securities issued by the U.S. government. Because these securities have no credit risk, the yield curves represent the term (maturity) structure of riskless interest rates as of each date. Yield curves can also be drawn for corporate bonds of various risk classes or ratings. At any given time, these corporate yield curves would tend to have the same general shape as a yield curve using U.S. government securities, but would show higher yields for comparable maturities.

Figure 10–3 demonstrates that many different shapes for the yield curve can exist, depending on the time chosen to draw the yield curve. The potential bond investor can use the yield curve to decide whether to purchase short-term bonds rather than long-term bonds. The investor has a picture of the differences in yields for the various maturities under consideration. Explanations for the various shapes have been proposed and are known as the expectations hypothesis, the liquidity preference hypothesis, and the market segmentation hypothesis.

The first explanation is called the *expectations hypothesis.* If one-year bonds are selling to yield 8 percent and two-year bonds are selling to yield 9 percent and the investor is planning to invest for two years, one of two basic strategies could be followed. The investor could buy the two-year bonds and simply hold them to maturity. Excluding credit risk, the investor would be assured of a 9 percent return.

An alternative strategy would be to invest in the one-year bond and, at the end of the first year, purchase another one-year bond. Whether the investor picks this alternative will depend on the investor's expectations regarding interest rates at the end of the first year. Suppose that the investor expects one-year interest rates to be 12 percent in one year instead of the current 8 percent. If this expectation materializes, an investment of $1,000 would grow to $1,209.60, which is the compound value of 8 percent for one year and 12 percent for the second year. With $1,000 invested at 9 percent for two years, the compound value at the end of the second year would be only $1,188.10.

Figure 10–3
Yields on U.S. Government Securities, Various Dates

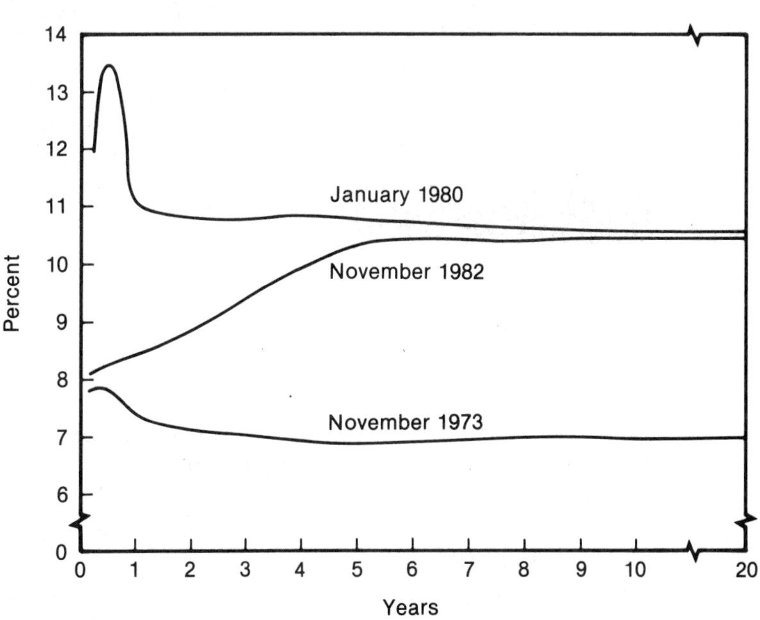

In this example, the investor's expectations differ from those of the market. Recall that the market rate for one-year bonds was 8 percent and that the two-year rate was 9 percent. The implication is that the market expects one-year rates to be approximately 10 percent one year from now. A two-year investment will produce a compound value of $1,188.10 if the 9 percent, two-year bonds are purchased. In order for an equivalent return to be made from the strategy of purchasing consecutive one-year bonds, the rate of interest in the second year must be 10.01 percent.[2]

The expectations hypothesis concludes that the yield curve's shape exists because of different expectations regarding the course of future interest rates. If short-term rates are expected to increase, the yield curve will be upward sloping. If interest rates are expected to decline, the yield curve will be downward sloping.

It is fair to conclude that a long-term bond is more risky than a short-term bond from the investor's viewpoint and less risky from the corporation's viewpoint. Consequently, the investor demands a higher yield on the long-term bond and the corporation will be willing to accept the higher rate in order to obtain the less risky funds. This recognition that risk may vary with maturity goes under the general name of the *liquidity preference hypothesis.*

The uncertain course of future interest rates and *purchasing power risk* will make a long-term bond less desirable for the investor than the short-term bond. With the long-term bond, an investor can "lock in" the current interest rate. If interest rates rise, the investor must wait to reinvest at the higher rate. In addition, the uncertainties regarding the fortunes of the issuing corporation are considerably greater in the long run than in the short run. A one-year bond may be paid with the liquidation of short-term assets, but a long-term bond must be paid from the earning power of the firm. These risks to the investor imply that long-term interest rates will be greater than short-term rates.

Some bond market analysts suggest a third explanation of the yield curve, which has been labeled the *market segmentation theory.* This theory suggests that our capital markets are segmented in that investors tend to purchase certain types of securities and ignore others. The segmentation theory implies that some investors will buy and sell only short maturities while others will trade only long maturities. The segmentation hypothesis is typically not confined to maturities, but also claims segmentation among various types of financial securities. In support of this, we note that several bond investors, such as life insurance companies, must purchase long maturities because their assets require such a strategy. They must match the maturities of their assets and liabilities. In addition, many investors must confine their investments to certain types of instruments by law or tradition or both. Trust departments usually confine their in-

2. The rate of 10.01 percent is calculated as follows:

$$(1.09)^2 = (1.08)(1 + i)$$

$$(1 + i) = \frac{(1.09)^2}{(1.08)}$$

$$i = \left(\frac{1.1881}{1.08}\right) - 1 = 10.01\%$$

vestments to legal list securities, savings and loan associations to home mortgages, commercial banks to short- and intermediate-term loans, and so on. Finally, many large investors find that specialization in a particular type of corporate bond is beneficial because of the high cost of information and analysis of the data.

We have little doubt that segmentation exists along the lines suggested. However, to conclude that interest rates are influenced by such segmentation is an extremely large step that is probably not supportable. Basically, segmentation assumes that investors specialize but does not take into account investors who specialize in arbitrage between markets. Many investors buy nothing but short-term securities, and others buy nothing but long-term securities. However, many investors exist who specialize in taking advantage of differences between rates. To support the segmentation theory, one would have to show that arbitrage either does not exist or is done poorly. We find no evidence to support such a conclusion. Market segmentation supporters cite facts that could imply segmentation but do not show an actual influence on interest rates.

A general explanation for the shape of a given yield curve seems to be a combination of the expectations and liquidity preference hypotheses. In essence, yield curves express investor expectations and the preference by investors to own short-term bonds coupled with the preference by borrowers to issue long-term bonds. Because of this dual causation, determination of market expectations is more difficult than would be the case if the expectations hypothesis were the only explanation. We cannot determine precisely the market consensus regarding future rates. If the yield curve is downward sloping or flat, we can conclude that the market expects declining rates. A rising yield curve is much less informative given the liquidity preference hypothesis, because we could have a rising yield curve with an expectation of no change in interest rates. The expectations are reflected in how rapidly the yield curve rises. If the rate of increase is greater than the historic norm, an increase in yields can be expected. If the yield curve rises slightly, it may be reflecting an expectation of a slight interest rate decline.

Purchasing Power Risk

Purchasing power risk, as we have seen, involves the possibility that the proceeds of an investment will not purchase the goods and services expected because of a change in the general price level. We speak of a real rate return, which is the return after consideration of changes in the price level. The usual method of estimating the real rate of return is to take the difference between the actual monetary return and the inflation rate. For example, during the 1926–86 period, the average annual rate of inflation was 3.1 percent and the return from treasury bills was 3.5 percent resulting in a real return of .4 percent. The return from long-term corporate bonds was 5.3 percent, which is a real return of 2.2 percent after subtracting the inflation rate. Hence, it appears that the shorter the maturity of a fixed-income security, the less likely it is to provide protection from purchasing power risk.

Unfortunately, an adjustment for the inflation rate is not the only problem associated with purchasing power risk. If you are not planning to hold a bond to maturity, changing rates of inflation can affect the market price of your bond drastically. Suppose you have purchased a twenty-year, 8 percent bond for $1,000 and at the time of your purchase you and the market were expecting an inflation rate of 4 percent. You purchased a bond with a monetary return of 8 percent and a real return of 4 percent, provided inflationary expectations are realized. If, a year later, the market concludes the future inflation rate will be 6 percent rather than 4 percent, you will not be able to sell your bond for $1,000. For investors to obtain the same real return of 4 percent, the monetary yield must be 10 percent. The bond now (one year after you purchased it) has a nineteen-year maturity and must sell for a price of $831.30 in order for the yield-to-maturity to be 10 percent. This value is found on a bond table and is the present value of all the future returns from the bond discounted at 10 percent. Even if you plan to hold the bond to maturity, you have still suffered from purchasing power risk. You have an opportunity loss in the sense that you could have invested a year later at ten percent but now own an investment earning only 8 percent.

The price change potential resulting from interest rate changes is precisely why it is often said that a constant rate of inflation does not trouble the fixed-income investor. As long as the rate of inflation is constant in the future, no inflation risk exists, provided the monetary return is high enough to compensate the investor for the rate of inflation. What the bond investor is worried about is a changing rate of inflation. If a bond investor can predict a change in the inflation rate accurately and ahead of the market, the profit potential may be large.

Interest Rate Risk

The maturity (or duration) of a fixed-income security has a profound impact on the price of the security for any given change in interest rates. The general rule is that an increase in interest rates is associated with fixed-income security price declines and an interest rate decrease is associated with fixed-income security price increases. Prices and interest rates move in opposite directions. This general rule is important, but we must be more specific. A given interest rate change will produce the greatest price change for fixed-income securities with the longest maturities. The longer the maturity, the greater the price change associated with a given interest rate change.

Figure 10–4 shows the price change for a bond with an 8 percent coupon interest rate and varying maturities and for market interest rates of 6, 8, and 10 percent. An investor wishing to maximize price changes resulting from interest rate changes would select a fixed-income security with a long maturity. Hence, an investor expecting the market interest rate to decline would follow the investment strategy of buying long-term bonds to obtain capital gains. However, the investor need not buy maturities much beyond thirty years to obtain a reasonable approximation of the maximum price change because the present value of cash flows to be received many years in the future is quite small.

Let's consider an actual situation facing an investor at the beginning of 1979. Commonwealth Edison (CWE), a Chicago utility, has the two following bonds outstanding:

CWE 9% August 1, 1983 bond selling for 99 on 2/7/79
CWE 9⅛% October 15, 2008 bond selling for 95 on 2/7/79

Which of these two bonds should be purchased? The answer depends to a considerable extent on what the investor expects to happen to interest rates. Exhibit 10–4 shows the current yield and yield-to-maturity for each of these two bonds. It also shows what will happen to the price if

Figure 10–4
Bond Prices for an 8 Percent Bond for Market Rates of 6, 8, and 10 Percent by Maturity

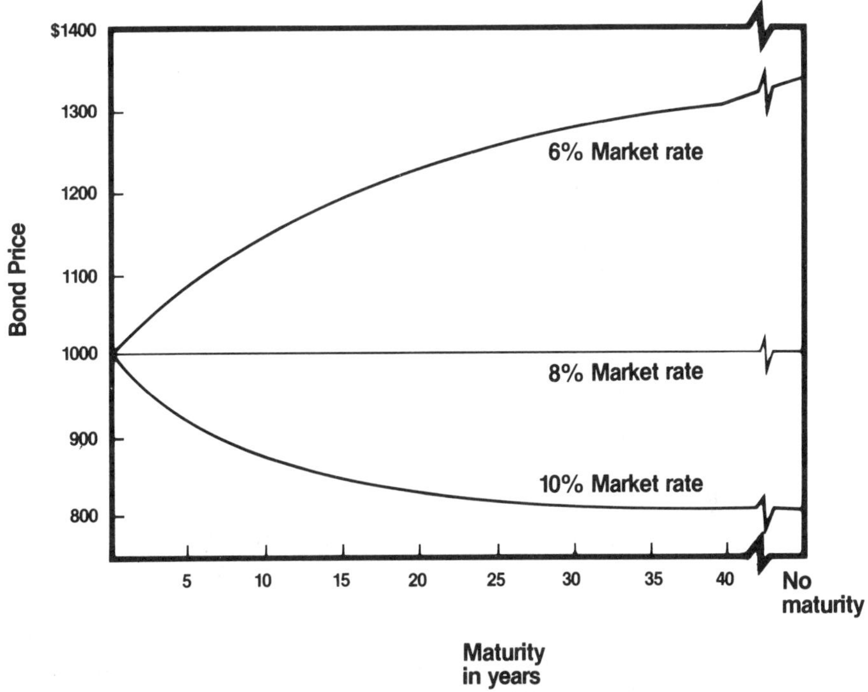

Exhibit 10–4 **Impact of Changing Interest Rates on Two Commonwealth Edison Bonds**

Bond	*Price Feb. 1979*	*Current Yield*	*Yield-to-Maturity*	*Price (percentage change in price) if Interest Rates = 7%*	*12%*
CWE 9%, 1983	99	9.09%	9.28%	107.61 (+ 8.7)*	89.90 (− 9.3)
CWE 9⅛%, 2008	95	9.61%	9.64%	126.37 (+33.0)*	76.81 (−19.1)

*Ignores the impact of any potential call provisions.

market interest rates immediately decline to 7 percent or increase to 12 percent.

The coupon rate of any fixed-income security will also influence the price change resulting from an interest rate change. The higher the coupon rate, the smaller will be the price change for a change in market interest rates. If both bond A and bond B have a twenty-year maturity, but A's coupon is 8 percent while B's is 4 percent, a decrease in the market rate of interest from 10 percent to 8 percent will produce the following results:

Bond Price with Market Interest Rate of			
	10%	**8%**	**Capital Gain**
Bond A (8%)	$828.40	$1,000.00	20.71%
Bond B (4%)	485.20	604.10	24.51

The 4 percent bond produces larger capital appreciation because it sells for a low price relative to the 8 percent bond. When the market interest rate declines, the lower-priced bond increases by a greater percentage because of the smaller size of the initial base price. If one's objective is to maximize the percentage capital appreciation, bond B with its lower coupon rate should be purchased.

Marketability Aspects

A potential purchaser of a bond should not ignore marketability. In this regard, a number of questions need to be considered.

1. Can you, as the purchaser of the fixed-income security, hold the security until its maturity?
2. Is there a good secondary market for the fixed-income security if you have to sell before its maturity? Is the bond traded over the counter or listed on an exchange?
3. What type of order should you place with your broker for the purchase and sale of fixed-income securities?
4. Should you buy new issues of fixed-income securities or already outstanding bonds?

Some fixed-income investment alternatives provide their best return if held to their maturity. For example, a thirty-month certificate of deposit at a local financial institution might provide a return of 10 percent if held for thirty months. If redeemed prior to maturity, a substantial interest penalty is applied that typically is the loss of three to six months of interest. Premature redemption of the certificate of deposit is costly in terms of yield lost, and these certificates should normally not be purchased unless you can hold them to maturity.

The availability of a good secondary market is often a consideration in whether a fixed-income security needs to be held to its maturity date. If no secondary market trading exists for the security, the investor has no choice but to hold until maturity. However, secondary markets for fixed-income securities differ from the standpoint of their ability to provide the investor with a relatively quick sale without much change in the market price. Some bonds are listed for trading on one of the major exchanges, but the vast majority of bond trading occurs in the over-the-counter market.

Two potential problems result for the investor because of the nature of the secondary market for many fixed-income securities. First, many bonds are traded in the over-the-counter market, and an investor owning a small amount of a given bond may not receive good price execution because he or she is essentially dealing in an odd-lot of bonds rather than a round-lot of bonds. For example, the round-lot for many municipal bonds is $100,000 and not the $5,000 or $10,000 that many individuals purchase. Two, the "thin" market for many listed bonds means that the spread between bid and asked prices will often be large. For example, the last trade of a bond may have occurred a week ago at 92 ($920). The closest current bid and asked may be as follows: two bonds bid at 89 ($890) and five bonds offered at 94½ ($945). The investor may have trouble getting bond orders executed at a price that seems reasonable.

The "thin" nature of the market trading for some bonds has implications for the type of order the investor should use in attempting to buy or sell them. For all but the largest bond issues having considerable trading volume each day, the investor should use limit orders. For example, if the investor has five bonds to sell and the market quotation is the one given previously (bid at 89 and asked at 94½), the investor could enter the following order: Sell five bonds at 91½. This would be a reduction of ½ from the last sale at 92, but more than the current bid price of 89 for only two bonds. The investor has to wait and see if another investor comes along willing to buy the bonds at the limit price of 91½. The limit order should be made good until cancelled as it might take two or three weeks for this order to get executed, if indeed it is ever executed. Clearly, the investor is in a better position in this sale attempt if the proceeds from the bond sale are not needed immediately.

Should the investor purchase new issues rather than bonds already outstanding? New issues provide both advantages and disadvantages to the investor. The investor can examine a prospectus for the issue and be well informed about the type of security purchased. In addition, the investor pays no brokerage commission because the issuing organization pays the issuing expenses for the issue. The investor also might get a slightly higher interest rate for a new issue than for a comparable issue in the secondary market. The interest rate on the new issue has to be attractive enough to draw new money from investors, whereas a secondary market trade simply occurs betweeen two investors. The primary disadvantage of buying new issues relative to outstanding issues is that some of the objectives of the bond investor may be more difficult to meet by buying only new issues. For example, an investor desiring bonds with maturities in the three-to-seven-year range might find that new issues with these maturities are scarce. Finally, it is sometimes easier to stagger maturities and find the exact quality bond one desires in the secondary market. Suppose an investor in 1988 has $80,000 to invest in fixed-income securities and desires to space maturities in the following manner: $8,000 in a savings account for liquidity with $8,000 in bonds maturing every two or three years (i.e., 1990, 1993, 1996, 2000, and so on). The secondary market provides many opportunities to accomplish this maturity spacing objective.

Summary

Fixed-income investing is an important activity for many investors. Fixed-income investments can provide liquidity, high returns, risk-reduction possibilities, tax benefits, and capital appreciation potential. Not all of these potential benefits come at the same time or from the same fixed-income investment, but these benefits are important enough that any investor might be interested in considering fixed-income investments.

The purchaser of fixed-income securities is mainly interested in the expected return from the investment in light of its quality, its maturity, and its marketability considerations. As with common stocks, the risk of fixed-income securities spans a wide range from U.S. government securities to extremely speculative corporate bonds of companies in bankruptcy.

A major risk that investors in fixed-income securities typically face is that interest rates will change during the time the security is owned. The level of interest rates could change. For example, long-term U.S. government bond yields could go from 8 percent to 12 percent. This upward movement in the level of rates will cause a decline in the price of these bonds. In addition, an investor could encounter a change in the shape of the yield curve. Short-term interest rates might remain unchanged while long-term rates increase for the same quality fixed-income security. In this instance, an investor could avoid the capital loss associated with the rising long-term rates by investing in short-term securities. Finally, an investor needs to think not only about what rates are at the time of the investment but also about what rates might be when either interest or principal payments become available for reinvestment. Careful thought about the future course of interest rate movements is essential for investment success in the fixed-income area.

Suggested Readings

ALTMAN, EDWARD I. "The Anatomy of the High-Yield Bond Market." *Financial Analysts Journal* (July–August 1987): 12–25.

ALTMAN, EDWARD I., and SCOTT NAMMACHER. "The Default Experience of High Yield Corporate Debt." *Financial Analysts Journal* (July–August 1985): 25–41.

BLUME, MARSHALL E., and DONALD E. KEIM. "Lower-Grade Bonds: Their Risks and Returns." *Financial Analysts Journal* (July–August 1987): 26–33.

EDERINGTON, LOUIS H. "Why Split Ratings Occur." *Financial Management* (Spring 1986): 37–47.

FABOZZI, FRANK J., and IRVING M. POLLACK, eds. *The Handbook of Fixed Income Securities.* Homewood, IL: Dow Jones-Irwin, 1983.

FOGLER, H. RUSSELL, and MICHAEL JOEHNK. "Deep Discount Bonds: How Well Do They Perform?" *Journal of Portfolio Management* (Spring 1979): 59–62.

FONG, H. GIFFORD. *Bond Portfolio Analysis.* Charlottesville, VA: Financial Analysts Research Foundation, Monograph No. 11, 1980.

Questions

1. Why have fixed-income security yields increased so much over the last twenty years?
2. What is the relationship between the call feature and the sinking fund provision on a fixed-income security and the maturity of that security?
3. How do capital gains and losses result from trading fixed-income securities?
4. Why might the addition of fixed-income securities to a portfolio reduce the risk of a portfolio?
5. Using Exhibit 10–1, determine the yield-to-maturity of a 10 percent coupon bond for the following maturities and prices:
   - **(a)** 19 years $1,100
   - **(b)** 20 years 935
   - **(c)** 21½ years 1,147
   - **(d)** 22 years 980
6. What risks are especially important to investors in fixed-income securities? Explain.
7. Define *yield curve.* Discuss the three hypotheses that attempt to explain the shapes of the yield curve.
8. Explain the two dimensions of purchasing power risk.
9. What is a "junk" bond? What risks are important in this type of investment?
10. What problem can result from buying bonds with poor secondary markets?
11. What reasons might prompt an investor to buy new issues of bonds? Why could this decision to buy a new issue be detrimental?

Problems

1. As of July 10, 1987, a Commonwealth Edison bond with an 8 percent coupon rate of interest and a maturity date of 2003 was selling for 86.
   - **(a)** What is the current yield for the bond?
   - **(b)** Calculate the yield-to-maturity using both the approximation method and the present-value method assuming annual interest payments.
2. What will be the price of the Commonwealth Edison bond from Problem 1 in July 1990 if the market rate of interest is at 10 percent? At 16 percent?
3. Using Exhibit 10-1, a twenty-two year bond sells for $910. What is its yield to maturity? Three years later, the bond sells for $880. What is the yield to maturity at that time? If instead of selling at $880 in

three years, the bond sells for $980, what will happen to its yield-to-maturity at that time?

4. Based on the following data and price quotations for three AT&T bonds, what are the factors an investor would want to consider before making a purchase?

Bond	Current Yield	Daily Volume	Closing Price
AT&T 3⅞s 90	4.1	32	94¼
AT&T 8.80s 05	9.2	267	95¾
AT&T 7¼s 03	8.8	408	81

5. The LML Company bond with ten years to maturity pays 8 percent interest annually.
   (a) If the current market interest rate is 12 percent, calculate the duration of the bond. Show all your work.
   (b) What happens to the duration for the bond if the market interest rate increases to 16 percent? Decreases to 0 percent?
   (c) For part a, what would be the duration if the bond's coupon rate were 4 percent instead of 8 percent?

6. After five years have passed, calculate the duration for the bond in Problem 5a. For example, calculate the duration of a bond with five years remaining to maturity paying 8 percent annually at a market interest rate of 12 percent. What do you observe to be the relationship between the decline in years to maturity and duration?

7. You observe the interest rates on a series of bonds to be increasing steadily over the next four years. However, the series does not include a bond with a three-year maturity.

Year	Interest Rate
1	8%
2	10
3	x
4	11

   (a) Calculate the yield to maturity for a three-year bond.
   (b) What is the expected interest rate for a one-year bond to be issued at the beginning of year three?
   (c) Given that the real interest rate is 4 percent and is expected to remain at that level for the next four years, approximately what inflation rate is implied by the above analysis for year three?

Chapter 11

Money Market Securities and Government Bonds

Key Concepts

- agency bond
- assessment bond
- bank discount rate
- bankers' acceptances
- certificate of deposit
- commercial paper
- "flower" bonds
- general obligation bond
- money market security
- municipal bond
- revenue bond
- savings bond
- tax anticipation security
- taxable equivalent return
- treasury bill
- treasury bond
- treasury note

Chapter Outline

Liquidity and quality are two of the most important aspects of any fixed-income security. This chapter examines short-term, high-quality debt obligations known as money market securities. Some money market securities are issued by the United States government or its agencies, although state, local, and foreign governments may also issue money market securities. Expanding from a discussion of these short-term securities, we conduct an examination of the longer-term securities, notes and bonds, issued by governmental bodies. The next chapter explores corporate short-term securities and longer-term bonds.

Money Market Securities

The predominant feature of a money market security, regardless of the issuer, is its highly liquid nature. This characteristic is implied in the name *money market security,* and investors generally consider holdings in this type of investment to be a good substitute for cash. As previously noted, liquidity as associated with an investment means that it can be sold quickly at a price close to the price of the last sale. Their relatively high quality and short maturity (one year or less) make money market securities relatively "safe" investments. The price of the security should vary little from its redemption value. If the price did fall, the investor could choose to wait the short period of time until the security matured in order to receive the full redemption value.

For investors to be able to sell a money market security quickly without much impact on the market price implies that the market trading in money market securities is very large. We will see as we discuss the various types of money market securities that both the amount of securities outstanding and the volume of trading is indeed huge, giving these fixed-income securities their justified reputation for liquidity. The liquidity of the marketplace for money market securities may vary, depending on the size of the investor. Large institutional investors may get better price execution and possess greater liquidity than investors with modest holdings of money market securities.

Money market securities may be purchased directly or indirectly by investors. Investors with large sums of money to invest, such as over $100,000, will often buy money market securities directly from the issuer or from the investment banker assisting the issuer with the sale. Investors with small sums of money to invest may purchase money market securities directly under certain circumstances such as when his or her investment time horizon equals the maturity of the security. However, investors with modest amounts to invest may be attracted to a number of indirect methods of participating in the market for these short-term securities. Two of the major indirect alternatives are money market investment companies and money market deposits available at financial institutions. Investment companies are discussed in Chapter 16.

Treasury Bills and Tax Anticipation Securities

Treasury bills are issued by the federal government and have a maturity of up to one year. The more typical maturities are periods of three and six months. Bills are issued on a book entry basis with a minimum denomination of $10,000. Figure 11–1 shows the amount of treasury bills outstanding at year-end from 1968 through 1986. With $400 billion in treasury bills outstanding, the market is well equipped to provide liquidity to the investor.

Figure 11–1 also shows the average yield available from three-month treasury bills for the 1968–86 period. Bills carry no coupon or interest payment and are issued at a discount from their redemption value. Treasury bills are quoted on a *bank discount* basis as are the yields presented on Figure 11–1. For a ninety-day (three-month) treasury bill quoted at 8 percent, the price would be determined with the following equation:

Figure 11–1
U.S. Treasury Bills, 1968–86

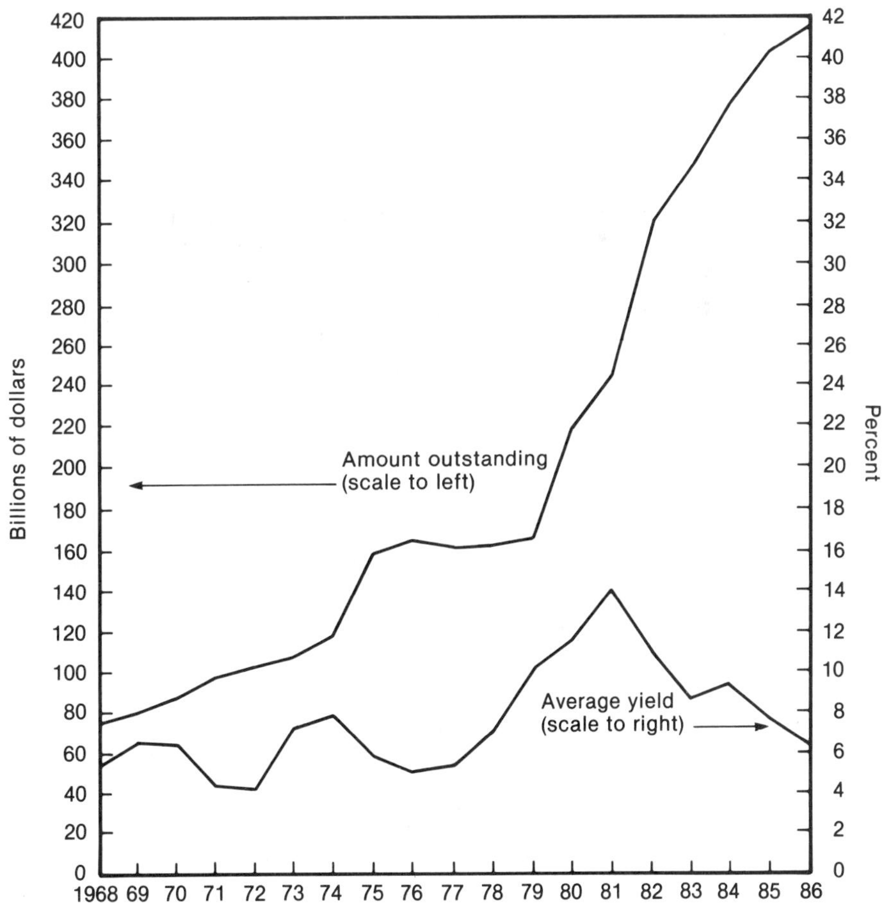

Source: Federal Reserve Bulletin.

$$P = 100 - \left[Y\left(\frac{M}{360}\right)\right]$$

$$= 100 - \left[8\left(\frac{90}{360}\right)\right]$$

$$= 98$$

where Y = quoted yield
M = days of maturity

The quoted yield is not the actual investment yield. The investment yield is approximately the ratio of the quoted yield to the price. Thus, the 8 percent treasury bill is a security with an investment yield of 8.16 percent: the ratio of 8 to 98. This calculation is an approximation because the quoted yield is based on a 360-day year. To adjust for this, one would multiply the restated yield of 8.16 percent by the ratio of 365 to 360. Using this exact technique, the investment yield becomes 8.27 on the ninety-day bill. In practice, the quoted bank discount rate (8.16 percent in our example) is used and is usually very close to the actual yield. The actual yield (8.27 percent) will always be slightly higher than the quoted rate. Like all income from U.S. government securities, the gain made on treasury bills is exempt from state and local taxes.

The typical procedure for issuing three- and six-month treasury bills is a weekly auction usually held on Monday. Delivery of the bills and payment for them is normally made the following Thursday. Investors may enter noncompetitive bids (without a stated price) in person or by mail at the Bureau of the Public Debt or at any of the thirty-six banks and branches of the Federal Reserve System. A noncompetitive bidder pays the average price of all competitive bids accepted and is assured of getting the treasury bills. Some brokerage firms will enter a noncompetitive bid for their customers for a modest fee. The brokerage firm will keep the securities in the customer's account and collect the principal at maturity.

Tax anticipation securities, as their name implies, are short-term securities that can be used to pay one's income taxes. Assume an investor owes $10,000 in federal income tax that is due in four weeks, the investor could purchase a tax anticipation bill at a discount and use the face amount of the bill to pay the tax liability when due. The motivation for wealthy investors and for corporations to use tax anticipation bills is that the maturity of these bills is set several days after the tax due date, but the Internal Revenue Service allows the bills to be redeemed at par on the tax date. Thus, the earnings on a tax anticipation bill will be earned over a somewhat shorter period of time than the stated maturity.

Short-Term Municipal Securities

State and local governments issue short-term debt obligations in anticipation of the receipt of funds from some source. The short-term municipal securities provide working capital to the issuer and are the tax-exempt version of commercial paper, which we discuss below. Three basic types of short-term municipal securities exist. Each takes its name from the anticipated source of funds for the repayment of the debt obligation. Tax anticipation notes (TANs) are issued to provide funds for a government or governmental body until such times as specific tax receipts are expected. Short-term obligations whose repayment is expected from other sources of revenue are known as revenue anticipation notes (RANs). If the short-term debt obligation is to be repaid from the proceeds of the issuance of a long-term municipal bond, they are called bond anticipation notes (BANs).

Short-term municipal bonds are rated by Moody's with the following classifications available:

MIG 1 Best quality with least risk

MIG 2 High quality with little risk

MIG 3 Favorable quality but lacking in the strength of the two higher ratings

MIG 4 Adequate quality and the most risky

The typical minimum denomination for short-term municipal securities is $5,000, but the investor planning to invest less than $25,000 may encounter price concessions in getting orders executed. In other words, an investor planning to sell $5,000 or $10,000 in short-term municipal securities may receive a lower price than an investor selling $25,000 or more. This might not be a practical problem for an investor who buys less than $25,000 when the bonds are originally issued and holds the securities until they mature. However, even in this situation, individuals may experience trouble buying the securities because many of the better quality short-term municipal bonds are purchased by commercial banks and other corporate investors.

Commercial Paper

Short-term promissory notes issued by private corporations are called *commercial paper.* The issuing corporation generally belongs to the "honor roll" of financially sound organizations. The amount of commercial paper outstanding in recent years has expanded rapidly, as shown by Figure 11–2. During the 1970–86 period shown on the graph, the amount of commercial paper outstanding rose from about $32 billion to about $331 billion, for an annual growth rate of approximately 16 percent. Commercial paper is sold directly to the investor by the issuing organization, or the sale is assisted by a dealer. Figure 11–2 shows the growth of both types of commercial paper.

The commercial paper issue is often backed by unused lines of bank credit. This means that a firm with $100 million in commercial paper outstanding will have borrowing capability of at least $100 million at a commercial bank. Typical maturities for commercial paper range from a few days to 270 days. Commercial paper is usually issued in bearer form and sold on a discount basis. However, some commercial paper has been issued recently on an interest-bearing basis. In general, investors in commercial paper are other large corporations, since the minimum round-lot transaction is $250,000 and the typical minimum denomination is $100,000 of face value.

The yields available on commercial paper are usually 30 to 100 basis points above the yields on treasury bills with equivalent maturities. Figure 11–3 shows the difference in yield between six-month commercial

Figure 11–2
Commercial Paper Outstanding, 1970–86

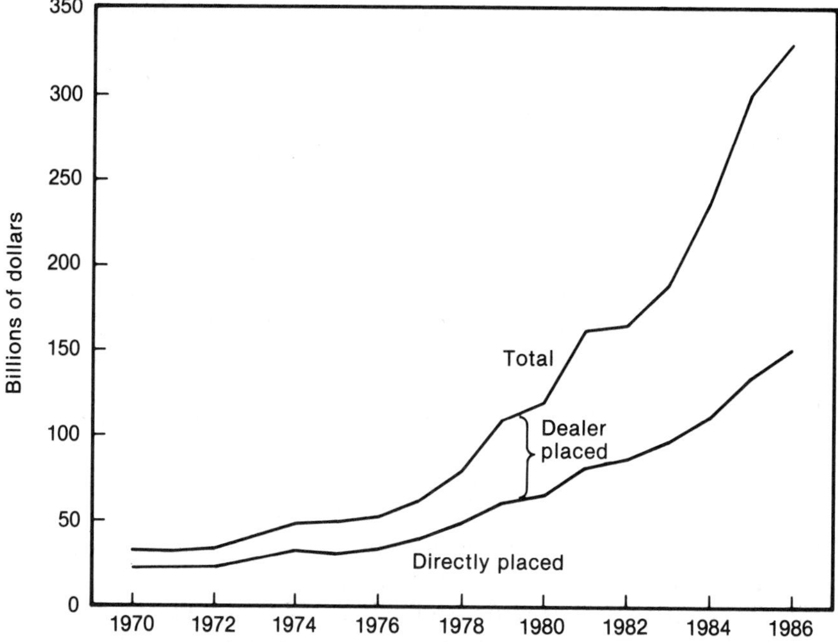

Source: Federal Reserve Bulletin.

Figure 11–3
Six-Month Commercial Paper Yield Less Six-Month Treasury Bill Yield, 1970–86

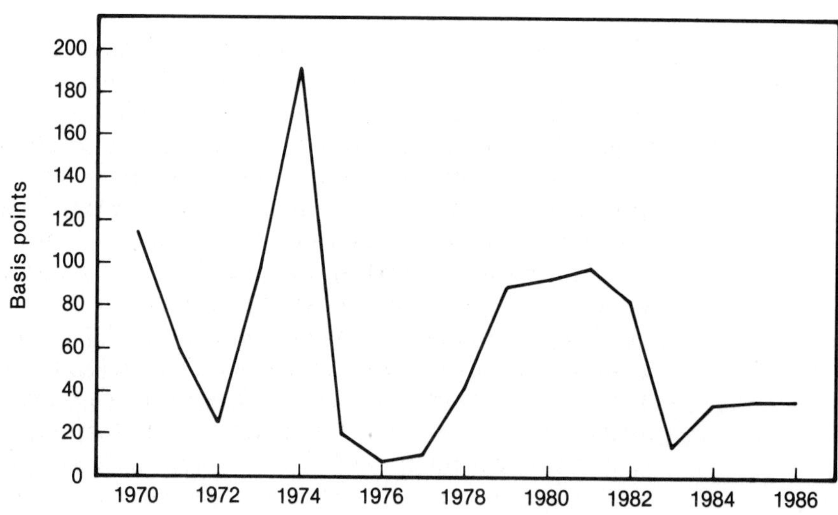

paper and treasury bills on an annual basis from 1970 through 1986. Notice the large difference in 1974, which expanded to as much as 300 basis points during the summer of 1974. Concern on the part of investors about the quality of commercial paper outstanding and a strong demand for short-term funds by corporations were responsible for the widening yield differential.

Although the risk associated with commercial paper is greater than that associated with treasury bills, in most cases the risk is insignificant and need not be given a great deal of consideration. Risk is not absent, however; witness the 1970 default on the approximately $80 million of commercial paper issued by the Penn Central Corporation.

Negotiable Certificates of Deposit

Another important money market instrument of recent vintage is the *certificate of deposit,* which is popularly known as a CD. Money market CDs are *negotiable* time deposits issued by large commercial banks. Since 1970, Federal Reserve controls have been gradually suspended on CDs of $100,000 or more, so that the rates today generally follow the rates on all other uncontrolled money market securities. CDs generally come in denominations of $100,000 to $1,000,000, and are usually traded in lots of $1,000,000. They can be issued with virtually any maturity, but most frequently, maturities are in units of 30, 60, or 90 days, with some 180-day maturities. The market for CDs is quite liquid, with several large banks actively making a market in CDs. As with commercial paper, the risk is only slightly higher than that of treasury bills, and yields in May 1987 were approximately 40 basis points above short-term U.S. government securities. Risk is not absent, however, as the failure of the Penn Square Bank of Oklahoma City during July 1982 illustrates.

Bankers' Acceptances

Money market investors also have available to them *bankers' acceptances,* which can be used for short-term, low-risk investments. Bankers acceptances are usually created as the result of a foreign trade transaction. If a large retailer in the United States wishes to purchase a shipment of toys on credit from an English firm and the English firm would like payment immediately, the usual arrangement is for the U.S. firm to arrange a letter of credit with a local bank made out in favor of the exporting firm. The letter of credit is sent to the English firm, which negotiates it at a local bank receiving payment in British pounds. The letter of credit along with the shipping documents is then sent to the U.S. bank where the letter is stamped "accepted." This means the U.S. bank has accepted responsibility for payment. The letter of credit becomes a bankers' acceptance that is usually sold to an acceptance dealer. The proceeds of the sale are returned to the foreign bank. The toys are turned over to the retailer, and the transaction is complete. The credit has been provided by the accep-

Table 11–1
Money Market Rates, May 21, 1987

Security	**Maturity in Days, Rate (%) for Various Maturities**							
	30	*60*	*90*	*120*	*150*	*180*	*270*	*360*
Treasury bills May 18 auction			6.03			6.34		
Commercial paper								
Finance co., direct issue	6.95	6.90	6.85	6.75	6.70	6.70	6.70	
Major corp., dealer placed	6.95	7.05	7.10					
Certificates of deposit	6.37	6.49	6.58			6.72		6.95
Bankers' acceptances	6.95	7.01	7.15	7.22	7.31	7.33		

Source: Wall Street Journal, May 22, 1987.

tance dealer, or more properly by the money market investor purchasing the acceptance from the acceptance dealer.

At year-end 1986, about $65 billion in bankers' acceptances were outstanding with maturities usually set at 180 days. The denominations vary but are often over $100,000. The purchase and sale of acceptances is done on a discount basis in the same manner as treasury bills and commercial paper. At maturity, the acceptance is presented to the accepting bank for payment. The bank collects from the original importing firm in the form of payments to the bank as the toys are sold. The risk associated with bankers' acceptances is directly related to the risk of the accepting bank becoming insolvent. Interestingly, a principal loss to investors from an investment in bankers' acceptances has never occurred, and these instruments have been available in the secondary money market since the early 1920s. Because of the low risk, the returns on bankers' acceptances have been close to those available from treasury bills.

Summary of Money Market Rates

Table 11–1 shows the interest rates available in the money market for the various direct money market investments examined in this section. Treasury bill yields are the lowest for the various maturities shown in Table 11–1, as would be expected on the basis of their low risk. The interest rates for other money market securities are close to but higher than the yields available from treasury bills. The precise rate offered by a money market security issuer will depend on how badly the issuer wants the money and how quality conscious the money market participants are at the time.

Federal Government and Agency Notes and Bonds

Fixed-income securities having a maturity over one year and issued by various governments or governmental agencies are called government bonds. We examine federal government bonds in this section and state and local securities (municipal bonds) in the next major section. As with money market securities, investor interest in government bonds has increased in recent years. We will concentrate on the direct means of purchasing these long-term debt obligations, deferring the indirect means to the chapter on investment companies.

Nature of the Market and Ownership

The U.S. government bonds that are marketable (some are not, as we shall see) hold a special place in our economy, because they are the most liquid of all long-term debt obligations. Virtually all trading in U.S. government bonds is conducted in the over-the-counter market. The Association of Primary Dealers in Government Securities represents important dealers in these financial securities. These dealers make the market in government securities and are regularly in contact with buyers and sellers. Large institutions and corporations may deal directly with one of these firms, while other investors may make transactions through a local bank or brokerage firm.

The large volume of over-the-counter activity assures the investor that a holding can be liquidated in minutes at a price very close to that of the previous trade. The spread between the bid and asked price is often less than 25 cents per $1,000 of par value. Most transactions are made on a net basis, which means that no commission is involved. Occasionally, a service charge will be made for small transactions, and the price execution for the small investor may not be as good as for the larger investor.

As of June 1986, the federal government had outstanding over $2,059 billion (face value) of fixed-income securities. The ownership of these securities is widespread, with the largest single owner being the federal government itself. If we include the Federal Reserve System, government ownership is approximately twenty-seven percent of the total outstanding federal issues. The large portion of the federal debt owned directly by the federal government is held in a variety of investment accounts. These accounts include reserves for the Social Security System, the insurance reserves of the Federal Deposit Insurance Corporation, and the retirement plan for federal government employees.

Although the various government investment accounts are extremely large, they are much less significant as a market force than might be indicated by their size, since the securities in the accounts are typically not traded. They are purchased at the time of issue and redeemed at maturity. The redemption process often does not involve cash, but merely the exchange of the maturing issue for a new issue.

The private ownership of U.S. government securities is strongly influenced by the stage of the business cycle. In expansionary times, commercial banks, insurance companies, and other financial institutions tend to be heavy sellers of federal government issues in order to invest in the private sector of the economy. During a contraction in the economy, the reverse occurs; financial institutions tend to accumulate government securities. The individual investor tends to accumulate government securities when the rates are better than the rates of return available on the time deposits of commercial banks and other financial institutions.

Risks of Federal Government Bonds

The changes in the ownership of U.S. government securities during various stages of the business cycle are directly related to the characteristics of these securities. In our general examination of fixed-income securities in Chapter 10, we noted three elements of risk: (1) interest rate risk, (2) purchasing power risk, and (3) credit or quality risk. In the case of U.S. government bonds, the element of credit risk is absent because no credit risk is associated with fixed-income securities of the federal government. The owner can be completely certain the principal and interest will be paid in full and on time. The reason for the absence of credit risk lies neither in the financial condition of the federal government nor in its taxing power. An understanding of both the financial condition of the government and its taxing power is vital to an understanding of the economy, but it is not important to the safety of the principal and interest of U.S. government bonds. The federal government has the constitutional power to issue and create money. In the final analysis, new money can simply be issued in order to meet the obligations of the federal debt. With this power, defaults on U.S. government issues will not occur unless the government is overthrown and previous debt issues are not honored.

The act of creating money may help to create inflationary economic conditions so that the face value of the bonds will purchase less than originally expected. But this situation has to do with purchasing power risk and perhaps interest rate risk; it is not credit risk. The return of principal and interest may represent a real income loss, but in monetary terms, the investor can be assured of the absence of defaults.

Types of Long-Term Federal Government Securities

Several types of federal government bonds are available for the investor. This section identifies federal government notes and bonds in addition to two varieties of federal bonds, savings bonds and "flower" bonds, available to investors. Bonds issued by agencies of the federal government are also discussed in this section.

Treasury Notes and Bonds

The federal government's long-term marketable securities issued at a stated or coupon rate are called treasury notes and bonds. Notes have an initial maturity of one to ten years. Notes are typically sold in registered form and sometimes carry a minimum denomination as low as $1,000. As was true for treasury bills, an investor's bid for newly issued notes or bonds may be competitive or noncompetitive.

Bonds carry initial maturities of five years or more, with the typical issue having a maturity longer than five years. Since mid-1971, all new issues of marketable U.S. government bonds carry a minimum denomination of $1,000. With the many issues of both notes and bonds outstanding, an investor can usually arrange virtually any maturity schedule desired, up to about twenty-five years, either by purchasing new issues or by trading issues in the secondary market.

When purchasing bonds or notes, an investor must be aware of the method of quoting U.S. government bonds in the financial press. Prices are reported and traded in increments of $\frac{1}{32}$. The usual method of reporting prices is in decimal form as follows: $8\frac{1}{4}$s 2000–05 May 92.10 Bid 92.18 Asked. The asked price for this bond is 92 and $\frac{18}{32}$. Occasionally, a quotation may be made in increments of $\frac{1}{64}$, and the price might be reported as 92.18+, which would be interpreted as 92 and $\frac{37}{64}$.

Treasury bonds are often callable at par during the last five years of their maturity. For example, the $8\frac{1}{4}$ percent bond maturing in 2005 is callable at par beginning in 2000. In order for the investor to be aware of this feature, the bond is described as $8\frac{1}{4}$, 2000–05; the first date refers to the initial call date and the later date the maturity. In reporting prices for this bond, the financial press retains this label.

Savings Bonds

With some very minor exceptions, bills, notes, and bonds represent the total marketable debt issued directly by the federal government. Of the nonmarketable issues, the most important for the individual investor is the U.S. savings bond, which has the attractions of small denominations and safety. Two categories of savings bonds are currently being sold, the series EE and the series HH. These two bond series replaced the series E and H bonds sold prior to 1980.

Important differences exist between these two types of savings bonds, as noted in Exhibit 11–1. The minimum denomination for the series EE is $50 of par value, while the series HH can be purchased in multiples of $500. The income from series EE bonds comes in the form of appreciation in the value of the bond, as opposed to the current income received every six months from series HH bonds. Series EE bonds carry a maturity that is fixed by U.S. Treasury regulation when the bonds are purchased, while series HH bonds have an initial maturity of ten years. However, series HH bonds cannot be bought for cash, but only received by swapping a series E or EE bond for them.

The income from a series EE bond comes in the form of price appreciation, and the bonds are purchased from the treasury at a discount of 50 percent of the face value of the bond. If you were to purchase a $100 series EE bond, the purchase price would be $50. Effective November 1, 1982, series EE bonds pay a variable rate of interest equal to 85 percent of the five-year U.S. government securities rate. The bond must be held for five years to get this entire rate. A guaranteed minimum yield of 6 percent accrues if the bonds are held for five years.

Like all U.S. government issues, the income from savings bonds is exempt from state and local taxes, but not from federal income taxes. However, in the case of series EE bonds, the tax payment need not be made until the bond is redeemed. This may be an advantage to the saver if redemption occurs after retirement or in a low income year. In addition, a series EE bond may be exchanged, at its current redemption price, for a series HH bond without having to pay taxes on the accrued income of the series EE bond. With such a conversion, the tax payable is postponed until either the redemption or final maturity of the newly acquired series HH bond.

"Flower" Bonds

The investor also has available for purchase a number of somewhat unusual securities. For example, several U.S. government bonds are known as flower bonds. The advantage of these bonds is that a flower bond purchased at a discount can be used at par in the payment of estate taxes. If death were to occur shortly after a person purchased a flower bond at 90, the person's estate would benefit because this bond is accepted at 100 for the payment of estate taxes. However, the Tax Reform Act of 1976 diluted some of these potential tax benefits, making a portion of the benefit taxable as a capital gain. Because no new bonds with this special provision have been issued since March 1971, the supply of these bonds gets smaller each year as outstanding bonds are used to pay estate taxes and older bonds mature.

Flower bonds tend to sell at substantial yield discounts because of

Exhibit 11–1 **Comparison of Series EE and HH Bonds**

Characteristic	*Series EE*	*Series HH*
Denominations	\$50, \$75, \$100, \$200, \$500, \$1,000, \$5,000, \$10,000	\$500, \$1,000, \$5,000, \$10,000
Purchase price	50% of denomination	Denomination value
Interest rate	85% of average five-year U.S. government securities rate—if held at least five years	Depends on issue date; currently 6%
Maturity	Set upon purchase	Ten years
Payment of interest	Increase in redemption value	By semiannual check to holder
Tax status of interest	Taxed as current income or may be deferred until redemption	Taxed as current income
Redemption	Any time after six months from issue date	Any time after six months from issue date
Exchange provision	May be exchanged for Series HH bond; \$500 minimum from six months after issue until one year after maturity	None

Investment Highlight

Series EE Bonds (A Rush to Buy a Government Investment)

The ability of the American investing public to recognize a sound, high-yielding investment is discussed in this investment highlight.

Description

At the end of October 1986, investors started to line up outside of selling agencies such as the commercial banks. Some sellers even ran out of some of the more popular denominations. What was this highly sought-after investment? It was none other than U.S. Government Series EE bonds.

Rumors had been prevalent for several weeks that the minimum guaranteed five-year rate of 7½ percent on Series EE bonds would be reduced on the semiannual rate-setting date of November 1, 1986. After all, interest rates in the market had declined over the past few years, and a rate of 7½ percent on a five-year investment in a government guaranteed security appeared to be a real bargain. Five-year U.S. government notes were yielding only 6.75 percent in late October.

Near the end of October, the U.S. Treasury announced that the guaranteed minimum rate for a five-year investment in Series EE bonds bought on or after November 1, 1986, would be only 6 percent, although these bonds would continue to pay a rate equal to 85 percent of the market average on five-year treasury securities. The forthcoming demise of the 7½ percent guaranteed minimum yield coupled with the ability of investors to defer taxation on the interest income from these bonds until they are redeemed caused a "buying panic." During October 1986, the U.S. Treasury sold $1.4 billion of these bonds, up substantially from the $.65 billion sold during June 1986.

Conclusion

Various financial advisors have criticized Series EE bonds in the past as a poor investment from the standpoint of the risk and return trade-off. This example shows clearly that no investment should be eliminated permanently from the set of potential investments. Market conditions can change rapidly, and in October 1986, Series EE bonds became a relatively attractive investment for conservative investors. Investors must be aware of these types of situations as they develop in order to make good risk and return decisions.

the estate tax feature. In late May 1987, the two following U.S. government bonds were quoted in the *Wall Street Journal:*

7% May 1993–98	87.13 asked	to yield 8.81%
3½% Nov. 1998	93.16 asked	to yield 4.22%

An institutional investor having no estate tax motive would have no interest in the 3½ percent bond of November 1998. However, for a person whose death could be anticipated within the next few weeks, the 3½ percent bond would be useful for estate planning purposes.

Agency Bonds

An increasingly important investment alternative exists in the market for federal agency securities. Over $300 billion of these securities are outstanding as of December 31, 1986. Figure 11–4 shows the growth of federal agency debt obligations since 1960 when only about $7 billion of these securities were outstanding.

We should distinguish between two types of agencies: federal agencies and federally sponsored agencies. Federal agencies, such as the Farmers Home Administration and the Postal Service, are a part of the federal government. Federally sponsored agencies, such as the Federal National Mortgage Association, are privately owned but have a definite public purpose. Most of the federal agency debt outstanding has been issued by federally sponsored agencies. Table 11–2 shows the principal agencies of both varieties and the amount of debt each has outstanding as of December 31, 1986.

In terms of return, federal agency securities will sometimes sell for as much as seventy-five basis points more than an equivalent maturity bond issued directly by the U.S. Treasury. Most of the debt obligations of federal agencies are also obligations of the United States, although those of the Postal Service and the Tennessee Valley Authority are not. In other words, if you owned bonds issued by the TVA, the principal and interest payments would be paid from the earnings of TVA. If these earnings were insufficient, the bondholder could not look to the taxing power or money-creating power of the federal government as a source of funds to meet the obligation of the TVA bonds.

The lack of a direct government guarantee is a problem in theory only. Although no explicit guarantee by the U.S. Treasury exists, a strong government guarantee is implied. In fact, the TVA has backstop funds available from the U.S. Treasury. Most federally sponsored agencies also have some emergency borrowing authority from the U.S. Treasury. It is difficult to imagine the federal government allowing TVA or some other

Figure 11–4
Debt of Federal and Federally Sponsored Agencies, 1960–86

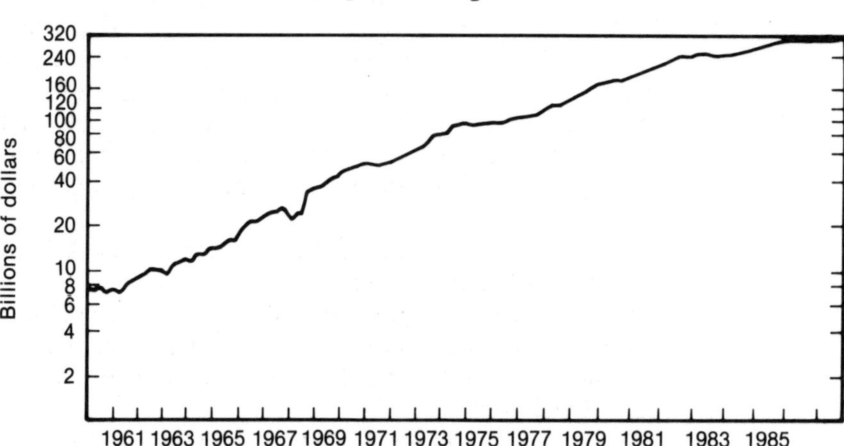

Sources: U.S. Treasury Bulletin and *Federal Reserve Bulletin.*

Table 11–2
Debt of Principal Federal Agencies, December 1986

Federal Agencies	
Export-Import Bank	$14.2 billion
Government National Mortgage Assoc.	2.2
Postal Service	3.1
TVA	17.2
Federally Sponsored Agencies	
Federal Home Loan Banks	88.8
Federal National Mortgage Assoc.	93.6
Farm Credit Banks	62.3
Federal Financing Bank[a]	157.5

[a]Started in 1974 to incur debt to lend to other agencies

Source: Federal Reserve Bulletin.

Table 11–3
Representative U.S. Government and FNMA Bonds

Security			May 21, 1987 *Bid*	*Asked*	*Spread*	*Yield*
U.S.	6.50%	11/91	92.19	92.23	.4	8.49%
FNMA	7.00	9/91	93.21	93.25	.4	8.76
U.S.	7.25	11/96	89.17	89.21	.4	8.89
FNMA	7.60	1/97	88.16	88.18	.2	9.43
U.S.	7.25	5/16	84.5	84.9	.4	9.03
FNMA	8.20	3/16	84.12	84.24	.12	9.79

agency to enter the bankruptcy courts because of the inability to meet principal and interest obligations on outstanding debt. The only real credit risk lies in potential delayed payments. Financial problems might cause a delay in payments, but it seems doubtful that the U.S. Congress would allow the liquidation of the assets of one of the agencies. In essence, the purchase of a federal agency bond requires the sacrifice of a slight amount of protection in return for an added yield. We note the bid-asked spread differences and the yield-to-maturity differences between U.S. government bonds and Federal National Mortgage Association bonds in Table 11–3.

The interest earned on federal agency bonds is subject to federal income tax. The taxability at the state and local level depends on the federal agency issue in question. Many agency securities are subject to state and local taxes, with the major exceptions being securities of the Federal Home Loan Banks and the sponsored farm credit agencies such as Federal Land Banks.

As with direct debt obligations of the U.S. Treasury, the investor with modest amounts to invest faces the same problems. The standard unit of trading in agency securities is \$100,000, and the investor purchasing a smaller amount than this should be prepared to hold the bonds to maturity or incur relatively large commission fees and get relatively poor price execution.

Municipal Bonds

Government units besides the federal government issue marketable fixed-income securities. State and local governmental units also issue debt securities that are generally referred to as *municipal* or tax exempt bonds. Municipals basically include all fixed-income financial instruments issued by a governmental unit other than the federal government.

Tax Status and Taxable Equivalent Returns

Municipal bonds have a variety of characteristics that separate them from U.S. government bonds, but the most outstanding feature is their tax status. The income received by the owner of most municipal bonds is exempt from the federal income tax. In addition, most states will allow a tax exemption on the interest received from its own state and local issues. However, the federal exemption is by far the most important of the tax exemption features.

To see the significance of the tax exemption feature, let us suppose that an investor filing a joint return has taxable income of \$48,000. This places the investor in the 28 percent marginal tax bracket. Suppose this investor can purchase a corporate bond that returns 10 percent. What would a municipal bond of comparable risk and maturity need to offer for the investor to be indifferent? We can answer this question by using the following equation:

$$R_{at} = R_{bt}(1 - t)$$

where R_{at} = after-tax rate of return
R_{bt} = before-tax rate of return
t = investor's marginal tax rate

The answer is 7.2 percent, determined as follows:

$$R_{at} = R_{bt}(1 - t)$$
$$x = 10\%(1 - .28)$$
$$x = 7.2\%$$

The problem could be stated in a different manner. Suppose an investor can purchase a municipal bond with a rate of return of 8 percent. What yield (often called the *taxable equivalent yield*) would the investor need to obtain on a corporate bond to prefer buying the taxable corporate bond? We can solve this problem as follows:

$$R_{at} = R_{bt}(1 - t)$$
$$8\% = x(1 - .28)$$
$$x = 11.1\%$$

At a return of 11.1 percent, the investor would be indifferent between the two investment alternatives. With a return greater than 11.1 percent for the corporate bond, the investor in the 28 percent marginal tax bracket would prefer the corporate bond, assuming all the other bond features for the two bonds are reasonably comparable.

Categories of Municipals

The risk associated with the purchase of municipals is typically much different from the risk associated with U.S. government bonds. In order to examine the risk associated with a municipal, we must understand three basic categories of municipals: general obligation, revenue, and assessment bonds.

General obligation bonds, or full-faith-and-credit bonds, are backed by the overall financial and taxing power of the issuing political entity. The risk of default is tied to the resources of the entire state, county, city, or other political entity issuing the bonds. These bonds typically carry high credit ratings with corresponding low risk and low returns. We need to recognize, however, that even general obligation bonds carry credit risk because taxing power is limited and state and local governments do not hold the power to create money.

Revenue bonds form the second large category of municipal bonds. The principal and interest payments on these bonds can be made only from the revenues generated by the assets financed from the proceeds of the issue. The building of a bridge, for example, may be financed with revenue bonds. The revenue bonds issued will be serviced from bridge tolls for the life of the bond. If the income from the bridge is not sufficient to meet the debt obligation, the bondholder has no recourse to state or local authorities. However, if the assets built with revenue bonds are indispensable to the particular state or other political entity, the political entity would be likely to intervene in the case of a revenue bond in default. Generally speaking, however, revenue bonds are more risky than general obligation bonds, although some revenue bonds are of very high quality.

Bonds in the much smaller third category are usually issued for the purpose of improving existing governmental facilities. These *assessment bonds* take their name from the fact that principal and interest will be paid from the proceeds of specific assessments on the property in the political entity. The property tax is set up so that a certain portion will go to meet the debt obligation. If the value of the assessed property declines, the bonds may be in risk of default.

The Market for Municipals

The market in municipal bonds is large. Out of nearly 100,000 governmental bodies capable of selling municipal bonds, at least 40,000 have some debt outstanding. In recent years, most municipal bonds have been issued in $5,000 units. Like corporate bonds, the large municipal issues are given a credit rating by Moody's or Standard & Poor's; essentially the same letter grade notation is used for municipals as for corporate bonds. We will discuss these ratings in more detail in Chapter 12. The credit rating techniques are complex, with consideration given to the aggregate tax burden of the community, the per capita income, the trend of expenditures, the stability of employment in the community, and the growth of the community. The quality of credit ratings for municipal bonds is quite good, and an independent credit analysis of the credit standing of a given municipal bond would usually produce a rating close to the rating given by Moody's or Standard & Poor's.

Although the ratings are generally reliable, many municipal issues are too small to merit attention by the rating agencies. Consequently, many investors choose from among only the larger issues. Thousands of smaller issues are available, but these are usually for the local investor only. To purchase or attempt to gain information on the small issues is usually impractical, unless one has a special interest in the community issuing the bond. Even with issues that have received a rating, most investors should limit their holdings to large issues of high-quality municipals with ratings of at least single A. Like corporate bonds, municipals with lower ratings are more appropriate for investors with either special expertise in the analysis of fixed-income municipal securities or sufficient capital to diversify widely.

Problems for Investors in Municipal Bonds

Liquidity

The secondary market is almost entirely over the counter, and unless the issue is large and well known, the investor may face a liquidity problem when attempting to sell. The sale of a holding of a small municipal bond may require several days and a considerable sacrifice in price. Even with larger issues, an investor probably should not consider the purchase of less than a round-lot, which is $25,000 of face value, unless planning to hold the issue to its maturity. Anything less than a round-lot will normally produce liquidity problems that will be manifested in a price sacrifice. The round-lot advice has nothing to do with commissions because no commissions are charged in the municipal bond market. Rather, the dealer earns a fee through a price difference between the buyer's price and the dealer's cost.

Maturity Structure

Many municipal bonds are issued in the form of serial bonds. A serial bond issue exists when the individual bonds under the indenture have their own special maturity. Exhibit 11–2 is the front page of a prospectus for a Municipal Assistance Corporation bond offering. The offering consists of varying dollar amounts of serial bonds maturing from 1982 through 1985 and a term bond issue maturity in 1995.

NEW ISSUE

In the opinion of Bond Counsel, under existing statutes and court decisions, interest on the 1978 Series JJ Bonds is exempt from Federal income taxes, and shall at all times be free from New York State and New York City personal income taxes.

$250,155,000

MUNICIPAL ASSISTANCE CORPORATION FOR THE CITY OF NEW YORK

(A Corporate Governmental Agency and Instrumentality of the State of New York)

1978 SERIES JJ BONDS

(Issued pursuant to the First General Bond Resolution)

Dated January 1, 1978 **Due February 1, as shown below**

Principal of and interest on the 1978 Series JJ Bonds are payable at the corporate trust office of Citibank, N.A., New York, New York, or at the option of the holder at Bank of America NT & SA, San Francisco, California, unless registered. Interest on the 1978 Series JJ Bonds is payable August 1, 1978 and semi-annually thereafter on each February 1 and August 1. The 1978 Series JJ Bonds will be issued as coupon bonds in the denomination of $5,000 each, registrable as to principal only, or as fully registered bonds in the denomination of $5,000 or any integral multiple of $5,000. Coupon and registered bonds are interchangeable as more fully described herein.

The 1978 Series JJ Bonds will be issued for the purpose of refunding the previously issued 1975 Series B Bonds of the Corporation. For information which may affect the market or market prices for and sources of payment of the 1978 Series JJ Bonds, see "PART 1—INTRODUCTION" and the references included therein.

The 1978 Series JJ Bonds due February 1, 1982 through 1985, are not subject to redemption prior to maturity. The 1978 Series JJ Bonds due February 1, 1995, are subject to redemption at the option of the Corporation on and after February 1, 1988, as a whole on any date, or in part by lot on any interest payment date or dates, at an initial redemption price of 102% of the principal amount thereof, and from mandatory sinking fund installments on and after February 1, 1989, at a redemption price of 100% of the principal amount thereof, plus, in each case, accrued interest to the redemption date, all as more fully described herein.

The Trustee under the First General Bond Resolution (pursuant to which the 1978 Series JJ Bonds are to be issued) is United States Trust Company of New York.

Due	Amount	Rate	Price	Due	Amount	Rate	Price
1982	**$13,250,000**	**7¼%**	**@100%**	**1984**	**$40,280,000**	**7¾%**	**@100%**
1983	**52,745,000**	**7½**	**@100**	**1985**	**83,880,000**	**8**	**@100**

$60,000,000 8¼% Term Bonds due February 1, 1995 @ 99¼%

(Accrued interest to be added)

The 1978 Series JJ Bonds are payable out of certain revenues of the Corporation, including revenues derived from certain sales and compensating use taxes imposed by the State of New York within The City of New York and, under certain conditions, the State stock transfer tax. The State is not bound or obligated to continue the imposition of such taxes or to make the necessary appropriations of the revenues derived from such taxes. The Corporation has no taxing power. The 1978 Series JJ Bonds do not constitute an enforceable obligation, or a debt, of either the State or the City, and neither the State nor the City shall be liable thereon. Neither the faith and credit nor the taxing power of the State or the City is pledged to the payment of principal of or interest on the 1978 Series JJ Bonds.

The 1978 Series JJ Bonds are offered when, as and if issued by the Corporation and received by the underwriters and subject to approval of legality by Hawkins, Delafield & Wood, New York, New York, Bond Counsel to the Corporation. Certain legal matters will be passed on for the Corporation by its General Counsel, Paul, Weiss, Rifkind, Wharton & Garrison, New York, New York. It is expected that the 1978 Series JJ Bonds in definitive form will be available for delivery on or about January 10, 1978.

MERRILL LYNCH, PIERCE, FENNER & SMITH

INCORPORATED

Members New York Stock Exchange and other Principal Security Exchanges

The date of this Official Statement is December 22, 1977.

Investment Highlight

"Whoops" (The Washington Public Power Supply System Bonds)

This highlight tells the story of a financial "China Syndrome," or the meltdown of the value of a municipal bond. It illustrates the hazards of grandiose plans financed by huge amounts of debt.

Description

The Washington Public Power Supply System (WPPSS) was established in 1957 by nineteen public utility districts and four cities to build a small hydroelectric project. In the early 1970s, the WPPSS agreed to construct three nuclear power plants. The Bonneville Power Administration agreed to participate in these plans by lending its triple-A credit rating to the WPPSS. Later, two more plants were planned. In December 1980, the WPPSS No. 4–5 12½ percent bonds due 2010 were issued at 100. In May 1981, construction cost estimates were increased and a construction slowdown for plants 4 and 5 was recommended. In January 1982, termination of plants 4 and 5 was announced, at which time the 12½ bonds were selling for about 65 percent of face value.

In January 1983, eighty-one utilities failed to make the monthly payments for the abandoned plants. In June 1983, a Washington court effectively eliminated the financial backing for the WPPSS No. 4–5 bonds by stating that the utilities involved did not have to pay. On July 22, 1983, the WPPSS acknowledged that it could not meet obligations on these plants as they became due, which represented a default under the bond resolution. At that time, the 12½ percent bonds were selling at a bid price of 19. As of the middle of 1987, the bonds were selling for only 12½.

Conclusion

The decline in the demand for electric power in the late 1970s along with rapidly growing costs and perhaps a poorly conceived strategic plan caused this investment debacle. As *Fortune* noted: ". . . the WPPSS has poured $8.3 billion of bondholders' money into five nuclear power projects and hasn't a volt to show for it." *Fortune* (July 25, 1983): 46.

Most toll road bonds are term bonds in which each bond issue matures at one time instead of serially on an annual basis. The difference between a serial bond arrangement and the typical sinking fund in a corporate bond issue, which provides for periodic retirement of corporate bonds, is that the indenture for the municipal bond issue stipulates particular bonds for the annual maturities. The advantage for the investor is that the purchase of a municipal bond can be made without the risk that the investment will be called prior to the expected maturity.

As can be noted in the Municipal Assistance Corporation offering shown in Exhibit 11–2, the serial bonds do not normally maintain a constant coupon interest rate for all maturities. This is no problem for the investor. The secondary market adjusts the prices of the various maturities to reflect the difference in coupon rates relative to the market interest rate for that quality and maturity bond. At the same time, a low coupon rate may cause the bond to sell at a discount, depending on the general level of interest rates.

Quality Determination

Another potential problem for the investor is determining the quality of the municipal bonds offered in the market. With some issuers, bonds may be unrated or the investor may not want to rely on the ratings or attempt to do any independent analysis. An alternative is available. Local governments and governmental agencies can sell municipal bonds insured by the Municipal Bond Insurance Association (MBIA). MBIA is the largest bond insurer in the United States. Several major insurance companies share the liability assumed by insuring municipal bonds. MBIA typically accepts fewer than one-third of the municipal bond issuers that apply for insurance guaranteeing that their interest and principal repayments will be made on time. The issuers pay an insurance premium of from \$9–\$20 per \$1,000 of face par value of the bond at the time the bond is sold. The exact insurance fee depends on the quality and marketability of the bond being insured. As a result of these strict insurance standards, MBIA insured bonds have achieved an automatic triple-A rating from Standard & Poor's.

Summary

Short-term, high-quality money market securities, purchased either directly or indirectly, provide investors with an important means of obtaining an attractive yield when short-term interest rates are high. These securities also provide a useful "parking place" for funds awaiting reinvestment in the stock market or in the long-term bond market. For those investors with large amounts to invest, the direct purchase of money market securities is feasible. Treasury bills, for example, are sold with a minimum denomination of \$10,000. Other money market securities, such as commercial paper, bankers' acceptances, and negotiable certificates of deposit, typically require about \$100,000 if an investor is to invest directly.

Government bonds are issued by the federal government, federal agencies, or state, local, or foreign political entities. Huge quantities of government securities are outstanding, representing the issues of thousands of political entities. The quality ranges from securities issued by the U.S. government that are free of credit risk to municipal bonds of a very speculative nature.

U.S. marketable long-term securities include treasury notes and bonds. Notes have a maturity of from one to ten years, while bonds mature in five or more years. The interest income of federal securities is exempt from state and local income taxes. Securities issued by federal agencies are also available and usually carry slightly higher yields than do the direct issues of the federal government. Savings bonds are considered a nonmarketable U.S. government security because the holder must present them for redemption in order to liquidate the investment.

State and local issues are called municipals or tax-exempt securities (their interest is exempt from federal income taxes in most instances). The three main categories of municipal bonds are general obligation bonds, revenue bonds, and assessment bonds. General obligation bonds are backed by the taxing power of the issuing political entity. Revenue bonds must rely on the revenue produced by projects financed by the proceeds of the bond issue, unless the revenue issue is also backed by the full faith and credit of a political entity. Assessment bonds are serviced by property taxes collected to finance a specific improvement to government services, such as a sewage system.

When investing in money market securities and in government bonds, investors must examine the yields available on the various alternative investments, the amount of money needed to purchase the security, the risk of the various alternatives, and their tax and liquidity positions. Tax advantages are especially critical in municipal bond investing because the interest from most municipal bonds is exempt from federal income taxes.

Suggested Readings

ABKEN, PETER A. "Commercial Paper." *Economic Review,* Federal Reserve Bank of Richmond (March–April 1981): 11–21.

CHANG, ERIC C., and J. MICHAEL PINEGAR. "Return Seasonality and Tax-Loss Selling in the Market for Long-Term Government and Corporate Bonds." *Journal of Financial Economics* (December 1986): 391–415.

COOK, TIMOTHY Q. "Determinants of Individual Tax-Exempt Bond Yields: A Survey of the Evidence." *Economic Review,* Federal Reserve Bank of Richmond (May–June 1982): 14–39.

Fundamentals of Municipal Bonds. New York: Public Securities Association, 1981.

GRIEVES, ROBIN H. *Cash Management.* New York: Financial Analysts Research Foundation, 1982.

GULTEKIN, N. BULENT, and RICHARD J. ROGALSKI. "Government Bond Returns, Measurement of Interest Rate Risk, and the APT." *Journal of Finance* (March 1985): 43–61.

MAYERS, DAVID, and CLIFFORD W. SMITH, JR. "Death and Taxes: The Market for Flower Bonds." *Journal of Finance* (July 1987): 685–98.

STIGUM, MARCIA. *The Money Market,* rev. ed. Homewood, IL: Dow Jones-Irwin, 1983.

YAWITZ, JESS B. "Risk Premia on Municipal Bonds." *Journal of Financial and Quantitative Analysis* (September 1978): 475–85.

YAWITZ, JESS B., and WILLIAM J. MARSHALL. "Risk and Return in the Government Bond Market." *Journal of Portfolio Management* (Summer 1977): 48–52.

Questions

1. What is the effect of the maturity of money market securities on their degree of interest rate risk?

2. Why would an investor consider the purchase of short-term, fixed-income securities issued by the federal government?

3. What are the advantages and disadvantages of treasury bills as an investment for the individual investor?

4. What major types of securities are considered to be money market securities?

5. What types of markets exist for long-term government bonds? How good are these markets?

6. What risks are inherent in long-term government securities? Explain.

7. Discuss the general characteristics of
   (a) treasury notes and bonds
   (b) savings bonds (series EE and HH)
   (c) agency bonds

8. What is the meaning of the following U.S. government bond quotation taken from the *Wall Street Journal?*

   8s, 1996–01 Aug. 91.6 Bid   91.14 Asked + .2 Change

9. What general sort of investor should purchase U.S. savings bonds? Should any difference distinguish the investors who purchase series EE bonds from those who purchase series HH bonds?

10. What is a flower bond? What type of investor might want to purchase such a bond?

11. What are the two main categories of municipal bonds?

12. What factors are important in the determination of the quality of a municipal bond?

13. What type of market exists for municipal bonds? What improvements have been made in this market from the viewpoint of the individual investor?

14. An investor has taxable income of $55,000 and files a joint return. The investor can purchase a triple-A corporate bond at par to yield 9.5 percent. Assuming a marginal tax rate of 28 percent, what yield would this investor require from a municipal bond of comparable quality before it would be purchased?

15. What return would an investor require on an equally risky corporate bond if he or she is in the 40 percent marginal tax bracket and can obtain a 6 percent tax-exempt return from a municipal security?

Chapter 12

Corporate Bonds and Preferred Stocks

Key Concepts

accrued interest
antidilution clause
arrearages
bond rating
bond value
charges coverage ratio
combined premium
common stock substitute
consol
conversion premium
conversion price
conversion ratio
conversion value
convertible security
coverage ratio
cumulative dividends provision
cumulative method
loss premium
noncumulative dividends provision
par value
preferred stock
split rating
straight value

Chapter Outline

Corporate Bond Trading and Statistics
Corporate Bond Ratings
Preferred Stock
Convertible Securities
Summary

Whether to buy or avoid long-term fixed-income investments issued by corporations is an important decision facing investors. Bonds and preferred stocks may very well have a place in an investor's portfolio. This chapter concentrates on investing in both corporate bonds and preferreds.

Corporate Bond Trading and Statistics

Exhibit 12–1 shows selected bond quotations from the NYSE, as reported in the financial press for December 16, 1986. The first item is the name of the issuing corporation followed immediately by the coupon rate and bond maturity. The AT&T bond shows a coupon rate of 7 percent and maturity of 2001, shown as 01.

Corporate bonds are generally issued in units of $1,000. The $1,000 is the face value, or par value, of the bond and is the amount to be received when the principal is repaid. However, we should note that bond quotations in the financial press are listed in $100 units. The *Wall Street Journal* prices of December 16, 1986, show the last sale of the AT&T bond at $88⅜. This means that an investor wishing to purchase one of these bonds should pay about $883.75. The price quotation should be multiplied by ten to arrive at the actual price of the last trade.

Following the identification of the bond in Exhibit 12–1 is the current yield. For the AT&T 7 percent issue to mature in 2001, the current yield is shown as 7.9 percent (7 ÷ 88.375; numbers above 10 are rounded to the nearest whole number, numbers below 10 to the nearest tenth). The current yield would be the investor's return if the bond were purchased for $883.75 and later resold for the same price and if all coupon payments were made on time during the investment's holding period. For the AT&T bond, the current yield may represent a poor measure of the rate of return expected from holding this bond because the current yield ignores any potential capital appreciation or loss. An investor holding this bond to maturity would receive a capital appreciation of $116.25. The financial press routinely reports current yields, but the investor should exercise caution in using these yield figures. The lower the price compared to the bond's par value and the shorter the maturity of the bond, the more misleading is the current yield compared to the yield-to-maturity.

Following the current yield is the number of bonds traded that day. One hundred and sixty-four of the AT&T 7 percent bonds traded on December 16, 1986. The next set of figures indicates the highest price, the lowest price, and the closing or last transacted price of the trading day, respectively. The final figure is the difference between the current closing price and the closing price of the previous day on which a trade occurred. Thus, the net change for the AT&T bond was +¼, or an increase of $2.50 per bond.

Two of the bonds shown on Exhibit 12–1 have *cv* listed in the current yield column. The *cv* stands for convertible bond. Calculate a current yield for a convertible bond in the same manner just discussed. For example, the current yield for the USX 5¾ percent bond of 2001 is 9.13 percent, determined by dividing $57.50 by $630. We will discuss convertible

Exhibit 12–1 **Selected Corporate Bond Price Quotations, December 16, 1986**

Bonds	*Cur Yld*	*Vol*	*High*	*Low*	*Close*	*Net Chg*
Alcoa 9s 95	8.9	10	101⅛	101⅛	101⅛	. . .
ATT 7s 01	7.9	164	88¾	87⅞	88⅜	+¼
Citicp 5¾ 00	cv	4	133	133	133	+11
vjLTV 11s 07f	. . .	412	16	15¼	16	+¼
PacTT 7⅝ 09	8.5	47	90⅜	89⅝	90	−1
USX 5¾ 01	cv	91	63½	62¾	63	. . .

Source: Wall Street Journal.

securities in detail later in this chapter and will see that the current yield is an important calculation in the analysis of a convertible.

The typical corporate bond trades on the basis of price plus *accrued interest.* The AT&T 7 percent bond makes interest payments on February 15 and August 15. Because interest payments are made only every six months, sale of the AT&T bond for $883.75 on December 15 would deprive the seller of four months of interest to which the seller is entitled. A coupon of 7 percent means an annual payment of $70 and an equivalent monthly payment of approximately $5.83. Thus, buying the bond at $883.75 on December 15 requires paying an additional $23.32 for accrued interest. The total cost would be $907.07 plus commission. The investor will recover the $23.32 on February 15 when he or she receives interest of $35 for the entire six-month period.

Accrued interest calculations can become rather complex. The basic rule is that any full month is counted as thirty days and any partial month is calculated as the exact number of days. Sometimes bonds are traded *flat,* which means that trading is conducted without regard to accrued interest. Corporate bonds are traded flat when receipt of the scheduled interest payment is in doubt because of such events as bankruptcy, indicated by *vj* for the LTV bonds listed in Exhibit 12–1. Bonds traded flat are noted with an *f* after the maturity date.

Corporate Bond Ratings

Determination of the credit risk of the bonds of any corporation is a complex task involving many of the analytical techniques used in the evaluation of common stocks. Because of the complexities, many bond investors rely on the credit evaluations of two prominent *bond rating* agencies, Moody's and Standard & Poor's. These rating agencies do not place an absolute value on the credit risk of corporate bonds but rank bonds from the highest credit risk to the lowest credit risk. The ranking takes the form of risk categories. The highest quality bonds are designated Aaa by Moody's and AAA by Standard & Poor's. These bonds are often referred to as triple-A bonds. As the credit risk increases, both rating agencies assign lower ratings.

Moody's rates bonds as Aaa, Aa, A, Baa, Ba, and so on, down to C.

Exhibit 12–2 **Standard & Poor's Bond Ratings**

Rating	*Description*
AAA	Highest rating, which indicates extremely strong financial capacity to pay principal and interest
AA	High-quality debt obligation with very strong capacity to pay
A	Strong capacity to pay principal and interest. Somewhat susceptible to adverse changes in the company or in the economy
BBB	Adequate capacity to pay, but adverse circumstances are likely to lead to weakened capacity to pay
BB	Predominately speculative with large uncertainties or major risk exposures present in the debt obligation
B	A more speculative bond than BB-rated debt obligations
CCC	A more speculative bond than B-rated debt obligations
CC	Highest degree of speculation
C	An income bond on which no interest is presently being paid
D	A bond in default on the payment of either principal or interest

A plus (+) or a minus (−) is used for ratings AA to B to indicate relative standing within the rating classification.

Standard & Poor's rates defaulted bonds as low as D. The rating of defaulted bonds indicates the relative salvage value. Moody's does not rate defaulted bonds. Exhibit 12–2 is a description of Standard & Poor's Corporate and Municipal Bond Rating Definitions. The descriptions used by Moody's are comparable to those of S & P.

Bond investors generally consider the first three categories (triple, double, and single A) to be the highest quality where the risk of default is low. Bonds rated triple B or higher are often considered to be investment-quality bonds because they are generally eligible as commercial bank investments. The poorer quality bonds are those with the next two ratings, double and single B. These bonds are for more aggressively managed bond portfolios, but are still normally less risky than some common stocks.

The two rating agencies do not always agree on the rating of a given bond. When this occurs, it is known as a *split rating.* Split ratings are not uncommon, but the rating agencies rarely disagree by more than one rating category. In addition, not all bonds are rated by the agencies. This is especially true of the debt issues of financial concerns such as bank-holding companies and consumer finance companies.

Ratings are not carved in stone. Although the ratings are assigned with a long-term perspective, bond ratings are changed as the fortunes of the firm change. Boston Edison's bonds are an example of extremely swift downward rating revisions, as can be seen from the following Standard & Poor's ratings from various monthly issues of the *Standard & Poor's Bond Guide:*

January 1970	**AAA Rating**
July 1970	Changed from AAA to AA
May 1973	Changed from AA to A
June 1974	Changed from A to BBB

Why were the bonds of Boston Edison downgraded so swiftly? Part of the answer to this question concerns the problems the utility industry faces, such as rapidly increasing costs of fuel and the difficulty of obtaining rate relief (often called "regulatory lag"). Moody's also downgraded Boston Edison's bonds in June 1974 from A to Baa. In announcing this decision, Moody's referred to a deterioration of the firm's financial condition in the past few years.[1] For example, from 1968 to 1973, interest coverage fell from 4.88 to 1.94 times interest earned. Moody's opinion was that this deterioration resulted from an increase in the percentage debt in the capital structure without adequate rate relief to support the level of the debt. However, by 1987, the rating of Boston Edison's bonds had been raised to A+ as its interest coverage increased to about 3.00.

Coverage Ratio

The potential corporate bond buyer should examine the extent to which the firm is capable of satisfying the obligations of the bond. A measure of repayment ability is the *coverage ratio,* an important factor to consider along with the bond rating. This ratio is designed to indicate the extent to which earnings of the firm can deteriorate before the firm is unable to meet its creditor obligations. Times interest earned, introduced in Chapter 9, is the ratio of earnings before interest and taxes (EBIT) to the interest obligation. In Exhibit 12–3, the interest obligation is $4.5 million and EBIT is $15 million. The exhibit shows a times interest earned ratio of 3.33. The interpretation is that the firm's earning power is presently 3.33 times the interest obligation.

In Exhibit 12–3 we have two bond obligations, one of which is junior to the other. The senior bond must be paid before the junior bond. Coverage ratios could be calculated for each bond obligation. The senior bond is first in line, so the firm's first obligation is to earn the interest necessary to pay the senior bondholders. Hence, the coverage ratio is the ratio of EBIT to the interest payment for the senior bond. The senior obligation has a times interest earned of 4.69 (15/3.2).

In order to pay the junior bondholders, the firm must earn both the junior and senior interest payment. Thus, we use the *cumulative method* of calculating the coverage ratio for junior bonds. The EBIT remains the same, but we add the junior interest payment to the denominator of the ratio. The coverage ratio for the junior bond is 3.33. In this example, the coverage ratio for the junior bond is identical to the ratio for the entire firm. The junior bond is last in line for interest payments, and generally the ratio for the most junior bond will be the lowest ratio and equal to the overall interest coverage ratio.

We use the cumulative technique because junior bonds may appear to be less risky than the senior bonds if we don't. In our example, if we simply used the junior bond interest of $1.3 million and the EBIT after the senior interest payment ($15.0 less $3.2 million), we would obtain

1. *Moody's Bond Survey,* June 3, 1974, p. 856.

Exhibit 12–3 **Income Statement—Hypothetical Company**

Sales	$200,000,000
Expenses	185,000,000
Earnings before interest and taxes (EBIT)	$ 15,000,000
Interest*	4,500,000*
Net income before taxes	$ 10,500,000
Taxes at 50 percent	5,250,000
Net income	$ 5,250,000

$$\text{Times interest earned (before taxes)} = \frac{\text{EBIT}}{\text{Interest}} = \frac{\$15 \text{ million}}{\$4.5 \text{ million}} = 3.33$$

*Composed of the following:
$40 million, 8% senior mortgage bonds (interest = $3.2 mil).
$13 million, 10% junior mortgage bonds (interest = $1.3 mil).

Annual sinking fund payment of $1 million for each bond ($2 million total). Paid with after-tax income.

$$\text{Charges coverage ratio} = \frac{\text{EBIT}}{\text{Interest} + \text{Before-tax sinking fund payment}}$$

$$= \frac{\$15}{\$4.5 + \$2/.5}$$

$$= 1.76$$

a coverage ratio of 9.08 (11.8/1.3). This coverage ratio is greater than the coverage ratio for the senior bonds. This calculation is obviously incorrect and should not be used.

Many bond investors employ a *charges coverage ratio* as well. This ratio is identical to the times interest earned except that it is designed to reflect both interest and principal payments that must be made by the firm. It is the ratio of EBIT to the interest and sinking fund payments. Suppose that each of our bonds in Exhibit 12–3 has a $1 million annual sinking fund requirement designed to retire the bonds by the final maturity date. In order to meet the sinking fund obligation from earnings, the firm must earn $4 million before taxes (the illustrative tax rate is 50 percent). In our example, the charges coverage is 1.76, which is the ratio of EBIT to the sum of the interest payments and the before-tax sinking fund payment.

Can a generalization be made regarding the minimum acceptable times interest earned for a given bond or firm? An absolute standard such as three or four is often inappropriate because the adequacy of a given coverage ratio will depend on such factors as the industry, the stage of the business cycle, and the efficiency of management. Although the coverage ratio must be judged in light of the business risk faced by the firm, the rating agencies often tend to require a given interest coverage to maintain a specific rating (i.e., 3 for a utility to maintain a triple-A rating).

Table 12–1
Yields by Moody's Corporate Bond Rating, May 14, 1987

Moody's Rating	**Bond Yields (%)** *Corporate*	*Industrial*	*Railroads*	*Public Utilities*
Aaa	9.24	9.26	[a]	9.22
Aa	9.53	9.55	9.00	9.51
A	9.80	9.73	9.41	9.87
Baa	10.46	10.60	10.19	10.32

[a]Series discontinued December 18, 1967.

Source: Moody's Bond Survey, May 18, 1987, p. 6,536.

Returns by Rating

Investors typically require higher rates of return as bond quality decreases. Thus, triple-A bonds will typically have the lowest yield-to-maturity, and the yield will increase as one moves down the rating scale. Table 12–1 lists yields-to-maturity for several of Moody's rating classifications as of May 14, 1987. The data in Table 12–1 contain the assumption that interest will be paid when due and the principal repaid at maturity. For triple-A bonds, the probability of default is so small that the assumption is valid. For the lower quality bonds, a higher probability of default becomes a factor. If default occurs, the actual yield will be lower than the yields presented in Table 12–1.

The risk of a particular bond, summarized in its agency rating, is important to the investment decision, but risk in the portfolio context is probably even more important to most investors. The beta of corporate bonds must be evaluated in the same light as we have suggested for common stocks. William Sharpe has provided us with some evidence regarding the beta of "high-grade" corporate bonds. As can be expected, these financial instruments have a beta that is substantially below one. Using the Dow Jones Industrial Average as the market portfolio, Sharpe found betas on the order of .25 during the period 1946–71. In other words, high-grade corporate bonds are not only less risky than common stocks on an individual basis but also less risky than common stocks when considered within the context of one's portfolio.

Preferred Stock

"The preferred-stock *form* is fundamentally unsatisfactory."[2] Why did the fourth edition of *Security Analysis* by Graham, Dodd, and Cottle make such a bold and uncompromising statement? The statement was made

2. Benjamin Graham, David Dodd, and Sidney Cottle, *Security Analysis*, 4th ed. (New York: McGraw-Hill, 1962), p. 375.

primarily because *preferred stock* is a hybrid security with certain undesirable features. However, this does not imply that investment in preferred stocks should be avoided at all times by investors.

Preferred stock is a hybrid security combining elements of both the common stock (equity) and bond forms of investment. This form of security gets its name because of its preference both with regard to dividends and to the distribution of assets upon liquidation of the corporation. The preferred shareholder receives dividends prior to any payment to the common shareholders. The preferred shareholder also receives payments upon liquidation of the firm before payments are made to common shareholders.

Legally, preferred stockholders are considered owners of the firm because no debtor-creditor relationship exists such as between the firm and bondholders. Preferred dividends are declared by the board of directors in the same fashion as cash dividends on common stock. While legally an owner, the preferred stockholder does not share directly in the growth and prosperity of the firm, as the common shareholder can. No opportunity to receive a growing stream of dividend income is available to preferred stockholders.

Because the preferred stockholder receives a fixed-dividend payment, the holder's position is much like that of the bondholder. The bondholder receives a fixed contractual amount of interest, while the preferred stockholder looks forward to a noncontractual fixed amount of preferred dividends. The preferred dividend is stated either as a percentage of the par value or as a dollar amount. If stated as a percentage of par, the dollar figure is arrived at by multiplying the par value by the stated percentage.

Interest Rate Risk

The fixed-dividend payment associated with preferred stock means preferreds are subject to interest rate risk. The present value concepts previously discussed suggest that the longer the period of time before receipt of the principal repayment, the less its present value. Preferreds are similar to bonds because they have a fixed stream of future benefits. Unlike most bonds, they have no maturity. Hence, preferred stocks are similar to *consols,* which are bonds with no maturity.

Table 12–2 shows the impact of varying market rates of interest on a fixed-income obligation having a stated or coupon rate of 8 percent. The maturity of the obligation is of no consequence as long as the market interest rate is at 8 percent—corresponding to the stated rate on the fixed-income obligation.

If the market interest rate moves upward to 10 percent, the stream of expected future benefits must be discounted at the 10 percent rate. The future benefits in this example are the $80 yearly income plus the principal repayment. As the maturity lengthens, the present value (price) of the security declines. For a security with no maturity, the price would be only the present value of the dividend income, or $800, as shown in Table 12–2.

Table 12–2
Impact of Changing Interest Rate on Various Maturity Fixed-Income Obligations ($1,000 par with 8% stated rate)

Maturity	*Present Value (Price with Market Level of Interest Rates)*		
	8%	10%	6%
1 year	$1,000	$981.40	$1,019.10
5 years	1,000	922.80	1,085.30
10 years	1,000	875.40	1,148.80
20 years	1,000	828.40	1,231.10
30 years	1,000	810.70	1,276.80
40 years	1,000	804.00	1,302.00
50 years	1,000	801.50	1,316.00
No maturity (preferred stock or consol)	1,000	800.00	1,333.33

Source: Expanded Bond Values Tables, *Publication No. 83* (Boston: Financial Publishing Company, 1970), p. 355.

The $800 preferred stock price in the above illustration may be computed by using the following equation:

$$\text{Preferred stock price} = \frac{\text{Annual preferred dividend in dollars}}{\text{Market rate of interest}}$$

$$= \frac{\$80}{.10} = \$800$$

A decline in the market interest rate to 6 percent produces an increase in the present value of the security. The longer the maturity, the greater the increase in the present value of the obligation. For a preferred stock, the price would increase to $1,333.33. This would be the result of dividing $80 by .06 in the equation above.

Of what practical value is all this to the investor? If an investor has strong expectations regarding a pronounced decline in interest rates, Table 12–2 shows that the investor should seek a fixed-income obligation *with the longest possible maturity.* In this manner, interest rate risk will work to the maximum benefit of the investor. Because preferred stocks do not normally have a maturity date, they become a suitable investment for realizing capital appreciation during interest rate declines. Table 12–2 suggests, however, that bonds with thirty or more years to maturity are good securities with which to speculate on interest rate movements.

Par Value and Call Prices

While the par value of most corporate bonds is $1,000, preferred stocks have traditionally had a *par value* of $100 per share. However, in recent years, companies have tended to issue preferred stock with low par values (around $25 per share) or no par values. The preferred stock price

Table 12–3
Selected Preferred Stocks

S&P Rating	Issue	Call Price	Par Value	Number of Shares Outstanding (thousands)	5/27/87 Price	Yield
AA	ATT pfd A $3.64 cum	52.18*	$1	600	50¼	7.2%
AA	General Motors pfd B $5 cum	120	None	1,530	66¾	7.5
A	Kansas City Southern Ind. 4% non cum	None	25	284	12	8.3
BBB+	Commonwealth Edison pfd C $1.90 cum	25.25	None	4,250	20⅜	9.3
BB	Ohio Edison 7.36% cum	104.68*	100	350	71	10.4
C	Long Island Lighting pfd W $3.52 cum	32*	25	2,600	29¼	—

*Call price changes over time.

Source: Standard and Poor's Corporation, *Security Owner's Stock Guide,* May 1987.

quotation just examined would be applicable no matter what the par value because the annual preferred dividend is stated in dollars. Near the end of the chapter, we will examine the implications for the investor of the trend toward lower par values for preferred stocks. Most preferreds also have call prices as indicated on Table 12–3, which shows statistics for selected preferred stocks.

Dividend Payment Methods

Preferred stocks have dividend provisions that are either cumulative or noncumulative. Most preferred stocks have the *cumulative provision,* which means that any dividend not paid by the company accumulates. Normally, the firm must pay these unpaid dividends prior to the payment of dividends on the common stock. These unpaid dividends are known as *dividends in arrears* or *arrearages.*

Noncumulative dividends do not accumulate if they are not paid when due. Under the noncumulative provision, unpaid dividends are lost forever. The Kansas City Southern Industries 4 percent preferred in Table 12–3 has a noncumulative dividend provision. Hence, an investor contemplating the purchase of a preferred stock with a noncumulative dividend provision needs to be especially diligent in the investigation of the firm because of the investor's potentially weak position with regard to dividends. Actually, the holder of a preferred stock with a cumulative dividend provision is not in a much stronger position, as we shall see shortly.

Tax Considerations

A provision exists in the tax laws allowing a corporation to exempt from taxation eighty percent of all dividends received as a result of holding the stock of another corporation. Although this provision applies to dividends paid on both common and preferred stock held by a corporation, it is especially important for preferred stocks. Because preferred stocks have a fixed-dividend payment, they tend to compete with bonds for the fixed-income investment dollars of a portfolio. This tax provision has produced a market for preferred stocks that favors the institution as opposed to the individual. This can be seen from the following example of an 8 percent preferred and an 8 percent bond held by a corporation and by an individual. We are interested in the after-tax yield from each security.

	Corporation Holding		Individual Holding
	Bond	**Preferred**	**Bond or Preferred**
A. Pre-tax yield	8.0%	8.0%	8.0%
B. Nontaxable portion of yield	0	6.4	0
C. Taxable portion of yield (A–B)	8.0	1.6	8.0
D. Tax—34% corporate*	2.7	.5	2
Tax—28% individual*			2.2
E. After-tax yield (A–D)	5.3	7.5	5.8

*Assumed marginal tax rates.

Three conclusions may be drawn from this example. First, the tax benefits for a corporation from owning a preferred stock rather than a bond can be substantial, as indicated by the difference of 2.2 percentage points in after-tax yield. At any positive marginal corporate tax rate, benefits would still exist, although the higher the marginal rate, the larger the benefits. Second, because of the high after-tax yield, insurance companies and other financial institutions tend to be large purchasers of preferred stock. These institutions may be willing to accept a lower before-tax yield than they would accept for a bond of comparable quality. This results in a situation in which the yield on the preferred stock of a company may be either equal to or less than the yield on a bond *of the same company*. For example, in mid-1987, Duke Power had the following securities outstanding:

Issue	Price—5/29/87	Current Yield*
9½% bond, due 2005	99	9.60%
$8.70 preferred	95	9.16
8.20 preferred	90	9.11
7.80 preferred	86	9.07
8.28 preferred	91	9.10

*Dollar interest or preferred dividend divided by the price.

The risk-premium concept would indicate that securities with more financial risk should sell at higher yields. On this basis, one would not anticipate that a preferred stock of a company would sell for a lower yield than the firm's bonds.

Table 12–4
Weekly Trading Volume for Cincinnati Gas & Electric Preferred and Common Stocks, Week of May 29, 1987

Issue	Trading Volume (hundreds)	Number of Shares Outstanding (thousands)	Price
Common	3,388	44,470	24½
Preferred*			
9.30	7,860*y*	350	91
9.28	177*z*	400	93¼
9.52	140*y*	450	97

*All are $100 par value
y indicates ex-dividend and sales in full
z indicates the actual number of shares traded (120*z* = 120 shares traded).

Sources: S&P Stock Guide, May 1987, and *Barron's,* June 1, 1987.

A third conclusion to be drawn from the example is that an individual investor would be indifferent between the 8 percent bond and preferred stock because of the identical after-tax yields. However, if institutions seek preferred stock and drive the before-tax yields down, the individual should choose the bond because it would have a greater rate of return. If the bond and preferred were issued by the same company, the bond would normally represent a more secure investment. Hence, preferred stocks are not normally an attractive investment for individuals because of yield considerations.

Marketability

The investor should never ignore the marketability of a security. This advice is especially appropriate for the potential preferred stock investor. Table 12–4 shows the trading activity for Cincinnati Gas & Electric's common stock and its various preferred stocks that are listed on the NYSE for the week ending May 29, 1987. The significant aspect of this table is the small trading volume for many of the preferred stocks. One of the preferred stocks listed did not even have any trades that week despite the fact that the issue had 500,000 shares outstanding. The small trading volume is the result of two basic factors—the relatively small size of many preferred stock issues and the fact that institutions are a major force in the preferred market because of the tax aspects already examined. Although rules of thumb may not be practical in this area, any preferred stock issue with less than one million shares outstanding should be carefully studied by the potential investor to see if trading activity is sufficient to provide acceptable marketability for the investor.

Sinking Funds

Another aspect to be considered by the potential preferred stock investor is whether the preferred stock has a sinking fund. If the preferred stock has a sinking fund, the stock should be considered more as a bond from the viewpoint of pricing. Consider the Burlington Northern 5½ percent $10 par preferred stock issued in 1970. This preferred stock has a sinking fund that became effective January 1, 1976, requiring Burlington Northern to retire 4 percent of the par value of the outstanding preferred stock through redemption each year. The sinking fund also allows the firm to retire an additional 4 percent a year on an optional basis. As a result of the operation of this sinking fund provision, the number of preferred shares outstanding has decreased.

In contrast to preferred stocks without a sinking fund, the Burlington Northern 5½ percent preferred will eventually be eliminated in much the same fashion as a bond's principal is eventually repaid. We cannot determine precisely the average life of this preferred, but it probably was around four years as of mid-1987. The sinking fund's impact accounts for the fact that this preferred sells for $9 to provide a current yield of 6.1 percent despite the fact that its S&P rating is A−. Using Table 12–3 as a guide, we find that the Burlington Northern issue should yield about 8.5 percent in the absence of the sinking fund provision.

Preferred Stocks with Arrearages

Should an investor buy a preferred stock with dividends in arrears? What has been investor experience with stock of this nature? On an intuitive basis, investors should not seek out preferred stocks with dividends in arrears. The inability to pay preferred dividends is a sign of financial distress. Additionally, preferred shareholders have a weak bargaining position compared to bondholders because they cannot force the company into bankruptcy. Considering these factors, it would appear that preferreds with arrearages represent an attractive investment only under special circumstances. If the firm's financial condition is improving rapidly, the firm may want to eliminate preferred arrearages so that it may make dividend payments on the common stock and improve its credit standing.

Investor experience during the 1961 to 1975 period with preferred stocks having arrearages was more favorable than one perhaps might expect. An investor purchasing all AMEX- or NYSE-listed preferred stocks with arrearages at the beginning of 1961, holding them to the end of the year (or the resolution of the arrearage if it occurred first), and repeating the process each year would have achieved the results shown in Table 12–5. This table also shows the returns from the S&P 500 *Stock Index* and Moody's Aaa *Bond Index*, calculated on the same basis as the preferred returns. All returns include dividends or interest as well as capital gains or losses.

The mean annual arithmetic return of 12.8 percent compares favorably with the 7.9 percent from common stocks and the 3.5 percent from bonds. However, when the returns from preferred stocks with arrearages were adjusted for risk, these securities were not a superior portfolio holding during that period of time. In effect, the market for preferred stocks with arrearages was found to be an efficient market in terms of pricing the securities.

Table 12–5
Returns from Preferreds with Arrearages, S&P 500, and Moody's Aaa Bonds, 1961–75

	S&P 500	Aaa Bonds	Preferreds in Arrears
Mean arithmetic annual return	7.9%	3.5%	12.8%
Standard deviation	18.1	4.8	29.2
Maximum annual return	36.9	12.2	84.9
Minimum annual return	−24.8	−3.5	−28.9
Correlation coefficients			
S&P 500 to preferreds =	.60		
Aaa bonds to preferreds =	.05		

Source: Richard A. Stevenson and Michael Rozeff, "Are the Backwaters of the Market Efficient?" *Journal of Portfolio Management* (Spring 1979): 31–4.

Convertible Securities

A *convertible security* can be exchanged, at the holder's option, for a fixed or determinable number of shares of a security junior to it in rank. This normally means that the convertible bondholder or convertible preferred stockholder receives common stock in the same firm upon exercise of the conversion privilege. Because the convertible security may eventually become common stock, the convertible has features of both a debt and an equity security. In essence, the convertible is a hybrid security. The basic form of the analysis does not differ markedly whether the convertible is a preferred stock or a bond. Consequently, we discuss both in this section.

Convertible securities are attractive to the investor because they are hybrid securities in which the investor effectively has an option on the common stock. The investor hopes to combine the stability of a fixed-income security with the growth potential of a common stock investment. The convertible security, if analyzed properly, can provide a limit on the amount of loss, while giving the investor an opportunity for capital appreciation.

Conversion Price

The *conversion price* is usually stated as a formal part of the terms of the issue. Xerox issued a convertible bond in 1970, and IT&T issued a convertible preferred in 1968. The Xerox bond has a par value of $1,000 and a conversion price of $92. The ITT preferred stock has no par value and a conversion price of $61.32. (ITT's preferred does have a stated value of $100 per share.)

When the investor finds the conversion price, the next step is to divide the conversion price into the par or stated value of the security to obtain the *conversion ratio*, as shown in the following formula:

$$\text{Conversion ratio} = \frac{\text{Par value of bond or preferred stock}}{\text{Conversion price}}$$

Using the conversion ratio formula to determine the conversion ratio for these two securities results in the following:

$$\text{Xerox conversion ratio} = \frac{\$1{,}000}{\$92} = 10.87 \text{ shares per bond}$$

$$\text{ITT conversion ratio} = \frac{\$100}{\$61.32} = 1.63 \text{ common shares per preferred stock}$$

The conversion ratio and the conversion price are actually two different ways of measuring the same thing. Should the holder of a $1,000 par value, 6 percent Xerox convertible bond maturing in 1995 elect to convert this bond to common stock, he or she would receive 10.87 shares of Xerox common stock. Some investment advisory services give the investor the conversion ratio, but others do not.

The Xerox bond has a constant conversion price until its maturity date of 1995. However, this price will change if Xerox splits its common stock, issues a stock dividend, or takes other action, such as the acquisition of another company by merger, that results in an increase in the number of shares outstanding. In other words, the Xerox bondholder is fully protected by an *antidilution clause.* Although most convertible securities are fully protected against dilution, the investor should check the antidilution feature because some securities do not change the conversion price for stock dividends below a certain percentage. A convertible security may have a conversion price that changes over time. The potential purchaser should carefully examine a convertible security that has a changing conversion price because this feature can influence the value of the security over its life.

Bond or Preferred Stock Value

The analysis of convertible securities also uses what is known as the *bond* (or preferred stock) *value.* The bond or preferred value is an estimate of the market value of the convertible if it were not convertible. This value is often referred to as either the straight value or the investment value. The term *straight value* is used because the investor is looking at the convertible as a nonconvertible or straight bond or preferred stock.

Like many corporate bonds, convertibles have a credit rating. The investor needs to be aware of the credit rating of a given convertible before attempting to calculate the bond or preferred value. In essence, the bond value reflects what the security would reasonably be expected to sell for in the market with the conversion feature stripped from it. The investor can attempt to calculate a bond or preferred value or use the investment advisory services that often make these estimates. The determination of the bond or preferred value of most convertible securities is far from an exact science, however, primarily because of the low ratings carried by many convertibles.

The relatively low bond ratings reflect two major factors. First, a company needing to sell a bond issue will often attach a convertible feature to the bond to enhance its marketability. Companies with low bond ratings are the firms most likely to do this. Second, convertible bonds are usually subordinated debentures having a rank in the liquidation of the company equal to that of other unsecured creditors and superior only to the common and preferred stock. Whatever the cause, the low bond ratings make an estimate of a given convertible's bond value a difficult task because of the existence of considerable business and financial risk.

If an investor must calculate a bond value, he or she needs to know such items as the convertible bond's rating, its maturity, and what comparable bonds yield in the market. Xerox's 6 percent convertible bond is rated A+ and matures in 1995. Once the investor finds the yield-to-maturity on comparable bonds, a bond table can be used to estimate the selling price. Naturally, a change in market yields or the business or financial risk of the firm results in a different bond value.

ITT's $4 preferred K stock sold for $90¾ per share on December 16, 1986. What is the preferred stock value? Unfortunately, ITT has no other preferred stock outstanding that is nonconvertible. However, Georgia Pacific has several preferred stocks outstanding rated BBB, the same ranking as ITT's preferred. Georgia Pacific's preferred stocks yield about 9.5 percent. Hence, we would anticipate that ITT's $4 preferred would also yield 9.5 percent if it were nonconvertible. By dividing the dollar dividend ($4) by the yield (9.5 percent), the estimated value of $42.11 for ITT's $4 preferred as a nonconvertible security is obtained.

Conversion Value

The *conversion value* of a convertible security is obtained by multiplying the conversion ratio by the current market value of the common stock. The resulting figure is the market value of the convertible if it were immediately exchanged for the common stock. On December 17, 1986, Xerox common stock closed at $60⅞. ITT's common stock closed at $53⅜ the same day. The conversion values for these two securities are determined as follows:

Xerox: $10.87 \times 60.875 = \$661.71$

ITT: $1.63 \times 53.375 = \$\ 87.00$

The Minimum Market Value

To judge the value of a convertible, we must establish the minimum market value. By definition, the price of a convertible should never fall below the greater of its bond or preferred value and its conversion value. For the

Xerox bond, the bond value was estimated to be $820, and the conversion value was $661.71. Hence, the minimum price of the Xerox convertible bond must be $820 on December 17.

We can illustrate this concept graphically if we assume that the bond value is $1,000 for any given bond and that it will remain unchanged. Figure 12–1 shows the bond value constant at $1,000. The straight upward sloping line in Figure 12–1 is the conversion value determined by multiplying the various stock prices by the conversion ratio. The heavy portion of these two lines represents the convertible's minimum market price, given a particular stock price. The price of the convertible should never drop below these theoretical values, because the convertible can always trade as a pure bond or as a pure stock. Of course, the bond value line may shift up or down as interest rates change.

A convertible rarely sells for exactly its theoretical minimum value. Convertibles normally sell at a price higher than the minimum value, as represented by the dashed line on Figure 12–1. Why would anyone pay more than the bond or stock value? Probably the most important reason has to do with the reduced risk resulting from the bond value of the convertible bond. Suppose we are examining a convertible bond with a conversion ratio of fifty shares, a stock price of $22, and a bond value of $1,000. The minimum market price of the convertible would be $1,100, its conversion value. Its actual market price is likely to be somewhat higher than $1,100, as explained below.

The alternatives facing the investor may be viewed as purchasing the convertible bond or fifty shares of the common stock. In either situation,

Figure 12–1
Stock and Bond Values for a Convertible Bond

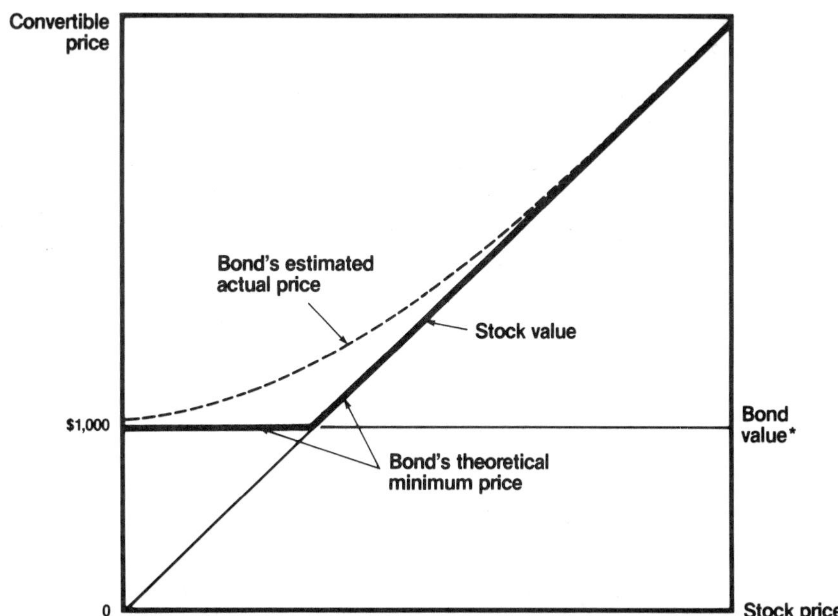

*Subject to shifts as interest rates change.

the investor will profit from an increase in the price of the stock. What happens if the price of the stock declines? If the price declines to $15, the loss will be considerably less for the bond because the convertible should sell for no less than its $1,000 bond value. In summary, an investment of $1,100 in the stock would produce a loss of $350, given a stock price of $15, but the same investment in the convertible bond would produce a loss of only $100.

Most investors are willing to pay more than the $1,100 stock value for the convertible bond in order to obtain the loss protection provided by the convertible. The purchase of fifty shares of the stock exposes the investor to all of the potential losses of the stock, while the purchase of the convertible exposes the investor to losses which cannot exceed the difference between the purchase price and the bond value. Whatever happens to the price of the stock, the convertible should not drop below its bond value. This "floor price" provides the investor with an element of risk protection. With lower risk, the price must be higher. Hence, the convertible bond should sell for a price that exceeds the stock value.

Premium Calculations

The investor can calculate three values to assist in the investment decision regarding convertibles, the *loss premium,* the *conversion premium,* and the *combined premium.* Xerox's 6 percent convertible bond and the ITT $4 preferred serve as examples for the calculation of these premiums and their interpretation.

Loss Premium

The loss premium measures the amount of loss an investor would suffer if a convertible security were purchased at its current price and the price fell to the security's bond value. This might happen if the underlying common stock fell in price. Xerox's bond sells for $970 and has an estimated bond value of $820. Hence, the bond investor could lose $150 (15.5 percent of the purchase price) by buying this bond, provided interest rates remained unchanged. ITT's preferred stock sells for $90¾, with an estimated nonconvertible preferred value of $42.11. The loss premiums for the Xerox bond and for the ITT preferred stock are shown below:

$$\text{Loss premium} = \frac{\text{Market value} - \text{Bond or preferred stock value}}{\text{Market value}}$$

Xerox Bond

$$\frac{\$970 - \$820}{\$970} = 15.5\%$$

ITT Preferred

$$\frac{\$90.75 - \$42.11}{\$90.75} = 53.6\%$$

As the loss premium becomes larger, the less "bondlike" the convertible becomes. If the common stock into which the convertible security is converted rises in price, the price movements of the convertible security will become more like those of the common stock. In this situation, the convertible feature dominates the fixed-income aspect of the convertible security. The loss premium will also become larger if everything remains the same except for an increase in interest rates. We noted previously that bond values drop if interest rates increase. If the bond value for the Xerox bond were to decline to $700, the loss premium would increase to 27.8 percent ($270/$970). The bond value is expected to cushion the fall of the price of the convertible bond even if the common stock falls, but rising interest rates reduce the bond value.

Conversion Premium

To calculate the conversion premium, we view the convertible security solely as the purchase of the common stock. The Xerox bond is viewed as the purchase of 10.87 shares of Xerox common stock having a conversion value of $661.71 for a cost of $970. This is a conversion premium of $308.29. The conversion premium of 46.6 percent can be calculated as follows.

$$\text{Conversion premium} = \frac{\text{Market value} - \text{Conversion value}}{\text{Conversion value}}$$

Xerox Bond

$$\frac{\$970 - \$661.71}{\$661.71} = 46.6\%$$

ITT Preferred

$$\frac{\$90.75 - \$87.00}{\$87.00} = 4.3\%$$

An investor will often encounter a small conversion premium such as in the case of the ITT preferred. Investors may even encounter a small negative premium. The current yield could explain any negative premium, as the yield on a preferred could be below that of the common stock. In addition, the common and the preferred trade separately and are subject to their own supply and demand conditions.

Combined Premium

The investor may add the loss premium to the conversion premium to obtain the combined premium. The Xerox convertible has a combined premium of 62.1 percent compared to 57.9 percent for ITT's preferred.

The combined premium becomes a useful starting point for an analysis of the attractiveness of any convertible security. Table 12–6 shows selected statistics, including the combined premium for four different convertible bonds. An investor would desire a loss premium of zero and a conversion premium of zero, resulting in a combined premium of zero. With all these premiums at zero, the investor would purchase a convertible security at bond value that was also worth the bond value in common stock. Naturally, this situation is unlikely to exist, because both the risk protection of the bond value and the possibility of participating in the growth of the common stock are valuable to the investor. Consequently, both these valuable features are unlikely to be available at a zero cost.

The combined premium should be low to obtain both benefits of a convertible security, the risk limitation feature and the capital apprecia-

Table 12–6
Convertible Bond Statistics, Selected Bonds

Description (Name, Rate, Maturity)	S&P Rating	Amount Out-standing	April '87 Price	Con-version Value	Estimated Bond Value	Premiums		
						Loss	*Con-version*	*Com-bined*
Bally Mfg. 6, 1998	B+	$34 mil.	$ 880	$ 668	$ 600	32%	32%	64%
Ford Motor Credit, 4⅞, 1998	A+	54	3,423	3,423*	550	84	0	84
IBM 7⅞, 2004	AAA	1,285	1,252	978	1050	16	28	44
USX Corp. 5¾, 2001	BB−	236	722	448	610	16	61	77

*Convertible into Ford Motor Company common stock.

Sources: S&P Bond Guide, April 1987, plus estimates by authors of the bond values.

tion potential. A useful rule of thumb is that the combined premium should be no more than approximately 40 percent. This is based on a 20 percent loss premium and a 20 percent conversion premium. The investor stands to lose only 20 percent of the investment if interest rates remain unchanged. In addition, the investor pays only a 20 percent premium to obtain the conversion feature. By staying within the suggested guideline of 40 percent, the investor purchases convertibles having relatively limited risk as well as capital appreciation potential obtained at a modest conversion premium.

The investor may want to trade some risk for some growth potential and purchase a convertible with a loss premium of 30 percent and a conversion premium of 10 percent. The suggested 40 percent guideline gives investors the flexibility to satisfy different risk preferences while remaining true to the desirable hybrid nature of a convertible security—a reasonable risk limitation and a capital appreciation possibility.

For the Xerox bond, the combined premium of 62.1 percent is higher than the 40 percent we recommend. Should this bond automatically be ignored by the investor? Whether the purchase of a Xerox bond with a combined premium of 62.1 percent is a reasonable purchase depends on many factors associated with the company and the convertible issue itself. Likewise, the 57.9 percent combined premium for the ITT preferred stock does not automatically disqualify the preferred for investor purchase, especially in light of the stock's low conversion premium.

Determinants of Convertible Premiums

Current Yield Differences

A consideration in the premium determination is the current income of the convertible relative to the income of the common stock. The current yields for the Xerox and the ITT common stocks along with the current yields for the convertibles we have been analyzing are as follows:

	Xerox	ITT
Common stock	4.9%	1.9%
Convertible	6.2	4.4

A portion of the conversion premium for both convertible securities can be attributed to their higher current income relative to the common stock.

Brokerage Commissions

Convertible bonds may carry a positive combined premium, resulting from differences in the brokerage commissions for stocks as opposed to bonds. The commission for the purchase of a bond is around $5 to $10 per bond, while the commission to purchase approximately $1,000 worth of common stock is in the neighborhood of $25 to $40. Thus, the purchase and sale of a convertible requires around $10 to $20 in commissions, while the purchase and sale of the equivalent stock requires approximately $50 to $80. The relevant stock commission for comparative purposes would depend on the conversion value of the bond, but a difference of about $30 to $40 is representative.

This commission savings from purchasing the convertible should be reflected in the combined premium, with the size of the premium a function of the difference between the two commission rates. Both yield and commission differences may appear to be much ado about very small values. However, relative to the loss premium or the conversion premium, they can assume considerable significance.

Growth Potential

A crucial element in determining whether the loss and conversion premiums are reasonable is the growth potential for the common stock to be obtained upon conversion. Because of Xerox's past record of growth and prospects for future growth, the investor may accept a combined premium greater than the suggested 40 percent standard. This decision will, of course, require a complete analysis of Xerox's desirability as a common stock investment.

Other Terms of the Convertible

Several other factors may influence the premium, but their impact is usually small. The duration of the conversion option and the period of time over which the option can be exercised can influence the size of the premium. The longer the duration of the conversion feature, the greater the period over which the expected growth of the firm can be realized in the marketplace.

The extent to which the conversion ratio declines over time may influence the size of the premium investors are willing to pay. However, the effect of both duration and a changing conversion ratio appears small.

Nevertheless, if we are close chronologically to either a change in the conversion terms or to the expiration of the conversion feature, these factors may assume considerable importance.

The convertible bond buyer should also study the antidilution clause previously mentioned. We noted that antidilution clauses have not been standardized, and that an unusual clause may have a profound impact on the price of a given convertible security.

Call Provisions

Convertible bonds are almost always callable in some form, and the typical corporation will insist on a call provision. The typical call provision for a convertible security is for the convertible to be callable immediately upon issuance, with thirty days in which to convert after the notice of conversion is given.

A firm is able to force conversion with the use of the call provision. The Xerox 6 percent bond has a call price of $1,012. We previously calculated in an earlier section of this chapter that this bond is convertible into 10.87 shares of Xerox common stock. If the price of Xerox common stock increases to $110, the conversion value becomes $1,195.70. If Xerox calls this bond when the common stock is selling for $110, the investor has the choice of either accepting the call or of converting the bond into common stock. The choice is obvious: Accepting the call would mean receiving $1,012, whereas conversion would mean receiving common stock with a market value of $1195.70.

By forcing conversion, the firm has converted the bond into common stock. The possibility of a forced conversion is an important consideration to the convertible bondholder. The investor considering the purchase of the Xerox convertible bond, with the common stock selling for $110, would need to consider carefully what price should be paid for the bond. If the investor pays more than $1,195.70 for the bond, he or she runs the risk that Xerox will soon force conversion of the bond. Then, the difference between the price paid and the conversion value will be a loss for the investor. For example, if the investor were to pay $1,300 for the Xerox bond and the bond were called, the investor would convert the bond into common stock worth only $1,195.70, incurring a loss of about $104. As a result, the convertible is not likely to sell much above the conversion value of $1,195.70.

If a convertible security is selling at a substantial premium over its conversion value and the conversion value is greater than the call price, the investor will need to determine the probability of a call actually occurring. Many questions need to be answered. Has the firm called convertible bonds in the past? Does the firm have a need to sell more debt? If so, does the firm need to call the convertible to alter its debt-to-equity ratio to facilitate the sale of a new debt issue? What is the coupon rate on the convertible bond compared to the rate the firm will have to pay on a new debt issue? The firm might not be willing to give up a low interest rate debt security unless compelled to do so by pressing needs to raise new capital by selling a new debt issue.

Convertibles as Fixed-Income Investments

An investor may view the purchase of a convertible only as the purchase of a fixed-income security. The conversion feature is effectively ignored in this situation, and the bond or preferred stock is analyzed only on its merits as a fixed-income security. This situation occurs when the loss premium is at a relatively low level, indicating that the convertible security is essentially a bond.

In Table 12–6, the IBM and USX bonds have small loss premiums. An extremely small loss premium means the bond is selling for about its bond value and little consideration is being given by the market to the convertible feature. Those bonds could be viewed as the purchase of a pure bond.

An investor could follow the strategy of buying bonds such as the USX bond. This means the investor looks for convertible bonds with low loss premiums (about 15 percent or less) and gets the conversion feature thrown in at very little additional cost. The investor actually buys a straight bond and a conversion feature of dubious value. However, the conversion feature might be of value at some future date.

Convertibles as Common Stock Substitutes

The strategy of buying convertible securities as a substitute for the common stock may be a better strategy than buying convertibles for their bond value, considering that convertible bonds are generally of rather low quality. The Ford Motor Credit 4⅞ percent bond of 1998 listed on Table 12–6 is a good example of the possibility of buying a convertible security as a *common stock substitute.* The bond sells for $3,423, but the conversion value of the bond is also $3,423. If the investor is willing to accept the risk inherent in the purchase of Ford Motor common stock, the bond is attractive as a common stock substitute. Not only is the Ford Motor Credit bond selling at no premium from its conversion value, but the bond is also rated A+ by Standard & Poor's. We previously observed that the commission for purchasing one bond would be substantially less than for purchasing an equivalent dollar amount of common stock ($3,423 in this case). However, the current yield from the stock is greater than from the bond, as shown below:

Current Yield from	
Bond	**Common Stock**
$\frac{\$48.75}{\$3,423} = 1.42\%$	$\frac{\$3.00}{\$84.375} = 3.55\%$

One thing has become evident as a result of examining the Ford Motor convertible bond. If an investor discovers a common stock that appears to be an attractive investment, the capital structure of the firm should be examined to determine if a convertible security exists that provides an even better investment alternative.

Summary

Corporate bond investing is, in some ways, easier than investing in common stocks. Once the potential bond investor has studied the terms of the issue and its quality, the investor need only determine if the promised yield-to-maturity is satisfactory for the particular issue. The quality of a bond issue is expressed in a rating given to the bond issue by a bond rating agency. These bond ratings are extremely useful guides to bond quality, but the investor should also do some credit risk assessment. Even bonds having the same rating often have different characteristics.

Most investors generally are not "turned on" by preferred stock. But we observed that preferred stocks are attractive investments for corporate holders because of the tax provision that makes 80 percent of dividends tax exempt for the corporate holder. In some instances, this has the effect of reducing before-tax yields on preferreds below the level existing for bonds of comparable quality.

For the individual investor, preferred stocks have several disadvantages, which tend to reinforce the investor's dislike of preferred stock. The yield is normally equal to or less than what can be obtained on comparable quality bonds. The purchaser of a preferred also owns a hybrid security that is part common stock and part bond, but it lacks the principal advantages of each form. Moreover, the commission cost of buying and selling preferred stock may be greater than for a comparable dollar amount of bonds.

Despite the generally undesirable nature of preferred stocks for investment by individuals, one should not conclude that the individual investor should own no preferred stock. Preferred stocks are sensitive to interest rate fluctuations because they lack a maturity date. Therefore, an investor expecting a pronounced decline in interest rates might seek a high-quality preferred stock to attempt to maximize interest rate risk and achieve capital gains.

The number of convertible issues has increased recently, and convertibles have become an important area for investors. The basic attraction of a convertible security is the possibility of having your cake and eating it too. As a hybrid security, a convertible is part fixed-income security and part equity. The fixed-income element of a convertible is important because of the stable income it provides. In addition, the fixed-income element is supposed to act as a means of reducing the risk of investing in a convertible compared to a direct investment in the common stock. The convertible should not decline in price below its value at that specific time as a fixed-income security. Because the convertible has a common stock aspect, its price may increase as the price of the stock into which it is convertible increases.

In analyzing a convertible, the investor should determine its bond or preferred value, the price for which the security would sell if it were nonconvertible. Of course, this value will change as interest rates change: increasing interest rates will cause the bond value to decline, and vice versa. In addition, the generally low quality of convertible securities means that considerable business and financial risk as well as interest rate risk may be present in any given situation.

The loss premium is a measure of the possible loss from buying a convertible if both interest rates and the quality of the convertible remain unchanged. The loss premium is the difference between the convertible's current price and its bond or preferred stock value, expressed as a percentage of the current price. The higher the loss premium, the greater the potential loss if the underlying common stock declines in price.

The conversion value is determined by multiplying the number of shares to be received upon conversion by the market price of each share. Once the conversion value has been determined, the investor can calculate the conversion premium. The conversion premium relates the conversion value to the price of the convertible to determine the price paid for the convertible feature as opposed to buying the common stock directly. A conversion premium of twenty percent would mean that the investor is paying twenty percent more for the shares into which the convertible can be converted than what these shares could be purchased for directly. The investor is willing to pay a premium mainly because of the risk-reduction feature of the convertible.

By adding the loss premium to the convertible premium, the investor obtains a combined premium. A very high combined premium means the convertible is effectively either mostly fixed income security or mostly a common stock substitute. As a result, the convertible may not provide both a risk reduction function and an opportunity to participate in the growth of the common stock. The investor might buy a convertible with a high combined premium in that situation where the high combined premium results from a high loss premium and a low conversion premium. In this case, the investor is essentially purchasing the convertible as a substitute for the common stock.

Suggested Readings

ATKINSON, THOMAS R., and ELIZABETH T. SIMPSON. *Trends in Corporate Bond Quality.* New York: National Bureau of Economic Research, 1967.

BRENNAN, M. J., and E. S. SCHWARTZ. "Convertible Bonds: Valuation and Optimal Strategies for Call and Conversion." *Journal of Finance* (December 1977): 1699–715.

BRIGHAM, EUGENE F. "An Analysis of Convertible Debentures." *Journal of Finance* (March 1966): 35–54.

BUSER, STEPHEN A., and PATRICK J. HESS. "Empirical Determinants of the Relative Yields on Taxable and Tax-exempt Securities." *Journal of Financial Economics* (December 1986): 335–55.

FERRI, MICHAEL G. "How Do Call Provisions Influence Bond Yields?" *Journal of Portfolio Management* (Winter 1979): 55–57.

FITZPATRICK, JOHN D., and JACOBUS T. SEVERIENS. "Hickman Revisited: The Case for Junk Bonds." *Journal of Portfolio Management* (Summer 1978): 53–57.

HICKMAN, W. BRADDOCK. *Corporate Bonds Quality and Investor Experience.* Princeton, NJ: Princeton University Press, 1958.

JENNINGS, EDWARD H. "An Estimate of Convertible Bond Premiums." *Journal of Financial and Quantitative Analysis* (January 1974): 33–56.

KAPLAN, ROBERT S., and GABRIEL URWITZ. "Statistical Methods of Bond Ratings: A Methodological Inquiry." *Journal of Business* (April 1979): 231–61.

MCENALLY, RICHARD W. "What Causes Bond Prices to Change?" *Journal of Portfolio Management* (Spring 1981): 5–12.

NUNN, KENNETH P., JR., JOANNE HILL, and THOMAS SCHNEEWEIS. "Corporate Bond Price Data Sources and Risk/Return Measurement." *Journal of Financial and Quantitative Analysis* (June 1986): 197–208.

REILLY, FRANK K., and MICHAEL D. JOEHNIK. "The Association Between Market-Determined Risk Measures for Bonds and Bond Ratings." *Journal of Finance* (December 1976): 1387–403.

SOLDOFSKY, ROBERT M. "The Risk-Return Performance of Convertibles." *Journal of Portfolio Management* (Winter 1981): 80–84.

SOLDOFSKY, ROBERT M., RICHARD A. STEVENSON, and SUSAN M. PHILLIPS. "Convertible Securities: New Issues, Conversions, and Performance Record." In Stevenson and Phillips, eds., *Investment Environment, Analysis, and Alternatives.* St. Paul, MN: West Publishing Co., 1977, 199–214.

SORENSON, ERIC H., and JAMES E. WERT. "A New Tool for Estimating New Issue Bond Yields." *Journal of Portfolio Management* (Spring 1981): 42–45.

STEVENSON, RICHARD A. "Deep-Discount Convertible Bonds: An Analysis." *Journal of Portfolio Management* (Summer 1982): 57–64.

STEVENSON, RICHARD A., and MICHAEL ROZEFF. "Are the Backwaters of the Market Efficient?" *Journal of Portfolio Management* (Spring 1979): 31–34.

Questions

1. (a) What type of risk do credit ratings attempt to measure?
   (b) What firm-specific variables are key in determining bond ratings?
   (c) What is the historical relationship between ratings and returns?
2. Given the following bond price quotation information, tell all you can about this bond issue:

Bonds	Cur. Yld.	Vol.	High	Low	Close	Net Chg.
Gm 8⅝ 05	8.7	10	99½	99½	99½	+1⅝

3. What is the significance of a deferred call provision as far as the investor is concerned?
4. Some preferred stocks have par values and some do not. Does this matter to the investor?

5. We might say that a time and purpose exists in an investor's portfolio for virtually every form of investment security. Under what circumstances would an investor desire to hold preferred stock? What qualities would the investor desire to have associated with the preferred stock in the portfolio?

6. Distinguish among the different types of dividend provisions associated with preferred stock, and note their importance for the investor.

7. What impact do marketability and a sinking fund have on the valuation of preferred stocks?

8. Discuss the general significance of tax considerations that are important in the analysis of preferred stock.

9. Why is preferred stock referred to as a hybrid security? Of what significance is this to the investor?

10. What are the main reasons why an investor would purchase a convertible security?

11. What are the determinants of convertible premiums, and how does each determinant influence the size of the premium?

12. How do call provisions affect the price of convertibles?

13. Is it possible to lose a greater percentage of your investment in a convertible bond than you could lose by investing directly in the common stock into which the bond is convertible?

14. In comparing two convertible securities, the investor finds that one of the securities has a high loss premium while the other security has a low loss premium. What does this tell the investor?

15. Why would an investor purchase a convertible security rather than the related common stock if the convertible's bond value is far below the current market price of the convertible security?

16. An investor can voluntarily convert a convertible security into the common stock at any time during the life of the convertible provision. Under what circumstances would the convertible security holder want to do this?

17. Both a current yield and a yield-to-maturity can be calculated for a convertible bond. Some have suggested that the yield-to-maturity calculation is not an appropriate yield concept to apply to a convertible bond. Do you agree?

18. An article in *Business Week* of September 28, 1974, stated: "Some portfolio managers are loading up on convertible debentures in hopes of double-barrelled action." What do you think the article had in mind by "double-barrelled action"?

19. A special type of convertible security, referred to as an exchangeable security, will sometimes be encountered by the potential investor in convertible securities. For example, Dart Industries has a convertible security outstanding that is convertible into 10.75

shares of Minnesota Mining and Manufacturing Company common stock per $1,000 par value bond. Would the investor need to modify the standard form of analysis for convertible securities in considering this security for purchase?

Problems

1. A 9½ percent bond pays interest on January 1 and July 1. If an investor purchases this bond on September 15, how much accrued interest will the buyer need to pay?

2. Assume you are making the choice between the two bonds listed below as of October 1974. If you expect the yield-to-maturity on AT&T bonds of this maturity to drop to 7 percent by the end of 1977, which bond would you purchase?

Coupon Rate	Maturity	Call Price	Market Price	Yield-to-Maturity
8.70%	12/1/2002	107.09*	$930	9.41%
7.125	12/1/2003	105.55**	770	9.45

*Not callable until 1975
**Not callable until 1977

3. On August 21, 1979, Northwestern Bell Telephone issued $300 million of bonds with an unusual call provision. The bonds carried an interest rate of 9½ percent and were sold at a price of $995 resulting in a yield to maturity of 9.53 percent. However, these bonds were callable at the end of five years at a call price of $1,047.50 rather than at more than $1,080, which would have been a common provision for bonds of this type.
   (a) Why do you think Northwestern Bell wanted such a low call price?
   (b) What do you anticipate would be the effect of the low call price on the yield-to-maturity for this bond compared to bonds of comparable quality and maturity but with a more standard call price?
   (c) What is the yield to first call assuming annual interest payments? In this case, which is a better indicator of the return for bond investors, the yield-to-maturity or the yield-to-first call?

4. Major Company has a 7¾ percent bond outstanding with a final maturity of March 2006. It is now March 1987, and the bond has nineteen years until its final maturity.
   (a) What is the bond's current yield if it sells for 86⅝?
   (b) What is the bond's yield-to-maturity assuming annual interest payments?
   (c) The bond is callable starting in March 1991 at $1,058.90 per $1,000 par value bond. What is the bond's yield-to-first call date? Is the bond likely to be called?
   (d) The bond has a sinking fund starting in 1992 that requires an annual payment of $7.5 million each year until 2005. Presently,

$150 million of the bond is outstanding. What percentage of the bond will be retired by the sinking fund?

5. A $50 par value preferred stock is paying an annual dividend of $3 and is selling in the market at $30 a share. If the market rate of return desired on this quality preferred stock falls to 8 percent, what will happen to the price of the preferred stock? What will happen if the market demands an interest rate of 12 percent?

6. Given that AT&T's $4 preferred stock is selling for 68½, calculate the after-tax yield for an individual in the 28 percent marginal tax bracket and for a corporation in the 34 percent marginal tax bracket.

7. XYZ Corporation has outstanding a $200 million issue of a 5 percent convertible bond that matures on August 1, 2009. This bond is convertible at a price of $70.50 for the common stock. On October 18, 1987, the convertible bond's closing price is $1,270, and the common stock closes at $90.75 per share.

   (a) What is the conversion ratio for this bond?

   (b) What is the bond's conversion value and the conversion premium?

   (c) As of October 21, 1987, the bond value was estimated at $590. Using this bond value, calculate the loss premium and the combined premium.

8. Straights Oil Company called its 5 percent convertible bond for redemption on November 29 at a price of $1,042.50. On November 22, Sue King knew she would soon have to make a decision regarding the bond she purchased on October 18. On November 21, the bond closed at $1,160 and the common stock closed at $83.50. The bond is convertible at $70.50 per share.

   (a) What alternatives are available for Sue King?

   (b) What would you recommend that she do?

9. On May 20, General Instrument called to redeem its 10¼ percent convertible bond of 1996. A holder of this bond has until June 20 to either convert the bond or accept the call price of $1,080 for the investment. As of May 27, the common stock of General Instrument is selling for $38 a share. The convertible bond is convertible into 36.47 shares of common. What courses of action are open to the investor? What would you recommend?

10. The three following convertible bonds are all selling for about their par values:

Issue		Price	Rating	Conversion Price	Amount Outstanding
Chemical Bank NY	5% '93	99½	none	$47.33	$28.5 mil.
American Motors	6% '88	99½	CCC	8.16	21.2
PSA 11⅛% '04		100	B	30.00	29.1

The common stocks and the dividend payments per share are as follows:

Chemical Bank sells for 47¾ and pays $3.24 per share.
American Motors sells for 7¾ and pays no dividend.
PSA sells for 21 and pays $.60 per share.

What are the advantages and disadvantages of purchasing each of these convertible bonds rather than the common stocks if the bond values are estimated as follows: Chemical Bank $600; American Motors $600; and PSA $750?

11. ABCD Company has the following securities outstanding:

Issue	Market Price	Convertible into (Shares)	Call Price
Common	42⅛	—	—
$4 Pfd. K	67⅝	1.624	100.00
$5 Pfd. O	63	1.696	102.30
$4.50 Pfd. I	70½	1.447	100.00

Preferred stocks of this rating are currently selling in the market to yield 12 percent if they are nonconvertible. Calculate the following:

(a) The loss premium for each preferred issue

(b) The conversion value and conversion premium for each preferred issue

(c) The combined premium for each preferred issue

(d) The yield on each preferred issue

(e) ABCD's common stock pays a dividend of $2.76 per share. What are the investment merits of each preferred stock compared to the common stock?

(f) What other information would you like to have before making an investment decision?

12. U.S. Steel sold ten million shares of new convertible preferred to the public on June 9, 1983, at a price of 25. The preferred is convertible into .8658 shares of common stock for each preferred share and is also exchangeable beginning June 15, 1986, for $25 par value per preferred share of U.S. Steel's 9 percent convertible subordinated debt issue of 2013. As of August 1983, when you find out about this issue, the common, with 23.89 million shares outstanding, is selling at 28 and paying a dividend of $1 per share. The preferred is selling at 27⅝ and paying a dividend of $2.25.

(a) Determine the attractiveness of buying this preferred as opposed to the common stock if nonconvertible preferreds of comparable quality are yielding 11.4 percent.

(b) Of what significance to you is the fact that this preferred is also exchangeable into a convertible bond? What additional information would you want to seek concerning this feature?

Chapter 13

Fixed-Income Innovations and Investment Management Strategies

Key Concepts

- active management
- bond swap
- collateral
- commodity-backed bond
- complete market
- contingent immunization
- coupon
- denomination
- duration
- efficient market
- floating rate note
- immunization
- maturity
- original-issue, deep-discount bond
- passive management
- price risk
- reinvestment rate risk
- risk management
- stock-indexed bond
- zero coupon note

Chapter Outline

TIGERS, CATS, CARS, SPINS, DATES, and DARTS. These represent just a few of the many innovative fixed-income securities offered to the investing public in recent years. The number and variety of new forms of fixed-income securities has certainly taxed the analytical abilities of professional investors and may have hopelessly confused individual investors. This chapter examines the factors that have been responsible for this creative burst of energy and what they mean for the investor.

The first section of the chapter examines the process of financial market innovation. We are mainly interested in the marketing and financial motivations involved in this innovative effort. The second section of the chapter deals with the importance of innovation to investors and issuers of securities. It seeks an answer to the question: Of what benefit is this innovative activity to investors? Ways to modify the risk of a "standard" fixed-income contract by using either the provisions of the bond itself or fixed-income investment management strategies are covered in sections three and four.

The Process of Financial Market Innovation

The process of financial market innovation involves an interesting melding of marketing and finance. New varieties of fixed-income securities tend to have a product life cycle very much like a standard consumer product. The product is introduced, becomes known as a result of promotional activities, and then tends to stagnate or is phased out.

Product or Process Involved

James Van Horne lists the following six factors as being responsible for innovations in the financial markets: (1) volatile inflation and interest rates, (2) regulatory aspects, (3) tax changes, (4) changes in technology, (5) varying levels of economic activity, and (6) research work of academics in finance.[1] According to Merton Miller, most of the innovative activity has been the result of either regulatory influences or tax law changes.[2] More specifically, Miller attributes innovations to the desire to circumvent the burden of regulation or to take advantage of provisions of the tax law that have innovative potential not recognized previously.

We can relate the process of innovation in financial markets to the concept of an *efficient market* and the ultimate desire for a *complete market.* An efficient market should provide investors with those securities that will be useful in their investment activities and should provide

1. James C. Van Horne, "Of Financial Innovations and Excesses," *Journal of Finance,* July 1985, pp. 620–31.
2. Merton H. Miller, "Financial Innovation: the Last Twenty Years and the Next," *Journal of Financial and Quantitative Analysis,* December 1986, pp. 459–76.

issuers of securities with the ability to raise funds in a timely and low-cost manner. The concept of a complete market is linked to the notion of an efficient market in the sense that a complete market will also be efficient. The process of innovation in a financial market is a continuing search for securities that will complete the menu of security offerings so that the raising of capital will become increasingly efficient. For example, interest rate changes that make it difficult to sell the available variety of fixed-income securities and the desire to exploit tax loopholes have produced significant new fixed-income securities.

Terms of Fixed-Income Securities

We can identify four basic features, or terms, of a fixed-income security that can be easily altered to create a new type of security. These four terms are the security's maturity or duration, its coupon rate of interest, its collateral backing, and its denomination.

Maturity or Duration

We noted in earlier chapters that as interest rates rise, two fundamental things happen to fixed-income securities. First, the securities decline in price, and the security with the longest maturity declines the most. Second, the duration of a fixed-income security becomes shorter as the discount rate increases. After a pronounced rise in interest rates, such as the rise that occurred during the 1977–81 period when long-term U.S. government rates went from 7.5 percent to 13.3 percent, investors may desire to invest in long-duration bonds, thereby maximizing their exposure to interest rate risk. In order to market bonds, issuers must design securities that satisfy the desires of investors for long-duration securities. This is true even though the issuers might prefer to issue short-term securities in the hope that interest rates will decline, making the raising of long-term money more inexpensive at a later date. Taking advantage of a tax loophole, issuers conceived the first original-issue, deep-discount corporate bonds in 1981. These securities will be discussed in detail below.

Coupon

As interest rates rose in the early 1970s, investors in long-term, fixed-income securities suffered substantial capital losses. Tired of suffering losses, investors started to think of ways to reduce their exposure to interest rate risk. Perhaps this desire was ill-advised, but that is not our concern here. At the time, investors were attracted to the idea of variable-rate securities rather than fixed-rate securities, their motivation being to reduce interest rate risk. The variable interest rate would protect investors from volatile price changes. If enough investors desire a particular type of security, a market exists for that security and innovative activity should create the proper investment opportunity.

Collateral

We noted earlier in this book that real assets provided investors with a much better rate of return than financial securities during most of the 1970s. Interest rates had risen, and investors were happy with their real assets. In order to enhance the marketability of fixed-income securities, issuers added "sweeteners" that allowed holders to receive upon redemption a certain amount of a real asset such as silver or oil rather than mere dollars. These *commodity-backed bonds* allowed firms to raise capital at favorable rates of interest during a period when it was difficult to raise capital—especially for companies with low bond ratings.

Denomination

Sometimes, firms attempt to broaden the market for a security issue by selling that issue to different types of investors. For example, if institutional investors are the typical purchasers of a firm's securities and capital is difficult to raise, the issue might be redesigned to appeal to individual investors. One way of doing this is to decrease the denomination associated with the security. We saw in the previous chapter that some issuers reduced the par value of new preferred stocks from the $100 a share that was the standard for the institutional market down to $25, for example, in order to sell preferred stock to individuals.

Why Innovate in Fixed-Income Securities?

Several reasons explain why the financial markets should tolerate the innovative activity that has occurred in recent years. The principal reason is that this innovation has produced the tools that investors need to manage risk more efficiently. We have also observed that when organizations attempt to raise capital during difficult economic periods, the desires of investors for new and different securities may be satisfied. Innovative activity in the issuing of securities sometimes involves taking advantage of tax loopholes. When these inequities in the tax laws surface, they can be corrected.

Efficient Management of Risk

The ability to manage risk, such as the risk associated with fluctuating interest rates, may be valuable to both the issuer and the purchaser of a security. An organization might be interested in issuing a security with a short call period so that the issue could be redeemed if interest rates fall. An investor might be willing to agree to a short call period if he or she feels that the call premium associated with the issue provides adequate compensation for the risk of early redemption of the security. Floating, or variable, interest rates also provide a vehicle for *risk management.* The organization might desire to issue a variable-rate security if interest rates are likely to fall. Individuals and institutions might desire variable-rate securities to hedge against the risk that interest rates will continue to increase. Obviously, both parties to the transaction will not be right, but because each views the variable rate as the appropriate tool for managing risk, the marketability of the security is enhanced.

Development of the market for futures and options is another manifestation of the motivation to manage risk. The next two chapters discuss options and futures in detail. For our purposes in this chapter, it is sufficient to know that these financial instruments allow the purchaser to alter the risk configuration of an initial position. For example, if a portfolio manager of common stocks thinks that the stock market is going to decline, he or she could sell the stocks. This action clearly alters the risk position of the portfolio manager. However, this action may also involve transaction costs in the form of substantial brokerage commissions as well as potential difficulties in selling large holdings of some stocks. The existence of a futures market, such as treasury bond and stock index futures, provides the portfolio manager with another instrument to change the risk of the portfolio. The portfolio manager can simply sell enough futures so that the amount short in the futures market equals the value of the portfolio. Because the amount short equals the amount held in common stocks, a zero position similar to the actual sale of the stocks has been created.

Better Marketing of Securities

Many financial market innovations are attempts to offer a security investors will purchase. We previously noted that variable-rate securities and small denominations are examples of marketing-driven innovations. Bonds incorporating options features have been popular in recent years. Some of these securities can be complex, but a simple version is a convertible bond. These bonds essentially give holders call options on the firm's common stock.

Convertible bonds have been around for many years and could hardly be considered a recent financial market innovation. However, fixed-income securities have recently incorporated both put and call options in rather unique ways. For example, IBM Credit issued a bond in late 1984 that had a variable rate plus a call and a put option. The call option was relatively standard in that the company could call the bond after two years at a premium of 1 percent ($10 per $1,000 par value bond). In fact, IBM Credit did call this bond for redemption in December 1986. The nature of the variable rate and the put provisions were quite innovative, however. At the end of this twelve-year bond's second year, IBM Credit had the right to determine the interest rate that would be paid for the next interest payment period. The holder of the bond also had the right to exercise a put provision that required the firm to redeem this bond at a stated price. In effect, after the initial two-year period, the maturity of this security would be very difficult to calculate because the company had the right to call the bond and the holder had the right to require the firm to redeem the bond if other investments appeared more promising. Although it initially appeared to be a twelve-year bond, this bond's innovative features incorporated characteristics of a two-year renewable certificate of deposit.

Tax Aspects

Original-issue, deep-discount bonds initially were created to take advantage of a little-noticed provision in the tax laws. Under the law existing in 1981 when the first issues were sold, any discount from par was amortized on a straight-line basis. For example, if a firm issued a seven-year, $1,000 par value bond with a zero coupon rate of interest for $500, the implied rate of interest would be approximately 14 percent. The firm could claim $500 divided by seven years, or $71.43 per year, as interest expense, even though no cash outlay for interest was made until the end of the seventh year. This was attractive to "cash-starved" companies during the high-interest, tight-credit conditions of 1981. It allowed companies to effectively claim a tax refund equal to $71.43 multiplied by the firm's marginal tax rate. These bonds posed some important investment considerations to individuals and institutions that will be covered in the next section.

Risk Modification via Bond Provisions

"Sweeteners" added to bonds help to overcome fears investors have of buying fixed-income securities that may produce capital losses. This section presents a detailed discussion of several bond provisions that tend to modify the traditional risk-return relationship of fixed-income securities.

Commodity-Backed and Stock-Indexed Bonds

Commodity-backed and *stock-indexed bonds* are marketed to investors as inflation hedges. A commodity-backed bond has an interest rate or principal repayment tied in some fashion to the price of a physical commodity. In 1980, Sunshine Mining sold two different 8½ percent bond issues, due at different times in 1995, that were redeemable for the greater of $1,000 in cash or the cash equivalent of fifty ounces of silver. Also in 1980, Petro Lewis sold a twenty-year bond with an interest rate tied in part to the price of west Texas crude oil.

Oppenheimer & Company's $25 million issue, marketed in 1981, carried an interest rate indexed in a limited fashion to the volume of trading on the New York Stock Exchange. The original interest rate of 18 percent could rise to a maximum of 22 percent at high stock market trading volume levels.

Floating Rate Notes

In June 1974, Citicorp, the one-bank holding company controlling the First National City Bank (New York), proposed selling a floating rate note. *Floating rate notes* are unsecured debt obligations issued by corporations. The interest rate paid on these notes varies from time to time. In addition, the holders of these notes may redeem them at their face value at preset dates.

Citicorp's issue provides a good example of the operation of floating rate notes. The issue was to mature on June 1, 1989. It carried an interest rate of 9.7 percent from issuance to November 30, 1974, and a minimum rate of 9.7 percent from December 1, 1974, to May 31, 1975. Starting December 1, 1974, the interest rate was determined for six months and set at 100 basis points above the three-month U.S. Treasury bill rate (minimum rate of 9.7 percent). The rate would be determined every six months thereafter until the note reached maturity. On June 1, 1975, the interest rate was set at 100 basis points above the three-month treasury bill rate that existed during the first three weeks of May 1975. No minimum interest rate provision would apply to rates starting with the June 1, 1975, period. Beginning on June 1, 1976, and every six months thereafter, the holders of the Citicorp notes had the right to redeem them on any semiannual interest date, at the holder's option, by giving thirty days' notice to Citicorp. While the initial minimum purchase applicable to this $650 million issue was $5,000, the bonds were traded on the NYSE in units of $1,000.

What are the advantages of floating rate notes for the investor? First, if inflation rates increase, causing interest rates to go higher, the investor will probably receive a higher interest yield on the note because the rate is reset every six months. Second, the notes are actually renewable short-term obligations once the first redemption (put) date is reached. Every six months, the investor can decide whether the money should be left in the Citicorp issue or plaçed in more attractive investments. Third, because of the short-term character of the notes, interest rate risk is minimal. The price of the notes is unlikely to vary much from the $1,000 par value when that value can be obtained by redemption every six months once the first redemption date is reached.

On the other hand, floating rate notes may not be a desirable security for an investor. An investor who expects a decline in interest rates would not be attracted to floating rate notes. Long-term, high-quality bonds would be a better holding because of the potential for capital appreciation. The holder of a floating rate note might also be adversely influenced by changes in the shape of the yield curve if short-term interest rates drop faster than long-term rates. In fact, long-term rates may remain unchanged or increase slightly. In this situation, the investor would do better with a long-term bond than with a floating rate note.

The disadvantages of floating rate notes as they were issued during the mid-1970s led to the issuance of *second-generation* floating rate notes in 1979. This variety of floating rate notes is convertible into a long-term debt obligation. Continental Illinois Corporation issued what is believed to be the first convertible floating rate note in April 1979. The Continental Illinois floating rate issue allowed holders of the eight-year notes to convert into twenty-five-year debentures paying a fixed annual rate of 8½ percent.

The advantage of the convertible floating rate note issued by Continental Illinois was that the note provided the investor with some protection against falling short-term interest rates. If the floating rate falls substantially below the long-term rate of 8½ percent, the investor can convert and move into the long-term debenture. By converting to a longer-term debt obligation, the investor takes on more interest rate risk. Hence, if interest rates should increase after conversion, a capital loss would be incurred. In addition, the conversion process is not reversible. The investor wanting to invest for the short term would have to sell the long-term security and incur transaction costs. Although a convertible floating rate note is an interesting form of debt obligation, the investor is still called upon to make important decisions regarding interest rate movements and maturity timing decisions.

Original-Issue, Deep-Discount Fixed-Income Securities

In the early 1980s, a large number of securities known as original-issue, deep-discount securities were sold to investors. These fixed-income securities carried coupon interest rates ranging from 0 to about 7 percent at a time when market rates were in the 13 to 16 percent range. These bonds were sold at prices substantially below par—often for only 25 to 40 percent of par. The precise offering price naturally depended on the coupon rate, quality, and maturity of the fixed-income security. For example, in 1982, BankAmerica issued *zero coupon notes,* which they called "money multiplier notes," that would double, triple, or quadruple the original investment by 1987, 1990, or 1992, respectively. These notes promised rates of return in the 13 to 13.5 percent range, or approximately one percentage point (100 basis points) below the required rate of return demanded by the market at that time on a standard or "plain vanilla" note of comparable quality and maturity.

As with most "gimmick" fixed-income securities, these original-issue, deep-discount bonds were not for every investor. The BankAmerica zero coupon notes of 1987 were issued in 1982 for $500 for each $1,000 principal amount of bond. Each year, BankAmerica reported that, for tax purposes, holders earned about $100 in interest income per bond. However, investors received no annual cash flow with which to pay income taxes on this interest income because the entire $500 in interest was paid at the note's maturity. Hence, these bonds are suitable only for those investors in a zero-marginal tax bracket. This would include some corporate pension plans, some individuals such as minor children, Keogh plans, and IRAs. With a Keogh plan or an IRA, taxes are deferred until withdrawals are made during retirement. These original-issue, deep-discount securities also have profound fixed-income investment management strategy considerations, which are examined in the next section. In any event, investors need to be very cautious and make sure they fully understand the varied ramifications of any new fixed-income security such as a zero coupon bond.

Risk Modification via Fixed-Income Investment Strategies

With the fluctuations in interest rates noted in Figure 10–2, investors have been forced to devote more attention to fixed-income investment management. This section presents an introduction to some of the investment strategies used in recent years. We first distinguish between active and passive fixed-income management strategies. The nature and rationale for bond swaps is then discussed. Finally, we examine immunization as a fixed-income investment management technique. The use of interest rate futures as an investment management technique is covered in Chapter 15.

Active and Passive Management Strategies

When interest rates were in the 4 to 5 percent level in the late 1950s and early 1960s, a *passive* approach to fixed-income investment management was probably close to optimal. A buy-and-hold strategy is the epitome of a passive investment strategy. Investors buy bonds and simply hold those bonds until maturity, unless a sale is required because of severe quality deterioration of one or more of the bonds. In an attempt to get better investment performance from fixed-income investments and as a reaction to increasing interest rate volatility, *active* strategies have been used more frequently in recent years. With an active strategy, purchases and sales are made as circumstances change.

Bond Swaps

An active strategy often involves *bond swaps*, which means that the investor sells one bond and purchases another bond in an attempt to improve some aspect of portfolio performance. The following are some of the general reasons why an investor would want to swap bonds:

1. To increase the current yield of the portfolio.
2. To increase the yield-to-maturity of the portfolio, given the desire to maintain a given level of risk. In other words, to attempt to achieve a more efficient fixed-income portfolio.
3. To increase the interest rate sensitivity of a fixed-income portfolio in an attempt to get more capital appreciation.
4. To realize a loss for tax purposes.

Investment Highlight

Merrill Lynch and the POs (The Pieces Are Different from the Whole)

The significance of the manner in which a GNMA security is offered to the investing public is analyzed in this investment highlight.

Description
During the first half of 1987, Merrill Lynch reported a $250 million loss on its trading operation in mortgage securities. Part of this loss resulted from the innovative manner in which GNMA securities were being marketed to the investing public.

GNMA securities are government guaranteed, mortgage-backed securities. They pass on to investors both the principal and the interest paid by mortgage holders. Recently, GNMA cash flows have been divided into those involving only the interest income (IOs) and those involving only the principal repayment (POs). Each separate stream of anticipated cash flows, the interest only or the principal only, is then sold to investors at the appropriate discounted present value. The investment attributes associated with each of these two separate components are different from an undivided GNMA interest and principal cash flow stream—especially with regard to interest rate sensitivity.

Investors cannot predict the life of a mortgage because the mortgage holder typically has the right to prepay the mortgage and will typically do so when moving to a new residence or if interest rates decline sufficiently to justify refinancing the existing mortgage. Interest rate risk becomes especially important for IOs and POs. If market interest rates fall, the eleven-year average life of a mortgage with a thirty-year final maturity might fall to five years. Investors would desire the POs because they would get their money back faster than they anticipated. If interest rates rise, the average life of a mortgage might rise from eleven to fifteen years, and investors would desire IOs in order to receive interest payments for four years longer than they originally anticipated.

In early 1987, investors desired IOs because they expected market rates to rise and were reluctant to buy POs. These POs remained in dealer inventories, and Merrill Lynch lost money. Consistent with investor expectations, market rates rose and the POs declined in value. Their effective maturity had been increased by the rising interest rates.

Conclusion
Securities sell for the discounted present value of their anticipated cash flows. When a security's cash flows are altered, as when GNMAs are split into IOs and POs, interest rate changes may become especially important to brokers as well as to investors.

5. To improve the quality of the portfolio.
6. To improve the marketability of the portfolio.

The area of bond swapping can become complex because of the calculations involved. However, let us examine some of the major types of bond swaps and what the investor hopes to accomplish from these swaps.

Maturity or Time Horizon Swap

In this type of swap, the investor anticipates a change in the shape of the yield curve. For example, assume that an investor is presently holding six-month treasury bills yielding 8 percent. Twenty-year government bonds are yielding 7 percent. The investor expects short-term rates to fall substantially in the next two months to 5 percent while long-term rates will fall only slightly to 6 percent. If the investor waits for the six-month treasury bills to mature, the rates available for reinvestment are only 5 percent for six months and 6 percent for twenty years. Hence, the investor makes the following trade to lock-in the long-term rate now:

Sell: Six-month treasury bill yielding 8 percent
Buy: Twenty-year government bond yielding 7 percent

With this swap, the investor increases interest rate risk in that interest rates are expected to fall. Not only is the 7 percent long-term rate locked-in, but the longer maturity increases the possibility of obtaining capital appreciation from the bond portfolio. It also increases the possibility of getting capital losses if interest rates increase rather than decline.

Quality Bond Swap

This swap involves selling one quality of fixed-income investment and purchasing a different quality. In order to accomplish successfully a swap of this type, an investor needs to monitor carefully the yield spread between fixed-income securities of different qualities. For example, assume the typical historical spread between long-term government bonds and the highest quality corporate bond is twenty-five basis points so that if a U.S. government bond is selling to yield 9.25 percent, an IBM bond should be priced to yield 9.50 percent. However, if an investor holding the government bond yielding 9.25 percent sees the IBM bond yielding 9.75 percent, the following bond swap might be undertaken:

Sell: U.S. government twenty-year bond yielding 9.25 percent
Buy: IBM twenty-year bond yielding 9.75 percent

The investor improves the yield relative to risk for this portfolio by twenty-five basis points. Of course, the investor needs to make certain the quality of the IBM bond has not actually deteriorated relative to a U.S. government security, which could account for the bigger yield spread. Transaction costs would also need to be considered.

Nature-of-Rate Swap

This type of swap involves swapping a bond having a fixed rate of interest for a bond having a floating rate of interest or vice versa. If an investor is holding a fixed-rate bond in a portfolio and decides interest rates are likely to increase, one strategy is to make the following swap:

Sell: X company's ten-year 9 percent bond selling at par
Buy: Z company's ten-year floating-rate note presently yielding 8.75 percent

This swap allows the investor to accomplish two things: (1) to preserve the principal of the investment better because the rate on the floating-rate bond will increase and the note should sell closer to par than is true for the fixed-rate note and (2) to get a current rate of return that tracks the return available in the market. Notice that the investor has to give up twenty-five basis points, assuming the bonds are of equal quality, to gain the two potential advantages just cited.

Summary

Bonds swaps are probably more feasible for institutional investors than for individual investors. Most institutions are better able to monitor conditions in the financial markets and spot situations that result in good swapping opportunities. Institutions also tend to deal in large quantities of bonds, and transaction costs are less of a consideration than is true for many individuals. We have only mentioned some of the potential swapping opportunities that might be available to the astute investor. However, clearly, a buy-and-hold strategy must be carefully examined to determine if some swaps might produce better results. This is true for both individuals and institutions.

Although we have described various bond swaps, the investor should be alert to the fact that considerable variation in the terminology is used in investments literature to describe swaps. The important things to determine are what the swap is attempting to accomplish and whether this seems reasonable under anticipated financial market conditions.

Immunization Strategies

Immunization strategies are designed to protect the fixed-income investor from the risk associated with fluctuating interest rates. We are mainly concerned with the impact of rising interest rates on the price of long-term bonds. In fixed-income investing, we can identify two major risks associated with changing interest rates: (1) *price risk* and (2) *reinvestment rate risk* from having to reinvest the periodic interest payments at rates different from what we originally anticipated. Immunization strategies are concerned with both of these risks.

If we purchase a bond and interest rates do not change during the life of that bond, neither the price of the bond nor the reinvestment interest rate changes. If interest rates rise during the life of the bond, the price of the bond will decline, resulting in a capital loss. However, this price risk is offset to some degree by the fact that interest payments received from the bond can now be reinvested at higher rates of return. Immunization strategies seek to determine the point at which the price risk is effectively offset by the reinvestment rate risk. If we set the duration of our bond portfolio equal to our investment time horizon, we have immunized. Interest rate fluctuations during the time horizon will not alter our terminal wealth position significantly.

Exhibit 13–1 shows how immunization would work for a 5 percent

Exhibit 13–1 Immunization Example

Original situation: Coupon rate = 5%
Maturity of bond = 15 years
Current market interest rate = 7.5%
Duration of bond = 10.1 years
Investment time horizon = 10 years

	If interest rate stays at 7.5%	*If interest rate goes to 9% at once*
1. Bond price in year 10 (price risk)	$ 89.73	$ 84.17
2. Interest received in years 1–10	50.00	50.00
3. Reinvestment income at existing rate	22.54	28.43
4. Total value received	$162.27	$162.60

bond with a maturity of 15 years if the current market rate of return demanded on this bond is 7.5 percent. The duration of this bond is 10.1 years, and the investment time horizon is 10 years. If interest rates remain unchanged at 7.5 percent over the life of the bond, the total value at the end of the period is $162.27, which comes from the price of the bond in year 10, the coupon interest received of $5 a year per $100 par value and $22.54 received from reinvesting the coupon interest at 7.5 percent. If the market interest rate jumps immediately to 9 percent and remains at that level for the next 10 years, the total value at the end of the 10-year period is $162.60—virtually unchanged despite the rise in interest rates. Notice, the $5.56 decline in the price of the bond is offset by added reinvestment income of $5.89. The same type of analysis could be done if interest rates are expected to decline. The increase in the price of the bond could be offset by lower reinvestment income. However, we would probably not want to immunize if we expect interest rates to decline, but would rather lengthen the maturity of the fixed-income portfolio in an attempt to seek large capital appreciation.

One version of an immunization strategy is known as *contingent immunization.* Suppose a portfolio manager is told by actuaries for the pension plan being managed that a return of 8 percent is required. However, the going rate of return from high-quality bonds is now 10 percent. The investment manager decides to follow a strategy of active bond management including such things as the bond swaps discussed in the previous section. The manager is allowed to pursue an active management strategy until the interest rate drops to 8 percent. At the 8 percent interest rate level, the manager immunizes the portfolio so that the 8 percent return persists during the investment time horizon. At times, institutions dedicate the income from a portfolio to meet a specified portion of the firm's pension plan liabilities. An article in the *Wall Street Journal* related this immunization strategy:

> GAF Corp. recently cut $8 to $10 million off its yearly pension bill with an immunized portfolio. The chemical and building materials concern in a single day sold $150 million in stocks and bonds, bought $125 million in

high-yielding bonds and dedicated the 14% yield to pension expenses. It had earlier assumed that pension funds would earn only 7%.[3]

Given interest rates that have existed in the market in recent years, investors may find bonds having durations of a maximum of about ten years. Hence, investors can immunize for only about ten years, at which time they would have to reinvest the principal repayment at whatever interest rates exist in the market. Zero coupon bonds tend to have durations equal to their final maturities because they have no periodic interest payment inflows. Hence, these bonds were attractive to investors in 1981 and 1982, when they thought interest rates were high and likely to fall.

Summary

Many of the more creative minds in finance have been engaged in recent years in designing innovative aternatives in the types of securities available to the investing public. This innovative activity has occurred to bypass regulation and to take advantage of tax laws. In addition, the need to provide solutions to some of the difficult financing problems that faced organizations needing capital during the past decade was another major impetus.

Innovative activity has altered the maturity of securities, the coupon rate offered, the collateral backing the issue, and the denomination. Some of these innovations have allowed investors to manage risk more efficiently, while other innovations were simply designed to create a security that could be sold. In any event, the knowledge and skills required of successful investors has changed substantially in the past decade.

Innovation has occurred not only in the types and terms of securities being offered to investors but also in the area of investment management strategies. These investment management strategies, which range from passive to very active, attempt to alter the risk of a portfolio or to allow investors to quickly and easily manage the risk present in the current holdings. One type of relatively passive investment management strategy is immunization, which means the duration of the portfolio is set equal to the investment time horizon. Little trading in the fixed-income portfolio occurs once the portfolio is immunized. Active trading of a bond portfolio involves such activities as bond swaps to accomplish objectives, including an increase in current income, an improved yield-to-maturity, better quality, and better marketability.

The investor interested in fixed-income securities must be aware of the many alternatives available in the financial markets. The yields from many alternatives tend to change constantly, and what might be the best buy one month may be a poor buy just a few months later. In addition, the investor needs to be alert to the creation of new and inno-

3. Daniel Hertzberg, "Bond Investors Using a Textbook Strategy to Hedge Against a Drop in Interest Rates," *Wall Street Journal* (November 11, 1981):27.

vative fixed-income investment alternatives. Many very interesting opportunities, such as zero coupon bonds, have developed in recent years.

Suggested Readings

BIERWAG, G. O., G. G. KAUFMAN, R. SCHWEITZER, and A. TOEVS. "The Art of Risk Management in Bond Portfolios." *Journal of Portfolio Management* (Spring 1981):27–36.

BILLINGHAM, CAROL J. "Strategies for Enhancing Bond Portfolio Returns." *Financial Analysts Journal* (May–June 1983):50–56.

CHANCE, DON M. "Floating Rate Notes and Immunization." *Journal of Financial and Quantitative Analysis* (September 1983):365–380.

CHATFIELD, ROBERT E., and R. CHARLES MOYER. "'Putting' Away Bond Risk: An Empirical Examination of the Value of the Put Option on Bonds." *Financial Management* (Summer 1986):26–33.

GUSHEE, CHARLES H. "How to Immunize a Bond Investment." *Financial Analysts Journal* (March–April 1981):44–51.

LEIBOWITZ, MARTIN L., and ALFRED WEINBERGER. "The Uses of Contingent Immunization." *Journal of Portfolio Management* (Fall 1981):51–55.

MCENALLY, RICHARD W. "Duration as a Practical Tool for Bond Management." *Journal of Portfolio Management* (Summer 1977):53–57.

PAVEL, CHRISTINE. "Securization." *Economic Perspectives,* Federal Reserve Bank of Chicago (July–August 1986):16–31.

RAMASWAMY, KRISHNA, and SURESH M. SUNDARESAN. "The Valuation of Floating Rate Instruments: Theory and Evidence." *Journal of Financial Economics* (December 1986):223–72.

REILLY, FRANK K., and RUPINDER S. SINDU. "The Many Uses of Bond Duration." *Financial Analysts Journal* (July–August 1980):58–72.

SANTOMERO, ANTHONY M. "Fixed versus Variable Rate Loans." *Journal of Finance* (December 1983):1363–80.

TUTTLE, DONALD L., ed. *The Revolution in Techniques of Managing Bond Portfolios.* Charlottesville, VA: Institute of Chartered Financial Analysts, 1983.

YAWITZ, JESS, HOWARD KANFOLD, THOMAS MACIROWSKI, and MICHAEL SMIRLOCK. "The Pricing and Duration of Floating Rate Bonds." *Journal of Portfolio Management* (Summer 1987):49–56.

YAWITZ, JESS, and WILLIAM J. MARSHALL. "The Shortcomings of Duration as a Risk Measure for Bonds." *Journal of Financial Research* (Summer 1981):91–102.

Questions

1. What are the causes of financial market innovation? 360
2. What is a complete market, and what is its relationship to the development of financial market innovation? 361

3. What are the two basic ways in which investors can modify the risk presented to them by the financial markets?

4. If someone said that maturity and coupon are the most important terms when creating innovative securities, would you agree? Why or why not?

5. How do financial market innovations help firms to raise capital more efficiently?

6. Two so-called functional business disciplines, marketing and finance, are closely linked when it comes to the area of innovative securities. Why is this the case?

7. What is portfolio immunization? Why can it be considered an investment innovation?

8. Rising interest rates and their increasing volatility over the past decade have resulted in the addition of new provisions to some bonds. How have these "sweeteners" (as they are called) helped to make bond investment more attractive?

9. What are original-issue, deep-discount securities? Why should an investor be wary of such investments?

10. Give reasons why an investor would want to swap bonds.

11. Discuss the different types of bond swaps that an investor can perform while actively managing a bond portfolio.

12. Suppose an investor undertakes the following transaction:

    Buy: Twenty-year, AAA-rated 8 percent bonds, price $100, yield to maturity 8 percent.
    Sell: Twenty-year, A-rated 8 percent bonds priced at $95.5, yield to maturity 8.5 percent.

    Buy: Six-month, T-bills, to yield 10 percent.
    Sell: Twenty-year government bond to yield 11.00 percent.

    Buy: Twenty-year, A-rated 4 percent bond priced at $60 to yield 8 percent.
    Sell: Twenty-year, A-rated 7 percent bond priced at $90 to yield 8 percent.

    For each of the above *swaps*, what are the underlying motivations and the associated risks?

Part

Specialized Investments and Investment Approaches

5

This part of the book deals with securities that have unique characteristics, such as options and futures contracts. The other major topic considered is the use of specialized investment approaches by investors. Investor interest in specialized investments and specialized investment approaches has increased dramatically in the last decade. This increased attention has been the result of high and volatile interest rates and a more intense examination of the ways in which risk-return trade-offs can be changed for the benefit of the investor. Investors have increasingly utilized options and futures to control the risk of their portfolios.

Chapter 14 examines leverage-inherent securities, with most of the emphasis on put and call options. Chapter 15 discusses financial futures and how they may be used for both speculation and hedging. The use of both interest rate and stock index futures to control risk is of significance to investors. Investment companies, both mutual funds and closed-end investment companies, are the subject of Chapter 16. In recent years, we have seen a great increase in the number and variety of investment companies available to the investing public. Chapter 17 examines the nature of global investing and the role of foreign securities in the portfolio of an investor.

Chapter 14

Leverage-Inherent Securities

Key Concepts

- arbitrage
- at-the-money option
- call option
- CD warrant
- covered option writing
- exercise price
- expiration date
- external leverage
- financial leverage
- hedge ratio
- hedging
- in-the-money option
- index option
- inherent leverage
- naked option writing
- operating leverage
- option buyer
- option premium
- option seller
- option spread
- out-of-the-money option
- put option
- skewed return distribution
- speculative premium
- striking price
- theoretical value
- underlying security
- warrant

Chapter Outline

- Nature of Leverage
- Options
- Exchange-Listed Option Trading
- Option Valuation
- An Overview of Option Trading Strategies
- Warrants
- Summary
- Appendix

Leverage-inherent securities come in a variety of forms that help to expand the investment outcomes available to investors. These securities can be used to alter the risk and return characteristics offered by real and financial assets. By using leverage-inherent securities, investors are supplied with a more complete set of risk and return trade-offs than are generally available through investing in the underlying securities alone. Portfolio managers have found leverage-inherent securities to be cost-effective in implementing strategic portfolio adjustments and in controlling risk. This chapter examines the concept of leverage and analyzes the most popular leverage-inherent securities: options and warrants. The following chapter presents the features of futures that allow risk and return alterations.

Although option trading has been going on for centuries, the practice was not widespread until the 1980s. In 1973, the Chicago Board Options Exchange (CBOE) started trading listed options. In recent years, option trading activity has skyrocketed, and over 300 stock options are listed on the major exchanges. To see why options have become so popular, we need to develop an understanding of the leverage and insurance potential provided by options.

Nature of Leverage

In an elementary physics class, a student may learn that a large rock can be moved by inserting the end of a lever under the rock and using a fulcrum to multiply the student's power. The student can move the rock because the fixed point, the fulcrum, has the ability to increase the force exerted by the student.

Operating and Financial Leverage

In finance, leverage works in a way quite similar to the concept illustrated in the physics example. A small change in one variable—the firm's revenues—produces a larger change in a second variable—the firm's profits. Any leverage situation has a fixed element present corresponding to the fulcrum in the physics example. Two types of leverage are discussed in the basic business finance course, operating leverage and financial leverage. Operating leverage exists when the fixed operating costs of a firm become important in relation to the total costs of the firm. Airlines typically have cost structures with fixed costs as a substantial proportion of total costs because of their heavy investment in fixed assets such as airplanes and support facilities. Because the revenues of an airline tend to change by a greater percentage than do the fixed costs, its profits are sensitive to small changes in revenues; airlines could be said to have a high degree of *operating leverage.*

The other type of leverage used by businesses is financial leverage. *Financial leverage* exists when a firm incurs fixed financial expenses in a form such as interest. A firm with a large amount of debt in its capital structure typically must make large interest payments. Interest payments are a fixed financial expense and operate (as the fulcrum in the physics example) to magnify small changes in the earnings before interest and taxes (EBIT) into larger changes in the earnings after taxes. Some of the major U.S. airlines have a high degree of both financial and operating leverage and are likely to have earnings after taxes that are quite volatile over the business cycle.

Upon taking a broad view of leverage, we can see that it results from the existence of a fixed element in the company, the security, or the portfolio being examined. Our concern is with the investment aspect of leverage, and we will focus on the possibility of leverage in individual securities and portfolios. To do this, we must distinguish between *external leverage* and *inherent* (built-in) *leverage.*

External versus Inherent Leverage

Margin buying is the simplest way to add leverage to a security or portfolio. If this is done, leverage of the *external* variety is added. Purchasing securities on margin increases both the expected return on a portfolio and its risk. We demonstrated in Chapter 6 that a portfolio's risk and return characteristics could be moved to a preferred position on the capital market line by investing in the market portfolio and by either borrowing or lending at the risk-free rate. Margin buying was assumed to occur at the risk-free rate.

An alternative to buying securities in margin accounts is purchasing securities that, because of their terms, already have built-in leverage. Options, warrants, and futures are examples of these leverage-inherent securities. Because the existence of leverage requires that a fixed element be present, we expect to find a fixed element associated with the terms of these securities. The fixed element occurs in the form of either a fixed exercise price for the securities or a fixed redemption value. Next, we will focus our discussion on the nature and use of two popular leverage-inherent securities, options and warrants.

Options

"To my mind, this Exchange is unquestionably the most exciting and potentially important experiment now occurring in the securities industry."[1] U.S. Senator Harrison A. Williams, Chairman of the Securities Subcommittee of the Senate Banking Committee, made these remarks on the first anniversary of the opening of the Chicago Board Options Ex-

1. Chicago Board Options Exchange, Reprint of Senator Williams's speech.

change (CBOE) and prophesied the emergence of a very popular investment vehicle, the option.

Options on financial assets have become so popular that the dollar value of trades in some options often exceeds that of their underlying securities. Options are available on different types of underlying securities, including (1) stocks, bonds, and market indexes, (2) currencies, (3) futures contracts, and (4) precious metals. The evolution of trading on a wide variety of option contracts provides a more complete financial market so that investment opportunities are available to meet a broader range of investor preferences for risk, return, and liquidity.

Option Terminology

To understand the nature and use of options, we must define the key characteristics of options and option trading. The definitions in this section apply to options on common stock. An option is often called a derivative security or contingent claim because its value is determined by the option's claim on the value of another security. An option is simply a contract between two investors. A *call option* gives the holder the right to purchase a specified number of shares of a given stock from another investor at the specified exercise price at any time through the exercise date. A *put* is an option similar to a call except that it gives the holder the right to sell (rather than buy) shares in the future to another investor. Call and put options traded on organized exchanges typically have a maximum life of nine months.

The option *seller* is the party to the contract who promises to fulfill the call (put) option if asked to do so. The seller is often referred to as the option writer. The option *buyer,* or holder, is the party to the contract with the right to exercise the call (put) option or to let it expire unexercised.

The stock into which the option can be exercised is known as the *underlying security.* To demonstrate option features, we will discuss the stock of Reebok Corporation and the July Reebok 50 call option. On March 31, 1987, the call option sold for 4½ while the stock sold for 46¾, as shown in Table 14–1 below. (Throughout this chapter, both stock and option price quotes will be given without leading dollar signs.)

Option premium	The price paid by the option buyer to the option seller. For the Reebok option, the premium was 4½.
Exercise price	The price at which the common stock is bought (sold) if the call (put) is exercised. To exercise means to execute the right guaranteed by the option contract to buy (sell) the stock at the exercise price. The price is often referred to as the *striking price.* The Reebok option's exercise price was 50.
Expiration date	The last date on which the holder can exercise the option. After the expiration date, the option is worthless. The Reebok option expired on the Saturday following the third Friday in July 1987.

Theoretical value	The larger of (1) the stock price minus the exercise price or (2) zero. If the theoretical value is positive, the stock is said to be *in the money*. If the stock price equals the exercise price, the stock is said to be *at the money*, and if the stock price is less than the exercise price, the stock is said to be *out of the money*. The minimum price for an out-of-the-money option is zero because negative prices are impossible. We calculate that the Reebok option was out of the money by subtracting 50 from 46¾, which equals −3¼.
Speculative premium	The difference between the option's price and the option's theoretical value. The premium for the Reebok option was 4½. Table 14–1 shows the Reebok call and put options that were traded on March 31, 1987. For example, the July 50 put gave the holder a right to sell Reebok stock through the Saturday after the third Friday in July at 50 per share. For that privilege, the holder paid 7 per option. Exhibit 14–1 shows the calculations of the theoretical values and speculative premiums for a series of July Reebok options.

Table 14–1
Calls and Puts for Reebok Traded on March 31, 1987

Reebok Stock Price	*Strike Price*	**Call Price** *April*	*May*	*July*	**Put Price** *April*	*May*	*July*
46¾	25	20⅞	s*	20½	1/16	s	r*
	30	17	s	16½	r	s	r
	35	11¾	11¾	12½	⅛	5/16	¾
	40	7	7½	9¼	¼	1 1/16	2⅛
	45	3⅜	4½	6⅝	1⅜	3	4
	50	1 3/16	2½	4½	5⅜	6¼	7
	55	5/16	1¼	3	r	r	r

**s* means that no option contract exists, and *r* means that the option was not traded on March 31, 1987.

Exhibit 14–1 Reebok Call and Put Option Premiums

	July Call			**July Put**		
Exercise Price	*Option Price*	*Theoretical Value*	*Speculative Premium*	*Option Price*	*Theoretical Value*	*Speculative Premium*
45	6⅝	1¾[a]	4⅞	4	0[a]	4
50	4½	0	4½	7	3¼	3¾

[a]The Reebok common stock was quoted at 46¾ on March 31, 1987. The theoretical value equals the larger of (1) the stock price minus the exercise price (for calls; reverse calculation for puts) or (2) zero.

Levering Returns with Options

An option is a leverage-inherent security because of its fixed exercise price. If an investor had been lucky enough to purchase Reebok common stock on January 2, 1987, at 24⅞, he or she would have profited when the price increased to 46¾ by March 31, 1987. However, if instead the investor had wisely paid the 2⅝ premium for an April Reebok call option with an exercise price of 25, the investor would have earned an incredible 695 percent return when the option price increased to 20⅞ over the same period. This is in contrast to the healthy return on the common stock of 87.9 percent. An investment of $2,625 in the April Reebok 25 call to buy 1,000 shares of Reebok stock would have been worth $20,875 in less than three months. This is the power of leverage possible with options.

If, on the other hand, an investor had purchased an April Reebok 25 put option on January 2, 1987, for 2⅛, the price would have shrunk to 1/16 by March 31, 1987, for a loss of 97 percent. For every option that expires out of the money, the loss on the investment to the option holder is 100 percent. We will concentrate most of our discussion on call options, but put options are subject to similar reasoning.

Exchange-Listed Option Trading

Prior to the opening of the CBOE, an investor who desired to purchase either a put or a call option would have a brokerage firm contact a special put and call broker to obtain a price for the desired option. The put and call broker would arrange to have the option written by an investor whose portfolio contained the desired stock. If and when the buyer of the option contract decided to exercise it, the writer of the option had to immediately fulfill the contract.

Exchange-listed trading has had a dramatic effect on the option market. Major developments include (1) standardization of the option contract with respect to the number of shares under option, expiration date, striking price, and trading practices, (2) establishment of good secondary markets for options, including continuous public reporting of prices and volume similar to that existing for common stocks, and (3) establishment of clearinghouse corporations to act as go-betweens for buyers and sellers and to guarantee delivery on the contracts. Every business day, the *Wall Street Journal* carries almost two full pages of option price quotes for actively traded contracts on the Chicago, America, Philadelphia, Pacific, and New York exchanges.

Options on Individual Stocks

Standardization of the expiration date and the striking price was critical to the development of a good secondary market for options. In most cases, options expire on the third Friday of the month of January, April,

July, or October (or every three months following either February or March). Trading in any given option starts approximately nine months before the expiration date. As a result, trading in three different expiration months usually occurs at any given time. For example, in March 1987, trading occurred in the following options: April 1987, July 1987, and October 1987. About the time that the April 1987 option expired, trading opened in the January 1988 option.

When trading opens in a new expiration month, the exercise price is set at a dollar figure that approximates the market price of the common stock. If the market price changes during the period of the option, trading may start in a new option that has the same expiration date but a different striking price. Table 14–1 shows that this occurred in the case of the Reebok options. On March 31, 1987, call options expiring in April 1987 were traded for Reebok with the following exercise prices: 25, 30, 35, 40, 45, 50, and 55. Each of these call options allowed the holder to purchase 100 shares of Reebok common stock at the exercise price stipulated in the option through the Saturday settlement date following the third Friday of April.

Index and Other Options

In March 1983, the CBOE started trading what is called the CBOE 100 Index option, or simply the OEX option. This investment alternative allows investors to trade options based on the cash equivalent of the 100 stocks comprising the index. Since then, trading in a variety of *index option* contracts has become very active. Exhibit 14–2 gives an example of the daily trading activity for the CBOE S&P 100 and 500 stock index options.

Settlement of an index option contract is made on the basis of cash instead of the physical delivery of the underlying securities. An investor purchasing an index option contract must pay an amount equal to the quoted option premium multiplied times 100. Exhibit 14–2 shows that for a CBOE S&P 100 Index June call option with a striking price at 280, an investor would pay a call premium of 13¼ times 100, or $1,325, plus commissions.

Investors and portfolio managers use the CBOE S&P 100 index option to adjust portfolio risk and to time stock market cycles instead of using individual stock options. As stock market conditions change, investors can adjust portfolio risk and return characteristics quickly and dramatically, and at minimal transaction cost. Consequently, index options have become extremely popular instruments with investment managers as a means of timing portfolio adjustments.

By 1982, trading in foreign currency options had become well established on the Philadelphia Exchange. Also in 1982, an exchange had begun trading in options on U.S. Treasury issues. A somewhat more complex option that gained popularity in the mid-1980s was the option on bond futures contracts. New option contracts are continually being introduced by the exchanges, but many are discontinued because of the low volume generated.

Exhibit 14–2 Options on Market Indexes, Selected Quotes, March 31, 1987

Chicago Board

S&P 100 INDEX

Strike	Calls–Last			Puts–Last		
Price	Apr	May	Jun	Apr	May	Jun
235	48⅜	....	....	....	⅛	....
240	43	....	....	....	¼	....
245	38½	....	....	1/16	⅜	....
250	34	35	....	1/16	9/16	....
255	27½	29½	....	1/16	1	....
260	23	24 3/16	26 3/16	¼	1 7/16	2⅝
265	18½	20	24	½	2½	3¾
270	12⅞	16⅞	20	1 3/16	3⅝	5¼
275	9	12⅞	15½	2½	5	7
280	5¾	9½	13¼	4⅜	7¼	9⅜
285	3⅜	7⅛	10½	7	9½	12¼
290	1⅜	5⅛	8½	11	12¾	14
295	⅜	3½	6½	14⅛	16⅝	18¾
300	⅜	2⅜	4⅜	18⅛	20⅜	....
305	⅛	1 9/16	3½	23	23¾	....

Total call volume 177,623 Total call open int. 506,958
Total put volume 173,238 Total put open int. 668,975
The index: High 282.47; Low 279.29; Close 282.07, + 2.57

S&P 500 INDEX

Strike	Calls–Last			Puts–Last		
Price	Apr	May	Jun	Apr	May	Jun
220	....	....	....	....	....	1/16
225	....	....	....	....	....	1/16
235	....	....	....	....	....	¼
240	....	....	....	....	....	5/16
245	....	....	....	....	....	¼
250	....	....	....	....	....	⅜
255	....	....	....	....	....	¾
260	....	....	....	....	....	1⅜
265	....	....	....	....	....	2 5/16
270	21¾	....	....	¼	....	3¼
275	....	....	....	9/16	....	4¾
280	12⅛	15⅛	17½	1 3/16	4	5⅜
285	7⅞	11⅞	....	2 5/16	4⅞	7⅞
290	5⅞	8¾	12½	4¼	7½	9½
295	3	7¼	9½	7	10⅞	11¾
300	1¾	5	7½	10⅝	12⅜	14⅜
305	¾	3¼	6⅛	14⅛	17⅛	....
310	⅜	2⅜	4½	18¾	....	....
315	⅛	....	3½	....	....	....

Total call volume 14,255 Total call open int. 132,176
Total put volume 6,402 Total put open int. 125,978
The index: High 291.87; Low 289.07; Close 291.70, + 2.50

Source: Reprinted by permission of the *Wall Street Journal,*© Dow Jones & Company, Inc. (1987).

Option Valuation

A model to show how options should be priced in efficient markets was developed by Fisher Black and Myron Scholes in 1973. The Black-Scholes Option Pricing Model is based on arbitrage concepts similar to those used in deriving the CAPM and APT. Black and Scholes showed that the return on certain portfolios constructed by purchasing an option and the option's underlying stock should equal the risk-free rate.[2]

Arbitrage and Option Pricing

We will now show how *arbitrage* operates in the pricing of an option relative to its underlying security. The ratio between the stock position and the option position is determined by the variability of the expiration period returns on the two securities and is called the *hedge ratio.* A *hedge* can be defined as a combination of an option and the underlying security so that either the stock protects the option from loss or the option protects the stock.

Assume that we have a one-year option with an exercise price of 25 and the underlying common stock is currently selling for 30 per share. Also, assume that at the end of one year, the stock will be selling at either one of two possible prices, 20 or 40. Given that the current risk-free rate is 5 percent, we can derive the value of the option as 8.21. The calculation of the option's price is shown in Exhibit 14–3. The portfolio in Exhibit 14–3, consisting of an option and the underlying stock, creates a riskless investment with a return of $15 regardless of the stock price outcome. Observe that at the end of the year, the option is worth to the buyer either 0 or 15, depending on whether the common stock price is 20 or 40, respectively. If the stock price is 20, the option is worthless because no advantage results from buying stock at 25. If the stock price is 40, the option is worth 15 because stock valued at 40 can be purchased with the option at 25.

An astute investor can recognize that the return possibilities for the stock (20 or 40) are wider than those on the call option (0 or 15). In fact, .75 share of stock will have the same return range as one call option, that is, 15. Because .75 share of stock and one option are both dependent on the same set of circumstances (the stock price in one year), they are equivalent investments. Recognizing this, the investor can buy .75 shares of stock and write one call on the stock to produce a riskless investment with a return of 15—regardless of what stock price actually occurs.

The relationship between the interest rate and the option price can be seen directly: *The option price equals the current stock value minus the present value of the riskless ending value.* A higher interest rate results in a lower present value of the ending value. Because this factor is subtracted from the current market value of the stock to arrive at the option value,

2. Fischer Black and Myron Scholes, "The Pricing of Options and Corporate Liabilities," *Journal of Political Economy,* May–June 1973, pp. 637–54.

Exhibit 14–3 Option Valuation Using Riskless Arbitrage

Time 0	
Write call option and receive	+ 8.21*
Buy .75 share common stock	−22.50
Net investment	−14.29
Present value of $15 discounted at risk-free rate of 5 percent	14.29

*Call option value calculated below

Year 1	
If stock price rises to 40:	
Option value	−15.00
Value of .75 share stock at 40	+30.00
Value of investment	+15.00
If stock price declines to 20:	
Option value	0
Value of .75 share stock at 20	+15.00
Value of investment	+15.00

Call Value Calculation at Time 0
(Present Value of Riskless Return at Time 0)

Call value = Value of stock hedged − Present value of certain return at end of year 1
= 22.50 − [15/(1 + .05)]
= 22.50 − 14.29
= 8.21

the higher the discount rate, the lower the present value of the terminal value, and the higher the option price. Intuitively, the call option seller has a higher opportunity cost for the funds tied up in the security as interest rates increase and must be rewarded with a higher premium.

What is to guarantee that the option price will equal the value we have calculated? Assume that the option price varied from 8.21 to 9, for example. In this case, writing one call at 9 and buying .75 share of stock at 22.50 will result in a net investment of $13.50, which is immediately worth $14.29—the present value of the riskless investment. The arbitrageur simply borrows $13.50 at the risk-free rate, buys .75 share of stock at 22.50, and writes call options at 9 for as long as the opportunity is available. The $13.50 invested to equal $15 at the end of one year will earn an 11.1 percent risk-free return instead of 5 percent [($15/$13.50) − 1 = .111, or 11.1 percent]. Equilibrium is reestablished when the option price returns to 8.21, the return on the riskless hedge goes to 5 percent, and the present value of the riskless investment returns to $14.29.

Obviously, the example is too simple to reflect actual option pricing situations. Instead of only two possible future stock prices, a distribution of stock prices is possible at the expiration of the option. In order to maintain a perfectly hedged or riskless investment position, the arbitrageur must use a dynamic *hedging* strategy. This means that as time passes and security prices change, the hedge ratio between the option price volatility and the stock price volatility changes. Consequently, the investor must continuously recalculate the hedge ratio and adjust the investment positions so as to "roll the hedge forward" to the expiration date. Otherwise, the losses in one security will not be exactly offset by the gains on the other security at expiration.

Key Factors in Option Pricing

In general, the valuation of a stock option depends on the following key factors:

1. *The stock price.* The higher the price of the stock, the higher the premium, and the larger the potential losses.
2. *The length of time to expiration.* An option is a wasting asset. Its value will decline over time if the price of the underlying security remains unchanged, as indicated for the following ITT option:

   Speculative Call Premiums, March 31, 1987

Expiration Month	**June**	**September**	**December**
ITT 60 call	3⅛	5	6

   Figure 14–1 shows the potential decline in the speculative premium as an option approaches expiration. For example, an at-the-money, nine-month option is worth more than a four-month option. The four-month option is, in turn, worth more than the two-month option.
3. *The probability of a large price change in the underlying security.* The more volatile the price of the underlying security, the higher the speculative premium. For example, an October AT&T 22½ call sold for 2⅜ on March 31, 1987, when the common was at 23¾, for a speculative premium of 1⅛. The October 30 call on a more volatile stock, Avon, sold for a speculative premium of 2⅛ when the common stock was at 31⅛.
4. *The relationship between the exercise price and the market price.* This relationship can be seen in Figure 14–1. A *deep-in-the-money* call will sell for a lower speculative premium than a call at the money. The speculative premium tends to decline as the call goes deeper into the money. The minimum value rises as the theoretical value increases. The maximum value in Figure 14–1 is the stock's price. In other words, the option's price should never exceed the price of what can be obtained by exercising the option.
5. *Interest rates and dividend yields.* The relationship between the call value and the interest rate was shown in the arbitrage example: The

Figure 14–1
Option Valuation, by Time to Expiration

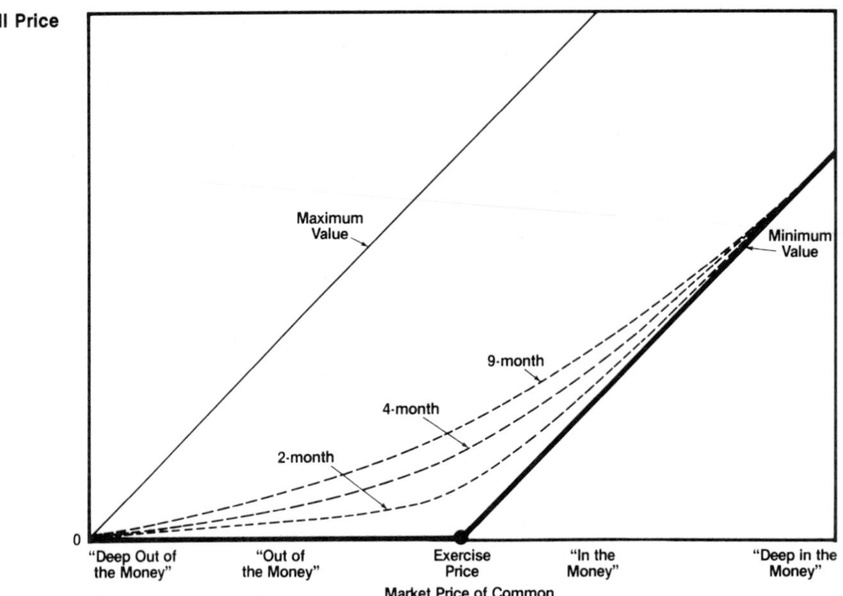

higher the interest rate, the higher the call value. If a common stock pays a dividend, the owner of the option does not participate in the dividend income as would the common stockholder. As a result, the higher the dividend yield on the underlying security, the lower the speculative premium. The exercise price of the option is not adjusted for any stock that goes ex-dividend—a fact that could be important to the option trader if the stock's dividend is a large amount per share.

An Overview of Option Trading Strategies

Options are becoming increasingly important to individual investors and institutional portfolio managers as a means of attaining portfolio performance that cannot be achieved by using the capital asset pricing model or arbitrage pricing theory strategies. In Chapter 6, we learned that CAPM and APT were concerned only with trade-offs between return and systematic risk variables. The returns on portfolios were assumed to be symmetrical and approximately normally distributed. Hence, all portfolio decisions were reduced to consideration of two variables, the mean and variance. However, few investors or portfolio managers view the trade-off between the chance of high returns and the chance of high losses as being equal. For example, a pension fund manager may want to avoid any large losses on a stock portfolio but would like to benefit at least partially from any "bull" markets occurring in the near future.

Investors' Preferences for Skewed Return Distributions

Portfolio objectives for some investors can be described as *skewed return distributions*. By skewed, we mean that the probability distribution of returns is not symmetrical and bell shaped but has a long "tail" for the distribution on one side of the mean that is not on the other side. Curve S in Figure 14–2 represents the normal return distribution typical of a well-diversified portfolio of common stocks. An investor might prefer to face a return distribution such as the one shown by curve PS in Figure 14–2. Notice that curve PS has a lower mean value, 6 percent, than curve S, 15 percent, but that curve PS has limited downside risk to −4 percent and curve S losses can range below −32 percent. For each level of return above 15 percent, the return on curve PS is slightly below the return on S.

Curve PS can be achieved by purchasing market index put options in combination with the portfolio of underlying securities. Notice that if the market declines, the gains on the market index put option offset the losses on the stock portfolio, thereby limiting the downside risk. On the other hand, if the market goes up, the gains on the stock portfolio are diminished only by the fixed premium cost of the put option. Investors can achieve a wide variety of return distributions in addition to PS simply by the way they package the options and the underlying securities to form

Figure 14–2
Normal versus Skewed Return Distributions

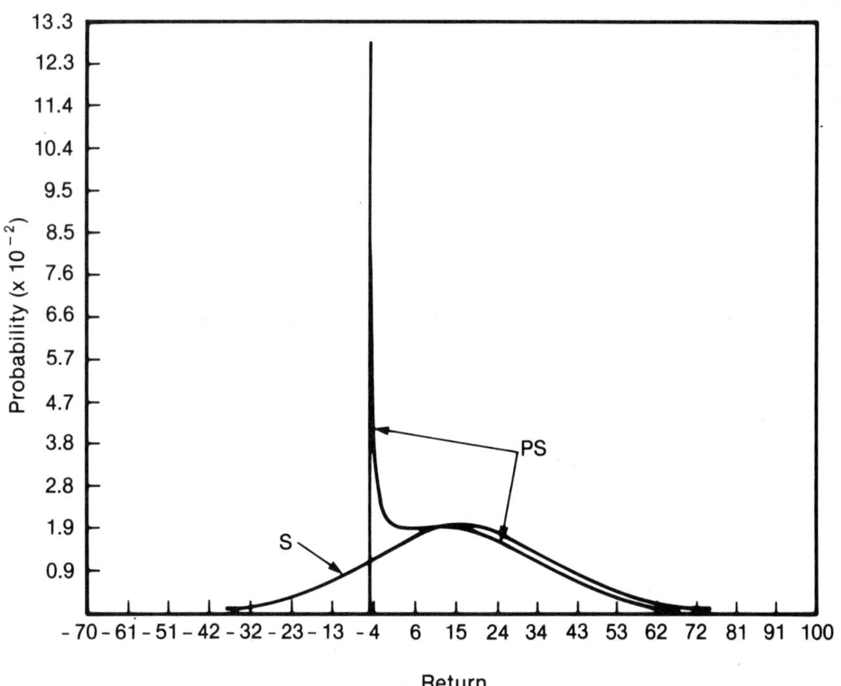

Source: Richard M. Bookstaber and Roger G. Clarke, *Option Strategies for Institutional Investment Management* (Addison-Wesley, 1983), p. 78. Reprinted by permission.

hedged portfolios. Determining the exact return distribution derived from various combinations of options, option prices, and portfolios of underlying securities is a mathematically complex task that we will not pursue in our discussion.

Let us summarize the three reasons why options are used for altering common stock return distributions. The first is the leverage potential inherent in option contracts. The second is the possibility of purchasing insurance for established portfolio positions. Options are important instruments used in transferring risk from one investor to another. The third is the creation of portfolios with return patterns that serve the investment needs of a segment of investors who are not satisfied by existing instruments.

In designing option strategies, the following five factors should be considered by portfolio managers and investors:

1. *General price direction expected for the stock market and individual stocks.* Certain strategies, such as buying calls, tend to be appropriate if a rising market is anticipated. Other strategies, such as buying puts, tend to be appropriate if a falling market is anticipated. Option trading strategies can also be designed for a neutral market in which neither a price rise nor fall is anticipated to any significant degree.
2. *Degree of risk undertaken by investors.* Trading strategies can be designed that range from relatively conservative to very speculative. Investors need to make risk assessments in order to select appropriate strategies.
3. *Capital and time devoted to option trading.* The degree of risk desired will determine, to a considerable extent, the amount of capital to be devoted to option trading. Because options are leverage-inherent securities, their prices can be very volatile relative to the price movements of the underlying securities. If investors decide to pursue aggressive option trading strategies, considerable time will need to be devoted to following the trading positions taken.
4. *Degree of complexity desired in trading.* Just as the degree of risk can vary greatly for different option trading strategies, so can the degree of complexity required in the initial analysis. Relatively simple strategies involve just the purchase or sale of a put or a call option. Combining a purchase or sale of an option with a holding of the underlying security introduces more complexity. Strategies involving the purchase or sale of two or more different options on the same underlying security are the most complex. Investors need to analyze strategies carefully in order to understand the profit and loss impact of a given change in the price of the underlying security.
5. *Commission costs incurred by investors.* As a percentage of the value of the trade, option commissions are much higher than commissions for buying common stock. An active options trading program can mean the trader will pay substantial commissions over time. However, a leveraged position may be worth the commissions paid in a stock that moves substantially in price.

Option trading activities can be classified by three main investment objectives: (1) to earn more current income via covered call writing; (2) to

Figure 14–3
Profit and Loss Position of Call Option Writer (Excluding Commissions)

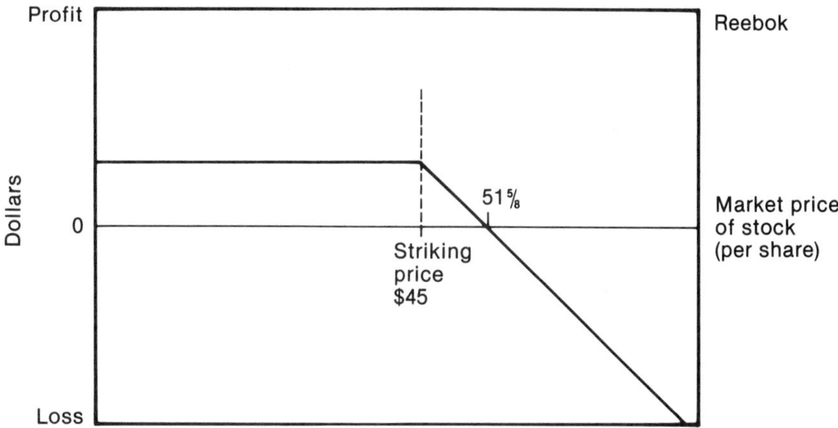

lever returns by buying or selling put or call options or combinations of options; and (3) to hedge or insure a portfolio position by purchasing puts. Let us now look at these various trading objectives and strategies in greater detail.

Option Writing

The objective of option writers is to increase the return on their portfolios by capturing option premiums. Investors will write call options to realize a return if the stock declines or remains unchanged in price. For a single option transaction, the option buyer and option writer will agree, through their respective brokers, to a price for the option. Let us assume that an investor writes an option for Reebok common stock with a striking price of 45 and a July expiration date. The premium agreed to is 6⅝—the closing price shown in Table 14–1. When the transaction is completed, the writer gets the premium less transaction costs.[3] If Reebok's stock price does not end above 45 on the third Friday of July, the writer will not have to fulfill the option agreement. The writer has earned $662.50 in the form of the premium paid for writing the option, less a commission.

The main risk assumed by the writer of the call option is an increase in the price of the common stock on which the option is written. In Figure 14–3 the profit and loss position of the option writer for Reebok is displayed on the expiration date. With a market price on the stock above 45, the writer loses a portion of the premium. As the market price of the stock passes the sum of the striking price and the premium (45 + 6⅝ = 51⅝), absolute losses are incurred.

---

3. Option transactions normally take place in a margin account.

A typical call writing situation occurs when the writer is "covered." In this case, the writer owns the stock required to satisfy the call option agreement. *Covered option writing* reduces the investor's risk because losses on the option will be offset by gains on the stock. Investors can also write "naked" call options, in which case the writer does not own the stock and must purchase it in the stock market if delivery is required. *Naked option writing* is riskier than covered option writing because investors are exposed to the losses depicted in Figure 14–3.

Naked option writing can be very harmful to an investor's financial health in situations where the common stock takes a large, unexpected price move. The announcement of a merger will often cause such unexpected price movements. When Cities Service was being sought via a tender offer by Mesa Petroleum on June 16, 1982, the stock rose from 37¾ to 53⅛ in two days with no trading taking place on the first day. The Cities Service June 40 call option was selling for 7/16 prior to the announcement. If an investor had written twenty-five naked options before the announcement, expecting the option to expire shortly as worthless and to net the writer a "quick $1,000" before commission, the net loss would have been $1,269 per option, for a total of $31,725. This loss would have happened because the option went immediately to its theoretical value of 13⅛, reflecting the new market price. The investor would have to buy at 13⅛ what was sold at 7/16.

Investors may also write put options. Table 14–1 shows put options traded on Reebok. The July Reebok 45 put allows the holder to sell 100 shares of stock at 45 a share through the Saturday after the third Friday of July 1987. A put option writer would agree to buy at 45 and receive the premium (less commissions) of 4 per put option. Looked at from the opposite side of the transaction, the holder of the put option contract sells the stock or "puts it to" the writer at the exercise price of the put option contract. In this case, the writer of the put wants the market price of the common stock to stay above 45.

Figure 14–4 shows the profit and loss position of the writer of the put option at 4. At a market price of 45 or higher for the Reebok stock, the

Figure 14–4
Profit and Loss Position of Put Option Writer (Excluding Commissions)

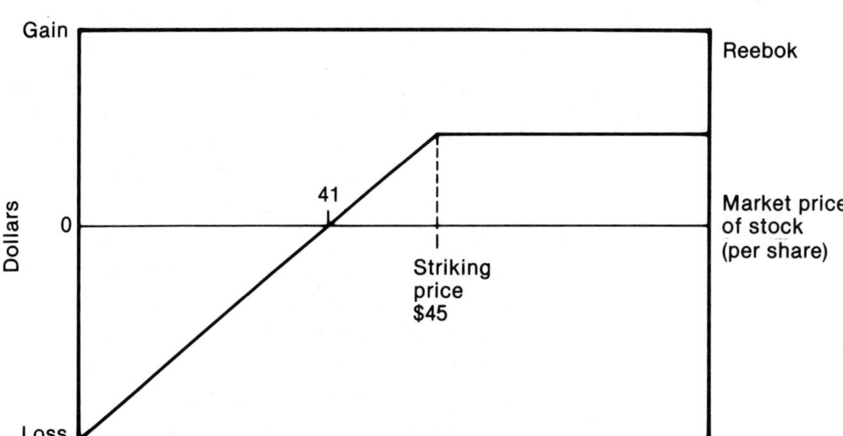

put expires with the writer keeping the entire premium of 4. At a price of 41 (45 − 4), the writer breaks even. The writer buys stock worth 41 a share in the market for a put price of 45 but also keeps the 4 premium for a total value of 45. Below a market price of 41 for the common stock, the put option writer loses money on the transaction.

The actual rate of return realized on any option-writing venture depends on the amount of premium received and the common stock's price movement before the option expires. During a bear market, call option writing is generally a profitable activity because the option writer is seldom called upon to make delivery of the stock. Likewise, writing put options during a bull market tends to be a desirable activity.

Option Buying

Purchasing options presents investors with an investment position opposite to that of writing options. As discussed earlier, the price (premium) of an option is composed of two elements—a theoretical value and a speculative premium. Consider the following two options:

Quotes for March 31, 1987
IBM July 150 call selling for 9⅜
IBM July 155 put selling for 9

With IBM common stock selling for 150½, the theoretical value of each of these two options can be calculated as follows:

Call option = Stock price less exercise price
= 150½ − 150 = ½

Put option = Exercise price less stock price
= 155 − 150½ = 4½

The theoretical value cannot be less than zero. Both the call and put options just examined are in-the-money options. The speculative premium for the IBM call is 9⅜ − ½ = 8⅞; the IBM put is 9 − 4½ = 4½. The potential buyer of an option should compare the speculative premium to the attractiveness of the option as a leveraged investment.

The principal attraction of purchasing options is the leverage potential from their fixed striking prices. An example of the leverage potential is given by the IBM July 150 call option shown in Figure 14–5. The price information was taken from the closing prices of the stock and the option on March 31, 1987. If the price of the common stock increased 25 percent by July 1987 from 150½ to 188⅛, the option would sell for at least its theoretical value of 38⅛. This minimum option price would mean an increase of 307 percent over the March 31, 1987, option price of 9⅜. Actually, the call option could sell for somewhat more than its theoretical value if time remained before the option's expiration date. Of course, if the common stock does not sell for at least 150 by the expiration of the option, the investor will suffer a total loss. The speculator might reduce the loss somewhat by selling the call before its expiration date.

Figure 14–5 also shows the profit and loss line for an investor pur-

Figure 14–5
Profit and Loss Position of Call Option Buyer versus Stock Buyer

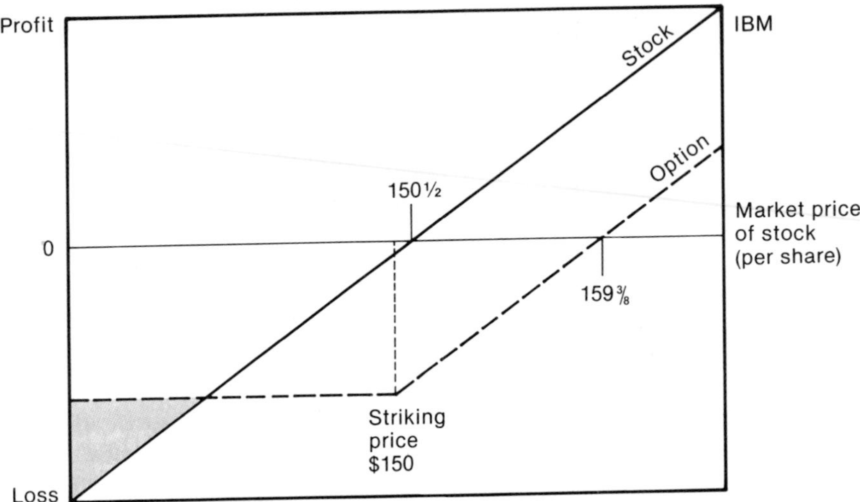

chasing the IBM common stock at 150½ versus buying the option. The shaded portion of the graph indicates the area in which the investor would lose more dollars with the stock than with the option. The common stock must advance to 159⅜ for the call option buyer to make money, but the percentage gains on the relatively low cost of the option then start becoming important. We previously noted that a 25 percent increase in the price of the common stock would mean a minimum increase of 307 percent in the price of the option because of the leverage inherent in the option.

Figure 14–6 shows the profit and loss position of the put option buyer. The buyer of a put option hopes that the price will decline for the common stock on which the option is written. For example, buying the IBM July 155 put option for 9 and then having the common stock decline to 150 implies the put option would sell for at least its theoretical value of 5, for a loss of only 4 per share. Hence, the lower the price of IBM common stock, the more money the put option buyer makes. Notice that as the stock price decreases to 146, the investor breaks even because the gain on the put position, 155 − 146, exactly offsets the price paid for the option of 9.

Often, investors want to protect an established gain in a portfolio or to insure against large losses but also want to participate in any future increases in portfolio value. Buying a put option can be used as a form of insurance, or hedge, against the decline in value of an asset or portfolio. If a stock price declines, a put will increase in value and serve as an offset to the decline in the stock's value. If a stock price rises, the put can be ignored as the hedger's maximum loss is the put option (insurance) premium. For example, if an investor held 100 shares of IBM at 150½, the October IBM 150 put could be purchased for 7½, which would guarantee the investor that the minimum value received on the investment would be 142½, the price at which the stock could be sold minus the put premium. The insurance protection provided by purchasing a put for the

Figure 14–6
Profit and Loss Position of Put Option Buyer

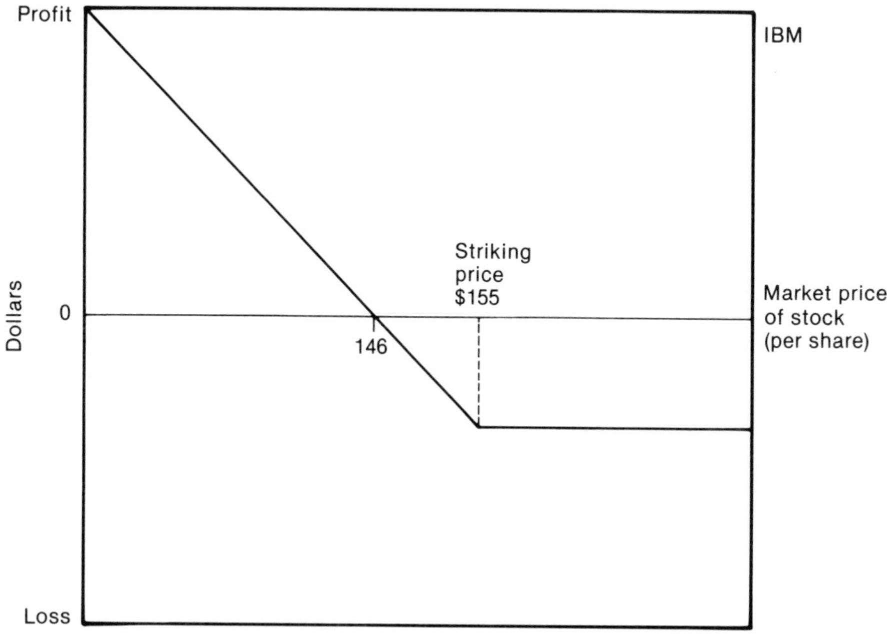

Figure 14–7
Hedging an IBM Stock Position with a Put Option

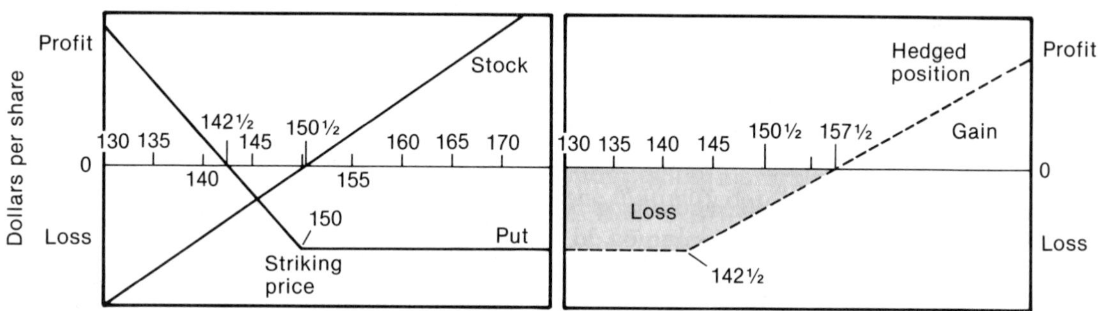

IBM stock is shown in Figure 14–7. As the stock price increases above 150, the profits on the stock position are diminished by the 7½ option premium. At 157½, the investor breaks even as the stock position profit exactly offsets the option premium. Above 157½, the investor makes a positive return on the hedged position.

Option Spreading

An *option spread* is created when an investor engages in two or more option transactions at the same time. The types of option spreads differ according to their degree of complexity. Although we are unable in this

Figure 14–8
Option Spread Profit and Loss Position

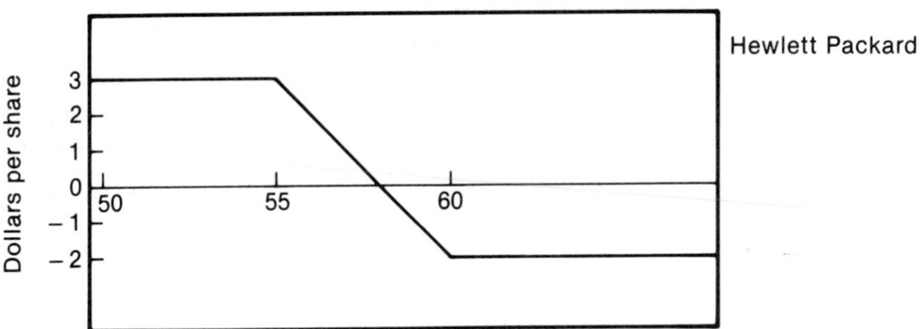

survey to examine all spreads in detail, one common type is of particular interest.

A spread often used by investors involves writing (selling) the in-the-money option and buying the out-of-the-money (having no theoretical value) option. The out-of-the-money option is bought as a hedge against an incorrect option-writing decision. For example, an investor could establish the following spread, based on price quotes for March 31, 1987:

Write (sell) Hewlett Packard November 55 call at 9¼
Buy Hewlett Packard November 60 call at 6¼

Figure 14–8 shows the potential profit and loss function for the option spread. If Hewlett Packard's common stock is at 55 or less, the writer of the November 55 call option keeps the premium of 9¼ and forfeits the premium of 6¼ associated with buying the November 60 call. The net result is a gain of 3 per share on the spread before commissions. If the Hewlett Packard common stock is at 60 or more, the maximum loss of 2 per share is incurred on the spread position. For example, consider the situation that occurs if Hewlett Packard common stock sells for 65 per share. The Hewlett Packard 55 call that sold for 9¼ will now sell for at least its theoretical value of 10, resulting in a loss of ¾ on writing that option. However, the Hewlett Packard November 60 call will sell for at least its theoretical value of 5 per share for a loss of 1¼ on the option purchase. The net result is the loss of 2 per share (losses of ¾ and 1¼).

Warrants

Warrants are long-term options to buy shares of a company's stock at a given price within a specific period of time. In recent years, these options have been used primarily by corporations as "sweeteners" to aid in the issuance of long-term debt or preferred stock issues, or they have been issued as part of the financial reorganization plan for distressed or bankrupt corporations. For example, Eli Lilly had an outstanding warrant that allowed the holder to purchase one share of common stock for 75.98 per share until March 31, 1991. As of March 31, 1987, the warrant sold for 37⅞ and the common stock sold for 91½.

Warrants are leverage-inherent securities in that stock can be purchased at a fixed exercise price. The major advantage of using warrants is that they provide the investor with the ability to engage easily in long-term leverage and hedging activities. The percentage increase or decrease in the market price of the warrant will tend to be greater than the percentage increase or decrease in the market price of the common stock. Figure 14–9 shows the price movements of both the Eli Lilly common stock and warrant from March 1986 through March 1987. A ratio scale is used for Figure 14–9 so that the percentage price changes may be read directly from the graph. Note the wider price movements for the warrant.

In most cases, the value of a "pure" warrant is approximated by the same techniques used to value options, for example, the Black-Scholes option pricing model. The major difference between warrants and call options is that warrants can extend for many years and the maximum maturity for most options is nine months. Because of the longer term to maturity for warrants, the speculative premiums (which increase with time to expiration) tend to be larger for at-the-money warrants. As with options, deep-in- and deep-out-of-the-money warrant prices approximate their theoretical values.

In valuing warrants, investors must be aware of some nonstandard

Figure 14–9
Prices of Eli Lilly Common Stock and Warrant, March 1986–March 1987

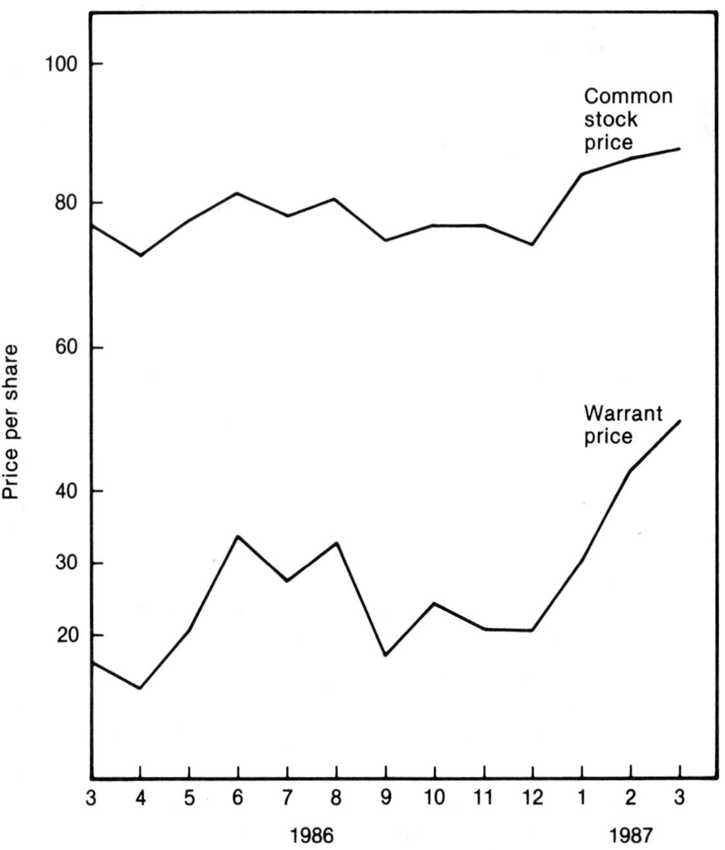

features that may be associated with individual warrants. Warrants are sometimes exercisable into more or less than one share per warrant. For example, Pier 1 Imports had a warrant allowing its holder to obtain 2.595 shares of Pier 1 Import stock for a total cost of 22. The effective exercise price per share was 8.4778 for this warrant.

Another form of warrant exercise provision effectively alters the warrant exercise price over time. This is the so-called *CD warrant,* for which the warrant holder can use either cash (the *C*) or the par value of specified debt (the *D*) in exercising the warrant. CD warrants are often referred to as senior security warrants because a senior security, a bond issue, can be used in the exercise of the warrant.

In some recent instances, corporations have extended the expiration dates of their warrants. This may be detrimental to an investor if the warrant is originally sold short in a reverse warrant hedge—the object of which is to profit from a decline in the premium on the warrant as expiration approaches. If the expiration date is extended, which happened with the warrants of Continental Telephone on March 4, 1974, the warrant price could increase because of the extended life. In fact, the price of the Continental Telephone warrants went from ⅞ to 1¾ from March 4 to March 5—much to the anguish of the short-seller.

Another problem is the treatment of the warrantholder in the event that two firms merge. In July 1974, Indian Head's warrants were selling for approximately 5, even though they had no theoretical value. The exercise price was 25, and the common was at 22. Another firm made a tender offer for Indian Head's common stock at 27 per share and also offered to purchase the warrants at their theoretical value of 2. The warrantholder suffered a severe loss as a result of this tender offer.

Summary

Leverage-inherent securities provide an interesting alternative for investors. Instead of purchasing securities on margin, investors can alter the risk of a portfolio by engaging in transactions involving options and warrants. Prices of options and warrants tend to be more volatile than those of the average security because they have a fixed exercise price or a fixed redemption price as part of their terms.

Options and warrants are similar in nature. They both give holders the privilege of obtaining shares of another security at a fixed or determinable price per share. The main differences between options and warrants are the party from whom the shares are obtained and the length of time during which the shares may be obtained. Options allow holders to obtain shares from other investors, and warrantholders obtain shares directly from the company. Options typically allow holders to exercise the option for a period of up to nine months, and warrants are initially written with much longer exercise provisions.

The option market has undergone a dramatic change as a result of the establishment of the Chicago Board Options Exchange in April 1973. In addition to providing a good secondary market for options, the CBOE standardized option terms. The expiration date is standardized along with the number of shares per option and the striking price of the option.

Options and warrants pose an interesting valuation problem for investors. What is the privilege of purchasing a security at some future time at a fixed price worth at the present time? The speculative premium is the value the market places on this privilege. This value combined with the theoretical value equals the security's market price. The theoretical value for a call is obtained by subtracting the exercise price from the price of the underlying stock, but is never less than zero.

A common use of options and warrants is to speculate on the price movements of the underlying stock to take advantage of the leverage inherent in these securities. Options and warrants can also be used to hedge other positions in the market. Hedging transactions are valuable because they tend to reduce the risk of the initial position taken in the market. Spread transactions are also possible with options.

Although not for all investors, leverage-inherent securities provide those investors willing to take above-average risks with a means of participating in a strong bull or bear market. A leverage-inherent security, if properly analyzed, will tend to change in price by a greater percentage than the underlying stock or market in general, producing possible good rates of return relative to the market. Of course, if investors are incorrect in making an investment judgment, the inherent leverage works to produce poor relative rates of return.

Suggested Readings

BLACK, FISCHER, and MYRON SCHOLES. "The Pricing of Options and Corporate Liabilities." *Journal of Political Economy* (May–June 1973): 637–54.

DAWSON, FREDERIC S. "Risk and Return in Continuous Option Writing." *Journal of Portfolio Management* (Winter 1979): 58–63.

EVNINE, JEREMY, and ANDREW RUDD. "Index Options: The Early Evidence." *Journal of Finance* (July 1985): 743–56.

FINNERTY, JOSEPH E. "The Chicago Board Options Exchange and Market Efficiency." *Journal of Financial and Quantitative Analysis* (March 1978): 29–38.

GASTINEAU, GARY L. *The Stock Options Manual,* 2d ed. New York: McGraw-Hill, 1979.

GOMBOLA, MICHAEL J., RODNEY L. ROENFELDT, and PHILIP L. COOLEY. "Spreading Strategies in CBOE Options: Evidence on Market Performance." *Journal of Financial Research* (Winter 1978): 35–44.

JARROW, ROBERT A., and ANDREW T. RUDD. *Option Pricing.* Homewood, IL: Richard D. Irwin, 1983.

JOHNSON, R. STAFFORD, RICHARD A. ZUBER, and DAVID LOY. "An Investigation into Currency Options and Market Efficiency." *International Review of Economics and Business* (October–November 1986): 1077–93.

Malkiel, Burton G., and Richard E. Quandt. *Strategies and Rational Decisions in the Securities Option Market.* Cambridge, MA: MIT Press, 1969.

Merton, Robert C., Myron S. Scholes, and Mathew L. Gladstein. "The Returns and Risk of Alternative Call Option Investment Strategies." *Journal of Business* (April 1978): 183–242.

Modest, David M. "On the Pricing of Stock Index Futures." *Journal of Portfolio Management* (Summer 1984): 51–57.

"Options—A Pension Management Tool for Controlling Risk and Return." *Financial Executive,* March 1979, 37–43.

Pounds, Henry M. "Covered Call Option Writing Strategies and Results." *Journal of Portfolio Management* (Winter 1978): 31–42.

Smith, Clifford W., Jr. "Option Pricing: A Review." *Journal of Financial Economics* (January–March 1976): 3–51.

Stoll, Hans R., and Robert E. Whaley. "Program Trading and Expiration-Day Effects." *Financial Analysts Journal* (March–April 1987): 16–28.

Yates, James W., Jr., and Robert W. Kopprasch, Jr. "Writing Call Options: Profits and Risks." *Journal of Portfolio Management* (Fall 1980): 74–79.

Yeasting, Kenneth L. "CD Warrants." *Financial Analysts Journal* (March–April 1970): 44–47.

Questions

1. Distinguish between financial and operating leverage.
2. An investor can add leverage to a portfolio by buying securities on margin. Why might the investor choose to purchase leverage-inherent securities instead?
3. Compare the put and call market as it existed prior to the establishment of the Chicago Board Options Exchange with the trading that occurs on the CBOE.
4. Distinguish between
   (a) calls and puts
   (b) option sellers and option buyers
   (c) an option's theoretical value and its speculative premium
5. What is the relationship between arbitrage theory and option pricing?
6. What would be the main objectives of an investor in trading options?
7. Why might an investor want to purchase a portfolio with a skewed distribution of returns rather than a portfolio having a normal return distribution?
8. Television advertisements shown during financial news programs

often stress the "limited and predetermined risk" investors have when they purchase options. What does this mean for the investor?

9. In options trading, what is the relationship among the risk desired by the investor, the capital that the investor has available for trading, and the degree of complexity that can be handled by the investor?

10. Option writing has often been considered a risky strategy. Distinguish the nature of the risk an investor would face in writing covered options, where the stock is owned, versus writing naked options, where the option writer does not own the underlying stock.

11. What does the investor hope to achieve in a strategy of option spreading?

12. What are the differences between purchasing call options and warrants?

13. In estimating the value of a call option, an investor should look at five underlying factors affecting the option's value. List and briefly discuss each of these factors, showing how each influences the price.

14. Define the following terms:
    (a) premium
    (b) exercise price
    (c) expiration date
    (d) at-the-money option
    (e) in-the-money option
    (f) out-of-the-money option

15. What is an index option? Why might an investor elect to use an index option rather than an option on an individual stock?

Problems

1. Given the following option prices as of mid-July 1987;
    (a) Determine the speculative premium and the theoretical value of each option.
    (b) Assuming you are going to write (sell) each of these options, what is the break-even point for each option? What percentage change does this represent for the price of the common stock? For the price of the option?
    (c) Assume that you are planning to purchase one of these call options. If you expect a 10 percent increase in the price of each of the common stocks by mid-October 1987, which is the best option to buy?

Company	Common Stock	Call Option Series and Price
Eastman Kodak	87¾	Oct. 90 at 3½
IBM	161	Oct. 160 at 7¼
Xerox	74⅛	Oct. 70 at 6

2. Cray Computer's common stock sells for 99⅝ on July 24. A speculator decides to buy the December 100 call option at a price of 9½. Compare at the expiration of the option the profit and loss function for both the option and the common stock, given common stock prices of 95, 100, 105, and 110. Assume the purchase of either 100 shares of the common stock or one call option. Assuming you pay cash for both purchases, calculate the profit and loss function both in dollars and in percentages of the initial investment.

3. Assume that in July 1987, you own 1,000 shares of Dayton Hudson stock and decide to write ten October 50 call options. When you write the options, the stock price is 48⅞ and the option price is 2⅝. In late July, Dayton Hudson is mentioned as a merger candidate, and shareholders receive a merger offer that immediately increases the price of the common stock to 52. Calculate the following:
   - **(a)** Your profit if you own only the common stock.
   - **(b)** Your profit if you own the covered option position.

4. Texas Instruments's common stock sold for 60¼ on July 24, 1987. A speculator decides to spread the Texas Instruments's October 58⅜ and 63⅝ call options. The "in the money" October 58⅜ option is sold at 5, and the "out of the money" October 63⅝ is bought for 3⅛. Calculate and draw the profit and loss function for this option spread for prices between 50 and 70.

5. In August, W. R. Wright is willing to bet that Syntex Corporation's stock price will not fall below the 45 level. The stock has been selling around 46¼, which is an all-time high. In fact, he is so sure of his bet that he will write a put option guaranteeing to purchase 100 shares of Syntex anytime during the next six months for 45 per share. Assume that cash is paid for all purchases. Syntex is not expected to pay a dividend in the near future.
   - **(a)** If W. R. receives $250 (2½ per share) for the option, calculate the speculative premium and theoretical value for the option.
   - **(b)** What is the break-even point for this put option?
   - **(c)** In five months, if the stock price is at 43, what is the return on W. R.'s position? What is his return if the stock is at 50?
   - **(d)** What would happen if instead of writing a put option, W. R. purchases a 45 call option for 4¼? Compare the differences in returns for the two positions if the stock price increases to 50 or falls to 40.

6. Bally Manufacturing's warrants went from 1⅝ on July 13, 1987, to 2⅞ on July 14, 1987. During the same day, the common stock went from 24½ to 25¾.
   - **(a)** Calculate the respective percentage changes in these prices and the *ex post* leverage factor (percentage change in warrants divided by the percentage change in the common).
   - **(b)** Why did the warrants go up so fast relative to the common?

7. A warrant hedge was established in Greyhound in early 1979 when the common was at 11⅛ and the warrant was at ⅜. By the end of

June, the warrant had risen to 1½ and the common was at 15¼. These warrants allowed the holder to buy 1 share at $23.50 until May 14, 1980.

(a) Calculate the profitability of this warrant hedge where the common is sold short and the warrant purchased (ignoring commissions and dividends) if equal dollar amounts had been executed on each side of the hedge.

(b) Calculate the profitability of this hedge (ignoring commissions and dividends) if a 100-share transaction had been executed in each security.

(c) Which hedging strategy would you favor? Would your answer change under different market circumstances?

8. Assume that you write a call option expiring in one year that requires you to sell a share of stock in the Cheek Company for 50. You know that at the end of the one year, the stock will sell for either 30 or 70. Currently, you are earning 6 percent on your risk-free investments.

(a) What are the possible values for the stock at the end of the year? For the option?

(b) What is the hedge ratio for a riskless stock-option position?

(c) If you take a riskless position by purchasing Cheek stock and writing a call option, what is the value of your position at the end of the year?

(d) What price should you receive for the option at the beginning of the year?

(e) If the option is currently selling at 14, what should you do?

(f) What would happen to the price of the option if the risk-free rate increases to 16 percent?

Appendix

Option Pricing

In this appendix, we will set forth an option valuation formula and discuss the application via an example.* As discussed in the chapter, option contracts are agreements that give the purchaser of the option the right (but not the obligation) to exercise the contract. Whether an option will be exercised depends on the price of the underlying security at expiration. (Hence, options are usually referred to as contingent claims.) An option is also viewed as a derivative security because it derives value from the underlying common stock. The basic option valuation formula that has resulted from the work of Black-Scholes states such a relationship.

The Black-Scholes Model

The formula for the valuation of a European call option (an option that can be exercised only at maturity) in the Black-Scholes model is as follows:

$$C = S[N(d_1)] - Ee^{-rt}[N(d_2)]$$

where $$d_1 = \frac{\ln\left(\frac{S}{E}\right) + (r = \frac{1}{2}\sigma^2)T}{\sigma\sqrt{T}}$$

$d_2 = d_1 - \sigma\sqrt{T}$
C = the current value of the call option
S = the current market price of the underlying common stock
E = the exercise price of the call option
T = the time remaining before expiration (in years)

*This material was written by Eric Chang and Richard A. Stevenson.

r = the current continuously compounded riskless rate of interest

σ = the standard deviation of the continuously compounded annual rate of return on the underlying stock

e = the exponential (i.e., e = 2.71828)

$\ln\left(\frac{S}{E}\right)$ = the natural logarithm of (S/E)

$N(d)$ = the probability that a derivation less than d will occur in a normal distribution with a mean of zero and a standard deviation of one

The use of the formula requires the input of the following five variables:

1. The stock price.
2. The exercise price.

   The first two variables are easily observable from the option contract and the *Wall Street Journal*

3. The time to maturity.

   The expiration date for an option is the Saturday after the third Friday of the expiration month. The time to maturity is obtained by counting the number of calendar days until that day and then dividing it by 365 to get the time to maturity in annual terms.

4. The market risk-free rate.

   The typical proxy for the riskless rate of interest is the annualized U.S. treasury bill rate that corresponds to the term of the option. However, some investors argue that the rate only reflects the risk-free lending rate and underestimates the applicable rate. Alternatives may be the certificate of deposit rate or the rate for top-quality commercial paper. These rates are quoted daily in the *Wall Street Journal.* Empirical studies have shown that option prices are not sensitive to small changes in interest rates.

5. The standard deviation of the annual stock returns.

   The volatility of the stock price is by far the most difficult variable to estimate. An easy approximation of the volatility of the stock can be obtained by using past data. However, care must be taken in doing so because empirical evidence shows that the volatility of individual stocks changes over time. Therefore, subjective adjustment in the estimates is not uncommon. Special attention needs to be given to changes in uncertainty concerning the market, specific industries, and stocks.

To calculate the standard deviation from historical stock price data, we first must obtain the past price quotes. The quotes should be evenly spaced. The interval used can be daily, weekly, biweekly, or monthly. We then convert prices into rates of return. The next step is to take the natural log of 1 plus the return in order to approximate the continuously compounded return. In Chapter 4, we discussed the calculation of the variance for a series of returns. The final step is to annualize the variance by multiplying the estimate by the number of intervals in a year.

An Application of the Black-Scholes Model

To demonstrate the formula, consider the AT&T October 65 call option selling for 2¼. The required data are taken from market quotes of June 29, 1983. The historical standard deviation of stock returns is estimated and used in the formula.

The basic variables are:

$S = \$63.125$
$E = \$65$
$r = .09$
$\sigma = .25$ (estimated)
$T = .315$ (i.e., 115 days to maturity)
$rt = (.09 \times .315)$, or $.02835$

Using the formula:

$$d_1 = \left[\frac{\ln(63.125/65) + (.09 + .5(.25)^2).315}{.25 \quad \sqrt{.315}}\right]$$

$$= \left[\frac{-.0293 + .0382}{.1403}\right]$$

$$= .0634$$

$$d_2 = .0634 - (.25)(\sqrt{.315})$$
$$= .0634 - (.25)(.5612)$$
$$= -.0766$$
$$N(d_1) = .5252$$
$$N(d_2) = .4695$$
$$C = S[N(d_1)] - Ee^{-rt}[N(d_2)]$$
$$= 63.125[.5252] - 65e^{-.02835}[.4695]$$
$$= 33.1533 - 29.644$$
$$= 3.489 \text{ (the Black-Scholes value of the option)}$$

With a cumulative normal distribution table, such as the one shown below, only a hand calculator is needed to estimate the value of an option using the Black-Scholes formula.

The Black-Scholes model was originally developed to value a call option of a nondividend-paying stock. If the AT&T stock is expected to go ex-dividend prior to the option exercise date, C should be adjusted downward. The call option's theoretical value will decline on the ex-dividend date. This is one of the reasons the unadjusted Black-Scholes model gives a value of $3.489 while the option is selling for $2.25.

AT&T's quarterly dividend is $1.35 per share, and one ex-dividend will occur in the 115-day option period. One way to take into account the dividend effect is to subtract the present value of the dividends likely to be paid before the option's expiration from the current stock price in the Black-Scholes formula. This may roughly reduce the call value by the anticipated quarterly dividend. Given the AT&T regular dividend of $1.35, the adjusted option price is about $2.14.

Table 14–A1
Cumulative Normal Distribution Table

d	*N(d)*	*d*	*N(d)*	*d*	*N(d)*
		−1.00	.1587	1.00	.8413
−2.90	.0019	−.90	.1841	1.10	.8643
−2.80	.0026	.80	.2119	1.20	.8849
−2.70	.0035	−.70	.2420	1.30	.9032
−2.60	.0047	−.60	.2743	1.40	.9192
−2.50	.0062	−.50	.3085	1.50	.9332
−2.40	.0082	−.40	.3446	1.60	.9452
−2.30	.0107	−.30	.3821	1.70	.9554
−2.20	.0139	−.20	.4207	1.80	.9641
−2.10	.0179	−.10	.4602	1.90	.9713
−2.00	.0228	.00	.5000	2.00	.9773
−1.90	.0287	.10	.5398	2.10	.9821
−1.80	.0359	.20	.5793	2.20	.9861
−1.70	.0446	.30	.6179	2.30	.9893
−1.60	.0548	.40	.6554	2.40	.9918
−1.50	.0668	.50	.6915	2.50	.9938
−1.40	.0808	.60	.7257	2.60	.9953
−1.30	.0968	.70	.7580	2.70	.9965
−1.20	.1151	.80	.7881	2.80	.9974
−1.10	.1357	.90	.8159	2.90	.9981

Problems

1. According to the Black-Scholes option pricing model, what should be the price of a Federal Express Corporation 65 stock option based on the following data for early August 1987?
   (a) The common stock price is 64¾.
   (b) The 90-day treasury bill rate is 6.31.
   (c) The estimated variance for the Federal Express stock price is .36.
   (d) The company is not expected to pay a dividend this year.
   (e) The option expires in 90 days.

2. How would each of these individual changes affect the option price for Federal Express as calculated in Problem 1?
   (a) The treasury bill rate decreases to 4 percent.
   (b) The estimated variance for Federal Express stock price increases to .64.
   (c) The option expires in 180 days.

Chapter 15

Futures Trading

Key Concepts

- basis
- capital management
- cash market
- commodity margins
- daily price limit
- forward contracting
- future
- futures option
- hedger
- intercommodity spread
- intracommodity spread
- long
- nonsystematic risk
- open interest
- profit and loss function
- short
- speculator
- spot market
- spread transaction
- systematic risk
- tick
- to-arrive contract
- zero-sum game

Chapter Outline

On September 11, 1986, the Standard & Poor's 500 Stock Index dropped almost 12 points, from 247.06 to 235.18. The same day, the Dow Jones Industrial Average fell over 86 points. Trading of futures could have been very useful and profitable on September 11. A speculator short the S&P 500 index futures contract that day would have made approximately $6,000, or an amount equal to the initial margin requirement at that time. Hedgers who were also short the index future could have helped to preserve the value of a diversified portfolio. The ability to make money by speculating or to preserve value by hedging is obviously important, as evidenced by the trading volume for the S&P 500 index future on September 11. Approximately 151,300 contracts changed hands, and this index future was created only four years earlier.

Futures trading involves forward contracting in an underlying asset. By forward contracting, we mean setting a price today for the delivery of an asset, real or financial, at a specified date in the future. Forward contracting exists in many forms, the most established being futures contracts. Gold, sugar, copper, and treasury bonds are just a few of the many commodities traded in the futures market. Commodity trading has grown rapidly in recent years, both in terms of the number of contracts traded in previously existing commodities and in the creation of new trading vehicles in areas such as interest rates and gold.

We first consider the nature of a future and the rationale for the existence of futures markets. Futures trading is then compared with stock investing. A detailed examination of speculative and hedging transactions is also presented. Finally, we discuss options on futures.

Nature of a Futures Market

An individual or the representative of an institution who desires to trade in a given commodity buys or sells a future. A *future* is a bona fide contract providing for future delivery of the actual commodity. Market participants include both speculators and hedgers. *Speculators* attempt to profit from price movements in the futures contract. Hedgers already hold a position, either long or short, in the underlying asset. *Hedgers* use futures contracts to establish a position opposite to that already attained in the asset. The holding of the asset is referred to as the *cash market* or *spot market* position. Although the futures contract calls for delivery at some time in the future, a trader can avoid accepting or making physical delivery by closing out the position prior to the time of delivery.

For many assets, markets exist simultaneously for the underlying asset and its futures contract or contracts. The difference between the price of a futures contract and the underlying asset is called the *basis*. If the basis is positive, investors generally expect the price on the spot market to rise over the life of the futures contract. If negative, they expect spot prices to fall.

A futures contract is standardized in many important ways. For example, the size of the contract is standardized. Treasury bill futures trade in $1 million denominations, while treasury bond futures have a par value of $100,000. Other standard features relate to the specification of the commodity deliverable to satisfy the contract, the delivery period, and approved delivery points. Some of the financial futures contracts allow for cash settlement in lieu of physical delivery. These standardized features make futures trading viable. Table 15–1 shows some of the contract specifications for selected futures contracts.

The major U.S. commodity exchanges are the Chicago Board of Trade

Table 15–1
Commodity Futures, Selected Statistics

Commodity	Major Exchange	Contract Size	Nearby Contract 3/31/87 Dollar Value
Grains			
Corn	CBOT	5,000 bushels	7,750
Soybeans	CBOT	5,000 bushels	24,400
Wheat	CBOT	5,000 bushels	14,875
Livestock			
Cattle—live	CME	40,000 pounds	25,448
Hogs	CME	30,000 pounds	13,380
Pork bellies	CME	40,000 pounds	26,020
Food			
Coffee	CSCE	37,500 pounds	39,938
Orange juice	CTN	15,000 pounds	19,575
Sugar—world	CSCE	112,000 pounds	9,038
Metals and petroleum			
Gold	CMX	100 Troy ounces	40,690
Platinum	NYM	50 Troy ounces	26,525
Silver	CMX	5,000 Troy ounces	27,735
Crude oil	NYM	42,000 gallons	18,350
Currencies			
British pound	IMM	25,000 pounds	39,675
Canadian dollar	IMM	100,000 dollars	75,610
Japanese yen	IMM	12.5 million yen	81,388
Swiss franc	IMM	125,000 francs	79,938
West German mark	IMM	125,000 marks	67,100
Equity and fixed income			
S&P 500	CME	500 times index	144,975
Value Line	KC	500 times index	132,900
Major market	CBT	250 times index	111,050
Treasury bills, 90-day	IMM	$1 million	985,750
Treasury bonds	CBT	$100,000	101,219

Exchanges: CBOT, Chicago Board of Trade; CME, Chicago Mercantile Exchange; CSCE, Coffee, Sugar & Cocoa Exchange; CTN, New York Cotton Exchange; CMX, Commodity Exchange; NYM, New York Mercantile Exchange; IMM, International Monetary Market at CME; and KC, Kansas City Board of Trade.

(CBOT), the Chicago Mercantile Exchange (CME), the New York Mercantile Exchange, the New York Cotton Exchange, the New York Coffee & Sugar Exchange, and the Commodity Exchange, Inc. Corn, soybeans, oats, other grains, and treasury bonds are the main commodities traded on the CBOT. Grains are also traded on the Midamerica Commodity Exchange, the Kansas City Board of Trade, and the Minneapolis Grain Exchange. The main commodities traded on the CME are live cattle, live hogs, pork bellies, lumber, and the S&P 500 index. Through its subsidiary, the International Monetary Market, futures on treasury bills, foreign currencies, and eurodollars are traded. The other exchanges trade futures in commodities such as platinum, cotton, orange juice, cocoa, sugar, silver, and gold.

Rationale for the Existence of Futures Markets

Only one rationale can explain the existence of any futures market—to shift risk. Hedgers desire to shift the risk of price movements to speculators. Speculators accept this risk shifting in an attempt to make trading profits. Society tolerates this speculative activity as the price it must pay to allow hedgers to shift price risk.

In the past, trading in futures grew to accommodate certain needs or problems that arose as the U.S. economy grew, and many of the needs still exist today. These problems include the need for capital, inventory management problems, pricing decisions, and the ownership risk involved in the movement of goods from the point of production to the point of consumption. As the nineteenth century U.S. economy grew, marketing areas ceased to be local and became regional or national. *To-arrive contracts* developed as a means of adjusting to the growth of these marketing areas. Grain might be sold now with arrival in Chicago to occur at a later date, perhaps in two or three weeks. The to-arrive contract had a number of defects, including unreliable delivery, nonstandardized quality, and the lack of a good secondary market for the contract. As a result of the experience with to-arrive contracts, the Chicago Board of Trade established in October 1865 general rules to govern trading in specified commodities. This date is considered the start of modern futures trading in the United States.

Some major requirements exist for a futures market to develop in any given commodity. The commodity should be homogeneous and capable of being graded. An uncertain and competitive supply-demand relationship for the commodity, and numerous producers and users of the commodity should be present. If one producer controls too much of the supply of a given commodity, the futures market could be manipulated and speculators would be reluctant to deal in that commodity. Further, the commodity traded is often in a raw or semiprocessed state. Exceptions include currencies, gold bars, sugar, lumber, interest rates, and common stock indexes. Also helpful is the participation of the major merchandising firms associated with the commodity in the futures market or at least the absence of their opposition to its establishment. This is quite an extensive list, but trading has been started in a number of new commodities over the years. For example, futures markets for pork bellies (1961), live cattle (1964), gold (1975), interest rates (1976), and common stock indexes (1982) have developed.

Stocks versus Commodities

A convenient method of discussing commodity trading is to compare it with investing in stocks. One must understand a number of differences before speculating in commodities. These differences involve the manner in which trading occurs, the risks involved, and the sources of information.

Market Participants

Hedgers use the futures market to establish a position opposite to the long or short position already held in the cash (spot) market. For example, a country grain elevator operator may agree in June to purchase, at the time of harvest, 5,000 bushels of corn at $1.80 a bushel from a local farmer. Essentially, the price is determined in June with delivery to take place in November. The elevator operator now has a *long* position in 5,000 bushels of corn. If corn sells for $1.50 a bushel in November, the elevator operator will lose $.30 a bushel because the farmer receives $1.80 a bushel.

To reduce this risk, the elevator operator will hedge by selling short one corn future contract at the time the price of $1.80 is agreed upon. If the price drops to $1.20 at harvest, the elevator operator makes money on the short position in the futures market. This should offset to a large extent the money lost by having to pay the farmer $1.80 a bushel in November. We will see hedging again in our examples dealing with financial futures.

Speculators perform an economic function by accepting the risk the hedgers want to avoid by taking positions in the market. When the country elevator operator wants to sell a corn future, a speculator may be the party purchasing it. The speculator helps to give the market liquidity by accepting the risks of commodity trading.

Margin

A margin transaction in the securities market involves the use of credit. The investor purchases a security by putting up equity and borrowing the rest of the purchase price through the use of a margin account. Margin accounts are regulated by the Federal Reserve Board.

In the futures market, the speculator is not buying or selling the actual commodity, but only agreeing to buy or sell at some future date. Because of this, the nature of margin in the futures market is quite different from that in the securities market. In essence, the *margin in a commodity transaction* is simply a security deposit to provide the brokerage firm with some protection from default on the contract by traders and to absorb trading losses.

Margins are also much lower for commodities than for securities. This makes commodity trading quite speculative because modest sums of money can control large commodity positions. For example, an S&P 500 index futures contract selling for $295 means that one contract at 500 times the value of the index is worth $147,500. The initial margin on this contract will be approximately $10,000. For every dollar put into margin, the speculator controls almost $15 worth of commodity. To find this kind of leverage with direct investment in the stock market would be difficult.

Margins in commodities do somewhat resemble those for securities in that an initial margin and maintenance margin are required. The initial margin requirement is set by the commodity exchange, although brokerage firms may require that their customers put up more margin than the exchange minimum. Margin calls typically come when the equity in the commodity trading account declines to about 75 percent of the initial margin requirement. If the purchase of an S&P 500 index futures contract were the only transaction, a margin call would come if the speculator lost $2,500 on the contract.

Daily Price Limits

The relatively low margins for commodities make commodity trading quite risky. The S&P 500 index futures contract needs to decline only 6.78 percent for the speculator's entire $10,000 margin to be wiped out. The protection of speculators and member firms of the exchange is the main reason why *daily price limits* exist for some commodities. However, if a series of limit moves occurs accompanied by no trading, the speculator could lose the entire margin amount and wind up owing the brokerage firm money before the position could be eliminated. Margin requirements and daily price limits are sometimes changed frequently, so the potential trader should check with the brokerage firm handling the account for more information.

Time Horizon

Even if an investor purchases a security after careful security valuation and attention to portfolio ramifications, an unfavorable market move may result in a loss. However, if the analysis was done properly, the investor should eventually get "bailed out" as the market improves. Such is not the case in the futures market.

Commodity futures have a maximum life of two years or less. If still in existence, the contract must be fulfilled by the end of the month in which it expires (delivery month). The holder knows when the contract expires and therefore should not be put into a position to accept delivery. In general, only the more experienced commodity traders should trade a future during the delivery month.

Zero-Sum Game

The futures market is what is known as a *zero-sum game.* For every long position, a short position exists. Thus, an upward price movement will cause one side of the market (the long position) to gain exactly what the other side (the short position) will lose. A downward market move will produce the opposite result. Taking into account commissions that must be paid, the market is often referred to as a zero-sum game less commissions.

The stock market is not a zero-sum game. A short position does not exist for every long position. Conceivably, virtually every participant in the stock market could make money if the market moves up or could lose money if the market moves down. This difference between stocks and commodities, coupled with the leverage available in commodity trading, means that a commodity trader needs superior skills to make money consistently.

Specialist versus Auction Market

We saw in Chapter 2 that each stock traded on the major exchanges is the responsibility of a specialist. The specialist is responsible for seeing that the trading in the security is conducted in a fair and orderly manner. No specialists operate in the commodities market; trading is conducted only by open outcry in conformity with the auction method used. However, scalpers exist on the floor of the exchange. They operate by buying and selling futures for very small price differences. In essence, they operate and function much like the specialists on the stock exchanges.

Fundamental and Technical Analysts

The manner in which one performs a fundamental or a technical analysis of a commodity differs little from the way one would analyze a stock. Fundamental analysis may be easier for commodities than for stocks because fewer commodities are traded and because the data needed are often provided at little or no cost by the U.S. Department of Agriculture or other government agencies. The commodity speculator does need to follow closely new information regarding a commodity. New information indicating a relatively small change in supply may result in large changes in price. A severe frost in Florida during early 1977 is a good example of how changes in supply projections can result in large changes in price. For example the May 1977 frozen orange juice future went from \$.389 per pound on January 11, 1977, to \$.705 on January 28, 1977—a gain of \$4,740 per 15,000-pound contract. This is a gain of 527 percent on the \$900 initial margin requirement existing at that time—if you were long.

Commissions

As with stock investments, full-service brokerage firms and discount firms serve the commodity markets. Some of the full-service firms are divisions of firms such as Merrill Lynch, and others deal exclusively in commodities.

The choice of a brokerage firm for futures trading is more critical than for making stock investments for two principal reasons. First, the price movements of these leveraged contracts can be rather dynamic, as we just noted in the case of orange juice. A good broker may be especially valuable in alerting an investor to a rapidly deteriorating situation. Speculators will need to decide whether the services provided by a full-service broker are worth the added commission cost. Second, the relatively short time horizon for most futures positions (typically a week or less) tends to generate a lot of trading activity that can run up total commission costs rapidly. For a fairly active futures trader to incur annual commission costs equal to 25 to 40 percent of the initial equity in the account is not unusual. A discount brokerage firm may help keep this cost down.

Speculative Transactions

Speculators can enter into outright positions or what we can call regular trades. The speculator either buys or sells a given futures contract in the hope of making a gain on the transaction. In effect, the speculator is either long or short.

In contrast to a single long or short position, a trader can engage in a spread transaction. A *spread transaction* is simultaneous purchase of a future for delivery in one month and sale of a future in the same commodity for delivery in another month. A straddle is a simultaneous trade across two different but related markets, such as corn and oats. Actually the terms spread and straddle tend to be used interchangeably. Hence, we will refer to all related transactions involving the purchase of one future and the sale of another future at approximately the same time as a spread.

Outright Positions

A speculator will purchase a futures contract if he or she expects the price of that contract to increase. Likewise, a future will be sold if the trader anticipates that the price of the contract will decline. The trader should understand fully the supply and demand elements involved in setting the price for a given commodity. We will examine trades in the S&P 500 stock index futures and in treasury bond futures.

Long the S&P 500 Index

On December 31, 1986, a trader faced the following prices for the S&P 500 stock index futures contract:

	Price	**Open Interest**
Actual index value	242.16	—
March 1987 future	242.15	92,211
June 1987 future	242.85	1,662

The trader expected the stock market to rise and desired to make money by going long the S&P 500 index contract. Each tick change in this futures contract is worth $5. A tick is the smallest price change. If the March future went up one point 242.15 to 243.15, the value of the contract would increase by $500 ($5 times the 100-tick change). The trader could reasonably buy either the March or June contract because the open interest indicates adequate liquidity in both of these contracts. *Open interest* is the number of contracts entered into by market participants and not yet liquidated by either closing out the positions or making or taking delivery on the contract. The trader would need to have $6,000 in margin deposited per contract in order to trade the March contract, which is currently worth $121,075 (242.15 times $500).

At the close of trading on February 24, 1987, the S&P 500 index had risen to 282.88, for a gain of 40.73 points. The speculator buying the March future could have gained $20,365 (40.73 times $500) on this position before commissions. Notice the leverage in this futures transaction. The index as measured by the March futures contract went up 16.8 percent, but the $6,000 margin deposit increased by 339.4 percent or $20,365.

Short Treasury Bond Futures

Investors may speculate in interest rate movements by trading interest rate futures. We will provide an example using treasury bond (T-bond) futures. T-bond futures have a denomination of $100,000 and trade in increments of 1/32 of a percentage point, just as in the trading of actual treasury bonds. Just before the close of trading on December 31, 1986, a speculator decided that long-term interest rates would rise. Checking the T-bond futures market, the trader found the March futures to be trading at 98–06, which implied a yield of 8.186 percent on the 8 percent treasury bond used as the standard for this contract. Because the trader expected interest rates to rise, she expected bond prices to decline. Hence, an expectation of rising interest rates would make the trader want to sell T-bond futures.

The trader sold one March T-bond future at 98–06 on December 31. However, interest rates started to decline, and on February 24, 1987,

March T-bond futures closed at 101–08, implying a yield of 7.875. Each 1/32 of a percentage (called a point) is worth $31.25, and the trader had lost 98 points, or $3,062.50. The speculator effectively sold the contract when it was worth $98,187.50 and could now buy it back for $101,250. However, because of margin call considerations, the speculator might have decided to sell before February 24.

Spread Transactions

Why would a commodity speculator enter into a spread transaction? The object is to profit from a change in the price difference between two futures contracts. A trader may find it easier to make judgments regarding the change in a price difference than to determine the direction of change in price as a speculator taking an outright position must do. We will examine two basic types of spread transactions: (1) the intracommodity spread and (2) the intercommodity spread.

Intracommodity Spread

An intracommodity spread involves the purchase of one future and the sale of a different future for the same commodity. Suppose that a speculator saw that the March 1987 silver contract was selling for 546.0 cents an ounce on December 31, 1986, and that the March 1988 silver contract was selling for 580.4 on the same day. For silver, the principal reason for this price difference is the carrying cost associated with the year's difference between these two contracts. The vast majority of this carrying cost is associated with the financing required to purchase silver for storage, and any spread transaction involving these two silver contracts is essentially an interest rate speculation. At the end of 1986, thirteen-week treasury bills were yielding 5.68 percent. Assuming that the trader expected short-term interest rates to rise during early 1987, what would be the proper spread position?

The price difference between the March 1987 and the March 1988 silver contracts is 34.3 cents an ounce. We can calculate an implied "interest rate" of 6.30 percent associated with these two contracts in the following manner:

$$\frac{34.3}{546.0} = 6.30\%$$

If the speculator expected interest rates to rise, the trader would also expect the price difference between these two silver contracts to widen as the financial cost of carrying silver for one year increases. Hence, the speculator would want to make the following transaction:

Sell March 1987 silver at 546.0
Buy March 1988 silver at 580.4

If the speculator was right about the direction of interest rate movements, March 1988 silver should increase in price relative to March 1987 silver. On February 24, 1987, the speculator closed out the position when

March 1987 silver was at 546.5 and March 1988 silver was at 582.6, a price difference of 36.3. We can summarize the results of this trade as follows:

	March 1987 Silver	March 1988 Silver
December 31	Sell at 546	Buy at 580.4
February 24	Buy at 546.5	Sell at 582.8
Gain or loss	−.5	+2.4
Net result = +1.9, or a $95 per contract gain at $50 a point		

The trader in this silver spread made a small profit, indicating that interest rates in the financial market probably rose slightly. In fact, the thirteen-week treasury bill rate declined from 5.68 percent on December 31, 1986, to 5.40 percent on February 24 when the silver spread was closed out. Obviously, other supply and demand factors influenced the price of silver, and our speculator appears lucky to have made a small profit, given that short-term interest rates actually fell.

Intercommodity Spread

An intercommodity spread involves the price relationship between two different but related contracts. An intercommodity spread of considerable interest to financial market participants is a yield curve spread. This spread involves taking long and short positions in treasury bill and bond futures contracts, depending on how the shape of the yield curve is expected to change over time. On December 31, 1986, a trader noticed the following prices for June T-bill and T-bond futures contracts:

T-bill contract 94.66 to yield 5.34%
T-bond contract 97–06 to yield 8.29%

The trader was unsure of which way interest rates would move but expected the difference between the T-bill and the T-bond yields to narrow from its December 31 difference of 295 basis points (a basis point equals .01 percent). In other words, the trader expected the yield curve to become less upward sloping. Hence, the trader started thinking about a spread transaction involving these two contracts.

In making an analysis of how a spread trade should be structured, assume that one leg of the spread will not change in price and focus on the other leg of the trade. For example, assume no change will take place in the T-bill price. The expectation of a decreasing yield difference between T-bill and T-bonds means that the long-term rate will fall and the price of the T-bond will increase. As a result of this analysis, the trader would want to buy the T-bond future while selling the T-bill future. Thus, the following trades were executed on December 31:

Sell T-bill future at 94.66
Buy T-bond future at 97–06

We have already noted that each point for a T-bond contract is worth $31.25. Each basis point movement for a T-bill future is worth $25. This information is essential in initially deciding on the trade to make and in determining the profit or loss when the spread transaction is finally completed. On February 24, the trader completed the spread transaction by making the following trades:

Buy T-bill future at 94.63
Sell T-bond future at 100–09

The yield spread between T-bills and T-bonds did narrow as the speculator anticipated. The yield on T-bills went from 5.34 percent to 5.37 percent, while the yield on T-bonds went from 8.290 percent to 7.972 percent. The spread went from 295 basis points to 260.2 basis points. We can summarize the results of this futures spread transaction as follows:

Dec. 31	Sell 1 T-bill at 94.66	Buy 1 T-bond at	97–06
Feb. 24	Buy 1 T-bill at 94.63	Sell 1 T-bond at	100–09
Gain or loss	.03		3–03
Gain or loss in dollars	75		3,093.75
Net result = A gain of $3,168.75			

Notice that this spread is slightly unusual in that both the T-bill and the T-bond legs of the spread made a profit. A more normal outcome is that one side of the spread loses money while hopefully the other side makes enough to more than offset the loss. Clearly, however, both sides of a spread can make money, and both sides can lose money.

An investor might spread in the anticipation that different sectors of the stock market will increase or decrease at uneven rates. For example, during 1986, the Dow Jones Industrial Average rose 23 percent, the S&P 500 rose 14 percent, but the *Value Line Composite* rose only 5 percent. This occurred because the high-quality Dow stocks did much better than lower-quality, secondary issues during 1986. Assume a trader anticipated that the same pattern of high-quality stocks outperforming lower-quality stocks would continue during early 1987. The trader could spread S&P 500 stock index futures against *Value Line* stock index futures. This trade becomes especially attractive because the S&P 500 index is value weighted and the *Value Line* index is equally weighted. Thus, the poorer price performance of the lower-quality stocks should show up clearly in the *Value Line* index.

As of December 31, 1986, the March S&P index was at 242.15, as we previously noted. The March 1987 *Value Line Composite* futures contract was trading for 224.00, representing a difference of 18.15 between the two contracts. Because the trader anticipated that the S&P 500 index futures contract would increase faster than the *Value Line* index futures contract, the trader purchased the S&P and sold the *Value Line*. On February 24, 1987, the March 1987 S&P 500 futures index contract was at 282.45, a rise of 16.6 percent. However, the March 1987 *Value Line Composite* index futures contract has risen only 15.3 percent to 258.25. The trader was correct in that the S&P 500 index contract did outperform the *Value Line* index. Let's see how much profit was made on this trade.

	S&P 500		***Value Line***	
December 31	Buy 1 March 1987 at	242.15	Sell 1 March 1987 at	224.00
February 24	Sell 1 March 1987 at	282.45	Buy 1 March 1987 at	258.25
Gain or loss		+40.30		−34.25
Net result = +6.05 times $500 equals $3,025				

We can see that although the spread position produced a profit of $3,025, the gain was dwarfed by the profit of $20,150 that would have been produced had the investor simply been long the S&P 500 stock index futures contract. However, remember that the spreader was not trying to forecast the direction of the movement of stock market prices but only the change in the price difference between these two stock market indexes that measure different sectors of the market. Spreads are often less risky than outright positions, so the fact that the profit in our spread is lower is not really surprising. On the other hand, spreads may be more risky than outright trades. Potential spread positions need to be carefully evaluated.

Requirements of Successful Speculation

Commodity speculation is not for everyone. Should you trade? This question is important and must be answered fairly and honestly. The answer involves a consideration of whether you have genuine risk capital, can manage your capital prudently, and have the temperament for commodity trading. All three are essential elements for successful speculating in commodities.

Genuine Risk Capital

"One must approach commodity trading as a business venture and apply good business techniques and judgment."[1] One important element in this business venture is whether or not you have sufficient capital to withstand a series of initial losses before a profit occurs. This capital should be available exclusively for trading in commodities and should not be needed for normal living expenses. Because of the leverage in commodity trading, the speculator should be willing to lose all risk capital committed and still be able to live in a reasonable fashion. Hence, many speculators (especially inexperienced ones) commit only a portion of their risk capital to commodity trading.

Temperament

If you do not know who you are, the futures market is a poor place to find out. These markets are very competitive, and a highly disciplined personality is required to trade in them. The trader has to have the ability to take loss after loss and not admit defeat. The trader must also have the ability to take a gain if circumstances warrant. We have seen that the time horizon for futures trading tends to be much shorter than for stocks and the leverage much larger. Quick, decisive action becomes very im-

1. Leo Melamed, "A Professional's View of Commodity Trading," in *Before You Speculate* (Chicago: Chicago Mercantile Exchange, August 1973), p. 16.

portant in this environment, or total ruin may result. The trader should not be vain or greedy. Every farmer knows that the greediest hogs get slaughtered first.

Capital Management

An essential task for the commodity trader is to establish trading objectives so that risk capital committed can be prudently managed. Many rules of thumb have been suggested to assist the trader in using proper capital management techniques. The number of commodities traded should be severely limited to about three or four. The placing of stop orders at the same time that the initial position is established should be seriously considered. The trader should add to an existing position only if a profit exists in the original position. An inexperienced trader should never carry more than three open contracts in any one commodity. If a margin call occurs, consider liquidating the position instead of meeting the call. Don't overtrade because this action will tend to warp your judgment. All of these rules of thumb and more that could be mentioned suggest that the potential commodity speculator should maintain a realistic and cautious attitude. The rewards can be substantial, but every dollar gained by one trader is lost by another.

Hedging Transactions

The objective in a hedging transaction is to lock-in the current price. This means the hedger is both long and short and that price movements will have little, if any, impact on the position of the hedger. We will use two hedging transactions as examples: a portfolio manager who hedged a bond against an increase in interest rates and an owner of a portfolio of common stock who hedged that portfolio against a drop in the stock market.

Hedging a Bond Holding

A portfolio manager owned $1 million par value of the 10¾ U.S. government bond of May 2003. This bond was selling at a bid price of 96–27 as of June 23, 1983. At this price of $968,438 for the bond, the yield-to-maturity would be 11.11 percent. However, the owner of this bond was afraid that interest rates were going to increase, which would cause a capital loss on the bond holding. The holder could sell the bond and reinvest in treasury bills. However, another possibility would be to hedge against this anticipated increase in interest rates by using the T-bond futures market, without disturbing the bond holding. Thus, as of June 23, the owner of the treasury bond sold ten September T-bond futures at 74–29. We have the following situation:

June 23 Own $1 million bond at $968,438 (long position)
Sell 10 September T-bond futures at 74–29 (short position)

By July 5, 1983, the interest rate for the 10¾ percent bond of May 2003 had increased to 11.41 percent, causing the price to decline to $945,625. If the investor had not hedged, the loss would have been $22,813 on this bond. However, the futures price had also declined, resulting in the following situation:

July 5 Loss of $22,813 on the bond holding.
Buy 10 September T-bond futures at 72–25 for a gain of 2–04, or 68 points (32 × 2 + 4). Each point is worth $31.25, as we noted earlier in the chapter, which means a gain of $21,250 for the ten contracts. This was not a perfect hedge, as we still lost $1,563, but this is better than losing $22,813.

Hedging a Stock Portfolio

We can use a stock index futures contract such as the S&P 500 to hedge the *systematic risk* in a stock portfolio. If a portfolio is well-diversified, this means that it has little *nonsystematic* risk, and our hedge can be quite effective. If our stock portfolio is not well-diversified, the hedge will be less effective because we will be unable to hedge against the nonsystematic risk. Let us assume that an endowment fund owned a $5 million, well-diversified common stock portfolio and that the portfolio manager expected the market to drop. The holdings could be sold and commission costs incurred, but it might be much easier and less costly in terms of commissions to sell some S&P 500 stock index futures to hedge the endowment portfolio. Near the close of market trading on September 10, 1986, the endowment fund's portfolio manager sold 40 December S&P 500 index futures contracts to create the following hedge in which the dollar amounts long and short are approximately equal:

Sept. 10 Long $5 million portfolio (S&P 500 index = 247.06)
Sell 40 December S&P 500 stock index futures at 248.65. This is a total short position of $4,973,000 (248.65 times $500 equals $124,325 per contract times 40 contracts).

The market dropped to 230.67 on September 12, and the December futures contract dropped to 229.70. These prices result in the following profit and loss situation:

Sept. 12 Portfolio now worth $4,668,299, assuming it "tracked" the market exactly
Buy 40 December S&P 500 index futures for $4,594,000 (229.70 times $500 times 40), for a gain of $379,000

The net result of this hedge was a profit of $47,299 consisting of a loss of $331,701 for the endowment portfolio and a gain of $379,000 on the 40 December futures contracts. Not all hedges are profitable, and certainly not all are as profitable as this trade. In this example, the endowment fund manager gained because the December futures contract went from a

Investment Highlight

Chase Manhattan Bank's Innovative CD (Ups but No Downs?)

This investment highlight examines a certificate of deposit issued by Chase Manhattan Bank that allows investors to participate in stock market movements.

Description
Can you have your investment cake and eat it too? That seems to be the question posed by the introduction by Chase Manhattan Bank of an innovative CD during the spring of 1987. This certificate is available with maturities of three, six, nine, and twelve months. By giving up part of the interest income normally expected from a CD with these maturities, investors can participate to some extent in the price movements of the S&P 500 stock market index.

This CD offers a risk and return trade-off. If investors decide to take no interest on the CD, they get to participate in 75 percent of any market rise, but are assured they will get their original investment back. A twelve-month CD paying interest of 4 percent allows investors to keep 40 percent of any gain achieved by the stock index during the period. If the market goes up 10 percent, the return on the CD is 8 percent, with equal parts coming from interest income and stock market gains.

Chase Manhattan can offer these CD terms because it engages in risk reducing transactions in the futures markets. These futures market transactions alter the distribution of returns achieved from stock investing, and the reduction in interest income is the cost associated with these hedging transactions. This is easiest to see in the situation in which investors receive no interest income on the CD. Investors trade-off 25 percent of any market gain and all interest income they would normally receive in exchange for suffering no loss should the stock market decline.

Conclusion
For investors with small amounts of capital or limited knowledge of the complex hedging transactions required in the futures markets, altering the normal risk and return trade-offs provided by the financial markets has been difficult. Chase Manhattan is providing its expertise in offering an innovative security. However, this CD does raise some interesting public policy questions regarding the dividing line between banking and brokerage businesses.

premium to the actual index on September 10 to a discount two days later.

Hedging will sometimes have the impact of reducing the return from a portfolio as well as the risk. This would clearly have been the case had the market risen from September 10, 1986, to September 12, 1986, rather than declined. The gains from being long the actual portfolio would have been offset to a large degree by the losses on the short futures position.

Another example is the return during the first quarter of 1987 on the Common Fund's unhedged and hedged South African Free Fund. The Common Fund is a money management group for nonprofit educational institutions. Investors generally believe that the South African Free portfolio has more price volatility than stocks in general because many large "blue chip" firms are not represented in this special portfolio. Thus, futures are used to reduce the volatility of the South African Free Fund. During the first quarter of 1987, the unhedged fund had a total return of 17.7 percent versus only 15.4 percent for the hedged fund. In this instance, hedging reduced both the risk and the return.

Options on Futures

Commodity option trading has had a rather checkered history. Options on domestic agricultural commodities were banned by law in 1936 because of abuses in option trading. Widespread abuses in commodities options in so-called London options (such as on gold and cocoa traded in London) during the early 1970s caused Congress to ban all option trading for commodities until an adequate regulatory framework could be established. However, a three-year pilot program for options on commodities, established in 1982, has been expanded so that active trading now occurs in more than twenty futures options.

The analysis of *futures options* is essentially the same as we noted for stock options in Chapter 14. In addition, the trading strategies are the same. Let's examine the purchase of a stock index call on the S&P 100 and the writing of a spread on both a call and a put.

Buying a Call

As of December 31, 1986, the S&P 100 index was at 231.09 and the February 235 OEX call option was selling for 3.75, or $3,750 a contract. A speculator purchased one of these options in the hope that the market would rise. The market would have to increase to at least 238.75 (235 plus 3.75) by the expiration of the option for the investor to make any profit. By January 29, 1987, the market had leaped to 263.21, for a gain of 13.9 percent. The option would sell for at least 28.21, which was its theoretical value (263.21 less 235). Because some time remained before expiration, the investor sold the option for 29, achieving a gain of 673 percent. The option paid $29,000.

Writing a Spread

On January 29, 1987, a speculator noticed the following price relationships in the market for OEX options:

Investment Highlight

The Triple Witching Hour (Which Way Will the Market Go?)

The simultaneous quarterly expiration of stock index futures, index options, and many options on individual stocks has become known as the triple witching hour because of the price volatility that may be associated with these expirations.

Description

During the last hour of trading on four Fridays a year, arbitrageurs unwinding their positions in futures and options sometimes cause wild price swings on huge volumes. This is the result of what is known as program trading.

Program trading is effectively a riskless arbitrage transaction. A buy program, for example, might involve a transaction in the S&P 500 stock index futures contract and related transactions in the individual stock components making up the index. At the expiration of the futures contract, its price by definition must equal the value of the stocks in the index futures contract, and this feature is what accounts for the risk arbitrage nature of the transaction. If professional investors discover in March that the S&P index is at 300 but the June S&P 500 futures contract is at 304, they can sell the futures contract and buy the appropriate amounts of the underlying stocks.

Program trading is normally done by large investment banking firms using computer monitoring to discover arbitrage opportunities. Computers may also be used to place orders to execute these programs. In the example, if the S&P 500 index remains unchanged at 300, the index future must be selling for 300 at its expiration in June. Unwinding the buy program means that the underlying stocks must be sold and the futures contract purchased. The unwinding of buy or sell (where the stocks themselves are originally sold and the futures contract purchased) programs near expiration may create price volatility. In an effort to eliminate some of this concentrated program trading volume, some of the futures and options will be settled at opening prices on Friday instead of at closing prices. Whether this will solve some of the problems associated with the triple witching hour is uncertain. See "This Triple Witching Hour Could Last All Day," *Business Week* (June 22, 1987): 126.

Conclusion

Although program trading and related price volatility that can result during a triple witching hour may cause some market observers concern, program trading may not alter long-term fundamental investment values.

OEX Index = 263.21
March OEX 265 call = 7½
March OEX 265 put = 9¼

The trader decided to write (sell) both the put and the call. What would the trader accomplish by this action? If the market stayed rela-

Figure 15–1
S&P 100 Spread Profit and Loss Function at Option Expiration

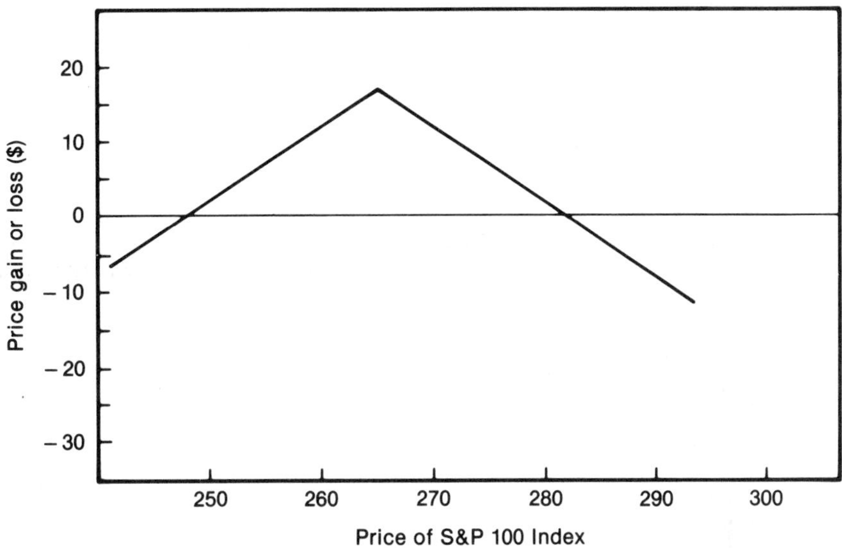

tively constant through the March expiration date, the trader would keep almost all of the premiums for writing these two options. The best possible outcome would be for the market to close at 265 on the expiration date of the option. In that event, both options would expire as worthless, and the investor would make 16¾ (7½ plus 9¼), or $16,750 per pair of option contracts. If the index were at 250 at the option's expiration, the call would be worthless, for a gain of 7½, and the put would sell for 15, for a loss of 5¾, resulting in a net gain of 1¾. Figure 15–1 shows the *profit and loss function* for this option-writing strategy. Ignoring commissions, we see that the break-even point on the downside is an index value of 248.25 and the upside break-even is 281.75. Below 248.25 and above 281.25, this spread starts to produce losses. Hence, if the trader anticipated that the market would be relatively stable (would not fall more than 5.7 percent nor rise by more than 7 percent) through late March, this trading strategy would produce profits.

Summary

Futures trading attracts investors because of the possibility of turning a small sum of money into a very large sum of money. Of course, the saying goes that the way to make a small fortune in the futures market is to start with a large fortune! Futures tend to be risky because they are typically purchased with relatively low margins compared to stocks. Hence, the leverage in trading commodities is substantial, and the resulting risk is clearly not acceptable to all investors. One way to reduce the risk is to trade with margins much greater than required by the exchanges.

Commodity trading differs from stock investing in a number of other important ways. The main difference is that a commodity trading position is limited to the life of the future, which is between one and two years, depending on the commodity. From a practical aspect, the liquidity in the nearby contracts is much better than in many of the distant contracts, making futures trading even more a short-term venture. Daily price limits exist for many futures contracts. Futures trading is a zero-sum game less commissions; any gain on a futures contract means a corresponding loss for other traders. A potential commodity speculator must carefully examine his or her personality to see if it is of the type that can stand the rigors of commodity trading.

Although hedging in the futures market cannot eliminate the risk associated with adverse price movements, risk shifting is possible. Futures provide a method for the quick and cost-effective establishment of positions opposite to those held in the cash (spot) market. The ability to be both long and short, if a difficult market environment is anticipated, justifies the tremendous interest investors have shown in futures-related transactions in recent years.

Suggested Readings

BARRO, ROBERT J. "Futures Markets and the Fluctuations in Inflation, Monetary Growth, and Asset Returns." *Journal of Business* (April 1986): S21–S38.

BELONGIA, MICHAEL T., and G. L. SANTONI. "Hedging Interest Rate Risk with Financial Futures: Some Basic Principles." *Review of the Federal Reserve Bank of St. Louis* (October 1984): 15–25.

BRENNAN, MICHAEL. "A Theory of Price Limits in Futures Markets." *Journal of Financial Economics* (June 1986): 213–34.

CHANG, ERIC. "Returns on Speculators and the Theory of Normal Backwardation." *Journal of Finance* (March 1985): 193–208.

CHANG, ERIC, and RICHARD A. STEVENSON. "The Timing Performance of Small Traders." *Journal of Futures Markets* (Winter 1985): 517–27.

ELTON, EDWIN J., MARTIN J. GRUBER, and JOEL RENTZLER. "Professionally Managed, Publicly Traded Commodity Funds." *Journal of Business* (April 1987): 175–99.

FIGLEWSKI, STEPHEN, and STANLEY J. KON. "Portfolio Management with Stock Index Futures." *Financial Analysts Journal* (January–February 1982): 52–60.

FISHE, RAYMOND P. H., and LAWRENCE G. GOLDBERG. "The Effects of Margins on Trading in Futures Markets." *Journal of Futures Markets* (Summer 1986): 261–71.

GAY, GERALD D., and STEVEN MANASTER. "The Quality Option Implicit in Futures Contracts." *Journal of Financial Economics* (September 1984): 353–70.

GOLDFARB, DAVID. "Hedging Interest Rate Risk in Banking: Financial Futures, Fixed Rate Loans, Variable Rate Loans and Asymmetric Risks." *Journal of Futures Markets* (February 1987): 35–47.

Grant, Dwight. "How to Optimize with Stock Index Futures." *Journal of Portfolio Management* (Spring 1982): 32–36.

Grieves, Robin. "Hedging Corporate Bond Portfolios." *Journal of Portfolio Management* (Summer 1986): 23–25.

Harlow, Charles V., and Richard J. Teweles. "Commodities and Securities Compared." *Financial Analysts Journal* (September–October 1972): 64–70.

Hartzmark, Michael L. "The Effects of Changing Margin Levels on Futures Market Activity, the Composition of Traders in the Market and Price Performance." *Journal of Business* (April 1986): S147–S180.

Hilliard, Jimmy E. "Hedging Interest Rate Risk with Futures—Portfolios Under Term Structure Effects." *Journal of Finance* (December 1984): 1547–70.

Lee, Cheng F., Raymond M. Leuthold, and Jean E. Cordier. "The Stock Market and the Commodities Futures Market: Diversification and Arbitrage Potential." *Financial Analysts Journal* (July–August 1985): 53–60.

Martell, Terrence F., and Avner S. Wolf. "Determinants of Trading Volume in Futures Markets." *Journal of Futures Markets* (June 1987): 233–44.

Moriarty, Eugene, Susan Phillips, and Paula Tosini. "A Comparison of Options and Futures in the Management of Portfolio Risk." *Financial Analysts Journal* (January–February 1981): 61–67.

Pashigian, B. Peter. "The Political Economy of Futures Market Regulation." *Journal of Business* (April 1986): S55–S84.

Powers, Mark, and David Vogel. *Inside the Financial Futures Market.* New York: John Wiley & Sons, 1981.

Ramaswamy, Krishna, and Suresh M. Sundaresan. "The Valuation of Options on Futures Contracts." *Journal of Finance* (December 1985): 1319–40.

Roll, Richard. "Orange Juice and Weather." *American Economic Review* (December 1985): 861–81.

Telser, Lester. "Futures and Actual Markets: How They Are Related." *Journal of Business* (April 1986): S5–S20.

Trainer, Francis H., Jr. "The Uses of Treasury Bond Futures in Fixed Income Portfolio Management." *Financial Analysts Journal* (January–February 1983): 27–34.

Whaley, Robert E. "Valuation of American Futures Options: Theory and Empirical Tests." *Journal of Finance* (March 1986): 127–50.

Questions

1. What economic role does the futures market play in the U.S. economy?
2. Compare the concept of margin as it applies to common stocks and

to commodities. Do important differences exist as far as the investor is concerned?

3. What are daily price limits, and why do they exist in the commodity markets? What happens when they are reached?

4. What is the relationship between margins in commodity futures transactions and the existence of daily price limits?

5. What is a spread transaction in the commodities market? What is the rationale one would use in establishing an intercommodity spread?

6. What personal characteristics are necessary for an individual to be a successful commodity trader? Are there any reasons why a successful investor in common stocks might not be successful as a commodity trader?

7. What is basis, and why is it so important in futures trading?

8. Why is futures trading a zero-sum game, and what implications does this have for traders?

9. In spreading silver contracts, an implied interest can be calculated. Why is this the case?

10. Discuss the theory behind spreading stock index contracts based on the different methods used to construct the indexes. Give an example of a common trade of this variety.

11. Investors often state that hedging reduces risk as well as return. Would you expect this to be the case? Can you give an example in which this would happen?

12. An investor's portfolio has a coefficient of determination of .65 with the Standard & Poor 500 stock index. What difficulties would the investor encounter in attempting to hedge this portfolio with a stock index future?

Problems

1. Herman Pickett bought a December 1987 gold futures contract in late March 1987 at $422.40, making the contract worth $42,240. Herman's broker required a 10 percent margin deposit. By late July, this contract was selling for $468.80.
   (a) What was Herman's dollar profit on the contract if he sold in July?
   (b) He held the contract for four months. What was his annualized rate of return?
   (c) If he had originally sold this contract rather than buying, what should have happened?

2. When the stock market experienced a major rally in January 1987, Trudy Roush believed that the market would increase even further

in the next months. Therefore, she decided to investigate speculating with S&P 500 index futures contracts. On February 16, she received the following information:

	Price	Open Interest
June future	283.50	12,319
September future	284.65	246
Index value	279.70	

She decided to buy a September contract, which required her to deposit $6,000 to her account with her broker.

(a) What was the contract worth on February 16?

(b) On July 30, she received the following information:

	Price	Open Interest
September future	319.70	109,606
Index value	318.05	

Ignoring commissions, how much did Trudy make on her speculative position if she chose to close out her position on July 30? What rate of return did she make on her $6,000 margin?

3. Brad speculated that interest rates were in for a strong increase after the beginning of the year. He decided to speculate in the interest rate movement by selling treasury bond futures. On December 19, he decided to short a September treasury bond futures contract at 97²²⁄₃₂. The underlying treasury bonds were selling at 110²⁄₃₂ and yielding 7.68 percent.

(a) If the September T-bond futures closed on February 24 at 97¹⁸⁄₃₂, what was Brad's gain or loss?

(b) Brad did not close out his position in February because he still believed that interest rates would soon climb. On July 30, September T-bond futures were quoted at 89³¹⁄₃₂. Brad decided to close out his position. Ignoring commissions, what was his gain or loss on this speculative trade?

4. Duncan, a bond manager for Permanent State Insurance Company, was concerned about the movement of interest rates in the coming year. On December 19, 1986, he had a $50 million portfolio consisting entirely of 8⅜ August 03–08 treasury bonds. The bonds were quoted at 106.24 and were yielding 7.65 percent. Duncan gathered the following information:

Treasury bond	106.24
June future	98²³⁄₃₂
September	97²²⁄₃₂

(a) How should Duncan set up a hedge to protect his bond portfolio from changes in interest rates? Use the September future in the hedge.

(b) On February 16, on the basis of the following information, Duncan considered lifting the hedge and covering his position:

Treasury bond	105.20
June future	$98^{16}/_{32}$
September future	$97^{18}/_{32}$

Ignoring commissions, what would have been his gain or loss on the futures contract? On the bond position? On his net position?

(c) Assume Duncan left the hedge on until July 30. On that day, he gathered the following information:

September future $89^{31}/_{32}$ Treasury bond 94.08

Ignoring commissions, what would have been his gain or loss on the futures contract? On the bond position? On his net position? What was the amount of basis risk in this transaction?

(d) What would have been his position if he had lifted the hedge on February 16 and left the bond position unhedged until July 30?

5. Marion manages a highly liquid portfolio of government securities for a major financial institution. In December 1986, Marion's director informed her that she would receive a $3 million inflow into her portfolio on August 1 and would have the funds to invest until October 31. She observed that interest rates had been volatile in recent months, but she expected them to decline gradually during 1987. On December 19, 1986, she obtained the following quotes:

	Price	**Open Interest**
December 87 T-bill future	94.55	919 contracts
13-week T-bill rate	5.55%	

(a) How could Marion lock in the current interest rates for the $3 million she would receive in August?

(b) On July 30, 1987, Marion observed the following quotes:

December 87 T-bill future	93.62
13-week T-bill rate	6.14%

Ignoring commissions, how well would Marion do on her investment?

6. Harriet Fitzgerald faced the following soybean futures prices in August 1979:

September	733
November	729
January 1980	741
March	754
May	764

Carrying charges for a bushel of soybeans are an estimated seven cents per month per bushel including interest.

(a) If Harriet expects the price difference to widen between the November and the January soybeans, what spread should she establish?

(b) What is a reasonable expectation for the maximum profit that may be made on this spread?

(c) Ignoring commissions, what would be Harriet's gain (loss) if the spread is closed out when November soybeans are 715 and January soybeans are 723?

7. The prices of the futures shown in Problem 6 reveal that the November contract was priced four cents below that of the September contract. It would seem that a spread should be established in the expectation that the September contract would fall relative to the November contract. Can you detect any potential difficulties with this spreading opportunity?

8. Sing Lee is considering the establishment of a spread between gold and silver. As of July 1987, the December 1987 gold future sells for $468.80 (100-ounce contract) while the December silver contract sells for 822.1 cents (5,000-ounce contract). Sing is thinking of buying five silver contracts and selling four gold contracts.

   (a) What does Sing expect will happen to the prices of the two metals?

   (b) What might Sing expect the metal prices to move in this direction?

   (c) Why would Sing trade four gold contracts but five silver contracts?

   (d) Do you feel that this is a bona fide spread opportunity?

9. In August 1983, March wheat on the Chicago Board of Trade is selling for 424 ($4.24 per bushel). You expect prices of wheat to rise in the future and buy three contracts (15,000 bushels).

   (a) Assuming that your broker requires a 15 percent margin, how much must you deposit?

   (b) In November 1983, the price of wheat is at 440 ($4.40 per bushel). Ignoring commissions, compute the annualized rate of return if you close out this contract. Does leverage have any impact on your return?

   (c) Suppose, however, that the price of wheat is 404 and that you want to close out. Compute your annualized return.

   (d) Compute your annualized rate of return for part *b* if the margin is 10 percent rather than 15 percent. Discuss the leverage effect between these two different margin requirements.

10. As of March 18, 1987, Debbie Robinson owned a diversified portfolio worth $500,000. The S&P 500 stock index had already increased from 242.17 to 292.78 since the beginning of the year for a gain of about 20 percent. Debbie decided to use S&P 500 index future contracts to hedge the market risk component of her stock position through July rather than simply selling her stocks. The September S&P 500 index future was selling for 296 on March 18.

    (a) How many contracts did Debbie need to buy or sell to be hedged?

(b) The margin on each S&P 500 index future contract is $6,000. How much margin money did Debbie need to deposit?

(c) Debbie was wrong! On July 30, the S&P 500 index was up 4.4 percent to 315.65 while the S&P 500 index future was at 317.05. Ignoring commissions and margins, how did Debbie's hedge work out?

11. On February 16, 1987, Cathy Sorvick obtained the following price quotes from her broker.

S&P 500 index future	June	283.50 (500 times the index)
S&P 500 index		279.70
Value Line index future	June	256.10 (500 times the index)
Value Line index		260.35

Cathy believed that a major market move was about to take place but was unsure of the direction.

(a) Calculate the basis for both index futures.

(b) Set up an intermarket spread involving one futures contract for each market index.

(c) On June 10, 1987, Cathy decided to close out her futures positions. The quotes on that day were as follows:

S&P 500 index future	June	297.75
S&P 500 index		297.28
Value Line index future	June	265.25
Value Line Index		264.35

Ignoring commissions, calculate Cathy's profit or loss on the intermarket spread. What is the equivalent annual rate of return?

(d) If, instead of investing in the spread, Cathy had purchased the S&P 500 index futures contract only, what would have been her return? Why might Cathy have invested in the intermarket spread instead of taking a direct position in the futures contract?

12. In February 1987, Sally Warder expected that long-term interest rates would soon increase relative to short-term rates. On February 16, 1987, she obtained the following quotes for treasury bill futures contracts.

	Treasury Bill Futures
June	94.38
September	94.41
December	94.38
March 88	94.29
June 88	94.15

(a) How would she set up a spread with T-bill futures to benefit from an increase in the slope of the yield curve? Show how to set up the spread using the June 87 and June 88 futures contracts.

(b) On May 30, 1987, the following prices existed for treasury bills and treasury bill futures contracts.

	Treasury Bill Futures
June 87	93.91
June 88	93.17

Ignoring commissions, calculate the profit or loss on the spread given that each basis point gain or loss equals $25.

13. Suppose Alex saw that the September 87 silver contract was selling for 564.5 cents an ounce on February 16, 1987, and that the September 88 silver contract was selling for 602.0 on the same day. The thirteen-week treasury bill rate was 5.79.

(a) Assuming that Alex expected short-term interest rates to rise during early 1987, what would be the proper spread position?

(b) What is the implied interest rate on this spread?

(c) On July 30, Alex closed out his spread position. The September 87 future was selling for 836.5, and the September 88 future was selling for 904.2. Ignoring commissions, calculate the gain or loss on the spread given that each point equals $50.

(d) The thirteen-week T-bill rate on July 30, 1987, was 6.00. Explain what produced the results obtained in part c.

14. On July 30, 1987, the OEX 100 index was at 311.57; Tony observed the following price relationships for OEX 100 index options:

October OEX 100 Index Options		
Exercise Price	**Call**	**Put**
305	12¾	5⅝
310	10	7½
315	7⅝	10

Tony thought that the stock market index would be around the 310 level through October and wanted to write both a call and a put at the 310 level.

(a) Derive a profit and loss function for the 310 October spread on the OEX 100 index option. Show this on a graph for values from 290 to 320.

(b) What are the break-even values for this option-writing strategy?

(c) Assuming Tony closed out his position on October 1, 1987, what was his gain or loss on the spread (ignoring commissions)? (Note: you will have to obtain the closing prices for the 310 October 87 options and the OEX index for October 1, 1987.)

Chapter 16

Investment Companies

Key Concepts

- accumulation plan
- characteristic line
- closed-end investment company
- exchange provision
- front-end load fund
- Keogh plan
- letter of intent
- load charge
- load fund
- mutual fund
- net asset value
- no-load fund
- open-end investment company
- operating expenses
- portfolio turnover
- reinvestment plan
- right of accumulation discount
- withdrawal plan

Chapter Outline

It won't be long. Soon investors will have as many different investment companies from which to select as there are companies listed on the New York Stock Exchange. Investment companies are available in an incredible assortment of shapes and sizes. This wide variety is consistent with a complex financial system and the new product marketing orientation we noted in our previous discussion of fixed-income innovations.

Hardly a week passes without a new investment company fund being offered to the public. Some of these funds are large. In September 1986, the Zweig Fund managed by Martin Zweig sold its initial public offering of 34 million shares at $10 each. In January 1987, Merrill Lynch sold $1.2 billion of the Duff & Phelps Selected Utilities Fund. This investment company, designed mainly for individual investors, plans to invest in utility stocks and bonds.

An investment company may be generally defined as any company whose assets consist primarily of the securities of other companies. The Investment Company Act of 1940 defines an investment company as a company with over 40 percent of its assets in securities other than United States government obligations or minority-owned subsidiaries. An investor should be able to find the appropriate investment company to satisfy virtually any investment objective.

Functions of Investment Companies

Investment companies have at least four primary functions: (1) diversification, (2) professional management, (3) liquidity, and (4) allocation of equity funds within the economy. The first three functions are directly beneficial to the investor, and the fourth concerns the functioning of the economy as a whole.

Because the investment company allows the purchase of a fractional interest in a diversified portfolio, an individual investor can achieve the risk-reducing properties that diversification provides. As previously noted, owning ten to fifteen properly selected stocks is sufficient to substantially reduce diversifiable risk. This implies that an investor without sufficient funds to purchase ten to fifteen separate securities may find investment companies useful investment vehicles. But investment companies offer more than just the opportunity to invest in a number of securities. An investor might purchase ten securities with a total of $10,000, but this would entail a substantial commission. The exact commission would involve considerations such as minimum charges per order, but between $400 and $800 could be spent on commissions at the time the securities are bought and when they are sold. The purchase of an investment company share may involve a transaction cost, but selling the share normally does not. However, investment company fund ownership sometimes requires the payment of management expenses. The value of the diversification service then becomes a trade-off between commission rates and investment company charges. In the authors' opinion, an investor with less than about $25,000 to invest may find the diversification service of an investment company valuable.

The second function of an investment company is to provide the investor with professional management. The investment decisions of a professional investor may be better than the decisions of most of the investing public. The professional may have greater interpretative skill, more and better information, and greater economies of scale in processing the information. Hence, an investment company will be beneficial to an investor insofar as the decisions of the individual investor can be expected to produce lower returns or higher risk or both compared to the decisions of the investment company management.

Some investment companies stand ready to redeem shares upon written notice by the investor, while the shares of other investment companies must be sold in the open market. Rarely will an extended delay be encountered in attempting to liquidate all or a portion of an investor's holdings. This does not imply that investors will be able to liquidate at a particular value, only that the current value can be turned into cash almost immediately.

To the extent that these three services are desired by the community at large, the existence of investment companies within the economy probably has generated a larger portion of investable funds than would otherwise be the case. As such, the allocation of real resources is probably more efficient than it would be without an investment company industry. At the same time, this conclusion is extremely difficult to prove in any absolute sense.

Types of Investment Companies

Only two major types of investment companies are significant at the present time—open-end investment companies and closed-end investment companies. *Open-end investment companies* are commonly called *mutual funds.* Exhibit 16–1 presents a detailed classification of investment companies, showing many of the varied major portfolio holdings.

Investment companies trace their origins to the early nineteenth cen-

Exhibit 16–1 Classification of Investment Companies

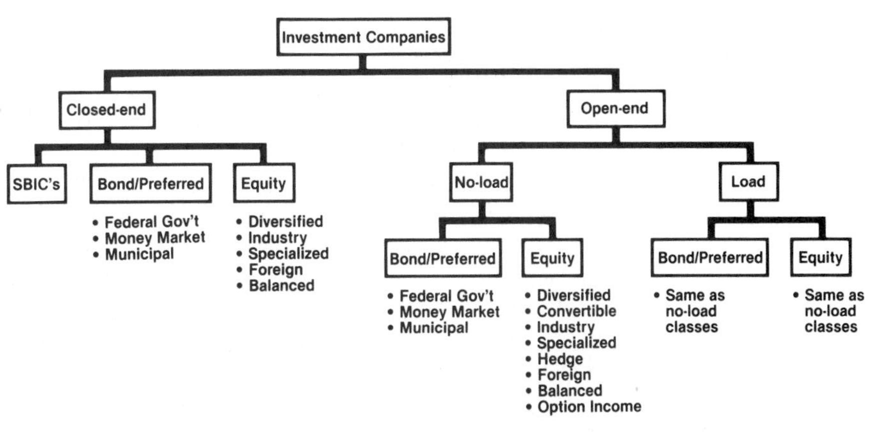

tury in Europe. Investment trusts were quite popular in England and Scotland in the period from 1870 to 1890, until a financial crisis slowed their rate of growth. Early American investment companies were either fixed trusts or *closed-end investment companies.* The first open-end investment company, as we know it today, was the Massachusetts Investors Trust formed in March 1924. However, open-end investment companies ran a very poor second to the closed-end funds. The SEC estimated that only nineteen open-end investment companies having assets of $140 million were in existence as of December 31, 1929.

Many of the closed-end investment companies of the 1920s were heavily margined and very speculative. As a result, their investment performance during the 1930s was a disaster. This poor performance of closed-end funds seriously damaged the reputation of the whole investment company concept for many years to follow.

Open-End Investment Companies

Open-end investment companies are named for their capital structure. New shares are continually sold by the investment company to any interested purchaser, unless the fund closes sales to new investors. A few of the more successful mutual funds sell shares only to existing holders as a means of controlling the size of their portfolios. If these funds did not curtail their growth by closing up, management flexibility and portfolio control might be lost. Outstanding shares are redeemed by the investment company for cash at the option of the shareholder. Sales and redemptions take place at net asset value plus any sales commission or less any redemption fee that may be imposed.

Net asset value is determined by valuing the assets in the investment company's portfolio and subtracting any liabilities. The net asset value is divided by the number of shares outstanding at the time to determine the net asset value per share. For many funds, the per-share net asset value is determined daily and published in the financial section of many newspapers. Exhibit 16–2 shows part of the mutual fund section from the *Wall Street Journal* of May 29, 1987.

Load Funds

Mutual funds may be classified as either load or no-load funds. Load funds, such as the Rochester Funds in Exhibit 16–2, have a sales commission called a *load charge,* which is paid when buying the shares. The fee is usually a sliding load charge based on the amount of the purchase. Not all load funds have the same loading fee schedule, although larger purchases will mean a lower percentage load charge. The dollar amount at which the load fee declines may differ from fund to fund. Often, no redemption fee is required when liquidating a mutual fund holding, although investors may encounter a modest fee. For example, the Nicholas Fund charges a redemption fee of 1 percent for funds invested for less than ninety days. This redemption fee is meant to discourage short-term investors.

Exhibit 16–2 **Selected Mutual Fund Prices Reported in the *Wall Street Journal* for May 29, 1987**

	*NAV**	*Offer Price*	*NAV Chg*
Rainbw Funds	6.18	N.L.	+.03
Rochester Funds:			
Conv Gr	10.94	11.28	−.01
Conv Inc	8.46	8.72	+.01
Growth	10.60	11.58	+.10
Scudder Funds:			
Cptl Gro	18.48	N.L.	+.13
Devl Fd	24.53	N.L.	+.10
Income	12.57	N.L.	+.06
Intl Fd	40.93	N.L.	+.12
Muni Bd	8.25	N.L.	+.03

*Net asset value

Load charges are stated as a percentage of the offering price. For example, an investor placing $1,000 into the Templeton Growth Fund would be credited with an investment on the fund's books of $915 and would pay a load fee of $85. If the net asset value of this fund were $10, the investor would buy 91.5 units. Expressed as a percentage of the amount actually invested in the fund's shares, the load fee would be 9.3 percent ($85/$915).

Over the years, the SEC has been interested in the level of load fees and the manner in which they are charged. As a result of the Investment Company Amendments Act of 1970, the National Association of Securities Dealers is responsible for promulgating rules regarding the sales charges of an investment company. Legally, these sales charges shall not be excessive.

Sales charges by contractual *front-end load funds* have also been studied carefully by the SEC, and new requirements were incorporated in the 1970 amendments. Contractual front-end load funds require an investor to make periodic payments over the life of the plan. An investor, for example, may agree to pay $50 per month for ten years for a total investment of $6,000. It is important to emphasize that a contractual plan does not represent a legal contract because the investor is not compelled to maintain scheduled payments and may drop from the plan at any time. The investor may perceive the contractual plan as having a beneficial "forced" savings element, but experience shows that a substantial number of investors drop out of contractual plans in their early years.

If an investor pays $50 a month for ten years, the sales commission for the whole transaction might be in the neighborhood of 8½ percent of the investment ($510). Prior to the 1970 legislation, 50 percent of the payments during the first year ($300) could be taken as commission, with the remaining sales commission ($210) spread over the remaining nine years. Investors dropping out of the contractual plan within the first year or two would incur high sales commissions because no provision existed for a sales commission refund.

Front-end load funds may now select either of the following methods for calculating sales charges. No matter which method is used, the investor has the right to a complete refund of sales fees during a forty-five-day period following the mailing of the investor's certificate.

Contractual Load Fee Method One

This method includes a 50 percent sales charge in the first year, but the investor has a right of refund upon withdrawal for a period of eighteen months. The refund would be equal to the net asset value of the shares in the account plus an amount equal to sales charges in excess of 15 percent of gross payments. No refunds are made for custodial charges or insurance payments.

If an investor paid $600 during the first year and then dropped the plan, the refund would be calculated as follows under method one:

Investment: $600 at an average net asset value of $10 per share
The number of shares purchased would be calculated as follows:
$600 − $300 commission = $300/$10 = 30 shares

If the investor drops the plan when the net asset value per share equals $9, the total amount of the check including the sales charge refund would be calculated as follows:

Value of share = 30 shares at $9 per share	=	$270
Sales charge refund = $300 less 15%	=	255
Total amount of the check	=	$525

Contractual Load Fee Method Two

Sales charges are limited to 20 percent of any payments and an annual average of not more than 16 percent for the first forty-eight monthly payments.

No-Load Funds

A number of mutual funds, known as no-load funds, do not charge a load fee. No-load funds have no sales charge because they sell directly to the investor and compensate no salesperson for a sales effort. Investors must normally initiate contact with the fund to obtain a prospectus and to transact business. Investors may find that determining which mutual funds are truly no-load funds is becoming more and more difficult. This is because of what is known as a 12b–1 plan. About 100 mutual funds that belong to the No-Load Mutual Fund Association have 12b–1 plans. These plans are named after the Securities and Exchange Commission's 1980 rule, which allows mutual funds to make a charge against the assets of the fund to pay for certain distribution and marketing expenses. Some mutual funds use the money that is produced by these charges to print sales literature, and other funds use this money to compensate salespersons over a period of time for sales efforts. These charges are typically justified by the fund's management as being necessary to help the fund grow. This growth would allow smaller funds to spread their fixed costs over a larger asset base.

A charge against assets under a 12b–1 plan is sometimes combined with a redemption fee or a so-called back-end load. An investor can expect to encounter great variety in both the 12b–1 charge and any redemption charge. For example, the Gabelli Asset Fund has an annual 12b–1 charge equal to .3 percent of average daily assets and a redemption fee of 2 percent if the fund is held less than one year. However, the Hutton Investment-Option Income Fund has a 12b–1 charge of 1 percent of assets and a redemption fee that starts at 5 percent and reduces gradually to zero in six years. Although the Scudder Income Fund in Exhibit 16–2 is a no-load fund, as shown by the *N.L.* in the offering price column, it behooves the investor to determine if a 12b–1 plan is in effect or if a redemption fee is charged. A careful reading of the prospectus is more important than ever, as it allows potential investors to ascertain the true nature of mutual fund charges to be levied on their investment dollars.

Closed-End Investment Companies

Want to make an investment sojourn in France or Italy? Want an investment that concentrates in financial companies? If you answered yes to either of these questions, a closed-end investment company may be an appropriate investment vehicle for you. Closed-end investment companies are pooled investment alternatives that have a fixed number of shares outstanding. Trading takes place in these shares, which are often listed on a stock exchange. No continuous offering and no redemption of shares occurs with closed-end investment companies.

Investors have shown increased interest in closed-end investment opportunities. One reason for this is that these funds are well suited to specialized types of investments. The fund managers do not have to worry about shareholders taking their funds away. Once the closed-end fund shares have been sold, investors have to sell their shares to other investors via market transactions rather than present them to the investment company for redemption. The specialized nature of some closed-end investment companies means that they may not be well-diversified investments. Investors should probably view them as only a potential part of a larger portfolio.

Closed-end investment companies can be classified according to their portfolio composition, the method by which their price is determined, and their capital structure.

Portfolio Composition

Table 16–1 shows some of the closed-end investment companies available for the investor. Some closed-end investment companies, such as the Tri-Continental Fund, hold a diversified portfolio of common stocks. In a similar fashion, the Lincoln National Convertible Securities Fund provides the investor with a portfolio containing many different convertible securities.

Table 16–1
Statistics of Selected Closed-End Funds as of November 1986

Type and Fund Name	Net Assets (in millions)	Price	Discount or Premium
Diversified Common Stock			
Lehman	$ 811	$16.00	− 5.3%
Tri-Continental	1,213	30.63	− 4.9
Zweig Fund	281	10.00	+ 7.3
Fixed-Income			
Ellsworth Convertible	42	10.25	+ 7.9
Lincoln Nat'l Convertible	85	15.88	+11.7
Sector Fund—Country			
First Australia	58	8.75	−18.3
France Fund	99	10.00	−23.7
Germany Fund	74	9.88	− 2.5
Italy Fund	74	10.50	−27.3
Japan Fund	515	15.88	−18.0
Korea Fund	130	31.50	+55.2
Mexico Fund	73	3.25	−29.2
Scandinavia Fund	60	7.00	−26.0
Sector Fund—Other			
First Financial	79	6.75	−22.8
Pilgrim Regional Bankshares	86	8.00	−15.8
Regional Financial Shares	86	7.75	− 9.4

Source: "Where's the Bargain?" *Forbes* (November 17, 1986): 268.

A relatively recent development is the proliferation of sector funds. Such funds limit investments to a part of the economy, as does the Pilgrim Regional Bankshares Fund, or to a particular country. The Japan Fund was created in 1962, and the other country funds shown on Table 16–1 were created in the 1980s. For example, the Mexico Fund was started in 1981, and the France and Italy Funds were first sold to the public as recently as 1986. The surge in the issuance of country-specific closed-end funds occurred as investors became more interested in the risk and return benefits of global investing.

Price Determination

The price of the shares of a closed-end investment company is determined by the forces of supply and demand in the marketplace. The market price will only by coincidence equal the net asset value per share. In fact, many closed-end investment companies sell at discounts from net asset value as can be seen from Table 16–1. Of the sixteen closed-end investment companies listed on this table, only four sell at a premium to net asset value and some sell at a deep discount from net asset values.

The quality of the net asset value figure appears to be an important factor in the size of the discount. *Quality* relates to the ability of the closed-end investment company to obtain a given value upon liquidation of the holdings in its portfolio. Large blocks of stocks and securities with no active markets or relatively inactive (thin) markets may cause large discounts from net asset value. This liquidity explanation probably explains part of the discount noted on Table 16–1 for the France, Italy, and Scandinavia funds. The massive premium noted on Table 16–1 for the Korea Fund also relates to the nature of that market. In the case of Korea, tightly enforced Korean governmental restrictions limit the access of foreign investors to the Korean stock market. Therefore, individuals who want to participate in the robust growth of the Korean economy have to use an investment company. The result is that the shares of the Korea Fund have been bid up to a sizable premium. In the case of country funds, the risk of exchange rate fluctuations unfavorable to the investment position may also cause a deep discount.

Should investors buy closed-end funds simply because they are selling at a discount? Should investors purchase new issues of closed-end funds? Both of these questions address the topic of how persistent closed-end fund discounts are and when premiums will appear. A closed-end fund that is selling at a discount may not achieve its net asset value in the future and may never produce a premium. Rex Thompson found that from 1940 to 1971, an investor buying closed-end investment companies at a premium would have lost approximately 8 percent relative to a comparable risky combination of NYSE stocks.[1] However, he found that buying closed-end investment companies at a constant 20 percent discount would have resulted in a relatively high risk-adjusted return. New issues of closed-end funds automatically sell for a premium when they are issued. The Zweig Fund, for example, went public at $10 a share with an underwriting fee of 6.5 percent, or $.65. This underwriting fee resulted in a net asset value for the Zweig Fund of $9.35 a share immediately following the completion of the initial offering. One would expect this closed-end investment company to eventually sell at a discount unless Martin Zweig exhibits exceptional performance in his management of this fund.

Capital Structure

Although open-end investment companies generally do not have senior securities such as bonds or preferred stock in their capital structure, closed-end investment companies are allowed by the Investment Company Act of 1940 to issue bonds and preferred stock up to the legal limits. Asset coverage following the sale of a senior security must be at least 300 percent if a bond is issued and 200 percent if a preferred stock is issued. A provision also restricts dividend declarations if the asset coverages fall below the minimums required. Thus, to classify closed-end investment companies into those that are levered by the issuance of a senior security and those that have not issued senior securities and remain unlevered is possible.

1. Rex Thompson, "The Information Content of Discounts and Premiums on Closed-End Funds," *Journal of Financial Economics*, June/September 1978, pp. 165–8.

Over the years, investment companies have developed many ways to accommodate the desires of investors. This section discusses the more important features developed because their presence or absence may be significant.

Accumulation, Withdrawal, and Reinvestment Plans

An *accumulation plan* allows the investor to make periodic, noncontractual purchases of investment company shares. After a stipulated initial investment, payments may be sent to the fund at any time to purchase additional shares at the existing net asset value plus any applicable sales charges. These periodic payments may need to be of a certain dollar size.

Along with the accumulation plan, some load funds have two other features known as the *letter of intent* and the *right of accumulation discount.* With a letter of intent, an investor planning to purchase more than a specified dollar amount of fund shares within a thirteen-month period may receive reduced sales commissions that apply to all purchases within the letter-of-intent period. Letters of intent usually include provisions for retroactive sales charge adjustments if the investor eventually qualifies for lower sales charges. A letter of intent may normally be terminated by the shareholder at any time. The right of accumulation discount allows an investor to combine the value of existing holdings with the amount of the current purchase in order to determine the loading fee applicable to the purchase.

Withdrawal plans allow an investor whose account has a minimum specified dollar value to request that monthly or quarterly payments be sent from the fund. These plans are often used as a means of supplementing other sources of retirement income, although withdrawal plans do not provide a guaranteed annuity. If payments cannot be made from the fund's dividends, shares in the account are redeemed to make up the difference. In declining markets, these redemptions could deplete an investment account.

A fund shareholder might elect to have dividends and capital gains paid in cash or *reinvested* at the existing net asset value. Many shareholders who do not need current income elect to have the fund reinvest for them at net asset value. Loading fees are normally not charged on these reinvestments.

Keogh Plans, Individual Retirement Accounts, and Group Investment Plans

Keogh plans are designed to assist self-employed persons in providing for their retirement years, with a tax deferral privilege as the main incentive. Individuals may use investment company shares as one of the qualifying investment alternatives and are allowed to contribute a portion of their income from self-employed activities to an investment company under the Custodial Agreement required by the act. Income taxes on these contributions are deferred until the individual receives payment from the fund or other qualifying alternative at retirement. Individual Retirement Accounts (IRAs) provide a tax-deferral investment retirement plan for qualifying individuals, and investment company shares may also be used for these investments.

Investment companies typically charge either a small fee upon opening these special accounts or an annual maintenance fee or both. Some mutual funds charge a small fee for each distribution under the plan. Many mutual funds have corporate pension and profit sharing plans, which have been approved by the Internal Revenue Service. Corporate contributions to these plans on behalf of the participants quality as a tax-deductible expense for the corporation. All contributions accumulate dividend income and capital gains, the taxes on which are deferred until retirement.

Exchange Provisions

If two or more funds are managed by the same management group, such as the Rochester Funds in Exhibit 16–2, investors will normally be allowed to *exchange* shares of one fund in the group for shares of another fund in the group. As a result of improved technology and marketing considerations, investment companies often allow telephone transfers through the use of a toll-free number. The exchange takes place at net asset value, although a small service fee is sometimes charged. Restrictions may require that the shares to be exchanged have been held a specified length of time or have a specified dollar value.

To what extent should investors use the telephone exchange capabilities of mutual fund management groups? The answer to this question depends on whether or not investors are good market timers. Trying to pick "hot" funds or decide when to make substantial shifts of money from common stocks to fixed-income securities and vice versa are high-risk transactions at which many investors may not excel. Additionally, the ease of buying and selling shares over the telephone may well induce actions inconsistent with long-run investment strategies involving fundamental value considerations.

Performance Evaluation

The evaluation of the typical investment company is similar in concept to the evaluation of any investment portfolio. The rate of return determination requires not only beginning and ending market values but also income and capital gains distributions made during the period. The formula for determining the rate of return is as follows:

$$\text{Rate of return} = \frac{(\text{NAVeop} - \text{NAVbop}) + \text{Income dividends} + \text{Capital dividends}}{\text{NAVbop}}$$

where NAVbop and NAVeop are the net asset values at the beginning and at the end of the evaluation period, respectively.

Using data in the Wiesenberger write-up for the Nicholas Fund shown in Exhibit 16–3, the rate of return for 1985 can be calculated as follows:

$$ROR = \frac{(32.18 - 25.84) + .575 + .61}{25.84} = .291, \text{ or } 29.1\%$$

Performance Criteria

We can evaluate mutual funds on the basis of the following four performance criteria: (1) diversification, (2) maintenance of the risk level desired, (3) selection of undervalued securities or "picking winners," and (4) market projections.

Diversification

Without exception, every study that has considered diversification has found that funds do an excellent job of eliminating diversifiable risk. Clearly, an investor who is unable to purchase the ten to fifteen securities required to substantially eliminate diversifiable risk will be able to achieve the required diversification through the purchase of a mutual fund.

Risk Level

The majority of the evidence regarding risk level tends to suggest that the actual risk level is generally consistent with the fund's stated policy toward risk. A fund that claims to invest in growth stocks will generally have a beta greater than one. The fund that maintains that it is an income fund will generally have a low beta. However, this observation cannot be taken as law because a good deal of variation exists.

Table 16–2 shows performance results for no-load and full-load funds for time periods of five and ten years. These returns are generally consistent with the notion that risk for a mutual fund is what it is advertised to be. For the full-load funds during the ten-year period, where the time is sufficient for measurement and the number of funds large enough for statistical reliability, a steadily declining rate of return can be noted as one goes from aggressive growth funds to income funds.

Security Selection

With regard to picking winners, we can be virtually certain that funds do not consistently outperform randomly selected portfolios of equivalent risk. Empirical evidence suggests that only a few investors have been able to select securities that generate an above-average, risk-adjusted re-

NICHOLAS FUND, INC.

Nicholas Fund was organized as the Nicholas Strong Fund in July 1968 and in August of the same year acquired the assets of Bradley Investment Club, a private investment partnership. Initial public offering of its shares was on July 14, 1969. The present name was adopted in 1974. Under the same management is Nicholas Income Fund and Nicholas II, Inc. The fund's investment policy stresses capital appreciation as an objective, with income a secondary consideration. Investments for the most part will be in common stocks.

At the end of calendar 1985, the fund had 42.7% of its assets in net cash and equivalent, 0.7% in senior securities and 56.6% in common stocks. Major industry representations in common stock investments were banks & savings & loan (7.6% of assets), insurance (7.2%), consumer products (6.9%), energy (6.4%) and health care (4.7%). The largest common stock commitments were Combined International (1.4% of assets), Pic 'n Save and First Union Corp. (1.3% each) and Community Psychiatrics and Dillard Department Stores (1.2% each). The rate of portfolio turnover in the latest fiscal year was 13.8% of average assets. Unrealized appreciation in the portfolio at the calendar year-end was 16.2% of total net assets.

Special Services: A voluntary accumulation plan requires an initial investment of $500; subsequent investments may be $100 or more. Automatic dividend reinvestment is available; fractional shares resulting from reinvestment may be paid in cash, at the option of the fund. Shares of the fund may be exchanged at net asset value for those of Nicholas Income Fund and Nicholas II Inc. A Keogh plan and Individual Retirement Account plan are available.

Statistical History

	AT YEAR-ENDS							ANNUAL DATA				
					% of Assets in							
Year	Total Net Assets ($)	Number of Shareholders	Net Asset Value Per Share ($)	Yield (%)	Cash & Equivalent	Bonds & Preferreds	Common Stocks	Income Dividends ($)	Capital Gains Distribution ($)	Expense Ratio (%)	Offering Price ($) High	Low
1985	764,895,215	85,287	32.18	1.8	43	1	56	0.575	0.61	0.82	32.26	25.57
1984	214,963,888	19,694	25.84	3.0	24	—	76	0.828	1.39	0.87	26.43	21.62
1983	163,689,636	16,216	25.84	2.4	19	—	81	0.638	1.074	0.95	27.48	22.10
1982	97,841,141	10,409	22.28	2.6	26	—	74	0.615	1.014	1.03	22.39	15.18
1981	59,813,152	8,504	18.12	2.8	22	—	78	0.522	0.835	1.06	19.81	16.17
1980	54,261,168	7,754	17.91	2.2	11	—	89	0.389	—	1.11	18.18	11.51
1979	48,516,830	8,572	13.64	2.3	16	—	84	0.31	—	1.04	13.64	10.67
1978	40,310,846	9,500	10.69	1.7	9	—	91	0.184	—	1.01	12.11	8.13
1977	39,580,413	10,944	8.68	0.8	27	1	72	0.07	—	1.00	8.69	6.83
1976	34,256,757	10,700	7.28	0.4	10	—	90	0.03	—	1.01	7.28	5.98
1975	37,832,765	13,600	5.96	0.8	6	—	94	0.051	—	1.08	6.76	4.09

Note: Figures adjusted for 2-for-1 split effective 6/15/79.

Directors: Albert O. Nicholas, Pres. and Treas.; Robert H. Bock; Melvin L. Schultz; Richard Seaman.

Investment Adviser: Nicholas Company, Inc. Compensation to the Adviser is 0.75% annually on the first $50 million of average monthly net assets, 0.65% on assets over $50 million.

Custodian, Transfer And Dividend Disbursing Agent: First Wisconsin Trust Company, Milwaukee, WI.

Distributor: None; shares are sold directly by the fund.

Sales Charge: None. Minimum purchase is $500; subsequent purchase must be at least $100. There is a redemption fee of 1% on shares held 90 days or less.

Distribution Plan: (12b-1) None.

Dividends: Income dividends and capital gains, if any, are paid annually within two months after the close of the fund's fiscal year.

Shareholder Reports: Issued quarterly. Fiscal year ends March 31. The current prospectus was effective in July.

Qualified for Sale: In all states and DC.

Address: 700 N. Water St., Milwaukee, WI 53202.

Telephone: (414) 272-6133.

An assumed investment of $10,000 in this fund, with capital gains accepted in shares and income dividends reinvested, is illustrated below. The explanation in the introduction to this section must be read in conjunction with this illustration.

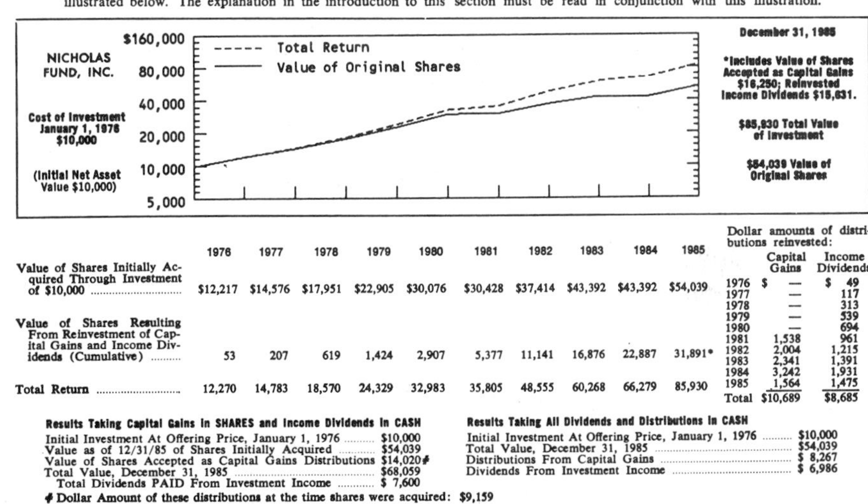

	1976	1977	1978	1979	1980	1981	1982	1983	1984	1985
Value of Shares Initially Acquired Through Investment of $10,000	$12,217	$14,576	$17,951	$22,905	$30,076	$30,428	$37,414	$43,392	$43,392	$54,039
Value of Shares Resulting From Reinvestment of Capital Gains and Income Dividends (Cumulative)	53	207	619	1,424	2,907	5,377	11,141	16,876	22,887	31,891*
Total Return	12,270	14,783	18,570	24,329	32,983	35,805	48,555	60,268	66,279	85,930

Dollar amounts of distributions reinvested:

	Capital Gains	Income Dividends
1976	$ —	$ 49
1977	—	117
1978	—	313
1979	—	539
1980	—	694
1981	1,538	961
1982	2,004	1,215
1983	2,341	1,391
1984	3,242	1,931
1985	1,564	1,475
Total	$10,689	$8,685

Results Taking Capital Gains in SHARES and Income Dividends in CASH

Initial Investment At Offering Price, January 1, 1976	$10,000
Value as of 12/31/85 of Shares Initially Acquired	$54,039
Value of Shares Accepted as Capital Gains Distributions	$14,020#
Total Value, December 31, 1985	$68,059
Total Dividends PAID From Investment Income	$ 7,600

Dollar Amount of these distributions at the time shares were acquired: $9,159

Results Taking All Dividends and Distributions in CASH

Initial Investment At Offering Price, January 1, 1976	$10,000
Total Value, December 31, 1985	$54,039
Distributions From Capital Gains	$ 8,267
Dividends From Investment Income	$ 6,986

Source: Wiesenberger Investment Companies Service, division of Warren, Gorham & Lamont, Inc.

Table 16–2
Investment Company Rates of Return, by Load Status and Time Period

Nature of Fund	**Five Years Ended 9/30/86** *No-Load*	*Full-Load*	**Ten Years Ended 9/30/86** *No-Load*	*Full-Load*
Aggressive growth	14.19 (6)*	17.50 (17)	18.26 (6)	17.25 (14)
Growth	17.12 (55)	17.41 (75)	16.05 (45)	15.69 (68)
Growth and income	19.91 (16)	19.07 (40)	14.12 (11)	14.37 (37)
Balanced	19.83 (3)	20.75 (12)	12.38 (2)	13.86 (10)
Income	20.17 (10)	18.32 (22)	15.66 (8)	13.47 (17)
Other				
International	24.80 (3)	22.02 (11)	17.51 (1)	16.60 (7)
Small company	14.44 (6)	12.15 (7)	18.73 (6)	17.60 (3)
Specialty	16.57 (7)	6.87 (9)	16.38 (5)	12.04 (5)
All-Average	17.77	17.66	16.06	15.13

*Numbers in parentheses indicate the number of funds in the category.

Source: Wall Street Journal (December 1, 1986): 7D.

turn, commonly measured by Jensen's *alpha*. This alpha is the same as the alpha derived from the characteristic line, except the risk-free return has been subtracted from both the portfolio and market returns. In general, investment company managers have not picked winners. Some evidence implies that low beta funds have a positive alpha and high beta funds have a negative alpha, but the evidence is weak. In essence, outperforming the market on a risk-adjusted basis by purchasing mutual funds does not appear to be a reasonable investment outcome.

Market Projections

Mutual funds apparently are not able to predict the market and adjust the risk level accordingly. Superior or inferior market timing should result in a *characteristic line* that is curved instead of linear. Figure 16–1 shows hypothetical curved characteristic lines along with other characteristic line configurations. Empirical studies find no such curvature suggesting that fund managements did not make superior market predictions. However, the data do not tell us whether the average performance observed was due to average market predictions or an inability to act on any superior predictions actually made.

Other Investor Considerations

In considering the performance record of an investment company, investors should consider the size of the fund and its operating characteristics.

Figure 16–1
Hypothetical Mutual Funds Characteristic Lines

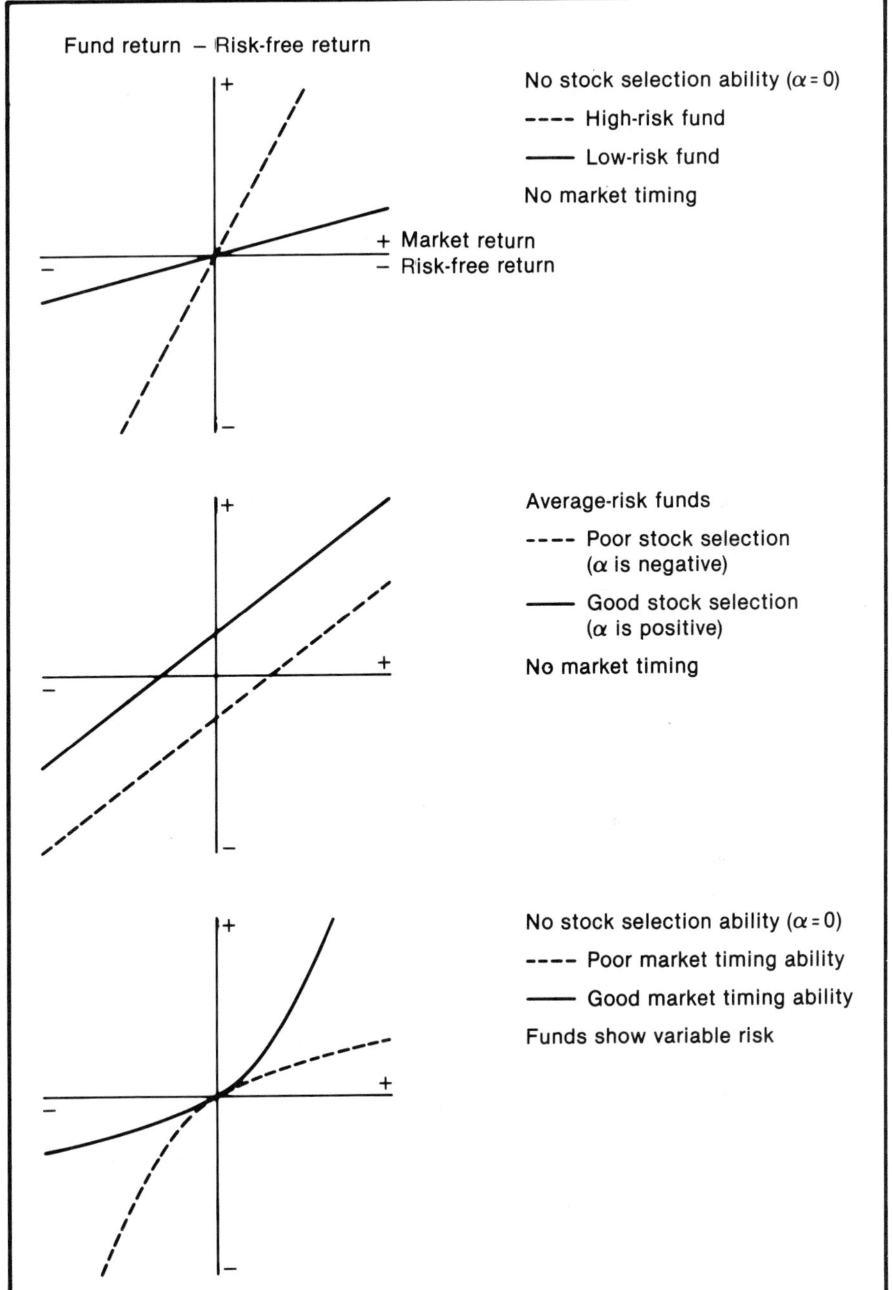

Size

What is the ideal size of an investment company? Can funds be too large or too small? What has been the performance of small funds as opposed to large funds? These are important questions for the potential investment company investor.

Small funds may have problems recruiting and retaining a competent managerial staff. A fund with $10 million in assets at an annual investment advisory fee of ¾ percent will have only $75,000 to support its activities. This will not hire many competent financial specialists. Other expenses for small funds tend to be proportionately high. While small funds may have considerable market trading flexibility, their transactions may not be large enough to qualify for substantial discounts on brokerage commissions. Small funds may also have high *portfolio turnover* rates. The brokerage fees resulting from trading activity impact directly on investment performance.

Large funds also have their managerial problems. The main problems result from the need to invest large sums of money in individual stocks. Large blocks of stock may be difficult to acquire and dispose of at a price reasonably close to the current market price. Large funds, when they do take positions in small securities, may only be able to invest a relatively small percentage of the total assets of the fund so that performance is not really affected very much even if the small company's stock does well in the market. On the positive side, large funds have the advantage of large research staffs, lower brokerage costs, and economies of scale in operating costs and management advisory fees.

Operating Expenses

Potential fund shareholders should determine whether the fund is managed in such a way that its operating expense ratio is consistent with funds of comparable size. Consider the Nicholas Fund in regard to the expense ratio. Exhibit 16–3 reports its expense ratio at .86 percent of net assets for 1985. According to the *Forbes* annual mutual fund issue of September 8, 1986, the expense ratio for no-load mutual funds in the over $300 million asset category range from a low of .51 to a high of 1.30 (if one excludes the Vanguard Index Trust at .28 and another statistical outlier at 2.10). The mean expense ratio is .84. The Nicholas Fund is just above the mean and seems to manage its expenses reasonably well. An investor who is satisfied that the fund will provide good performance and who is happy with its investment philosophy might choose to invest in this fund.

A Performance Appraisal

A brief example of measuring mutual fund performance will demonstrate the general nature of our conclusions. During the period from 1972 through 1986, The Nicholas Fund increased 361 percent in value compared to only 333 percent for the S&P 500. Did the Nicholas Fund per-

Figure 16–2
Nicholas Fund Performance, 1972–86

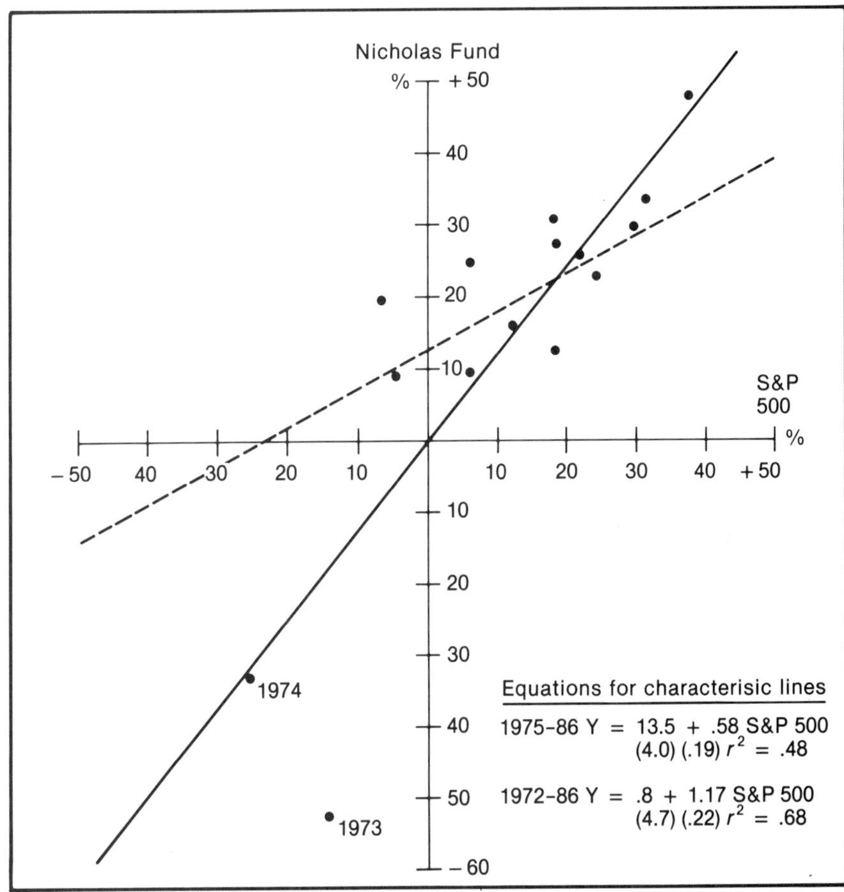

form well? Perhaps it did. To tell for sure, we must make a risk-adjusted performance evaluation.

Figure 16–2 shows the Nicholas Fund's characteristic line for the 1972–86 period, based on the annual returns from the fund and for the S&P 500 index.[2] The fund's beta was 1.17, which makes it more risky than the market. However, the standard error of the beta was .22, suggesting the "real" beta probably falls within a range of .73 to 1.61 (plus or minus two standard deviations of the beta estimate). For practical purposes, Nicholas is equal in risk to the market.

Nicholas did a fair job in eliminating diversifiable risk, as indicated by the coefficient of determination of .68. Thirty-two percent of the fluctuations in Nicholas's return were due to lack of diversification. This fund could be combined with other assets in a portfolio to achieve more complete diversification.

2. The characteristic line can be calculated using returns either adjusted or unadjusted for the risk-free rate. R_f is not subtracted from either the Nicholas Fund returns or the S&P 500 returns in Figure 16–2.

Regarding the possibility of superior security selection or market prediction, the regression analysis indicates an alpha of .78 percent. Recall that average performance would be indicated by an alpha of zero (if beta equals 1). However, a conclusion of superior performance is unwarranted because the actual value for alpha is not statistically significant from zero, as indicated by the standard error of 4.7 percent for alpha. On the basis of picking winners for this fifteen-year period, Nicholas did no better and no worse than the average, for all practical purposes.

A problem in evaluating characteristic line performance is indicated on Figure 16–2. In addition to the characteristic line for the fifteen-year period, 1972–1986, the characteristic line for the twelve-year period, 1975–1986 is shown. The slope and the intercept (alpha) for the twelve-year characteristic line are quite different from those of the fifteen-year line. Which is representative of the future performance of this fund? The beta for the 1975–1986 period is only .58 versus a beta of 1.17 for the 1972–1986 period. In addition, the alpha of 13.5 for the twelve-year period represents a statistically significant excess return above the equilibrium alpha of 3.4 (that is: $R_f(1 - \text{beta}) = 8.2(1 - .58) = 3.4\%$). The principal difference between these two periods is the results for 1973 and 1974. The poor performance of the Nicholas Fund in 1973, when it declined 53 percent versus only a 15 percent decline for the market, is discouraging as well as being crucial for the regression results. Could history a la 1973 repeat itself for the Nicholas Fund?

Summary

Investment companies exist in so many different forms and have such differing investment objectives that an investor should be able to find an appropriate fund after a reasonable amount of searching. For investors whose resources are too small to allow adequate diversification or to make stock purchases large enough to avoid paying relatively high brokerage commissions, investment companies may be the solution. Investment companies may also be attractive to an investor unable to analyze individual stocks or to assume the risks of direct stock ownership.

Special features have been developed by investment companies over the years to accommodate the desires of the investing public. Most mutual funds have a voluntary accumulation plan, which allows the investor to make periodic payments to the fund. Many mutual funds have withdrawal plans, allowing the investor to obtain periodic payments from the fund to supplement other sources of income. In addition, most mutual funds have qualified as tax-deferred pension plan alternatives. All of these special features make many investment companies especially attractive to some investors.

Before an investor purchases the shares of any investment company, a careful analysis of the most recent annual report and prospectus should be undertaken. Investors must make practical decisions regarding the size of the investment company, the reasonableness of the expense ratio, the proper investment objective, and the desirability of a load fund as opposed to a no-load fund. Many of these practical decisions relate directly to the risk preference of the investor.

A portfolio approach should be taken to evaluate the performance of an investment company. An annual rate of return can be calculated by considering changes in the net asset value of the investment company and any dividends (either income or capital) declared by the investment company. To compare the performance of one investment company against other investment companies, the investor needs to develop a risk-adjusted return analysis.

Suggested Readings

ALEXANDER, GORDON J., GEORGE BENSON, and CAROL E. EGER. "Timing Decisions and the Behavior of Mutual Fund Systematic Risk." *Journal of Financial and Quantitative Analysis* (November 1982): 5479–602.

BOUDREAUX, KENNETH J. "Discounts and Premiums on Closed-End Mutual Funds: A Study in Valuation." *Journal of Finance* (May 1973): 515–22.

CALDERWOOD, STANFORD. "The Truth About Index Funds." *Financial Analysts Journal* (July–August 1977): 36–47.

CHANG, ERIC C., and WILBUR LEWELLEN. "Market Timing and Mutual Fund Investment Performance." *Journal of Business* (January 1984): 57–72.

JENSEN, MICHAEL. "The Performance of Mutual Funds in the Period 1945–1964." *Journal of Finance* (May 1968): 389–416.

KON, STANLEY J. "The Market-Timing Performance of Mutual Fund Managers." *Journal of Business* (July 1983): 323–47.

KON, STANLEY J., and FRANK C. JEN. "The Investment Performance of Mutual Funds: An Empirical Investigation of Timing, Selectivity, and Market Efficiency." *Journal of Business* (April 1979): 263–89.

LEHMAN, BRUCE N., and DAVID M. MODEST. "Mutual Fund Performance Evaluation: A Comparison of Benchmarks and Benchmark Comparisons." *Journal of Finance* (June 1987): 233–65.

MALKIEL, BURTON G. "The Valuation of Closed-End Investment-Company Shares." *Journal of Finance* (June 1977): 847–59.

RICHARDS, R. MALCOLM, DONALD R. FRASER, and JOHN C. GROTH. "Winning Strategies with Closed-end Funds." *Journal of Portfolio Management* (Fall 1980): 50–55.

ROENFELDT, RODNEY L., and DONALD L. TUTTLE. "An Examination of the Discounts and Premiums of Closed-End Investment Companies." *Journal of Business Research* (Fall 1978): 129–40.

THOMPSON, REX. "The Informational Content of Discounts and Premiums on Closed-End Fund Shares." *Journal of Financial Economics* (June–September 1978): 151–186.

TREYNOR, JACK L. "How to Rate Management of Investment Funds." *Harvard Business Review* (January–February 1965): 63–75.

TREYNOR, JACK L., and KAY K. MAZUY. "Can Mutual Funds Outguess the Market?" *Harvard Business Review* (July–August 1966): 131–36.

Questions

1. Why have investment companies had good asset growth in the past twenty-five years?
2. Discuss the areas of investment company performance evaluation, and outline how you would go about making a performance appraisal.
3. What is the value of an exchange provision for a potential mutual fund purchaser?
4. Distinguish between
   (a) open-end and closed-end investment companies
   (b) net asset value and price for investment companies
   (c) load and no-load funds
5. Why has it become increasingly more difficult for investors to find true no-load mutual funds?
6. How may investors use the withdrawal plans offered by mutual funds?
7. Why do you think the closed-end investment company format has been used so extensively for developing portfolios of the securities of firms in a single country (i.e., the Italy Fund) for sale to investors?
8. What are the factors that appear to explain the premiums or discounts that closed-end investment companies have relative to their net asset values?
9. Discuss why the following might influence mutual fund performance:
   (a) company size
   (b) operating expenses and portfolio turnover
   (c) load fee
   (d) risk class
10. Certain mutual funds belong to a category of funds known as closed-up funds. These funds originally had a continuous sale and redemption of shares to anyone interested in purchasing them. However, when they reached a predetermined size, sales were suspended except for sales to current shareholders. What would be the motivating factor(s) for closing-up a fund?
11. What factors have resulted in the growth of investor interest in index funds?
12. Discuss the performance of the following fund:

Characteristic line: $Y = \underset{(.82)}{2.04} + \underset{(.30)}{1.29}\ \text{S\&P 500} \qquad r^2 = .64$

Reward-to-risk ratio: fund = .13
market = .10

Problems

1. Sara Gray has heard that common stock returns have been close to 10 percent over long periods of time. She has been investing in the Universe Investors Fund for several years in anticipation of retirement.

   At the close of 1983, Sara decided to stop making payments and established an annual withdrawal plan with the fund. Universe Investors makes this plan available without charge to accounts valued at $10,000 or more. Sara's account is valued at $60,000 at Universe Investors' 1983 year-end asset value of $10.68 per share.

   Sara instructs Universe Investors Fund to send her $6,000 annually beginning with December 31, 1983. She feels that her principal should remain reasonably intact if the fund can earn close to 10 percent annually in the future.

   The following figures show the record of Universe Investors since Sara established her withdrawal plan.

Year-End NAV per Share	
1984	$7.51
1985	5.31
1986	5.50
1987	6.07

   No capital gains distributions were made during the 1984–87 period. Modest income dividends were paid, but they may be ignored since they do not significantly alter the performance results of the fund.

   (a) Calculate the value of Sara's account at the end of each year under the withdrawal plan she set up after she had withdrawn her $6,000

   (b) Why do you think Sara's account fared the way it has?

   (c) Has Sara gained any benefits by establishing the withdrawal plan?

2. The Keystone Group allows holders of shares to exchange them for shares of any other fund managed by the group for a $5 service fee. A record of the year-end net asset values of K–1 and K–2 is shown in the following table:

	Net Asset Value			Net Asset Value	
Year-End	K–1 (Income)	K–2 (Growth)	Year-End	K–1 (Income)	K–2 (Growth)
1976	7.84	5.27	1981	7.25	5.96
1977	7.46	4.89	1982	8.19	7.18
1978	7.15	5.07	1983	8.95	7.37
1979	7.19	5.69	1984	8.08	6.18
1980	7.54	7.02	1985	9.26	7.65

   If an investor owned the growth fund at the end of 1976, would an exchange between K–1 and K–2 have been advantageous during the 1976–85 period? Under an optimal exchange arrangement with exchanges made at year-end (no exchanges may be optimal), how would an investor with $10,000 in K–2 at year-end 1976 fare relative to another investor making no exchanges but retaining a position in K–2? You may ignore the $5 exchange fee for ease of calculation.

3. The Japan Fund is a large, closed-end investment company. During October 1985, Lewis purchased 1,000 shares of the Japan Fund paying 11¾ per share when the net asset value per share was 13.68. At the beginning of 1987, the Japan Fund was selling for 15 but the net asset value had risen to 20.27. The graph in Figure P16–1 shows the market price premium or discount above the fund's net asset value for the period January 1981 through February 1987.
   (a) Lewis does not understand what happened to his investment and asks you to help provide an explanation.
   (b) In 1987, the directors of the Japan Fund asked the shareholders to vote on a proposal to convert the Japan Fund from a closed-end to an open-end mutual fund. Should Lewis vote for or against the proposal?
   (c) On July 31, 1987, Lewis sold his shares of the Japan Fund for 21¾ per share. The net asset value per share was 22.89. Ignoring the transaction costs, how well did the Japan Fund perform for Lewis over the investment period, October 1985 through July 1987?
   (d) On August 14, 1987, the Japan Fund became open-ended at 23.49 net asset value per share. Ignoring transaction costs, how much would Lewis have gained by waiting for the fund to become open ended?

Figure P16–1
Japan Fund Premium/Discount: January 1981 through February 1987

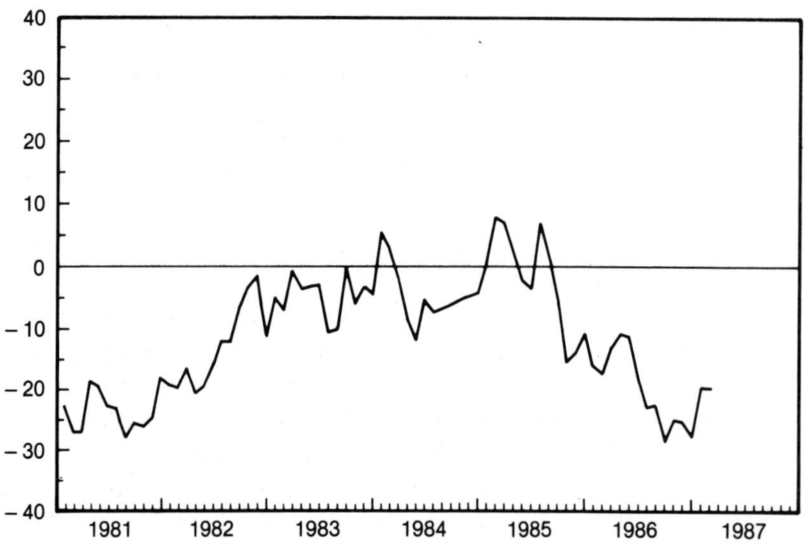

Table P16–1

	Acorn Fund	Founders Special Fund	Pioneer Fund	Market
1973	−22%	−19%	−3%	−15%
1974	−27	−20	−17	−26
1975	31	1	38	37
1976	65	17	37	24
1977	18	14	4	−7
1978	17	7	12	7
1979	50	53	28	18
1980	31	52	31	32
1981	−7	−13	−3	−5
1982	18	30	13	21
1983	25	23	25	22
1984	4	−12	−1	6
1985	32	15	26	32

Table P16–2

	Zeus Fund	Market
1972	21.4%	19.0%
1973	−11.4	−14.7
1974	−28.3	−26.5
1975	18.7	37.2
1976	14.4	23.8
1977	−7.4	−7.2
1978	8.8	6.6
1979	17.2	18.4
1980	27.9	32.4
1981	−6.0	−4.9
1982	14.6	21.4
1983	15.8	22.5
1984	.2	6.3
1985	29.9	32.2
1986	18.6	18.5

4. Given the data in Table P16–1 for the Acorn Fund, the Founders Special Fund, and the Pioneer Fund, do a performance evaluation of the results they have achieved.

5. The annual performance of the Zeus Fund for the 1972–86 period is given in Table P16–2.

(a) Examine this performance for the 1972–76 period, the 1977–82 period, the 1983–86 period, and for the entire fourteen-year period. As part of your evaluation, determine how much an initial investment of $10,000 would be worth at the end of each period for both the fund and the market.

(b) In your opinion, what happened to the performance of the Zeus Fund for the years of 1975, 1976, 1982, 1983, and 1984?

(c) What would you expect the performance of the Zeus Fund to have been in 1987 assuming the market return is 25 percent?

6. In June 1983, George Diamond's broker brought the Keystone S–4 mutual fund to his attention. The fund was considered an aggressive stock fund seeking growth of capital, and the load fee on this fund had just been eliminated. However, in accordance with the 1980 SEC rule, Rule 12b-1, Keystone now deducts 1.25 percent annually from this fund's assets. This deduction is used to pay a 4 percent commission to brokers for new investments they bring to the fund. In addition, the broker gets .25 percent for each additional year the investor is in the fund. A contingent deferred sales charge may be imposed at the time of redemption for shares redeemed within four years. For example, 4 percent is charged if redemption occurs during the calendar year of purchase, but only 1 percent is charged during the third year following purchase.

   (a) Keystone S–4's performance, expressed as the total percentage change in net asset value for the period shown, is given in the following table. What impact does this performance record have on your decision to purchase this fund?

Period	**S–4**	**Open-End Fund Average**
Jan.–June 1983	72.7%	21.7%
1982	20.2%	25.3%
1978–82	173.0%	110.0%
1973–82	80.0%	125.5%

   (b) What is the impact on your decision regarding the annual percentage deduction rather than the former load fee?

   (c) What is the investment management impact of the contingent deferred sales fee upon redemption of shares? Is there any relationship between the fund's past performance and this new redemption fee?

7. Table P16–3 shows the statistical history for the Sentinel Common Stock Fund as listed in the 1985 Wiesenberger Mutual Fund Report.

Table P16–3
Statistical History

Annual Data					**At Year-Ends**		
Year	*Total Net Assets ($ million)*	*Number of Shareholders*	*Net Asset Value per Share ($)*	*Yield (%)*	*Income Dividends ($)*	*Capital Gains Distribution ($)*	*Expense Ratio (%)*
1984	340.5	25,541	17.01	4.6	.895	1.00	.72
1983	331.1	26,341	16.93	4.7	.915	.78	.71
1982	303.0	25,649	15.54	5.8	1.00	.37	.89
1981	265.0	27,550	13.18	6.5	.95	.31	.88
1980	282.7	30,550	13.64	5.5	.838	.40	.91

Source: 1985 Wiesenberger Mutual Fund Report, p. 480.

(a) Calculate the rate of return for the Sentinel Common Stock Fund for each year, 1981 through 1984.

(b) The fund's primary objective is to achieve long-term growth of capital; income is only a secondary consideration. Compare the performance of the Sentinel Common Stock Fund with that of the mutual funds shown in Problems 4 and 5 and of the S&P 500 index.

Chapter 17

Global Investing

Key Concepts

- American Depositary Receipt
- American share
- Association of International Bond Dealers
- Eurobond
- foreign exchange rate risk
- foreign-listed securities
- multinational corporation

Chapter Outline

Global investing is a way to participate in the growing economies of the world. Many economies around the world can either match or exceed the growth rate of the United States economy. More and more foreign firms have become competitive in the world marketplace. Some foreign firms have even established operations in the United States. Names such as Toyota, Sharp, TDK, and Michelin are well known to U.S. consumers. Improvements in communication and travel facilities have fostered better understanding of the world by Americans. This improved understanding and the trend toward the globalization of domestic business have motivated domestic investors to consider global financial markets. The sheer size of the non-U.S. equity and bond markets, as indicated in Table 17–1, is reason enough for considering international investments.

To accommodate the needs of internationally minded investors, many stock exchanges around the world have listed foreign company stocks for trading purposes. Hundreds of foreign firms have their shares traded on the NYSE, AMEX, and the OTC markets in the United States, and several hundred U.S. firms are listed on international exchanges such as the Toronto Stock Exchange, the London Stock Exchange, and the Bourse de Paris. Almost 50 percent of all stocks listed on the Amsterdam Stock Exchange are foreign companies. Thus, the global financial markets are increasingly interwoven. To add to this trend, recent technological advances have encouraged the NYSE and the London Stock Exchange to explore the possibility of linking the two exchanges electronically to provide better price information for traders. In 1983, the Japanese government approved adding a selective group of foreign brokerage firms as members of the Tokyo Stock Exchange. These recent events all point toward more integration of the world financial markets in the future.

Table 17–1
Estimated World Bond and Equity Markets, U.S. Dollars, 1986

	Bonds	% of Total	Equities	% of Total
U.S.	3,660	47.1	2,202	41.3
Non-U.S.	4,116	52.9	3,133	58.7
Japanese Yen	1,530	19.7	1,783	33.4
U.K. Sterling	232	3.0	384	7.2
Deutsche Mark	849	10.9	217	4.1
Canadian Dollar	147	1.9	163	3.1
French Franc	245	3.2	128	2.4
Italian Lira	382	4.9	112	2.1
Swiss Franc	106	1.4	97	1.8
Dutch Guilder	161	2.1	77	1.4
Australian Dollar	55	.7	69	1.3
All Other	409	5.3	103	1.9
Total	$7,776	100.0	$5,335	100.0

Source: Salomon Brothers, Inc., *Prospects for Financial Markets in 1987* (December 16, 1986): 22.

Figure 17–1
Risk Reduction from International Diversification

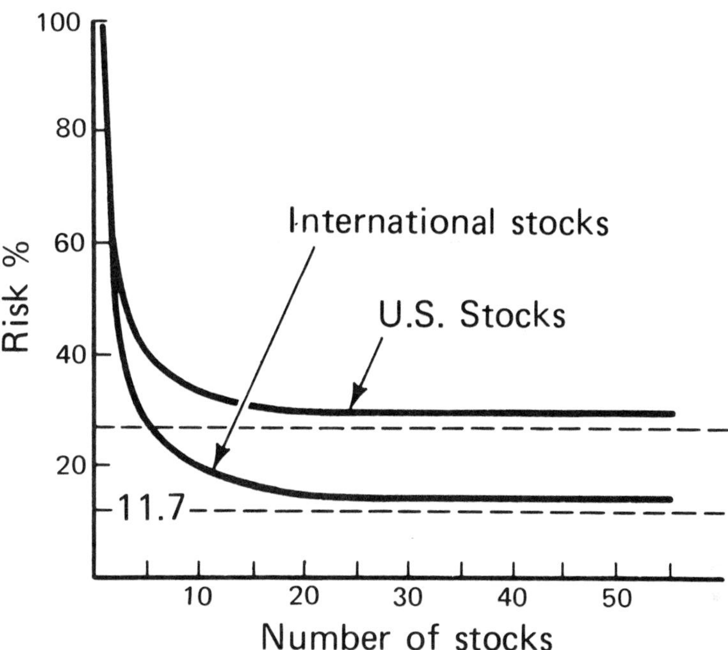

Source: Bruno H. Solnik, "Why Not Diversify Internationally Rather Than Domestically?" *Financial Analysts Journal* (July–August, 1974): 51.

Motives for Global Investing

A global investment for risk-minimizing investors was advocated almost twenty years ago. The recommendation was based on the simple notion of correlation between foreign stock prices and U.S. stock prices. Because the degree of correlation was low, many argued that U.S. investors could reduce their systematic investment risk by diversifying investments globally. A number of articles in recent years have addressed the potential benefits of international diversification. The general conclusion from all these studies is that important benefits may be gained. For example, Bruno Solnik writes:

> The gains from international diversification are substantial. In terms of variability of return an internationally well-diversified portfolio would be one-tenth as risky as a typical security and half as risky as a well-diversified portfolio of U.S. stocks (with the same number of holdings).[1]

Figure 17–1 shows the risk reduction achieved by Solnik by combining stocks from eight different countries compared to a portfolio con-

1. Bruno H. Solnik, "Why Not Diversify Internationally Rather Than Domestically?" *Financial Analysts Journal* (July–August 1974): 51.

Table 17–2
Returns for Equities, by Country

	Annual Returns (in U.S. Dollars)			
	Geometric Mean	*Arithmetic Mean*	*Standard Deviation*	*Terminal Wealth Index**
U.S. Equities	8.7%	10.2%	17.7%	5.78
Total Non-U.S. Equities	10.6	11.8	16.3	8.23
Japan	15.6	19.0	31.4	20.86
United Kingdom	10.0	14.7	33.6	7.39
Canada	10.7	12.1	17.5	8.47
Germany	8.3	10.1	19.9	5.32
Australia	9.8	12.2	22.8	7.12
France	6.2	8.1	21.4	3.56
Switzerland	10.2	12.5	22.9	7.74

*1959 = 1.00

Source: Roger G. Ibbotson, Richard C. Carr, and Anthony W. Robinson, "International Equity and Bond Returns," *Financial Analysts Journal* (July–August 1982): 65.

sisting of only U.S. stocks. The internationally diversified portfolio is constructed by assuming an equal chance of holding a security from eight different countries. The systematic risk from the internationally diversified portfolio is 11.7 percent compared to 27 percent for the portfolio consisting of only U.S. stocks.

A recent study of annual returns from investing in the equities and bonds traded in the United States and seventeen other countries confirms the general conclusions of Solnik. The study by Ibbotson, Carr, and Robinson covered the twenty-one-year period from 1960 through 1980.[2] They concluded that U.S. equities slightly underperformed the world equity market portfolio when adjusted for risk.

Table 17–2 presents some of the returns calculated by Ibbotson, Carr, and Robinson. This table shows the geometric mean, the arithmetic mean and its standard deviation, and the terminal wealth index, assuming that the investor started at 1.00 at the end of 1959. U.S. equities had a geometric mean of only 8.7 percent during this period compared to 10.6 percent for all non-U.S. equities. The standard deviation of the arithmetic return is slightly lower for non-U.S. equities, indicating a better risk-return combination in light of the better arithmetic return. The terminal wealth index is 8.23 for non-U.S. equities compared to only 5.78 for U.S. equities. Results are also presented for countries representing large portions of the world equity market. The returns available in the Japanese equity market stand out on Table 17–2, but one cannot assume the next two decades will produce comparable performance. Germany is the country whose equity market seems to provide about the same returns

2. Roger G. Ibbotson, Richard C. Carr, and Anthony W. Robinson, "International Equity and Bond Returns," *Financial Analysts Journal* (July–August 1982): 61–83.

Table 17–3
Correlation Matrix of Equity Returns, U.S. Dollars, 1960–80

	U.S. Equities	Non-U.S. Equities	Japan	United Kingdom	Canada	Germany	Australia	France	Switzerland
U.S. Equities	1.00								
Non-U.S. Equities	.67	1.00							
Japan	.22	.69	1.00						
United Kingdom	.62	.72	.17	1.00					
Canada	.71	.59	.23	.36	1.00				
Germany	.21	.47	.30	.26	−.04	1.00			
Australia	.70	.70	.18	.67	.58	.32	1.00		
France	.21	.65	.36	.43	.44	.27	.50	1.00	
Switzerland	.46	.64	.24	.45	.35	.70	.43	.44	1.00

Source: Roger G. Ibbotson, Richard C. Carr, and Anthony W. Robinson, "International Equity and Bond Returns," *Financial Analysts Journal* (July–August, 1982): 71.

and risk as the United States. France shows the lowest equity returns for those countries listed on the table. In fact, Italy had the lowest returns of all the countries examined in the study, with a geometric return of only 2.4 percent and a terminal wealth index of 1.63. The total market value of Italian equities amounted to only $25 billion, however, compared to $1,381 billion for the United States.

Table 17–3 presents the correlation matrix of the annual returns for U.S. equities, non-U.S. equities, and returns from seven countries other than the United States. A low correlation coefficient indicates risk-reducing potential. Not only did Japanese stocks provide high returns during the 1960–80 period, they also had a low correlation coefficient with returns from all the other countries shown. For example, the correlation between U.S. returns and Japanese returns was only .22. Of major significance is the fact that the correlation between the U.S. equity returns and non-U.S. equity returns was only .67, indicating that foreign securities added to a portfolio of U.S. holdings would provide some risk-reduction potential.

Global Equity and Bond Markets

Most U.S. investors are knowledgeable about the way domestic stock and bond markets operate. Many investors, however, are not well informed about foreign financial markets. The volume of trading in overseas markets has been growing significantly in recent years. The NYSE is still the largest stock exchange in the world in terms of total market capitalization and the number of securities listed. The Tokyo Stock Exchange ranks a close second, and the London Stock Market occupies a distant third place. In addition to these exchanges, many other financial markets exist around the world.

It is important for the global investor to know about the similarities and dissimilarities among the various foreign financial markets and those of the United States. Many foreign stock exchanges have unique attributes that may influence the way prices respond to buying and selling pressures. We will now compare the Tokyo Stock Exchange with the NYSE.

Tokyo and New York Stock Exchanges

Both the Tokyo and the New York stock exchanges account for a substantial portion of the securities traded in their respective countries. The Tokyo Stock Exchange (TSE) accounts for about 80 percent of all trading in Japan, with the remaining 20 percent shared by seven other exchanges. Initially founded in 1878, the TSE resumed trading in May 1949 following the end of World War II. Operations since 1949 have been conducted under a law modeled after the U.S. Securities Exchange Act of 1934.

About 1,500 companies are listed on the TSE. They are classified into approximately 1,000 in the first section and 500 in the second section. The listing requirements for the first section are somewhat stricter than for the second section, and the companies are more seasoned.

International companies are listed on the TSE. Only eleven non-Japanese corporations were quoted on the TSE at the end of 1984. This number jumped to fifty-two by the end of 1986 and will probably continue to increase. By comparison, fifty-nine foreign firms were listed on the NYSE.

Two major types of members trade on the TSE: Regular members, who buy and sell for their own accounts and the accounts of their clients, and Saitori members, who serve as intermediaries for regular members. Saitori members are unlike the marketmaking specialists on the NYSE in that they are unable to buy or sell for their own accounts, but receive a monthly commission from the regular members. About eighty-three securities firms own Regular memberships, and twelve firms are Saitori members. Each TSE member is allowed to have as many as ten floor traders.

Individual investors dominate trading activity in Japan, and they have shorter-term outlooks and more aggressive risk-reward trade-offs than large institutions. Odd-lot trading is allowed in Japan. Odd-lot shareholders are not issued stock certificates. Instead, their ownership is recorded on the company's books. Interested odd-lot owners may sell their shares back to the company at the prevailing market price.

Fixed brokerage commissions were eliminated in the United States in May 1975, but they are still in effect on the TSE. The commission schedule is as follows:

Less than Y200,000	Y2,500
Y200,000–1 million	1.25%
Y1 million–3 million	1.05% + Y2,500
Y3 million–5 million	.95% + Y5,000

Unlike the practice of the U.S. stock exchanges, the TSE has limits on daily price fluctuations. The size of the limit move on a stock depends on the price level of that stock. For example, the total daily fluctuation allowed is Y30 for a stock with a price level of less than Y100 per share, while the limit move is Y500 for a stock with a price per share that is between Y3,000 and Y5,000.

Some Japanese researchers have tested the efficient market hypothesis in Tokyo markets. The empirical test of informational efficiency revealed that stock prices in Japan did not respond to new information as fully and as instantaneously as they did in the United States. The TSE was found to be relatively efficient in an operational sense in that security buyers and sellers could obtain transaction services at a relatively low cost.

Eurobond Market

Eurobonds are bonds underwritten by an international syndicate of investment bankers and sold outside of the country of the currency in which it is denominated. A Eurobond denominated in West German marks, for instance, "taps the pool" of marks owned by investors who are not residents of West Germany. London merchant banks pioneered the concept of the Eurobond issue in the early 1960s, and London became the central market for these bonds. Many foreign governments, supranational organizations like the World Bank, and U.S. and foreign corporations have floated Eurobonds in the past. The size of the Eurobond market is estimated at over $500 billion. Institutional investors such as insurance companies, pension funds, central banks, and trust funds are the largest purchasers of Eurobonds.

Eurobonds have a number of special features that attract investors: (1) no withholding tax on interest, (2) higher yields than are often available on comparable domestic issues, (3) short maturities from five to ten years, (4) attractive sinking fund features, (5) issuance in bearer form, and sometimes (6) conversion features. The anonymity of the bearer form is often valuable to many wealthy investors residing in countries with lenient tax collection agencies.

Almost 65 percent of the existing Eurobonds are denominated in U.S. dollars. The West German mark, Japanese yen, and other major currencies account for the rest of the issues. In 1985, the Japanese Ministry of Finance attempted to internationalize the yen and allowed foreign firms doing business in Japan to float Eurobonds outside of Japan. American firms such as TRW, Sears, and Dow Chemical have sold Eurobonds in recent years.

Most Eurobonds are listed on the Luxembourg Exchange or some other recognized exchange. However, very little trading takes place on the floor of the exchanges because secondary trading is done primarily over the telephone between dealers around the world. Consistent with its historical development, most trading originates in London. Trading in Eurobonds has become more orderly and systematic since the formation of the *Association of International Bond Dealers* in 1974. The Association publishes market prices and yields for Eurobonds issues, which are reprinted in the *Financial Times* of London.

Eurobond investors usually receive interest and principal payments in a foreign currency, and exchange rate fluctuations can significantly influence investors' actual returns. Suppose that during October 1985 a U.S. investor purchased at par a Dow Chemical 7 percent Eurobond in the secondary market. Further assume that this bond was denominated in West German marks (DMs). At the time of the purchase, the mark was worth .387 dollars and a 1 million DM issue was worth $387,000. A year later, the mark was worth .498 dollars. The same bond could be sold, and the marks converted into $498,000. This 28.7 percent increase in the dollar value of the Dow Chemical Eurobond combined with the 7 percent coupon would result in an annual return of approximately 35 percent, assuming no change in market rates of interest. If the DM's value had declined, however, the investor would have suffered a foreign exchange loss instead of a gain.

Eurobonds are exposed to an element of default risk as well as to interest rate and *foreign exchange rate risk.* Eurobond investors generally do not rely heavily on bond rating services or detailed analyses of financial statements. Instead, they seem to depend on the general reputation of the issuer. Although many Eurobonds are rated by rating agencies, some issues do not want their ratings published. This is especially true for issuers with mediocre ratings.

Approaching Global Investments

Global investing can be accomplished in either a direct or an indirect manner. In the indirect method, investors effectively hire professional investment managers to perform the analysis and handle the transactions and custodial duties. This section first examines direct global investing and then considers indirect investing.

Direct Global Investments

Direct global investment has two basic forms. Investors can purchase (1) real assets located in foreign countries or (2) financial securities issued by foreign firms and governments either individually or in a portfolio. Our discussion considers only the direct purchase of financial securities of firms located in another country. Two basic methods may be used to purchase these securities. First, investors may purchase shares listed on a foreign stock exchange. Second, investors may purchase *American Depositary Receipts* (ADRs), or *American shares.* American shares are issued in the United States by a transfer agent acting on behalf of the foreign company.

Foreign-Listed Securities

Large institutional investors may purchase securities listed on a foreign stock exchange, but this is not recommended for smaller institutions and individuals because of a number of potential problems. For example, limits may exist on the amount that may be invested in a particular foreign security. The more important problems, however, arise from the transaction being conducted in a foreign currency. This involves the acquisition or sale of a foreign currency and the need to take physical delivery of the securities or arrange for custodial services. These transactions require specialized knowledge, and even those investors with such specialized knowledge are exposed to risk resulting from fluctuations in relative currency values. A hedging transaction in the foreign currency can reduce foreign exchange risk, but again, this requires specialized skills and may be expensive. Finally, tax problems may result because taxes may be collected in the foreign country as well as in the domestic country. A way to avoid many of the problems investors could encounter with foreign-listed securities is to purchase ADRs.

American Depositary Receipts

Many of the larger foreign companies have their shares traded either on a major U.S. securities exchange or in the U.S. over-the-counter market. Of the fifty-nine listed foreign stocks on the NYSE as of December 31, 1986, twenty-three were in the form of ADRs, including such companies as British Petroleum and Sony Corporation.

Guaranty Trust Company, the predecessor to the Morgan Guaranty Trust Company, first issued issued ADRs in 1927. ADRs look much like a standard stock certificate but actually represent shares of the foreign company being held by the bank issuing the ADRs. In essence, the foreign shares have been Americanized by the use of the ADR. ADRs may be issued by a bank when it perceives that sufficient investor interest in the particular stock will make the effort worthwhile.

The use of ADRs gives foreign shares good marketability, especially if they are actively traded on a major U.S. securities exchange. The list of firms with ADRs outstanding consists primarily of large foreign firms. However, size is no guarantee of performance. Investors must still analyze the investment merits of the firm whose ADRs are being considered. Global investing involves some expertise even if one purchases an ADR. Accounting variations from country to country, especially in the area of accounting reserves, may be a consideration. The role of the foreign government in its economy may be quite different from the role of the U.S.

government in the U.S. economy. Many commonly accepted financial ratios may have little use when applied to a foreign company. The capital structure of a foreign company may be quite different from that of a U.S. firm in the same industry. The influence of inflation and foreign exchange rate fluctuations may be more important in global investing, especially when the foreign firm has heavy export sales.

Indirect Global Investments

For many investors, an indirect approach to global investing is more practical than a direct approach involving either the purchase of physical assets or a financial security such as an ADR. We will discuss two indirect approaches to global investing: domestic multinational firms and investment companies involved with global investments.

Multinational Corporations

By purchasing the shares of a domestic firm operating in many foreign countries, investors may achieve many of the benefits of foreign investments made directly in real assets. In the years following World War II, many U.S. firms made substantial global capital expenditures, especially in such industries as petroleum, retailing, and drugs. The purchase of the common shares of domestic multinational firms reduces the need for obtaining expertise regarding the investment environment in foreign countries. Investors must identify firms having a significant international business and then examine the nature of the global sales of the firm to determine the risks involved. Is the capital investment in danger of being nationalized? Will adequate compensation be made if nationalization does occur? Is the foreign country experiencing unique problems with its economy? While questions of this type should be considered, one can also reduce the business risk by deliberately diversifying across U.S.-based multinational firms. Combining firms having few global sales with those firms having strong international business might also be desirable.

How is the investor to identify those firms having large global sales and profits? Some of the reference sources mentioned in Chapter 3 carry feature articles relating to global investments. Of course, just because a firm has global sales does not necessarily mean that these sales are profitable. In addition, the profitability of global business may change dramatically within a relatively short period of time.

Despite potential risks related to the unique problems of global investment, the indirect method of using U.S.-based multinational firms has several advantages for the investor. Most of these firms are listed on a major American stock exchange. This carries the benefits of marketability and liquidity. In addition, the global investments are handled by the management of the U.S.-based firm. One should be able to achieve reasonable international diversification if one gives some attention to the geographic and product mix of U.S.-based firms.

Investment Company Approach

Several open-end and closed-end investment companies exist that invest primarily in foreign securities. The various types of investment companies and the benefits of this institutional form of investing were discussed in detail previously. Exhibit 17–1 lists eight mutual funds and two closed-end investment companies one might want to consider for direct foreign investing. Both closed-end investment companies are listed on the New York Stock Exchange.

The purchaser of shares in an investment company shown in Exhibit 17–1 obtains the general benefits associated with investment companies. Special consideration needs to be given, however, to the portfolio composition of an investment company that specializes in foreign securities because the portfolio may not be well diversified from the standpoint of geography or industry participation. For example, ASA Limited invests almost exclusively in South Africa gold mining securities, while Japan Fund invests only in Japanese securities. These specialized investment companies may not provide the degree of risk-reducing diversification provided by the typical investment company. In this context, viewing these specialized investment companies as essentially a one-security input to the investor's portfolio may be appropriate. Exhibit 17–1 also demonstrates the need to analyze the investment company being considered. Be aware that the performance of these investment companies varies considerably.

Exhibit 17–1 Investment Companies for Global Investing

		Percentage Change in Net Asset Value		
	Net Asset Value December 1986 (millions of dollars)	*1986*	*1981–86*	*1977–86*
Mutual Funds				
Canadian Fund	21	2.8	53.7	169.7
Keystone International	99	49.3	145.2	280.2
Merrill Lynch Pacific	419	77.8	258.9	599.0
Putnam Int'l Equities	411	37.6	221.4	483.6
Scudder International	711	50.7	191.0	417.4
Templeton Growth	1,133	21.2	133.1	433.3
Transatlantic	93	52.6	125.1	340.5
United Int'l Growth	214	30.3	179.8	405.1
Closed-End Investment Companies				
ASA Limited	705	87.7	62.4	539.2
Japan Fund	584	77.4	209.4	486.8
Standard & Poor 500 Stock Index		18.6	146.7	263.5

Source: Wiesenberger Services, Inc. "Management Results," *Supplement to Investment Companies* (December 1986).

Specialized Problems and Risks in Global Investing

In this section, we expand and summarize our discussion as it relates to the special features of global investing that should be of concern to investors. These problems and risks can be classified into those that are specific in nature to a given country or type of investment and those that are of a more general nature.

Specific Problems and Risks

The internal aspects of the investment being considered are important to investors. Accounting and financial practices and standards may vary from one country to another as well as from one industry to another. For example, Japanese firms typically carry higher debt loads in relation to their equity bases than many U.S. companies. This type of capital structure appears to be encouraged by the Japanese government. Restrictions on either individual or institutional trading may vary from country to country. We noted in the previous chapter that the Korea Fund sells at a very high premium over its net asset value because trading of securities in Korea is quite restrictive with regard to foreign investors. Finally, tax rules in a foreign country as well as custodial charges need to be considered. London custodial banks will charge about 1 percent a year of the market value just to hold shares for a foreign investor.

General Problems and Risks

One of the major reasons for global investing is that growth rates in various countries vary over time. Table 17–4 shows the annual growth rate of

Table 17–4
Annual Growth Rates in Real GNP for Selected Countries, 1961–86

	1961–70	1971–80	1981–83	1984–86
Developed Countries				
Canada	5.2	4.0	.7	4.0
France	5.6	3.7	1.0	1.7
Japan	9.0	4.8	3.3	2.6
United Kingdom	2.8	1.9	1.2	3.9
United States	3.8	2.8	1.0	2.8
West Germany	4.4	2.7	.2	3.0
Others				
Developing Countries	6.5	6.2	.9	3.0
China	4.0	5.8	7.4	10.3
USSR	4.8	2.6	2.5	2.0

Source: Statistical Abstract of the United States, 1987, p. 368.

Investment Highlight

Australian Dollar Bonds (An Investment "Down Under")

This investment highlight discusses the investment merits of Australian bonds sold in the United States but denominated in Australian dollars.

Description

Investors in the United States in early 1987 were attracted by the 13 percent rates quoted for five-year Australian dollar bonds. At the time, U.S. Treasury five-year notes were yielding about 6.7 percent. Whether these Australian dollar bonds are an attractive investment depends on the sophistication of the investor and the ability of that investor to bear exchange rate risk.

The primary reason investors are offered such an attractive coupon interest rate is that the Australian dollar might well decline in value against the U.S. dollar. If the exchange rate decline is sufficiently large, the loss of principal when converting back to U.S. dollars at the end of five years could offset the high coupon rate received and possibly even result in an investment with a negative total rate of return. In early 1987, the Australian dollar was worth about 67 U.S. cents. During 1986, its value had declined over 3.2 percent against the U.S. dollar.

Investors in these bonds are at risk if Australian inflation stays high relative to U.S. rates of inflation. In early 1987, inflation in Australia was running almost 10 percent a year versus about 3 to 4 percent in the United States. If these relative rates of inflation stay about the same over the next five years, investors could anticipate giving up about 6 percentage points of the 13 percent yield, resulting in a net yield of about 7 percent adjusted for exchange rate losses. The market appears to be valuing these bonds correctly if relative inflation rates do not change and the current inflationary rates continue to be reflected in exchange rates.

The question is whether Australia is solving its inflationary problems with austere monetary and fiscal policies. By mid-1987, the Australian dollar had risen to 72 U.S. cents, and the exchange markets apparently concluded the answer to the question is yes. This made the bonds excellent investments over this short period because an exchange rate gain of about 7 percent was achieved in addition to the 13 percent coupon rate.

Conclusion

Australian dollar bonds provided an attractive coupon interest rate but presented investors with an Australian dollar exchange rate speculation. The high coupon rates, however, provided some cushion against a decline in the value of the Australian dollar.

real Gross National Product for selected countries for the 1961–86 period. The growth rate for Japan as well as for the developing countries of the world has slowed during the 1980s, according to Table 17–4. Yet price-to-earnings ratios on Japanese stocks were about three times the level of P/E ratios for U.S. stocks as of the middle of 1987.

Mainland China has shown extraordinary growth during the 1980s. However, those firms located in noncommunistic countries who want to do business in China may encounter many unique marketing, cultural, and political problems. Japan is often cited as a classic case of special marketing problems. With a homogeneous population base, a heavy emphasis on quality, and a long-term orientation, Japanese consumers may not respond to marketing techniques that work well in the United States. In mid-1987, a U.S. tobacco company shipped some cigarettes tainted with a weed killer to the Japanese market. Considerable concern exists among U.S. firms about the negative long-run consequences that the marketing of this poor-quality product may have had. The concerns are especially significant, given that Japan only recently opened its borders to more imports of foreign-produced cigarettes.

Exchange rate fluctuations and the coordination of business cycles are also risks of a general nature. As world commerce becomes increasingly interdependent, the positive aspects noted in past studies regarding diversification benefits may be less valid. If the domestic economy of the United States is in a recession, many of the economies of the major developed nations may also be in a recession. This could cause interest rates and stock prices worldwide to move in roughly the same manner. We already noted that increasingly volatile foreign exchange rates have the potential for making otherwise profitable investments unprofitable and vice versa.

Summary

As the world becomes more and more economically interdependent, global investments become a more viable investment alternative. Developments favorable to one country or a group of countries may be detrimental to other countries. This provides risk-reducing possibilities from a strategy of international diversification. In addition, the growth of countries has varied in the past, and future variations in growth rates by country are likely, thus creating potentially profitable investment opportunities.

Several ways of making foreign investments are possible. By deliberately seeking domestic firms that have strong positions in foreign countries, investors should be able to obtain many of the risk-reducing benefits of international diversification. Investors may also purchase shares of foreign firms that are traded in the United States. Most of these shares come in the form of American Depositary Receipts (ADRs). ADRs are issued by banks and are backed by foreign shares held in the bank's custody. The investor is essentially buying an Americanized foreign security. The investor may also purchase shares of an investment company whose objective is to invest in foreign securities. One should analyze the past performance of these investment companies in the same manner as one would analyze any investment company. Direct purchase of shares on a foreign stock exchange is a difficult venture for investors lacking specialized knowledge and is generally not recommended.

Although a number of risks exist for the investor in global investments, especially the risk of expropriation without adequate compensation, numerous studies have observed that foreign securities can potentially reduce the risk of a portfolio of domestic securities. The systematic risk of the portfolio may be reduced considerably as a result of international diversification. One or two investment companies specializing in global investments would appear to be a worthwhile holding for an investor seeking to achieve risk reduction in a portfolio.

Suggested Readings

CHOLERTON, KENNETH, PIERRE PIERAERTS, and BRUNO SOLNIK. "Why Invest in Foreign Currency Bonds?" *Journal of Portfolio Management* (Summer 1986):4–8.

COHN, RICHARD A., and DONALD R. LESSARD. "The Effect of Inflation on Stock Prices: International Evidence." *Journal of Finance* (May 1981):277–89.

ERRUNZA, VIHANG R., and BARR ROSENBERG. "Investment in Developed and Less Developed Countries." *Journal of Financial and Quantitative Analysis* (December 1982):741–62.

FINNERTY, JOSEPH E., and KENNETH P. NUNN, JR. "Comparative Yield Spreads on U.S. Corporate Bonds and $Eurobonds." *Financial Analysts Journal* (July–August 1985):68–73.

GRAUER, ROBERT R., and NILS H. HAKANSSON. "Gains from International Diversification: 1968–1985 Returns on Portfolios of Stocks and Bonds." *Journal of Finance* (July 1987):721–39.

GULTEKIN, N. BULENT. "Stock Market Returns and Inflation: Evidence from Other Countries." *Journal of Finance* (March 1983):49–65.

HILLIARD, JIMMY E. "The Relationship Between Equity Indexes on World Exchanges." *Journal of Finance* (March 1979):103–14.

IBBOTSON, ROGER G., RICHARD C. CARR, and ANTHONY W. ROBINSON. "International Equity and Bond Returns." *Financial Analysts Journal* (July–August 1982):61–83.

ITTENSOHN, JACQUES. "How to Structure Efficient International Portfolios." *Journal of Portfolio Management* (Fall 1976):62–66.

JACUILLAT, BERTRANT, and BRUNO SOLNIK. "Multinationals Are Poor Tools for Diversification." *Journal of Portfolio Management* (Winter 1978): 8–12.

KIDWELL, DAVID S., M. WAYNE MARR, and G. RODNEY THOMPSON. "Eurodollar Bonds: Alternative Financing for U.S. Companies." *Financial Management* (Winter 1985):18–27.

LESSARD, DONALD R. "World, Country, and Industry Relationships in Equity Returns." *Financial Analysts Journal* (January–February 1976):32–38.

LEVY, HIAM, and MARSHALL SARNAT. "International Diversification of Investment Portfolios." *American Economic Review* (September 1970):668–75.

Mantell, Edmund H. "How to Measure Expected Returns on Foreign Investments." *Journal of Portfolio Management* (Winter 1984):38–43.

Officer, Dennis T., and J. Ronald Hoffmeister. "ADRs: A Substitute for the Real Thing?" *Journal of Portfolio Management* (Winter 1987): 61–65.

Senchak, Andrew J., Jr., and William L. Beedles. "Is Direct International Diversification Desirable?" *Journal of Portfolio Management* (Winter 1980):49–57.

Shohet, Ruben. "Investing in Foreign Securities." *Financial Analysts Journal* (September–October 1974):55–72.

Solnik, Bruno H. "The Relationship between Stock Prices and Inflationary Expectations: The International Evidence." *Journal of Finance* (March 1983):35–48.

———. "Why Not Diversify Internationally Rather Than Domestically?" *Financial Analysts Journal* (July–August 1974):48–54.

Questions

1. Despite the risks involved in foreign investments, securities of foreign firms may be a desirable holding for the investor. Why?
2. Foreign investments may be made indirectly using U.S.-based multinational firms. What are the advantages of this approach?
3. What is an ADR? What are the advantages of purchasing ADRs rather than shares listed on a foreign securities exchange?
4. How will fluctuations in foreign exchange rates influence foreign investments?
5. Solnik suggests the development of a multinational mutual fund in which investments are proportional to the source of the investment capital. For example, if German residents bought 15 percent of the fund's shares, the portfolio would contain 15 percent German securities.
   - **(a)** What do you see as the advantages of this arrangement?
   - **(b)** Do you foresee any difficulties with the arrangement? What are they?
6. Special knowledge is often needed in foreign investing to judge the risk involved. What are the risks that require this expertise?
7. We stated in the text that a low correlation exists between the rates of return from domestic and foreign securities. How is this beneficial to an investor?
8. Identify the differences that exist between the Tokyo Stock Exchange and the New York Stock Exchange?
9. What are the features associated with Eurobonds that attract investors?

Problems

1. Brigette has 100,000 French francs to invest in the stock of a U.S. company. She decides to purchase Control Data at a price of $30 per share.
   (a) How many shares can she purchase if the exchange rate is .16 $US/franc?
   (b) After holding the stock for three months, Brigette sells the stock for $33 per share. At that time the exchange rate is .14 $US/franc. What rate of return did Brigette earn on her investment for the three-month period? Assume no dividends were paid during the period.
   (c) How much of the return was due to the stock price increase and how much to the change in exchange rates?

2. Hans is a student at a university in the United States. During the summer, he borrows 10,000 West German marks from his bank in Frankfurt at an interest rate of 6 percent. Upon arriving in the United States, Hans converts the marks into $5,600 and invests the money in a mutual fund to earn 19 percent. At the end of the year, he sells his mutual fund, converts the proceeds into marks, and uses the proceeds to retire his loan.
   (a) If the exchange rate is .52 marks/U.S. dollar at the end of the year, how many marks will he have after paying his loan?
   (b) If Hans borrows the $5,600 from a U.S. bank at an interest rate of 10 percent and not from his bank in Frankfurt, invests in the mutual fund to earn 19 percent, sells the fund at the end of the year, and pays the loan plus interest, how many marks will he have when he returns home?

3. International diversification can be achieved easily by investing in mutual funds consisting of securities issued by companies from different countries. The following table lists the returns for four internationally diversified mutual funds for the 1976–85 period.

	Keystone International	Putnam International Equity	Scutter International Fund	Trans Atlantic Fund	S&P 500 Index
1976	11%	24%	6%	2%	24%
1977	−1	−1	0	6	−7
1978	6	23	21	26	7
1979	25	20	19	16	18
1980	21	25	27	49	32
1981	−2	0	−3	−15	−5
1982	13	10	1	−16	21
1983	14	28	30	33	22
1984	−8	1	−1	−14	6
1985	39	65	49	54	32

   (a) Show the diversification potential between each pair of the funds by constructing a correlation matrix. Include the S&P 500 index as a fifth security in the correlation matrix.

(b) Calculate the mean and standard deviation for a portfolio consisting in equal proportions of the four mutual funds. Compare the portfolio performance with that of the S&P 500.

(c) Form a *world* portfolio in which half is invested in the portfolio from step *b* and half in the S&P 500 index. Calculate the mean and standard deviation for the world portfolio. Compare the performance of the world portfolio with that of the S&P 500.

Part

Investment Planning and Portfolio Construction

6

The theoretical and practical aspects of portfolio construction are discussed in this part. The purchase of any individual security or asset should be evaluated from the viewpoint of what adding that security or asset to an existing portfolio will do to the portfolio risk-return relationship.

Chapter 18 examines the elements that are important in planning for a portfolio. Institutional investment management is discussed in Chapter 19. The management decisions of an actual endowment fund over time are presented in this chapter. The last chapter in the book presents a detailed examination of how investment performance may be measured and evaluated. The goal of this evaluation is to produce more favorable investment decisions in the future than was true for the past.

Chapter 18

Planning for a Portfolio

Key Concepts

- efficiency criterion
- efficient market theory
- ERISA
- information flow
- investment policy statement
- investment time horizon
- major mix decision
- portfolio
- return requirement
- tolerance for risk

Chapter Outline

Our study of the investment process has concentrated thus far primarily on the analysis of individual financial assets. However, few investors make decisions regarding a single common stock or other investment without considering their existing investments and other available opportunities. In the first section of this chapter, we examine the nature of a portfolio. Next, we discuss the rationale for constructing portfolios. In section three, the efficient market approach to portfolio construction is presented. Policy considerations in portfolio construction are discussed in section four. Finally, we present an analysis of the relationship between the expected returns on either individual assets or asset classes and portfolio construction techniques.

Nature of a Portfolio

A *portfolio* consists of one or more assets that are held by the investor for investment purposes rather than consumption. We could speak of one-security or one-asset portfolios, but few individuals actually have such portfolios. Most individuals and institutions own many different types of securities and other assets such as real estate. Hence, we will generally assume that a portfolio has two or more assets. To achieve the best possible performance, constructing a portfolio with careful consideration of how portfolio assets relate to one another is important.

A number of decisions must be made prior to constructing a portfolio. One of the major decisions is the type and diversity of assets to be held. This decision will, of course, depend to some extent on the experience, education, and training of the individual planning the portfolio. This decision as to the type of assets and proportion of various assets to hold in the portfolio may be referred to as the *major mix decision*. Naturally, an important aspect of the major mix decision is the amount of risk the investor is willing to take on in the portfolio.

Constructing Portfolios

A portfolio in a general sense includes all of an individual's real and financial assets, plus intangibles such as education. Almost everyone can be said to own a portfolio of some sort. Various types of insurance, which act to reduce risk, pension plan benefits, and real assets such as automobiles, personal residences, and furniture are part of the portfolios of most U.S. citizens. Haphazardly accumulating assets is not likely to produce the most desirable portfolio, and this is one of a number of important reasons for a carefully planned and constructed portfolio.

The fundamental reason for constructing a portfolio is to alter the risk and return relationship to fit the preferences of an individual investor or an institution's portfolio manager. Private or institutional investors assemble portfolios to obtain diversification and to achieve the best possible risk-return combination. We previously noted that the relevant decision rule, known as the *efficiency criterion,* may be stated in either of the two following ways:

1. Select the highest return portfolio for any given level of risk.
2. Select the lowest possible risk level for any given rate of return.

The efficiency criterion essentially means that investors attempt to own the best possible portfolio in terms of the anticipated rate of return and the risk they are willing to assume in seeking that return. As a result, some investors will own low-risk, low-return portfolios, and other investors will own high-risk, high-return portfolios. In seeking the optimum portfolio as conditions in the economy and in the financial markets change, investors may alter the risk-return attributes of their portfolios in order to keep them optimum or on the efficient frontier that we discussed previously.

The Efficient Market Approach to Portfolio Construction

Although much has been written about *efficient market theory,* the subject continues to be controversial. This section reviews the theory and the concept of market efficiency. A portfolio approach that is consistent with this concept is then presented.

Efficient Market Theory

In its most general form, an efficient market is one that fully reflects all relevant information. In such a market, a security or commodity will be priced in accordance with all relevant information. When the information is complete, the price will be the best estimate available of the true or intrinsic value of the security.

An efficient market does not mean that the optimum investment strategy is to select securities by price alone or randomly—popularly known as throwing darts at the *Wall Street Journal.* Nothing could be further from the truth. Rather than implying that the returns and risk of each security will be the same, the existence of an efficient market suggests that security analysis is being done extremely well and that all relevant knowledge is being applied. An efficient market is entirely consistent with the proposition that security analysts are generally proficient in their analytical abilities and that they perform an important function for the investor by selecting appropriate securities, given the investor's characteristics.

Implementing the Efficient Market Approach

The efficient market concept can be used to plan a portfolio. The four steps presented below involve determining a suitable risk level and buying enough securities to provide adequate diversification.

Step One: Determine the Appropriate Risk Level

In the efficient market approach, as in other portfolio construction approaches, the first step is to determine the appropriate risk level. This risk level determination should be based on the investor's unique characteristics. It should be carefully considered, as the implication under the efficient market approach is that the investor's desired risk level will not change often. The individual investor needs to weigh such factors as age, employment status, marital status, income stability, wealth and debt levels, and the psychological ability to assume risk. For an institutional investor, the risk of the portfolio should reflect the institution's goals as determined by the nature of the obligations supported by the portfolio.

Step Two: Diversify to the Risk Level Chosen

We previously identified systematic and nonsystematic risk. The goal of this step is to eliminate nonsystematic risk to the extent possible. Hence, the portfolio manager assumes only systematic risk at the risk level deemed appropriate. Mutual funds are a useful means of achieving diversification for the individual investor. Most institutional investors have enough investment capital to achieve a proper level of diversification without using such investment vehicles as mutual funds. Institutions often engage the services of outside investment managers to gain benefits other than diversification.

Step Three: Buy and Hold the Portfolio

Because the risk level determination is made for a relatively long period of time, investors should be able to buy enough securities to eliminate most of the nonsystematic risk in the portfolio. Once these securities have been selected and the portfolio manager is confident the risk level of the securities chosen will not change appreciably over time, little reason exists to trade the securities purchased. A benefit of buying and holding is the reduction of brokerage commission costs compared to actively trading a portfolio.

Naturally, investors occasionally might wish to alter the composition of the diversified portfolio chosen. A fundamental change in the economy or the world situation might make a group of securities that originally seemed of average risk suddenly more risky. For example, a change in the availability and cost of energy might change the riskiness of the airline stocks. In addition, the investor should watch for securities in the portfolio that might be candidates for bankruptcy. In essence, the efficient market approach is a strategy of passive portfolio management.

Step Four: Adjust the Risk Level When Necessary

As the circumstances of the individual investor gradually change over time, the original risk level may need to be adjusted. This risk level change might be the result of a change in employment, a change in family status, a sudden large inheritance, the approach of retirement, and similar situations. Effectively, this step requires the investor to return to step one to repeat the first three steps in implementing the efficient market approach. Some of the securities held might be appropriate for the new risk level, but many of them might need to be changed. In a similar fashion, a risk level change in an institutional portfolio such as a pension fund might be necessary if the age mix of the employees changed dramatically. This might happen if the firm were forced to discharge workers because of a change in the long-term outlook for the company.

Policy Considerations for Portfolios

An institution managing a portfolio should have a formal, written investment policy statement or, at the very minimum, should carefully address the factors that will impact on how the portfolio is constructed. A written investment policy statement might cover such areas as unauthorized investments, security safekeeping procedures, and order execution. However, these are not the things that really count from the standpoint of achieving good portfolio performance. The following items need to be carefully considered:

1. Tolerance for risk
2. Return requirements
3. Investment time horizon
4. Information flow and reporting requirements
5. Taxation
6. Regulatory or legal constraints
7. Impact of external developments

Tolerance for Risk

Institutions will vary greatly in their ability to bear risk in seeking a higher return from their portfolio management activities. For example, a life insurance company's liabilities are stated as specific dollar amounts under many of the policies issued. The company is committed to pay an amount, such as $100,000, at the time of the insured's death. Hence, the insurance company need not worry greatly about keeping the return on its investments high enough to offset any decline in the purchasing power of the dollar. This task is effectively the job of the individual purchasing the life insurance policy in his or her investment management practices. Of course, to the extent that the competitiveness of a given life insurance company's products depends on the return it can earn on its investments as well as its operational efficiency, seeking high rates of return cannot be completely ignored.

An endowment fund, on the other hand, may have a widely ranging tolerance for risk, depending on the objectives of the fund. If the principal objective of the fund is to provide current income to support scholarships or some other worthwhile expenditure, the portfolio of the fund should contain many fixed-income securities. This will allow the fund to attempt to maximize current income subject to only modest risk of changes in the value of the fund. However, even in this case, the fund assumes purchasing power risk. An endowment fund with a current income of $100,000 at the present time will provide less valuable scholarships in terms of purchasing power than the same $100,000 of current income ten years ago. If the current income needs of the endowment fund are relatively modest for many years into the future, then capital growth can be sought by taking on more risk.

Return Requirements

The *return requirements* will influence the risk assumed by the institution. If a pension fund requires a high rate of return because of benefit improvements granted to employees over the years, the risk level will have to reflect these return requirements. For such institutional portfolios as pension plans and life insurance company investments, actuaries may determine the rate of return required for the portfolio to handle the liabilities that will eventually need to be met. In the case of a pension fund, if the rate of return falls below the actuarially determined rate of return, the plan's sponsor may have to increase its contribution to keep the fund in sound financial condition.

In a life insurance company, an actuarially assumed rate of return is determined for each contract written. Any failure to meet this rate of return could cause the life insurance company's regulatory agencies to require an increase in the reserves of the firm. Fortunately, this has been of little consequence in recent years because the interest rates existing in the market have far exceeded the minimum return for most life insurance contracts.

Time Horizon Considerations

Spending sufficient time defining the time horizon appropriate for a given institutional portfolio is an activity that should pay rich dividends. The ability to bear risk is closely related to the *investment time horizon.* If liquidity is an important consideration, this may dictate a short time horizon. The need to be able to meet unexpected withdrawals from the fund being managed means the investments must be planned with safety of principal as a key portfolio objective. If liquidity is not an important portfolio objective, the ability to bear risk tends to increase because short-run market fluctuations can be ignored, as would be the case with a life insurance company's portfolio. In essence, a long time horizon would allow a more passive approach to investment management.

A portfolio's investment time horizon is also closely connected with its return requirements. If we generally expect to face an upward-sloping yield curve in the financial markets, a relatively high return requirement may force us to concentrate most of our investments in long-term, fixed-income issues. Whether this implied long time horizon is appropriate, given our risk tolerance, is a question that may force the portfolio manager to seriously reconsider the required rate of return.

Although an investment's maturity might well be timed to match a specific payment date for a liability of the organization, such is not often the case in institutional investment management situations. The investment time horizon is not usually a precise point in time, but a variable length of time. An endowment fund providing financial aid to college students will typically have a relatively long investment time horizon, but we would not normally define its time horizon as ten years. Rather, we would likely say its investment time horizon is about seven to twelve years.

The significance of the notion of a somewhat flexible time horizon is that it allows for flexibility in making investments. For example, the investment manager for an endowment fund might want to purchase a fixed-rate GNMA security with an average life of twelve years. The manager will need to recognize that twelve years is just an average life calculation, not a precise maturity for the investment. If mortgage interest rates fall substantially, home owners will seize the opportunity to refinance their mortgages at lower rates. These refinanced mortgages will mean that the GNMA security will return its principal faster than implied by the original twelve-year average life calculation. Likewise, if mortgage interest rates rise in the market, mortgage holders may be reluctant or unable to move to a new or bigger residence. Hence, they will not prepay their mortgages, and the GNMA's life may turn out to be thirteen or fourteen years. If the fund's investment manager has determined that the endowment fund's investment time horizon is flexible enough to handle a potentially variable cash-flow pattern, the GNMA could still be considered for inclusion in the portfolio based on its risk and return characteristics.

Information Flow and Reporting Requirements

An institutional investment manager needs to organize the flow of information in several areas so that good investment results are possible. We will discuss *information flow* as it applies to the areas of research, characteristics of the portfolio being managed, and cash-flow patterns associated with the organization that will impact on the construction of the portfolio.

One of the more difficult tasks for an institutional investment manager is to obtain sound, creative ideas for new security additions to the existing portfolio. Research provided by brokerage firms is often a good source for new ideas as are some of the sources discussed in Chapter 3, such as the *Standard & Poor's Outlook* and the *Value Line Investment Advisory Service.* In arranging for an orderly information flow, the investment manager must also consider whether a particular information source is cost effective.

For an investment manager to know the financial demographics of the portfolio being managed is critical. Information needs to be collected so that elementary questions relating to both common stocks and fixed-income securities can be answered. For equities, the investment manager would want to know such basic information about the portfolio as its dividend yield and beta. For all the companies in the portfolio, the manager would want to know such information as the anticipated growth of both earnings and dividends per share, the rate of return on net worth, and the firm's financial strength. For fixed-income securities, the manager would be interested in the current yield, the yield-to-maturity, and the portfolio's weighted average maturity or duration. Many of the computerized data bases are valuable for constructing a financial profile for the investments being managed.

Having a sound operating knowledge of the cash flow associated with an organization is exceedingly important for the investment manager. The basic pattern associated with the cash flow gives the manager a good idea of the liquidity requirements imposed on the portfolio. The manager should know as far in advance as possible when substantial new sums of money will be coming under management. Adequate time and thought can then be given to how this new money should be invested in light of the present portfolio composition and other relevant considerations. The timing of substantial cash outflows should be known as far in advance as possible so that hasty and potentially costly portfolio liquidations do not occur.

An investment manager has to organize the information flow so that portfolio performance can be reported to whatever individual or group has overall responsibility for the investment management area. The nature of reporting is closely associated with the concept of an investment time horizon. The investment manager of an endowment fund with an investment time horizon in the area of ten years should not logically have to report his or her performance on a weekly or a monthly basis because performance may be affected by random elements in such short periods of time. However, this does not mean that ten years should elapse before performance is reviewed. Periodic measurements about the progress made toward portfolio risk and return objectives may serve a useful purpose. If quarterly or annual portfolio performance reviews are undertaken, however, the examination must take into account that the investments may have been made with a much longer time horizon in mind. What would be a reasonable period of time for getting a reliable measurement of the performance of an investment manager of an endowment fund or a pension fund with a relatively long investment time horizon? A complete business or stock market cycle would seem to be a logical answer, and this might easily involve four to six years.

The relevant reporting period is also related to the marketability and the risk of the assets being managed as well as legal requirements. Generally speaking, the more illiquid the assets in a portfolio are, the less frequently performance reviews need to be made. Real estate investments are good examples because appraisals are often required to determine how investments are performing. The more risky an investment, the more closely it should be watched and the more frequently performance should be reviewed. Investments in stocks involved in complex merger or takeover situations or in firms involved in major lawsuits need to be monitored carefully. Finally, the investment manager may have reporting requirements imposed by a state or federal law or by some regulatory authority. However, legally mandated timing for the reporting of performance results may or may not bear much relationship to the investment time horizon or the nature of the assets being managed.

Taxation

Taxation may be a significant factor in the management of an institutional portfolio. The degree to which the institutional portfolio is taxed will be an important determinant for several investment management decisions. Many institutional portfolios are tax-exempt. An endowment fund at a university would be a typical example. Such a tax-exempt institution would not normally pay a premium price for a municipal bond offering tax-exempt interest income.

Some institutional investors are effectively fully taxed at the corporate tax rate (34 percent in 1987). For example, property and casualty insurance companies may have this rate applied to profits from their insurance underwriting activities and to their investment income. For these institutions, municipal bonds are often a desirable holding because the after-tax returns will exceed the returns available from comparable fully taxable corporate bonds. Dividends received by one corporation on holdings of the common and preferred stock of another corporation are 80 percent exempt from taxation. This means the effective tax rate on dividend income is only 6.8 percent (20 percent times the tax rate of 34 percent). Thus, a property and casualty insurance company might give considerable weight to the dividend yield available from the stocks in its portfolio, especially preferred stocks. If a company eliminates or substantially reduces its dividend per share, the property and casualty company's portfolio manager should seriously consider whether this stock should remain in the portfolio.

Regulatory and Legal Considerations

Regulatory or legal constraints on an institutional portfolio may be very important in its management. These portfolio management considerations may arise from regulatory or legal constraints at either the state or federal level. In most cases, the impact of these rules and regulations is either to prevent the portfolio manager from engaging in certain activities or to establish a minimum acceptable amount of portfolio diversification.

Although it is difficult to determine what might be a binding constraint on a given institutional portfolio without a detailed investigation of its regulatory and legal environment, we will examine two specific legal constraints as examples of how important this area may be for portfolio management activities. The *Employee Retirement Income Security Act* of 1974 (*ERISA*) is concerned with protecting the retirement income of pension fund participants. First, ERISA requires that pension fund managers use the same care, skill, prudence, and diligence that a prudent person acting in a like capacity and familiar with such matters would use in the conduct of an enterprise of like character and with like aims. The prudent-person standard in this instance is applied to the total portfolio. Second, ERISA requires that the portfolio of the pension fund be diversified to minimize the risk of a large loss unless it would clearly be prudent not to diversify. State laws often generate rules and regulations for such institutional portfolios as endowment funds, a consideration that will be almost overwhelming when we discuss the restructuring of an endowment fund in the next chapter.

Impact of External Developments

Clearly, institutional portfolio managers do not operate in a vacuum. This is certainly the case when it comes to the policy implications of new developments in any industry served by the portfolio manager. For example, as innovative investment products are developed for the public, portfolio managers must react to the challenges posed by these new products. Whether the marketing personnel in a financial services company are responsible for creating a new investment concept or form of investment or whether the financial personnel in the organization suggest that a particular type of investment portfolio can be marketed is unimportant. What matters is that portfolio managers must be willing and able to adapt to the changing needs of their institutional clients. For example, new life insurance products such as universal life contracts or guaranteed income contracts may well require the investment of funds in relatively new ways compared to traditional life insurance investments. Universal life contracts may mean life insurance companies will want to invest a higher percentage of their funds in short-term debt obligations because these insurance contracts contain some of the characteristics of money market funds. Guaranteed income contracts in which the holder of the contract is guaranteed a specific rate of return for a period of years, perhaps in the range of six to ten years, may mean investing in zero coupon bonds or implementing bond portfolio management strategies designed to lock-in that guaranteed rate of return.

Asset Returns and Portfolio Construction

In constructing portfolios, the investor usually starts by examining the expected return and risk characteristics of individual securities. Then, various combinations of securities are examined to determine the optimal portfolio. We discussed this approach in the first part of the book.

Investors often construct portfolios by combining holdings from various asset classes. Individual investment opportunities within an as-

Table 18–1
Annual Rates of Return, Selected Asset Classes, 1971–86

Year	T-Bills	Long-Term Corporate Bonds	Common Stocks	Single Family Dwelling	Gold	Portfolio
1971	4.4	11.0	14.3	4.9	13.3	9.7
1972	3.8	7.3	19.0	6.3	42.1	13.6
1973	6.9	1.1	−14.7	10.5	66.9	6.3
1974	8.0	−3.1	−26.5	9.6	63.3	1.4
1975	5.8	14.6	37.2	8.1	1.1	17.2
1976	5.1	18.7	23.8	13.2	−22.4	13.1
1977	5.1	1.7	−7.2	12.4	18.3	4.3
1978	7.2	−.1	6.6	14.1	30.5	10.0
1979	10.4	−4.2	18.4	13.8	58.9	16.0
1980	11.2	−2.6	32.4	10.7	98.6	23.4
1981	14.7	−1.0	−4.9	8.4	−24.5	.1
1982	10.5	43.8	21.4	.6	−18.4	14.6
1983	8.8	4.7	22.5	8.7	12.8	12.5
1984	9.9	16.4	6.3	6.1	−14.9	6.5
1985	7.7	30.9	32.2	5.5	−11.9	17.1
1986	6.2	19.9	18.5	8.9	16.4	14.5
Mean	7.9	9.9	12.5	8.9	20.6	11.3
Std. Dev.	2.9	13.6	18.0	3.7	36.8	6.3

set class may not promise the same return-risk combinations. However, some investors find that classifying investments into categories such as common stocks, bonds, real estate, and other asset classifications is a useful approach. Let's look at some of these asset classes to see what rate of return they provided from 1971 through 1986. Table 18–1 shows annual rates of return for U.S. Treasury bills, long-term corporate bonds, common stocks, houses, gold, and a portfolio comprised of the five asset classes.

Treasury Bills

Treasury bills provided a relatively stable positive return each year from 1971 through 1986. Showing the lowest standard deviation of all the asset classes on Table 18–1, treasury bills are often used as a proxy for the risk-free rate.

Bonds

The annual returns from investing in long-term corporate bonds have not fluctuated as much as those from common stocks. From a portfolio perspective, adding bonds to a common stock portfolio tends to reduce the risk of the portfolio. What adding bonds to a common stock portfolio does to the risk and return *combination* of the portfolio depends on the time period being considered and the exact common stocks and bonds bought for the portfolio.

Common Stocks

The highest common stock return for the 1971–86 period was 37.2 percent, and the poorest annual return was −26.5 percent. However, the risk of investing in common stocks can be reduced in two basic ways. One way is to invest in common stocks that appear to be much less risky than the average common stock. Another way to reduce the risk of investing in common stocks is to invest in other asset classes. Let's look at the annual returns from the other asset classes shown in Table 18–1 and attempt to determine the portfolio implications of combining asset classes.

Houses and Gold

Both houses and gold represent investment in real assets. Table 18–1 estimates the annual return from owning a personal residence during the 1971–86 period by calculating the yearly change in the price of a one-family house. As in the situation with common stocks, the return earned on a particular house is unique and will depend on the type and location of the house. Owning a personal residence contains both investment and consumption attributes, and the relative importance of these attributes may change over time.

An interesting aspect of Table 18–1 is that the estimated annual rate of return from investing in gold is quite different from that earned by owning a personal residence. However, during the inflationary period, 1971–81, investors appeared to benefit from holding real assets in their portfolios. The annual returns from the real assets, houses and gold, were generally positive. Although the returns from owning a house were consistent from year to year, returns from gold were volatile. Nothing guarantees that this situation will recur in future years. However, the owner of a personal residence during the 1971–86 period could take comfort from the fact that the value of the personal residence increased in such years as 1973 and 1974 when common stock values declined substantially.

The portfolio return column on Table 18–1 was constructed for the 1971–86 period using the following realistic portfolio percentages:

Treasury bills	10 percent
Long-term corporate bonds	20 percent
Common stock	30 percent
Single-family dwelling	30 percent
Gold	10 percent

Investment Highlight

Chrysler's Pension Fund Management (A Lesson in Asset Allocation)

This investment highlight analyzes the "daring" decision of Chrysler's treasurer to radically alter the mix of stocks and bonds in the company's pension plan.

Description

In July 1984, Frederick W. Zuckerman, Chrysler's treasurer, decided that long-term interest rates were going to decline. He directed the pension plan to sell all its stocks and buy $1.1 billion in high-quality bonds yielding 14.2 percent. During the next two years, interest rates fell 500 basis points and Chrysler's bonds increased greatly in value.

This major asset allocation move on the part of Zuckerman was probably not as "daring" as it appeared. Over long periods of time, total returns from stocks will exceed those from fixed-income securities, but they may not over short periods of time. In fact, Chrysler probably did as well or better in total returns from the bonds through the end of 1986 than if it had retained the stocks. Why did this happen?

The driving force for both the strong bull market in stocks and the large capital appreciation from bonds was the 1984–86 interest rate decline. Chrysler's pension plan would be better off with a lower-risk investment if both bonds and stocks were to be strongly influenced by interest rate movements. Using the historical risk premium of about 6 percentage points between stocks and bonds, Zuckerman needed to earn about 20 percent on Chrysler's stocks to equal, on a risk-adjusted basis, the 14 percent anticipated return on the fixed-income securities.

In March 1987, Zuckerman decided to return to stocks, and as of mid-1987, the pension fund was about equally invested in stocks and bonds. His timing in getting back into stocks was not nearly as good as his timing had been getting into long-term bonds in 1984 because he missed the bull market of January and February 1987. However, interest rates increased by mid-1987, causing bonds to decline while stocks reached new highs.

Conclusion

Major changes in the asset allocation percentage, if timed properly, can produce favorable investment results. Chrysler's asset allocation shift was probably not as daring as it first seemed, given the high yield available from bonds.

The interesting feature of the returns from this particular portfolio is that they were never negative, although 1981 returns came close. The returns from the financial assets and the real assets seemed to complement each other most of the time. The only year in which both financial and real assets tended to do poorly was in 1981. Also interesting is that treasury bill returns exceeded those from the portfolio in five out of the fifteen years.

Summary

Most investors hold portfolios containing various types of assets. Important from both a risk and a return standpoint is the examination of each financial and real asset to determine its portfolio effect. An individual asset might be risky when analyzed in isolation. When considered with other assets, a seemingly risky asset may be capable of reducing the risk of a given portfolio. This important observation implies an enormous problem because the number of potential portfolios is almost limitless even if only a few assets are considered by the investor. In recognition of this problem, we noted that the efficiency criterion says the investor need consider only those portfolios that maximize expected return for a given level of risk or minimize risk for a given level of return. This set of all efficient portfolios is referred to as the efficient frontier.

In planning for a portfolio, policy considerations are extremely important. Investors should give serious thought to the risk that can comfortably be assumed in seeking returns and the length of time for which investments can be made. The risk and the investment time horizon together tend to determine the return that the portfolio actually earns. Portfolio managers also need to be aware of the relevant tax status as well as any legal or regulatory constraints that might limit either the type of investment or the quality of asset that may be purchased.

In seeking to apply basic portfolio construction concepts, an investor typically focuses on certain characteristics of individual assets. Each asset considered for addition to the portfolio needs to be examined from the viewpoint of what it will do to the risk and return anticipated from the entire portfolio. If the investor finds a highly risky common stock and anticipates a high return from that stock, it could probably be added in modest amounts to a fairly low-risk portfolio without doing much to change the overall portfolio risk. In seeking to achieve the best risk-return combination from a portfolio, the investor might well concentrate on the types of assets in the portfolio because this approach may be easier than focusing on individual securities and real assets.

Suggested Readings

BEN-HORIM, MOSHE, and HIAM LEVY. "Total Risk, Diversifiable Risk, and Non-Diversifiable Risk: A Pedagogic Note." *Journal of Financial and Quantitative Analysis* (June 1980): 289–98.

BERNSTEIN, PETER L. "Markowitz Marked to Market." *Financial Analysts Journal* (January–February 1983): 18–22.

CHEN, SON-NAN, and STEPHEN J. BROWN. "Estimation Risk and Simple Rules for Optimal Portfolio Selection." *Journal of Finance* (September 1983): 1087–94.

ELLIS, CHARLES D. "Conceptualizing Portfolio Management." In *Managing Investment Portfolios, A Dynamic Process* by John L. Maginn and Donald L. Tuttle, eds. Boston: Warren, Gorham & Lamont, 1983, 11–23.

HAGIN, ROBERT. *Modern Portfolio Theory.* Homewood, IL: Richard D. Irwin, 1980.

KWAN, CLARENCE C. Y. "Portfolio Analysis Using Single Index, Multi-Index, and Constant Correlation Models: A Unified Treatment." *Journal of Finance* (December 1984): 1469–84.

MAGINN, JOHN L., and DONALD L. TUTTLE, eds. *Managing Investment Portfolios, A Dynamic Process, 1985–1986 Update.* Boston: Warren, Gorham & Lamont, 1985.

MARKOWITZ, HARRY H. "Portfolio Selection." *Journal of Finance* (March 1952):77–91.

———. *Portfolio Selection: Efficient Diversification of Investments.* New York: John Wiley and Sons, 1959.

MILLER, EDWARD M. "Portfolio Selection in a Fluctuating Economy." *Financial Analysts Journal* (May–June 1978):77–83.

SWALM, RALPH O. "Utility Theory: Insights into Risk Taking." *Harvard Business Review* (November–December 1966): 123–36.

ZINBARG, EDWARD D. "Modern Approach to Investment Risk." *Financial Executive* (February 1973):44–61.

Questions

1. How might one reduce the risk of investing in common stocks?
2. What is the nature of the major mix decision?
3. What are the advantages for investors of examining returns from different asset classes?
4. Discuss the nature of portfolio management.
5. Why would an institution need a formal statement of investment policy? What types of things are typically covered in such a statement?
6. What is the nature of the relationship between the tolerance for risk and the return requirements of an institutional investor?
7. Why is the proper determination of the investment time horizon so important to an institutional investor?
8. Assuming an institutional investor is tax-exempt, what is the impact of this characteristic on investments to be made in common stocks, preferred stocks, and fixed-income securities?
9. Your friend wants your help in managing a portfolio. As a firm believer in the efficiency of the capital market, how would you manage the portfolio? Be specific.

Problems

These problems apply material in the text to personal investment situations. Some of them may require library research to understand the precise nature of the financial situation and the alternatives being considered.

1. Warren Hennis graduated from Southeastern University two years ago. He is twenty-three years of age, unmarried, and works for a medium-size company in Columbus, Georgia. His annual salary is $17,000, from which he pays Georgia state income tax of 3 percent and Social Security tax of 7 percent. He rents an apartment for $170 a month with utilities taking another $80 per month. His employer's pension plan vests after ten years of service and does not carry a death benefit provision. He is covered by Social Security. His employer provides Blue Cross/Blue Shield coverage in addition to a major medical policy.

   Warren owns a late model automobile with a current market value of $5,000, on which payments of $160 per month are due for the next thirty-six months. He carries automobile liability insurance of $25,000/$50,000 and has collision coverage with a $50 deductible. He has no home-owner's insurance coverage. His employer provides a group life insurance policy of $15,000. Warren's only other asset is $1,000 in a savings account.

   Warren has learned that you are taking a course in investments and wonders if you have any comments regarding his present financial situation. He is also interested in establishing some form of investment program to increase his assets for those years when he is no longer "free and reckless."

2. David Bartow, one of Professor Phillips's students, approached her after class one day to ask if she had a few minutes to talk about the financial situation facing his seventy-seven-year-old grandmother. David explained that his grandmother is a widow who receives $250 a month in Social Security benefits after deductions for Medicare premiums. She lives alone in a modest apartment, which requires expenditures of $160 a month for rent and utilities. Other living expenses bring her monthly expenditures to $380. David's grandmother has $20,000 in a 5½ percent savings account. She uses the income from this account to supplement her Social Security check.

   Even with this interest income, David's grandmother is using her capital because her living expenses are about $40 a month greater than her income. David said she is concerned because she does not want to outlive her capital. In addition, she would really like to have the principal remain constant so that she could leave a "little something" to her grandchildren, as she puts it. David explained that his grandmother has never owned a stock or bond in her life and is somewhat afraid of the idea of buying securities. David wondered if Professor Phillips could talk to his grandmother for a few minutes and make some suggestions regarding her financial situation. If you were Professor Phillips, what would you recommend?

3. You have been asked to provide some financial advice to two college professors. This husband and wife team work for the same university and have two small sons, ages three and five. They are both tenured and are in their late thirties. Their marginal tax rate is 28 percent.

   In inquiring further on their financial condition, you discover the following facts:

(a) They both contribute to TIAA-CREF and have been paying income tax on their contributions even though the university allows them to defer tax on these contributions. They are both putting 75 percent into TIAA and 25 percent in CREF. The husband has a vested death benefit of $25,000; the wife's vested death benefit is $22,000.

(b) The husband has income (in the amount of $3,000) in addition to that paid by the university, and the wife had outside income of $5,000. They have no pension plan for this income.

(c) The university provides each of them with $63,000 in group life insurance. In addition, each of them has a $50,000 decreasing term policy with TIAA.

(d) The only common stockholdings they have are fifty shares of a local utility. This jointly registered stock provides them with dividend income of $100 per year.

Using the facts presented, recommend ways in which they might change the management of their financial resources.

4. In 1982, Helen Epson's husband died, and in August 1983, she came to you for personal investment advice. She has just settled the estate and knows what assets she has. In talking with her, you hear she is sixty years of age, which would mean she has an average life expectancy of about twenty more years. She has not worked in recent years and has no plans to join the labor force. She has the following assets:

Amount	Description	Income
$ 9,000	141 shares of AT&T common stock	$ 760
20,000	13.75% certificate of deposit maturity 1/85	2,750
100,000	IRA invested in 12% certificate of deposit maturity 3/85	12,000
90,000	Super NOW account paying a flexible rate of interest, which is now 8.5%	7,650
100,000	Insurance Company Guaranteed Income Contract (GIC), which pays 13% for the next four years and 14% for year five. After five years, the value can be withdrawn or reinvested for five more years at rates existing at that time	13,000
100,000	Market value of residence; no mortgage	0

In discussing Mrs. Epson's needs, you learn that she will need about $24,000 pretax income per year to maintain her standard of living. This amount does not include any extraordinary expenditures she might wish to make, such as buying a new automobile or making major repairs to the residence. Her Social Security amounts to about $6,000 per year. Design an investment management strategy for Mrs. Epson in light of her needs and the following facts:

(a) The stock market has gone from about 800 to 1,200 during the

1982–83 period as measured by the Dow Jones Industrial Average.

(b) Thirty-month certificates from financial institutions are yielding about 11 percent; treasury bills are at about 9 percent; and long-term U.S. government bonds are at about 11 percent.

(c) Withdrawals from the IRA account must begin when she is seventy and one-half years old, but could begin anytime since she is over fifty-nine and one-half. In fact, Mrs. Epson asks you whether she should start withdrawals from this account. The IRA account was established with the death benefits she received from her husband's pension plan.

(d) The income from the GIC is taxed on a current basis, but the IRA account earns tax-deferred income.

5. The following case was presented in the May 1987 Wiesenberger Mutual Funds Investment Report.

Gary and Sarah Williams have recently become empty-nesters. An aggressive savings program earmarked for funding the college costs of their three children has allowed them to emerge into empty-nesthood relatively unscathed in that they have no college loans to repay. On the other hand, much of their savings and investment portfolio has been depleted. Like many recent empty-nesters in their fifties (Sarah is fifty-three, and Gary is fifty-five), their thoughts now turn to planning for a comfortable retirement. Gary, who now earns $62,000, has been with his employer for almost twenty years, and his company has a good pension plan. Sarah is about to reenter the job market after a hiatus of more than twenty-five years, and she expects to earn approximately $25,000 in her first year.

Sarah and Gary have recently made some informal projections of their retirement resources (pension and Social Security) and have concluded that although they'll be able to get by, they do not have enough for a comfortable retirement. Gary's retirement annuity will be fixed. Therefore, what appears to be a reasonably good retirement at age sixty-five, when the couple plans to retire, will undoubtedly erode because of inflation over their retirement years. Thus, Gary and Sarah want to embark on a rather ambitious savings and investment program to provide the so-called third leg of the retirement income stool—income from personal savings and investments (pension and Social Security represent the other two legs).

The couple have been savers in the past, or they wouldn't have been successful in funding their children's education. They feel that with Sarah's additional income, they should be able to save 20–25 percent of their gross income, or approximately $20,000 per year. They feel this is a reasonable savings goal, which can be accomplished without depriving themselves of some self-indulgences, such as travel, which they can enjoy now that the children are on their own. (The fact that the couple has a $450 monthly mortgage payment doesn't hurt their savings prospects either.)

Gary and Sarah have limited experience in investing. The original nest egg they created for college tuition was generally invested in certificates of deposit and some individual common stock issues. The bear markets that occurred in the late 1960s and early 1970s soured them on the stock market, though they wish they had been participating in the recent bull market. Both of them seem intent on being more active in managing their retirement portfolio. On the other hand, they are not inclined to subject their hard-earned money to a great deal of risk. They realize how important this money will be for retirement purposes, particularly since they anticipate no windfalls—inheritance expectancies are minimal, and they don't play the lottery.

Analyze the Williams's situation and devise an investment program to achieve their objectives.

6. The following case was presented in the June 1987 Wiesenberger Mutual Funds Investment Report.

Mark Winbridge is a twenty-four-year old assistant manager at a large retail store. He has been with the store, a unit of a major chain, since his graduation from college. He now earns $26,000 plus a small bonus; in addition, he receives some annual cash gifts from his family amounting to about $3,500 each year. Mark has finally overcome the inevitable "start up" costs that are incurred by persons first embarking on their careers. His apartment is adequately furnished; he's made some headway in reducing his college loans; and his car loan will be paid off next year. As is typical in these situations, he hasn't been able to save very much, but he says he can now begin to "see some green" after all the monthly bills and living expenses are paid.

In discussing his future plans, Mark says he wants to buy a house or condo within the next few years. He knows he'll have to come up with most of the down payment, since his parents have made it clear that although they can help somewhat with his first home purchase, they still have substantial household expenses, including education costs for his younger sister. Furthermore, although there are no prime prospects at present, he expects eventually to get married and raise a family.

Based on an analysis of his current income and expenditures, Mark thinks he can save at least $5,000 per year. "I can now comfortably live on my salary, and, therefore, I should be able to save my bonus and cash gifts that I receive from my parents and grandparents. My relatives would be very happy if I saved their gifts."

Mark has some knowledge of mutual funds. He has an account with a large mutual funds family that holds essentially his entire savings: $1,400 in a maximum capital gains fund and $1,200 in a money market fund. He is aware of the multiplicity of investment opportunities offered by the mutual funds industry, but he is uncertain about how to approach his nascent investment program. He wants to do more than simply divide his money between a risk-oriented fund and a money market fund.

Design a financial strategy for Mark for the next ten years.

Chapter 19

Managing an Institutional Portfolio

Key Concepts

- active management
- asset allocation
- asset-based compensation
- buy-and-hold strategy
- incentive compensation
- index fund
- in-house management
- manager compensation
- passive management
- performance-based compensation
- portfolio management
- tilt index fund

Chapter Outline

Portfolio management is a process. The dictionary defines a process as the continuing development of a particular method of doing something that involves a number of steps or operations. Portfolio management is both a dynamic and a flexible process. As both economic circumstances and the needs and desires of the institution (or client being served by the institution) change, portfolio adjustments may be required. Hence, portfolio management is a continuous process as well as a systematic process, although the degree to which the process is formalized will vary from institution to institution.

The first section of this chapter discusses the general nature of the investment management decision process for an institution. Portfolio management strategies are presented in the second section. Portfolio management techniques that can be used to achieve good results for a given portfolio management strategy are examined in section three. Section four presents an example of an institutional portfolio in need of revision and how this revision was accomplished in light of the basic elements important to this decision.

Nature of Management Decisions

We can identify two basic decisions regarding the nature of institutional portfolio management. First, should investment management be done *in-house* or outside of the organization? Second, if the decision is made to employ outside managers, how many are needed, and how should they be chosen and compensated?

Internal versus External Management

One common justification offered for making in-house investment decisions is that the organization would save the cost of outside investment management fees. Another justification given is that performing investment management functions in-house would allow for a continual monitoring of the financial markets. This monitoring should lead to better investment management decisions as well as provide a basis for comparing how outside managers are performing if a portion of the portfolio is managed outside of the organization.

Before any decision can be made regarding how much, if any, of the portfolio will be managed in-house, an investment policy statement should be developed. Among the many benefits that flow from writing an investment policy statement is an appreciation of whether or not the required talent exists within the institution to handle the type of investments specified in the policy statement. If the talent already exists or can be readily developed, a case can be made for performing some or all of the investment management functions within the institution. However, the size of the institutional portfolio and the question of convenience also play a role in whether to manage funds internally. Managers of small portfolios may not be able to achieve sufficient economies of size in transaction costs to justify internal management. An investment management group outside of the firm may be able to negotiate lower commission rates. The size factor in conjunction with convenience is especially important in the management of liquid assets. Even a moderate-size institution may decide to "farm out" its short-term cash management to a money market fund because of the ability of the money market fund management to obtain good rates on large investments and to provide the portfolio manager the opportunity to make deposits and withdrawals, perhaps by check, of relatively small and uneven amounts.

Once the investment policy statement defines the asset classes appropriate for the institution and identifies general allocation procedures and percentages, the type and number of outside managers needed can be determined more easily. For example, if the policy statement identifies real estate, international stocks and bonds, small companies, and venture capital investments as appropriate asset classes for the organization, outside managers may possibly be needed to make these specialized investments.

The decision to employ an outside manager involves considerations of investment style, competence, personnel, and past performance record. The first question that needs to be addressed is the investment style of a potential outside manager. How does the manager operate within the market or the specialized segment for which expertise is claimed? Can the manager clearly define what investment management style is being employed and what investment objectives are being sought? For example, does the manager seek undervalued, small growth companies, or does the manager tend to seek superior performance by group rotation, shifting funds from drug stocks to energy stocks to food stocks, and so forth, as the manager assesses each group's potential? Does the outside manager have adequate personnel to accomplish the investment goals described, and are these people personally compatible with individuals within the institution? Last but not least, does the outside group being considered have a track record of good performance? How long a period of time has the group functioned under the same management, and does the record cover a complete business cycle? These questions and other similar ones are clearly important in the initial evaluation of any potential outside investment manager.

Investment Manager Compensation

The decision to employ outside investment managers means agreement will need to be reached on the nature and level of *manager compensation*. Three basic methods of compensation are (1) *asset-based compensation*, (2) *performance-based compensation*, and (3) a combination of asset-based and performance-based compensation.

Compensation based on a percentage of the assets under management is the most common form. Although the percentage will naturally vary depending on the type of asset being managed, annual compensation between .5 and .75 percent of assets is normal for common stock management. To find investment management compensation based only on the performance achieved is somewhat rare because an appropriate benchmark for measuring performance is difficult to find and the relevant time horizon for compensation purposes is difficult to define. However, some type of *incentive compensation* is usually desirable. We might find a combination of asset-based and performance-based compensation somewhat like the following:

If the manager's annual performance record is within 20 percent of the market as defined, the compensation will be .5 percent of average annual assets. Above 120 percent of the market return, the manager will receive .1 percent more for each percentage point that the portfolio beats the market with a maximum compensation equal to 2 percent. Below 80 percent of the market return, the manager will receive .1 percent less but will always receive .1 percent of average assets under management. With the market return at 10 percent, this compensation system, designed to achieve a good balance between reward for good performance and punishment for poor performance, would produce the following compensation levels:

Portfolio Performance	**Compensation Calculation (% of Assets)**			
(Market = 10%)	**Standard**	**Incentive**		**Total**
27% and above	.5	+1.5	=	2.0%
20	.5	+ .8	=	1.3
15	.5	+ .3	=	.8
8 to 12	.5	+ .0	=	.5
5	.5	− .3	=	.2
4 and below	.5	− .4	=	.1

Portfolio Management Strategies

We will consider portfolio management strategies as falling into two classes: (1) asset choice decisions and (2) the degree of portfolio management activity. Choosing strategies implies that broad goals and objectives have already been decided upon and that the portfolio is to be managed within these general guidelines. As such, portfolio management strategies are general in nature and do not deal with techniques for accomplishing specific risk and return objectives. Portfolio techniques are ways of implementing portfolio management strategies and are discussed in the next major section.

Asset Allocation

The main purpose of considering the elements that would go into constructing an investment policy statement is to be able to make a sound *asset allocation* decision. Three basic elements are involved in making this decision: (1) the objectives of the investor, (2) the constraints placed on the investor, and (3) risk and return expectations.

Investor Objectives

As we have noted often in this book, different investors may have widely differing objectives with regard to such fundamental factors as desired return, tolerable risk level, and liquidity. Because an institution's portfolio management essentially reflects the needs of its clients, one must look to their characteristics. For example, two pension funds may have different objectives, depending simply on the average age of the individuals covered by the pension plans. A pension plan in which the average age of the plan participants is thirty-five might be managed quite differently from a plan in which the average age is fifty because their investment time horizons could differ. The fund with the lower average age might have a common stock-to-fixed-income security split of 70 percent to 30 percent, and the other fund might have just the reverse split.

Constraints on the Investor

Constraints can be self-imposed or imposed by some external authority. As the result of careful consideration of its risk tolerance, return requirements, and other such factors, a pension fund might decide to invest no more than 50 percent of its portfolio in equities. On the other hand, a pension fund might have a maximum percentage of equity investments imposed on it. Many state and local pension funds have only recently been allowed to invest in common stocks or have only recently had their allowable allocation increased substantially. For example, until 1984, California's state pension fund was allowed equities up to only 25 percent of the portfolio's value. The fund's target equity percentage increased to 40 percent as of mid-1987.

Risk and Return Expectations

One way of forming risk and return expectations for asset allocation purposes is to use historical rates of return. Historical returns need to be meshed with the investment time horizon of the portfolio being managed. A relatively long time horizon, such as was the case with the pension fund having a thirty-five year average age for its participants, could more readily rely on the fact that common stocks have outperformed fixed-income securities over periods of about twenty years. This would mean that this fund should allocate a higher percentage of its portfolio to equity investment than would be the case for the pension fund having an average age of fifty for its participants.

Another method of arriving at risk and return expectations is to make explicit forecasts along the lines discussed in Chapters 7 and 8. One looks at the long-term growth potential for the economy and for various industries using fundamental factors such as demographic data, the rate of technological change in various industries, and the country's resource base. Present and anticipated financial market conditions should also be considered.

Passive Management

Passive management is essentially a *buy-and-hold strategy.* Fixed-income securities are bought with the idea of holding them to maturity or redemption. Common stocks are purchased with the prospect of a long holding period. Passive management keeps transaction costs at a minimum and eliminates the need to make major timing decisions. A common portfolio management approach for equity investing is known as indexing and involves use of an *index fund.*

An index fund is a portfolio constructed in such as way as to "track" the performance of a major stock market index. The Standard & Poor 500 stock index is often used because it contains about 75 percent of the market value of all NYSE-listed stocks. The index fund approach to investing is a form of the efficient market approach. The idea is to duplicate the performance of the market with acceptable variation levels.

Index funds have become popular in recent years as some professional investment managers have had difficulty matching or exceeding the rate of return from the market as represented by the S&P 500. An index fund would not have to own all 500 stocks in the S&P 500 in the percentage represented in the index. Evidence indicates that holding 200 to 250 properly chosen stocks out of the S&P 500 will enable the portfolio manager to keep the index fund roughly in line with the market. In addition, some managers monitor the firms in the S&P 500 for potential bankruptcies and eliminate these firms from their portfolios. Also possible is the construction of an international index fund to follow stock returns on an international basis rather than simply matching the S&P 500. Another idea is to index to the universe of small stocks rather than to the S&P 500. The rationale for this approach is that small companies appear to have outperformed large companies over the years.

Even if an investor likes the passive management approach of an index fund and is willing to settle for the market return, some investment questions are not answered by index funds. The index fund concept does not solve two of the important questions facing an investor, namely, how should investment funds be allocated among various major investment alternatives, and what risk is appropriate for the investor? A number of practical implementation problems are also encountered with index funds, such as the level of transaction costs required to keep the fund in line with the index. Despite these concerns, index funds have attracted considerable attention in recent years.

Active Management

Active portfolio management strategies attempt to achieve the highest return for the risk level accepted. Charles D. Ellis identifies three types of

Investment Highlight

Ivan Boesky (Insider Trading Arbitrageur)

This investment highlight examines the insider trading scandal involving Ivan Boesky and its ramifications.

Description

The investment community was shocked in November 1986 when Ivan Boesky pleaded guilty to insider trading. Insider trading involves the acquisition and use of nonpublic information to earn profits from trading in securities. This information often involves pending, but as yet unannounced, merger or takeover plans. Boesky paid $100 million to settle civil complaints and agreed to help federal investigators.

Boesky was well known for his risk arbitrage activities in merger situations and was something of a Horatio Alger. People often wondered how he was so successful in his trading activities and whether he could conduct his immense trading activities without receiving inside information. In November 1986, the question became, who would be next? Apparently, the Chinese Wall had cracked. The term *Chinese Wall* is Wall Street jargon for the controls designed to prevent confidential corporate information in an investment banking firm from being used in the firm's market trading activities.

Wall Street did not have to wait very long for the next development. On February 13, 1987, Martin Siegel, a former managing director and major stockholder of Kidder Peabody, pleaded guilty to two felony counts. On the previous day and based on Siegel's testimony, U.S. postal inspectors arrested Robert Freeman of Goldman, Sachs & Co., Richard Wigton of Kidder, Peabody & Co., and Timothy Tabor, formerly of Kidder Peabody. The New York division of the U.S. Postal Inspection Service became involved because it investigates mail fraud.

Conclusion

How are Washington authorities and the Wall Street community to prevent similar illegal insider trading activities in the future? The answer might include stiffer sentences for wrongdoing both at the individual and at the firm level, expanded enforcement activities, and speedier disclosures of stock holdings. One suggestion is that disclosure be required within twenty-four hours whenever ownership of more than 5 percent of a firm's stock is reached rather than the current ten-day reporting standard.

decisions that need to be made in actively managed portfolios: tactical, strategic, and philosophical.[1]

Strategic decisions have already been mentioned and deal with long-run decisions, such as the proper percentage of the portfolio to put into

1. Charles D. Ellis, "Conceptualizing Portfolio Management" in *Managing Investment Portfolios, A Dynamic Process*, ed. John L. Maginn and Donald L. Tuttle (Boston: Warren, Gorham & Lamont, 1983), 19–21.

common stocks. Tactical decisions deal with selecting securities. How do you go about determining the value of a security? Should you concentrate in emerging growth stocks or blue-chip stocks? Philosophical decisions are closely related to strategic decisions. The portfolio manager decides on a particular philosophy of investing and then sticks with that philosophy over a fairly long period of time. Investing fads are ignored. For example, the Babson Fund concentrates on high-quality growth companies. When these stocks were out of favor with investors in the mid-1970s, the Babson Fund did not alter its investment philosophy. Despite some relatively poor years, the Babson Fund has performed well recently. During the twelve months ending March 31, 1987, Babson's total return was 29.1 percent versus 26.2 percent for the S&P 500 stock index and 20.3 percent for the average capital appreciation fund.

Combined Active-Passive Management

A common portfolio management strategy, especially for large pension funds, is to combine an index fund with an actively managed portion of the fund. The College Retirement Equities Fund (CREF) is an excellent example of this strategy. Its portfolio composition as of year-end 1986 was as follows: $24.7 billion in U.S. stocks and $2.8 billion in international investments.[2] About 80 percent of the domestic holdings is indexed to the S&P 500. The remaining 20 percent is actively managed.

Another version of active-passive portfolio management involves some active portfolio management decisions within a passive investment management framework. In June 1981, Batterymarch Financial Management introduced what it called "FlexiTilt."[3] FlexiTilt indexes either to the entire S&P 500 or to the *Value Line* universe of about 1,600 stocks, at the option of the client. The major change, however, is that the client can select certain investment variables and *tilt* the fund. For example, a client could tilt the index fund to high-dividend yield stocks, low-P/E-ratio stocks, or high-beta stocks. In effect, the investor gets market performance, where the market is a designated portion of the entire equity market.

Portfolio Management Techniques

In putting portfolios together and in adjusting the composition of portfolios over time, portfolio managers can concentrate on three basic areas. These three areas are (1) type of portfolio asset, (2) quality of portfolio asset, and (3) the time horizon for the portfolio holdings. Let us briefly examine the nature and rationale for these portfolio management techniques.

2. *TIAA-CREF 1986 Annual Report.*

3. Richard Phalon, "Indexing: An Idea Who Time Has Gone," *Forbes* (October 12, 1981): 176ff.

Vary Type of Asset

We noted previously that the return from one type of asset varies on an annual basis from the return of other types of assets. Major switches that could occur in managing a portfolio would be between financial and real assets as well as between different types of investment alternatives within both the financial and real asset classifications. For example, a portfolio manager might decide to sell all common stock and bond holdings and buy real estate, antiques, and gold coins. Because many real assets cannot be bought and sold as readily as many financial assets, the investor contemplating such a switch would probably want to plan on being invested in the real assets for a fairly long period of time.

The portfolio manager has the option in the financial asset area of switching from common stocks to bonds and then back to common stocks at some later date. If the portfolio manager expects common stocks to perform poorly for the next year or two, the best move might be to sell the common stocks and buy fixed-income securities. Whether this would be desirable depends on the transaction costs incurred and on what one expects to happen to the price of the bonds over the period being examined.

Vary Quality of Asset

High-quality assets may well hold their value better than low-quality assets during poor economic conditions. U.S. government bonds may be a desirable portfolio holding during recessions because the investor need not be concerned with the ability of the federal government to pay the interest on the bonds and to repay the principal amount at maturity. On the other hand, bonds issued by smaller companies involved in manufacturing consumer durable goods might cause the portfolio manager some anxious moments as they decline in price because the business of the issuing company suffers from the recession.

The portfolio manager might deliberately seek low-quality common stocks and bonds if the economy is expected to stage a recovery. However, the investor has no guarantee returns will automatically be high from buying riskier assets in anticipation of improving economic conditions. The portfolio manager has to investigate the desirability of each potential portfolio addition.

Vary Time Horizon

In managing the fixed-income portion of a portfolio, varying the time horizon of the securities held may be helpful. Short-term, fixed-income securities such as U.S. treasury bills present little interest rate risk because the investor soon receives the principal amount of the investment. Fixed-income securities with a maturity of twenty years or more will vary more in price than a security such as a treasury bill.

If the portfolio manager expects interest rates to generally increase over the next few months, short-term securities should be bought and later switched over to long-term, fixed-income securities. In this manner, the principal of the investment is kept relatively intact and can be used to lock-in higher long-term rates when they appear to be at their peak. If the portfolio manager anticipates that interest rates will decline, long-term, fixed-income securities should be purchased to benefit from taking on interest rate risk. As interest rates decline, the investor with long-term, fixed-income securities may realize substantial capital appreciation. It should be noted, however, that interest rate forecasting in recent years has been a hazardous venture.

Another possible approach is to hold common stocks with varying investment time horizons. A portfolio manager might plan on holding a few "bedrock" stocks for a long time. If the stock market is expected to enter a period of rapid, upward price movements, the portfolio manager might add some speculative stocks with a view toward holding them only a few months. This technique, of course, increases the risk of the total portfolio and may result in poor performance if the portfolio manager is wrong on market timing.

Super Endowment Fund: *An Institutional Portfolio Management Example*

This section examines the portfolio of an endowment fund, the considerations involved in restructuring that portfolio, the revised portfolio, and the impact of a change in legislation. The material presented is based on an actual situation, although some modest changes have been made in the precise portfolio composition. These modest changes do not alter the basic thrust of the analysis that was actually performed.

The Portfolio and the Problem

Table 19–1 presents the portfolio of the fund as of April 7, 1983. The current income from this fund is used to provide scholarships to both undergraduate and graduate students. If this portfolio could be restructured to provide more current income, more financial aid could be granted. However, the growth of the fund's market value is also important so the dollar amount of the scholarships can be increased in the future. Let us now examine this portfolio from the viewpoint of some of the investment policy determinants that were discussed earlier.

Portfolio Management Considerations

This section looks at the risk, return, portfolio time horizon, taxation, and regulatory and legal considerations important to the portfolio management of this fund.

Table 19–1
Portfolio of Super Endowment Fund, April 7, 1983

Amount	Security	Dividend per Share	Price 4/7/83	Yield	Market Value	% of Total
300	CBS	2.80	66.500	4.2%	19,950	1.1
100	Delta Airlines	1.00	44.750	2.2	4,475	.3
700	Dun & Bradstreet	2.76	117.375	2.4	82,163	4.7
600	IBM	3.44	103.250	3.3	61,950	3.5
200	Mobil	2.00	28.000	7.1	5,600	.3
17,000	Raytheon	1.40	51.500	2.7	875,500	49.6
200	Texas Instruments	2.00	163.000	1.2	32,600	1.8
10,000	Union Carbide	3.40	58.250	5.8	582,500	33.0
	All Common Stocks				1,664,738	94.3
100,000	13% Gov't Agency Bond 12/83		101.000	13.0	101,000	5.7
	Total Portfolio				1,765,738	100.0

Risk

The portfolio shown on Table 19–1 is exactly as it was received from the donor. The portfolio had eight stocks, but 82.6 percent of the portfolio was invested in only two stocks. If these two stocks should decline significantly in value or reduce or eliminate their dividends, the fund could be severely injured. Eight stocks, if purchased in equal dollar amounts and carefully chosen with regard to their portfolio risk-reducing properties, would be adequate to get close to an efficient portfolio. However, the portfolio composition of the fund as of April 7, 1983, was clearly not efficient.

Return

The current income from the common stocks in the fund was $68,736. Combined with the $13,000 from the bond, the total portfolio income was $81,736, or a current return of 4.6 percent. To increase this yield to the range of 7 to 8 percent would be desirable because only current income can be spent for scholarships. Sufficient growth potential should still exist in the portfolio if this current yield objective is achieved.

Time Horizon

The time horizon for this portfolio is relatively long, and little need for liquidity exists in this fund. With the long time horizon and the low need for liquidity, a fairly passive portfolio management approach seems feasible.

Taxation

As an endowment fund, the income from this portfolio is not subject to taxation. The common stock portion of the portfolio should probably be tilted toward current income versus capital appreciation because of the fund's tax status.

Regulatory and Legal Considerations

Legal considerations are absolutely crucial to this analysis. Under the state law regulating this portfolio, only purchases of U.S. Treasury and agency issues are authorized investments. The fund can continue to hold its present portfolio of common stocks because "gifts-in-kind" may be kept, but any proceeds from common stock sales must be reinvested in government issues. The endowment fund's common stock portfolio cannot be restructured by selling certain common stocks and purchasing more common stocks.

Recommendations for Portfolio Revisions and Final Results

The inability to reinvest in common stocks is a severe portfolio management constraint. This constraint is so severe that any portfolio revision will likely result in a portfolio that is still an inefficient portfolio. Any suggestions for revising the portfolio must reconcile the various competing considerations we just discussed (i.e., the desire for both current income and capital appreciation) while improving the risk-return characteristics of the portfolio. Obviously, a substantial amount of judgment is involved in this portfolio revision decision. The following portfolio revisions were suggested and implemented:

1. Reduce the percentage of the portfolio invested in Raytheon and Union Carbide by selling 10,000 shares of Raytheon and 4,000 shares of Union Carbide. These sales would provide $748,000 for reinvestment and would also reduce the portfolio investment in these two stocks to $710,000, or 40.2 percent of the value of the entire portfolio. The total investment in all common stocks would be about 52 percent.
2. Reinvest roughly one-third of the $748,000 for five years, one-third for ten years, and one-third for fifteen years. This would keep interest rate risk at a manageable level. The yields available are as follows: 10.5 percent for five years, 10.9 percent for ten years, and 11.9 percent for fifteen years. This recommendation would provide an average return of 11.1 percent on reinvested funds.

The results of these recommendations are as follows:

1. A better common stock to fixed-income mix of 52 percent to 48 percent.
2. The current income changes as follows:

	Old	Revised
Income from stocks	$68,736	$68,736
Less income lost	0	27,600
	68,736	41,136
Bond interest	13,000	96,028
Total income	$81,736	$137,164

Some dividend income is lost when we sell the Raytheon and Union Carbide shares, but we gain 11.1 percent ($83,028) on the reinvestment of the proceeds. The total current income increases by $55,428, and the current yield goes from 4.6 percent to 7.8 percent ($137,164 ÷ $1,765,738).

3. Adequate growth potential still exists in the portfolio. The percentage invested in Raytheon and Union Carbide is still on the high side, however. More sales of these two stocks can be made in the future if the common portfolio increases in value.
4. Although the resulting portfolio is certainly not efficient, an improvement has clearly taken place.

The saga of the Super Endowment Fund up to this point clearly illustrates the problems that can be caused in a portfolio by restrictive legislation. The legislation, which was probably initially enacted in an attempt to protect the Super Endowment Fund, actually caused severe problems in the attempt to restructure this grossly inefficient portfolio. This inefficiency arose because the common stocks were initially received as a gift and gifts-in-kind could be held. A lobbying effort to change the state law was appropriate in this situation in order to accomplish two main goals. First, because the long-run total return from common stock has been greater than that available from fixed-income securities, the portfolio has limited growth potential as a result of not being able to purchase common stocks. Second, as indicated by the Super Endowment Fund story, any desired portfolio restructuring would be far easier to accomplish and the risk-return results much better if common stocks could be purchased. However, our story as it relates to the Super Endowment Fund is not yet complete.

A Law Change

While fund managers considered a lobbying effort to produce a less restrictive investment environment, change was about to occur shortly anyway. As a result of student political pressure, the state passed a law relating to divestment of the common stock of firms operating in South Africa. Effectively, the new law required the sale of common stock of companies doing business in South Africa.

Table 19–2 presents the portfolio of the Super Endowment Fund as of June 28, 1985. This table assumes the common stocks that existed in April 1983 were simply retained following the partial sale of Raytheon and Union Carbide. Although the portfolio probably still contains too

Table 19–2
Portfolio of Super Endowment Fund, June 28, 1985, After April 1983 Restructuring

Amount	Security	Price	Market Value	% of Total
300	CBS	116.250	34,875	2.0
100	Delta Airlines	49.000	4,900	0.3
1,400	Dun & Bradstreet*	79.125	110,775	6.3
600	IBM	123.750	74,250	4.2
200	Mobil	30.125	6,025	0.3
7,000	Raytheon	50.000	350,000	19.8
200	Texas Instruments	95.625	19,125	1.1
6,000	Union Carbide	46.250	277,500	15.7
	All Common Stocks		877,450	49.8
100,000	Money Market Fund	1.0000	100,000	5.7
249,333	10.5% U.S. Gov't Bond 8/88	103.6875	258,527	14.7
249,333	10.875% U.S. Gov't Bond 2/93	103.4400	257,910	14.6
249,333	11.75% U.S. Gov't Bond 2/01	108.1875	269,747	15.3
	All Fixed-Income Securities		886,184	50.2
	Total Portfolio		1,763,634	100.0

*Adjusted for two-for-one stock split.

much Raytheon and Union Carbide, the allocation between common stocks and fixed-income securities is about even. This table assumes the purchase at par of three different bonds in 1983 and the reinvestment of the $100,000 government agency bond that matured in December 1983 into a money market fund. The market value of the total portfolio is virtually unchanged from April 1983 to June 1985. As we noted earlier, however, the current income from the portfolio would have increased. The bonds purchased in April 1983 have increased in value, but the two biggest equity holdings, Raytheon and Union Carbide, decreased in value. Clearly, our restructuring in April 1983 was imperfect in achieving adequate diversification in the common stock area.

The South African divestiture had a serious impact on this portfolio. Table 19–3 shows the portfolio composition after selling all the stocks of companies doing business in South Africa. Almost no common stock is left, and new common stock cannot be purchased! Because no common stock can be purchased, Table 19–3 assumes the proceeds from the sale of stock, ignoring commission costs, were initially invested in the money market fund.

As the legislation relating to South African holdings was being considered in the state legislature, it became apparent that this divestiture would have a detrimental impact on this endowment fund as well as other portfolios being managed. Thus, the state passed a law, effective July 1, 1985, allowing investments to be made in accordance with a prudent-person standard. However, what investments would be prudent for an endowment fund such as the Super Endowment Fund still had to be determined. In effect, an investment policy statement needed to be drafted and agreed to by the institution's board of trustees. In the meantime, no change would be made in existing investments until the new investment policy statement was approved. It took until late April 1986 to draft and get agreement on what would be prudent investments. This period of over nine months during which the divestment proceeds could not be reinvested in other common stock caused a significant loss of market value for the Super Endowment Fund.

Table 19–4 shows the market value of the Super Endowment Fund as of March 27, 1986, assuming the divestment proceeds were simply left

Table 19–3
Portfolio of Super Endowment Fund, July 1, 1985, after South African Divestiture

Amount	Security	Price	Market Value	% of Total
100	Delta Airlines	49.000	4,900	0.3
200	Texas Instruments	95.625	19,125	1.1
	All Common Stocks		24,025	1.4
953,425	Money Market Fund	1.0000	953,425	54.1
249,333	10.5% U.S. Gov't Bond 8/88	103.6875	258,527	14.7
249,333	10.875% U.S. Gov't Bond 2/93	103.4400	257,910	14.6
249,333	11.75% U.S. Gov't Bond 2/01	108.1875	269,747	15.3
	All Fixed-Income Securities		1,739,609	98.6
	Total Portfolio		1,763,634	100.0

Table 19–4
Portfolio of Super Endowment Fund, March 31, 1986, Assuming No Common Stock Reinvestment

Amount	Security	Price	Market Value	% of Total
100	Delta Airlines	44.500	4,450	.2
200	Texas Instruments	122.000	24,400	1.3
	All Common Stocks		28,850	1.5
953,425	Money Market Fund	1.0000	953,425	51.1
249,333	10.5% U.S. Gov't Bond 8/88	105.0937	262,033	14.0
249,333	10.875% U.S. Gov't Bond 2/93	116.9375	291,564	15.6
249,333	11.75% U.S. Gov't Bond 2/01	133.0000	331,613	17.8
	All Fixed-Income Securities		1,838,635	98.5
	Total Portfolio		1,867,485	100.0

Table 19–5
Portfolio of Super Endowment Fund, March 31, 1986, Assuming Reinvestment on July 1, 1985, in Stocks

Amount	Security	Price	Market Value	% of Total
100	Delta Airlines	44.500	4,450	.2
200	Texas Instruments	122.000	24,400	1.2
853,425	S&P 500 Index	1.226	1,046,299	50.8
	All Common Stocks		1,075,149	52.2
100,000	Money Market Fund	1.0000	100,000	4.9
249,333	10.5% U.S. Gov't Bond 8/88	105.0937	262,033	12.7
249,333	10.875% U.S. Gov't Bond 2/93	116.9375	291,564	14.2
249,333	11.75% U.S. Gov't Bond 2/01	133.0000	331,613	16.1
	All Fixed-Income Securities		985,210	47.8
	Total Portfolio		2,060,359	100.0

in the money market fund. The fund's value increased over $100,000 from July 1, 1985. However, Table 19–5 shows what the market value of the fund would have been if the divestment proceeds had been reinvested in common stocks, as represented by the Standard & Poor's 500 stock index. From July 1, 1985, to March 27, 1986, the S&P 500 index rose 22.6 percent. The divestment proceeds of $853,425 would have increased in value to $1,046,299. The market value of the total portfolio of the Super Endowment Fund would have been $2,060,359, or $192,874 more than with reinvestment in the money market fund assumed in Table 19–4. The timing delay, which was essentially of a political nature, not only resulted in a much lower value for the endowment portfolio, but meant that the process of rebuilding the equity portion of the portfolio would have to begin following a substantial rise in the stock market.

Summary

This chapter examined portfolio management as applied in an institutional setting. Portfolio management is a systematic and continuous process. The appropriate risk, return, and investment time horizon need to be determined within the legal and regulatory framework facing the institution. The tax situation of the institution may also have an important part to play in its portfolio management.

In managing an institutional portfolio, a decision has to be made regarding how much, if any, of the portfolio's assets will be managed by external managers. Potential economies of scale, the talent available within the organization, and the type of investments authorized for the institution will determine to a considerable extent the need to employ external managers. These external managers can be evaluated based on their management style, their compensation requirements, and their track record.

We can distinguish between portfolio strategy and portfolio techniques. Strategies are broad goals for the portfolio decided upon as a result of long-term planning considerations. The two major strategic decisions are (1) how to allocate portfolio assets over various classes of assets and (2) what degree of activity to use in managing the portfolio. Portfolio management techniques are used to implement portfolio strategy. We can vary the type and quality of the portfolio assets. In addition, we can alter the time horizon implied in our portfolio.

Suggested Readings

AMBACHTSHEER, KEITH P., and JAMES L. FARRELL, JR. "Can Active Management Add Value?" *Financial Analysts Journal* (November–December 1979): 39–47.

ELLIS, RICHARD M., and ROBERTA L. PARKHILL. "South African Divestment: Social Responsibility or Fiduciary Folly?" *Financial Analysts Journal* (July–August 1986): 30–38.

FARRELLY, GAIL E., and WILLIAM R. REICHENSTEIN. "Risk Perceptions of Institutional Investors." *Journal of Portfolio Management* (Summer 1984): 5–12.

FONG, GIFFORD. "An Asset Allocation Framework." *Journal of Portfolio Management* (Winter 1980): 58–66.

GROSSMAN, BLAKE R., and WILLIAM F. SHARPE. "Financial Implications of South African Divestment." *Financial Analysts Journal* (July–August 1986): 15–29.

JOEHNK, MICHAEL D., ed. *Asset Allocation for Institutional Portfolios.* Homewood, IL: Dow Jones-Irwin, 1987.

WAGNER, WAYNE H., ALLEN EMKIN, and RICHARD L. DIXON. "South African Divestment: The Investment Issues." *Financial Analysts Journal* (November–December 1984): 14–22.

WILLIAMS, DAVE H. "Organizing for Superior Investment Returns." *Financial Analysts Journal* (September–October 1980): 21–23ff.

Questions

1. What are two basic decisions an investor needs to make regarding the management of a portfolio?

2. What reasons can be advanced for handling the investment management "in-house" rather than employing outside managerial talent?

3. What is the relationship of the investment policy statement to the decision whether or not to employ outside investment managers?

4. What factors should investors consider in selecting outside investment managers?

5. Distinguish between portfolio management strategies and techniques.

6. What advantages exist in using an index fund to implement a passive investment strategy?

7. Even under a passive portfolio management approach involving the use of an index fund, certain investment management decisions need to be made. What are these decisions?

8. What are the three types of decisions that need to be made in an actively managed portfolio?

9. What is the theory behind an investor using a combination of passive and active investment management strategies?

10. What are the three basic elements to be considered in making sound asset allocation decisions in the management of an institutional portfolio?

11. When an investor varies the time horizon for a fixed-income portfolio, the investor is really making an adjustment for what type of risk?

Problems

1. The Carriage and Buggywhip Makers Union has a pension fund with a book value of $200 million. The fund has been managed for many years by a committee of union members. However, none of the committee members has had any formal training or experience in either security analysis or investment management. The committee has relied largely on security salespersons for advice.

   Although additions to the portfolio are currently being made as the result of a positive net annual cash inflow, the committee recognizes the union members are in a profession that will die with them. The majority of the union members will reach retirement age within five years and will die within twenty-five years. In view of these circumstances, the committee feels the portfolio may not be well structured. You have been approached for assistance as a professional investment manager.

   The portfolio is presently structured as follows:

   5% short-term (less than one year) notes
   5% medium term (about five years) notes
   15% long-term bonds (more than twenty years) selling at relatively large discounts and offering ten-year call protection
   15% tax-exempt municipal bonds
   10% residential real estate mortgages; average life of fifteen years
   20% growth stocks
   10% cyclical stocks mainly of natural resource companies
   20% preferred stocks

(a) Discuss the suitability of this portfolio given the circumstances facing the union.

(b) Justify any portfolio changes you would like to recommend.

2. On December 31, 1980, Susan Megan received a telephone call from Henry Winters, the city treasurer of Union Center. Susan had been recommended as an investment expert. Henry wanted Susan to make a presentation on ways in which the portfolio management of the Union Center Pension Fund might be improved.

Union Center is a midwestern city with a population of about 40,000. The Union Center Pension Fund covers all municipal employees. The city has experienced moderate growth over the prior decade, and the pension plan contains fixed-income securities with a face value of slightly over four million dollars.

In planning for the forthcoming meeting, Susan visited Henry's office and obtained a listing of the securities in the Union Center Pension Fund. Exhibit P19–1 is a summary of the bonds in the fund classified by maturity date. By state law, the Union Center Pension Fund's investments are limited to federal government fixed-income

Exhibit P19–1 Union Center Pension Fund Assets, December 31, 1980

					Cost			
	Issue		*Date Purchased*	*Face Amount ($000)*	*Total ($000)*	*Per Bond**	*Market Price**	*Yield to Maturity*
	1/02/81	T-Bill	11/80	104	102.7	—	—	—
7.35%	3/81	FNMA	3/79 & 6/80	505	496.4	98.10	98.02	17.45%
	4/30/81	T-Bill	12/80	430	409.3	—	—	14.69%
	8/13/81	T-Bill	10/80	1,290	1,171.7	—	—	13.67%
6.375%	2/82	T-Bond	9/76	25	25.3	101.06	93.16	12.77%
6.80%	9/82	FNMA	11/74	310	286.4	92.12	90.20	12.88%
7.75%	3/83	FNMA	3/78	200	198.8	99.13	90.04	12.80%
9.25%	4/83	FNMA	7/78	50	51.0	102.00	92.24	12.76%
3.25%	6/78–83	T-Bond	5/53 & 12/71	17	14.9	87.21	82.08	11.80%
7.25%	2/84	T-Note	2/77	130	130.3	100.07	86.10	12.70%
6.375%	8/84	T-Bond	8/72	139	138.2	99.14	81.28	12.78%
7.25%	8/84	T-Note	8/77 & 9/77	274	274.0	100.00	84.30	12.55%
3.25%	5/85	T-Bond	8/76	80	72.6	90.24	81.13	8.42%
4.25%	5/75–85	T-Bond	12/71 & 8/76	55	46.8	85.03	81.16	9.52%
8.80%	10/85	FNMA	10/78	192	188.4	98.04	85.20	12.61%
8.00%	8/86	T-Note	8/76	40	40.0	100.00	82.28	12.31%
6.125%	11/86	T-Bond	8/76	28	27.9	99.21	77.18	11.48%
7.00%	3/92	FNMA	8/72; 10/72; 2/73	70	69.0	98.18	66.28	12.16%
7.05%	6/92	FNMA	9/72; 3/73; 6/73	110	107.1	97.12	67.00	12.13%
4.25%	8/87–92	T-Bond	11/65	5	4.9	98.00	82.10	6.43%
3.00%	2/95	T-Bond	7/55	21	21.0	100.00	81.16	4.82%
				4,075				

*Quoted in standard government bond price format.

securities, fixed income securities guaranteed by the federal government, and insured deposits at financial institutions. Consequently, all the securities shown in Exhibit P19–1 are federal government obligations or government-guaranteed obligations such as those issued by the Federal National Mortgage Association (FNMA). The month each security was purchased, the face amount of the security, the cost basis associated with the security, its market price as of December 31, 1980, and the yield to maturity are also presented in Exhibit P19–1.

Susan learned that the management of the fund was being handled by a seven-person advisory board composed of Henry Winters, five city employees appointed by the Union Center's city manager, and a business person from the community also chosen by the city manager. Over the years, the advisory board had followed essentially a buy-and-hold strategy. Funds for the new purchases of securities came from maturing securities and the quarterly receipt of contributions from Union Center itself and the employees. Henry also related that the Union Center Pension Fund appeared to be in a position similar to that of many other pensions funds in that inflows to the fund could be expected to exceed outflows for many years. This was the result of the number of active contributors relative to the number of people for whom retirement could be anticipated in the near future. In addition, since Union Center was growing, the municipal labor force provided new pension plan contributors.

Various investment banking firms and pension fund management groups were being asked to make presentations since Henry was interested in determining if the Union Center Pension Fund should be managed by an outside group rather than by the present advisory board. As a resident of Union Center, Susan had agreed to donate her services for her initial presentation. However, she wondered if she might eventually be retained as a portfolio consultant to the fund. In any event, Henry had asked Susan to comment on the desirability of employing an outside investment manager at an annual cost that would approximate .3 percent of the fund's assets.

In preparing her presentation to Union Center Pension Fund's advisory board, Susan wanted to discuss the nature of the fund and basic investment management considerations that should receive the board's attention. Susan felt there were three basic portfolio management approaches the board could follow, and she wanted to be prepared to comment on the desirability of each of the following approaches:

1. Turn over the entire portfolio management to one or more outside portfolio managers
2. Have the present advisory board assume a somewhat more active portfolio management role
3. Continue with the present portfolio approach

Henry also wanted Susan to make some brief comments to the advisory board regarding how one might go about measuring the portfolio performance no matter which portfolio management ap-

Exhibit P19–2 **Yields of Treasury Securities, December 31, 1980, Based on Closing Bid Quotations**

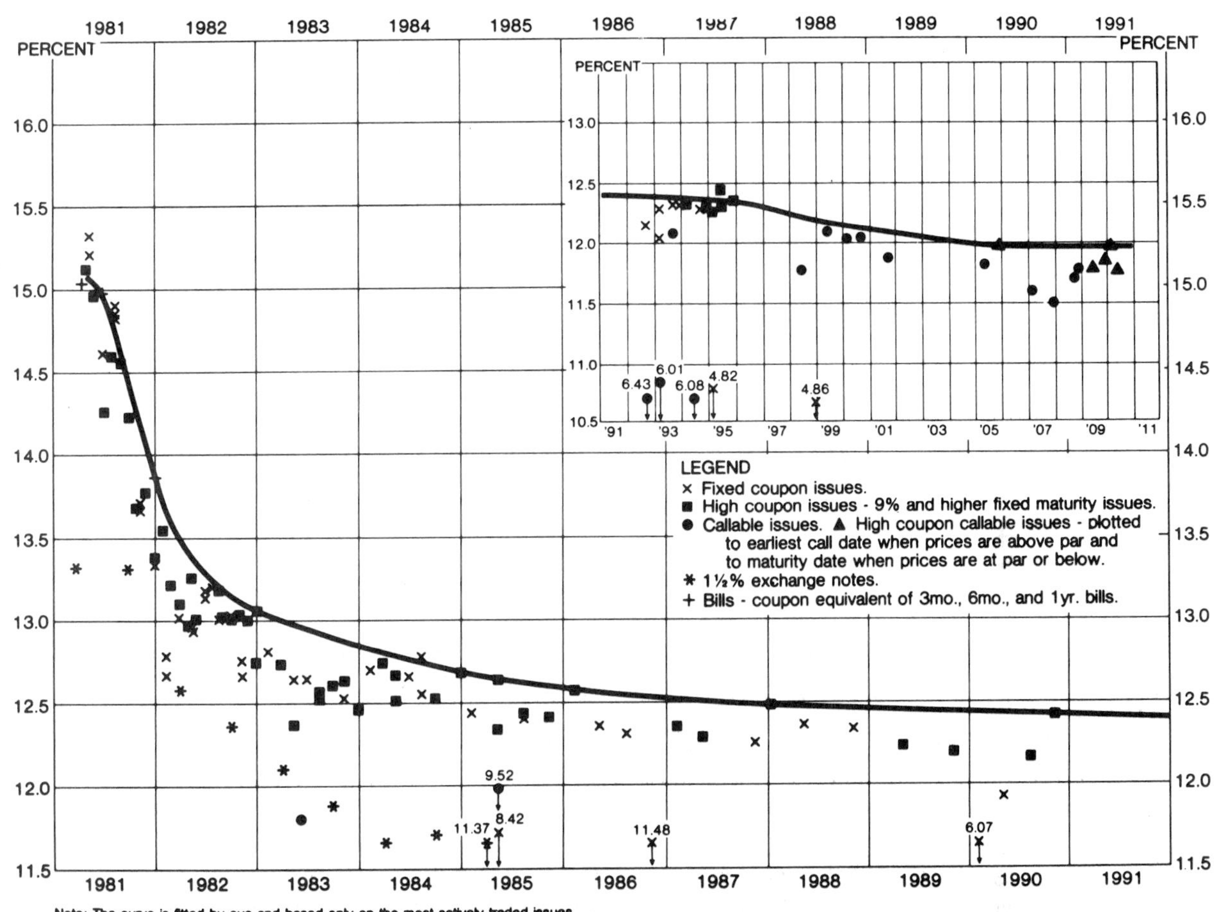

Note: The curve is fitted by eye and based only on the most actively traded issues.
Market yields on coupon issues due in less than 3 months are excluded.

proach was finally chosen. In this regard, the development of some practical portfolio management guidelines would be of considerable help to the board members since they are relatively unsophisticated in portfolio management matters.

Exhibit P19–2 is the yield curve for U.S. government securities as of December 31, 1980. Susan felt this might be useful in recommending a portfolio maturity structure for the Union Center Pension Fund. Exhibit P19–3 provides a historical review of the yields available on U.S. treasury bonds as well as other types of fixed-income securities since 1970. Exhibit P19–4 shows market quotations for treasury bonds outstanding as of December 31, 1980.

Prepare Susan's comments for her presentation to the advisory board.

Exhibit P19–3 **Average Yields of Long-Term Treasury, Corporate, and Municipal Bonds**

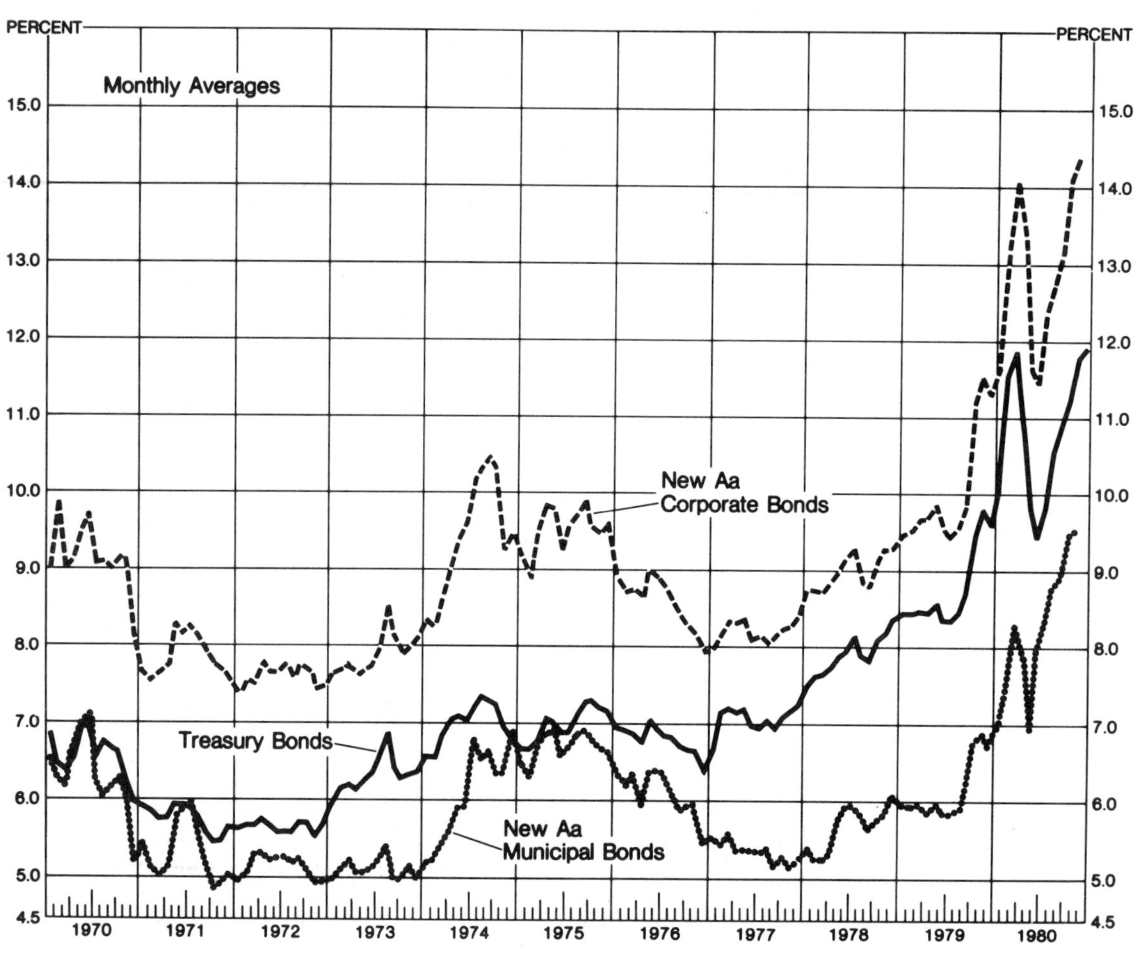

Exhibit P19–4 Market Quotations on Treasury Securities, December 31, 1980

(Price decimals are 32nds)

Amount out-standing (millions)	Description	Price		Yield		Issue date	Price range since first traded 1/			
							High		Low	
		Bid	Change from last month	To first call or maturity 2/	Change from last month		Price	Date	Price	Date
$ 807	7% - 8/15/81	95.16	+.24	14.83%	-.23%	8/15/71	110.02	11/15/71	89.06	3/17/80
2,702	6-3/8 - 2/15/82	93.16	+1.23	12.77	-1.22	2/15/72	101.14	3/09/72	86.10	3/06/80
1,185	3-1/4 - 6/15/78-83	82.08	-.02	11.80	+.32	5/01/53	111.28	8/04/54	62.02	5/26/70
2,203	6-3/8 - 8/15/84	81.28	+.14	12.78	-.04	8/15/72	100.10	12/03/76	77.04	3/06/80
641	3-1/4 - 5/15/85	81.13	-.05	8.42	+.14	6/03/58	101.04	5/11/58	61.08	5/26/70
963	4-1/4 - 5/15/75-85	81.16	-.24	9.52	+.33	4/15/60	105.28	5/05/61	69.02	3/12/80
1,196	6-1/8 - 11/15/86	77.18	+3.12	11.48	-.90	11/15/71	100.20	11/05/71	73.02	2/26/80
2,152	3-1/2 - 2/15/90	82.07	-.01	6.07	+.03	2/14/58	106.26	4/21/58	59.20	5/26/70
1,247	8-1/4 - 5/15/90	79.18	+1.02	11.93	-.20	4/07/75	111.05	12/31/76	74.18	12/16/80
2,422	4-1/4 - 8/15/87-92	82.10	-.08	6.43	+.04	8/15/62	104.10	12/26/62	63.00	5/26/70
1,504	7-1/4 - 8/15/92 3/	69.28	+1.26	12.16	-.36	7/08/77	99.10	6/29/77	65.09	2/26/80
143	4 - 2/15/88-93	82.28	+.18	6.01	-.06	1/17/63	100.11	1/16/63	62.18	5/26/70
627	6-3/4 - 2/15/93 3/	66.21	+.21	12.05	-.12	1/10/73	99.22	1/04/73	61.27	12/16/80
1,501	7-7/8 - 2/15/93 3/	72.18	+1.28	12.29	-.36	1/06/78	99.22	12/30/77	66.24	2/26/80
1,914	7-1/2 - 8/15/88-93	70.24	+3.12	12.07	-.68	8/15/73	104.14	9/28/73	64.14	12/11/80
1,768	8-5/8 - 8/15/93 3/	76.18	+1.18	12.33	-.30	7/11/78	102.15	9/12/78	70.22	2/26/80
1,509	8-5/8 - 11/15/93 3/	76.14	+1.10	12.32	-.24	10/10/78	100.13	10/13/78	70.18	2/26/80
3,010	9 - 2/15/94 3/	78.20	+1.16	12.33	-.27	1/11/79	101.17	7/02/79	72.28	12/11/80
902	4-1/8 - 5/15/89-94	82.08	-.09	6.08	+.04	4/18/63	100.26	8/28/63	61.26	8/26/74
1,506	8-3/4 - 8/15/94 3/	76.27	+1.23	12.29	-.32	7/09/79	99.15	7/02/79	71.08	12/11/80
1,502	10-1/8 - 11/15/94 3/	85.24	+1.22	12.29	-.29	10/18/79	103.26	6/13/80	79.14	12/11/80
423	3 - 2/15/95 3/	81.16	-1.10	4.82	+.15	2/15/55	101.12	6/18/55	59.20	5/26/70
1,502	10-1/2 - 2/15/95 3/	88.09	+1.29	12.27	-.31	1/10/80	106.24	6/16/80	81.22	12/11/80
1,504	10-3/8 - 5/15/95 3/	87.06	+1.20	12.30	-.27	7/09/80	101.10	7/08/80	80.14	12/11/80
1,503	12-5/8 - 5/15/95 3/	101.04	+1.28	12.45	-.29	4/08/80	121.30	6/16/80	94.06	12/11/80
1,482	11-1/2 - 11/15/95 3/	94.07	+1.19	12.36	-.25	10/14/80	100.14	10/15/80	87.04	12/11/80
692	7 - 5/15/93-98 3/	65.08	+.14	11.78	-.07	5/15/73	99.22	9/28/73	59.18	12/11/80
1,592	3-1/2 - 11/15/98 3/	83.29	+.21	4.86	-.05	10/03/60	95.14	5/12/61	59.20	5/26/70
2,414	8-1/2 - 5/15/94-99 3/	73.24	+1.24	12.09	-.30	5/15/74	112.16	12/31/76	67.12	2/26/80
2,771	7-7/8 - 2/15/95-00 3/	69.04	+1.24	12.04	-.31	2/18/75	107.04	12/31/76	62.21	12/11/80
4,662	8-3/8 - 8/15/95-00 3/	72.20	+1.24	12.04	-.30	8/15/75	111.16	12/31/76	66.12	12/11/80
1,575	8 - 8/15/96-01 3/	70.11	+2.01	11.88	-.36	8/16/76	108.10	12/31/76	63.19	12/11/80
4,246	8-1/4 - 5/15/00-05 3/	71.20	+2.00	11.82	-.34	5/15/75	110.24	12/31/76	65.02	12/11/80
4,249	7-5/8 - 2/15/02-07 3/	67.18	+2.00	11.60	-.35	2/15/77	100.28	6/28/77	61.10	2/21/80
1,495	7-7/8 - 11/15/02-07 3/	69.31	+1.07	11.51	-.20	11/15/77	100.23	11/23/77	64.14	12/11/80
2,103	8-3/8 - 8/15/03-08 3/	72.23	+2.01	11.71	-.34	8/15/78	100.06	9/12/78	65.29	12/11/80
5,230	8-3/4 - 11/15/03-08 3/	75.10	+1.28	11.78	-.31	11/15/78	100.20	11/16/78	68.00	12/11/80
4,606	9-1/8 - 5/15/04-09 3/	78.08	+2.00	11.79	-.32	5/15/79	103.13	7/02/79	70.20	12/11/80
4,201	10-3/8 - 11/15/04-09 3/	88.00	+2.10	11.85	-.33	11/15/79	108.04	6/13/80	79.31	12/11/80
2,647	11-3/4 - 2/15/05-10 3/	98.04	+2.10	11.98	-.30	2/15/80	120.24	6/16/80	89.26	12/11/80
2,987	10 - 5/15/05-10 3/	85.13	+2.07	11.78	-.32	5/15/80	105.02	6/16/80	77.27	12/11/80
2,160	12-3/4 - 11/15/05-10 3/	106.06	+2.26	11.97	-.34	11/17/80	108.08	12/22/80	96.29	12/11/80

1/ Beginning April 1953, prices are closing bid quotations in the over-the-counter market. Prices for prior dates are the mean of closing bid and ask quotations. "When issued" prices are included in the history beginning October 1941. Dates of highs and lows in case of recurrences are the latest dates.

2/ On callable issues market convention treats the yields to earliest call date as most significant when an issue is selling above par, and to maturity when it is selling at par or below.

3/ Included in the average yield of long term taxable Treasury Bonds as shown under "Average Yields of Long Term Bonds."

Chapter 20

Measuring Investment Performance

Key Concepts

- benchmark portfolio
- beta
- buy-and-hold strategy
- characteristic line
- diversifiable risk
- fully diversified risk premium
- gross security selection
- index fund
- investment time horizon
- Jensen's alpha
- naive opportunities
- net security selection
- reward-to-variability ratio
- risk-adjusted performance
- sector index
- Sharpe index
- standard deviation
- Treynor measure

Chapter Outline

Measuring Portfolio Performance
Risk-Adjusted Performance Measures
Investment Performance Attribution
Summary

To complete our study of the investment process, we must undertake the task of evaluating investment performance. Performance evaluation is necessary whether we hire professional managers or manage our own funds. If a professional manager is investing our funds, we want to know whether that manager is achieving better performance than we could achieve by investing ourselves. If we are investing our own funds, we need to determine whether our investment objectives are being accomplished. In this chapter, we will discuss procedures used to evaluate investment performance that take a total portfolio perspective and assess return on a risk-adjusted basis.

Measuring Portfolio Performance

We can approach the area of performance measurement by concentrating on the four key questions presented below. These questions will provide the foundation for our discussions throughout this chapter.

Four Key Questions

The first question we need to ask is, What should be measured? This seemingly simple question can lead to major problems when we try to focus on performance. For example, what portfolio is to be measured? Ideally, the performance of the entire portfolio of assets owned by the investor should be the object of analysis. However, problems can often arise when trying to measure the value of certain assets, and this would preclude the total portfolio approach for many investors.

What should performance be judged against? This second question identifies the need to have a standard of comparison for use in making judgments about investment performance. Portfolio returns are usually compared with the average performance of other investments in the same category or risk class. By setting *benchmarks,* a portfolio's performance can be ranked relative to similar investments. Usually, actively managed portfolios are compared to the performance of "naively" managed portfolios.

Problems arise, however, when trying to derive useful benchmarks for portfolios having complex asset structures. Should a portfolio containing both common stocks and fixed-income securities be judged as one or two portfolios? For an institutional portfolio, how should performance be measured when responsibility for fund management is distributed among several managers?

The third major question is, How are risk-adjustment factors to be calculated and applied? Given the elusive nature of risk, risk adjustment is not always an easy or an unambiguous task. For example, the portfolio being evaluated may not actually be achieving the desired risk level. A manager might have wanted a portfolio beta of 1.1 but ended up with a portfolio having a beta of .9. The return actually achieved may have been appropriate for the .9 beta portfolio, but the performance was poor in light of the risk objective of the portfolio. As another example, all investors do not hold fully diversified portfolios containing only systematic risk. If a portfolio is not fully diversified, many statistical and conceptual problems arise that make beta a less-than-perfect measure of risk. Perhaps the investor did not diversify deliberately because certain stocks were especially attractive as they were considered undervalued. Some measure of the lack of diversification needs to be considered in risk-adjusting the portfolio to measure performance.

What caused the superior or inferior performance? This fourth question is important because we need to identify what caused above- or below-average performance so the information can be used in making future investment decisions. Just because risk-adjusted performance is above or below what investors anticipated does not mean the manager should be praised or blamed. The manager may have actually picked undervalued securities, and this may have helped to account for the good performance. On the other hand, the manager may have shown poor market timing, and this would be a negative factor. In considering these two factors together, how should a portfolio manager be evaluated when investing in undervalued, low-beta securities just before a strong bull market when high-beta securities would have been desirable? The manager would be half right and half wrong. Finally, the element of luck can not be disregarded. The manager might have just been lucky in being able to show superior performance over the period examined. Over long periods of time and over many investors, the element of chance or luck should cease to be an important influence, but it might be important for a single investor over an investment period of a few years.

Portfolio Perspective

Any performance measurement needs to examine the overall behavior of the portfolio. Stories abound about the investor who purchased 100 shares of common stock for a low price, say $5 per share, and sold them a year later at ten times the original price. This would certainly be an outstanding return, but the evaluation of performance must consider all the investor's securities and not just the result of a single investment. Portfolio performance is the critical ingredient when attempting to determine the wisdom of investing. Investing in the stock market can be quite profitable, but to conclude that the investor would consistently achieve superior performance on the basis of the one-year return on one stock alone would be foolish.

Return from Professional Management

Professional fund managers often do not have control over the amount of funds they have to invest. This is especially true for open-ended mutual funds in which participants can make contributions to and withdrawals from the fund at any time. For example, assume that an investor purchased 100 shares of a mutual fund with a \$50 net asset value (NAV) and watched them rise to \$100 NAV per share by the end of year one. Also at the end of year one, assume the investor decided to buy an additional 50 shares at \$100 per share only to have the value drop to \$60 per share by the end of year two. At the end of year two, the total value of the holdings would be \$90,000 (150 shares × \$60 per share). The internal rate of return on the investor's holdings for the two-year period would be −6.8 percent.

Period	Cash Flow	
0	(\$50,000)	
1	(50,000)	IRR = −6.8%
2	90,000	
Net	(\$10,000)	

The untimely investment of \$50,000 in the fund at the end of year one is not the fault of the mutual fund manager. If the effect of the \$50,000 contribution is "neutralized," the fund manager's performance can be judged better. In this case the return for the first year was

$$(1 + R_1) = \$100/\$50 = 2 \qquad R = 100\%$$

and the return for the second year was

$$(1 + R_2) = \$60/\$100 = .6 \qquad R = -40\%$$

The average return over the two-year period was

$$(1 + R_1)(1 + R_2) = 2 \times .6 = 1.20 \qquad \bar{R} = 9.5\%$$

Although the knowledge that the fund manager produced an average annual return of 9.5 percent may not soothe the investor who lost \$10,000 over the two-year period, the reason for the loss can be easily assessed. For managed portfolios, the value of the portfolio should be recalculated each time that contributions or withdrawals occur so that the investment decision process can be isolated from the decisions by investors to change their dollar commitments to the fund.

Benchmark Portfolios

Reviewing actual portfolio returns is critical to the evaluation process, but performance should be judged within the context of the opportunities available. Most of us would conclude that an average annual return for common stock of 12 percent over a twenty-five-year period is adequate performance considering that an investment of \$10,000 twenty-five years ago would now be worth \$170,001. Such a return may be adequate but does not necessarily suggest good performance.

We might ask, what could have been accomplished during the same period had we invested in a broadly diversified fund and left the funds for the entire period? For example, had the 12 percent return been achieved during the period from 1941 through 1965, we would have to conclude that performance was mediocre. The New York Stock Exchange (NYSE) stocks averaged a 16 percent return during that same period. Had the investor purchased a portfolio consisting of all the NYSE stocks at the beginning of 1941, $10,000 would have grown to $408,742 by the end of 1965. Performance must be judged relative to the opportunities available.

The opportunities used as a benchmark are referred to as *naive opportunities.* Any performance comparison should be made to a portfolio that could have been selected by an investor without any special skills, information, or foresight. One way to construct such a portfolio would be to assume a *buy-and-hold strategy.* With the buy-and-hold strategy, an initial *benchmark portfolio* is purchased and held to the end of the investment period. All cash proceeds are invested in securities similar to the initial portfolio. The buy-and-hold strategy might be used primarily by bond investors seeking to maximize income over a long period of time.

Another technique would be to select an *index fund* as the benchmark portfolio. The most obvious common stock portfolio falling into this category would be an index fund that replicates the performance of a broad stock market index, such as the S&P 500 index. For bonds, the Shearson/Lehman Corporate Bond Index provides a standard for a large universe of bond investments. This index consists of over 3,000 bonds. Because the return on a market index such as the S&P 500 shows the average portfolio return earned for common stock investors, average investment skills should produce a return equal to the market index fund.

No matter what index is chosen for making comparisons, the investor must use judgment in ranking various portfolios. We pointed out in Chapter 3 the problems that can arise from the way various market indicators are constructed. For more specialized portfolios and investment strategies, a benchmark may need to be tailor-made to capture the particular circumstances of a given portfolio or investment style.

Portfolio Management by One Manager

Let us look at a portfolio recently held by an endowment fund. This portfolio is known as the Market Portfolio and has a stated objective of at least matching the total market return over time. The holdings for this portfolio as of the end of March 1987 are shown in Exhibit 20–1. The weighted-average Value Line beta estimate for the stocks in the portfolio is 1.01. Diversification of unsystematic risk is accomplished mainly by holding nineteen stocks that each account for at least 1 percent of the fund's total market value.

The performance of the endowment fund portfolio over the nine-month period, June 1986 through March 1987, is provided in Exhibit 20–2. The S&P 500 index is used as a benchmark for judging the short-term performance of the endowment fund. Over the nine-month period, the average monthly return for the market fund underperformed the S&P by .57 percent.

What can we say about the performance of this endowment fund? What other things would we like to know before making a performance assessment? We should first recognize that nine months is a rather short time period for making a valid assessment of the performance of a port-

Exhibit 20–1 **Endowment Fund, Market Portfolio, March 1987**

Stock Name	*Shares Held*	*Price*	*Market Value*	*Weight*	*Beta*	*Dividend Income*
American Stores	51	$65.75	$ 3,353	.17%	1.00	$ 43
Amoco	2,564	79.75	204,479	10.51	1.05	8,461
Banc One	3,000	26.25	78,750	4.05	.70	2,520
Bell South	2,715	39.75	107,921	5.54	1.10	5,973
Campbell Soup	400	69.13	27,650	1.42	.85	576
Comsat	2,500	32.50	81,250	4.17	1.00	3,000
Consolidated Freight	990	35.00	34,650	1.78	1.00	812
CSX	120	31.75	3,810	.20	1.30	139
Federated Dept. Sts.	500	99.00	49,500	2.54	1.15	1,480
Fuqua	1,784	32.50	57,980	2.98	1.10	428
Georgia Pacific	209	49.13	10,267	.53	1.40	209
Interlake Steel	2,496	42.38	105,768	5.43	.70	3,245
K mart	1,000	62.63	62,625	3.22	1.15	1,740
Maytag	2,200	57.88	127,325	6.54	.90	3,916
Mellon Bank	1,000	50.25	50,250	2.58	.95	2,760
Norfolk Southern	800	93.50	74,800	3.84	1.00	2,880
Penney	500	99.00	49,500	2.54	1.05	1,480
Perry Drug Stores	4,000	13.63	54,500	2.80	1.00	880
Quaker Oats	2,797	46.75	103,526	6.71	.85	2,234
Sears	4,896	50.88	249,084	12.80	1.25	9,792
Security Pacific	3,208	35.00	112,280	5.77	1.15	4,748
Syntex	3,200	75.50	241,600	12.41	.90	5,120
Union Pacific	240	75.25	18,060	.93	1.20	480
Woolworth	210	50.13	10,526	.54	1.05	235
Total			$1,964,455			$63,151
Average					1.01	

Units = 168,821.16 Value/unit = 11.53 Dividend/unit = .37

Exhibit 20–2 **Market Fund versus S&P 500 Benchmark, June 1986–March 1987**

	Net Asset Value of Fund		**Percentage Monthly Change**		
Month	*Market*	*S&P 500*	*Market*	*S&P 500*	*Difference (Market – S&P 500)*
6/86	10.49	250.84			
7/86	9.70	236.12	−7.53	−5.87	−1.66
8/86	10.27	252.93	5.88	7.12	−1.24
9/86	9.46	231.32	−7.89	−8.54	.65
10/86	9.90	243.98	4.65	5.47	− .82
11/86	10.13	249.22	2.32	2.15	.17
12/86	9.67	242.17	−4.54	−2.83	−1.71
1/87	10.82	274.08	11.89	13.18	−1.29
2/87	11.72	284.20	8.32	3.69	4.63
3/87	11.53	291.70	−1.62	2.64	−4.26
Geometric Mean Monthly Return			.95%	1.52%	

folio such as this fund. The market was mostly going up during this period, and this portfolio has not been tested by a strong bear market. The stocks in this portfolio were purchased with an *investment time horizon* of three to five years as is consistent with the time horizon for an endowment fund. Hence, three to five years may be required before we can make a valid assessment of this fund's performance, although periodic measurements are useful. The current yield on the endowment fund is about 40 basis points greater than on the S&P 500, so a comparison of total returns rather than simply price movements might be more realistic. Finally, this fund does not invest in any companies doing business in South Africa. This means that a value-weighted index composed mainly of large companies might be a poor benchmark for performance measurement purposes. According to the Standard & Poor's *Outlook,* a large percentage of the top firms by market value were not eligible investments for this fund during early 1987. The figures are as follows:

	Top 50	**Top 100**	**Top 150**
Cumulative market value of firms as % of total S&P 500 index	44.8%	61.9%	73.1%
South African firm statistics			
Number of firms in South Africa	26	45	54
SA firms as % of number of firms	52%	45%	36%
Market value of SA firms			
As % of total S&P 500 index	26.1%	32.3%	34.4%
As % of value of top firms	58.2%	52.3%	47.1%

We can note that the top 50 firms in the S&P 500 index in terms of market value account for 44.8 percent of the market value of the entire index. Of these 50 firms, 26 are not eligible for investment by the endowment fund, and these companies account for 26.1 percent of the market value of the total S&P index and a large 58.2 percent of the market value represented by the top 50 firms in the index. Perhaps an equally weighted index, such as the *Value Line Composite Index,* might be a better benchmark for measuring performance as far as this endowment fund is concerned.

Portfolio Management by Multiple Managers

For many institutional portfolios, investments are balanced, or mixed, and invested in more than one asset class. In these cases, establishing a benchmark portfolio can become a difficult task. This problem becomes especially acute, for example, when trying to measure the overall performance of pension funds.

Many pension funds hire a group of portfolio managers instead of one manager to make all investment decisions. Each individual manager has a portion of the pension fund to invest independently of the other managers. The individual managers are selected for their specialization in a specific segment of the financial markets or their "style" of investing. For example, one manager may be a bond specialist, another a small capitalization stock specialist, while a third might be a growth stock specialist. In effect, the pension fund sponsor picks managers instead of investments per se. By rotating the investment funds among the managers, the pension fund executes its overall investment strategy.

At the individual manager level, performance is often measured by comparison to indexes developed for the specific *sector* or by comparison with other managers operating in the same investment style. At the fund level, the pension plan sponsors must integrate the diverse set of benchmarks into an overall standard that can be used to give an indication of total fund performance. The global benchmark becomes very important in helping the fund sponsors make decisions regarding manager selection and fund rotation.

In the benchmark approach discussed in this section, performance for a portfolio or manager is judged against the average performance for investments of the same class. Perhaps, a more precise approach used by many investors in performance evaluation is to specify benchmarks based on risk-adjusted security pricing models.

Risk-Adjusted Performance Measures

The discussion of *risk-adjusted performance* measurement centers on the four basic functions of the portfolio manager, including (1) market risk level selection, (2) diversifiable risk, (3) security selection, and (4) responses to market projections. All of these items may be summarized by using the ratio of return to risk. As we have discussed in Chapter 6, no single measure of risk has proven to be "best" for pricing securities. To the extent that CAPM is *not* a reasonable way to describe market tradeoffs between risk and return, the relative conclusions of the analysis below are subject to bias and error.

We have seen in Chapter 6 that our optimal portfolio strategy involves the selection of a portfolio with the maximum return per unit of risk. For example, if we have a fully diversifiable portfolio, the risk might be measured with *beta.* If the portfolio is not fully diversified, the risk might be better measured with the *standard deviation* of the return. Whatever the "appropriate" measure of risk, the "best" portfolio will be the portfolio with the maximum return per unit or risk. When the risk measure is the standard deviation, we call the return per unit of risk the *reward-to-variability ratio.* When beta is used to measure risk, the return ratio is referred to as the *characteristic line.*

We present four techniques based on CAPM that are available for measuring the overall performance of a portfolio. They are the characteristic line approach, the Sharpe index, the Treynor measure, and Jensen's alpha.

Characteristic Line Approach

The *characteristic line* is the result of comparing the performance of the portfolio to the market index. As presented in Chapter 4, the performance is often graphically compared and the linear least square regression (characteristic) line best fitting the data is calculated.

Let us consider the performance of K mart and an equally weighted portfolio of four stocks (Chrysler, IBM, A&P, and U.S. Tobacco) for the 1970–86 period. The following are summary statistics for these two investment alternatives along with market statistics as represented by the S&P 500 stock index. K mart can be viewed as a single-security portfolio.

	K mart	Equally Weighted Portfolio	Market
Rate of return	12.8%	17.2%	12.0%
Standard deviation of return	36.1	48.9	17.5
Beta	1.20	1.28	1.00

The risk-free rate as measured by ninety-day treasury bills was 7.8 percent during this period. From these data, investors should be able to draw an initial impression about the performance of the two alternatives compared to the risk-free rate and the market index portfolio.

Figure 20–1 is a graph comparing the returns of K mart and the equally weighted portfolio with the returns for the S&P 500 index portfolio. By examining the characteristic line for each investment alternative, some conclusions can be made regarding how they performed

Figure 20–1
Characteristic Lines

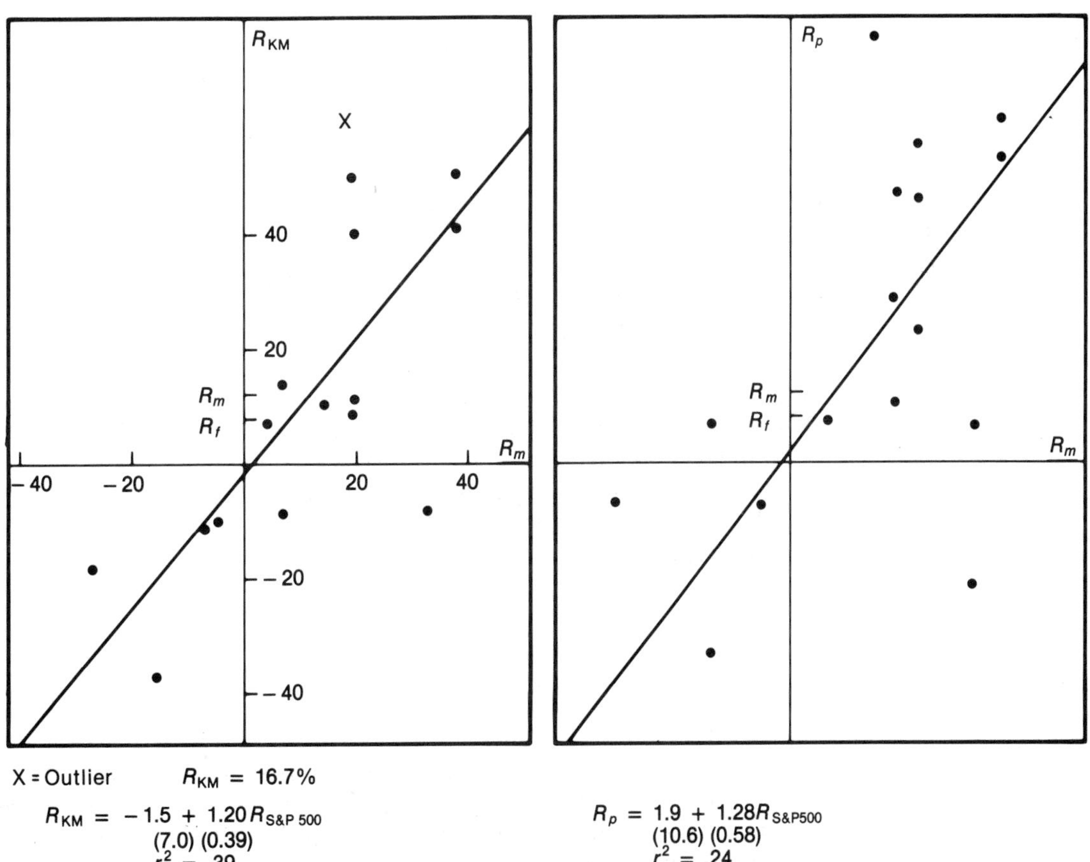

during the 1970–86 period. The characteristic lines in Figure 20–1 were determined by regressing the annual holding period returns for each of the investment alternatives against the annual holding period returns for the S&P 500 index. Where the actual intercept, a_j, exceeds the market equilibrium alpha estimate, $R_f(1 - \text{beta})$, the investment outperformed the market index. The opposite is true where a_j is less than $R_f(1 - \text{beta})$.

K mart

The a_{KM} of -1.5 shows that K mart performed about equal to the market index on a risk-adjusted basis. The equilibrium alpha for K mart is 7.8 percent $(1 - 1.2)$ or -1.6 percent. The standard error for the intercept estimate, a_{KM}, is 7 percent, which indicates that the alpha estimate of -1.5 percent does not differ significantly from -1.6.

K mart's beta of 1.2 shows that the stock was probably more risky than the market index, although the beta estimate did not differ statistically from zero. The coefficient of determination of 39 percent shows that, for an individual security, this stock had fluctuations that were reasonably like those of the average stock in the market. A coefficient of determination of 1.00 would indicate perfect correlation with the market index portfolio.

Equally Weighted Portfolio

The rate of return from the equally weighted portfolio performance was superior to the market index, although its beta of 1.28 was higher than the market index. The 1.9 value for alpha, α_p, is not statistically different from the equilibrium alpha, $7.8\%(1 - 1.28)$ or -2.2%. The r^2 of 24 percent means that 76 percent of the return fluctuations are not explained by market movements.

Sharpe Index

The *Sharpe index* is a performance measure that calculates the excess return per unit of risk where risk is defined as the standard deviation of the portfolio returns. Sharpe's reward-to-variability ratio (*SI*) is calculated as follows:

$$SI = (\bar{R}_p - \bar{R}_f)/\sigma_p = (12.0 - 7.8)/17.5 = .24$$

where $\bar{R}_p$ and $\bar{R}_f$ are the average annual returns for the portfolio and the risk-free rate, respectively, over the historical period. The *SI* measure for the S&P 500 index for the 1970–86 was .24.

Applying the SI formula to evaluate K mart and the equally weighted portfolio produces the following results:

$$SI(\text{K mart}) = (12.8 - 7.8)/36.1 = .138$$
$$SI(\text{portfolio}) = (17.2 - 7.8)/48.9 = .192$$

The poor performance of K mart is reflected in its .138 *SI* value compared to the S&P 500 *SI* value of .240. Both K mart and the equally weighted portfolio provided less return per unit of risk than the market index portfolio. The equally weighted portfolio was ranked higher than the K mart stock by the *SI* measure.

Treynor Measure

The *Treynor measure* is a performance measure that is similar to the Sharpe index in that it calculates the excess return per unit of risk. However, risk is defined as the portfolio's beta. If a portfolio is poorly diversified, as indicated by a low coefficient of determination between the portfolio's returns and those of the market index, the Treynor measure could give a different performance ranking compared to that of the Sharpe index. The Treynor measure could even yield a different order of ranking if the performance of several portfolios is being evaluated. The Sharpe index uses a more comprehensive measure of risk than does the Treynor measure. The Sharpe index uses the portfolio's total risk and not simply its systematic risk, as indicated by the beta of the Treynor measure.

The Treynor measure (T) is calculated by the following equation:

$$T = (\bar{R}_p - \bar{R}_f)/\beta_p$$

Applying the Treynor measure to the S&P 500 index, we get a T value equal to 4.2.

$$T = (12.0 - 7.8)/1.00 = 4.2$$

The Treynor measures for K mart and for the equally weighted portfolio are as follows:

$$T(\text{K mart}) = (12.8 - 7.8)/1.20 = 4.2$$
$$T(\text{portfolio}) = (17.2 - 7.8)/1.28 = 7.3$$

From the Treynor measure, K mart's performance shows up as equal to the market index. Meanwhile, the equally weighted portfolio appears to be far superior to the performance of both the market index and K mart.

Jensen's Alpha

This statistic measures the portfolio's excess return compared to the market index's excess return. The risk-free return *in each period j* is subtracted from the corresponding portfolio return to produce the excess return on the portfolio, $(R_{p,j} - R_{f,j})$, for period j. The risk-free return is also subtracted from the market index return to produce the excess return on the market, $(R_{M,j} - R_{f,j})$, for period j. The following linear regression is then calculated between the annual excess returns for the portfolio and the S&P 500 index.

$$R_{p,j} - R_{f,j} = \alpha_j + \beta_j(R_{M,j} - R_{f,j}) + e_j$$

The "alpha," called *Jensen's alpha,* is expected to be zero for the average portfolio. We are interested in seeing if the alpha, defined as the intercept of the regression line, is statistically different from zero. A positive (negative) value for alpha would indicate that the portfolio earned a positive (negative) risk-adjusted return. The statistics below are for K mart and the equally weighted portfolio.

	K mart	Portfolio
Alpha	−.3%	4.1%
Standard deviation	7.0	10.6
r^2	.43	.23

K mart's performance is indicated by the alpha of almost zero. The alpha of the equally weighted portfolio is 4.1 percent, which is not statistically different from zero, given the standard error of 10.6 percent. Neither K mart nor the equally weighted portfolio could be said to have earned a significant excess risk-adjusted return over the period.

The four measures in this section provide ways to develop rankings of aggregate portfolio performance on a risk-adjusted basis. However, they do not give us an indication of the aggregate return components—in other words, what went into producing the level of return.

Investment Performance Attribution

Let us now break down the aggregate performance into the investment decisions or attributes that helped to produce the observed returns. The investment results of our equally weighted portfolio are presented in Exhibit 20–3. The portfolio's actual return was a respectable 17.2 percent, including dividends and capital gains. In an absolute sense, the portfolio outperformed the market index portfolio by over 5.2 percentage points per year. The investors did quite well, but this is merely a surface comparison. We must investigate further.

Market Risk Adjustment

Initially, the investigation should concentrate on the risk accepted by the investor. Exhibit 20–3 shows that the portfolio had an actual beta of 1.28, suggesting the need to adjust our benchmark, the market index portfolio, to reflect the higher level of risk. Given a beta of 1.28, the portfolio risk premium should be 28 percent higher than the market risk premium. We know that the market risk premium is the difference between the market return and return on the risk-free asset. Adjusting the market risk premium ($\bar{R}_M - \bar{R}_f$) for the actual portfolio beta of 1.28 results in an expected *fully diversified risk premium* of 5.4 percent, as shown in the center column of Exhibit 20–4.

Exhibit 20–3 Investment Results of Hypothetical Portfolio

	Risk-Free Asset	*Market Index Portfolio*	*Four-Stock Portfolio*
Annual rate of return	7.8%	12.0%	17.2%
Standard deviation σ_p	0	17.5%	48.9%
Variance σ_p^2	0	3.07%	23.94%
Coefficient of determination with market index portfolio	0	1.00	.24
Portfolio beta	0	1.00	1.28

Exhibit 20–4 Summary of Risk-Adjusted Performance Measurement (*A*)

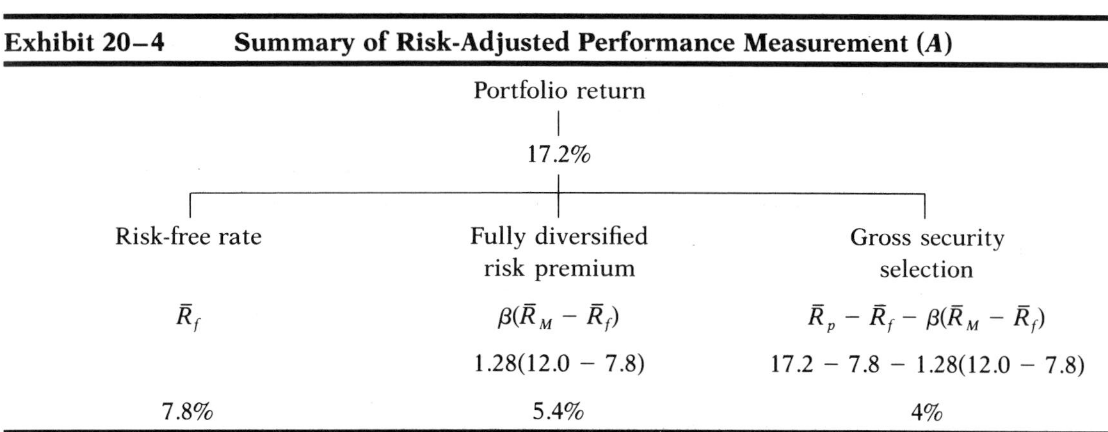

A risk premium of 9.4 percent, determined by subtracting the risk-free rate of 7.8 percent from the total portfolio return, indicates the investor outperformed the riskless investment standard. The investor could have achieved a risk premium of 5.4 percent simply by purchasing a fully diversified portfolio with a beta of 1.28. In this case, the investor not only outperformed the riskless alternative but also showed superior performance after adjusting for risk. The investor beat the risk-adjusted standard by 4 percent per year, which is labeled *gross security selection* in Exhibit 20–4.

Exhibit 20–4 summarizes the risk-adjustment process by showing the three return components we have separated at this stage of our analysis. The actual portfolio return of 17.2 percent included 7.8 percent for the risk-free asset, 5.4 percent to reflect the market's return for the actual beta for the portfolio, and 4 percent to represent the investor's excess return from security selection. At this stage, we conclude that the investor earned 4 percent from the selection of undervalued securities.

Gross Security Selection and Diversifiable Risk

Concluding that the investor picked winners is appropriate even though the difference of 4 percent is not large. However, the analysis of the actual return is not complete because the utilization of beta assumes a fully diversified portfolio. From Exhibit 20–3, we see the portfolio was not very close to being fully diversified. The coefficient of determination was only .24. A fully diversified portfolio would have had a coefficient of determination equal to 1.

A coefficient of determination less than 1 means the investor accepted more risk than accounted for in the beta measure. Perhaps this was done deliberately in order to purchase some securities believed to be undervalued. Indeed, a failure to diversify completely in this case was seemingly wise in view of the fact that the investor actually achieved a return in excess of the risk-adjusted market index return.

To see whether or not the failure to diversify completely was wise, we must determine what sort of return could have been obtained from a benchmark portfolio that *was fully diversified and had the equivalent total risk of the portfolio under examination.* Could the investor have achieved the 17.2 percent return with a fully diversified portfolio and not have had to engage in the security analysis required to isolate the undervalued securities? In Chapter 6, we saw that the beta of a fully diversified portfolio will be the ratio of the standard deviations for the portfolio and the market-index. In our example, this ratio is 2.79 (48.9/17.5). The implication is that our hypothetical portfolio was equivalent in risk to a fully diversified portfolio with a beta of 2.79. The difference between the 2.79 and the actual beta of 1.28 reflects the lack of perfect diversification.

Added risk is perfectly acceptable provided the compensation forthcoming in the form of added return is consistent with the amount of added risk. In our example, the added risk from a lack of diversification is represented by the difference between the actual beta (1.29) and the fully diversified beta (2.79). Because beta is related to the market risk premium, the added amount of return needed is the product of the market risk premium $(\bar{R}_M - \bar{R}_f)$ and the difference in betas $(\sigma_f/\sigma_M - \beta)$. In our example, the failure to diversify fully should have produced a 6.4 percent per year return, calculated as follows:

$$(\bar{R}_M - \bar{R}_f)(\sigma_p/\sigma_M - \beta) = (12.0 - 7.8)(48.9/17.5 - 1.28) = 6.4\%$$

We previously concluded that 4 percent was earned from the selection of undervalued securities (*gross security selection*). We see now that the earnings were not sufficient to compensate the investor for the added risk accepted in the form of *diversifiable risk.* The investor could have purchased a fully diversified portfolio with a beta of 2.79 and earned an additional 6.4 percent instead of the 4 percent actually earned from security selection.

Exhibit 20–5 summarizes this adjustment for diversifiable risk. Exhibit 20–5 is identical to Exhibit 20–4 except that gross security selection has been separated into two parts. The first part is the return required to compensate for diversifiable risk, and the second part is *net security selection,* or the difference between gross security selection and the return required for diversifiable risk. Net security selection is the added return the investor achieved by choosing undervalued securities. In the example, this activity produced a minus 2.4 percent return, indicating that although added returns were obtained, they were insufficient to compensate for the added risk.

Exhibit 20–5 Summary of Risk-Adjusted Performance Measurement (*B*)

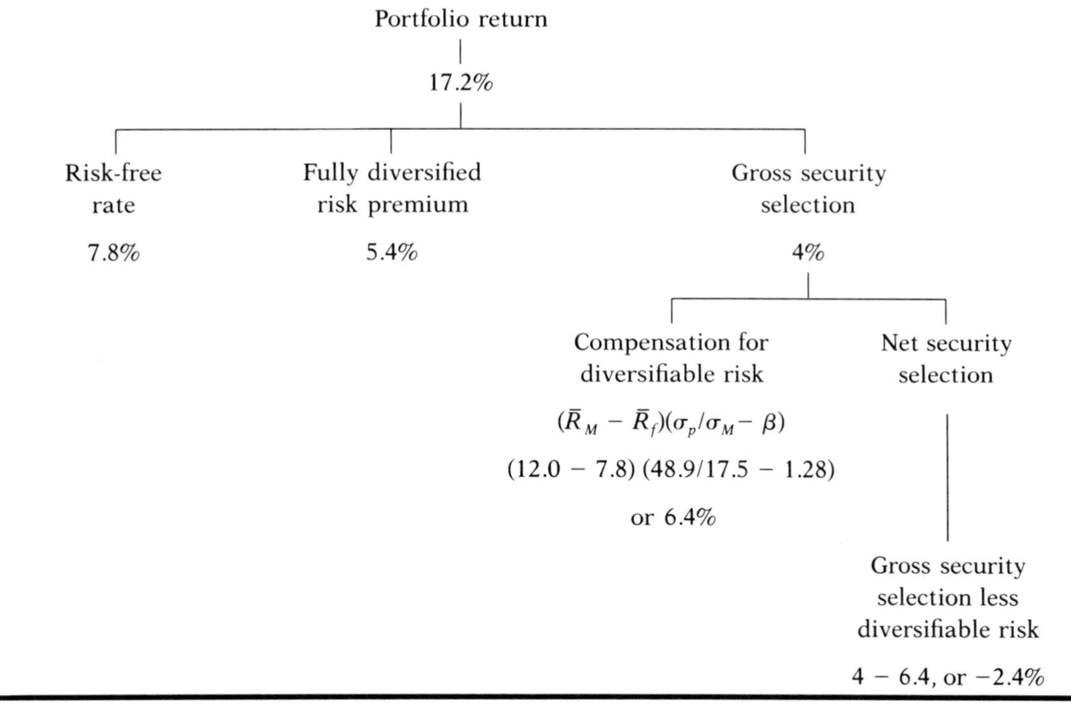

Risk Level Selection

We should also examine the performance of the portfolio manager in the context of whether the actual risk of the portfolio was consistent with the risk expected. Was the portfolio in the right location on the security market line? Suppose an investor actually sought a portfolio with a beta of 1.10. The actual risk achieved in our example was 1.28, suggesting that the manager underestimated the actual risk of the portfolio. The consequences of this "mistake" can be evaluated on the basis of return achieved due to the higher risk. In Exhibit 20–4, we saw that the portion of the investor's return attributable to market risk was 5.4 percent per year. Had the investor achieved the desired beta of 1.1, the 5.4 percent would have been 4.6 percent (the desired beta of 1.1 times the market risk premium of 4.2 percent). The difference of .8 percent represents the return gained as a result of not obtaining the 1.1 beta.

Like gross security selection, the fully diversified risk premium of Exhibits 20–4 and 20–5 has the two components summarized in Exhibit 20–6. The first component is the return associated with the market risk premium and the desired beta. The second component is the return associated with the market risk premium and the difference between the desired beta and the actual beta.

Exhibit 20–6 Components of the Fully Diversified Risk Premium

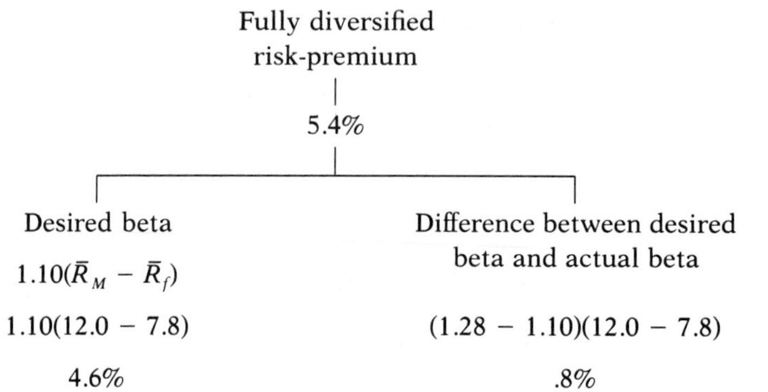

Market Projections

The difference between actual market risk and desired market risk may not have been a mistake. Suppose that, under normal conditions, the investor prefers a portfolio with a beta of 1.1. If the investor predicts the market will perform unusually well over the time period under consideration, the purchase of a portfolio with a higher level of risk may be considered. A more pessimistic prediction might dictate a lower level of risk. If the predictions are correct, gains will result from the decision to accept higher or lower risk based on market projections.

By breaking out the return attributable to differences in the actual risk and the desired risk level, we are isolating the benefits or losses that result from variations in the portfolio risk that may have been made in response to estimates of the market return. However, this breakdown will operate only during the time period of the estimated market movement. Over long periods of time, the changes will average out, and we will not be able to detect the benefits of shifting the risk level by examining differences in the return from the actual risk level and the desired risk level. If shifts are made on purpose, the actual and desired risk should be the same over long periods. Nevertheless, benefits will show up. They will be reflected in the net security selection portion of the return. (See Figure 16–1 for the curved characteristic line that would be expected if investors were able to successfully time their investments.)

The net security selection portion will be positive even if no undervalued securities are selected. In other words, over long periods of time, net security selection reflects both the picking of undervalued securities and portfolio shifts in response to market predictions. At this point, no way exists to separate which is occurring merely by looking at the figures. The only way of making the separation is to examine the period-by-period association between the actual beta and the desired beta. In our example, it appears that the selection of a beta of 1.28 instead of the desired beta of 1.10 was wise. When the market risk premium is positive, shifts into higher risk generally produce higher returns.

Exhibit 20–7 **Summary of Performance Components for Hypothetical Portfolio**

Risk-free return		7.8%
Fully diversified risk premium		
Desired beta	4.6	
Actual beta	.8	
		5.4
Gross security selection		
Diversifiable risk	6.4	
Net security selection	−2.4	
		4.0
Total Return		17.2%

Summary of Measurement Components

Exhibit 20–7 summarizes the performance measurement attribution by depicting the return for each item discussed. The actual total return was 17.2 percent per year. By accepting no risk, the investor could have obtained the risk-free rate of 7.8 percent. However, risk was accepted in the form of market and diversifiable risk. Desired market risk should have produced a return of 4.6 percent, and the actual market risk another .8 percent. The fully diversified risk premium should have totaled 5.4 percent. Accepting diversifiable risk should have produced a return of 6.4 percent. The returns from security selection are found by taking the difference between the sum of the returns assigned to each of the risk measurement categories. In the example, the investor chose winners but accepted too much diversifiable risk, producing a loss of 2.4 percent from net security selection.

Summary

The measurement of investment performance must consider several aspects of the investment decision. We started by insisting that any measurement technique concentrate on the performance of the entire portfolio. Single assets that do well contribute to outstanding performance, but the indicator of a manager's or investor's skill still resides in the outcome of the portfolio. We also noted that performance must be judged in light of available opportunities. The performance must be compared to an appropriate benchmark portfolio. One conventional technique employs the use of market index portfolios to represent the investor's opportunities. A more refined analysis specifies that the benchmark portfolio be adjusted for risk. Often, we need to risk-adjust returns to be able to make an evaluation of the performance for a given portfolio. The characteristic line, the Sharpe index, the Treynor measure, and Jensen's alpha were suggested as ways to make this risk-adjusted appraisal.

Measuring investment performance was shown to be important in providing feedback to the investor about the wisdom of prior decisions. We gain valuable insight by decomposing the aggregate return earned on a portfolio into its component parts or investment attributes. We identified several performance attributes for a hypothetical portfolio of four stocks. As the first step in the attribution process, we showed that if the portfolio is fully diversified, the risk adjustment can be accomplished with beta, where the portion of the investor's return required to compensate for risk is simply the product of beta and the market risk premium. However, when diversifiable risk exits, we indicated that an additional adjustment must be made. By taking the ratio of the standard deviations for the portfolio and market index, we get an equivalent beta. We are then able to see whether the investor had any superior ability in security selection.

We also emphasized that a comparison must be made between the actual beta of the portfolio and the beta desired by the investor. If the actual beta exceeds the desired beta in an up market, a net benefit will result; if the market moves down, a net loss results. With the actual beta less than the desired risk level, gains will be produced in a down market and losses in an up market. The differences between actual and projected betas could be the result of mistakes or of deliberate portfolio shifts in response to market projections. Over long periods of time, the measure of security selection shows both returns of wise security choices and wise portfolio shifts based on market projections.

Suggested Readings

ANTHONY, ROBERT N. "How to Measure Fixed-Income Performance Correctly." *Journal of Portfolio Management* (Winter 1985): 61–65.

BROWN, KEITH C., and GREGORY D. BROWN. "Does the Market Portfolio's Composition Matter?" *Journal of Portfolio Management* (Winter 1987): 26–32.

CONNOR, GREGORY, and ROBERT A. KORZJCZYK. "Performance Measurement with the Arbitrage Pricing Theory: A New Framework for Analysis." *Journal of Financial Economics* (March 1986): 373–94.

COPELAND, THOMAS E., and DAVID MAYERS. "The Value Line Enigma (1965–1978): A Case Study of Performance Evaluation Issues." *Journal of Financial Economics* (November 1982): 289–321.

DYBRIG, PHILIP H., and STEPHEN A. ROSS. "Differential Information and Performance Measurement Using a Security Market Line." *Journal of Finance* (June 1985): 383–99.

FERGUSON, ROBERT. "The Trouble with Performance Measurement." *Journal of Portfolio Management* (Spring 1986): 4–9.

FRENCH, D. W., and GLENN V. HENDERSON, JR. "How Well Does Performance Evaluation Perform?" *Journal of Portfolio Management* (Winter 1985): 15–18.

GOOD, WALTER R. "Measuring Performance." *Financial Analysts Journal* (May–June 1983): 19–24.

JAGANNATHAN, RAVI, and ROBERT A. KORAJCZYK. "Assessing the Market Timing Performance of Managed Portfolios." *Journal of Business* (April 1986): 217–35.

JOBSON, J. D., and BOB KORKIE. "Potential Performance and Tests of Portfolio Efficiency." *Journal of Financial Economics* (December 1982): 443–66.

MOSES, EDWARD A., JOHN M. CHEYNEY, and E. THEODORE VEIT. "A New and More Complete Performance Measure." *Journal of Portfolio Management* (Summer 1987): 24–33.

Questions

1. What four key questions need to be addressed in measuring the performance of a portfolio?
2. What type of portfolio do we usually select as a benchmark against which to compare the performance of a specific portfolio?
3. What problems might an investor encounter with using beta as a risk measure for determining the causes of good or poor portfolio performance?
4. How should one adjust for the timing of cash inflows and outflows in making a portfolio performance evaluation?
5. What is the importance of the concept of an investment time horizon in making a portfolio valuation?
6. What additional problems arise in the performance evaluation of multiple investment managers versus having only a single manager?
7. Evaluate the problems associated with adjusting returns for risk, including
   (a) the difference between actual and expected risk
   (b) the diversification achieved
8. In evaluating performance, should the problem of chance be considered? Why?
9. Discuss the differences in computing the characteristic line and the reward-to-variability ratio. Which is the more appropriate measure for an inefficient portfolio? Why?
10. Discuss several criteria you might use in selecting the risk level of your portfolio. Which beta should your portfolio have, and why do you expect to change your portfolio beta over time?

Problems

1. At the end of 1983, Steve invested $50,000 in a retirement fund for college professors. At the end of 1987, Steve had $67,630 in his retirement fund.
   - (a) What average rate of return did he earn over the four-year period?
   - (b) The fund manager indicated that over the four-year period, the fund had earned a return on each investment share in the following amounts: −13%, 26%, −10%, and 37.1%. What was the average of the annual return on a fund share?
   - (c) Reconcile the difference between the return on the investment by Steve and the average of the annual returns on a fund share.

2. Vera has been asked to evaluate the performance of four portfolio managers. The portfolios managed by the four managers have had the following characteristics for the past five years:

Portfolio Manager	Return	Standard Deviation	Beta
Ann	18%	20%	1.25
Bev	16	15	.80
Carrie	22	25	1.45
Darla	11	15	.20

   Over the same five-year period, the returns on the risk-free asset and the market portfolio were 8 and 16 percent, respectively.
   - (a) Calculate the Treynor measure for each portfolio. How did the managers rank?
   - (b) Calculate the Sharpe measure for each portfolio. How did the managers rank?
   - (c) Why is there a difference in the rankings according to the Treynor and Sharpe measures?

3. Over a period of two years, investors A and B achieved the results listed below. During the same period, the market had a return of 4.3 percent with a standard deviation of 30 percent. Treasury bill rates averaged 7.9 percent over the same period. You are asked to evaluate the performance of A and B. Would you hire either investor to manage your portfolio?

	A	B
Annual return (R)	5.1%	4.2%
Standard deviation	28.0%	40.0%
Actual portfolio beta	.90	1.10
Desired portfolio beta	.75	1.35

4. In the two years following the period described in Problem 3, the market had an annual return of 14.7 percent and a standard deviation of 30 percent. The annual treasury bill rate was 5.4 percent during the same period. You are asked to reevaluate investors A and

B using the results for the most recent two years as noted below. Would these results change your assessment of the competence of investors A and B?

	A	B
Annual return (R)	11.8%	13.9%
Standard deviation	25.0%	43.0%
Actual portfolio beta	.70	1.40
Desired portfolio beta	.75	1.35

5. In comparing the results of the evaluation of investors A and B in Problems 3 and 4, why was the compensation for diversifiable risk negative in Problem 3 and positive in Problem 4?

6. Mabel is interested in purchasing either Portfolio Y or Z. She has collected annual rate of return data for the 1977–86 period for (1) both portfolios, (2) the market represented by the S&P 500, and (3) the risk-free rate. Using these data, determine the following for both portfolios:

(a) Sharpe Index

(b) Treynor measure

(c) Jensen's Alpha

Year	Portfolio Y	Portfolio Z	Market	Risk-free Rate
1977	29%	6%	–7%	5%
1978	24	1	6	7
1979	43	1	18	10
1980	42	2	32	11
1981	3	3	–5	15
1982	50	28	21	11
1983	30	15	23	9
1984	15	3	6	10
1985	16	12	32	8
1986	32	24	18	6

Appendix

Appendix A–1
Present Value of One Dollar at End of Period

Period	1%	2%	3%	4%	5%	6%	7%	8%	9%	10%	11%	12%	14%	16%	18%	20%	25%	30%
1	.9901	.9804	.9709	.9615	.9524	.9434	.9346	.9259	.9174	.9091	.9009	.8929	.8772	.8621	.8475	.8333	.8000	.7692
2	.9803	.9612	.9426	.9246	.9070	.8900	.8734	.8573	.8417	.8264	.8116	.7972	.7695	.7432	.7182	.6944	.6400	.5917
3	.9706	.9423	.9151	.8890	.8638	.8396	.8163	.7938	.7722	.7513	.7312	.7118	.6750	.6407	.6086	.5787	.5120	.4552
4	.9610	.9238	.8885	.8548	.8227	.7921	.7629	.7350	.7084	.6830	.6587	.6355	.5921	.5523	.5158	.4823	.4096	.3501
5	.9515	.9057	.8626	.8219	.7835	.7473	.7130	.6806	.6499	.6209	.5935	.5674	.5194	.4761	.4371	.4019	.3277	.2693
6	.9420	.8880	.8375	.7903	.7462	.7050	.6663	.6302	.5963	.5645	.5346	.5066	.4556	.4104	.3704	.3349	.2621	.2072
7	.9327	.8706	.8131	.7599	.7107	.6651	.6227	.5835	.5470	.5132	.4817	.4523	.3996	.3538	.3139	.2791	.2097	.1594
8	.9235	.8535	.7894	.7307	.6768	.6274	.5820	.5403	.5019	.4665	.4339	.4039	.3506	.3050	.2660	.2326	.1678	.1226
9	.9143	.8368	.7664	.7026	.6446	.5919	.5439	.5002	.4604	.4241	.3909	.3606	.3075	.2630	.2255	.1938	.1342	.0943
10	.9053	.8203	.7441	.6756	.6139	.5584	.5083	.4632	.4224	.3855	.3522	.3220	.2697	.2267	.1911	.1615	.1074	.0725
11	.8963	.8043	.7224	.6496	.5847	.5268	.4751	.4289	.3875	.3505	.3713	.2875	.2366	.1954	.1619	.1346	.0859	.0558
12	.8874	.7885	.7014	.6246	.5568	.4970	.4440	.3971	.3555	.3186	.2858	.2567	.2076	.1685	.1372	.1122	.0687	.0429
13	.8787	.7730	.6810	.6006	.5303	.4688	.4150	.3677	.3262	.2897	.2575	.2292	.1821	.1452	.1163	.0935	.0550	.0330
14	.8700	.7579	.6611	.5775	.5051	.4423	.3878	.3405	.2992	.2633	.2320	.2046	.1597	.1252	.0985	.0779	.0440	.0254
15	.8613	.7430	.6419	.5553	.4810	.4173	.3624	.3152	.2745	.2394	.2090	.1827	.1401	.1079	.0835	.0649	.0352	.0195
16	.8528	.7284	.6232	.5339	.4581	.3936	.3387	.2919	.2519	.2176	.1883	.1631	.1229	.0930	.0708	.0541	.0281	.0150
17	.8444	.7142	.6050	.5134	.4363	.3714	.3166	.2703	.2311	.1978	.1696	.1456	.1078	.0802	.0600	.0451	.0225	.0116
18	.8360	.7002	.5874	.4936	.4155	.3503	.2959	.2502	.2120	.1799	.1528	.1300	.0946	.0691	.0508	.0376	.0180	.0089
19	.8277	.6864	.5703	.4746	.3957	.3305	.2765	.2317	.1945	.1635	.1377	.1161	.0829	.0596	.0431	.0313	.0144	.0068
20	.8195	.6730	.5537	.4564	.3769	.3118	.2584	.2145	.1784	.1486	.1240	.1037	.0728	.0514	.0365	.0261	.0115	.0053
21	.8114	.6598	.5375	.4388	.3589	.2942	.2415	.1987	.1637	.1351	.1117	.0926	.0638	.0443	.0309	.0217	.0092	.0041
22	.8034	.6468	.5219	.4220	.3418	.2775	.2257	.1839	.1502	.1228	.1007	.0826	.0560	.0382	.0262	.0181	.0074	.0031
23	.7954	.6342	.5067	.4057	.3256	.2618	.2109	.1703	.1378	.1117	.0907	.0738	.0491	.0329	.0222	.0151	.0059	.0024
24	.7876	.6217	.4919	.3901	.3101	.2470	.1971	.1577	.1264	.1015	.0817	.0659	.0431	.0284	.0188	.0126	.0047	.0018
25	.7798	.6095	.4776	.3751	.2953	.2330	.1842	.1460	.1160	.0923	.0736	.0588	.0378	.0245	.0160	.0105	.0038	.0014
26	.7720	.5976	.4637	.3607	.2812	.2198	.1722	.1352	.1064	.0839	.0663	.0525	.0331	.0211	.0135	.0087	.0030	.0011
27	.7644	.5859	.4502	.3468	.2678	.2074	.1609	.1252	.0976	.0763	.0597	.0469	.0291	.0182	.0115	.0073	.0024	.0008
28	.7568	.5744	.4371	.3335	.2551	.1956	.1504	.1159	.0895	.0693	.0538	.0419	.0255	.0157	.0097	.0061	.0019	.0006
29	.7493	.5631	.4243	.3207	.2429	.1846	.1406	.1073	.0822	.0630	.0485	.0374	.0224	.0135	.0082	.0051	.0015	.0005
30	.7419	.5521	.4120	.3083	.2314	.1741	.1314	.0994	.0754	.0573	.0437	.0334	.0196	.0116	.0070	.0042	.0012	.0004
35	.7059	.5000	.3554	.2534	.1813	.1301	.0937	.0676	.0490	.0356	.0259	.0189	.0102	.0055	.0030	.0017	.0004	.0001
40	.6717	.4529	.3066	.2083	.1420	.0972	.0668	.0460	.0318	.0221	.0154	.0107	.0053	.0026	.0013	.0007	.0001	.0000

Appendix A–2
Present Value of One Dollar Each Period for N Periods

Number of Periods	1%	2%	3%	4%	5%	6%	7%	8%
1	0.9901	0.9804	0.9709	0.9615	0.9524	0.9434	0.9346	0.9259
2	1.9704	1.9416	1.9135	1.8861	1.8594	1.8334	1.8080	1.7833
3	2.9410	2.8839	2.8286	2.7751	2.7232	2.6730	2.6243	2.5771
4	3.9020	3.8077	3.7171	3.6299	3.5460	3.4651	3.3872	3.3121
5	4.8534	4.7135	4.5797	4.4518	4.3295	4.2124	4.1002	3.9927
6	5.7955	5.6014	5.4172	5.2421	5.0757	4.9173	4.7665	4.6229
7	6.7282	6.4720	6.2303	6.0021	5.7864	5.5824	5.3893	5.2064
8	7.6517	7.3255	7.0197	6.7327	6.4632	6.2098	5.9713	5.7466
9	8.5660	8.1622	7.7861	7.4353	7.1078	6.8017	6.5152	6.2469
10	9.4713	8.9826	8.5302	8.1109	7.7217	7.3601	7.0236	6.7101
11	10.3676	9.7868	9.2526	8.7605	8.3064	7.8869	7.4987	7.1390
12	11.2551	10.5753	9.9540	9.3851	8.8633	8.3838	7.9427	7.5361
13	12.1337	11.3484	10.6350	9.9856	9.3936	8.8527	8.3577	7.9038
14	13.0037	12.1062	11.2961	10.5631	9.8986	9.2950	8.7455	8.2442
15	13.8651	12.8493	11.9379	11.1184	10.3797	9.7122	9.1079	8.5595
16	14.7179	13.5777	12.5611	11.6523	10.8378	10.1059	9.4466	8.8514
17	15.5623	14.2919	13.1661	12.1657	11.2741	10.4773	9.7632	9.1216
18	16.3983	14.9920	13.7535	12.6593	11.6896	10.8276	10.0591	9.3719
19	17.2260	15.6785	14.3238	13.1339	12.0853	11.1581	10.3356	9.6036
20	18.0456	16.3514	14.8775	13.5903	12.4622	11.4699	10.5940	9.8181
21	18.8570	17.0112	15.4150	14.0292	12.8212	11.7641	10.8355	10.0168
22	19.6604	17.6580	15.9369	14.4511	13.1630	12.0416	11.0612	10.2007
23	20.4558	18.2922	16.4436	14.8568	13.4886	12.3034	11.2722	10.3711
24	21.2434	18.9189	16.9355	15.2470	13.7986	12.5504	11.4693	10.5288
25	22.0232	19.5235	17.4131	15.6221	14.0939	12.7834	11.6536	10.6748
26	22.7952	20.1210	17.8768	15.9828	14.3752	13.0032	11.8258	10.8100
27	23.5596	20.7069	18.3270	16.3296	14.6430	13.2105	11.9867	10.9352
28	24.3164	21.2813	18.7641	16.6631	14.8981	13.4062	12.1371	11.0511
29	25.0658	21.8444	19.1885	16.9837	15.1411	13.5907	12.2777	11.1584
30	25.8077	22.3965	19.6004	17.2920	15.3725	13.7648	12.4090	11.2578
35	29.4086	24.9986	21.4872	18.6646	16.3742	14.4982	12.9477	11.6546
40	32.8347	27.3555	23.1148	19.7928	17.1591	15.0463	13.3317	11.9246

Appendix A–2
Continued

9%	10%	11%	12%	14%	16%	18%	20%	25%	30%
0.9174	0.9091	.9009	0.8929	0.8772	0.8621	0.8475	0.8333	.8000	.7692
1.7591	1.7355	1.7125	1.6901	1.6467	1.6052	1.5656	1.5278	1.4400	1.3609
2.5313	2.4869	2.4437	2.4018	2.3216	2.2459	2.1743	2.1065	1.9520	1.8161
3.2397	3.1699	3.1024	3.0373	2.9137	2.7982	2.6901	2.5887	2.3616	2.1662
3.8897	3.7908	3.6959	3.6048	3.4331	3.2743	3.1272	2.9906	2.6893	2.4356
4.4859	4.3553	4.2305	4.1114	3.8887	3.6847	3.4976	3.3255	2.9514	2.6427
5.0330	4.8684	4.7122	4.5638	4.2883	4.0386	3.8115	3.6046	3.1611	2.8021
5.5348	5.3349	5.1461	4.9676	4.6389	4.3436	4.0776	3.8372	3.3289	2.9247
5.9952	5.7590	5.5370	5.3282	4.9464	4.6065	4.3030	4.0310	3.4631	3.0190
6.4177	6.1446	5.8892	5.6502	5.2161	4.8332	4.4941	4.1925	3.5705	3.0915
6.8052	6.4951	6.2065	5.9377	5.4527	5.0286	4.6560	4.3271	3.6564	3.1473
7.1607	6.8137	6.4924	6.1944	5.6603	5.1971	4.7932	4.4392	3.7251	3.1903
7.4869	7.1034	6.7499	6.4235	5.8424	5.3423	4.9095	4.5327	3.7801	3.2233
7.7862	7.3667	6.9819	6.6282	6.0021	5.4675	5.0081	4.6106	3.8241	3.2487
8.0607	7.6061	7.1909	6.8109	6.1422	5.5755	5.0916	4.6755	3.8593	3.2682
8.3126	7.8237	7.3792	6.9740	6.2651	5.6685	5.1624	4.7296	3.8874	3.2832
8.5436	8.0216	7.5488	7.1196	6.3729	5.7487	5.2223	4.7746	3.9099	3.2948
8.7556	8.2014	7.7016	7.2497	6.4674	5.8178	5.2732	4.8122	3.9279	3.3037
8.9501	8.3649	7.8393	7.3658	6.5504	5.8775	5.3162	4.8435	3.9424	3.3105
9.1285	8.5136	7.9633	7.4694	6.6231	5.9288	5.3527	4.8696	3.9539	3.3158
9.2922	8.6487	8.0751	7.5620	6.6870	5.9731	5.3837	4.8913	3.9631	3.3198
9.4424	8.7715	8.1757	7.6446	6.7429	6.0113	5.4099	4.9094	3.9705	3.3230
9.5802	8.8832	8.2664	7.7184	6.7921	6.0442	5.4321	4.9245	3.9764	3.3254
9.7066	8.9847	8.3481	7.7843	6.8351	6.0726	5.4510	4.9371	3.9811	3.3272
9.8226	9.0770	8.4217	7.8431	6.8729	6.0971	5.4669	4.9476	3.9849	3.3286
9.9290	9.1609	8.4881	7.8957	6.9061	6.1182	5.4804	4.9563	3.9879	3.3297
10.0266	9.2372	8.5478	7.9426	6.9352	6.1364	5.4919	4.9636	3.9903	3.3305
10.1161	9.3066	8.6016	7.9844	6.9607	6.1520	5.5016	4.9697	3.9923	3.3312
10.1983	9.3696	8.6501	8.0218	6.9830	6.1656	5.5098	4.9747	3.9938	3.3317
10.2737	9.4269	8.6938	8.0552	7.0027	6.1772	5.5168	4.9789	3.9950	3.3321
10.5668	9.6442	8.8552	8.1755	7.0700	6.2153	5.5386	4.9915	3.9984	3.3330
10.7574	9.7791	8.9510	8.2438	7.1050	6.2335	5.5482	4.9966	3.9995	3.3332

Glossary

Accrued interest
Interest accrued (due) on a debt since the last payment was made. Purchasers of bonds pay a market price plus accrued interest.

ADR
American depositary receipt. A means of investment in foreign companies.

Agent
An individual or other party acting on behalf of another person. Many investment transactions are handled on an agent basis.

Alpha
A measure of the above or below average risk-adjusted return from a security. It provides an indication of the ability to select undervalued securities.

Annuity
A series of annual payments or receipts.

Antidilution clause
A provision of a bond indenture that protects the relative position of the holders in the event of the issuance of additional common stock or debt obligations.

Arbitrage
The simultaneous purchase and sale of assets or their equivalents at prices that differ temporarily. The objective is to make a profit when the prices converge.

Arbitrage pricing theory (APT)
An asset pricing model that states that the return from a security will equal the risk-free rate plus a return from assuming one or more types of systematic risk.

Arithmetic return
Average (mean) of a series of returns.

Arrearage
In preferred stocks, the accumulation of unpaid preferred dividends.

Asked price
The price a marketmaker is asking for selling shares or units of a security. An indication of what an investor will have to pay in purchasing a security.

Asset
Property, money, or other valuable items owned by an organization, an individual, or a government.

Asset allocation
The determination of how to invest over major asset classes, such as the decision as to how much to invest in common stocks versus fixed-income securities. Also referred to as the major mix decision.

Balance sheet
A financial statement showing the nature and amount of an organization's assets, liabilities, and capital as of a given date.

Basis
In commodity trading, the price difference between two contract months or commodities.

Basis point
One-hundredth of one percentage point, .01%. Used mostly to describe changes in yields.

Bear
An individual who believes the market will decline.

Bear market
A market which is declining.

Bearer bond
A bond that does not have the owner's name registered on the books of the issuer. The bond is payable to the holder or bearer of the bond.

Benchmark portfolio
A portfolio of a given risk level used to measure the performance of a portfolio manager. The Standard & Poor's 500 stock index is often used for common stocks.

Best efforts
An offering of securities to investors where the investment banker provides only a marketing effort.

Beta
A measure of the risk of a security. Beta is obtained by measuring the variability of returns relative to some market measure.

Bid price
The price at which marketmaker is willing to buy shares or units of a security. An indication of what an investor will be able to sell a security for.

Block
A trade of 10,000 or more shares of stock.

Blue sky laws
State security laws which regulate the registration and sale of securities.

Bond
Essentially an IOU or promissory note of a corporation or government. Usually issued in multiples of $1000 or $5000.

Bond rating
An indication of the independently determined quality of a debt obligation.

Book value
The value of a corporation according to its accounting records. Book value is equal to the assets less the liabilities.

Broker
Registered representative who carries out investment orders for customers.

Bull
An individual who believes the market will rise.

Bull market
A rising market.

Call loan rate
The rate of interest paid on margin account borrowings.

Call option
A financial instrument allowing the holder to buy 100 shares of stock from another investor during a specified period for a specified price.

Callable
A bond issue or other security, all or part of which may be redeemed by the issuing organization before the security's final maturity.

Capital gain
Monetary gain achieved by the sale or exchange of a capital asset.

Capital structure
Long-term debt, preferred stock, and common stock accounts of an organization. The sources of financing for an organization.

Cash account
A brokerage account where the settlement for securities purchased is in cash.

Certificate of deposit
A money market instrument, which is evidence that the holder has funds on deposit at a financial institution.

Characteristic line
A visual indication of how an investment has performed relative to the market. It provides a measure of the security's risk and return characteristics.

Closed-end investment company
A form of pooled investment alternative whose capitalization remains fixed. Trading occurs in the shares outstanding.

Coefficient of determination
In a regression program, a measure of the degree to which the independent variable explains the dependent variable. The r^2.

Collateral value
The amount a security is worth in securing a loan.

Commercial paper
Short-term promissory notes issued by large firms.

Commission
The broker's basic fee for executing a purchase or a sale transaction as an agent.

Common stock
Financial securities representing ownership of a corporation.

Compound interest
Interest paid on both the principal and on interest paid in previous periods.

Consol
A fixed-income security having no maturity date.

Convertible security
Financial security which allows its holder to convert it into another security (often common stock) under specified conditions.

Coupon bond
A bond with interest coupons attached. These coupons are clipped and presented for payment of interest when due.

Covariance
A measure of the degree to which two securities move together.

Current assets
Cash, marketable securities, and other assets which are readily converted into cash within a one-year period.

Current ratio
A measure of the firm's ability to pay its current debts from its current assets. Current assets divided by current liabilities.

Current yield
The dollar return in the form of interest or a dividend divided by the present market price.

Death benefit
The payment to be made from a pension plan or an insurance policy upon the death of the individual covered.

Debenture
Unsecured long-term debt obligation issued by a firm.

Discount bond
A bond that sells for less than its par value.

Diversification
Risk reducing strategy in which investors hold assets of varying quality, type, maturity, and/or size.

Dividend
The income payment made to stockholders on a common or preferred stock.

Duration
The cash flow maturity of a security measured in present value terms.

Efficient market
A market in which all assets are priced in accordance with their intrinsic or true value.

Equity
The ownership of a firm as represented by the common stock accounts. The percentage actually owned of an asset.

Eurobond
A form of international debt obligation that is sold in a country different from the country of the currency in which the bond is denominated. Most trading in these obligations occurs in Europe.

Exercise price
Price per share at which a warrant or an option may be exchanged for common stock.

Financial asset
A claim on the assets of an organization in the form of a "piece of paper."

Financial ratio
Number expressing the relationship between two items on a financial statement.

Fiscal policy
The expenditures and receipts of the government and their impact on the economy.

Floating rate
An interest rate that varies over time depending on what another benchmark rate does.

Flower bond
A special type of U.S. government bond that allows its use at par in the payment of estate taxes.

Fourth market
An agent market for the trading of securities off the floor of an exchange.

Fundamental approach
Investor determines the value of a security by using information relating directly to the health of the firm and the economy.

Futures contact
Instrument which requires the delivery of a specified quantity of a specified commodity at a specified future time.

Geometric return
The time-weighted rate of return on a security; its internal rate of return.

Hedger
An individual or organization that takes a risk-reducing position opposite to that held in the cash (spot) market.

Immunization
A fixed-income portfolio management strategy where the investor's time horizon is set equal to the duration of the portfolio; virtually eliminates interest rate risk over the time horizon.

Indenture
A written agreement under which debt obligations are issued. It sets forth the essential terms of the debt issue.

Index fund
A portfolio constructed so that its performance over time will closely match a given market indicator.

Individual retirement account
Voluntary pension plan for individuals having earned income. Allows tax-exempt contributions until the benefits are withdrawn from the plan.

Interest
The periodic dollar payment made to owners of bonds and other fixed-income investments.

Intrinsic value
Security's value based on financial and other characteristics of the firm. Its "true" worth.

Investment banker
Financial intermediary which accepts and invests funds of investors or otherwise facilitates financial market transactions.

Investment company
A company or trust fund that uses its capital to invest in other companies. Individuals buy units in the investment company and own part of the portfolio.

Keogh plan
Voluntary pension plan for self-employed individuals. Contributions are tax-deferred.

Leverage
The existence of a fixed element in a security. Increases the price variability of the security.

Liability
Debt owed by an individual or an organization including governments.

Limit order
Security purchase order specifying the maximum or minimum price for the order's execution.

Liquidity
Ease with which a security can be converted into cash at a price close to the last market trade.

Load charge
The transaction payment an investor makes when purchasing a mutual fund.

Long
A position in the market where the investor owns the security or other asset.

Major medical policy
A form of health insurance coverage that pays for large and unexpected medical expenses—supplements basic health insurance.

Margin account
A brokerage account which allows the purchase of securities partly on credit.

Marginal tax rate
The tax paid on the last dollar of income.

Margin requirements
Federal Reserve imposed regulations which state what percentage of a security purchase must be paid for in cash. Other margin requirements are imposed by the exchanges and the brokerage firms to keep the account in good standing.

Marketability
A characteristic of an investment relating to how quickly and easily that security can be sold.

Market order
Order instructing brokerage firm to obtain the best available price in the market at the time the order is executed.

Maturity
The date on which a loan comes due or a bond is to be paid off.

Mean
Arithmetic average of a data series.

Median
Midpoint of a data series that is arranged from highest value to the lowest value.

Monetary policy
The management by the Federal Reserve of the nation's money supply.

Money market fund
Institutionally managed portfolio of money market securities such as treasury bills, commercial paper, and certificates of deposit.

Municipal bond
Debt obligation issued by governmental bodies other than the federal government and its agencies.

Mutual fund
Open-end investment company. Fund continually accepts new investment funds and stands ready to redeem shares previously purchased.

NASD
National Association of Security Dealers. An association of brokers and dealers in the over-the-counter market.

NASDAQ
An automated network for information providing brokers and dealers with price quotations on securities traded over-the-counter.

Net asset value
The value of shares of an investment company as determined by valuing the securities in the portfolio and subtracting any liabilities.

NOW account
A negotiable order of withdrawal account which pays interest but on which drafts (or checks) can be written.

Odd-lot
An amount of stock less than the established trading unit of 100 shares (sometimes ten shares).

Open-end investment company
An investment company (mutual fund) that continually accepts new funds and redeems previously issued shares.

Option
A financial instrument that gives the holder the privilege of buying or selling a fixed number of shares at a fixed price for a fixed period of time.

Ordinary (whole) life insurance
Provides both insurance protection in the event of death and a savings feature. Al-

lows for the gradual buildup of the policy's cash value.

Original issue, deep discount bond
A new fixed-income security sold to investors at a price substantially below its par value. These securities carry coupon interest rates below those available on par bonds.

Over-the-counter market
A communications network allowing for the trading of securities not traded on an organized exchange.

Par value
An arbitrary value assigned to stock for purposes of accounting for it on the firm's books.

Payout percentage
The relative amount of earnings paid out as dividends to stockholders.

Pension plan
Funds periodically provided by employees and/or employers for group investment or retirement savings. Benefits are paid out during retirement.

Portfolio
A combination of all assets or investments owned by an individual or an organization.

Preferred stock
A form of equity security that pays a fixed dividend rate per share.

Premium bond
A bond that sells for more than its par value.

Present value
The current value of funds that are to be received at some time in the future. Determined by discounting at a discount (interest) rate.

Price-earnings ratio
The valuation of a stock determined by dividing the market price of the stock by the earnings per share.

Price limit (daily)
On the futures exchanges, the amount which the price of the contract can move up or down in any given trading day.

Primary market transaction
Transactions which create new assets and bring funds into the organization.

Principal
A dealer buying or selling for his or her own account. The term also refers to the face amount of a bond.

Put option
A financial security that allows the holder to sell 100 shares of a specified stock at a specified price for a specified period of time.

Real growth
A measure of the growth in a variable after removing the influence of inflation.

Redemption price
The price at which a bond or preferred stock may be redeemed before its final maturity.

Red herring
A preliminary prospectus for a security offering.

Registered bond
A bond which is registered on the books of the issuing organization as belonging to an individual.

Registered representative
See Broker.

Retained earnings
The income of the firm that is kept and reinvested.

Right
A certificate that gives the holder the opportunity to participate pro rata in a new issue of equity securities issued by a firm.

Risk-free rate
An interest rate that an investor earns from a security that has no variance (risk); usually proxied by the U.S. treasury bill rate.

Risk premium
Extra return required to compensate an investor for taking on additional amounts of risk.

Round-lot
The standard unit of trading on an exchange, usually 100 shares.

SEC
Securities and Exchange Commission, the federal regulatory agency for the securities industry.

Secondary market
The marketplace for securities after they have initially been issued.

Sector fund (or index)
A portfolio designed to allow investor participation in only a portion of the entire market.

Short
A position in the financial markets where the investor sells an asset that is not owned.

Short sale
The sale of stock not owned by an individual, but believing that the price of the stock will decline. The hope is to cover the sale later at a lower price.

Sinking fund
A device for the orderly reduction of the principal of a loan prior to its final maturity.

SIPC
Securities Investor Protection Corporation. This federal agency insures customer's accounts at brokerage firms.

Specialist
A New York Stock Exchange member with two functions: 1) to maintain an orderly market; 2) to act as a broker's broker and execute limit orders.

Speculator
An individual or an organization that takes on risk in an asset position in an attempt to earn a profit; the opposite of a hedger.

Spot market
The cash market for the actual commodity being traded. The opposite of a futures market.

Spread
The difference between the bid and the asked price for a security.

Standard deviation
A statistical measure of the dispersion or variability of a return of a security or any other data series.

Stockholders' equity
Net worth or owners' investment as reported on the books of the firm.

Stop order
An order to buy at a price above or to sell at a price below the current market price.

Striking price
See Exercise price.

Sustainable growth
A measure of how fast a company can grow without selling new issues of common stock, but only by using retained earnings and debt.

Systematic risk
The risk of a security or other asset which comes from the system (market). This risk can not be eliminated by diversification.

Technical analysis
Study of the behavior of the market or an individual security by charting price movements or using other measures of supply and demand.

Term insurance
Temporary insurance that provides only protection from the financial consequences of death.

Thin market
A market in which there are relatively few orders to buy or sell. Hence, price movements may be large on relatively little trading activity.

Third market
A principal market for trading of securities off the floor of an exchange. The term is sometimes used to indicate all trading in the over-the-counter market.

TIAA-CREF
A pension plan for educational institutions. TIAA is the fixed-income portfolio and CREF is the common stock portfolio.

Trustee
A financial institution or individual having responsibility for the enforcement of the provisions of a bond contract.

Unit trust
A portfolio that is constructed and then sold to the investing public in pieces called units; each unit is a proportional interest in the portfolio.

Unsystematic risk
The risk of a security or other asset which is unique to the security and which can be diversified away since it is not a part of the system.

Variance
A statistical measure of the difference between anticipated results and actual results. A measure of the risk of a security.

Vesting
The acquisition of ownership rights to an asset; usually applied to pension plan participation.

Warrant
A security giving the holder the privilege of buying a specified number of shares from a firm at a specified price for a specified period of time.

Wealth relative
A value determined by dividing an ending (terminal) security or portfolio value by the beginning value. May include dividend or interest income as well as price changes.

Whole life policy
See ordinary life insurance.

Withdrawal plan
A mutual fund provision that allows holders to receive periodic payments from the fund.

Yield
The dividend or interest received from an investment. Sometimes known as return, indicating the total amount of profit or loss achieved from holding an investment asset.

Yield curve
A graphic representation of the relationship between maturity and yield for fixed-income securities of the same risk class.

Yield tilt
A portfolio where the objective of receiving current income is more important than achieving capital appreciation.

Yield-to-maturity
The yield of a bond if the holder keeps it until its final maturity date. This yield calculation takes into account any premium or discount on the bond.

Zero-coupon bond
A fixed-income security that offers no periodic cash payments of interest, but only offers a cash payment (including interest) at the final maturity of the security.

Index